HEGEL'S
DEVELOPMENT

❋

Toward the Sunlight
1770-1801

HEGEL'S
DEVELOPMENT

*

Toward the Sunlight
1770-1801

BY

H. S. HARRIS

OXFORD
AT THE CLARENDON PRESS

This book has been printed digitally and produced in a standard specification
in order to ensure its continuing availability

OXFORD
UNIVERSITY PRESS

Great Clarendon Street, Oxford OX2 6DP

Oxford University Press is a department of the University of Oxford.
It furthers the University's objective of excellence in research, scholarship,
and education by publishing worldwide in

Oxford New York

Auckland Bangkok Buenos Aires Cape Town Chennai
Dar es Salaam Delhi Hong Kong Istanbul Karachi Kolkata
Kuala Lumpur Madrid Melbourne Mexico City Mumbai Nairobi
São Paulo Shanghai Singapore Taipei Tokyo Toronto

with an associated company in Berlin

Oxford is a registered trade mark of Oxford University Press
in the UK and in certain other countries

Published in the United States
by Oxford University Press Inc., New York

ISBN 0-19-8243588

Viel hat von Morgen an,
Seit ein Gespräch wir sind und hören voneinander,
Erfahren der Mensch; bald sind wir aber Gesang.
Und das Zeitbild, das der große Geist entfaltet,
Ein Zeichen liegts vor uns, daß zwischen ihm und andern
Ein Bündniß zwischen ihm und andern Mächten ist.

HÖLDERLIN

'I exhort myself always in the words of the *Lebens-läufe*: "Strive toward the sun, my friends, that the salvation of the human race may soon come to fruition! What use are the hindering leaves? or the branches? Cleave through them to the sunlight, and strive till ye be weary! Tis good so, for so shall ye sleep the better!"'

(HEGEL *to* SCHELLING, *16 April 1795*)

ACKNOWLEDGEMENTS

M OST of the first draft of this book was written in 1964–5 during
a year of sabbatical leave from York University, Toronto. In that
year I was awarded a Senior Fellowship by the Canada Council,
together with a travel grant which enabled me to spend some time
in England and to make a short visit to the *Hegel-Archiv* (then in
Bonn, now in Bochum). In England I discussed my project with
Sir Malcolm Knox and Warden G. R. G. Mure, and received
valuable advice from both of them. In Bonn I was given access to
typed transcripts of a handful of fragments from Hegel's Frankfurt
period that have not yet been published. I was also able to consult
a number of books which are not easily obtainable elsewhere; and
the kind assistance of Dr. Gisela Schüler and Dr. Heinz Kimmerle
enabled me to clear up several points of difficulty or uncertainty.
Had it not been for the contribution that these two scholars have
made to the task of ordering and dating Hegel's manuscripts in
terms of the handwriting, which was begun by Hermann Nohl and
carried on most notably by Franz Rosenzweig, my undertaking
would have been both more difficult and more perilous than it is.

In an undertaking of this kind one cannot hope to remember all
that one owes to others. I have not even tried to list all the books
that I had occasion to consult. But the enormous extent of my
debt to previous students of Hegel's development will be apparent,
I hope, from my footnotes. There are many to whom I might have
owed more had I been more industrious; but I trust that my notes
will make it clear that I have not approached my task lightly. In
singling out for special mention here the work of three scholars on
whom I have depended heavily I should like to underline the
limitations of my own scholarship. No one can read everything;
not even Hegel did that. But he tried conscientiously to absorb
everything significant in the culture and the heritage of his own
time and his own people. I cannot claim to have done that; were
it not for the more heroic efforts of Carmelo Lacorte in that

direction, and the learned zeal of Johannes Hoffmeister in editing Hegel, and of Adolf Beck in editing Hölderlin's Letters, my work would be even more imperfect than it is.

The making of a book from a manuscript is a process to which many people contribute in different ways. There is, to begin with, the often far from mechanical labour of the typist. My first protector against slips, errors, and oversights was Mrs. Marja B. Moens, who typed the whole of my original manuscript. She also typed most of the final draft, though Miss Beatrice M. Oliver and Miss Betty Yacoubian also helped with this. My son David helped me make the analytical index, and Miss Lorraine Fadden typed it.

The book was brought to the notice of the Clarendon Press by the sympathetic interest of Professor J. N. Findlay; and the final stages of its development were greatly influenced by the comments of the adviser to whom it was submitted by the Press. Not only did he make many valuable suggestions on points of detail, and help me to remove a number of errors and blemishes; but also his more general critical reactions alerted me to some of the dangers of false perspective that exist in a work conceived on the present scale. I have tried to obviate these dangers in my Prelude–Coda; if I have succeeded the Press adviser must have a large share of the credit.

H. S. H.

Glendon College, York University
Toronto
Gebhard's Day, 1970

CONTENTS

NOTE ON REFERENCES AND ABBREVIATIONS

IN referring to the fragmentary texts of Hegel's juvenilia I have followed the convention set by Gisela Schüler and Heinz Kimmerle of identifying each fragment by its opening phrase or *incipit*. This practice avoids all the ambiguities of titles supplied by editors, and it also enables us to distinguish at need between the different drafts or stages in the composition of any single essay. The source references indicate clearly where the most accurate published texts are to be found (except for a few pieces which have never yet been printed); and wherever an English translation is known to me I have referred to it. The chronological index (supplemented by Appendix 2 to Chapter I) provides a full conspectus of all the juvenilia that can be dated.

Almost all references to sources, whether primary or secondary, have been abbreviated in the footnotes. In general I have given the author's (editor's, translator's) name with the page number of the work referred to. The remaining details can be found quickly and easily in the Bibliographical Index which is arranged alphabetically by author (including all necessary cross references). It seems to me that this is preferable to hunting for the first occurrence of a work which recurs perpetually as 'op. cit.'. A few books which are cited incidentally (and usually only once) are given their full description in the footnote (but they are also included in the Bibliography).

The following abbreviations are employed regularly:

Akad.   *Kants gesammelte Schriften*, herausgegeben von der Königlich Preußischen Akademie der Wissenschaften, Reimer, Berlin, 1902–38.

Briefe   *Briefe von und an Hegel*, herausgegeben von Johannes Hoffmeister und Rolf Flechsig, F. Meiner, Hamburg, 1961.

Dok.   *Dokumente zu Hegels Entwicklung*, herausgegeben von Johannes Hoffmeister, Frommann, Stuttgart, 1936.

GSA   Hölderlin, *Sämtliche Werke* (Große Stuttgarter Ausgabe), herausgegeben von Friedrich Beißner und Adolf Beck, Kohlhammer, Stuttgart, 1946ff.

Jub.   Hegel, *Sämtliche Werke*, Jubiläumsausgabe in 20 Bänden, einer Hegel-Monographie und einem Lexicon, herausgegeben von Hermann Glockner, Frommann, Stuttgart, 1927–35.

PRELUDE AND CODA

This book contains the whole of a story, half of a story, and the beginning of a story. Considered as a whole it is a tale of the pursuit of an ideal, and of how that ideal, when at last it was clearly seen and grasped, did not avail against the stubbornness of actual life. But this is not the whole story, and for this reason there is nothing tragic in the defeat of the ideal by reality. My story is, after all, only the first half of an *Erziehungsroman*, a tale of a real, live, Wilhelm Meister; and the whole of *that* story—which I do hope to complete eventually—is still only a part, perhaps not even a proper half, of the full story of a great philosopher, which I have no thought of trying to tell as a whole.

This book tells only of how that philosopher discovered philosophy; indeed it does not even quite do that, for the discovery of philosophy was, properly speaking, the sequel to the failure of the quest with which we are here directly concerned. In other words, the discovery of philosophy is really the subject of the other half of my *Roman*, the half that has still to be written. We are here concerned rather with Hegel's discovery that he must become a philosopher.

But my story is a true story, not a romance at all; and I have striven above all else not only to tell the whole truth but to show that it is the truth. I have tried to present all of the evidence, to indicate clearly where the evidence is defective, and not to go beyond the evidence into the realms of fancy and conjecture. No philosopher—except perhaps Plato—has tempted so many sober, black-gowned scholars into such wild flights of fancy, such extraordinary feats of imagination, as Hegel. One might almost say with justice about Hegel's followers what Hobbes said of his own predecessors, that there is no opinion so absurd that you will not find it advanced and defended by one of them as the gospel truth. Yet Hegel himself, for all his Puck-like capacity to make sober men lose their senses, was no hero of romance, but a model of solid

bourgeois common sense, outwardly remarkable only for his un-
remitting industry in the pursuit of understanding. And this book
is the plainest chronicle that I can contrive of the first stages in
that industrious pursuit. Only my title, and this prelude, are in any
way fanciful.

Since it has been the historic fate of Hegel to be identified in the
English-speaking world, and perhaps not only there, as the greatest
of the sophists, a veritable wizard of words who was able to deprive
men—even, and quite notably, Englishmen—of their reason and
their common sense; and since there is, as I have said, some
justice in this verdict if we accept history as our court of judgement,
it may seem imprudent to let fancy intrude in this way on my title-
page and at the beginning. For why, when my primary concern is
to lift the spell, should I begin by writing like one of the bewitched?
Why must I insist on presenting this rather subjective concluding
synthesis, which is for me only the coda to my plain chronicle, as a
prelude?

On the level of prudence, my defence is simple. Only a reader
who is already familiar with most of my material could possibly be
expected to follow the thread of my story as the chronicle unrolls
in all of its detail from the middle of the second chapter onwards;
some sort of prospectus is absolutely essential. And I cannot think
of a better way of providing it than by making a sort of general
summary of my own beliefs about the course of Hegel's intellectual
development, indicating as clearly as I can what elements in the
account are tainted by conjecture, but not seeking to justify any of
my assertions for the present. Written out in this way and in this
place it will be obvious, I trust, that my outline neither has nor
claims for itself any authority or independent validity. It simply
serves as a help in need for the uninitiated reader who is about to
embark upon the book, and as a confession of assumptions or
prejudices that may not always have been made explicit in the
course of the argument to the critical reader who has finished the
book. My hope is that if it does successfully explicate the book,
the book in turn will justify it.

The justification of my title must wait till the end of this Prelude.
But I can begin by explaining it. The metaphor of the sunlight,
which I have borrowed from a long-forgotten philosophical novel
that Hegel studied as a student, refers with apt ambiguity to all
the main sources of his youthful inspiration; and the young Hegel

himself used it to express the goal of all his endeavours. The reader should think first of the actual sunlight of Greece, the light that is so brilliantly evoked in Hölderlin's *Hyperion*. For this is the same sun that shone in the Athens of Aeschylus and Sophocles, of Pericles and Socrates. And then, secondly, he should think of the sunlight of Plato's ideal City, the sunlight outside the Cave to which Plato compared Athens after the death of Socrates. Thirdly, and most obviously of all to the young Hegel and his contemporaries, there is the sunlight of the *Aufklärung*, the light of reason shining in the community of free men. And if, finally, we extend this Platonic metaphor of the light of reason to embrace the 'inner light' of the Christian tradition, we can understand why Hegel chose to speak, with von Hippel, of 'striving toward the sun' as the way to the 'salvation of the human race'.

If we would picture once more the sun toward which the young Hegel strove we must allow all these lights to blend into one. We cannot even begin to understand the culture in which he grew up unless we are willing to let them blend, however odd the result may at times appear. For instance when Hegel read the *Phaedo* of Moses Mendelssohn as a schoolboy of fifteen, he did not distinguish between the historical Socrates, the Socrates of Plato, and the Socrates of Mendelssohn. To have done that would have been, in his eyes, an insult to all three of them, and to their authors human and divine. He was perfectly well able to make the distinctions, for he spent most of his time working on original texts and he displays from the first a quite sophisticated interest in historiography. But he saw himself as a student of the history of mankind seeking to define his own vocation as a man, and Socrates as *the* great teacher of mankind. He could appreciate that 'Socrates' did not use the same forms of argument in Plato's dialogue that he does in Mendelssohn's; but the essential doctrine (of human immortality) was the same, and this great truth about human nature and human destiny was what mattered, not the technicalities of argument and proof.

This belief that, as long as one has the right attitude, theoretical differences do not matter, was the essential error that Hegel had to overcome before he could begin seriously to be a philosopher in his own right. It was a belief that was widely prevalent in, indeed typical of, the Enlightenment; and it goes a long way to account for the fact that the age produced so little philosophical work of the first importance. Only Hume, who used theoretical reason with such extraordinary wit and subtlety to show us why we cannot rely on it, and Kant, who made 'the right attitude' (the moral law) into the fundamental form of reason itself, escaped the general mediocrity. Through his long struggle with Kant, Hegel finally found the way to justify and defend the pragmatic rationalism of his earliest mentors. We could properly name the young Hegel as one of the most important thinkers in the main stream of the Enlightenment, if it were not for the fact that, in finding his way, he transcended the boundaries of Enlightenment thought altogether, and provided us rather with a very carefully thought out statement of the Romantic position.

It may be that I have not brought out the classical humanist character of Hegel's education clearly enough—though I have tried to show how sound the scholarship involved in the formulation of his Greek ideal was. The body of evidence that has survived from his earliest studies is unrepresentative in this respect; it serves much better to illustrate his heritage from the philosophical culture of his own time. But it is clear from his school essays on classical themes that Hegel's relative indifference, not to say actual hostility, toward theoretical philosophy was nourished even more by his classical studies than by his readings in contemporary thinkers. His fundamental concern was to comprehend why knowledge was 'living' (practically effective) in some minds and 'dead' (merely theoretical) in others. He found his answer to this problem by contrasting the direct experience of the Greeks, with the indirect, verbally mediated, experience of his own culture. This contrast was so familiar as to be a cliché in writers like Lessing, and in lesser-known authors like Garve. But, even while he was still a schoolboy, Hegel endowed it with a depth and import that was hitherto unparalleled. The theory of two kinds of abstraction, which he deliberately injected into an excerpt that he made from Garve, is the first germ of his mature concept of the concrete universal. This was his first independent step as a philosopher, and the *only* important positive step that he took until his last summer in Berne (1796).

This significant fact points up one of my reasons for devoting careful attention even to Hegel's Stuttgart excerpts. But his schoolboy essays and excerpts merit the detailed attention which Lacorte was, as far as I know, the first to give them, even apart from this discovery, for which Lacorte must take the credit. For the attitude toward philosophy which these early papers reveal explains why Hegel made no important philosophical progress for such a long time.

When Hegel went to Tübingen he had to come to grips with that aspect of his own culture to which the 'enlightened' attitude was, either openly or secretly, opposed—the orthodox religious tradition. He had by this time defined his own vocation fairly clearly: he knew that he was going to be, like Socrates, a teacher, an enlightener of his own people in his own time, and ultimately of mankind. His new circumstances did not affect this resolve. He made it clear from the start that for him the study of Judaism and of Christian origins was simply an extension, a new dimension of, his study of human nature through cultural history, 'the philosophical history of humanity'. He went serenely on collecting and arranging his materials to the amusement of his friends and the irritation of at least some of his teachers.

At the beginning of his second year in the university (and his twentieth in the world) came the news of the Revolution in France. To Hegel, and to many of his fellow students, it appeared that the battle for enlightenment had now moved from the study to the market-place. For the first time his vocation as a scholar was called in question; he had already met, in Hölderlin, someone who shared his ambition to be a *Volkserzieher*, but who intended to answer the call in the high Greek fashion as a poet. Now, like Hölderlin, he thought of fulfilling his destiny through a career in the law. But his father would not listen to his plea; and he had to go on to the study of dogmatic theology—which was much less adaptable to the advancement of his own interests than Old and New Testament history.

The evidence for Hegel's development in these years is almost all indirect; and much that is necessary for a balanced understanding of the intellectual life of the *Tübingerstift* is still unpublished. It is possible, therefore, that I have given to Hegel's proposal to transfer to law after the completion of the Master's Degree a focal importance that it did not really have. I do not think this is likely, however, for my view rests on the only consistent and intelligible interpretation of the testimony of Hegel's friend Leutwein; and while the long brooding of that disappointed old man certainly distorted his judgement I think it also ensured the reliability of his factual memories.

Leutwein tells us that Hegel was not much interested in the current discussions of Kantian philosophy in the *Stift*. This is confirmed by remarks made and attitudes adopted later by Hegel himself in his letters. But he certainly *studied* Kant carefully in these years. During his second year he read the *Critique of Pure Reason* and quite a lot of other philosophical works. If he had not already read the *Critique of Practical Reason* by then he certainly read it before very long. The second Critique was, after all, the latest, and by universal consent the best, new statement of those fundamental practical doctrines that the great teachers of humanity have always preached. For this reason, if for no other, the would-be *Volkserzieher* realized that he must master and learn to use the theoretical structure of concepts in which the latest gospel of reason was embedded. So Hegel appropriated the doctrine of the first Critique as the basis for his own articulation of human psychology. (The evidence for this is in his *rewriting* of his notes in 1794; but there is no reason to suppose that his attitude was different when the notes were first made.)

His study of dogmatic theology under Storr compelled Hegel for the first time to examine carefully the theoretical foundations of his own position. This was Storr's great merit, that he forced Hegel to examine the assumptions of the critical philosophy carefully. For Storr and his followers claimed that Kant's arguments really supported a set of conclusions which absolutely undermined and overthrew the comfortable faith that there was an invisible church to which all rational men belonged, and that to follow reason as well as one could was all that was necessary to salvation. In defence of this fundamental conviction—which was the basis for his complacent acceptance of the variety of philosophical opinions—Hegel had to enter the lists on behalf of the particular opinion that he had himself espoused. In due course his efforts to formulate the right interpretation of Kant brought him face to face with those aspects of Kant's doctrine that were irreconcilable with his Hellenic ideal. And so, as he turned from defending Kant to criticizing him, he stumbled backwards and almost involuntarily, into the attempt to provide a more adequate philosophical basis for the expression of that ideal.

This gradual retreat from Kant was a retreat from the *Critique of Practical Reason*; and specifically from Kant's formulation of the 'postulates of practical reason'. There was no corresponding retreat from the *Critique of Pure Reason*: on the theoretical side the philosophical expression of the ideal involved rather an advance from a merely pragmatic adoption of Kant's position (for purposes of argument and effective communication) to its justification as the highest expression of reflective thought. But even so the standpoint of reflection was still subordinated to the higher standpoint of life itself. Hegel's ideal was not in the end a philosophical but a religious-aesthetic one; and, though we cannot prove it, there is every reason to believe that that is what it was at the beginning too.

Just how this ideal of human existence was articulated into the 'theory' of the ἐν καὶ πᾶν in its earliest form I cannot tell. It is just barely possible, I suppose, that at the very beginning the ἐν καὶ πᾶν was more of a philosophical theory than anything we find in the Frankfurt manuscripts. But in view of the way in which Hegel subsequently borrows his theoretical terminology wholesale from Kant and Fichte, from Schelling, and then from Hölderlin it seems certain that he began simply with a contrast between two kinds of religious experience. At any rate this is all that appears explicitly in the first major essay that we have—the so-called Tübingen fragment. This is an important and interesting essay, but it can only be called 'philosophical' in a very extended sense. All of the important practical conclusions are taken for granted. The problem is how to make these conclusions existentially effective, and the answer, so far as it is explicit at all, is that they must be existentially acquired, they must be lived. The only constructive philosophical argument in the essay is the defence of the three essential conditions for an effective folk-religion; but these canons are not applied in any recognizably logical way. We have to infer what they really mean from what Hegel says about his great historical exemplar, the Greeks. Thus it is not instantly obvious how 'the teachings' of Greek religion 'are grounded in universal reason'; and it is fairly clear that Kant's 'religion within the bounds of reason' does 'send fancy, heart and sensibility empty away'. But in the body of the essay the first of these problems is virtually ignored, and the second is glossed over with only the faintest hint of a blush. The real appeal is to a kind of aesthetic intuition by which we read off the ideal from the historical record, and a kind of creative imagination by which we can reintegrate the fugitive glimpses that the record supplies into a unified and stable vision.

Hegel explicitly tells us that in analysing out the three canons of folk-religion ('Its teachings must be grounded on universal reason', 'Fancy, heart and sensibility must not be sent empty away', and 'It must be so constituted that all the needs of life—the public affairs of the state are tied in with it') he is treating the concept 'objectively'. There is from the beginning a gulf between philosophical argument and reasoning—which is bound to be 'objective'—and the 'subjective' reality of religion with which he is concerned. But although 'reason*ing*' belongs to the 'objective' plane, 'Reason' itself does not. Socrates talking to his friends on his last day is a model of *subjective* rationality, for he knows his audience well, and his arguments simply bring out the meaning of their actual life-experience. The young man who packed up his papers for the journey to Berne no longer believed, like the Stuttgart schoolboy, that the Deism of the enlightened moderns was an advance over the polytheism of the unenlightened ancients. He was even prepared to say that Lessing's *Nathan* was a work of *Verstand*. But he held firmly to the faith in *Vernunft* as opposed to *Verstand* which he owed, in great part, to *Nathan*. There might be a gulf between theoretical philosophizing and actual religion; but it was nevertheless true that actual religion came to its final fruition in practical philosophy.

For this reason the abstract 'canons' which are so far removed from the living experience of religion, continue to dominate and determine the whole course of Hegel's subsequent reflections; and for this reason too, the first canon—which seems farthest of all from the living experience of *Greek* religion—must come first. When Hegel wrote in 1795 that 'the aim and essence of all true religion, our religion included, is human morality' he was merely explaining what the first canon means and why it is placed first. But the course of his reflections, and particularly the *form* that he sought to give to his results, is determined also by the fundamental imperative of the *Volkserzieher*—that what is *objectively* known must be made *subjectively* effective. At the end of the Tübingen essay he is about to enliven his living image of the Greek spirit still further by presenting us with a contrasting image of the modern spirit. But he stops himself and turns aside; and from his struggles over the next few months we can see why. The moral effect of *that* contrast would merely be to induce despair; for the Greek spirit has 'flown', we cannot bring it to life *in practice*. Our

religion has its origins in a different tradition, and our religious
teacher is not Socrates but Jesus.

The true character of Jesus, and the relation of his message to
that of the modern apostle of reason, Kant, was a focus of controversy in the intellectual life of the *Stift*. Storr emphasized the
Messianic character of Jesus, his fulfilment of prophetic promises;
and he underlined the *prophetic* aspect of the Gospel message,
presenting it as a promise, or complex of promises, guaranteed by
miraculous deeds. On the other side, the 'Kantian *enragé*' Karl
Diez went so far as to claim that Jesus was a deceiver and Kant
himself was the true Messiah. Hegel only became involved when
Storr appealed to Kant's newly published essay on *Religion* as
evidence for his own view that *Vernunft* actually *needed* the supernatural guarantees of the Gospel promise. At this point Hegel
clearly felt that both Jesus and Kant must be defended, if the unity
and self-sufficiency of Reason was to be preserved. He shared the
conviction of all those 'enlighteners' who recognized their own
debt to the Gospel, that Jesus was a true teacher of mankind; but
he shared also their contempt for superstition, and he regarded all
heteronomous ethics, with its twin pillars of reward and punishment, as a merely transitional, though inescapable, aspect of the
growth of *Vernunft*. The pitch of Kantian orthodoxy to which his
Jesus rises is probably a reaction to the attacks of Diez, just as
much as the rigorous exclusion of everything prophetic and miraculous is a response to the claims of Storr. But Hegel's picture was
meant to be true to life in the same sense that Mendelssohn's
Socrates was meant to be true to life.

Hegel was not the only one in his own circle in the *Stift* to
conceive the idea of giving a Kantian interpretation of the Scriptures. Hölderlin toyed with the same idea and among the earliest,
still unpublished, manuscripts of Schelling are Kantian commentaries on some of the Pauline Epistles. But unlike Schelling Hegel
was no longer in the *Stift* when he wrote his *Life of Jesus*. His essay
was the first step in the reintegration of Christianity as a folk-
religion; the restored portrait of its founder as one of the true sages.
Any Christian who accepted this 'restoration' would be bound to
ask how the initial corruption of the record had come about. If
Hegel was to maintain his claim that 'the practical teachings [of
Christianity] are pure' he had to answer this question. And in
essence the problem was very like that of interpreting Socrates'

last words, a problem which recurs several times in Hegel's early manuscripts. It differed only in the magnitude of its practical import. In order to understand Socrates' last words we have to comprehend Greek religion, especially the place of sacrifice in it, and the character of Asclepius as the god of healing. In order to understand why Jesus assumed the Messianic role we have to comprehend the authoritarian character of Judaism: the only way in which the autonomy of the free rational agent could be asserted in this situation of absolute heteronomy was by claiming an authority equal to that of God himself and directly received from him. The Messianic hope offered the one way for Jesus to do this, so he seized on it; but at the same time he strove to make clear in every way possible that he was not claiming divine authority for himself exclusively, and he did not exercise authority over others at all.

In the society of the enlightened there can be no authority at all save that of reason. Hence the spirit of true religion is opposed to all institutionalized authority. Since all the institutions of his culture were authoritarian Jesus could not be blamed for turning away from the public life of his people altogether. But this was the moment of his failure. For a healthy folk-religion is necessarily a public religion; it invests and embraces all the normal activities and institutions of a healthy public life, i.e. a political society of free citizens. Political freedom, however, is freedom within the bounds set by a law which is enforced by external authority where necessary. So how can a genuinely rational religion be *public* at all?

This was the problem which Hegel was faced with, when he completed his purging of Christian doctrine. Christianity was born in a tyrannous society; it triumphed in a tyrannous world. How could it take the place proper to true religion in a free world? Reason, as Hegel understood it, was the synthesis of freedom with law. Every free man arrives at his conclusions and decisions for himself; but in their imperative aspect these autonomous conclusions are all expressions of one law. Thus great diversity, even contradiction of opinions, can subsist along with uniformity or harmony in action. Religion is the power by which, ideally, the variety of individual talents and tendencies are harmonized and reconciled, so that they do not conflict harmfully with one another or with the law. Reason itself can show us that there must be conflict of opinion and there must be freedom of conscience; but what sort of religion is it, then, that can save us from anarchy?

The Greek answer, already given in the Tübingen essay, was: a religion of the imagination, a religion of *myth*. When I wrote the main body of my text, I did not even suspect, still less believe as I do now, that Hegel was the author of the 'earliest system-programme of German idealism'. But even without that clinching piece of evidence I could see that the writing of *Eleusis* was linked with the 'continuation' of the essay on 'The Positivity of the Christian Religion' by Hegel's sense of the superiority of myth as the medium for the expression of religious truth. In mythical form the objective truth becomes subjective: it takes hold of us and moves us to action because 'fancy, heart, and sensibility are not sent empty away'. But no less important is the fact that in a conflict of myths we are not forced to choose as we are in a conflict of opinions. We are not obliged to sacrifice one or the other or else both for the sake of a third which is better than either. We can reconcile and harmonize them by perceiving different aspects of the truth in each. This was the point whose significance Hegel had not fully grasped in the Tübingen essay, or he would never have let religion become merely 'an old friend in the house' of the Greek spirit in its maturity. *Eleusis* is Hegel's testimony that the Greek spirit has not after all 'flown'; the Gods of Olympus are still there to answer the greeting of their fully enlightened worshipper. And so within a few months of his first explicit recognition of Kant's *theoretical* achievement (in the postscript of the 'Positivity' essay written in April 1796) the star of Kant's *practical* philosophy, long in the ascendant in Hegel's mind, begins to set. The highest act of *Vernunft* is no longer a practical one—it is *aesthetic*.

To find the right *application* of his new insight, to make his objective knowledge subjective, was still a problem for Hegel when he went to Frankfurt. He found his answer when he stopped concentrating on the myths in which folk-religion is expressed, and began to study the history of the religious experience of different peoples in its relation to their political experience. For in this context the aesthetic object of the folk-religion is revealed as the object of the people's *love*. The 'philosophical history of humanity' which Hegel had dreamed of as a schoolboy now peeps out from behind his sketches and studies of the 'spirit and fate' of Judaism and Christianity in the shape of an ideal pattern of cultural development

analogous to the life cycle of the rational individual. Thus the
religion of Abraham is the absolutely exclusive consciousness of the
tribe or blood-clan, which corresponds to the 'primitive unity' of
the undeveloped seed; and the 'fate' of the culture that persists in
this 'oneness' is to be alienated from all other life and to become
slavishly dependent upon the divine source of life—the ἐν και παν
of the Tübingen years—conceived as an absolute Lord and Master.
When a culture is in this disrupted state, *Vernunft* takes the form of
Verstand: that is to say it takes reflective cognizance of the gulf
(*Trennung*) between man's 'fallen' state and his 'natural' or ideal
condition, and strives to overcome it by postulating the conditions
for the healing of the rupture and the establishment of universal
peace and harmony. But reason cannot by its own power do away
with the rupture which it has already acknowledged and justified;
and hence all forms of reflective religion—even the highest form,
the religion of reason as we find it in Kant—are forms of *positive*
religion. It is the peculiar nemesis of the 'religion of reason',
through which man is at last set free from all arbitrary and alien
authorities, that in this form of absolute consciousness the *Trennung* is made absolute. The light of reason is the light in which no
man living can be justified. Every man becomes his own judge, but
in every case the judge can do nothing but utter sentence of eternal
condemnation. So even Kant must conceive the Divine Lawgiver
as a focus of arbitrary power, for reason cannot reconcile man with
the fate that arises when his nature is once ruptured, and it cannot
comprehend the reconciliation when it occurs.

   The power that does enable man to rise above fate, and above
the justice or 'righteousness' that is the absolute object of reflective
rationality, is called by Hegel simply 'love'. For anyone who wants
to understand or to expound Hegel's 'philosophy' at this stage of
its development this is a cause of difficulty, since, on the one hand,
all forms of religion are forms of 'love', and on the other hand, what
Hegel calls the spirit of 'love' absolutely still falls short of what he
calls the spirit of 'religion' absolutely. But Hegel, though he does
now have a 'philosophy' of his own, and is no longer a client of
Kant or of the Enlightenment generally, is still not directly concerned with it, and attaches merely instrumental importance to it.
He now has a second-order theory to account for the gulf between
abstract doctrine and concrete experience in the Tübingen essay,
but he still regards it as a product of mere reflection; and what

matters to him is to show us how to rise above the level of reflection altogether. For this the stark contrast between the morality of reason and the spirit of love is quite sufficient.

The spirit of absolute love is the spirit of Jesus—who thus emerges as a greater sage than Kant after all, and indeed as something more than a sage altogether. Jesus is reconciled with all life, and the source of all life is for him no longer a 'Lord' but a 'Father'. He is thus the exact antithesis of Abraham; and his 'fate'—for though he rises above fate, and does not fight against it, yet he does not escape it—is to lose his own life, the one thing that was guaranteed to Abraham, in his seed, forever. Forfeiture of life is in Hegel's view the universal fate of Christian love, though the mode of forfeiture varies with the degree of self-consciousness and actual effectiveness of the love itself.

The religion of love is the absolute consciousness of that moment of consummation in individual life when a new life, a human child, is begotten; and the community of love is the community of the 'sons of God', the divine power that 'acts and creates' in the moment when a human union 'has become unsundered' in the offspring (my little echoes here come, of course, from the celebrated fragment on 'Love'). Against this consciousness of unsundered life it would seem that fate cannot arise; and in one sense this is true. Jesus does not encounter his own acts risen up against him in the guise of an alien power. But he suffers, none the less; and his 'fate' in the ordinary sense is to die in circumstances of extreme suffering. This actually is a limiting case of 'fate' in Hegel's sense, for although Jesus does not do violence to the integrity of life in the sense of acting against it, he is guilty of absolute violence towards it because he *refuses* to act or to live his life within the natural bounds of life at all. The 'Son of God' denies his human parentage, he does not marry or have children, and he tells his followers to ignore the 'unwritten law' that Antigone obeys in the burial of her brother. He preserves the innocence of 'oneness', and so incurs the guilt of doing violence to *every* facet of his nature by denying its development. The torture of his body in every part which he undergoes in the Crucifixion is a strikingly exact image of what he himself does to the 'manifoldness' of life— the manifoldness of which the infant body as it takes shape in the womb of the mother is only the primal expression.

The fate of the 'Kingdom of God' is analogous to that of the

'Son of God'. The community of beautiful souls is marred by any activity that sets one of them or any group of them apart from the rest. All that they can really do together is to eat and drink to maintain life; and all that any of them can do on behalf of the community as a whole is to 'preach the Gospel'. As Jesus had been a 'private' person, fleeing from life in 'the world', so his Church was bound to be a private association. But the zeal for purity and for the Gospel is easily corrupted into fanaticism and persecution: Jesus himself was betrayed by one of the supposedly pure souls, and his Church took the image of the crucified man, who ought to have been forgotten in the glory of the risen Christ, as its image of divinity.

The presence of the divinity in a permanent and sensible form is vital to any religion that expresses the consciousness of a harmonious and fully developed life. This is one of the crucial ways in which the extreme of 'love', like the extreme of 'hostility', falls short of 'the middle course of beauty between the extremes'. But also, as Hegel showed in his brief analysis of the marriage tie, the love that generates life cannot express itself in the material aspects of life; in particular all forms of property rights are alien to it. Thus when *this* love is raised to the level of religion it becomes an 'otherworldly' thing, and is as impoverished as the 'worldliness' of the Jewish spirit.

Life itself develops in a non-living environment; and it needs this opposed material world to work on and to express itself in. This is what Hegel meant by the dictum, which is almost as celebrated as it is obscure, that 'life is the union of union and non-union'. The love which is the perfection of *this* union, the love that is the fulfilled harmony of life, is the love that creates beauty; and the paradigm of the absolute consciousness of this love is Greek religion—the 'religion of art' as Hegel will call it in the *Phenomenology*. It is fairly clear that the last great Frankfurt manuscript was indeed a statement of Hegel's 'system'. It contained at least a summary account of Hegel's philosophy, his theory of 'reflection' and of 'life', and it culminated by giving at least the abstract outline of a new Christian mythology in which the Holy Family replaced the Crucified Jesus as the focal image. I think it likely that between these two elements came an outline of Hegel's political philosophy in its religious aspects, so that the treatise as a whole showed how Christianity could be reinterpreted to satisfy not only the second canon of folk-religion but the third as well.

If so then we may hazard the further surmise that it is only the loss of this manuscript that has caused any doubt to arise about the authorship of the 'earliest system-programme'.

In what remains from Hegel's early political and economic writings there is very little that relates directly to the third canon of folk-religion. But we have the second half of the 'Positivity' essay, and some reports of his subsequent reflections on the relation of Church and State; and in the *Verfassungsschrift* we have enough discussion of the problem of the 'religious rights', both of citizens and of states within the Empire, to enable us to appreciate the practical function of Hegel's new Christian mythology. And it is worth noticing in this connection that Hegel's ultimate theoretical position, which puts religion on a higher plane than philosophical reflection altogether, coheres with the claim of the 'system-programme' that there is a realm of spiritual freedom above and beyond the authority structure of the State altogether; just as, on the other side, the initial formulation of the third canon confirms the essentially political character of religious experience.

For the most part, however, Hegel is concerned in his early political writings with the establishment of constitutional structures capable of sustaining the political freedom of the Germans as a single 'folk'. The basic practical premise of all his labours for the reform of Christianity was the belief that the French Revolution signalled the birth of a new age for all of Europe. The conditions for political change, and specifically for the re-establishment of popular freedom, already existed; and the transformation of existing authority-structures might begin at any moment. If Germany was to escape the agonies of France in the Terror, it would be at least partly because her religious thinkers could produce better food for the soul than the French revolutionaries with their Goddess of Reason. It is very noticeable that when the political crisis seems imminent, Hegel sets aside everything else in order to throw what weight he can into the scales. And in all of these unpublished manuscripts he has something of the air, which Marx retained all his life, of a man straining not to be overtaken by events that are already in train.

But never was there such a liberal-conservative revolutionary as the young Hegel. Unlike many of the 'enlighteners' whom he revered, he did not admire the English constitution. He felt that it was decadent, that it had become the cloak of ministerial tyranny;

and he felt the same way about the constitution of his native Württemberg, which was so often compared with that of England. So his programme of political action for Württemberg was rather more radical than was fashionable. He wanted to see power placed in the hands of a group of 'independent citizens', without too much regard for the constitutional niceties until such time as a reform had been carried through and stabilized. One is reminded here of such ancient institutions as the Dictatorship at Rome, and of the legislators or legislative commissions in Greek cities. And the parallel is an apt one, because the object of Hegel's proposed commission would have been the restoration of the 'ancestral constitution'. The new gospel of universal equality was not for him. His ideal was not Athenian democracy but a corporate body in which the different 'estates' had differing rights and responsibilities. He probably knew fairly exactly just who was to be on his Württemberg reform commission; but in spite of the precedent of Georg Forster at Mainz it was probably rather utopian to hope—if indeed he did hope—that a French army was going to put that group into power and then let them do as they thought fit. It is more likely, I think, that Hegel hoped that the fear of French arms and the spectre of a more radical revolution would scare the Duke and other interested parties in the establishment into accepting a 'rectification' in the way in which the reforms of the legislator or dictator were accepted in ancient times.

It was his programme for the Germans as a nation, however, that was integral to his work as a religious reformer. Here he was at once more radical and more conservative; and his proposed *modus operandi* in this arena was one that was not merely written about, but actually employed, in the politics of the Enlightenment. The constitution of Württemberg, whether one admired it or not, was still functional, whereas the political structure of the Empire was in the last stages of ossification and decay. As Hegel said, 'Germany is a state no longer'; and as he showed in his analysis, it never had become a modern state at all. But he nevertheless believed that out of the ruins of the old feudal state a unique synthesis of local spontaneity and central authority could be built; and he looked to Austria for an enlightened despot to carry out the plan. In view of the reforms achieved by Joseph II within Austria itself this was not an impossible hope. But it presupposed victory for the armies of Austria with resultant prestige and authority for Archduke Karl.

In fact the French triumphed in the field, and were even more effective in manipulating the German Estates at the conference table; the material conditions for the realization of Hegel's dream perished at the hands of Napoleon.

I believe that the triumph of Napoleon within France itself convinced Hegel, soon after the turn of the century, that the revolution was not going to take the course that he and his friends had assumed. He recognized that the *kairos*, the moment of opportunity within which his vocation as a *Volkserzieher* had been conceived and defined, had passed. If this belief is correct, there is a deeper irony in Hegel's famous remark in 1806 that he had seen 'this world-soul' riding through Jena to a review, than has generally been recognized. For in 1806 'this world-soul' merely happened in an accidental way to deprive Hegel temporarily of his means of subsistence. But in his actual emergence as 'world-soul' he had already prevented the birth of the world to which Hegel sought to give a soul.

Whether Hegel laid down his pen in 1802 because he actually perceived this, we shall never know. It may very well be that he stopped his work for the time being because of the pressure of his other concerns, and never returned to it because by the time he was able to do so, which may have been a long time later, he could see that the moment for it was gone. I feel sure, in any case, that the reason for his failure to publish any of the manuscripts of these early years is that he became convinced that his work was not after all of any practical use. He had striven from the beginning to 'apply' philosophy—first a philosophy borrowed largely from others, and then a philosophy that was largely his own—to the realization of an ideal that was very much his own, but which was always historical and imaginative rather than philosophical. A reader who is attracted to the kind of existential thinking that Hegel did in these early years may object to my refusal to give it the title of 'philosophy'. But I am only following the lead of Hegel himself. He began, certainly, by using philosophical terminology for it. He distinguishes for a long time between the theoretical reflection which is the work of *Verstand*, and concrete meditation upon the *Ideen* of practical reason. But this concrete meditation is always more intuitive and imaginative than it is logical and discursive. Historical imagination is always more important than reasoned understanding in Hegel's 'philosophical history of mankind'. And when Hegel arrives at full consciousness of the imaginative, aesthetic character of his own method he firmly denies that this level of consciousness should be called philosophical. He calls it religious—thus preserving its practical import—and asserts that religion is *higher* than philosophy, i.e. that aesthetic intuition is higher than either practical reason or theoretical understanding.

With this full consciousness of his own method, however, we have reached a moment of equilibrium of the kind that can prove to be either a resting-place or a watershed, a point of radical conversion. For Hegel it proved to be the latter. For in order to achieve an adequate theoretical understanding of his own undertaking he had to take theoretical philosophy far more seriously than he had done to begin with. The few pages of the *Systemfragment* in which he discusses the way in which religious experience transcends all forms of reflective reason are written not only in a style that strikes all readers as prophetic of his maturity, but in a vein of *theoretical* earnestness that we have hardly encountered before in Hegel's manuscripts. It is no surprise to find that at Jena the religious-aesthetic intuition that we meet here, first becomes a theoretical or intellectual intuition, and then develops into the discursive mode of expression that typifies Hegel's later systematic works. When he wrote the *Systemfragment* Hegel had already decided to become a professional philosopher if he could. I think it is fair to say that already, about two years before he surrenders his old vocation, he has heard the call of the new one. He has heard it but he does not yet know what it is, or where it leads. He stands on the brink of becoming a philosopher in the full sense, committed to understanding the world, rather than to changing it. But he does not yet know that this is his sun, he has not yet come out of the Cave into the world of Absolute Knowledge, the sunlight of the Absolute Idea. It is a steep and difficult slope that he has yet to climb—as everyone knows who has tried to read the Jena manuscripts. The present book is the story of his sojourn among the shadows and the picture-makers. It is only meet and right that its title should be a picture-maker's metaphor. And all of us who find the slope of Hegel's theoretical works precipitous, and the aether of the Absolute generally rather hard to breathe, will never cease to be grateful that Hegel did not lose, forget, or ever quite neglect, the image-making skill that he learned as a cave-dweller, in the days when he believed that it was his destiny to be an interpreter of the shadows.

I. STUTTGART: 1770-1788

The Vocation of a Scholar

1. The background of home and school

GEORG WILHELM FRIEDRICH HEGEL was born at Stuttgart on 27 August 1770. He was the eldest son of Georg Ludwig Hegel, who was a minor financial official in the court of the Duchy of Württemberg. The family had been in Swabia for nearly a hundred and fifty years, ever since an artisan named Johannes Hegel left Carinthia for the sake of his Protestant faith, when the Austrian emperors sought to stamp out heresy in their dominions after the Council of Trent. The strength of this ancestor's Lutheran convictions is less important, however, than the fact that the Duchy to which he came was itself a Protestant enclave almost entirely surrounded by Catholic territories. For this circumstance not only helped to keep alive in his descendants something of the fervour that brought him there; it also ensured that the young Wilhelm would grow up with a keen awareness of the existence of religious differences and with the conviction that these differences have momentous consequences.

Johannes's descendants were, for the most part, minor civil servants, teachers, and Lutheran ministers. One of Wilhelm's uncles was a teacher at the Stuttgart Gymnasium, and the nine-year-old professor-to-be duly passed through his class.[1] It seems

[1] Was it perhaps this uncle Göriz of whom the fifteen-year-old student was thinking when he wrote the obituary notice for the much loved and admired teacher of his first two years, Löffler, in which he comments that Löffler 'was not low minded, like some others who think, now they have got their living made, they need not study any more'? Hegel must surely have had some one or more of his teachers in the higher grades in mind, for he goes on to bewail the ill luck that compelled Löffler to work 'entirely beneath his proper level' [*ganz unter seine Sphäre*]' (*Dok.*, p. 12). It is more probable, however, that he was thinking of Jonathan Lenz, under whose tutelage he passed his fourth school year (1780–1). For Lenz was an avowed adherent of the old-fashioned ways and an apologist

C

to have been clear from the beginning that Wilhelm was destined for an academic career, or for the Church. He received his first lessons in Latin from his mother even before he went to the 'Latin school' at the age of five; and he was an apt and eager learner. His mother, who was better educated than most women of her time and station, was delighted with his rapid progress and encouraged him in all his studies. She died in 1781, when Wilhelm was eleven, of a 'bilious fever' which threatened also for a time to carry off Wilhelm and his father. The family by then numbered three children, the other two being a sister Christiane (born 1773) and a younger brother Ludwig who grew up to be a soldier. Christiane always watched the career of her older brother with deep interest and sisterly affection. It is from a letter of hers written to Hegel's widow shortly after his death that we learn what a model student he was at the Gymnasium, heading his class regularly year after year from the age of ten until he went to the University of Tübingen when he was eighteen.[1]

His gastric illness at eleven was Wilhelm's second serious sickness; he had already been near to death with the smallpox when he was six. He was a clumsy child, ungainly in movement and in speech, a fact which was regretfully noted by his teachers as a serious hindrance to a career in the ministry. His physical ineptitude may well have helped to fix his scholarly inclinations, and to stir his ambitions in that direction; but he was never shy or withdrawn, being rather social and friendly by nature, and cheerfully equable in disposition.

In his school years he would seem to have been an omnivorous student, who managed to enjoy everything put before him, and accepted it generally at the valuation placed upon it by his instructors. Christiane wrote that his favourite science in his last years at the Gymnasium was physics; but she also remarked on his early love of Greek tragedy, and from the diary that he kept sporadically from fourteen to sixteen we can see that a love of history and

---

for the precept 'Spare the rod and spoil the child'. (On Lenz see Klaiber, pp. 75 ff., or Lacorte, p. 65; and for a correction of Hoffmeister's surmise in *Dok.*, p. 402, about the identity of C. F. Göriz see Lacorte, p. 61 n. 6.)

[1] For the letter of 7 Jan. 1832 and other notes about Hegel's youth that stem from Christiane, see *Dok.*, pp. 392–4. (Most of the letter is translated in Wiedmann, pp. 11–12.) It appears that Christiane misremembered the year of her mother's death. According to the family tree given by Hoffmeister (at the end of *Briefe*, iv), she died on 20 Sept. 1781 (not 1783).

literature was one of his earliest passions. The teacher who did much to mould his early interests in this direction was a man named Löffler, who was his first instructor at the Gymnasium for two years (from 1777 to 1779) and gave him special lessons in Latin and Greek at intervals in following years. Löffler died about two months before Hegel's fifteenth birthday, and the young Wilhelm purchased from the widow a number of his teacher's books. He recorded these purchases in his diary (with the prices paid), and on the following day he added an account of the classes and private instruction he had received from Löffler. Finally, the next day, he concluded with an obituary judgement of Löffler's character and worth. Hegel praised Löffler for being open-minded (*unparteiisch*) and for always keeping up his own studies instead of sinking into a repetitive classroom routine. One of the most interesting and indicative comments in the whole record is the afterthought in which he remarks that Löffler made him a present of eighteen volumes of Shakespeare's plays (in a German translation) when he was still only eight.[1]

The eleven years that Hegel spent at the Stuttgart Gymnasium Illustre (1777–88) belonged to an important period of transition in the history of the school. A full-scale reform of the curriculum only came in the years 1794 to 1796, some six years after he had gone on to the University of Tübingen; but the great pedagogical impulse of the Enlightenment and the first stirrings of reform were felt much sooner, and piecemeal 'modernization' of the curriculum began about 1775. The basic classical emphasis in the curriculum remained untouched, but there was an attempt to make it serve 'pragmatic' purposes: for instance, it was decreed that passages for translation should be concerned with 'useful and pleasant' subjects

[1] *Dok.*, pp. 11–13 (Diary for 5–7 July 1785). The number 'eighteen' is certainly a mistake of some sort. Rosenkranz says (p. 7) that the Shakespeare gift was Wieland's edition (Zürich, 1762–6, 8 vols.). Hoffmeister thinks this is another mistake but I do not see how he can be so sure of this, merely on the basis of Christiane Hegel's remembering (in 1832) that the gift was the Eschenberg edition (Zürich, 1775–7, 12 vols.). After all, Rosenkranz had Christiane's letter in front of him, and was continually referring to it in this part of his work; so we might well argue that he would not have departed from what she says without having solid reasons for believing that she was mistaken (e.g. he may have found the books in Hegel's library). Of course, Rosenkranz may simply have decided that "XVIII Bände" was meant to be read as "VIII Bände"; and if he was right about that—which could perhaps be determined by a re-examination of the manuscript—the gift may still have been *eight* volumes of the Eschenburg edition.

related to ordinary life, and the teachers of theology and philosophy were asked to concentrate especially on the formation of character (*die Bildung des Herzens*). The sciences were given a greater place in the curriculum than before, and the study of German literature, along with mastery of the native tongue, gradually assumed a position of fundamental importance. But the 'modern spirit' (*Genius der modernen Zeit*) to which official directives often referred —and the champions of reform doubtless did so even more often— was not without its opponents; and our 'model student' Wilhelm must certainly have been forced to use his own judgement about it, for among the teachers at the Gymnasium were several, notably Balthasar Haug and one Jonathan Lenz, whose class Hegel passed through in 1780–1, who were its declared foes.[1]

A deep concern with what might be called the 'education of humanity' in the widest sense forms the main nerve of Hegel's earliest philosophical speculation, and this concern remained always one of his fundamental interests. It is tempting to trace the birth of it to his early awareness of his vocation as a scholar, combined with his recognition of the great gulf that lies between the living pursuit of scholarship, and pedantic insistence upon traditional authority. At the very least we must recognize that from the time that Löffler's death caused him to reflect upon the matter, Hegel consciously felt that the pursuit of scholarship must be enlivened by a moral purpose. Just a few months before this he had begun to make a systematic record of his studies in and out of school, thereby establishing a habit which he maintained steadily for the rest of his life.[2] Only a part of this early record has come down to us, but we have from Rosenkranz, his first biographer, a

---

[1] These summary remarks are based on the discussion in Lacorte, pp. 61–5; some details have also been derived from Klaiber, pp. 71–82.

[2] The earliest excerpts from his reading that have come down to us are dated 22 Apr. 1785 ('Plan der Normal-Schulen in Rußland' from Schlözer's *Staats-Anzeigen*) and 5 May 1785 (the only date given for the long series from Feder's *Neuer Emil* which must certainly have occupied him for a week or two). These two are the only ones which are earlier than the dramatic script 'Unterredung zwischen Dreien', which was written for submission to a teacher and which Rosenkranz (p. 17) calls 'the earliest, first product of Hegel's authorship'. From one or two indications—such as the incompleteness of the dating and the fact that Feder's *Emil* is excerpted continuously rather than topically, so that Hegel was later obliged to put a cross-reference slip to certain parts of this excerpt into his files under a new heading, we may fairly infer that these two extracts were among the first that he made (see *Dok.*, pp. 54, 55, and for the cross-reference slip, *Dok.*, p. 140 n. 1.).

fairly complete description of the collection of notes and extracts which Hegel made at school and University, and which was still preserved among his papers at the time of his death.[1]

The fact that Hegel preserved so carefully the accumulated results of his own first steps in scholarly research, taking them with him from place to place in later years, along with the manuscripts of his lectures and all his other academic papers, could, of course, be dismissed as merely another manifestation of that same obsessive concern with the systematic deployment of all his knowledge and all his experience, which caused the precocious and rather priggish would-be professor to begin his records at the age of fourteen. From this point of view, we should have to regard it as a mere foible—one of the pedantic frailties of a remarkably comprehensive intelligence. But the more carefully we examine the actual content of this early record, the more clearly we see that its preservation was justified by the fact of its essential continuity with all of Hegel's later work. It was, in a fairly literal and self-conscious sense, the beginning of a life's work, and in all the subsequent phases of development that we shall discover in his thought, Hegel remained always so close to the programme which seems to have guided his earliest researches, that he could reasonably expect to find many of his schoolboy records useful.

He made his records by carefully excerpting from the books that he read, or studied, the passages that seemed important for his purposes. Almost from the beginning he seems to have recognized that these purposes might vary, or rather (I believe) that the execution of his purpose would be facilitated if he made his record in the most flexible way. So he copied the passages that interested him on to separate sheets of paper with index headings to show as clearly and conveniently as possible the subject-matter or point of the extract. He also noted carefully the source of each one and the date on which he had copied it out. The main idea that guided him in his selection and arrangement of passages, was the desire to gain a clear understanding of human nature in all its aspects, and to understand the historical development of different cultures. As he would most probably have expressed it himself, he was assembling materials for a 'philosophical history of humanity'.[2]

---

[1] Rosenkranz, pp. 12–15; reprinted in *Dok.*, pp. 398–400. For an analysis of Rosenkranz's account see Table 1 at the end of this chapter.

[2] Compare the discussion in pp. 26–30 below; cf. also p. 52 n. 3.

Behind this project lay a personal concern. Hegel was in all respects a model student. He did his school work with tremendous thoroughness, and he enjoyed it. He was almost by instinct a scholar, and while still young he was accepted as a friend on more or less equal terms by older men, not only among his teachers, who were themselves scholars or appreciated scholarship.[1] He imbibed both from them and from his reading the general conviction of the Enlightenment that proper education was the great instrument of human progress; and both by temperament and by upbringing he was disposed to believe that each individual must strive to be useful to society and contribute to its advancement. He recognized his own vocation as a scholar, and he wished to clarify it for himself: that is to say he wished to understand the social use and purpose of the kind of education that he was receiving and enjoying. Rosenkranz remarks that 'Hegel's education [*Bildung*] belonged entirely to the Enlightenment with respect to principle, and entirely to classical antiquity with respect to curriculum'.[2] This judgement needs to be interpreted with caution, for we must not be led into the mistake of thinking that the 'principles' of the Enlightenment are clearly distinguishable from those of the classical humanistic tradition. In one of its aspects the Enlightenment was a continuation and development of Renaissance humanism; and it is to this branch of the Enlightenment—for which the names of Montesquieu and Gibbon may well serve as representative symbols—that Hegel's education and earliest inspiration belongs. Nevertheless Rosenkranz's way of putting the matter is accurate and illuminating in the sense that it brings clearly into focus the tension for which this aspect of the Enlightenment provided a resolution. A humanist imbued with the *Genius der modernen Zeit* was bound to face the question 'What use is all your historical and literary erudition to the progress of the human race?' This was the question from which Hegel's independent philosophical and scholarly researches began.

Of course, the young Hegel did not merely want to understand the use of humanistic scholarship; he wanted to be a good scholar. He laboured with passionate assiduity at his Greek and Latin authors, acquiring in the process an impressive control of both

---

[1] For Hegel's friendship with his professors Cless and Hopf and with C. F. Abel of the *Karlsakademie* see p. 9 n. 3 below.

[2] Rosenkranz, p. 10.

languages; and he took delight in accumulating information about subjects like mathematics and physics, which were not immediately germane to his 'philosophical' problem, simply because it interested him, and no doubt helped him to get good marks in school.[1] But in the main the record of his independent reading is directed towards the formation of a general conception of human nature, and particularly towards the understanding of the function of cultural and literary values in human history. We can see that this problem was very much in his mind when he began to make his collection of excerpts, because it recurs several times in the first entries in the *Tagebuch* that he began to keep very soon afterwards.

2. The Tagebuch

What moved Hegel to begin keeping a diary is, of necessity, a matter for surmise rather than for definite conclusions. The writing of diaries was a widespread fashion certainly, but Hegel was not introspective enough to be a natural diarist; and it is scarcely plausible to suggest that he may nevertheless have aspired to be one, for even in his earliest entries he made no attempt either to analyse his feelings or to describe the events of the day. His very first entry records the historical facts that he had learned from a sermon on the Augsburg Confession; and next day he noted his approval of Schrökh's *Lehrbuch der Weltgeschichte* for concentrating on the really important events of world history and not giving long lists of kings and of wars. Hegel was especially pleased that Schrökh took account of literary and cultural history: 'The best thing of all is that he connects the realm of scholarship [*das Lehrreich*] with history; likewise he takes care to refer to the condition of the scholars and of the sciences in general.'[2] This is not

[1] The mature Hegel had an intense interest in the nature and limits of mathematical reasoning as a specifically *human* power; and of course the 'philosophy of nature' occupied an important place in his thoughts from 1801 onwards. Just how far this aspect of his philosophy is capable of explanation and interpretation in terms of his earlier humanistic concerns we shall see in due course. But the absence of these topics in his philosophical reflections before the Jena period strongly indicates that he had no ulterior object in his earliest studies and excerpts in these areas beyond the acquiring of knowledge or technical mastery.

[2] 27 June [1785]; *Dok.*, p. 7. Hegel also knew and at some time in this period made excerpts from Meiners's *Geschichte der Menschheit*, but we cannot, of course, conclude that he was already acquainted with it at this time. Most probably he was comparing Schrökh's book with the official history textbook of the Gymnasium, which was the *Kurze Einleitung zur allgemeinen weltlichen Historie* of J. G. Essich (cf. Rosenkranz, p. 14; Lacorte, p. 69).

actually an independent verdict on the book itself, but only on the programme and criteria which the author sets forth in his introduction.[1] But the fact that Hegel believed Schrökh's book to be the best of its kind that he had come across *for these reasons* tells us a great deal about the interests and motives of this young reader of a manual intended for the use of his teachers.

Four days later we find him reflecting upon the problem of what 'pragmatic history' is. He records that although he has thought about it for some time and cannot now remember where he got the idea from, he is still unclear about it.

We have a pragmatic history, I think, when the author does not merely narrate facts, but brings out the character of a famous man, or of an entire nation, their customs and mores, their religions etc., and the notable variations and deviations in these matters from the ways of other peoples; when he investigates the ruin [*Zerfall*] and the up-springing of great kingdoms; when he shows what consequences this or that event or change of government [*Staatsveränderung*] had for the constitution of the nation, for its character etc., and so on.[2]

It seems clear that in this definition Hegel is trying to pull together what he knows (probably still only indirectly) about the great 'pragmatic' historians—Montesquieu, Hume, Voltaire, and Gibbon. Lacorte has drawn attention to the defence of pragmatic history in Schrökh's *History of the Christian Church* (1768), which may quite conceivably have been the occasion of some of the young Hegel's ponderings, for it contains many of the same ideas.[3] If it is reasonable to suppose that his present attempt to come to a conclusion on the subject was sparked off by his reading of the *Lehrbuch*, then we may well begin to suspect that the purpose of his diary in the author's eyes was to serve as a repository for his

---

[1] Cf. Hoffmeister's note in *Dok.*, p. 401; and Lacorte, pp. 72–3.

[2] 1 July 1785 (*Dok.*, pp. 9–10) Hoffmeister reads *Zufall*, not *Zerfall*, but I have accepted the correction of Glockner (vol. ii, p. 11) and Haering (vol. i, p. 16). There seems to be a clear reference here to Gibbon's *Decline and Fall*. The reference to Montesquieu in the following clause is scarcely less transparent; and surely Hume's *History of England* is in Hegel's mind in the first clause, as well as Voltaire's *Essai sur les mœurs*. This is not to say that Hoffmeister's note (*Dok.*, pp. 401–2) is altogether justified. We cannot assume that Hegel has already read, or begun to read, any of these famous authors. The direct influence that is to be looked for here is rather that of Schrökh, as Lacorte (pp. 75–7) has recognized.

[3] *Christliche Kirchengeschichte* (2nd edn., 1772), pp. 268 ff. My remarks are based on the citations and discussion in Lacorte, pp. 74–6.

own reflections upon his reading and excerpting, as well as a supplementary record of information and events which he conceived to have some significance for himself as a would-be scholar. Almost all of the early entries fit very conveniently into the context of this hypothesis. We are offered reflections on the relativity of men's interests, and how men's pleasures vary with their ages;[1] a hypothesis about the death of Socrates;[2] notes about, and reflections arising from, walks with Professor Cless, who was at this time his form master and also his philosophy teacher, and with other professors and school friends;[3] lists of books bought from Löffler's library and reflections on his own debt to Löffler as a teacher;[4] reflections on the nature of woman;[5] reflections on, and examples of, superstition;[6] notes about his visits to the ducal library.[7]

He had not consciously formulated this purpose when he began his diary, however, and the conflict between the keeping of a real diary on the one hand, and his sense of what was worth recording on the other, soon forced him to adopt a new plan. It was a point of conscience for someone as methodical as the young Hegel that in a 'day-book' every day should have its entry—though he soon

[1] 28 June [1785] (Dok., pp. 8–9). Compare also the walk on 3 July (Dok., p. 10: see n. 3 below).

[2] 2 July [1785] (Dok., p. 10). For Hegel's interest in the death of Socrates cf. 15 July (Dok., p. 15) and the excerpt of 6 Apr. 1786 (Dok., pp. 86–7). 'Socrates' cock' was one of Hegel's index headings.

[3] See 4, 15, 21, 22 to 25 July for walks with Professor Cless (Dok. pp. 10–11, 15, 16–18); 14 July (Dok., p. 15) for a walk with Professors Abel and Hopf; 3 July (Dok., p. 10) for the most interesting walk—probably with classmates since Hegel admits to dominating the conversation—on which the proposition that 'every good has its bad side' was discussed. The other recorded walk with classmates (29 June, Dok., p. 9) appears to have been quite unacademic.
Cless taught philosophy to the sixth class only one hour a week. His main responsibility was to teach them Latin. The recorded topics on his walks with Hegel are the physics of the solar system, and solid geometry (a topic which Hegel pursues in the following days). This squares well with Christiane Hegel's memory of his 'Freude an Physik' at the Gymnasium. The teaching of physics was the particular responsibility of Hopf (who also taught Greek to the sixth class, and was the form master of the seventh).
J. F. Abel was professor of philosophy at the Karlsakademie, the other important gymnasium in Stuttgart. But in 1790 he was called to the University of Tübingen where he thus became one of Hegel's teachers.

[4] 5–7 July (Dok., pp. 11–13). These entries are discussed on p. 3 above; compare also the entry for 11 Dec. (Dok., p. 24).

[5] 8 July [1785] (Dok., p. 13); cf. 24 Jan. [1786] (Dok., pp. 30–1).

[6] 9–12 July [1785] (Dok., pp. 13–14); cf. 11 Mar. 1786 (Dok., pp. 35–6).

[7] 13 July and 20 July (Dok., pp. 14–15, 16).

began to fail in this respect. But on the other hand he felt it was wrong to fill his pages with things of no importance. His record for 29 and 30 June 1785 reveals the conflict in his mind very clearly. These two entries are just the sort of thing that we should expect to find in any diary: the news of a riot, and some reflections on his weaknesses as a chess player, with resolutions for future improvement in this game that he enjoys so much. But in the first entry he adds a note: 'To-day was a holiday; but I did not go to Church, I went walking with Duttenhofer and Autenrieth [two school friends] in the Bopser Wald.' This seems to be intended as an explanation for his having nothing more serious to record; and in the entry about chess which is the nearest thing to a self-examination in the whole diary, the note of apology becomes explicit, for Hegel ends: 'I have said so much about chess playing, only *in fugam vacui*, in order that the last day of this month should not be left empty.'[1] He did not regard personal considerations and private details as worthy of record, unless they occurred to him as illustrations of some general philosophical principle.[2] We may reasonably suppose, for instance, that the mind of a fifteen-year-old would be occupied at fairly frequent intervals with thoughts about girls and his relations with them; but all we find on this topic in Hegel's diary is some rather frigid abstract moralizing.[3]

Hegel resolved his difficulty by making his diary-keeping subservient to the pursuit of scholarship in another way. After he had been keeping it for just one month, three days were allowed to pass without a record; then on 29 July 1785, he began to make his entries in Latin. Doubtless the end of the summer vacation and his return to school was the direct cause of this change in the character of the diary. Hegel needed to practise writing in Latin as often as he could, and during the week his schoolwork took up much of his time, and almost all of his attention. But any material would serve *exercendi stili et roboris acquirendi causa* [for stylistic exercise and to gain strength in the language]; so Hegel writes notes on Roman

[1] *Dok.*, p. 9. (His political bias against the peasantry should be noted.)

[2] For instance when he contrasts his own delight in the sight of a fine house with that of the women and married men in the company at the news that a confinement has terminated in successful delivery (28 June 1785, *Dok.*, p. 8).

[3] See p. 9 n. 5 above; the first entry concerns a quotation from Horace and the second is a Latin essay by Hegel himself. For a contrast compare the remarks about watching pretty girls in the real diary chronicle which Hegel kept for the first week of 1787 (*Dok.*, p. 39).

history and retells the story of Adrastus the Phrygian from the first book of Herodotus—*deficiente alia quadam materia* [for lack of other material]. After a week of this sort of thing he finally has something of his own that he thinks worth recording again—a visit to a Catholic church to hear Mass—a ceremony which, he says, displeased him as it would any sane man. He went again the following Sunday, however, and found the erudition and clarity with which the Catechism was expounded very admirable; he was sorry to have missed the sermon that morning 'on virtue'. In the intervening week there are only two entries, both concerned with Professor Cless's class on Livy. Livy and the Persian Wars continued to supply his material for three more days before the diary was interrupted for three months by preparations for an examination, immediately followed by several weeks of sickness.[1]

Hegel took up his pen again in December, on the ninth to be precise, or 'A.D.V. Id Dec. A. MDCC LXXXV' as he now begins to date his entries. The few days remaining before the end of the school semester on the fourteenth are filled with notes about happenings in the interval: his own sickness, the departure of his *carissimus amicus* Duttenhofer to the *Tübingerstift*, whither he was himself to follow in three years time; the death of a local monument of learning, J. J. Moser, *qui tot, quot perlegere humana non sufficit aetas perscripsit libros*; the books added to his *bibliothecula*. In the following days we hear of a public concert, of a house burning down, and of the hard winter weather; then come moral reflections about the evils attendant upon the love of money, before we learn that the Christmas present which most delighted our young scholar was Scheller's Latin lexicon. On New Year's day 1786 he writes that he has himself bought Scheller's *Praecepta* (intended to aid the development of a Ciceronian Latin style) to go with it. Then the diary lapses again for six weeks.[2]

The next entry records an annual address at the Gymnasium on the Duke's birthday (11 Feb. 1786) which was concerned with the

---

[1] 29 July–24 Aug. [1785] (*Dok.*, pp. 18–23). Cf. also the excerpts from Gesner (*Dok.*, pp. 82–6).

[2] *Dok.*, pp. 23–7. It would seem that the young Hegel enjoyed concerts; cf. 1 Jan. 1787 (*Dok.*, p. 39). He continued to do so throughout his life; compare for instance Letter 22 (to Nanette Endel), *Briefe*, i, 52. His housekeeping records for 1811, and again for 1819, show that while at home he went to concerts frequently; and his letters from Vienna in 1824 are full of the delights of the Opera (*Briefe*, iv, 96 ff., 118–19, iii, 53 ff.).

scholarly and literary achievements of the Württemberg schools. Four more entries scattered over the next ten days were devoted to planning and composing a Latin oration on the conduct proper to a Gymnasium student, which he expected to have to deliver in school. The draft of the speech breaks off very near the close, and unless a page or more has been lost here (as has certainly happened further on) Hegel wrote no more for two weeks.[1]

What follows then is very curious. The Latin date for 6 March is given with all possible solemnity ('Prid. Non. Martii. A.C. N. 1786') and followed by an essay in German *Über das Excipieren*, which was continued on the 7th, 8th, and 15th and finally completed on the 21st (the last two dates being given in German). In the intervals Hegel wrote two diary entries in Latin (though the second is dated in German) but on the 22nd he finally reverts to German altogether. The essay is a well-argued attack on the practice of dictating a theme in German for transcription by a class in Latin. Hegel notes that some teachers approve of it, and use it, while the majority do not. He considers all the arguments he has heard in its favour but thinks there is little substance in them. It looks rather as if his own arguments to show that this practice is reactionary and liable to lead to the development of bad Latin style rather than a true command of the language (which must come rather from close and frequent reading and study of good authors) convinced him that his own habit of writing his random thoughts in Latin was likewise a bad one. One of the intervening diary entries is an interesting little meditation on pagan and Christian superstition, the other a brief sermon on the importance of always keeping one's temper.

The entry in German for 22 March 1786 concerns the universality of the desire for happiness. Like the next entry (on 'Enlightenment') it can be directly linked with some of the surviving 'excerpts', so it is especially unfortunate that both entries are fragmentary. Two or more sheets have been lost from the manuscript, so that we have only five or six lines of the entry on happiness, and the entry on enlightenment lacks both beginning and end, and cannot even be securely dated (except for the year), since Hegel wrote no more in his diary until New Year's Day 1787.[2]

[1] *Dok.*, pp. 28–31. (It is a pity we do not have the oration *De utilitate poeseos* instead.)

[2] *Dok.*, pp. 31–8. The entries about superstition, happiness, and enlightenment are considered further below.

The record for the first week of 1787 is a diary in the ordinary sense. We get from it a very clear picture of exactly how Hegel spent his days. He inserted his weekly time-table of school-work in the margin of the first entry, and contented himself with the word 'gewöhnlich' as a sort of shorthand for it thereafter. This first entry is a sort of review of his situation, and the regular entry for the events of the day follows separately. But after a week his New Year's resolution failed him; or perhaps he decided that he had better uses for his time than the maintenance of this record. The record itself would certainly have provided good grounds for this decision. On New Year's day he went to a concert after spending the whole afternoon reading *Sophiens Reise* because he could not tear himself away from it.[1] He talked with his friends and they all enjoyed looking round at pretty girls. But even this day had begun with trigonometry, and during the following week Hegel's free time was given up to trigonometry and to the making of notes about Virgil and Demosthenes. Even on the two mornings when he stopped working to visit his friends, he was still devoured by intellectual curiosity: he examined a musical clock and a star atlas and borrowed another mathematics book, which he promptly began to work on. He even spent most of Sunday on his trigonometry.[2]

The analysis that I have given shows, I think, that it is misleading to speak of the young Hegel's diary as if it were a single entity. Over a period of some eighteen months he kept very

[1] *Sophiens Reise von Memel nach Sachsen* was an enormously long picaresque novel (Lacorte says about 4,000 pages) by Johann Timotheus Hermes, giving a moralistic and sentimentalized picture of life in Germany in the period of the Seven Years War. It began to appear in 1770 and was completed in five volumes in 1772; it was immensely popular, reaching its sixth edition in 1778 (all editions after the first were in six volumes). Hoffmeister's note (*Dok.*, p. 39) refers to the second edition (Worms, 1776), so it may be that he had evidence that this was the edition read by Hegel. Haym underlines the fact that the novel (and its popularity) was a reaction against the new spirit and the new morality of the *Werther* generation. He uses Hegel's delight in it, together with his life-long appreciation of Hippel's *Lebensläufe* (on which see below, p. 184 n. 2), as evidence of his poor literary taste. Schopenhauer seized on Hegel's reading of *Sophiens Reise* and contrasted it with his own early love of Homer (as if the young Hegel read nothing but bad novels!); but his point is, to my mind, more significant than Haym's, for Hegel's fascination tells us more about his interests than about his taste. The attraction of Hermes's book for the young student of the 'philosophical history of humanity' was no doubt increased by the wealth of physiognomic descriptions that it contained, which are reported to have impressed Lavater himself. An abridgement was published by Reclam at Leipzig in 1941 (edited by Fritz Brüggemann). See Haym, p. 22; Lacorte, pp. 80–1.

[2] *Dok.*, pp. 38–41.

sporadically three different kinds of daily record, the first two of
which were scarcely diaries at all in the ordinary sense. At first he
set out more or less unconsciously to make a scholarly and philosophical commonplace book, and later he began rather to do
regular composition exercises in Latin. Then his earlier preoccupation gradually reasserted itself, and for at least a short time
he consciously and deliberately kept a commonplace book for his
own reflections.[1] Finally for the first week of 1787 he made an
exact chronicle of his daily doings, a diary in the most basic sense
of the word.

3. The collection of excerpts

The *exercitium styli* aspect of the *Tagebuch* is of little interest to us.
But as a commonplace book it supplements the collection of
excerpts and the school essays that remain to us; and as a chronicle
it both supplements and illustrates the account Rosenkranz gives
of the total collection of papers that still survived from the
Gymnasialzeit when Hegel died. From it we can see, for instance,
how 'Socrates' cock' came to be a distinct heading in his excerpt
collection. For he records on 2 July 1785 that Professor Offterdinger
had raised in class the question why Socrates wished to offer a
cock to Aesculapius as he lay dying. The professor's hypothesis
was that Socrates was by then stupefied and did not know what he
was saying; but Hegel himself suggests that Socrates was merely

---

[1] The sheet dated '14 May 1787' and bearing the title 'Some remarks on the
Vorstellung of quantity' forms a sort of pendant to this aspect of the *Tagebuch*.
It would seem from Hegel's own footnote to have been occasioned by a passage
from Meiners's *Briefe über die Schweiz* about the way a difference in the light
affects our impressions of distances and distant objects. Hegel generalizes from
this example, offering others of the same sort. He is primarily concerned to
identify the controlling factor in his different cases; and he goes on from
estimates of size and distance to consider estimates of time. In both cases we
need a criterion and we employ the one that we are used to or that lies nearest
to hand: we measure the passage of time by the succession of distinct impressions
or ideas that we can recall when we look back over it. Thus the time occupied by
a journey in which we notice everything on the way will seem longer than the
same amount of time occupied in reading a book, unless it happens to be one
with subject-matter of a historical type. (Here the overwhelming influence of
the Lockean tradition in psychology on Hegel's mind is apparent: for we may
be sure that when he sat down to read *Sophiens Reise* for a while, and could not
tear himself away till evening, the time did not in fact seem as long to him as
when he read some other books—even if he was the sort of model student who
would copy long extracts from a book on spherical trigonometry so as to be able
to work through them in his own time! Cf. *Dok.*, pp. 42–3 and 39.)

falling in with an established custom in order not to offend the religious sensibilities of the 'masses' (*Pöbel*, not *Volk*). Almost a year later he found and copied out from Dusch's *Briefe zur Bildung des Geschmacks* a conjecture of Racine's that in saying to Crito 'We owe a cock to Aesculapius' Socrates was using a proverbial expression ironically or jokingly, just as an enlightened Frenchman might say to a friend 'nous devons une belle chandelle' without implying any religious commitment.[1]

One might use this example to argue for the view, which lies behind Haym's characterization of the schoolboy Hegel as 'eine sammelnde und lernende Natur',[2] that the researches of this early period were not really organized and directed, but were the spontaneous outgrowth of whims, accidents, and scholastic tasks, and were ordered only in ways suggested by the school curriculum itself. No doubt many of the particular problems and topics that Hegel followed up in his reading and excerpting *were* suggested by questions raised or problems set for him by his teachers, or even by incidental similarities and contrasts that struck him and aroused his interest while he was reading. But he had nevertheless one continuous and controlling concern in all of his philosophical or semi-philosophical investigations, and closer inspection will show that his apparently whimsical interest in the explanation of Socrates' death-bed remark touches that concern very closely.

Socrates, we must realize, was for almost all the writers of the Enlightenment the type of the enlightened man, the rational seeker after knowledge; and any problem about the explanation of something that he said or did was for them not so much a matter of biographical fact as a question of fundamental principle. The underlying question in this instance is: 'What attitude should the enlightened man adopt toward established religious ritual?' Socrates could not really have believed that we ought to repay a god for his gifts with ours, since that belief is a superstition unworthy of the enlightened man. But what then was his attitude, or in other words, what *should* the attitude of the enlightened man

---

[1] *Dok.*, pp. 10 and 86–7.

[2] Haym, p. 20. It will not have escaped the attentive reader that I agree with the judgement there cited: 'Hegel ward zum Philosophen, indem er sich bildete wie ein Gelehrter.' But I think this was a much more deliberate development than previous critics have recognized, and that behind the 'objectivity' that has impressed all who have examined the record there was a conscious and often a controlling concern on Hegel's part with his own vocation as a scholar.

be? Should he quietly conform as long as the practice involved is harmless? This is the assumption that appears to lie behind the interpretation of 'Socrates' cock' that Hegel himself proposed in class. But in other contexts he seems rather to accept the assumption implicit in Racine's interpretation: that the enlightened man must be resolutely critical, striving always to unmask superstition as such, and if possible to destroy it. He is extremely scornful, for instance, about claims which local people made to have seen the 'mutige Heer' (the fairy army or hunting-party which appears in English folklore as 'Arthur's chase') and about reports of 'ghosts' in general.[1]

Of course, ghosts and fairies were a fairly safe target for enlightened contempt. But Hegel also waxes quite violent at times against superstitious aspects of the Christian faith itself. We have already noted how scornfully he expressed himself about the Mass;[2] and there is another passage in his *Tagebuch* in which he begins by remarking on the pagan origins of the popular conceptions of the Devil and his ministers, and of the guardian angels, and goes on to comment on the survival of the rite of sacrifice in Christianity. In this connection he declares the Catholic belief that one may acquire the grace of God by giving alms to the priests to be as superstitious as the sacrifices and offerings of the pagans. He admits that among Protestants the same superstitions endure still, but the main weight of his sarcasm falls on the Catholic priesthood and the laity who foolishly 'stuff their priests with food' in return for the pronouncement 'by these fat, luxuriating, most profane men of some words which neither side understand'.[3]

At Tübingen he later vented his sarcasm privately on many aspects of Protestant faith and doctrine likewise. But it is a mistake, nevertheless, to read this passage in the *Tagebuch* as evincing a basic antipathy, a polemical attitude towards religion as such.[4] In general Hegel's attitude as a young student towards religious belief of all kinds was neutral and objective; he wanted to understand it, because he was convinced that it is a major force in the

---

[1] *Dok.*, pp. 13–14.
[2] *Dok.*, p. 21; cf. above, p. 11.   [3] *Dok.*, pp. 35–6.
[4] The quietist view is expressed once more in Hegel's excerpts from Moses Mendelssohn of a few years later (*Dok.*, pp. 140–3, excerpt of 31 May, 1787). The seeming contradiction in Hegel's attitude is really only a reflection of the contrast between the private opinions and the public conduct of the enlightened man (which Mendelssohn's view allows for).

formation of culture, the primary instrument in social education, and hence in the eventual development of human nature towards enlightenment. Thus he was torn between two ideals of enlightenment: on the one side the theoretical ideal of understanding for which 'tout comprendre, c'est tout pardonner', and on the other side the practical ideal of reform, which is based on faith in the perfectibility of man through education. As a scholar he had to try to understand how everything fitted together; but as a human being 'formed for society' he had to use his knowledge to improve the state of his fellows:

> Every scholar must know the encyclopedia of positive [*gewisser*] sciences [he copied dutifully on 22 March 1787 from an essay on Kästner's lectures]. Most counsels that are given to young men are one-sided, and cannot help being so. But every head and every community of men must have its own plan. To restrict oneself to a single science is admirable: but since this science itself leads on to others, and since the soul of man has just this peculiar property, that it rapidly grows fatigued with only one type of occupation and must either have frequent changes or be idle, should we not therefore let the circle of the sciences open out?
>
> A natural talent [*Genie*] for the study of some particular aspect of the natural order, is soon of itself drawn to its object, as long as it has first gained enough experience to have discovered it in its place. And are we not worth more in the end as enlightened citizens, than as teachers of a particular science; and does not this enlightenment consist precisely in a certain manifoldness of our knowledge so that each part of it is explained and defined by the others?[1]

Hegel wrote down his own views on the meaning of *Aufklärung* in 1786 (probably in March or April) about a year before he copied out the views of Mendelssohn and Garve. His own reflections read as follows:

> ... I am speaking here of enlightenment through the sciences and arts. It is therefore confined merely to the class of scholars [*auf den Stand der Gelehrten*]. For to sketch the outlines of an enlightenment of the common man, I think is on the one hand a very difficult task even

---

[1] *Dok.*, pp. 138–9. This was the ideal of scholarship that Hegel was already seeking to achieve (most obviously, for instance, in his excerpts from Sulzer's *Kurzer Begriff der Gelehrsamkeit* two weeks earlier: *Dok.*, pp. 109–15). And Kästner's conception of enlightenment here chimes well with the doctrine that 'God has formed man for life in society' which he found in Feder's *New Émile* when he first began making his excerpts (*Dok.*, p. 63).

for the most learned people, and on the other far harder still for me in particular, since I have not yet studied history as a whole philosophically and thoroughly. But anyway I believe this enlightenment of the common man has always been governed by the religion of his time; it extends only to enlightenment through handicrafts [*Handwerke*] and the comforts of life. So I am giving my opinion only about the sciences and arts.

With respect to these, my view then is that they flourished first in the East and South and have spread ever more Westwards from there. Although at the present time the great fame of Egyptian learning has been justly diminished, at least with respect to philosophy, this much at least remains certain that at least with respect to the mechanical and fine arts Egypt had achieved such a level of perfection that the very ruins of her works of art are even now still a cause for wonder, and it is very likely that their deep and wide ranging practical knowledge had already been organized into an accurate theory.[1]

At this point the fragmentary diary entry is unfortunately broken off by the loss of one or more pages from the manuscript. But even the slight fragment that remains suffices to make three things clear: first the social and eminently practical yardstick by which Hegel felt that all enlightenment was to be judged; secondly the fact that for him the class of professionally learned men, the theorists of a culture, constitutes a special élite within it; and thirdly that the conception of the march of the spirit from East to West, which played such a large role in his mature thought, is rooted in his earliest readings and reflections about cultural development.

The distinction of different levels or senses of *Aufklärung* was common enough in the literature of the time. About a year later, in May 1787, Hegel copied out a passage from Mendelssohn's essay 'Was heißt Aufklären' in the *Berlin Monatsschrift* for 1784,

---

[1] *Dok.*, pp. 37–8. In Dec. 1786 (i.e. in the same year but probably some months after this diary entry) Hegel copied out a passage from Meiners's *Revision der Philosophie* (Göttingen and Gotha, 1772) in which Meiners gives arguments for minimizing the Egyptian heritage in Greek culture. We know that he made excerpts from several of Meiners's works—especially the *Grundriß der Geschichte der Menscheit* (1785)—so it is possible that he was already consciously taking up a position *vis-à-vis* Meiners's views in this passage.

The passage 'On the fame of the Enlightenment of other lands', in which Eberhard adduces Greek examples (Homer, Plato, Xenophon) of the tendency of enlightened leaders of thought to claim that the ideals they wish to see realized in their own societies have already been achieved elsewhere (Persia, Egypt) shows that Hegel was still reflecting on the question at issue here in 1787 (*Dok.*, pp. 144–5).

in which 'Bildung' was subdivided into 'Kultur' and 'Aufklärung' very much along the lines of his own distinction between the practical *Aufklärung* of the common man and the theoretical *Aufklärung* of the learned:

Bildung, Kultur and *Aufklärung* are modifications of social life, products of men's industry and of their efforts to improve their social condition.

The more the social condition of a people is brought by art and industry into harmony with the vocation of man [*die Bestimmung des Menschen*] the more *Bildung* that people has.

Bildung subdivides into *Kultur* and *Aufklärung*. The former appears to belong more to the practical side: it refers to goods, to refinement and beauty in handicrafts, arts and social *mores* (objectively speaking); and to aptitude, industry and ability in the former [i.e. handicrafts and arts], and to inclinations, impulses and habits in the latter [i.e. social *mores*] (subjectively speaking). The more these correspond in a given people to the vocation of man, the more *Kultur* that people is endowed with.— *Aufklärung* on the other hand appears to be related more to the theoretical side. To rational knowledge (objectively) and aptitude (subjectively) for rational reflection upon the circumstances of human life with a view to estimating their weight and influence upon the vocation of man.

A language achieves *Aufklärung* through the sciences, and *Kultur* through social intercourse, poetry and rhetoric. Through the former it becomes more apt for theoretical purposes, through the latter for practical. Both together give the *Bildung* of a language.

. . . The language of a people is the best index of its *Bildung*, of its *Kultur* and of its *Aufklärung* alike, and equally for its extent and its depth [*Stärke*].

The *Bestimmung des Menschen* may be subdivided into:

1. The vocation of man as man, and
2. The vocation of man regarded as a citizen.

As far as *Kultur* is concerned the two aspects coincide; since all practical perfections have worth only in relation to social life they must be referred only and solely to the vocation of man as member of society. Man as man needs no culture: but he needs *Aufklärung*.

. . . The *Aufklärung* that is the concern of man as man is universal without distinction of ranks [*Stände*]. The *Aufklärung* of man regarded as a citizen varies according to rank and calling [*Beruf*]. But the vocation of man provides here the criterion and end of his striving. . . .

Menschen-Aufklärung can come into conflict with *Bürger-Aufklärung*.

. . .

If the essential requirements of the human vocation [*die wesentlichen Bestimmungen des Menschen*] are unhappily brought into conflict with the accidental concerns of men [*mit seinen außerwesentlichen Bestimmungen*]; if some useful and humane [*den Menschen zierende*] truth cannot be published abroad without demolishing the currently prevailing principles of religion and social ethics, then will the virtue-loving *Aufklärer* act with prudence and discretion and put up with the prejudice rather than cast out along with it the truth fast entwined in it. Certainly this maxim has long been a shield for hypocrisy and we have it to thank for so many centuries of barbarism and superstition. Whenever men want to commit iniquities they turn them into holiness. But for all that the friend of man must always even in the most enlightened times pay attention to this aspect of things. It is difficult, but not impossible to find the boundary lines which even in this regard mark off proper use from misuse.

.   .   .   .   .

A civilized [*gebildete*] nation knows no other internal danger save for the overflow of its national happiness, which like the most perfect health of the human body, can already in and of itself [*an und für sich*] be called a sickness, or the point of transition to a sickness. A nation which through *Bildung*, has arrived at the highest apex of national happiness, is thrust into danger precisely for that reason, because it cannot rise any higher.[1]

A few months later, in August 1787, Hegel copied out two passages from Nicolai's *Beschreibung einer Reise durch Deutschland und die Schweiz* (1785) in which the same distinctions are employed and developed. The first of them just repeats Mendelssohn's distinctions. Hegel probably noted it because Nicolai goes into considerable detail about the relation between *Kultur* and *Politur* (which as Mendelssohn put it is '*Kultur* in externals'). *Politur* is on the one hand the highest level of *Kultur*; but it may also on the other hand be a mere façade borrowed from the culture of another nation. And what is true of nations is true likewise of individuals. As we shall see, this was a point which greatly exercised Hegel's mind.[2]

The second passage from Nicolai undoubtedly caught his eye because of the important role which it assigns to the middle class with respect to the spreading of enlightenment. To create a strong

---

[1] *Dok.*, pp. 140–3. Hegel transcribed the whole of Mendelssohn's article apart from the introductory paragraph and a few elaborative phrases or examples.
[2] *Dok.*, pp. 145–6.

middle class, freed from concern about the most basic needs of life and so able to be reflective and active, is declared to be the supreme task (*höchste Kunst*) of a ruler, for

Kultur and *Aufklärung* will very soon spread from the middle classes to the lower classes of the people if their spirit is not weighted down by poverty, superstition, rottenness and dulled sensibility; and it will spread from there to the higher orders [*Stände*], if they have not through riches, pride, superstition, rottenness and refined sensibility, become indifferent to the things that matter to mankind. If this is true as history everywhere confirms that it is, it is equally obvious that *Kultur* and *Aufklärung* alike do not need a capital city for a seed bed, but must at least be introduced from a court focus [*nicht notwendig in einer Residenzstadt zuerst aufkeimen am wenigsten aber vom Hofe aus eingeführt werden mussen*].[1]

One other excerpt concerning Enlightenment has come down to us, and it is the most revealing of all, for it throws the conflict between theoretical understanding and practical reform which is implicit in the concept itself, into high relief. It is the latest of Hegel's notes on the subject (February 1788), but it directly echoes his own obituary note on Löffler which is the earliest indication that we possess of his personal attitude on the question:

Fighting against prejudice is not what makes an *enlightened man*, and even less is it crying down the truth under the name of prejudice. When someone apes the impartial researcher and declares some opinion to be absurd or unprovable, since research has shown it to be so, is he not then himself guided by prejudice? And when someone else first degrades the plain truth with the name of prejudice and then takes the field against it, does he not give us to understand that he himself is under the domination of prejudices? A man is not enlightened in virtue of his acceptance or rejection of this or that proposition, but because he has so much reverence and respect for the truth, so much resolution and firmness that he strives with all his might [*mit männlichem Ernste*], and will not be put off by praise or blame, by outraged clamour or by scornful derision, to investigate calmly why he accepts or rejects something.[2]

The young Hegel did not always live up to this high ideal of scholarly objectivity as his remarks about Catholicism alone suffice

[1] *Dok.*, p. 147.
[2] *Dok.*, p. 147 (an extract from Zöllner's *Lesebuch für alle Stände* found by Hegel in the *Allgemeine Literatur Zeitung* for Jan. 1788. He noted it down with remarkable promptitude on 1 Feb. 1788).

to show. But we can see from his excerpts about Egyptian culture, which are opposed to his own beliefs on the subject, that he really strove to achieve it; and the general impression of calm objectivity, which all who have examined his schoolboy researches have remarked on, is probably justified. This makes it very dangerous to take his excerpts as evidence of his opinions rather than simply as indications of his interests. We can only regard the excerpts as evidence for his views in cases like the present one, i.e. where we have some statement made by Hegel himself *in propria persona* to begin from.[1]

This condition can be met in the case of another important topic that occurs in Hegel's excerpts: the concept of 'true happiness'. Here again some reflections in his *Tagebuch* show that he had already been pondering about this; but unluckily the manuscript is here again defective and this time it breaks off too soon to provide a reliable index of his attitude, so that the interpretation of the excerpts is more difficult.

All men [he wrote on 22 March 1786] have the aim of making themselves happy. About certain rare exceptions, who possessed such sublimity of soul, that they sacrificed themselves in order to make

---

[1] In this connection, however, it may be significant that the five passages dealing with the nature of scholarship and enlightenment are almost unique in that not one of them has an index heading from Hegel's own hand; this might be taken as evidence that he did not regard these passages as part of the objective collection of views and information which he was making for scholarly purposes, but rather as having a bearing on his own attitude and aims in making it.

The difficulty with this interpretation is that there are two other passages, one on the place of 'chance' in historical development, and another on the origin of deponent and middle forms in Greek and Latin, which are similarly unindexed. The suggestion that Hoffmeister makes about the first of these passages—that the young Hegel found difficulty in classifying it—may well be valid for both of them. But it is paradoxical to extend this explanation, as Hoffmeister does, to the passage about the duty of a scholar; and even Hoffmeister does not venture to suggest it in the case of the passages where words like *Aufklärung* and *Bildung* are underlined or marked out at the very beginning. Nevertheless Hoffmeister may have been on the right track. For it is easily demonstrated that Hegel was growing steadily more sophisticated in his indexing. Whereas earlier he would head his extracts *Hahn des Socrates, Wahre Glückseligkeit, Weg zum Glück in den großen Welt*, and leave it at that, he wanted now to classify according to the divisions and subdivisions of the sciences. The subheadings of his passages on enlightenment and scholarship were easy enough and could be picked up from the words marked in the early sentences; but what science did these topics belong to? If this is the right explanation, however, the suggestion in the text that Hegel was conscious of a difference in the nature of his concern with these passages can still stand. For a further discussion of the classification of these excerpts in Hegel's collection see pp. 28-9 below.

others happy, there is this to say: These men, I think, have still not sacrificed true happiness, but only temporal interests, temporal happiness, even including life. Thus they are not really exceptions here. But first I must define the concept of happiness. I understand thereby a ... [*the remainder is lost*][1]

This is a very slender guide to use in approaching the twelve and a half pages of printed text, concerning the happiness of the elect, that Hegel excerpted from Wünsch's *Kosmologische Unterhaltungen für die Jugend* three months later. But we must, in the first place, assume that a fifteen-year-old who reasons thus, and then spends several days writing out someone else's views on heavenly bliss, really does himself believe in heaven.[2] His commitment to enlightened scepticism and suspension of judgement, and his scornful disgust about superstition did not touch the essential tenets of the prevailing faith. The young Hegel may not have believed in salvation by faith, or in original sin, but he did believe in salvation by works.[3] 'Holy Scripture itself bears witness', he noted in Wünsch, 'that faith in Jesus without the exercise of virtue is dead, i.e., it avails us nothing, it is nothing worth.'[4] It was 'abhorrent and

---

[1] *Dok.*, p. 37. It is suggestive, I think, that the break in the manuscript occurs just here. I would hazard the guess that Hegel himself may have removed the next page for use in connection with some subsequent reflections about self-sacrifice at Tübingen or Berne.

[2] *Dok.*, pp. 87–100. In the light of all that has been said about Hegel's 'objectivity' one might argue that this does not follow, since he only claims that all men aim at happiness. But if he was such an enlightened sceptic as to doubt the existence of the blessedness for which he supposes men to have sacrificed even their lives, surely it would have occurred to him that even men as sceptical as himself might nevertheless have sacrificed their lives; and in that case his argument would fail. (The enlightened justification for his faith in this respect was most readily available to him in Mendelssohn's *Phaedo*; cf. *Dok.*, p. 15.)

[3] Lacorte is quite severely critical of earlier interpreters of the *Jugendschriften* who have spoken loosely of the 'Aufklärung allemande, et donc chrétienne' (the phrase is actually Asveld's). We may well agree with him that the relation between 'Enlightenment' and 'Christianity' in German culture needs careful analysis, not least in discussions of Hegel's background. But he himself is guilty of the same sort of loose oversimplification when he says that 'to defend this formula [of Asveld's] in the face of a reading of the texts, in which with respect to Christianity, in the sporadic notes that concern it at all, we find only polemical sarcasm, when we do not find commonplaces or complete indifference, the terms "Enlightenment" and "Christianity" end by being emptied of all definite significance capable of providing an adequate characterization' (Lacorte, pp. 112–13; cf. also 83–4). Lacorte, it may be noted, relegates the long excerpt from Wünsch to a short footnote (p. 82 n.).

[4] *Dok.*, p. 88. This is the first appearance of the contrast between 'dead' and 'living' religion which plays such a crucial part in Hegel's later reflections.

quite contrary to Christian teaching' that a sinner should be forgiven in his last hours, while a virtuous man who dies suddenly should be damned. God judges us according to our intentions, but we must use all possible foresight to make our virtues profitable to ourselves and others.

Altogether Wünsch represents quite adequately that near-Kantian confluence of Enlightenment and Christianity which Hegel later labelled 'das moralische Weltanschauung'. He declares that 'prudence [*Klugheit*] is the mistress of Virtue, as understanding [*Verstand*] is the father of wisdom'; but he also inclines to a kind of 'moral sense' theory according to which we shall not go wrong if we do what our 'heart' tells us is right, unless we have been badly educated or are blinded by hunger or some natural weakness. This same Rousseauian doctrine of the natural goodness and nobility of man Hegel had already encountered of course in Feder's *New Émile*.[1] The doctrine that the moral penetration which is the key to happiness and success in the world is something intuitive, having nothing to do with philosophical reflection, sceptical doubt, or suspension of judgement, he found more explicity formulated in the way in which he himself held it in his maturity, in Zimmermann's *Über die Einsamkeit* a few months later. One would like to know exactly how Hegel felt about the Zimmermann excerpt when he copied it out word for word; for it is not easy to reconcile it perfectly with the practical programme of spreading enlightenment by strictly rational criticism of existing institutions.[2]

The most interesting passage in the notes from Wünsch, however, is that in which he discusses the false concepts that men have of Heaven and the blessed life. For here we catch a glimpse of the first origin of some ideas which Hegel himself developed later at Berne and Frankfurt:

Certainly men make for themselves odd and mostly sensuous conceptions of the happiness of the future life . . . in that they expect to find there in the main the very same happiness that they most wished for on earth but could never achieve. All these mistaken images [*Vorstellungen*] are based on their false conception [*Begriff*] of Heaven [wrote Wünsch,

---

[1] Cf. *Dok.*, p. 92; and *Dok.*, pp. 63 ff. That Hegel himself was committed to acceptance of views of this sort we may, I think, legitimately infer from what Leutwein tells us about his attitude to Rousseau at Tübingen (*Hegel-Studien*, iii, p. 56, lines 123-30).

[2] *Dok.*, p. 100; see also pp. 26-8 below.

but in Hegel's notes it was transposed to read: 'These mistaken concepts are mainly based on the inverted image of Heaven'] and of the dwelling of God with the blessed, since God is really everywhere, in Him we ever live, in Him we move and in Him we have our being; so we do not only reach Him for the first time after death. God is here! We find ourselves in Him [Hegel omitted this sentence]. Our speaking, hearing, seeing, the beating of our hearts in our breast, the way one thought follows after another, this is God's doing, in Whom we live and are. What a sublime, awe-inspiring thought! And because of these inverted images [here Hegel wrote 'mistaken opinions'] men seldom grasp the right means for the achievement of true happiness. In short for thousands of years [Hegel inserted this claim on his own initiative] men have not reflected on the enlightenment of the understanding and the exercise of virtue, as the things that faith in Jesus consists in, and which are the unique means of human happiness, and in some religions men still have not realized this, a fact which has irrational and vicious consequences. Many men are indeed good even so, and we would be better and the name of man much worthier, if the wise made it their business to teach thoroughly and express vividly the great truth that we are made happy by our own good actions without any further act of God, and on the other hand we are made immediately unhappy by bad actions and ignoble impulses. . . . No, the seed of goodness is planted in all our hearts by a benevolent Providence; but it is up to us to care for its development and growth. Those who teach the contrary, lay a heavy burden on their conscience; and likewise those who teach that we must live virtuously not for our own sakes, but only because God would have it so. For it is contrary to the nature of a rational man, to do something, if he does not foresee or surmise that certain advantages for himself will in some way spring from it. It is contrary to the conception of God, which we have to form for ourselves, if we believe that He requires us to render Him a service by our good deeds, for He only wills that we should do good because it profits us not Him, and directly makes us happy. People who take the other view, are not heeding the warning voice of God in their own hearts, because someone has told them that their own heart too is itself by nature corrupt and utterly evil.[1]

[1] *Dok.*, pp. 92–4. Hegel's transpositions affect the sense little, and do not improve the style or clarity here. Perhaps they are the accidental result of haste. But, like the omission that Hoffmeister noted, they are symptomatic of the significance and importance that the terms *Vorstellung* and *Begriff* will come to have for him, of the interest that the idea of Heaven and the supersensible as a *verkehrte Welt* probably already has for him, and of the influence that the idea of God as a living presence in actual human experience exercised on his mind. In this connection it deserves also to be mentioned that where Wünsch often wrote 'sein Geist' or 'unser Geist' Hegel regularly substituted simply 'der Geist'.

The general tenor of this passage is very close to the tenor of Hegel's own attempt to rewrite the life of Jesus, in Berne. Wünsch is determined to make the Christian gospel consistent with the rational morality which appears to him to be the gospel of reason. Hegel's own insertion of the claim that men have not thought about the identity of the Christian doctrine of salvation and the doctrine of rational enlightenment 'for thousands of years' throws light both on his antipathy to Catholicism which undoubtedly prompted it, and on his later attempts to purify the Christian faith by stripping off the irrational accretions of later centuries.

Behind this obvious affinity lies an even deeper one which took longer to come to the surface. The sentence that Hegel omitted—'God is here! We find ourselves in Him'—contains the fundamental insight behind the essays of the Frankfurt period. The fusion of the ideal of rational enlightenment with the romantic ideal of direct experience and living intuition,[1] led Hegel eventually to a different and far deeper conception of reason itself. This transformation of the rationalist humanism of his Enlightenment heritage was Hegel's life-work and constitutes his essential achievement.

These two ideals were confused and mixed together in his earliest vague notions of 'the philosophical history of humanity'. Many of his excerpts seem to be inspired by the belief that there is an abiding rational essence or pattern of human nature which can be discovered by critical comparison and analysis of different institutions and of typical human behaviour in different situations. The task of the enlightened man is then to strip off all the accidental excrescences by which this fundamental human nature has been covered over and even choked; and to become enlightened is to strip oneself in this way, to be always aware of and always guided by this essential self. This conception is quite explicit for example in Feder's New Émile, which Hegel excerpted at great length at the very beginning of his researches;[2] and in studying Feder he came

[1] That Rousseau was one of the primary sources that inspired this ideal is apparent from the excerpt we are here considering. But Wünsch's own more traditional reflections on die Liebe as die erste und edelste unter den Leidenschaften are also worthy of study in this connection (cf. Dok., pp. 95–6).

[2] Dok., pp. 55–81. Hegel's notes on Book I chapters 5 and 6 (Dok., pp. 59–69), which are the most relevant sections in this connection, were made from the third edition which differed completely in content from the first edition at this point (cf. Hoffmeister's note in Dok. p. 417). Several indications suggest that he was re-examining these chapters in 1787 (he may even have made new excerpts then and substituted them for his earlier ones in this section). These are the

upon a reference to Garve's *Prüfung der Fähigkeiten* (*Examination of the Faculties*) which he excerpted nearly two years later in March 1787.[1] Between these two came his excerpts from Campe's *Kleine Seelenlehre für Kinder* (October 1786) which was altogether too elementary to be satisfactory for his purposes and which he never bothered to classify fully.[2]

On the other hand the unclassified excerpt from the review of Kästner's lectures, which discusses the nature of historical revolutions, and the place of chance and of great leaders in history, suggests the rather different view that human nature *develops* in history and the proper task of an enlightened man is to understand why things have happened as they have. This excerpt comes echoing back to our ears in all of Hegel's later writings, from the early essays on Christianity, from the Preface of the *Phenomenology*, and finally from the lectures on world history.[3] What is more to the point for us at this moment is that it chimes with Hegel's own reflections on the history of enlightenment, with his interest in the debt of the Greeks to Egyptian culture, and with his school essay on the religion of the Greeks and Romans, which we shall come to presently.

This same ambiguity can be found in the source from which the young Hegel most probably derived his conception of 'philosophical history', the *Grundriß der Geschichte der Menschheit* (1785) of C. Meiners. This presumably only came into his hands some

---

first chapters for which the titles are given, and at some time he inserted a slip, bearing the titles of these chapters, into his collection under the heading *Philosophie.Psychologie*. This slip was found by Thaulow and printed by him immediately after the excerpts from the essay on Kästner (22 Mar. 1787). My own hypothesis is that the reading of Kästner—following closely upon his reading of Sulzer, from whom he derived his classification of the philosophic sciences—inspired Hegel to reorganize his own indexing in a properly scholarly fashion. It was at this time, if I am not mistaken, that most of the excerpts received the double or triple headings that they now have. Thus Feder's *New Émile* was classified as *Philosophie.Pedagogie* at this time; but this heading did not suit Book I chapters 5, 6; he recognized this because the re-examination of his notes led him to Garve's essay which (although it was also an overtly pedagogical work) was classified by Hegel as *Philosophie.Psychologie/Prüfung der Fähigkeiten*.   [1] *Dok.*, pp. 115–36.

[2] *Dok.*, pp. 101–4. This excerpt was headed simply *Seele*. Of course Hegel may have felt the higher classifications, *Philosophie.Psychologie*, too obvious to need adding later.

[3] *Dok.*, pp. 139–40; for echoes in the *Jugendschriften*, see Hoffmeister's notes, ibid., pp. 424–6; for a direct confrontation with the Preface of the *Phenomenology*, Lacorte, pp. 107–8.

time after Schrökh's compendium with which he was so delighted in June of that year. His excerpt from it was the only one under the heading 'Philosophical History' that Rosenkranz thought worthy of mention, but of course we cannot safely infer anything from that.[1] Meiners distinguishes between 'History of Mankind' and 'Universal History'. Whereas the latter deals with the whole sequence of actions and events, with all 'that man has done and suffered', the concern of the 'History of Mankind' is with 'what man was and still is'. Thus chronological order and temporal sequence was unimportant in this kind of history, of which Herodotus might with justice be called the 'father', for it was really concerned with the comparative description of different races, culture types, political constitutions, etc., the data being derived from travellers' reports and other similar sources. The aim of this still rather primitive form of cultural anthropology was to provide an account of 'the whole man . . . as he is naturally constituted for all time and in all corners of the world'.[2]

Hegel himself made a collection of excerpts under the heading 'Erfahrungen und Physiognomik' in which Zimmermann's *Über die Einsamkeit* played a large part—probably the excerpt that we have concerning Egyptian monks belonged to this classification.[3] Rosenkranz also mentions in this connection Meiners's *Briefe über die Schweiz*, Wünsch's *Kosmologische Unterhaltungen* (so perhaps the excerpt on 'True Happiness' also belongs here), Rousseau's *Confessions*, and Nicolai's *Reisen* (from which two of our unclassified excerpts on Enlightenment were derived). If Hegel was originally inspired to put this collection together by his reading of Meiners one can see why he may have provisionally placed his excerpts on the relation of *Aufklärung* to *Kultur*, and even on the character of an enlightened scholar in this category, for he would think of it as a branch of, or at least as closely related to, 'Philo-

---

[1] Rosenkranz, p. 14 (cf. *Dok.*, p. 400). We have already discussed the passage from Meiners's *Revision der Philosophie*, 'Von der Gelehrsamkeit der Ägypter', (*Dok.*, pp. 108–9) which has only one higher heading 'Ägypten', but was presumably classified as *Philosophische Geschichte.Ägypten*. Meiners was one of Hegel's most favoured authors for he also excerpted the *Briefe über die Schweiz* (Rosenkranz, p. 13; *Dok.*, p. 399); cf. Hegel's own footnote to his brief essay on the idea of physical quantity (*Dok.*, p. 43), and his references to Meiners in the diary of his walking-tour in the Bernese Alps (*Dok.*, pp. 223, 228, 231, 232, etc.).

[2] These remarks are founded on the note of Hoffmeister (*Dok.*, p. 419).

[3] *Dok.*, p. 105; for Rosenkranz's description of this part of Hegel's collection see pages 13–14 of his biography, reprinted also in *Dok.*, p. 399.

sophical History', which was a category that he seems to have employed technically in a sense close to that of Meiners's 'Universal History'.[1]

The existence of this collection—and its probable significance in Hegel's eyes—is enough in itself to invalidate Haering's claim that 'supra-individual cultural manifestations' formed the central focus of interest in Hegel's schoolboy researches.[2] 'Philosophical History' as Hegel would have preferred to call it, and we may well agree with him, did gradually absorb more of his attention in 1787 and 1788; and as this happened he gradually moved further away from the conception of man as an individual possessing an unchanging, self-contained, rational essence. He became more and more consciously convinced that 'truth is the whole', and at the same time that the wholeness of truth was essentially a process of development. As this happened, the collection of data to illustrate 'human nature' in the manner of Lavater's science of 'physiognomy' or even of Meiners's 'history of mankind', lost most of its attraction for him. But this conviction was not present in his mind at the beginning. What *was* present was a rather different, though nearly related, conviction which he never abandoned or lost, a conviction of the essential unity and integrity of human nature in all its manifestations, a conviction that from every particular case or event, if we can only understand it rightly, we can discover the whole truth about man, his nature, and his destiny.

This conviction can express itself equally in an atomic or in a developmental conception of human nature. It came to Hegel from his books and his teachers in both forms; but the conception of man as a rational atom was much more clearly and explicitly formulated in the thought of the period, which generally took mathematical analysis, mathematical construction, and mathematical intuition as its conscious model of rationality. Historical inquiry certainly came into its own in the eighteenth century, but its genetic and biological canons of rationality and models of explanation were less self-consciously adopted, being in any case much harder to formulate explicitly. One of Hegel's main aims in the *Phenomenology* was

[1] *Dok.*, pp. 145–7 (discussed above, pp. 20–1). For examples of Hegel's use of the term 'Philosophische Geschichte' see *Dok.*, p. 144. Lacorte (p. 86) draws attention to the occurrence of the phrase 'die allgemeine Geschichte des menschlichen Verstandes' in Hegel's excerpts from Feder's *Neuer Emil* (*Dok.*, p. 60).

[2] Haering, i, 16 (cf. also 18, 21).

to formulate the ideal of historical reasoning as opposed to the earlier mathematical ideal; this accounts for the sustained polemic in his mature works against mathematical modes of reasoning in philosophy in spite of the fact that he greatly enjoyed mathematics as a boy, and the philosophical foundations of mathematics continued to fascinate him all his life.

The true focus of Hegel's researches throughout his life was always, properly speaking, *man*; and even when he became convinced, as he did around 1788, that the proper approach to the study of human nature was through the analysis of human social institutions in their genesis and interrelations, he never lost sight of the fact that the real object of his concern was the rational individual agent. His philosophical activity began, if I am not mistaken, as an attempt to clarify for himself his own social role as an enlightened scholar and future teacher; and even his mature philosophy can best be grasped and understood as a philosopher's attempt to clarify for himself the function of his own science in a society of free and rational individuals.

4. *The school essays*

We can observe the gradual emergence of a historical conception of human nature in the essay 'On the religion of the Greeks and Romans' which Hegel wrote as a school task in August 1787. Only a few of his school essays are mentioned by Rosenkranz and it is probable that Hegel himself deliberately preserved those few, and did not preserve the others, or at least not many of them. This view, which rests mainly on the care with which Rosenkranz seems to have analysed and described everything that he found among Hegel's papers from this period, is further supported by the fact that the essays which remain to us, or of which we hear, are easily linked to what we know of Hegel's collection of excerpts and to the reflections we find in his *Tagebuch*.

Before we consider the essay on Greek and Roman religion however, we must consider briefly the only other school manuscript that has come down to us complete, the *Unterredung zwischen Dreien* which Rosenkranz explicitly says is the earliest product of Hegel's pen that survived him.[1] This is dated 30 May 1785, and is cast in the form of a dramatic conversation between

[1] *Dok.*, pp. 3–6; Rosenkranz, pp. 17–18.

the members of the second triumvirate, Antony, Lepidus, and Octavius. Earlier critics have commented on two points: first the influence of Shakespeare's *Julius Caesar* which is fairly easily discoverable in it; and secondly the evidence that it provides of Hegel's early preoccupation with the role of the hero or great political leader. What really needs to be noticed are the young author's political attitudes and commitments which the essay reveals. Octavius, who is clearly Hegel's hero, consents only reluctantly to the proscription of Cicero, and is doubtful whether 'the free Romans' will bear a master. He himself declares 'My unslavish neck is not used to bend before the overbearing glance of a master' in his closing soliloquy. The idealization of Republican freedom is patent. This tendency was, of course, typical of the 'enlightened' attitude towards Roman history, and reflects the way the young student was taught. The attitude of at least some of the teachers at the Protestant Gymnasium Illustre towards their Catholic Duke Karl Eugen—a little model of the enlightened despot who had established a rival institution, the Karlsschule or military academy, as his own pedagogical experiment in the proper moulding of youthful minds—was not perhaps quite as enthusiastic as the ritual effusions on his birthday might have led outsiders to believe. This is a point worth remembering when we come to consider Hegel's own valedictory address.

The essay *Über die Religion der Griechen und Römer*[1] is the most important and the most original piece of work that Hegel produced in his school years. In it we can see the emerging outline of the concept of a 'national religion' (*Volksreligion*) as the defining characteristic of community life and culture which continued to dominate Hegel's thoughts for quite a number of years. The influence of his reading and excerpts is everywhere apparent, but the main line of thought is his own and represents a development of several entries in his *Tagebuch* made in the previous year.

With respect to religion [Hegel begins], the Greeks and Romans followed the way of all nations—the thought of a Godhead is so natural to man that it has been developed by all peoples. In their childhood, in the primitive state of nature [*Urstand der Natur*], they thought of God as an almighty Being, who ruled them and all things according to His whim [*nach Willkür*]. They formed their conception of Him on the model of the masters that they knew, the fathers and chiefs of families

[1] *Dok.*, pp. 43–8.

who held the power of life and death over their subjects absolutely at their pleasure, and whose bidding they followed blindly in everything, even in the execution of unjust and inhuman commands; who were angry as men are, acted rashly, and might be sorry for it. In just this way they conceived their Godhead, and the ideas [*Vorstellungen*] of the majority of men in our times of renowned enlightenment are no differently constituted.

At this stage men viewed physical and even moral evil as punishments from the Gods and sought to placate them with sacrifices:

These men had not the insight that the former evil is no real evil, that happiness and misfortune are dependent on themselves, that the Godhead never sends misfortune for the hurt of His creatures. Nor did they reflect on the fact that the Supreme Being will not be won over by the gifts of men, that men can no more increase than diminish His riches, His might, or His glory.

The smoke of the burnt offering reached the heavens where the gods dwelt; and the gods themselves each had a sensible shape and an individual name. Each tribe had its own image of God and when tribes were united for a common purpose their gods also came together in a Pantheon. This was one root of polytheism; but also men personified the elements and natural forces and the particular localities of their world. Finally, too, they deified their great benefactors and heroes. 'The great confusion in their mythology was greatly aggravated by the efforts of the learned to find out the meaning of each fable.'

Temples were built and holy places set aside, often on heights, because their natural sublimity and their nearness to the heavens made them fit resting places for the gods; but also because of the effect that a far-reaching landscape has on the sensibilities of a solitary man. All experiences of strangeness were interpreted fearfully, and so all unexpected events became revelations of the power of the gods for 'those men without enlightenment, but endowed with vivid imaginations'. Everything was an omen for a superstitious Greek, and 'even in our days men read in a comet the life's end of a monarch, and in the scream of an owl the approach of death for a man'.

The more astute and cunning members of a social group took note of these fears and these yearnings for knowledge of fate. They realized that the peoples 'would be guided by nothing so readily as by religion. So they set themselves to feed and cultivate these beliefs and impulses.' 'Against all the assaults of reason they armed themselves thus by involving religion with all their actions and so sanctifying them.' They withdrew the images of the gods into secrecy, and exercised influence by way of oracles.

But once a nation 'reached a certain stage of civilization [*Bildung*]', men of greater intellect begin to discover and publish 'better concepts of the Godhead'. Most of the literature that we have from classical antiquity belongs to this stage, but even the earlier writings are valuable at least from the point of view of the 'history of mankind'. Every poet handles popular beliefs in his own way and for his own ends but the common faith forms the basis for their work and this faith in a beneficent ordering providence is common to all times alike:

The ignorant mass [*Pöbel*] of all peoples [*Völker*] ascribes human physical characteristics to the Godhead and believes in arbitrary commands and punishments. These opinions are moreover the strongest bridle of their passions; the grounds of reason and a purer religion are not powerful enough against them.

The Greek philosophers and their students offer us

far more enlightened and sublime concepts of the Godhead, especially in respect of the fate [*Schicksal*] of man. They taught that God gives to every man sufficient means and power to achieve happiness, and has so ordered the nature of things that true happiness is achieved through wisdom and moral goodness.

About these fundamental propositions they agreed, although they developed different systems of thought about the ultimate nature of the divine 'and other things incomprehensible to men'. These excesses will seem more intelligible and less laughable when we remember that their authors are men like ourselves, endowed with the same faculties; from them we can learn how hard it is to reach truth undistorted by errors. From their history we see how habit and ancient custom make men accept the greatest nonsense as reason, and utter stupidity as wisdom.

This will make us look carefully at our own inherited and traditional opinions, ready to test even those about which the hint of doubt has never entered our heads, or the suspicion that they may perhaps be entirely false or only half true.

This sentence Hegel himself emphasized in his closing paragraph, thus marking it as his most important conclusion. But his closing sentences turn back to the lesson of tolerance that can be derived from the comparison of other cultures with our own:

Once these experiences have taught us to consider it possible, even *likely* that many of our convictions are perhaps errors, and many of those of others, who think differently, are perhaps truths, we shall not then hate them, we shall not judge them without charity. We know how easy it is to fall into errors so we shall seldom ascribe them to ignorance and baseness, and hence we shall become ever more just and humane [*menschenliebender*] toward others.

This essay is outwardly dominated by the *contrast* between 'folk-religion' and enlightened religious insight. But we should particularly notice the assumption that all folk-religion contains a solid core of rational faith, which is made explicit and separated from its superstitious overgrowth by enlightened reflection; and we should notice also that the purely theoretical speculations of the philosophers are themselves regarded by Hegel as a sort of overgrowth of rational superstition. Thus folk-religion and true enlightenment are essentially *identical* in his vision, and only accidentally opposed or distinct.[1] Once we grasp this identity the

[1] This is probably the best point at which to consider the two excerpts of 1788 from reviews written by followers of Kant. For the remarks about philosophical theories in this essay provide the best indications we can get of the light in which Hegel viewed these excerpts. The first sets forth the Kantian conception of moral freedom. We can safely assume that Hegel accepted this as being already implicit in his conception of the enlightened man, though it is not quite concordant with the ideal of tolerance and charitable insight that he derived mainly from Lessing and Mendelssohn, which was generally dominant in his mind and which eventually caused him to react quite violently against Kantian rigorism.

The second was concerned with 'the relation between religion and metaphysics' and was taken from a critical essay about an attempt to defend Spinoza's system along lines suggested by Jacobi. The reviewer attacks it mainly from the point of view of the *Critique of Practical Reason*, arguing that Kant has shown the futility of any theory that rules out the possibility of the three postulates of practical reason, God, Freedom, and Immortality. One can readily see that in this perspective the critical philosophy would appeal to Hegel as providing rational grounds for his own 'purer religion', and the criticism of dogmatic metaphysics would be concordant with his own distinction between what is sound and what is erroneous in the productions of the enlightened intellect.

Whether these two excerpts are sufficient to justify Hoffmeister's contention that even in the Stuttgart period Hegel was 'quite well oriented about the spirit of the Kantian philosophy' (*Dok.*, p. 427), is something each reader must decide for himself. Negri (p. 67 n. 27) thinks not; but perhaps Fichte would have agreed with Hoffmeister.

seemingly violent pendulum swings in Hegel's later development, before he reached maturity, become much easier to understand. At Tübingen, where he felt himself faced only with different varieties of superstition, his attention seems to shift away from Christianity altogether, and he looks with longing toward the healthy folk-religion of Greece and the original birth of enlightened reflection upon it. But even then his thoughts were already beginning to focus on the project of doing for the Christian religion what the philosophers had done for Greek religion, and at the same time avoiding their opposite error of purely theoretical speculation. In the essay of 1787 it is the parallel in cultural development that strikes him as important in the first instance, not the possibility of progress from one culture to another that succeeds it, although the acceptance of that possibility is more or less explicit in his concluding paragraph.

The idea of a *necessary* progress from classical culture to our own, was not one that could have occurred to the young Hegel as yet, any more than it would have entered the heads of his teachers. His whole education was based on the assumption that the heritage of Greece and Rome contains the highest models of culture and enlightenment that we possess. The Romantics and Hegel himself were soon to claim that the masterpieces of modern literature were in a sense superior to those of the ancient world, but for the young Hegel it was more natural to assume the superiority of the ancient models and take that as a datum for explanation. This was the position which he adopted in his school essay of August 1788, 'On some characteristics which distinguish ancient writers ⟨from modern ones⟩',[1] and indeed it was an assumption which he never abandoned as far as purely aesthetic values were concerned. In this essay he leaned heavily on his reading of an essay of Garve's on the same topic.[2] After speaking of the way the ancients managed to identify the interest of the local community with the interest of humanity, and of the advantage of this for the poet, Hegel goes on:

In our times the poet has no longer any such ready prepared field of

---

[1] *Dok.*, pp. 48–51. (For use of angled parentheses here and elsewhere, see p. 480.)

[2] 'Betrachtung einiger Verschiedenheiten in den Werken der ältesten und neuern Schriftsteller, ins besondere der Dichter' in *Neuen Bibliothek der Schönen Wissenschaften*, vol x (Leipzig, 1770), pp. 189–210. Hoffmeister has provided in his notes (*Dok.*, pp. 407–14) an exhaustive analysis of the parallels between Hegel's essay and Garve's text.

activity. The famous deeds of our ancient, or even modern, Germans are not entwined into our constitution, nor is the memory of them preserved by oral tradition. We learn of them only from the history books and partly from those of foreign nations, and even this knowledge is confined to the cultivated classes. The tales that entertain the common folk are adventurous traditions connected neither with our religious system nor with the truth of history.[1]

For this reason, says Hegel, 'our great German epic poet' could not hope to reach the whole community as a Greek poet could. He was referring here to Klopstock's *Messias*; a few years later he made an exactly analogous contrast between the availability of English history to Shakespeare and the relative unavailability of the German tradition to Klopstock and other native poets.[2]

An important characteristic of ancient writers was their *Simplizität*: they set the simple image of the thing before us without trying to be subtle or learned, or to make it more exciting and fascinating than it is. Whereas we are 'interested in the art of the poet, and no longer in the thing itself', ancient poets expressed even a complex sensation (*Empfindung*) simply, 'without separating the manifold elements within it that the understanding can distinguish, and without dissecting out what lies hid'.

This is the first appearance in Hegel's own writings of the understanding (*Verstand*) as the power by which we analyse a complex living entity—and in the process destroy its life. The concept comes directly from Garve's essay, but as Lacorte has pointed out, Hegel had already taken possession of it, and made a more precise and technical term out of it than it was for Garve himself, in the course of making excerpts from Garve's *Examination of the Faculties* a year earlier:

From these materials [supplied by sensibility and imagination] *Reason* constructs the system of general concepts by which man governs

[1] Doubtless Tacitus' *Germania* is the foreign history book of which Hegel was primarily thinking.

[2] In the continuation of the 'Positivity' essay written in Berne in 1796 (see Nohl, pp. 216–17; Knox, pp. 148–9), Hegel quotes from Klopstock's *Odes* the bitter cry 'Is Achaea then, the Teutons' fatherland?' against the Hellenization of upper-class culture. He comments that one cannot restore a lost tradition and its imagery to life, and points out that one might as well ask Klopstock himself 'Is Judaea then, the Teutons' fatherland?', since the only common ground between the educated and the uneducated in Germany is to be found in the history of their religion. This common ground is the basis of Klopstock's 'wise choice' of subject-matter which Hegel speaks of in his Gymnasium essay.

himself and his affairs. Reason abstracts; if this happens repeatedly it is called Reflection [*Nachdenken*]; and since language supplies the soul with these abstract concepts in association with words, before the soul itself is capable of making abstractions, the understanding [here Hegel used *Verstand* where Garve had written *Vernunft*] is in the first place concerned to determine the meaning of words and to seek out the true general idea of which the word should be a sign.[1]

We can see how from the excerpt cited above a doctrine of two types of abstraction—direct or legitimate abstraction of concepts from one's own experience, and indirect or illegitimate abstraction of meanings for the words that we have learned—can be derived. The contrast between the two resulting types of knowledge, personal experience and book-learning as we may call them for short, was the most primitive and intimate concern of Hegel as a budding scholar. Book-learning was his particular *bête noire*. Ancient 'simplicity' appealed to him as a secure defence against it:

Further, since their whole system of education and *Bildung* was so constituted that everyone had derived his ideas from direct experience [*Erfahrung selbst*] and 'the cold book-learning that is just expressed with dead signs in one's mind' they knew nothing of, but for all they knew they could still tell 'How? Where? Why? they learned it'; for this reason everyone had to have his own system of thought, his own peculiar form of spirit, each one had to be *original*. We learn from our youth up, the current mass of words and signs of ideas, and they rest in our heads without activity and without use; only bit by bit through experience, do we first come to know what a treasure we have and to think something with the words, although they are already forms for us according to which we model our ideas; they already have their

---

[1] As far as I am aware Lacorte was the first to appreciate the significance of this passage. His claim that Hegel's substitution of *Verstand* where Garve wrote *Vernunft* was deliberate, is strongly supported by the fact that Hegel has already affirmed that it is *Vernunft* which abstracts (Garve did *not* say this); and by the fact that he omits Garve's own definition of abstraction (which would fit very well with the activity Hegel assigns to *Verstand* but not with the activity which both of them assign to *Vernunft*). Garve's definition of *Abstrahieren* was: 'Comparing a number of impressions [*Empfindungen*] with one another, noting what is similar in them, collecting this in a concept, and letting everything else which is not similar go' (*Dok.*, p. 122 with Hoffmeister's notes ad loc.). It seems to me rather unsafe to assume that Hegel already has a clear notion of the abstraction that he ascribes to Reason. But I think that it is fairly clear that he did already want to use *Vernunft* and *Verstand* as technical terms for two attitudes toward experience.

established range and limits, and are relations according to which we are accustomed to see everything.[1]

This passage—all of which is based on more scattered assertions in Garve, except for the three lines of poetry which Hegel himself added from Lessing's *Nathan the Wise*, a work whose enormous influence on him is here for the first time explicitly documented—shows us that the modifications Hegel introduced while excerpting Garve's *Examination of the Faculties* were intended to establish a distinction between *Vernunft*, the faculty by which we acquire personal knowledge, and *Verstand* which is the capacity for correct linguistic behaviour. It would seem that, although Garve, like Lessing and Rousseau and other pedagogical theorists of the time, made much of the contrast between personal knowledge and mere book-learning, and although he connected it with the two different ways in which we acquire abstract ideas, he did not think of the two types of abstraction as the work of distinct rational faculties. But Hegel, for whom the contrast had a burning importance, felt from the beginning the urgent need to keep the two sorts of mental operation quite distinct, and hence designated them by different names, as soon as he recognized their existence. What we have before us is the distinction between concrete and abstract universals at the moment of its first conception. It is destined to undergo much further development, in the course of which all types of abstract idea, regardless of their process of origin, will eventually be assigned to the domain of *Verstand*. But the ideal of the concrete universal as here stated—the formation of one's own *Geist*, of one's own *Gedankensystem* by and for the interpretation of one's own experience—remained constant in Hegel's mind. As his thought developed, the requirement of 'concreteness'—that the connection between the system and the experience be essential and indissoluble—became ever more rigorous. Thus we can recognize immediately how right Haering was to call Hegel a 'spiritual empiricist'; and we can appreciate to the full the irony of Kierkegaard's eventual rebellion against 'the System' in the name of 'subjectivity'. 'Subjectivity' was the original object of Hegel's most passionate devotion; and he bore witness to the source of his

[1] *Dok.*, pp. 49–50; for the origins of the passage in Garve see Hoffmeister's notes, ibid., pp. 411–13. The verses come from Lessing's *Nathan der Weise*, Act V, Scene 6 (Everyman edn., pp. 210–11). Hegel refers to this scene again in the 'Tübingen fragment'; see below, p. 495.

inspiration when he repeated in the Preface to the *Phenomenology* the thesis that we have just quoted from his Gymnasium essay of 1788:

The manner of study of the ancient world differs from that of the modern world in this, that the former was the forming to perfection [*Durchbildung*] of the natural consciousness. Putting itself to the test in every aspect of its existence and philosophizing about everything that happened, it [i.e. the natural consciousness] developed itself into a thoroughly activated universality [*erzeugte es sich zu einer durch und durch betätigten Allgemeinheit*]. In modern times on the other hand the individual finds the abstract form ready made . . .[1]

The echo here is plain, although by 1807 Hegel has come to regard the 'modern' situation as a progress relative to the situation of 'natural' consciousness, because it makes possible the achievement of a higher kind of universality altogether. Even in the essay of 1788 we can see a hint of the development that is to come, for Hegel goes on to note as another of his distinguishing characteristics of ancient poetry an interest in the immediate outward appearance of things, whereas we moderns are interested in the inward causes of what appears on the surface. But in the 1788 essay the point is turned to the disadvantage of the moderns, whereas in the *Phenomenology* it is precisely in this that our progress lies.[2]

---

[1] *Phänomenologie*, p. 30; Baillie, p. 94. There are in the immediate context other echoes to which Hoffmeister has drawn attention (*Dok.*, pp. 412-13).

[2] The passage cited above from the *Phenomenology* continues thus:

'In modern times, on the other hand, the individual finds the abstract form ready made; the straining to grasp it and make it his own is more the unmediated drawing forth of the inward, and truncated production [*Erzeugen*] of the universal than its emergence from the concrete and from the manifoldness of existence. Hence nowadays the task is not so much to purify the individual from the immediate mode of sense consciousness, and make it an object of thought and a thinking substance, but rather to do the opposite: to actualize the universal and to bring it to life [*begeisten*] by superseding [*das Aufheben*] fixed determinate thought-forms. But it is much harder to bring fixed thought-forms into a state of flux than it is to do the same to sensible existence [as happens in the abstraction of a thought-form from sense experience]. The reason lies in what has been said already; the fixed thought-forms have the Ego, the might of the negative or the pure actuality, as their substance and the element of their existence; the determinations of sense on the other hand have only the impotence of abstract immediacy or being as such [as their substance etc.]. The thought-forms go into flux because pure thought, this inner immediacy, recognizes itself as a moment, or because the pure certainty of itself abstracts from itself—it does not let itself go, set itself aside, but it gives up the fixity of its self-positing, both the fixity of the pure concrete which is the Ego itself as opposed to distinct contents, and the fixity of the

The rest of Hegel's essay, or rather, the rest of the fragment that we have, reiterates and further illustrates the two points which mainly interest him: that the ancient poets could write for the people as a whole without having to think of a specific audience, and that they wrote spontaneously, creating the forms which suited them but which modern poets must now willy-nilly accept. The hypothesis that he has Klopstock in mind as his representative modern poet receives further confirmation when he comes to the conclusion of a very summary account of the history of Greek tragedy viewed as an illustration of his thesis: 'Had the Germans gradually civilized [*verfeinert*] themselves without foreign *Kultur*, their spirit would without doubt have taken another way, and we would have our own German drama instead of borrowing our dramatic forms from the Greeks.' We know that Hegel's excerpts included long passages from Klopstock's *Odes*, and we can hardly fail to be reminded here of the way he quotes the cry 'Is Achaea then the Teutons' fatherland' in his essay on 'The Positivity of the Christian Religion' at Berne. But the fact that his essay closed, according to Rosenkranz, with an 'encomium of the perfection of the Greeks' indicates that he did not really regret the foreign intervention that disturbed the natural course of German cultural development. The explicit doctrine of his essays is that the rational essence of humanity expresses itself in the *parallel* course of development in all cultures. Anyone who really held this view would tend to sympathize with Klopstock's complaint. But the implicit doctrine even in these early essays is that the nature of humanity expresses itself in cultural history as a whole, that is to say in the *progression* from one culture to another. From this point of view we expect to find each stage of cultural development perfectly instantiated only once. That one instance must then serve as the common heritage of all further development and the

distinct contents which, being posited in the element of pure thought, participate in that absoluteness [*Unbedingtheit*] of the Ego. Through this movement the pure thought-forms become notions, and are then for the first time, what they are in truth, self-movements, circles—[they are] what their substance is, spiritual essences.'

We are not yet in a position to throw much light on this passage. But we can at least understand one mysterious and paradoxical fact. We know how it has come about that Hegel describes the *concrete* universal as the result of a kind of *abstraction*; and we know what form of abstraction he meant to rule out in this connection, for the expression 'letting everything else go' occurred in Garve's definition (given above, p. 37 n. 1).

parallel aspects of more advanced cultures will be partly contaminated, partly reduced to irrelevance (like the folk-tradition in German popular culture according to Hegel), and partly cut off altogether. Greece already has for Hegel the status of a perfect exemplar of this type. It is the perfect fulfilment of natural religion (*Volksglaube* as Hegel called it in the essay of 1787), of natural spontaneity or *Simplizität* (as he describes it here in 1788). In the *Phenomenology* he explicitly calls it 'the *Durchbildung* of the natural consciousness'. In 1795 he is still not perfectly aware of the assumptions implicit in his position; but he does explicitly recognize the *futility* of Klopstock's lament, and that recognition is the crucial step in the transition from the 'history of humanity' as understood by his teachers to the 'phenomenology of the spirit' as Hegel came to understand it.[1]

A few months later Hegel's school career came to an end, and he was chosen to give the valedictory address for his class. Any student in this situation anywhere, is expected to show himself appropriately grateful for the education he has received, and appreciative of its virtues; and there is no reason to suppose that Hegel was in any way deficient in this regard. But the way in which he chose to praise and thank his teachers was certainly a remarkable one. He 'paid the institution a very fine compliment', as Rosenkranz sardonically put it, by describing the stunted state of the arts and sciences among the Turks in order to show how much better it was to have been educated at the Stuttgart gymnasium. 'The reverential-ceremonial way in which he was wont throughout his life to open such occasions, is already fully present here [wrote Rosenkranz]. The uprightness and the solid depth of his piety, and his sense of official duty so to speak was only satisfied by a certain breadth and exhaustiveness.'[2] The conclusion of his speech which

[1] Rosenkranz, p. 13 (for his excerpts from Klopstock); ibid., p. 461 (for the conclusion of the essay); cf. *Dok.*, pp. 398 and 51 respectively. For the quotation see Nohl, p. 217 (Knox, p. 149) and p. 36 n. 2 above. The hypothesis that in this essay Klopstock is taken as the representative of 'modern' poetry was first advanced by Dilthey (*Gesammelte Schriften*, iv. 7); but we should note that Hegel cites Lessing's *Nathan* himself in the essay, and that he analysed Schiller's *Fiesko* (a play which, like *The Robbers*, certainly illustrates the characteristics and problems of 'modern' poetry, so far as they can be gathered from the essay). Klopstock is 'our great epic poet' but both Lessing and Schiller are probably in Hegel's mind as the modern tragedians.

[2] Rosenkranz, p. 19; his extract from the speech which immediately follows, is reprinted in *Dok.*, pp. 52–4, but the personal comments I have quoted are not there given. (See further the *Note* on p. 56 below.)

Rosenkranz has preserved for us began thus:

So great an influence then, has education upon the general good of a state! How strikingly we see in this nation [the Turks] the frightful consequences of its neglect. If we consider the natural capacities of the Turks and then the crude roughness of their character and all that they lack in the sciences, we shall come thereby to know our own high good fortune, and learn to value at its true worth the fact that Providence caused us to be born in a State whose Prince, convinced of the importance of education, and of the general and extensive utility of the sciences, makes both of them together a principal object of his high care, and has established lasting and unforgettable monuments to his fame in this respect also, monuments which our distant posterity will still wonder at and bless. Of his admirable views and of his zeal for the good of the fatherland, the most eloquent proof and that which touches us most closely is provided by—the equipment of this institution, at the basis of which lies the noble intent to educate for the state good citizens capable of meeting its needs.

A certain element of comedy in the situation strikes all observers; and if something of the same sort had been credited to Schiller when he said farewell to the Karlsschule a few years earlier, the suspicion of a deliberate joke would have arisen very quickly, soon enough probably to have brought the wrath of that same Duke Karl Eugen of Württemberg upon him. But because the author of the deed was Hegel, with his lifelong record of reverential solemnity upon academic occasions, the assumption has always been that the prime humour of the situation arises from his complete unawareness of anything incongruous in it. Here is a young student, very earnest in his devotion to learning and inexhaustibly curious about the 'history of mankind' as opposed to 'natural history', who has been reading, and perhaps making long extracts from, a book about the Ottoman Empire,[1] and who has laid upon him a duty and an honour which he regards very seriously as something he must live up to by an appropriate display of his own learning. It

---

[1] Hoffmeister suggests Rycaut, *Histoire de l'État present de l'Empire Ottoman* (Paris, 1670), as a possible source for Hegel's information. If he was reading it (or something else like it) at the time that he prepared his speech, we need not assume that he made excerpts as well. He could keep the speech and put a cross reference to it (with an indication of the source) into his collection of notes. I suspect he may have done something of this sort with his essay on the ancient poets. But, of course, he may simply have kept the essay and speech because they were germane to his interests, without bothering to index their sources.

appears to him that he can at one and the same time do honour to his school, and exhibit the particular virtues and uses of the studies to which he is personally devoted; and the result is the speech of which Rosenkranz has given us the conclusion.

This is a plausible enough view. But to someone who examines carefully all the evidence that remains to us of Hegel's attitudes and interests as a schoolboy, beginning with the excerpt headed 'Education. Plan of the Normal Schools in Russia', which he made several months before his fifteenth birthday,[1] a rather different hypothesis suggests itself. This very serious young student is deeply interested in educational theory and practice; he is especially concerned about the social function and duties of professional scholars and teachers, because he means to become one or at least to make his education effective in some way calculated to lead to an increase in general enlightenment. Also he is a thoughtful Protestant, not noticeably devout and certainly not very emotional about his religion, but disposed to be contemptuous of Catholicism in general, and finding twin grounds for his contempt in the phenomena of 'superstition' and absolute authority, which he believes to be causally connected and mutually supportive evils. His ideal is the achievement of an enlightened society, and it is clear that he inclines towards the view that it must be achieved by 'republican' means, rather than by the Platonic absolutism of the enlightened despots.[2]

This young man has heard his teachers give ceremonial addresses on such occasions as the Duke's birthday which were not perhaps always perfectly sincere, and he would without doubt be sensible on any note of irony that could be detected. Now that it is his turn to perform, his reading suggests to him a way in which he can say what he believes in a form that will make perceptive listeners realize that although they should certainly be grateful for the benefits of life in the Christian city of Stuttgart, it is still far

---

[1] *Dok.*, pp. 54–5.

[2] This assertion must rest mainly on the general tendency of the authors who contributed most to Hegel's conception of 'Enlightenment', whom I take to have been Mendelssohn and Lessing. His father was a court official, and certainly no radical. But we need not assume that no word of criticism of the Duke was ever uttered in the home. I have argued above that signs of 'republican' feeling (I use the word in the sense found in Kant's *Perpetual Peace*) can be observed, in the 'Unterredung zwischen Dreien'; and we may well suspect that it lay behind the 'analysis' which Hegel made 'of the republican tragedy *Fiesco*' (Rosenkranz, p. 13).

removed from the New Jerusalem of the Enlightenment. To compare Württemberg and its Duke interested in pedagogical experiments, with the Ottoman Empire and the Grand Turk was a way of saying that a petty but enlightened despot is better than a great and unenlightened one. But to say *that* about a Catholic ruler to an academic audience of Protestants, was certainly to suggest, if not strictly to imply, that things would really be far better in a society which had dispensed with despotic authorities altogether.

The polite words that he goes on to address to his teachers we can pass over.[1] But a few words from his closing adjuration to his fellow students deserve quoting, because they seem to sum up so well his own experience and the convictions of his school years: 'The sense of how important your vocation is will always give you fresh heart and, little by little, a love for your occupation, which will reward you with a greater, truer, and more lasting pleasure and happiness than the finest devices [*Erfindungen*][2] of sense experience will afford.'

5. *The gaps in the record*

We have more evidence for the reconstruction of Hegel's formative years than we have in the case of most great thinkers. But of course all the evidence that we now have is only a fraction of what was available to his first biographer; and that in turn was only a partial record of his school-days, which Hegel himself had preserved. The manuscript of the *Tagebuch* still exists, having been preserved originally, no doubt, because of its personal character and associations. The essays are preserved for us only because Rosenkranz chose to quote them wholly or in part in his biography. The excerpts that we have were discovered in a single packet by G.

---

[1] As one reads the account of the organization of study and instruction at the Gymnasium given by Julius Klaiber (and quoted by Flechsig in Hegel, *Briefe*, iv. 156–9) one is almost inclined to wonder whether the educational chaos in that institution may not have been one of the targets of Hegel's irony (supposing that conscious irony was intended). But he did gain much from some of his teachers and one cannot tell how far the organization of things appeared chaotic to him—the only sign we have of such an opinion is the regret he expressed about Löffler's being forced to work so far 'below his proper sphere'. Of course his interest in the organization of the school system elsewhere (specifically in Russia) may have sprung from a conviction of this kind.

[2] I suspect that this is a misreading by Rosenkranz of *Empfindungen* (sensations) in Hegel's manuscript.

Thaulow in 1854 and first printed in that year. Thaulow claimed that they had been put together and in order by Hegel himself, but this view is hard to reconcile with Rosenkranz's description of the divisions of the collection as Hegel left it.[1] A more plausible view, I think, when we compare what Thaulow printed with what Rosenkranz wrote, is that the bundle which Thaulow discovered had been put in order by Rosenkranz or by someone else on his behalf, as a representative selection for the Stuttgart period from a larger collection which extended into later years, and which was not itself chronologically arranged. The purpose of the compiler, on this hypothesis, was to get a clear view of just what there was among the surviving excerpts, that, on the one hand, dated back to the Stuttgart years, and, on the other, was of interest for the purposes of a philosophical biography.

If this view is accepted, the fact that Thaulow, who believed that Hegel had made the selection himself, decided that the connecting thread that would indicate his purpose was to be found in the heading of the very first excerpt—*Erziehung*—is very suggestive. On the other hand, if the excerpts were in fact selected for a philosophical biography in the first place, the whole interpretation of the surviving evidence proposed above lies open to the criticism that it takes no account of the selective bias that has determined what was preserved. It thus makes Hegel out to have been consciously controlled by a purpose which in his actual working life as a student he may scarcely have entertained consciously at all, or at best only very intermittently.

I myself believe that Hegel consciously wished from an early age, certainly before he was fifteen, to become a good and useful scholar. He was interested in many things, including almost everything that he did at school, and some things that were not much attended to there. But his concern with the problem of what makes a scholar good and useful gradually caused his interest in the general theory of human nature, and particularly in the formative influences of culture and education upon it, to take on a focal

[1] Thaulow, *Hegel's Ansichten über Erziehung und Unterricht*, Dritter Teil (Kiel, 1854), pp. 33–146 (I quote from *Dok.*, p. 414). It is of course possible that Hegel himself took the excerpts from various parts of his collection and put them together for some purpose of his own. But if so he must have done so no later than 1789 (otherwise we should surely find excerpts made at Tübingen among them), and I am quite unable to imagine what purpose he could have had in mind in making this selection at that time.

position in his mind; most of his other major interests were literary and philological and could easily be made subservient to this one. He learned from Garve (who had in turn learned from Adam Ferguson) to think of language as the most fundamental and revealing of human cultural institutions;[1] and the pedagogical character of his interest in literature is apparent from virtually every reference to it that remains to us from the early period (or from later periods for that matter). He thought of the poets primarily as teachers;[2] and we may add that in his time the poets themselves, and most of their audience, thought the same way. So I cannot believe that the preservation of the literary and philological parts of his collection of notes and excerpts would have materially changed the picture of Hegel's mind that we get from what does survive.

Only one of his interests remained really outside his concern with his own vocation as an enlightened scholar, and with the cultural history of mankind in general. This was his interest in physics and mathematics. How absorbing he found it, and how it occupied his time for fairly lengthy periods to the exclusion of almost everything else, we can judge from passages in his *Tagebuch* for 1785 and 1787. These subjects always continued to fascinate him, but he was thirty years old before his interests in them began to coalesce with his cultural and pedagogical concerns; it was when this happened that his philosophy began to assume the form that it has in his mature system.

His industry is almost staggering to contemplate. But when we remember that he did his regular school work with considerable zeal, and that much of his independent reading and studying was directly connected with it, it seems plausible to suppose that the selection of excerpts that we have represents a fairly generous sample from those that he assembled on philosophy, psychology, and pedagogy during the Stuttgart years. In particular, we know from Rosenkranz that his excerpts from the major philosophers began at Tübingen. I shall end this chapter with two tabulations designed to indicate the extent and limitations of our evidence for Hegel's activities between the ages of fourteen and eighteen. The first table shows how far Rosenkranz's account can be matched by documents that we have; and the second shows how much of Hegel's time we can account for by what we know about his

[1] *Dok.*, p. 393.   [2] Cf. the title of the lost oration *De utilitate poeseos.*

activities. The first table alone will go far, I think, to confirm the hypothesis that the excerpts we have were originally picked out to serve as the basis for the detailed comments made by Rosenkranz; and I believe that when taken in conjunction with the second table it will support the further claim that the excerpts we have represent quite a large proportion of the notes that Hegel assembled in the Stuttgart period, on the topics that Rosenkranz surveyed in detail.

APPENDIX A

ROSENKRANZ'S DESCRIPTION OF HEGEL'S EXCERPT COLLECTION COMPARED WITH THE MANUSCRIPTS DISCOVERED BY THAULOW (AND OTHER SURVIVING EVIDENCE)

ROSENKRANZ	THAULOW AND OTHER EVIDENCE

I: *Philology and Literary History*

(a) 'One of the largest of these excerpt collections' containing descriptions in Latin of the 'life, writings and editions of almost all the ancient authors' (including such less-known ones as Polyaenus' book of the battles of famous generals).

In some cases the extracts amount to small books: e.g. the notes of Brunk on Sophocles are almost all copied out.

(b) *Präparationen:*

  for the Psalms (Oct. 1785)
  for the *Iliad* (July 1786)
  for Cicero, *Ad familiares* (Nov. 1786)
  for Aristotle, *Ethics* (May 1787)
  for Sophocles, *Oedipus Coloneus* (July 1787)
  for Theocritus (? possibly later at Tübingen)

None of this material has survived.

[The *Tagebuch* entry for 30 July 1785 is an indication of Hegel's budding interest in the *editions* of ancient authors.]

[The loss of Hegel's notes on and translations from Sophocles— see (c) below—is particularly regrettable in view of the influence of Greek tragedy upon his thought throughout life.]

ROSENKRANZ

THAULOW
AND OTHER EVIDENCE

Wordlist for Tyrtaeus (July 1786)

(c) *Translations:*

Sophocles, *Antigone*[1]
Epictetus, *Enchiridion*
Longinus, *On the Sublime* (Nov. 1786–Sept. 1787)

(Compare *Tagebuch*, 1 Jan. 1787: *Dok.*, 38.)

? Tacitus, *Agricola* (not seen and not precisely dated by Rosenkranz)

(The Tacitus translation may belong to the Stuttgart period; see *Moral Philosophy*, p. 51 below.)

Extensive selections from ? Thucydides (no date on the manuscript)

(The translation of Thucydides almost certainly belongs to the Berne or Frankfurt period. Compare the fragments of 'historical studies' printed by Rosenkranz, pp. 514–32.)

II: *Aesthetics*

(a) *Excerpts from prose writers:*

Dusch, *Briefe zur Bildung des Geschmacks* (particularly extensive excerpts)

Ramler
Lessing[2]

It would appear that nothing from this *Sammlung* has survived although Thaulow's Excerpt 4 on *Hahn des Sokrates* was taken from Dusch's *Briefe* on 6 Apr. 1786 (*Dok.*, pp. 86–7).

(Hegel's interest in Dusch and 'Ramler' (i.e. Batteux) can be documented and dated from the *Tagebuch*.)[3]

---

[1] Hegel worked on Sophocles for several years both at Stuttgart (see below, p. 56 n. 1) and at Tübingen. Rosenkranz speaks of 'the surviving translations' of the *Antigone*, which indicates that Hegel translated parts of the play several times. At Tübingen, probably under the influence of Hölderlin, he attempted metrical versions of passages from Sophocles, which were not very satisfactory.

[2] Hegel certainly derived some of his extracts on 'Lehrgedicht' from Dusch's *Briefe zur Bildung des Geschmacks* (see Hoffmeister's note in *Dok.*, p. 404). He tried twice to obtain the work of Dusch from the Ducal Library in July 1785. But he had then to be content with Ramler's translation of Charles Batteux, *Einleitung in die schönen Wissenschaften* (4 vols., Vienna, 1770, with additions by the translator; he read at that time the section concerning 'Epic' in volume ii: see his *Tagebuch* in *Dok.*, pp. 15–16). Rosenkranz follows Hegel in referring to this work as 'Ramler'.

[3] No excerpts from Lessing's prose or poetry survive (and this is another very regrettable gap). Hoffmeister (*Dok.*, p. 398) proposes the *Literaturbriefe* and the *Hamburgische Dramaturgie* as probable sources of Hegel's excerpts in this general category. But we should remember that Hegel himself quotes *Nathan* in his essay on the 'Characteristics of Ancient Poets' (see p. 37 above).

<table>
<tr><td>ROSENKRANZ</td><td>THAULOW
AND OTHER EVIDENCE</td></tr>
</table>

ROSENKRANZ	THAULOW AND OTHER EVIDENCE
Engel[1] Eberhard[2] (under topical headings such as *Epopöie, Lehrgedicht, Roman*)	

(b) *Excerpts from poetic sources:*

Horace, *Epistles* (in Wieland's translation, Dessau, 1782) Klopstock, *Odes* (extensively copied) Schiller, *Fiesco* (analytical summary) *Stammbuchsentenzen* (collected 1786)	(Hegel cites Wieland's Horace in his essay on the ancient poets (Aug. 1788): see *Dok.*, p. 51.)

(c) *Excerpts on Language and stylistics:*

Gottsched, *Kern der Deutschen Sprachkunst* (extensive excerpts)

Lexicon of German idioms[3]

III: *Erfahrungen und Physiognomik*

Extracts from:

Zimmermann, *Über die Einsamkeit*	See *Weg zum Glück* (*Dok.*, p. 100) and excerpts 8 and 9 (*Dok.*, pp. 104–7).
Meiners, *Briefe über die Schweiz*	See Hegel's footnote to *Einige Bemerkungen* (*Dok.*, pp. 42–3).[4]
Wünsch, *Kosmologische Unterhaltungen*	See excerpt 6: *Wahre Glückseligkeit* (*Dok.*, pp. 87–99).
Rousseau, *Confessions*	From Rousseau nothing survives.[5]

---

[1] Hoffmeister (loc. cit.) suggests J. J. Engel, *Ideen zu einer Mimik* (Berlin, 1785).

[2] Hoffmeister (loc. cit.) suggests J. A. Eberhard, *Theorie der schönen Wissenschaften* (Halle, 1783).

[3] Nicolai's *Reisen durch Deutschland und die Schweiz*, Part 9, was undoubtedly one of the main sources for this: cf. *Dok.*, p. 399 n.

[4] No actual excerpts survive, but there is other evidence of the influence of this book on Hegel's mind. For instance we know from his remarks in the diary of his own journey in the Bernese Alps that he was much impressed by Meiners's descriptions of scenery and of the physical features of the landscape (see *Dok.*, pp. 223, 228, etc.).

[5] I suspect that Hegel may not have read Rousseau until he went to Tübingen and that Rosenkranz noticed the excerpts in the collection but did not note the dates. Quite possibly the genuine Rousseau excerpts were not dated if they were

ROSENKRANZ	THAULOW AND OTHER EVIDENCE
Nicolai, *Reisen* (from here Hegel gathered detailed physiognomies for German regional types, such as Bavaria, Brandenburg, Tyrol, Vienna)	See excerpts 17 and 18 (*Dok.*, pp. 145–7).

IV: *Special Sciences*

Excerpts concerning:

(a) *Arithmetic, Geometry, and related mathematical topics*

Excerpts mainly from Kästner	No mathematical excerpts survive —but see the *Tagebuch* entries
School notebook for Geometry	for 22–5 July 1785, and Jan. 1787 (*Dok.*, pp. 16–18 and 39–41).

(b) *Physics, Mechanics, Optics*

School notebooks	Nothing survives. But Christiane
Excerpt on *Farbenlehre* from Scheuchzer, *Physica* (Zürich 1729)	remembered Hegel's 'Freude an Physik' as a schoolboy (*Dok.*,
Other excerpts	p. 394).

(c) *Psychology*

Campe, *Seelenlehre für Kinder* ('plays large role' in this category)[1]	See excerpt 7: *Seele* (*Dok.*, pp. 101–4).

(d) *Moral Philosophy* (Die Moral)

Garve Ferguson[2]	See excerpt 13: from *Prüfung der Fähigkeiten* (*Dok.*, pp. 115–36).

made at Tübingen. Rosenkranz might then have used the long excerpt from Feder's *New Émile* as a guide for dating them.

[1] There are two reasons for suspecting that at this point Rosenkranz's account is a little careless. In the first place, the excerpt that we have from Campe's *Seelenlehre*, although quite long, is not of very much importance, and almost certainly Hegel did not attach much importance to it when he began to make excerpts explicitly catalogued as 'Psychology'. In the second place, these later excerpts are classified by Rosenkranz under 'Die Moral', which is a category that Hegel does not appear to have employed. But his classification system evolved gradually and he may have begun to use this heading to cover Psychology and Ethics (and Pedagogy?) later on. In any case Rosenkranz is at fault for not indicating something which the surviving excerpts show quite clearly—that Psychology, Pedagogy, Philosophical History, and Theology were for Hegel branches of Philosophy. (Campe's *Theophron* was more influential on Hegel than the *Seelenlehre*—but he would hardly have spent time excerpting from a book that he possessed—see the *Tagebuch* for Dec. 1785, *Dok.*, p. 24; and the 'Tübingen fragment', pp. 137, 139, 490, and 493 below. Hoffmeister's surmise —*Dok.*, p. 405—about *Robinson der Jüngere*, should also be kept in mind.)

[2] Hegel was undoubtedly led to study Adam Ferguson through his reading of

ROSENKRANZ	THAULOW AND OTHER EVIDENCE
Plato Aristotle Tacitus Cicero } (categorized excerpts concerning nature of justice and the virtues)	Almost certainly these belonged to the earliest stages of Hegel's collection, like the *Definitions* listed below. One excerpt from Cicero on Happiness has come down to us dated 27 June 1786 (*Dok.*, p. 100).

(*e*) *Pedagogy*

'the ideal of tutorship' (long excerpts)	See excerpt 2: *Feder's neuer Emil* (*Dok.*, pp. 55–81).
Schlözer's *Staatsanzeiger* (copiously used)	See excerpt 1 (*Dok.*, pp. 54–5).[2]

(*f*) *Philosophical History*

Meiners, *Geschichte der Menschheit*	Cf. excerpt 11 (from another work of Meiners); see further excerpt 16 (review of Eberhard).[3]

(*g*) *Theology* (*Natural and Positive*)

Critical Journals (almost entirely)[4]	See excerpt 14: *Vorsehung* (*Dok.*, p. 137).

Garve, for Garve translated Ferguson's *Principles of Moral Philosophy* and it was published with his notes at Leipzig in 1772. This would be the volume from which Hegel made his excerpts. See Hoffmeister's notes (*Dok.*, pp. 420–3, and 407) for other works of Garve or translated by Garve that Hegel either read or may have read.

[2] To justify Rosenkranz's comment there must obviously have been a number of other excerpts from this source. The selection of the one that has survived is easy to understand if we assume, as seems highly probable, that it was the earliest dated excerpt in Hegel's collection.

[3] This is the only category in which there are more surviving excerpts than there are authors in Rosenkranz's catalogue; and the excerpt that he does mention does not survive. This is a point against my hypothesis. We can be certain, moreover, that this category was an important one in Hegel's collection in its earliest stages. Of course, he *owned* a number of books in this category— e.g. perhaps Schrökh—and he would only need to excerpt from these for special purposes (compare *Tagebuch*, 27 June 1785, and 'Philosophy' in the collection of *Definitions* which was made at the same time. Rosenkranz finds Hegel's dependence on Schrökh for his definition of philosophy—cited in the first note on the next page—amusing, and he may well have felt that the category of 'philosophical history' was not worth much attention; and of course it probably did not appear nearly as important in the context of the whole collection as it was in the early years. This may have led Rosenkranz to discount it somewhat in his account of the early years. It would be of particular interest to know what excerpts there were in this part of the collection and when they were made.

[4] In spite of the survival of excerpt 14, I cannot help suspecting that Rosenkranz is here guilty of running together Hegel's Tübingen and even Berne periods with his Stuttgart studies.

ROSENKRANZ	THAULOW AND OTHER EVIDENCE

(h) Philosophy

Sulzer

Definitions (small volume dated 10 June 1785). This is the first sign of philosophical interests but covers a great variety of subjects. The first three are:

See excerpt 12 for the *Allgemeine Übersicht* to which Rosenkranz specifically refers (*Dok.*, pp. 109–12; cf. also pp. 112–15).

Superstition (*Aberglauben*)
Beauty (*Schönheit*)
Philosophy (*Philosophieren*)[1] (from Schrökh)

(Cf. *Tagebuch*, 9–12 July 1785 (*Dok.*, pp. 13–14).)
(Cf. *Tagebuch*, 27 June 1785 (*Dok.*, p. 7).)

Others are:

Change (*Veränderung*)[2] (from Mendelssohn's *Phaedo*)
Logic (*Logik*)[3]
State (*Staat*)[4] (from Cicero)

(Cf. *Tagebuch*, 15 July 1785 (*Dok.*, p. 15).)

Many definitions were from Rochau[5]

APPENDIX B

THE CHRONOLOGY OF HEGEL'S EARLIEST MANUSCRIPTS (1785–1788)[6]

1785

22 Apr.   Excerpt 1 (from Schlözer's *Staats Anzeigen* (*Dok.*, p. 54)).

[1] The definition is 'bis auf den Grund und die innere Beschaffenheit menschlicher Begriffe und Kentnisse von den wichtigen Wahrheiten dringen'.

[2] 'Ein Ding heißt verändert, wenn unter zweien entgegengesetzten Bestimmungen, die ihm zukommen können, die eine aufhört und die andere anfängt, wirklich zu sein' (*habe sich* stands in place of *heißt* in Mendelssohn's text).

[3] 'Ein Inbegriff der Regeln des Denkens abstrahiert aus der Geschichte der Menschheit.'

[4] 'Concilia coetusque hominum, jure sociati' (Cicero, *Somnium Scipionis*, cap. iii).

[5] Hoffmeister conjectures that D. Rochow, *Catechismus der gesunden Vernunft* (Berlin, 1786) is meant. If so, Hegel either obtained it very promptly or else he continued collecting definitions for some time. His excerpts from Sulzer (Mar. 1787) rather tend to show that he still believed philosophical concepts could be dealt with in dictionary fashion. By the time he went on to Tübingen, however, he had abandoned this conception in favour of a historical approach (cf. Rosenkranz, p. 14).

[6] Strictly speaking the earliest academic labours that can be definitely dated

5 May	Excerpting of Feder, *Neuer Emil*, begun (*Dok.*, pp. 55–81).[1]
30 May	*Unterredung zwischen Dreien* (*Dok.*, pp. 3–6).
6 June	Letter to Haug (*Briefe*, i. 3–4).
10 June	Collection of *Definitions* begun; leads to categorization of views of ancient (and modern?) authors regarding Justice, the Virtues, etc.(?) (Rosenkranz, p. 14).
26 June–25 July	*Tagebuch* kept fairly regularly in German (*Dok.*, pp. 6–18).
July	Reading (and almost certainly excerpting) of Charles Batteux, *Einleitung in die schönen Wissenschaften*, especially the section on 'Epic' in vol. 2. Hegel was also seeking to obtain Dusch, *Briefe zur Bildung des Geschmacks* at this time (see *Dok.*, pp. 15–16).
29 July–24 Aug.	*Tagebuch* kept in Latin (mainly for stylistic exercise—one interval of ten days with no entry) (*Dok.*, pp. 18–23).
25 Aug.	Writing of *Tagebuch* (and most other 'outside' interests?) set aside in order to prepare for examination.
About 1 Sept.	Hegel begins to feel ill.
4–5 Sept.	Hegel takes examination—afterwards confined at home (*Dok.*, p. 23).
31 Oct.	'Präparationen' for Psalms begin (Rosenkranz, p. 11).
1 Nov.	Returns to school. (For several weeks he would have to devote his spare time to the school-work he had missed.)
14 Nov.–9–25 Dec.	'Präparationen' for Cicero, *Ad familiares* begun.[2] *Tagebuch* recommenced in Latin (*Dok.*, pp. 23–7).

1786

1 Jan.	Brief note in *Tagebuch* (last entry until 11 Feb.) (*Dok.*, p. 27).

are Hegel's studies with Löffler in 1780 and 1783 (see *Tagebuch*, 6 July 1785 in *Dok.*, p. 12). But we cannot assume that these studies produced anything in the nature of continuous manuscripts, still less that Hegel preserved them. Lacorte is mistaken if he supposes that what Rosenkranz says about Hegel's translation of Vida's *Christiad* (Rosenkranz, p. 51) implies that he had seen the manuscript or knew that Hegel had kept it (Lacorte, p. 111).

[1] It is obvious that this excerpt was not completed in a day. It may have been completed in as little as a week (cf. the length of the excerpt from Garve which was finished in five days) or it may have taken up more than two weeks.

[2] Rosenkranz (p. 11) gives 14 Nov. *1786* as the date here. But this must be a slip. If the 'Präparationen' were for the year 1786, they were for *De officiis* (see *Tagebuch* for 1 Jan. 1787). If, on the other hand, they were for *Ad familiares* then they almost certainly belong to Nov. 1785 (and following months). For about that time Hegel records the addition of Cicero, *Ad Atticum* to his library (*Tagebuch*, 11 Dec. 1785). See *Dok.*, pp. 24 and 38–9.

6–17 Feb.	Excerpts from Gesner's preface to Livy rewritten in Hegel's own Latin (*Dok.*, pp. 82–6).
11 Feb.	*Tagebuch* recommences (Duke's birthday and school holiday) (*Dok.*, p. 28).
15, 16, 18, 23 Feb.	*Tagebuch*: draft of Latin oration for future use in school (*Dok.*, pp. 28–31). After this the *Tagebuch* breaks off.[1]
6, 7, 8, 14, 21 Mar.	*Über das Excipieren* (essay in *Tagebuch*: Dok., pp. 31–5).
11, 15, 18 Mar.	*Tagebuch* entries in Latin (*Dok.*, pp. 35–7).
22 Mar.	*Tagebuch* entry in German (fragment). Some sheets are lost from manuscript here. One sheet survives with undated fragmentary entry on *Aufklärung* (*Dok.*, pp. 37–8).
6 Apr.	Excerpt from Dusch, *Briefe zur Bildung des Geschmacks* (*Dok.*, pp. 86–7).
5 May	Translation of Epictetus, *Enchiridion* begun (Rosenkranz, p. 11).
5 June	Excerpt from Cicero (on *Stoics*) (*Dok.*, p. 87).
17–22 June	Excerpts from Wünsch, *Kosmologische Unterhaltungen* (*Dok.*, pp. 87–100).
27 June	Excerpt from Cicero added on same sheet (*Dok.*, p. 100).
3 July	Word-list for Tyrtaeus begun (Rosenkranz, p. 11).
10 July	'Präparationen' for *Iliad* begun (Rosenkranz, p. 11).
During 1786	Collection of *Stammbuchsentenzen*.[2]
10 Oct.	Excerpts from Campe's *Kleine Seelenlehre für Kinder* (*Dok.*, pp. 101–4).
15 Oct.	Excerpts from Zimmermann, *Über die Einsamkeit* (*Dok.*, pp. 104–7).
16 Oct.	Excerpt from Zimmermann added to the Wünsch excerpt of June (*Dok.*, p. 100).
16 Oct.	Excerpt from Kästner, *Anfangsgründe der Arithmetik* etc. (*Dok.*, pp. 107–8).

[1] The break comes in mid sentence but the speech is at a point where the closing conventionalities follow automatically. It is not clear, therefore, whether the manuscript is defective at this point. The silence of Hoffmeister suggests that it did not appear so to him. Of course, if the essay *Über das Excipieren* begins directly on the same sheet, nothing can be missing. It is a pity however that he did not tell us this explicitly.

[2] The three-month gap in the record at this point is one period in which Hegel may have done quite a lot of work on projects of his own. Of course he may have begun collecting *Stammbuchsentenzen* earlier in the year.

Nov. 1786–   Study and translation of Longinus, *On the Sublime*
Sept. 1787   (Rosenkranz, p. 10).

23 Dec.   Excerpt from Meiners, *Revision der Philosophie* (*Dok.*, pp. 108–9).

Dec.   Excerpt from J. F. Lorenz's edition of Euclid (see *Tagebuch*, 1 Jan. 1787: *Dok.*, p. 39).

1787

1 Jan.   *Tagebuch* recommences. Hegel's review of his scholastic position makes clear that he is now making excerpts quite systematically for a certain period of time each day. (On New Year's Day itself he spent all afternoon reading *Sophiens Reise*.)

Dec. 1786 and   Excerpts from Heyne's Virgil (*Tagebuch*, 1–4 Jan.: *Dok.*,
1–4 Jan.   pp. 38–40).

5 Jan.   Excerpts from *Allgemeine Deutschen Bibliothek* on Demosthenes (*Tagebuch: Dok.*, p. 40).
Reading and study of Kästner's *Mathematik*, vol. ii, as well as of Lorenz (*Tagebuch: Dok.*, pp. 39–41).

9–10 Mar.   Excerpts from Sulzer, *Kurze Begriff der Gelehrsamkeit* (*Dok.*, pp. 109–15).

14–18 Mar.   Excerpt from Garve, *Prüfung der Fähigkeiten* (*Dok.*, pp. 115–36).[1]

20, 22 Mar.   Excerpts from *Neue Bibliothek der schönen Wissenschaften* (on Kästner's lectures) (*Dok.*, pp. 137–40).

14 May   *Einige Bemerkungen über die Vorstellung von Größe*: Reading (and excerpting?) of Meiners, *Briefe über die Schweiz* (*Dok.*, pp. 42–3).

31 May   Excerpt from M. Mendelssohn, *Berlin. Monatsschrift*, Sept. 1784 (*Dok.*, pp. 140–3).

1 June   'Präparationen' for Euripides begun (Rosenkranz, p. 11).

10 Aug.   *Über die Religion der Griechen und Römer* (*Dok.*, pp. 43–8).[2]

16, 23 Aug.   Excerpts from Nicolai, *Reisen* (*Dok.*, pp. 145–7).

28 Sept.   Excerpts from Eberhard, *Berlin. Monatsschrift*, July 1787 (*Dok.*, pp. 144–5).

1788

1 Feb.   Excerpt from Zollner's *Lesebuch* (in *Allg. Liter. Zeitung*, Jan. 1788) (*Dok.*, p. 147).[3]

---

[1] The source of this excerpt is the *Neue Bibliothek der schönen Wissenschaften* (vol. viii), as for the Kästner excerpts of the following days.

[2] Again there is a two-month gap in which Hegel may well have made quite a lot of excerpts.

[3] The break of more than four months here is the worst gap in the record.

18 Mar.	Excerpt from review of Kistenmaker (in *Allg. Liter. Zeitung*, Feb. 1788) (*Dok.*, pp. 148–9).
May	'Präparationen' for Aristotle, *Ethics* begun (Rosenkranz, p. 11).
29 July	'Präparationen' for Sophocles, *Oedipus Coloneus* begun (Rosenkranz, p. 11).[1]
31 July	Excerpts from review of Ulrich's *Eleutheriologie* (in *Allg. Liter. Zeitung*, Apr. 1788) (*Dok.*, pp. 149–55).
7 Aug.	*Über einige charakteristische Unterschiede der alten Dichter* (this presupposes study of Garve's essay in *Neue Bibliothek der schönen Wissenschaften*, vol. x) (*Dok.*, pp. 48–51 and 407–14).
25 Sept.	Valedictory speech (this presupposes study of Rycaut or some similar source-book on the Ottoman Empire) (*Dok.*, pp. 52–4; cf. Rosenkranz, p. 19).
29 Sept.	Excerpt from review of Rehberg (in *Allg. Liter. Zeitung*, June 1788) (*Dok.*, pp. 156–66).[2]
27 Oct.	Hegel matriculated at Tübingen.

But of course school work filled much of Hegel's time, and most of his excerpting would be from classical literature and mathematics, to judge from the record of 1786–7 for this period.

[1] Perhaps Hegel's earliest attempts at the translation of the *Antigone* should be placed mainly in the preceding summer months.

[2] Again, this excerpt was probably not made all in one day.

Note on Hegel's Valedictory Address

The publication by Günther Nicolin of a report from the *Schwäbische Chronik* of 1 Oct. 1788 has cleared up the main mystery about this speech. The subject of Turkey was dictated by the professor of Rhetoric, Balthasar Haug, who arranged the ceremony. Five students who were intending to proceed to the University, all spoke on the topic, some in Latin, others in the vernacular. Hegel, the official valedictorian, spoke last. Thus the hypothesis that he was responsible for the farcical aspect of the proceedings is mistaken; and my alternative suggestion that he was using the contrast of Turkey and Württemberg ironically is not necessary either, but it is still quite possible and I think it deserves consideration (Nicolin, p. 5).

One of the five, Karl August Braun, did not in fact go on to the *Stift*. But if he was intending to go thither at the time of this farewell ceremony, then we may reasonably infer that Leutwein's memory of Hegel as the first of *five* students from Stuttgart was not really mistaken. He was rather recalling with quite remarkable vividness the things that Hegel himself said about his priority in the group from the *Gymnasium* after the Inspectorate placed Maerklin above him (see below, pp. 65–6, 82–3).

(Another point cleared up by Nicolin (pp. 563–4) is the identity of the Städlin sister who suffered from Hegel's clumsiness as a dancer—see p. 59 n. 2 below. This was Christiane (Nanette). Nicolin connects the incident not with a Tübingen ball but with the Stuttagrt dancing class of Christiane Hegel's notes.)

II. TÜBINGEN 1788-1793

The Church Visible and Invisible

1. *The atmosphere of the* Stift

IN 1804 in connection with a request for a *curriculum vitae* on the part of the Weimar government Hegel prepared the following account of his education:

I, Georg Wilhelm Friedrich Hegel, was born at Stuttgart, Aug. 27 1770. My parents . . . took care for my education in the sciences, both through private schooling and through the public schooling of the Gymnasium at Stuttgart, where classical and modern languages as well as the elements of the sciences were taught. I was admitted at the age of 18 to the theological college [*Stift*] at Tübingen [Oct. 27, 1788]. After two years spent in the study of philology under Schnurrer, and of philosophy and mathematics under Flatt and Beckh, I became a Master of Philosophy [Sept. 27, 1790] and then studied the theological sciences for three years under Lebret, Uhland, Storr and Flatt. I passed the theological examination before the Consistory of Stuttgart and was admitted among the Theology Candidates, Autumn 1793; I had sought admittance to the ministerial class [*den Stand des Predigtamts ergriffen*] in accordance with the wish of my parents, and remained faithful to the study of theology by natural inclination on account of its connection with classical literature and philosophy. After being admitted to it, I chose from among the professions open to theology graduates [*der theologische Stand*] the one which, while free from the peculiar responsibilities and concerns of the ministry, secured for me equally the leisure to devote myself to classical literature and philosophy, and offered the opportunity to live in other lands and under foreign conditions. I found these advantages in the two house-tutor posts which I occupied, in Berne from Autumn 1783 to Autumn 1796, and in Frankfurt from January 1797 onwards, for my professional duties left me time enough to keep abreast of the progress of knowledge which I had fixed upon as my purpose in life [*mit den Gang der Wissenschaft zu verfolgen, die ich zur Bestimmung meines Lebens gemacht hatte*].[1]

[1] Nohl, pp. viii–ix. The manuscript of this *curriculum vitae* has been lost, but it

At this time Hegel was seeking a professorial appointment in philosophy at Jena, where he was then a *Privatdozent*; and in documents of this sort the candidate's account of his aims and purposes in the past is apt to be coloured by his present objective. But in this case all that we can discover about Hegel's feelings and attitudes while he was at Tübingen and immediately afterwards seems to show that he has here given an accurate and precise account of his motives from 1788 onwards. His attitude toward the study of orthodox theology was never better than neutral, and he never seriously intended to enter the ministry. Certainly his relative indifference hardened into firm opposition while he was at Tübingen.

According to the recollections of his sister, Hegel wished to proceed to the study of law, not theology, after his magisterial examination. Several of his fellow students, including Hölderlin, toyed with the same plan; and one or two of them—notably Hölderlin's close friend Bilfinger—eventually did make the leap. It seems clear that the idea was conceived, and began to be generally discussed, as a direct result of the visit of Duke Karl Eugen to the *Stift* in November 1789. The Duke was graciously pleased to make known at that time that the reform of the *Stift* was to be his next great project for the advancement of education in his dominions. In the context of all the exciting reports from Paris, it is not surprising that many of his young stipendiaries viewed this prospect with grave alarm, and began to look for a way of escaping from their cloister and taking a worthy part in the overthrow of everything which the Duke, through his 'reforms' was seeking to strengthen and preserve.[1]

Hölderlin's father had spent five of the happiest years of his life as a law student at Tübingen; and the young poet naturally made

was plainly only a rough draft; we cannot be sure that it was ever sent to anyone, though it is natural to assume that it was.

[1] The Duke's visit of 5 Nov. 1789 is described in the documents assembled and published by Beck (*GSA*, viii. 1, 404-9). Less than two weeks later Hölderlin was brought before the Ephor for a typical undergraduate trick—knocking a dame-school usher's hat off. The oddest thing about this little episode is the absolute indifference that Hölderlin displayed toward the prospect of punishment for it. He was 'incarcerated' for six hours. A few days later he applied for and was granted a month's leave on account of a foot wound (24/5 Nov. 1789). He wrote from home to Neuffer about his efforts to persuade his mother to let him follow in Stäudlin's footsteps (Letter 28, lines 32-6; compare also Letter 27 to his mother and Beck's notes to both letters: *GSA*, vi. 45-7 and 541-7). For more details about Bilfinger see p. 60 n. 1 below.

much of this precedent in pleading with his mother.[1] But the example that counted for most in his own mind was that of the Stüttgart lawyer G. F. Stäudlin (1758–96) who was already a well-known poet, editor of a successful literary journal, and a close associate of the great champion and martyr of liberty and enlightenment in Württemburg, the poet Daniel Schubart. Hölderlin first met Stäudlin in the spring or summer of 1789. I cannot find documentary evidence that Hegel met him before June 1793, but he was in all likelihood acquainted with him much earlier—long before Hölderlin. In any case the example of Stäudlin was hardly less relevant for a would-be *Volkserzieher* of the prosaic variety than it was for one with a poetic vocation; so I feel sure that the career of a lawyer, and the example of Stäudlin, were much talked of between Hegel and Hölderlin in the winter semester of 1789/90.[2] Hölderlin was obliged by his mother's opposition to give up the idea fairly quickly; Hegel, on the other hand, did not really begin to argue seriously with his father, until he found himself studying dogmatics under Storr.[3]

[1] See Letter 27, lines 9–12, with Beck's note (*GSA*, vi. 46 and 542).

[2] Neuffer arranged for Hölderlin to meet both Schubart and Stäudlin during the Easter holiday of 1789 (see *GSA*, vii. 1, 12). Hölderlin did meet Schubart at that time, but he did not mention Staüdlin when he commented on that encounter in a letter to his mother a little later (Letter 26, lines 17–24, *GSA*, vi. 44). He certainly had some converse with him before Dec. 1789, however, for he wrote to Neuffer then that 'Stäudlin ist warlich ein herrlicher Mann' (Letter 28, lines 32–3.).

Both Stäudlin and Matthisson wrote album leaves for Hegel when they visited the *Stift* in June 1793 (entries 42 and 61, *Briefe*, iv. 52, 58). It is virtually certain that the two families—not just Hegel and Stäudlin—were mutually acquainted before this, however. In later life one of Stäudlin's three sisters often told the tale of how she suffered from Hegel's clumsiness at a dance (*GSA*, vii. 1, 400). This was not Rosine Stäudlin who was engaged to Neuffer—they were married in 1793 and she died of consumption in Apr. 1795. But Rosine, at least, must surely have been at the dance in Tübingen in Sept. 1789 where Magister Klett danced so much with Christiane Hegel—see Bilfinger's letter to Niethammer, 29 Sept. 1789, *GSA*, vii. 402. One of the other sisters—Charlotte—would gladly have gone to this dance for the sake of Hölderlin's bright eyes: see Neuffer's letter to Hölderlin, 24 Oct. 1790, lines 11–17, *GSA*, vii. 1, 23; and Hölderlin's reply, Letter 35, line 28, with Beck's note, *GSA*, vi. 57 and 567–8. Perhaps she did go; but whether it was *she* who had to tolerate Hegel's clumsiness—as well as Hölderlin's courteous indifference—I have not been able to determine. The incident may not have happened in 1789, and it may have involved the third sister Nannette; but it must have occurred before June 1793. (In his *Tagebuch* for 27 June 1785, Hegel refers to a boy named Stäudlin who was either in his class, or—more probably—a year above him. Hoffmeister does not identify the boy further: *Dok.*, p. 8.) (See further the *Note* on p. 56 above.)

[3] The Duke's reforms were slow to materialize; almost every year a new

In postulating a fairly close friendship between Hegel and Hölderlin by the end of their first year in the *Stift*, I realize that I am setting myself against the received tradition. It appears to be generally assumed that Hölderlin only became especially friendly with Hegel after the departure of Neuffer and Magenau from the *Stift* in 1791. But this is a quite gratuitous and implausible supposition. Hegel and Hölderlin entered the *Stift* together as two of the best students in a class of thirty-one. Hölderlin belonged to the large group of twenty-seven who had already lived and worked together for years at Denkendorf and Maulbronn. But he already knew Magenau and was hoping to be in his room (where Neuffer surely was?). Within a year he had grown so close to Neuffer that Bilfinger, who had been his closest friend for years at school, was quite noticeably jealous.[1] Hegel, on the other hand, was one of only

commission arrived from Stuttgart until, after some transitional reorganization, the new order was officially proclaimed in May 1793. (See p. 113 n. 1 below. The interested reader can now find almost all of the story in *GSA*, vii. 1.) Thus, quite apart from their private desires, the *Stiftler* had continual occasion for public discussion of the need to escape. Bilfinger was only the first to go. A boy named W. C. G. Christlieb, from a lower *Promotion*, followed his example in Feb. 1792; and at that time Hölderlin spoke of doing manual labour if the new order proved as bad as he expected (Letter 49, with Beck's notes, *GSA*, vi. 74 and 598-600). My hypothesis about Hegel's taking up the idea as a way of escape from Storr's theology, in 1791, is based on the combination of Christiane's reminiscences (*Dok.*, pp. 393, 394) with the other evidence set forth below, p. 63 n. 1. Hegel's wish was certainly opposed by his father, just as Hölderlin's was by his mother; and I think it is reasonable to assume that Leutwein's memory of 'his father's opposition' was occasioned by *this* conflict (see *Hegel-Studien*, iii. 55, lines 100-2; with Henrich's note ad loc.).

[1] Magenau wrote to Hölderlin at Maulbronn (10 July 1788, *GSA*, vii. 1, 5-7); and a year later Bilfinger wrote to Niethammer—who also apparently had wished to be more intimate with Hölderlin than the latter was prepared to be with him—that '*Genius* Neuffer has influence over him [Hölderlin]. He goes with him to Stuttgart in a day or so and will honour him with his presence for about a week. It makes me sad to see the good fellow fall into such hands' (29 Sept. 1789: see p. 59 n. 2 above). Bilfinger seems to have thought of Hölderlin's plan to go into law as part of the war between himself and Neuffer for Hölderlin's soul. For he was already waiting for his own release (*Dimission*) from the *Stift*. There is an echo of this conflict between the old love and the new in Hölderlin's remark to Neuffer: 'Oh if only you had still been in Tübingen all this would never have happened! I would not have had cause [the usher's hat no doubt!] to press for my *Dimission* more urgently than ever, I would not be troubling my mother, I would not be a burden to myself with my despondency' (Letter 28, lines 10-14, *GSA*, vi. 47); and again in his self-comforting reflections after he gave in to his mother's wish: 'I have friends in my cloister such as I would hardly find anywhere. My Neuffer does his duty when the crickets [i.e. the blue devils] get at him' (Letter 29, lines 17-19, *GSA*, vi. 48).
At that moment (Jan. 1790) the 'friends in the cloister' still included Bilfinger

four candidates from the Gymnasium at Stuttgart; and Neuffer, who had come from there two years earlier, was one of the relatively few people in the *Stift* with whom we can be sure he was already acquainted. Thus, even if we ignore the one hundred and one ways in which Hegel and Hölderlin could accidentally have discovered very rapidly how much they had in common—for instance they sat regularly at the same table for meals—they were bound to be brought together almost immediately by the possession of a common mentor.

A 'mentor' was something that Hölderlin needed far more permanently than Hegel; and although his relation with 'Genius' Neuffer remained very close after the latter's departure in 1791, he may very well have come to lean on Hegel more then than he had earlier.[1] But if that was so, it was only because they were good

(*pace* Beck's note in *GSA*, vi. 495), for Hölderlin reports in the same letter that Bilfinger has hardly anything left to sell and is now wearing the same cassock all the time. Probably he was released in February. (Two other members of the class were released at their own request then; one of them, J. C. Klett, transferred to medicine. I cannot trace what became of K. G. Keller—see *GSA*, vii. 1, 317–18, and Hegel's *Stammbuch*, entry 36: *Briefe*, iv. 50.) But even then the release does not seem to have been official, for it did not affect Hölderlin's placing in the class as we would expect. Bilfinger was sixth and Hölderlin eighth. He became seventh only in July 1791 (immediately after Hesler's expulsion, which would surely have effect instantly in the *Lokation*?) and sixth in April 1792. Both the legal process of release from the *Obligation*, and the custom of the Inspectorate in re-ordering a *Promotion* are obviously in need of some clarification. Even Beck has been betrayed into a slip by the Apr. 1792 puzzle. He ascribes Hölderlin's advance to the departure of Autenrieth (see p. 62 n. 1), who was, of course, below him in the order. (For Hölderlin's quarterly reports see *GSA*, vii. 1, 383.)

[1] Neuffer writes to Hölderlin as 'Dein Genius' (20 July 1793, *GSA*, vii, 1, 33); and Hölderlin says in his reply; 'You're right brother-heart! [*Herzens-bruder* is a title he uses quite often for Neuffer, and never for anyone else outside of his own family, though all his friends are "brothers" to him.] *Dein Genius* was very near me in these last days.' Magenau calls Neuffer 'Meister *Genius*' in a letter to Hölderlin (Dec. 1789, *GSA*, vii. 1, 22); and Bilfinger refers to him sarcastically as '*Genie* Neuffer' (Sept. 1789; see the preceding note). It looks to me as if Neuffer (otherwise known as 'der Pelargide' on account of his Greek mother) adopted the title 'Genius' with specific reference to his relation with Hölderlin; and it may very likely have been bestowed on him, possessively ('you are my Genius'), by Hölderlin. The word does not occur in Letter 28 (*GSA*, vi. 46–7), but the relationship of dependence is evident: compare p. 60 n. 1 above.

Hölderlin actually says to Hegel (in a letter forwarded by Neuffer!): 'Du warst so oft mein Genius' (*Briefe*, i. 9: cf. Letter 84 with the postscript to Letter 83 in *GSA*, vi. 126–8). But the character of his reliance on Hegel is more graphically illustrated by his shocked reaction when Hegel spoke of accepting *his* 'guidance and leadership' in a letter of 1796: 'You have so often been my mentor when my faint heart was making me into a young fool, and you will often have to be so again' (*Briefe*, i. 45).

friends already. In the first two years they took several classes together, and in the magisterial examination of 1790 they were examined together on the same thesis.[1] They must certainly have discussed both their current projects and their plans for the future during that summer, and a firm friendship was definitely cemented by then, if not much sooner.

An attitude of not very secret rebellion against, and alienation from, everything that the institution stood for politically and socially, was quite widespread among the students in the *Stift*. E. F. Hesler, who stood second in Hegel's class, was expelled in June 1791; and K. C. Renz, the universally admired *primus* of the class, crowned his career in the *Stift* by absenting himself from the public examination of the graduands in 1793, in which he could hardly have failed to win—and receive from the Duke's own hands—the first prize.[2] Under the eyes of their *Repetenten*, the

[1] On the examination and the individual and common tasks involved in it see *Dok.*, pp. 435–8 (which supersedes Rosenkranz, pp. 35–8, because Rosenkranz was under the impression that Hegel himself wrote the thesis—of Bök—which was in fact publicly discussed by all the candidates). The other candidates involved, as well as Hölderlin, were J. C. F. Fink, who was certainly one of Hegel's closest friends thereafter, for they often spent vacation periods at one another's homes (Rosenkranz, p. 34), and J. C. F. Autenrieth, who is identified by Flechsig (*Briefe*, iv. 185) as the school friend from Stuttgart with whom Hegel went walking in the Bopser Wald in 1785 (*Dok.*, p. 9; Hoffmeister's note ad loc. less plausibly suggests the younger J. H. F. Autenrieth, who was later Chancellor of the University of Tübingen). J. C. F. Autenrieth transferred to the Karlsschule to study for the civil service in March 1792 and died in September of that year (see Hegel's *Stammbuch*, entry 1, *Briefe*, iv. 39; and Hölderlin, Letter 34, line 15, with Beck's note, *GSA*, vi. 80 and 611). Thus of the four of them only Fink actually became a pastor.

[2] For Hesler see Beck's note in *GSA*, vi. 686. After leaving the *Stift* he matriculated in law at Jena (where he was again in the company of Hölderlin in 1795). In the interim he corresponded with Hölderlin and perhaps with Hegel also (see for example the remarks in *Briefe*, i. 10–11).

K. C. Renz had been the *primus* of his class since a few months before his fifteenth birthday (*GSA*, vii. 1, 315); and most of his fellows had long been in what Leutwein (himself the *primus* of the previous year) correctly calls 'das Renzsche Promotion' (*Hegel-Studien*, iii. 54, line 61). Schelling (another *primus*) is reputed to have said in later years that he had never met anyone more talented than Renz (Plitt, i. 69). Hegel inquired at Christmas 1794 whether Renz had 'buried his talents', and added 'I hope not; it would certainly be worth the effort to make him reflect, and encourage him to collect together his very thorough-going investigations of really important topics; this might perhaps compensate him for the disgust he has suffered for so long' (*Briefe*, i, 12). His 'disgust' was plainly expressed in the affair of the prize examination; and to cure his 'self-will' he was obliged to remain in the *Stift* until the beginning of 1794 (*GSA*, vii. 1, 464–7). He was already a candidate for a *Repetentstelle* in Nov. 1795, actually became a *Repetent* in 1797, and could

stipendiaries donned their monkish cassocks, studied their appointed books, completed the required exercises or essays, and preached their statutory sermons, rehearsing the expected arguments in support of the approved doctrines and generally evincing the appropriate sentiments. Meantime in private they studied Voltaire and Rousseau, read French newspapers and journals, and preached the gospel of Liberty, Equality, and Fraternity to one another in speeches and gestures of all kinds. One of them came back from Strasbourg in 1792 fired by the example of the Jacobin clubs, and bearing with him the words and music of the 'Marseillaise'. He formed a club in the *Stift* and caused a public scandal by organizing a concert at which the new anthem of the Revolution was sung. The famous story of the 'Tree of Liberty' planted by a group of students that included Hegel, Hölderlin, and Schelling, on a fine Sunday morning in the spring of 1793—or alternatively on 14 July—is an appropriate myth for Hegel's part in this unrest, though it is almost certainly not grounded in historical fact.[1] Botany certainly interested Hegel more than theology in 1791 and 1792.[2]

very soon have become a Theology Professor had he chosen. Instead he became a pastor (Hölderlin, letter 107, line 28, with Beck's note, *GSA*, vi. 186 and 765–6).

[1] Most of the radical students were not really 'Jacobins' (the term was very freely and loosely applied by enemies of the Revolution in Germany, and hence perhaps accepted as a badge of honour by its friends); and not all of the 'French' journals referred to in our tradition were published in France. Hegel writes in his first letter to Schelling that he has encountered K. E. Oelsner, author of the 'Letters ⟨from Paris⟩ that you know so well in Archenholz's *Minerva*' (Letter 6, Christmas Eve 1794, *Briefe*, i. 11). For the (Girondist) politics and connections of this journal, and for evidence of Hegel's studies in it see D'Hondt's *Hegel secret, passim*. For further discussion of, and references for, Wetzel's 'political club', the 'Marseillaise' scandal, and the 'Tree of Liberty' legend, see below, pp. 113–15 and notes.

[2] Christiane recorded that in his *Studienjahre* Hegel spent several months at home recovering from a long attack of 'tertian fever' and devoting his good days to the reading of Greek Tragedy and to botany. This illness can definitely be assigned to the spring and summer of 1791 in the light of the following evidence:

(*a*) The Consistory records, which show that Hegel requested leave to remain at home for a 'cure' on 15 Feb. 1791 and that several extensions were granted (the last on 29 July for fourteen days) (*Briefe*, iv. 79–80).

(*b*) Hegel's *Stammbuch* shows by the number of entries for 12 and 13 Feb. 1791 that his friends were trying to give him a good send-off for his journey; and the entry of Magister Sartorius (7 Sept. 1791) documents his current interest in botany after his return (*Briefe*, iv. 39 ff.; esp. p. 56).

(*c*) Betzendörfer (p. 101) records that Hegel borrowed Linnaeus from the Library of the *Stift* in the summers of 1791 and 1792.

It would seem from his *Stammbuch* that Hegel had to return to Tübingen

In part this alienation of the students from their official teachers and their prescribed studies was a natural and healthy symptom of the growth of independence and personal judgement. In part too, it was simply a conformity of rebellion opposed to the conformity required by the institution. Doubtless many of them made their inflammatory speeches, and swore their vows of eternal loyalty to the ideals of the Revolution, and then went quietly off to their parsonages, to preach the gospel of the established order without ever feeling any great wrench or strain in passing from the one posture to the other. They would feel, perhaps, a sense of relief at being free from the cloistered life of the *Stift*—as Hegel did when he wrote 'Adieu Tubingue' on an album leaf for a fellow *Stiftler* in 1793, and as some of his friends did when they provided leaves for his *Stammbuch* dated 'Am letzten Tag meines *Kloster*lebens'. But that very relief would soon reveal that their rebellion was only against the degrading sense of being *compelled* to do and believe what they genuinely wanted to do and believe in any case.[1]

In the case of the three friends Hegel, Hölderlin, and Schelling, however, their reaction against the *Stift*, and their devotion to revolutionary ideals, amounted to more than this. All of them had entered the *Stift* only because by doing so they could receive their education at state expense. They did not mean to fulfil the obligation which they solemnly undertook upon entry, to follow a career in the Church or the schools of the Duchy of Württemberg.[2] They knew already that Württemberg was a very conservative place, in comparison with others not too far away; and they soon discovered

some time before the second week of May 1791 (see entries 12, 52, 50, 41, 60). Probably he borrowed the books for his new interest then. But he was soon sick at home again and he probably remained in Stuttgart until 15 Aug. (see entry 69). He was certainly back in Tübingen by 24 Aug. (entry 44: cf. entries 13, 15).

[1] See *Briefe*, iv. 65 for the *Stammbuchblatt* that Hegel wrote in 1793; compare in his own *Stammbuch* entries 25 and 39. The latter entry is by C. P. F. Leutwein, who never did, in fact, adjust successfully to his station and his duties as a pastor. See the article by D. Henrich in *Hegel-Studien*, iii. 43-50. (We should remember that by no means all of the *Stiftler* were radicals. This is attested in the political sphere by the report of Klüpfel—see *Briefe*, iv. 166—that they took sides and fought duels as 'Democrats' and 'Royalists'. No doubt it was true in most, if not all, areas of common concern.)

[2] See *Briefe*, iv. 74-6 for Hegel's *Obligation*. In the case of students who, like Hölderlin and Schelling, came from *Klosterschulen* the obligation was incurred even earlier. The fact of this 'obligation', which represented at once his mother's dearest wish, and the only means of obtaining an education and so escaping into a wider world, weighed particularly heavily upon the mind and conscience of Hölderlin.

that the *Stift* was the most conservative institution in a University where the great oak of the *ancien régime* flourished still too strongly for any new-planted saplings of the Goddess of Reason to take root in its shadow.[1]

Of the three Hegel was probably by natural temperament and acquired habit the least rebellious and the most disposed to a quietly industrious pursuit of learning. He could not match Schelling's precocious facility, but his school record was remarkable in its consistency. Yet his record at the *Stift* was far from outstanding, even if perhaps it was still rather better than average. At the Gymnasium he had stood first in his class for years, and he entered the *Stift* placed first among the candidates from Stuttgart. But the authorities of the *Stift* (very probably the Ephor himself, Professor Schnurrer) took that distinction from him about six months or a year after his matriculation, and he was always afterwards placed below J. F. Maerklin, who was half a year younger and a class behind him at Stuttgart. Leutwein in his reminiscences of Hegel at the *Stift* claims that this caused him great bitterness, and even goes so far as to suggest that his resentment was the main spur for his later achievements in philosophy. This latter suggestion is certainly quite untenable, but probably the bitterness was real enough.[2]

---

[1] As Hegel wrote to Schelling from Berne: 'Unless someone like Reinhold or Fichte gets a chair at Tübingen, nothing significant [*reelles*] will come from there; nowhere else is the old system so well and truly entrenched [*fortgepflanzt*] as there' (*Briefe*, i. 12). In defence of Tübingen Haering points out that it is scarcely legitimate to make the absence of outstanding genius in a University a ground of complaint. But this misses Hegel's point, which is that nothing less than outstanding genius would make a difference to the climate of the place. Anyone whose gifts were more modest and whose sympathies were liberal would only strive and suffer uselessly (cf. Haering, i. 51).

[2] Students were seated at meals—and presumably in their 'required' classes as well—according to their *Lokation*. Thus the top eight or ten students in any year would be thrown together continually in the routine of the day. (Compare Henrich's remark about Hölderlin and Klüpfel in *Hegel-Studien*, iii. 279.)

It was the task of the *Repetenten* to make up the 'location-list' for each class (*Promotion*) and submit it to the Inspectorate (the Ephor and two senior professors—at this time Schnurrer, Uhland, and Storr). The Inspectorate generally accepted the order recommended by the *Repetenten*, since they were the ones who had to read and mark the students' essays and exercises. Changes in the list once it had been established were very rare, and attracted universal notice. According to Henrich, Hegel was demoted at the Martinmas report of 1789 (10 Nov.), but this is not borne out by the semester reports as printed by Flechsig (*Briefe*, iv. 76; see further, p. 82 n. 2 below). Leutwein's reminiscences show that the demotion was generally believed to be a decision of the Inspectorate

The source of his difficulties, and the reason for his bitterness, are to be found, I think, in the unusual maturity and independence of judgement that he had gained from his years of self-directed study at Stuttgart. He had early learned at the Gymnasium what a world of difference there is between a good and a bad teacher, between enthusiastic devotion and the following of a routine, between creative scholarship and pedantry. But at Stuttgart he found most of the required work congenial, and he was always on terms of friendship and admiration with at least some of his teachers. At Tübingen everything was different. He was removed from home and subjected continually to a distasteful discipline, and a routine that was none of his own making. He was compelled to do quite a lot of work which he regarded as wasted; and worst of all there was no one among his teachers whom he could admire, or whom he felt was in sympathy with his aims and ideals. It will not do to say, as Haering does, that Schnurrer and Storr, who were certainly worthy and admirable enough as scholars and teachers, were too old. Age is no barrier to this sort of educational relationship. They were not in fact older than Professors Cless and Hopf with whom Hegel had been friendly enough at the Gymnasium. Schnurrer, the Ephor of the *Stift*, was internationally known as an orientalist; he had spent much time in England and France and had there made the acquaintance of Rousseau—who was Hegel's declared hero in these years. Schelling and Hölderlin both seem to have admired him. But he did not get on well with Hegel, or Hegel did not get on well with him—'whichever you like', as Christiane put it. Probably, as I suggested above, Hegel held Schnurrer responsible for his being placed below Maerklin. The difficulty must have been a personal one, for Schnurrer, together with councillor Georgii at Stuttgart, was known as a defender of educational enlightenment against the

rather than a recommendation of the *Repetenten*. Schnurrer was the only member of the board who was in any position to take such a decision, since Uhland and Storr would not have classroom contact with the students until they became *magistri*. Some students even suspected nepotism, since Maerklin's uncle was a colleague of Uhland and Storr on the Theology Faculty. But Hegel was under Schnurrer's eye in his private class on the *Psalms* for the whole year (Rosenkranz, p. 25). So no matter when the *Lokation* took place I do not think we need to look further for the explanation of Hegel's antipathy for Schnurrer. See Leutwein's account in *Hegel-Studien* iii. 54–5. (Two years later the fifteen-year-old Schelling had the opposite experience. He came from Maulbronn with a brilliant record but was placed second, probably by the decision of the Inspectorate on account of his youth. Then later, through the direct intervention of the Duke, he was made *Primus* of his *Promotion*.)

conservatism of the Duke.[1] On the other hand, Hegel clearly felt that Storr was on the wrong side of the battle between the *ancien régime* and the forces of the Enlightenment.

The 'testimonial' that Hegel received upon the conclusion of his studies recorded that his health was 'not constant' and his industry 'sometimes interrupted'.[2] The semester reports give 'bonum, diligens' as a constant verdict upon his *ingenium*; but the report on his conduct shows a quite dramatic deterioration in the spring of 1791, which was his first semester in the theology course, and also the term in which he received permission to go home on account of illness. The verdict on his *mores* for that term and the following one is 'languidi'. Thereafter, his record recovers into a steady respectability.[3] Of course the final report may not be directly related to the terminal reports at all in this respect, but it does seem plausible to suppose that after passing the magisterial examination Hegel began to neglect the prescribed tasks to the point where it was bound to be officially noticed.

Apart from the interest in botany, which we have already remarked on, this was also the spring and summer of Hegel's first recorded love-affair. He was enamoured of a girl named Auguste Hegelmeier, daughter of a deceased professor of Theology, who lived with her mother in the house of a baker. The baker also kept a wine-shop where the students foregathered to pay court to the beautiful Auguste. Hegel's passion was well known to his friends, but he was by no means the young lady's only admirer; and although it is recorded that he liked to get girls involved in kissing games, it would seem that he was quite shy with her. At any rate, she does not seem to have paid him any special attention, and it is quite likely that the whole affair was more an excuse for drinking the good baker's wine and for organizing a summer ball than

[1] *Dok.*, p. 393; a convenient summary of Schnurrer's career and achievements will be found in Lacorte (pp. 128–9). He gave signal proof of his courage in defence of liberal values in his treatment of August Wetzel in 1792 and 1793 (see below, pp. 113–14 and notes; for the career and attitude of Councillor Georgii see Beck's note on Hölderlin, Letter 49, lines 12–40, *GSA*, vi. 74 and 599). For the probable grounds of Schnurrer's attitude towards Hegel, see further pp. 69–70 below. It needs to be remembered, however, that coming from the Gymnasium at Stuttgart, Hegel was almost certainly not as well grounded in Hebrew as the best students from the *Klosterschulen*. He may well have felt that Schnurrer misjudged and underestimated him on this account.
[2] *Briefe*, iv. 87.
[3] *Briefe*, iv. 76–7.

anything else. Probably Hegel had a friendly rival for Auguste's affections in his close friend Fink. He wrote in Fink's *Stammbuch* in October 1791: 'The motto of last summer was: Wine; for this summer: Love!', and added the inscription 'V.A.!!!' as the symbol of his love ('Vive Auguste'). Fink for his part had done the same in Hegel's *Stammbuch* in August '2 days after the great Ball'. Hegel's note in Fink's *Stammbuch* is the last that we hear of the affair, which has the aura of a student imitation of the age of chivalry about it. Rosenkranz's report that 'Hegel began to fence with his boon companion Fink, but soon gave it up' probably refers to the previous winter, and belongs to this same context.[1]

Certainly Hegel's love of wine was more lasting than his affection for 'la belle Augustine'.[2] Leutwein believed that his conviviality helped to spoil his academic record. But whatever the authorities may have thought, his fellow students always seem to have recognized that 'the Old Man', as they called him, was the sort of scholar who belonged in Faust's study rather than in Auerbach's cellar; he may have been lax in his attendance at lectures and *Kollegien*[3]; but he was also a byword for spending half the night studying. And since he was not much more interested in 'Kant and metaphysics' than he was in his lectures and classes, it is no

---

[1] Rosenkranz, pp. 30-2, 34; Hegel's *Stammbuch*, entries 4, 15, 33. Fink's entry ends: 'Long live the *Ballgesellschaft*—long live also our *Kandidatengesellschaft*.' Of the three friends who refer to Auguste in the *Stammbuch* only one, the 'Mompelgarder' Bernard, explicitly indicates that his own affections are elsewhere engaged, for he wrote 'V. la belle Augustine—pour toi! / et la C... pour moi seul!'

The fact that there is no page contributed by Auguste in Hegel's *Stammbuch* would suggest either that he was too shy or not really interested enough to ask for one, and that she for her part was not interested enough to volunteer one. (Hölderlin's request that his foil should be sent on to him from home—Beck, Letter 39, mid Dec. 1790, *GSA*, vi. 61—points to the previous winter as a likely date for Hegel's fleeting interest in fencing.)

[2] Ten years later when he was contemplating a move from Frankfurt he stipulated that wherever he went there must be good beer (Letter 29 to Schelling, 2 Nov. 1800, *Briefe*, i. 59). He also liked to play cards from his youth onwards—in his *Tagebuch* he records a Saturday evening spent in playing 'the geographical card-game that is somewhat like Tarock' (*Dok.*, p. 41). In later years he preferred whist. At Frankfurt in 1798 he even wrote a short essay on the significance of card-playing as 'ein Hauptzug im Charakter unserer Zeit' (*Dok.*, pp. 277-8).

[3] The *ordinarii* lectured every term both 'publicly' and 'privately'; and the *Repetenten* similarly gave private classes as well as routine instruction connected with the prescribed curriculum. Students had some freedom in the choice of their 'private' classes (called *Collegia, Kollegien*); and they also paid special fees for them directly to the instructors concerned.

wonder that he gained the reputation of being a somewhat eccentric 'eclectic'.[1]

In the spring of 1793 Hegel was again at home in Stuttgart on account of his health. His regular *Kurzeit*—the leave that was granted to each student during the year—was extended for 'a few days' on 1 March. But subsequently he went home again for a large part of the summer. For in September Schnurrer wrote to J. E. H. Scholl in Amsterdam:

> Magister Hegel will be examined now at the close of the academic year, and at the same time granted freedom to take a post abroad. A little discretion would not hurt here. I doubt very much whether he has as yet learned to bear with patience the sacrifices that are always bound to be associated, at least at first, with a position as private tutor. He has been absent from the *Stift* almost all of this summer, on the pretext of a cure, and his long stay at home, where his own wishes perhaps are of more consequence than his father's, is surely no proper preparation for the not exactly unconstrained life of a house-tutor.[2]

From this letter it appears that the reason for the strained relations between Hegel and the Ephor of the *Stift* may well have been Schnurrer's feeling that he wanted too much of his own way, and

---

[1] See Leutwein's reminiscences (*Hegel-Studien*, iii. 56-7, lines 133-5, 151). The more famous phrase *lumen obscurum* in lines 55-6, like the colourful *Kneipenbehaglichkeit* in lines 45-6, has no manuscript authority. The irresponsible way in which Schwegler injected these terms into the text of Leutwein's letter would be easier to excuse if we could plausibly surmise that Leutwein used them in face-to-face conversation with him or with someone else to whom he had access. But in view of the unblushing way in which Schwegler pretended that Leutwein's letter to the younger Pressel was addressed to himself, we have to admit that the likeliest hypothesis is that he simply invented everything ascribed to Leutwein that is not to be found in the letter itself.

[2] See *Briefe*, iv. 82, for the extension of his *Kurzeit*. For Schnurrer's letter see Haering, i. 114-15. Compare also *Dok.*, p. 434, where Hoffmeister attempts to argue on the basis of this citation that Schnurrer's writing to a man in Holland 'otherwise still not known in connection with Hegel's biography or educational career' proves that Hegel was no *lumen obscurum*, that the Ephor was watching him with a keen eye, and that his irritation arose from some awareness of Hegel's gifts. But to take this view is not only to make Schnurrer very percipient (which he may have been); it is to make him also a foolish babbler (which he certainly was not). He would never have written this to a man in Amsterdam, even though he was a former *Stiftler*, about Hegel without some good reason. Claims like Hoffmeister's must be based on a fuller knowledge of the context; they cannot rest upon our ignorance. All we can say in the light of the quotation is that Schnurrer thought Hegel might have a rather unpleasant shock awaiting him, and he knew that Scholl (as a *Hoffmeister* himself) would appreciate his reasons for thinking so.

Schnurrer wrote to a number of his former students regularly; and his letters

was not above using his health as an excuse for avoiding things that he did not like. Whether Schnurrer had any very clear idea of just how this self-willed young man preferred to spend his time we cannot be certain. Quite possibly he did, for he certainly knew quite a lot about the revolutionary fervour of the students, their political clubs, and their opposition to the established order. According to one of the most trenchant student critics of the *Stift* Schnurrer protected freedom of thought as best he could by turning a blind eye upon it. But he could not turn a blind eye when he was faced by a student who neglected the curriculum in order to pursue his own researches. The young Hegel was beyond the limits of his tolerance, not to speak of his sympathies.[1]

How Hegel himself felt and what he did with his time can be inferred from two comically ironic contributions to his *Stammbuch* by unidentified 'cousins'. The first was written at Stuttgart on his birthday and probably belongs to 1791.

Naked came I into the world and naked go I again under the earth.
Naked from hence to go, that calls for sorrow and grief.

———

That, however, concerns the 100, so Herr Cousin need not be troubled about the above sayings; we know well he is in good hands. Yes?

are full of general news and gossip about events in the *Stift*. But we do know of one possible reason why Scholl may have expressed an interest in Hegel's progress and prospects. He succeeded Hegel as holder of the Hirschmann-Gomerischen Stipendium when Hegel relinquished it on receiving his Jena professorship in 1805 (*Briefe*, iv. 85). Was he already interested in the prospects of the four holders of this stipendium in 1793?

[1] Cf. the comments by C. F. Reinhardt in *Schwäbisches Museum*, I (1785): 'The present Ephor [Schnurrer] protects liberty of thought as far as he can, that is, he does not hinder it. . . . One may read what one will, and one need have nothing to fear, if one were caught with Voltaire even' (Betzendörfer, p. 15). Haering (i. 49–50) quotes this passage, but destroys its real import as a personal tribute to Schnurrer by making it mean that 'die allerweiteste Freiheit' reigned in the *Stift*, and that the new ideas of Hegel, Hölderlin, and Schelling were welcomed and nourished by their teachers. Betzendörfer himself says that even after the reform of 1793 'the personal freedom of the *Stiftler* was very limited'. We can now get a good idea of the actual situation, and of Schnurrer's efforts to improve it, from his correspondence with Scholl and other documents printed by Beck in *GSA*, vol. vii. It is fairly clear that *within the limits of the curriculum* Schnurrer did all he could to help his students develop their own interests. It may well have been he who suggested to Conz, and later to Hölderlin, the comparisons between classical authors and parts of the Old Testament that they offered as *Specimina* for the magisterial examination. (It should be noted that this sort of interest was far removed from the orthodox theology of G. C. Storr.)

Oh if only there were not the letters from the University!—It doesn't matter Herr Cousin, (*sage bis Georgii ganz richtig*) as sure as I am

St[uttgart]				Your
Written on	+	+	+	true and sincere friend and cousin
Gebhard's day[1]	+	+	+	M.H.—

The other entry is undated; but from internal evidence we can tell that it belongs to the 'summer of love' in 1791. It was signed with a pseudonym which cannot now be completely deciphered, but which may I think have been 'Voltaire'. We get from it a clear impression of the amused and friendly bewilderment with which his fellow students regarded 'the Old Man'. But we can also see that the young scholar of Stuttgart has by no means abandoned his high ambitions and that some of his friends at least understood them well enough to poke fun at them effectively:

> Experience, Part 396704510, Page 75146 in the Notes.

> Crooked are the ways of the old man even into old age and until he grows gray.—His legs wobble like the legs of singers and dancing girls. Therefore O Man, old or young, cast from thee the cloth all covered with fat drippings from the mouth, and take thee a new clean bib, that thou mayst go to thy heart's desire with firm step!—

> Herr Cousin—I am and shall be for all days that God shall bless me with, a lover of short and pithy moral proverbs. Herr Cousin!—When the heart is full, then runneth the mouth over—is it not so? Sapienti sat! Herr Cousin! [etc. etc.] . . . and so farewell my dear old acquaintance and comrade of the Gymnasium. Give X my greetings. Love strives with gray hairs, even with the Old One it plays its game—oh yes!—but one is then just as if struck upon the *Head* and just then one realizes that is time to take one's place in Charon's skiff. But see now if I

---

[1] Entry 64: *Briefe*, iv. 59. I assume that this leaf was written for Hegel on his birthday in 1791 just a few days after he had been obliged to return to Tübingen because of a 'letter from the University' informing him that no further extension of his sick leave would be granted. But the text of the last sentence is impossible to construe, and may have been misread by Flechsig. What I have taken to be a reference to the quarterly report of St. George's Day (23 Apr.), after which Hegel would be free to come home again for a month, may perhaps be a reference to Councillor *Georgii*. In that case the sheet could have been written in 1793 while Hegel was at home, but had not yet received permission to take a post in Switzerland.

Hegel's birthday, 27 Aug., was the feast of St. Gebhard, bishop of Constance in the tenth century. Even in maturity he was mindful of his patron saint—his friend Rösel, who would surely only have known that 27 Aug. was Gebhard's day because Hegel told him so, wrote a humorous poem for the occasion in 1825 (*Briefe*, iii. 93–4).

haven't written all the paper full! So it goes, if I once get deep in thought! I must do violence to myself, to commend you for your virtues? at last, and to assure you that I—for the rest see Rautenstrauch's Book of Compliments pages 17–34.[1]

2. *The philosophy course*

The *Magisterprogramm* made up when Hegel received his diploma in September 1790 certifies that *praeter consueta* he attended the lectures of C. F. Rösler *novellas tradentem*; of J. F. Flatt on Cicero's *De natura deorum* and on 'empirical psychology'; and of *Repetent* Bardili on the use of profane writings in theology. It further certifies that he gave his Baccalaureate oration, and defended a dissertation before Professor Bök 'On the limit of human duties, immortality being set aside'; and that he offered two specimen essays 'On the judgement of ordinary common sense regarding the objectivity and subjectivity of representations' and 'On the study of the History of Philosophy'.[2]

The first stage in this curriculum, after his matriculation in October 1788, was the Baccalaureate which Hegel received in December. For this he was examined in languages (i.e. Greek and Latin), History, Logic, Arithmetic, and Geometry, apart from delivering the oration already mentioned. Then began the two-year course for the degree of *Magister*. For this the regular requirements (*consueta*) were Logic, Metaphysics, Natural Law, Moral Philosophy, History, Greek and Hebrew, Mathematics, theoretical and experimental Physics. Instruction was partly in the formal public lectures and private classes given by professors, partly in small weekly classes (*Kollegien*) given by *Repetenten* in the *Stift* itself. The regular or required courses were normally devoted to explanation of, and commentary upon, an appointed *Kompendium* or textbook. Three lecture courses were ordinarily compulsory in the first year (the *Novizenzeit*): Logic and Metaphysics, Greek and Hebrew, and History; and two more were required in the second year (the *Complentenzeit*): Moral Philosophy and

---

[1] Entry 66, *Briefe*, iv. 60. Hoffmeister and Flechsig conjecture that the signature may be V.....rê. The author would seem to be an old friend who remembered Hegel from the Gymnasium. Perhaps Hegel took the nickname 'the Old Man' to Tübingen with him from there.

(I think also that further study of the manuscript might show that 'Grüßen Sie mir X' ought to be read 'Grüßen Sie mir A'. But in any case the reference to Auguste Hegelmeier is patent.)   [2] *Briefe*, iv. 169.

Physics. Students could choose for themselves among the *Kollegien*, for which they paid supplemental fees.[1]

In the light of these requirements and all other available indications it would seem that Hegel's programme of studies for the philosophy course was as follows:

Winter Semester 1788/9

Logic and Metaphysics: J. F. Flatt (public lecture).
History of the Apostles: C. F. Schnurrer (public lecture).
Universal History: C. F. Rösler (public lecture).[2]
The Psalms: C. F. Schnurrer (private class).
Repetition for the week.[3]

Summer Semester 1789

Cicero, *De natura deorum*: J. F. Flatt (public lecture).[4]
Empirical Psychology and Kant's *Critique*: J. F. Flatt (private class).[5]
The Catholic Epistles: C. F. Schnurrer (public lecture).
The Psalms (continued): C. F. Schnurrer (private class).
Repetition.

Winter Semester 1789/90

General Moral Philosophy: A. F. Bök (public lecture).[6]

[1] Betzendörfer, p. 39.
[2] Betzendörfer simply records that Rösler lectured on 'Universal History' throughout the two-year period. I have tentatively assigned Hegel's attendance at this compulsory course to his first term because the second term seems to have been filled by courses which were *praeter consueta*, but which either his *Magisterprogramm* or the manuscripts available to Rosenkranz show that Hegel attended.
[3] The weekly *Repetition* (two hours) for the *Novitii* and *Complentes* was given by a *Repetent* designated for each week. The topic was also frequently designated. A connection between the *Repetition* and one or another current lecture course is sometimes evident, but there was no systematic pattern of connections; and there is no detectable organic sequence or development in the list of designated topics for a semester. See Brecht and Sandberger, pp. 53, 54, 61–5.
[4] Betzendörfer's summary of the lecture lists—from which my lecture titles are derived—does not explicitly state that this was a public lecture course (Betzendörfer, pp. 40–4). But see the next note.
[5] Henrich has determined, on the basis of students' notes from this course which he has discovered and examined, that the central section of Hegel's 'Psychologie' of 1794 was excerpted from his notes on this class (*Hegel-Studien*, iii. 70–1 n.). Since Henrich calls this class a *Kolleg* I have inferred that Flatt lectured publicly on the *De natura deorum*.
[6] Again Betzendörfer simply records that Bök lectured on the topics of moral philosophy and natural law, both publicly and in private classes throughout the period. But in view of Hegel's own interests, and the part that Bök played in his *Magisterexamen*, I think it safe to assume that Hegel took his public lecture course at the beginning of the year (see further, p. 74 n. 2).

Job: C. F. Schnurrer (private class).[1]
History of Philosophy: C. F. Rösler (private class).
The Use of Profane Authors in Theology: *Rep.* C. G. Bardili.
Repetition.

Summer Semester *1790*

Natural Law: A. F. Bök (private class).[2]
Theoretical Physics: C. F. Pfleiderer (public lecture).[3]
Ontology and Cosmology (Ulrich's *Compendium*): J. F. Flatt (public
lecture).[4]
The Most Recent Political Changes: C. F. Rösler (private class).[5]
Repetition.

If we may assume that everything apart from the regular courses
(*praeter consueta*) would be mentioned on the printed programme
at the time of the examination, the above list can be regarded as
complete. In any case we can assume that Hegel did nothing else
that seemed to him important enough to be worthy of note.[6]

[1] Hegel's attendance at this class is not documented by anything in Rosenkranz
or by his *Magisterprogramm*. But Leutwein speaks of his 'particular enjoyment
of the book of Job on account of its unconventionalized natural speech'. I agree
with Henrich that we have here a fairly conclusive proof that 1789/90 was the
year of closest intimacy between Hegel and Leutwein (see *Hegel-Studien*, iii.
56, 63). See further, n. 6 below.

[2] For the reasons given above, p. 73 n. 6, I think we can be sure that Hegel
took Bök's private class during the year. The second semester seems the most
natural time for him to have taken it. (For the separation of Bök's public-lecture
and private-class topics see the lecture lists for Schelling's time published by
Fuhrmans, i. 19.)

[3] Hegel may have taken this required course in the first semester.

[4] Betzendörfer adds: 'und erklärte sich im Vorlesungsverzeichnis für dieses
Semester bereit, *"potiora Kantianae criticae capita"* zu erklären.' I take this to
refer to a private class that he gave in the same term. Putting together Leutwein's
reminiscences, with the *Magisterprogramm* and final testimonials of both Hegel
and Hölderlin, we can infer that Hölderlin attended this class and Hegel did not
(cf. *Dok.*, pp. 429–30; *Briefe*, iv. 87, 169; Betzendörfer, pp. 20, 22, 26–7, 40–5).
(Fuhrmans thinks that it is more probable that the class was never given in 1790.
Flatt certainly lectured on the Critical Philosophy from 1791 onwards.)

[5] This is what I take to be referred to by *novellas tradentem* in the *Magisterprogramm*. One wonders whether this class on 'Neueste statistische Veränderun-
gen' touched on the Revolution of France. If it did it was undoubtedly popular
with the students. But it was probably concerned in the main with constitutional
developments in the German Empire.

[6] Hölderlin's programme records his attendance at the class of Rep. Conz on
Euripides (as well as the class of Bardili on profane authors). It does not mention
Schnurrer's class on Proverbs which he almost certainly attended, just as Hegel's
does not list the classes on the Psalms (which we know he attended) or the class
on Job. But I assume that for the *Stiftler* Schnurrer's classes in general, like the

During his first semester he wrote a discourse 'On some advantages which the reading of ancient classical Greek and Roman writers secures for us', which according to Rosenkranz is merely a revised version of his Stuttgart essay on the distinguishing characteristics of classical poetry. The manuscript is dated December 1788 and was gone over by one of the *Repetenten*, so it was quite clearly submitted in fulfilment of some academic obligation. In view of the date it seems most probable that it was written up for the Baccalaureate examination; I think myself that it served as the oration recorded in the programme of 1790.[1] The basic thesis remains unchanged: through the study of classical authors we can recapture and appreciate the spontaneous novelty of experience in all its original freshness, and particularly we can grasp what the original invention of concepts was like in a natural language that has not already become ossified into a system of conventional signs. But the underlying assumption that a common human essence is revealed everywhere in the history of mankind, and that every people must therefore go through the same stages of cultural development, is more explicitly stated than before;[2] and so is the view that the proper task of the philosopher is to solve practical problems through the reconciliation of opposed views and the finding of a middle way to the truth.

In general the essay is a conflation of the views which Hegel expressed in his essay of 1787 on the religion of the Greeks and Romans with the views put forward in the essay on the classical poets, rather than a direct repetition of the latter—but of course we must remember that we possess only a fragment of that essay. In any case the only real novelty in this later version, relative to the two earlier essays taken together, is to be found in the heightening of certain earlier claims on behalf of classical culture, and

classes which other *ordinarii* held in direct connection with the required courses, could count as *consueta*.

[1] *Dok.*, 169–72. Hopf's verdict on the August essay would be bound to recur to Hegel's mind when he was faced with the task of giving his first public oration at the University: 'proprii Martis specimen et felix futurorum omen; vide ut declamatio commentationi respondeat' (Rosenkranz, p. 18). He was never able to live up to this final admonition, however.

[2] Hoffmeister notes that this view of history was not the one adopted by Garve himself—who thought of the relation of modern culture to that of the ancients as one of progress. Like the practical conception of the philosopher's task, it is one Hegel himself had adopted in 1787 in his essay on the religion of the Greeks and Romans (cf. *Dok.*, pp. 43–8, and Chapter I, pp. 31–5 above).

specifically of Greek culture. For Hegel accepts the view of Winckelmann, which was by now a commonplace, and declares that 'the Roman writings . . . are for the most part only imitations', whereas the Greeks . . . had in their language an astonishingly rich supply of words with which to express the appearance of changes in sensible objects and in the visible realm, even to the finest shadings, but particularly the distinct modifications of passions, of states of mind, and of character; our language has also, indeed, a great stock of such words; but it would be even greater if they were not mostly provincial, and some of them vulgar, and so in either case banned from the speech of polite society and from literature.[1]

The implied superiority of ancient Greek as against modern German in respect of expressions for passions and states of mind is contrary to Garve's view, which Hegel seems in general to have agreed with, that modern culture is superior in its psychological and mental vocabulary, its conceptions of the intelligible as opposed to the visible world. The presence of the Platonic contrast between visible and intelligible in this passage, which is evident from expressions like 'der sichtbaren Natur' and 'die feinsten Schattierungen', even lends some plausibility to Hoffmeister's suggestion that Hegel never really meant to imply Greek superiority in the intellectual realm.[2] Certainly in the end he came to hold that whereas perfection of outward form was achieved in the Hellenic world, the comprehension of inward meaning was a distinctively modern, Christian achievement. Nevertheless Hoffmeister is demonstrably mistaken, for the point that Hegel is making here is the very one with which the surviving fragment of the August essay began. He is contrasting the healthy, undivided, *natural* consciousness of the Greeks with the corrupt, divided, *artificial* consciousness of the moderns; and this, too, is a contrast that he never abandoned. At Tübingen his mind was increasingly dominated by this particular contrast, though it never produced in him—except perhaps momentarily at the end of the Berne period—the sensations of hopeless yearning toward the lost Arcadia that it seems to have induced in Hölderlin. He was always seeking to overcome the alienation and corruption of modern consciousness, and when he finally succeeded in doing so—at least to his own satisfaction—he was at last able to claim that modern Christian consciousness really is superior in its inwardness.

[1] *Dok.*, p. 171.   [2] *Dok.*, p. 441.

The present essay shows, however, that his entry into the *Stift* immediately intensified his sense of the corruption of modern consciousness, and of the consequent superiority of the Hellenic culture as compared with Christianity. The first hint of an explicit contrast between the two heritages of Achaea and Judaea in his mind is to be found in his claim that, in virtue of the constancy of human nature, the study of our classical heritage will enable us 'to explain more naturally and make more comprehensible a great deal of the culture, the habits, the customs, and the usages of the people of Israel, who have had, and still have, so much influence upon us'.[1]

Even now as at the end of the essay of 1787 Hegel assumes that enlightened Christianity represents a great progress over the religion of the Greeks and Romans. Doubtless he introduced the reference to Christian origins here only because it seemed obvious and appropriate as he was embarking on a five-year course in Hellenic philosophy and Judaeo-Christian theology. But the placing of the Jews on a level with the Greek and Roman heathens, in an essay with this title, has something defiant about it. Hegel is proclaiming fairly clearly, though perhaps not deliberately, that he prefers to seek his salvation by seeking among 'the many contradictions of the ancient philosophers, especially in their speculations about the practical part of philosophy . . . to find the middle way where the truth lies'.[2]

Of the essays that Hegel must have written in connection with his philosophy course, nothing remains except the titles of the two that he submitted as *specimina* for the *Magisterexamen*. About the effect that his teachers had upon him, therefore, we can only speculate. In the *curriculum vitae* of 1804 he mentions Schnurrer, Flatt, and Bök. But there are two reasons for suspecting that he mentions these names only because they are the most likely to carry weight in relation to his current purpose. First, we know that he disliked Schnurrer and that Schnurrer did not approve of him;

---

[1] *Dok.*, p. 171. Lacorte, p. 300, points out that this idea is to be found in Mendelssohn's *Jerusalem* (Berlin, 1783), ii. 26 ff.

[2] *Dok.*, p. 172. Hoffmeister in his note (*Dok.*, p. 445) says that this was precisely Abel's conception of philosophy and quotes a similar view from Schiller's 'Versuch über den Zusammenhang der thierischen Natur des Menschen mit seiner geistigen' (1780). In this connection it is important to note that Hegel first expressed this view in his essay of August 1787 at a time when he was still in frequent contact with Abel. Abel did not, of course, come to Tübingen until 1790 (cf. *Dok.*, pp. 15 and 47–8).

and secondly he says he did philosophy *and mathematics* under Flatt and Bök, which is obviously not accurate. He wishes to mention his mathematical training, but sees no point in giving the name of his professor (Pfleiderer). It is altogether likely, I think, that the two professors (Rösler and Pfleiderer) whom he does not mention, because they were not philosophers in the narrow technical sense, influenced him far more than the two whom he does mention because they were.

About Hegel's relations with Schnurrer I have already spoken in the preceding section, since he was the Ephor, the most immediately present authority, of the *Stift*. Hegel's attitude to Flatt it will be more convenient to discuss in detail in the next section, since he was primarily a theologian, the most prominent and probably the most intelligently faithful pupil and disciple of G. C. Storr, and he transferred to the faculty of theology in 1792. In the faculty of philosophy it would seem that he performed the necessary tasks of the professor of Logic and Metaphysics, Gottfried Plouquet, who died in 1790 but had ceased to lecture in 1782.[1] Flatt was greatly interested in, and much influenced by, the philosophy of Kant, about which he was generally regarded as an authority. In his lectures on metaphysics he used as a textbook the compendium of Ulrich, in which an attempt was made to combine the old metaphysics of Wolff with the new methodology of Kant. But Hegel doubtless got more out of his discussions of Cicero's *De natura deorum*, and of empirical psychology in relation to Kant. The factual content of these lectures no doubt appealed to him, even if, as seems probable, the general orientation of the lecturer did not.

A. F. Bök was, at least until the coming of J. F. Abel, which occurred only after Hegel had passed on to theology, the philosopher whose attitude and interests were closest to those of Hegel himself at this time. He was professor of moral philosophy, rhetoric, and

---

[1] Quite a lot of ink appears to have been spilt over the question of whether Plouquet formed a bridge between the logic of Hegel and the school-metaphysics of Wolff. It seems to me that this question has been decisively settled in the negative by Lacorte, pp. 130–5. A bridge might perhaps be found, if it is needed, in the compendium of Ulrich and the lectures of Flatt. But Hegel was being made to learn the elements of Wolff's metaphysics from the age of twelve onwards (see *Werke* (1832 ff.), xvii. 364) so the influence of any particular teacher in this respect would be hard to establish; and I cannot believe that any connection one might wish to make would be interesting enough to merit the labour involved.

poetry. In moral philosophy he used the compendium of Feder with which Hegel was already familiar at the Gymnasium; and in aesthetic theory he followed Mendelssohn. He was a man of consequence at Tübingen, being vice-rector of the University, but certainly not an original thinker. His most important work was a history of the University. Like Hegel himself at this time, he was not much interested in purely theoretical questions, and not much affected by the ferment aroused by the *Critique of Pure Reason*. Because of this he has generally been written off as unimportant by modern students. But there is no reason to suppose that Hegel thought the worse of him on these grounds. The real reason why we do not need to worry about his influence on Hegel, whether great or little, is that it did not and could not change anything; it could only reinforce what was already there. Bök was a typical product of just those tendencies in the Enlightenment which were already part of Hegel's background. There are some indications that Hegel may have felt this himself. It would seem from Rosenkranz's silence that Hegel kept no notes from his courses with Bök; and according to the report of Schelling's biographer Bök was not a stimulating or exciting teacher.[1] But, of course, no one who was unmoved by Kant would have been likely to excite Schelling.

C. F. Rösler, the professor of history, on the other hand, may well have exercised a really significant influence on Hegel's development. Only a close examination of his writings in relation to Hegel's juvenilia could establish whether this was so, and as far as I know the question has not yet been investigated. But in the light of Hegel's known interests before and after the Tübingen period the following purely external data are suggestive, to say the least. For his basic required course on Universal History he used the compendium of Schrökh, a fact which can hardly have failed to endear him to Hegel at the beginning; and like Schrökh he was certainly interested in 'connecting the *Lehrreich* with history', for the book that first established his reputation was on the *Lehrbegriff* of the early Church (1773). Again, like Schrökh, he was primarily a church historian; he spent many years editing a great collection of translated excerpts from the early fathers (10 vols., 1776–86) which according to Betzendörfer was probably the most frequently

[1] Cf. Betzendörfer, pp. 40–1; Rosenkranz, p. 25; Lacorte, pp. 128–219; Plitt, i. 27. Bök was a former *Stiftler*.

borrowed work in the *Stift* library. In the years in which Hegel was at Tübingen he had rather moved on to the study of the medieval church, but he was also deeply interested in the political and constitutional history of Germany and modern Europe. Although himself a *Stiftler* he was more an enlightened humanist than an orthodox Lutheran. Betzendörfer tells us that he lectured on classical bibliography (*Bücherkunde der alten Schriftsteller*), and although he does not appear to have done so in the period 1788–90—unlesss perhaps in connection with his class on the history of philosophy—this raises the question how much of Hegel's collection of material on this topic, ascribed by Rosenkranz to the Stuttgart period, may in fact have been assembled at Tübingen. His attitude both as a teacher and as a historian was one that would certainly have attracted the 'eclectic' Hegel with his consuming interest in concrete experience. For Betzendörfer reports that

The students prized his learning, his free spirit, and his lively and amusing way of lecturing. Rösler spoke mainly without notes, in Swabian dialect, and he knew how to make his lectures entertaining by remarks that were both relevant and witty. But he seems often to have got so involved in the telling of anecdotes that 'scientific understanding and deeper explanation' suffered. Every attempt to construe the course of history in accordance with an a priori principle was hateful to him; he saw in it the death of all historical research. Klüpfel marks him out as the first real historian that Tübingen ever had.[1]

There is thus some reason to doubt, in the case of Rösler at least, whether Lacorte is altogether correct when he concludes:

Of an active elaboration of contemporary literature and philosophy, as also of the personality of a *maestro* capable of guiding the concerns of the young Hegel in a definite direction, it would be vain to seek traces in the program and among the teachers of the faculty of philosophy.[2]

[1] Betzendörfer, pp. 41–2. It is not recorded that Rösler studied at the *Stift* but he began his academic career there as a *Repentent* in 1763. Once again it should be noted that the criticisms are not of the kind that would necessarily have led Hegel to think the worse of him.

[2] Lacorte, p. 135. Rosenkranz's cautious comment is surely more nearly correct: 'As Flatt stood between the Wolffian and Kantian philosophy . . . so Rösler, the editor of the *Library of Church-Fathers* . . . stood likewise between orthodoxy and heterodoxy, and he must have been a not unwelcome teacher for a young man already so deeply infected by the tendencies of the Enlightenment' (Rosenkranz, p. 26).

Finally C. F. Pfleiderer, professor of mathematics and physics, was a mathematician of some worth, whose principal interest was in analytical geometry. Betzendörfer says that he was an admirer of the Greek mathematicians. Hegel would have appreciated him for both of these reasons, but his interest in mathematics and physics remained largely extraneous to his more philosophical concerns for more than a decade still to come, so the question of Pfleiderer's possible influence upon him can scarcely concern us here.[1]

It does not appear likely that Hegel was much influenced by any of the *Repetenten* in the *Stift*. They were closer to his own age and he was certainly thrown into fairly continuous and intimate contact with them, but their interests were in the main oriented rather towards the orthodox theology which certainly did not appeal to him.[2] Partial exceptions should perhaps be made in the cases of Bardili and Conz.[3] These two had been students together at the *Stift* along with C. F. Reinhardt and K. F. Stäudlin (the younger brother of the lawyer poet). The four of them formed a 'company of poets', who were admirers of Schiller. Both Bardili and Conz certainly sympathized with the attitude that Hegel adopted in his baccalaureate oration—if that is indeed what it was—of December 1788; and it is not at all surprising that both Hegel and Hölderlin took Bardili's class on 'The Use of Profane Authors in Theology'. Conz had, of course, far more influence on Hölderlin, but contact with both of them doubtless helped to develop Hegel's interest in Schiller, which had probably been aroused in the first instance by Abel at Stuttgart.[4] Through

---

[1] Betzendörfer, pp. 42–3. Pfleiderer was once again a former *Stiftler*. Thus all of the Philosophy Faculty, except Abel when he came, had been associated with the *Stift* either as students or as teachers at the beginning of their careers.

[2] His own attitude toward orthodox theology was certainly influenced by the 'Kantian *enragé*', Karl Diez. But the influence may well have been mainly indirect, since Hegel only became actively involved in the controversy about Kant's theology after Diez had left the *Stift* (see below, pp. 107 ff.).

[3] Another possible exception is I. D. Mauchardt, whose primary interest was in descriptive psychology, and who may well have contributed significantly to Hegel's ideas in this area as well as to his stock of information—see p. 175 n. 3. (A full list of the *Repetenten* in Hegel's time with all available details of career and publications can be found in Brecht and Sandberger, pp. 58–61).

[4] Cf. p. 9 n. 3. Abel probably had friendly ties with several of the *Repetenten*. Mauchardt's *Phänomene der menschlichen Seele* (Stuttgart, 1789) was dedicated to him; and when he came to be professor at Tübingen (1790) Bardili took his place at the *Karlsschule*.

them also, he came to have a personal interest in the career of C. F. Reinhardt, who was like himself an enthusiastic admirer of Rousseau.[1]

At the end of the first term in the *Stift* the new students were 'placed' by the Inspectorate. Either now (in April 1789) or six months later in November, Hegel, who had entered the *Stift* placed first among the Stuttgart candidates, was ranked fourth in his class of twenty-seven, below J. F. Maerklin, who had been second to him in the Stuttgart group. Even without the testimony of Leutwein who shared a study with Hegel in the following year, we might fairly have surmised that this was a very grievous blow to the pride of a student who had always stood first in his class at the Gymnasium.[2]

---

[1] Compare *Briefe*, i. 11 where he writes to Schelling from Berne on Christmas Eve 1794; '[Oelsner] gave me news of some Württembergers in Paris, especially of Reinhard [*sic*], who has a post of great importance in the Département des affaires étrangères.' Reinhardt doubtless appeared to all of the young radicals in the *Stift* as a model of someone who was actually *doing* something to further the ideals in which they believed. He was in France when the Revolution began, and entered the diplomatic service there in 1791. In 1799 he became minister for external affairs under the Directory. Under Napoleon he served as an ambassador. Like Hegel, he went from Tübingen first to a post in Switzerland (*Briefe*, i. 187, 433).

[2] *Briefe*, iv. 76 (for the Semester Reports of the *Stift*); *Hegel-Studien*, iii. 54-6 (for the testimony of Leutwein). The further report of Schwegler that Hegel was spurred for a time into a fury of industry and did not properly go to bed for weeks at a time (see *Hegel-Studien*, iii. 60-1) must be dismissed as a plausible embroidery upon the very strained hypothesis of Leutwein that an enduring jealousy of the 'Erz Metaphysiker und Kantianer' Maerklin was the ultimate reason for Hegel's emergence as a major philosopher in his own right.

Henrich states explicitly in two places (*Hegel-Studien*, iii. 63 and 65, notes to line 7 and line 70 in Leutwein's letter) that Hegel was placed fourth at Martinmas 1789 (10 Nov.). But the Semester Report for St. George's Day (23 Apr.) records him as *fourth*; and Leutwein's testimony tells firmly against the hypothesis that Hegel was placed *third* in April and *fourth* in November. (*Hegel-Studien*, iii. 55-6, lines 104-5: 'Wäre er der dritte in der Promotion geworden . . .' strongly suggests that Hegel never was anything but *fourth* at Tübingen.)

There is, indeed, an ambiguity in the printed records of *Hölderlin* which might mean that the initial *Lokation in* April was regarded as tentative or unofficial. He is placed *eighth* in the *Semester* Report for April 1789 but is still listed as *sixth* (i.e. he is ranked only in relation to his fellow students from Maulbronn) in the quarterly testimonial for April. He is given his Tübingen rank at the Feast of St. James (25 July). But the quarterly ranking for April is probably just a slip. It may even be a misprint, since it is ignored by Beck in his note. He says that Hölderlin was placed below the two Stuttgart candidates, Hegel and Maerklin, 'in the spring of 1789' (*GSA*, vii. 1, 384); and in his note on the Semester Reports he says explicitly that the Tübingen location took effect 'nach den ersten Semester'. This is confirmed by Letter 32, which ought quite definitely

In his second term Hegel took Flatt's course on 'Empirical Psychology and Kant's Critique', and in all probability he studied and excerpted the *Critique of Pure Reason* with some care. It seems likely indeed that much of the excerpting from modern philosophers mentioned by Rosenkranz was done at this time.[1] The notes

to be assigned to the spring of 1789, and not, as Beck believes, to the spring of 1790. (The evidence for this claim is in the *Aufgabenliste* of Hölderlin's mother (*GSA*, vii. 1, 284.) Letter 32, like many others that Hölderlin wrote to his mother in these years, is very largely an appeal for more money. So Hölderlin has to explain where the money she had already given him has gone. He mentions first the fate of the last eight florins out of a sum of thirty (lines 9–11). These thirty florins cannot be directly identified with any amount mentioned in the *Aufgabenliste*. They must have come from the monies his mother gave him for his return to Tübingen after the Easter vacation, but they could equally well be the remainder—after travelling expenses?—from the 41 florins 12 Kreutzer he received in 1789, or from the 42 florins of 1790 (ibid. 285). A little later, however, Hölderlin explains what has happened to the '3 florins that I just now received' (lines 18–19): these *must* be the three florins sent on 5 May 1789—the first amount sent after Easter 1790 was eleven florins sent on 30 April. Thus letter 32 can be securely dated 'early May 1789', and all the remarks about trouble between Hölderlin and Louise Nast arising from his deference to his mother's wishes must refer to some lover's quarrel *before* the final break between them, and not to that breach itself—as Beck so plausibly argues. Even without the objective certainty provided by the *Aufgabenliste* I would myself have said that a love life with as many ups and downs in it as Hölderlin's is a much shakier ground for dating a letter than the reasonable assumption that a good student will react to his placement in his class *when it happens*—not a whole year, or even six months, later. Hölderlin was, as we might expect, rather upset by the decision of the Inspectorate: 'Daß ich in der Lokation um die zwei Stutgarder, Hegel u. Märklin hinuntergekommen bin, schmerzt mich eben auch ein wenig. Wie gut habens andre, die ununterbrochen durch solche Schulfuchsereien in ihren Studien fort machen können' (*GSA*, vi. 53, lines 24–8).
  [1] Rosenkranz, p. 14. Ever since Haering (i. 55) wrote 'es läßt sich mit Sicherheit sagen, daß hiernach von einem nennenswerten Einfluß der *theoretischen* Philosophie Kants in dieser früheren Zeit (und wir fügen sofort hinzu: auch späterhin wird es nicht anders sein), mindestens nur ein Wort, daß die Probleme der Kritik der reinen Vernunft ihn näher beschäftigt oder ergriffen hätten', there has been a tendency to ignore the evidence of Hegel's Kantian studies which Haering himself carefully records. Lacorte (p. 110) even tries to argue Hegel's excerpts out of existence by suggesting that Rosenkranz was probably referring to the manuscript of 1794 (discussed in the following note). But this is ridiculous. If Rosenkranz had known that Hegel took this class of Flatt's he would most certainly have said so. But he did not; and he certainly could not have known it from these notes. We only know it ourselves from the comparison of Hegel's *Magisterprogramm* with the lecture lists. Yet Rosenkranz (loc. cit.) is able to tell us explicitly that 'the earliest study of Kant's *Critique of Pure Reason* . . . falls quite definitely [*mit Bestimmtheit*] in the year 1789'. How did he know this? Surely because the 'Auszug' of which he speaks on pp. 86–7 was a normal excerpt, headed by the date as almost all of Hegel's excerpts were? What Haering says about the *influence* of Kant on Hegel is probably not far from the truth; but Lacorte's assertion (p. 135) that 'a systematic *study* of Kant on

from Flatt's course itself were not seen by Rosenkranz; it is probable that Hegel threw them away after incorporating all that he thought worth preserving in his own notes on 'Psychologie'— the so-called 'Materials for a philosophy of subjective spirit'—in 1794.[1]

In his third term Hegel was occupied with the book of Job, which certainly interested him, but probably not in the way in which it interested his professor (Schnurrer), for Leutwein says that Hegel 'had a special delight in the Book of Job on account of its unconventionalized [ungeregelter] natural language'.[2] From the way in which I have translated 'ungeregelter' it will be seen that I take this to mean that Hegel found in Hebrew poetry, and especially in this book, the same sort of spontaneous 'simplicity', the same direct and natural expression of immediate experience in concepts 'abstracted' there and then, rather than inherited in the conventionalized form of established usage, that he admired in the Greek poets. Obviously therefore he was quite serious in putting Israel *on a level* with the Greeks when he began his University course. In many respects, as we shall see, he soon came to feel that the Jewish consciousness was somehow impoverished by comparison with that of the Greeks, but his admiration for their poetic and prophetic heritage was as yet unstinted.

He was at the same time taking his first course in the history of philosophy with Rösler. But all trace of this has been lost—reabsorbed doubtless in his many later manuscripts. All that we have in this connection are reports of the fervour with which Hölderlin and he read Plato. Doubtless this reading went on all the time, but the study of Plato *together* is something that may well have begun in this term if they were at the same time taking Bardili's

the part of Hegel in these years can be absolutely excluded' is quite unjustified— indeed it is probably the exact reverse of the truth.

[1] See *Dok.*, pp. 195–217 for the text, and pp. 448–53 for Hoffmeister's notes on its origins. Several hypotheses have been put forward to explain this manuscript, but only one needs to be mentioned here. Lacorte (pp. 301–2) has suggested that it may simply be a revision of Hegel's notes from Flatt's course. There are both external and internal grounds for holding that this view is too extreme—the manuscript is assigned to 1794 by Schüler, and the discussion is based upon Hegel's own division of the faculties—see below, Chapter III, pp. 174–6. But Lacorte's conjecture has now been in a large measure confirmed by Henrich on the basis of his examination of another student's *Kollegienheft* from this class (*Hegel-Studien*, iii. 70–1 n.).

[2] *Hegel-Studien*, iii. 56, lines 130–3.

course, since of all the 'profane authors' Plato is the most obviously useful in theology.[1] Bök's lectures, on the other hand, would give him an excuse, if he felt the need of one, for studying the *Émile*, *Social Contract*, and *Confessions* of his hero Rousseau, and the other works governed by like sentiments, through which one could cast off the 'fetters' and generalized conventions of the understanding.[2] We cannot say just what these 'fetters' were, but one suspects that Rousseau's idea of natural spontaneous self-expression was what attracted Hegel, and that the structure of modern society may well have seemed to him to mirror in some way the artificiality that he found in modern thought and language.[3]

In the second term of this year (summer 1790) he must have been occupied quite a lot of the time with preparations for the *Magisterexamen*. He had to write his two *specimina*,[4] and to prepare his defence of Bök's thesis 'On the limit of human duties, immortality being set aside'. In connection with the latter task

[1] Rosenkranz (p. 40) says that Hegel, Hölderlin, Fink, Renz, and other friends read and discussed Plato, and that some Plato translations by Hegel dating from this time were still extant. Hegel's early concern with Plato is further attested by the biographical sketch in the Brockhaus *Conversation-Lexicon* (1827), which almost certainly stems from Hegel himself: 'He devoted himself with particular effort to the philosophy lectures, but did not find in metaphysics as it was then expounded to him, the hoped-for resolution of his deepest problems. This led him to seek out the writings of Kant, with the study of which he was now earnestly concerned, without laying those of Plato aside' (*Dok.*, pp. 395). This is surely a good example to that 'tenacious memory' recalling—with the aid of his *Kollegienhefte*—the lectures of Flatt, first on metaphysics, then on psychology (which led him to Kant); and in the following year the lectures of Rösler and Bardili (which brought him back to Plato).

Hölderlin's continuous concern with Plato and Kant is attested first by his leaving testimonial: 'Philologiae, inprimis graecae, et philosophiae, inprimis Kantianae . . . assiduus cultor' (*GSA*, vii. 1, 479); and secondly by his letters— though not as early as summer 1790—see p. 102 n. 2 below.

[2] See Leutwein's letter, *Hegel-Studien*, iii. 56, lines 123–30.

[3] The connection between the quality of aesthetic awareness and the character of actual social structures was always a close one in his mind. Cf. his laments about the alienation of German literature, both refined and vulgar, from their constitutional history in Aug. 1788 (*Dok.*, pp. 48–9), and the way in which the study of the '*Staatsverfassung* und des Systems ihrer Erziehung' is taken for granted in connection with Greek literature (*Dok.*, p. 169).

[4] Though he probably wrote the first draft for his essay 'On the study of the history of philosophy' in connection with Rösler's class of the previous term, and may also, conceivably, have used something he wrote for Flatt's class on empirical psychology the year before, as a basis for the essay 'On the judgment of common human understanding about the objectivity and subjectivity of representations'.

Bök held a number of practice disputations during the summer.[1] But this was the summer of which, as he wrote in Fink's *Stammbuch*, 'the motto was Wine!', so we may be sure that he did not take life too seriously.

We have some knowledge of the dissertation that Hegel defended, because Rosenkranz wrote an analysis of it under the impression that Hegel composed it himself.[2] It was in fact defended by Hegel in common with Hölderlin, Fink, and Autenrieth. We may assume that students had at least some measure of choice in this matter of thesis defence, and in the light of his own essays we can see why Hegel should have chosen this one. Indeed it is not difficult if one looks back at the essay of 1787 on the religion of the Greeks and Romans to see why Rosenkranz had no hesitation about accepting it as Hegel's own work. The Kantian distinction between reason and sensibility is accepted in the sense that morality is derived from the former, but no absolute separation is envisaged. Morality proceeds by stages in accord with the development of rational enlightenment, but moral goodness can never be separated from happiness. It follows that a man of nobility who has no belief in immortality will develop a utilitarian ethics containing (1) obligations of immediate necessity or instinct; (2) obligations of pleasure; (3) obligations of utility; and (4) obligations of perfection (from a sense of beauty or high mindedness). Belief in God will particularly strengthen the sense of these higher duties, for one who believes in an all-powerful creator and ruler will view himself as a citizen in the realm of the greatest and best of rulers. One can see how this structure would offer the young Rousseau enthusiast a welcome opportunity to sing the praises of the 'natural man'.

Of the two *specimina* that Hegel did write himself we have only the titles. We may reasonably suppose that his essay 'On the study of the history of philosophy' followed the line indicated by his remarks about the ancient philosophers first made in the essay of 1787 and repeated in December 1788: 'the many contradictions of the ancient philosophers, particularly in their speculation about the practical part of philosophy have at least lightened the labour

[1] Betzendörfer, p. 41.

[2] Rosenkranz, pp. 35–8. There was also a report of it in the *Tubingsche Gelehrte Anzeigen* (1790) which is reprinted in *Dok.*, pp. 436–7. Only rarely were candidates allowed to write their own dissertations, but the privilege was granted to the seventeen-year-old Schelling in 1792.

of finding the middle way, where the truth lies.'[1] It would be interesting to have the essay 'On the judgement of common human understanding about objectivity and subjectivity of representations', because we might perhaps have learned from it what Hegel made of the *Critique of Pure Reason*. A few moments' reflection on the title in the light of all that we know about his interests and his readings is sufficient to make us realize that in all probability several threads that we can trace separately earlier were brought together in this essay. Hegel had always been fascinated by the variety of human sensibility and the consequent differences in opinion and point of view. His concern with this problem is almost the only sign of a purely theoretical philosophical interest that can be found in his early papers. At the beginning of the *Tagebuch* in 1785 he was reflecting about the different impressions (*Eindrücke*) that things make on different people according to age, sex, and interest; and as a sort of tailpiece to it in 1787 we have his thoughts on the ideas (*Vorstellungen*) of quantity. It is not hard to see why problems of this sort worried him when we remember how his fundamental concern with the origin of our abstract ideas arose out of his sense of the difference between real scholarship and pedantic routine discipline, between living ideas and abstractions, between natural language and conventional expressions.[2] For while it was all very well to praise the Greeks for their originality and individuality, he could hardly help recognizing as a student of Plato that the formation of conventional standards of opinion was unavoidable unless some better way out of the Protagorean anarchy of sense experience could be provided. If he wished to preserve at all costs the living concreteness of original direct experience, it must somehow be reconciled and united with a rational standard of objectivity. The establishment of this union eventually became the controlling concern of his *Phenomenology*. The title of this essay makes one wonder whether, and how far, he was aware of the problem in 1790.

Having successfully completed the *examen rigorosum* in which he had to write a Latin essay and answer oral questions concerning the basic curriculum of the course, Hegel celebrated his new

---

[1] *Dok.*, p. 172; cf. *Dok.*, pp. 47–8. (This line of argument was probably suggested initially by Abel.)

[2] *Dok.*, pp. 8–9, 42–3; the first sign of his interest in the problem of the part played by language in the origin of our ideas is the essay *Über das Excipieren* of Mar. 1786: *Dok.*, pp. 31–5.

dignity at a dance and doubtless went home for the vacation quite well pleased with himself and with life.[1]

3. The theology course

When he returned to the *Stift* in October the prospect before him was not inviting. For three years he must read orthodox Lutheran theology of a distinctly conservative type. In the first year, as the inspectorate had just now decided, he was to take Dogmatics, Exegesis, and Moral Theology; in the second Polemics would be added to these three; and in the third there would be only Polemics and Exegesis.[2] From these indications it is not possible to identify with certainty more than a few of the courses that he took.[3] We should know, even if Rosenkranz had not confirmed it in the light of the remaining manuscripts, that he must have attended several of the courses of G. C. Storr, who did most of the lecturing on Dogmatics and New Testament Exegesis. We can be certain that he attended the lectures of Flatt on Moral Theology in the summer of 1792;[4] and it is probable that he took Chancellor Lebret's course on controversies concerning the means of grace in the summer of 1792, and the course on the history of the deistic controversy in the summer of 1793—but in this last summer

---

[1] Hegel refers to a ball arranged by Niethammer *am Magisterium* in a letter to Christiane in October 1814 (Letter 242, *Briefe*, ii. 44); he does so because Niethammer asked him to give her his greetings and to remind her of that occasion when they met. But if *am Magisterium* means 'at my Magisterium' then this was not the first occasion when they were together at a ball. There was a dance in Sept. 1789 when Christiane danced too long with Magister Klett; and Niethammer was certainly there (see Bilfinger's letter to him, 29 Sept. 1789, *GSA*, vii. 1, 401–2), though we do not know that he arranged it. It would have been a natural occasion for him to do something of the sort, since he completed his formal studies in Theology at that time. But he did remain in the *Stift* for another semester (studying Kant and Reinhold under Flatt—see the article of J. L. Doderlein in *Hegel-Studien*, iii. 284). After March 1790, as far as I can determine, he was at Jena. We shall know more about subsequent visits to Tübingen—if any—when his correspondence is published. It does at the moment seem to me quite likely that *am Magisterium* in Hegel's letter simply means 'at the time of the annual Magisterial examination', and that the reference is to the year 1789. Still there may have been a ball in 1790 anyway; and it is certainly clear that Niethammer had formed ties of friendship with Hölderlin, Hegel, Bilfinger, and others in the *Renzsche-Promotion* by the spring of 1789.

[2] Betzendörfer, p. 52.

[3] See Table on facing page.

[4] Since the regulation stipulated that students must take the course in moral theology given in the summer semester in their first and second years, he must also have been enrolled in Maerklin's course in 1791. But in this term he was absent for long periods on account of sickness.

Note 3 to p. 88: The lecture list for the period, reconstructed from the data given by Betzendörfer and Fuhrmans is as follows. (The courses which Hegel seems most likely to have taken in fulfilment of the regulations have been marked with an asterisk.)

Lecturer		Lebret (public 10 a.m. / private 3 p.m.)	Uhland (public 9 a.m. / private 4 p.m.)	Storr (public 8 a.m. / private 5 p.m.)	Maerklin/Flatt (public 11 a.m. / private 2 p.m.)
winter 1790/1	public	Controversien (nach Morus)	Micah, Habbakuk, Zephaniah*	Dogmatik (nach Sartorius*)	Moraltheologie* (Maerklin)
	private	Kirchengeschichte seit der Völkerwanderung (nach Schrökh)	Christliche Altertümer (nach Baumgarten)	St. John's Gospel	Homiletik (Maerklin)
summer 1791	public	Controversien (nach Morus)	Haggai, Malachi	Dogmatik (nach Sartorius)*	Moraltheologie* (Maerklin)
	private		Christliche Altertümer	Epistle to the Romans	Homiletik (Maerklin)
winter 1791/2	public	Controversien (nach Morus)*	Zechariah	Dogmatik (nach Sartorius)	
	private	Kirchengeschichte von 1100 an (nach Schrökh)	Einführung in die Symbol. Bücher der lutherischen Kirche*	Minor Pauline Epistles	Homiletik und Katechetik (Maerklin)
summer 1792	public	Polemik: Controversien de mediis gratiae und de novissimis*	Hosea	Dogmatik (nach Sartorius)	Moraltheologie nach Döderlein (Flatt)*
	private	Theologische Literaturgeschichte (nach Noesselt)	Einführung in die Symbol. Bücher (Forts.)*	Hermeneutik des Neuen Testaments (nach Ernesti)	Homiletik (Flatt)
winter 1792/3	public	Kirchengeschichte des 18. Jahrhunderts*	Isaiah	Dogmatik (nach Morus)	Intro. to Speculative Theology (Flatt)
	private	Kirchengeschichte vom Baseler Konzil bis zum Westfälischen Frieden (nach Henke)	Einführung in die lutherische Liturgie	Matthew, Mark, Luke*	Epistles (Flatt)
summer 1793	public	Geschichte der Deisten und Antideisten*	Isaiah (continued)	Dogmatik (nach Morus)	Moraltheologie nach Döderlein (Flatt)
	private	Geschichte der lutherischen Kirche des 18. Jahrhunderts	Einführung in die Liturgie (Forts.)	Matthew, Mark, Luke (continued)*	Von der richtigen Art, die christlichen Dogmen populär zu erklären OR Vergleich von Kants Kritik der praktischen Vernunft mit der Prinzipièn der christl. Lehre (Flatt)

he was absent much of the time. He will have heard some of Uhland's exegesis of the prophets, and very probably his introduction to the symbolic books (since one imagines that this fulfilled the requirement in Dogmatics and he could not go on for ever listening to Storr and studying Sartorius).[1]

Except perhaps for Lebret's class on deism, and the undecidable problem of whether Hegel attended Storr's class on St. John's Gospel in the first term of his course, none of these details is of any particular significance. Only the general tenor of the theology school at Tübingen is really of any concern to us. The senior professors were J. F. Lebret (Chancellor of the University) and Ludwig Uhland (grandfather of the poet) but the dominant figure was G. C. Storr, founder of the so-called Old Tübingen School. Chancellor Lebret was in many ways a model example of the enlightened Protestant ecclesiastic, for he had been a tutor in Venice and had worked many years in Italian libraries. He had written books on the history of the Jesuits and had been on friendly terms with Cardinal Ganganelli, who later became Clement XIV. He had been Karl Eugen's guide and companion on the Grand Tour and was still a trusted friend and counsellor of the Duke. He used Schrökh's history as the textbook for his own lectures. But he was not a great teacher or a deep thinker and he was certainly no match for Storr in either respect.[2]

L. J. Uhland had been professor of history and Ephor of the *Stift* before passing to the theology faculty, and his most important work was done in the field of local history. He lectured on the history of the early Church as well as expounding the prophets, so he may

---

[1] Storr lectured on the compendium of Sartorius until his own compendium was printed in 1793; and every year the whole compendium was covered section by section in the *Lokus* (*repetitio loci*) a two-hour class on Monday afternoons taken by a *Repetent* designated for the week. This session, with its rigidly fixed syllabus, took the place of the weekly *Repetition* in the philosophy course. Even that earlier *Repetition* was sometimes devoted to Sartorius; and even in the upper forms of schools Sartorius' compendium was studied (until it was supplanted by Storr's). Thus at the beginning of his three-year course in theology Hegel knew that he must three times 'repeat' a work with which he was already quite familiar—see Brecht and Sandberger, pp. 52–7, 65–71. (C. F. Sartorius was professor of theology and Rector of the University of Tübingen.)

[2] See Betzendörfer, pp. 52–3, and Lacorte, pp. 138–9; Lebret was also, it should be remembered, the father of Hölderlin's beloved Elise and of Christoph Lebret who had been at school with Hegel (*Briefe*, iv. 156). (The 'Geschichtetabellen' mentioned by Rosenkranz (p. 60) may have been made by Hegel between 1791 and 1793 in connection with one of Lebret's courses. But see further, p. 417 n. 4 below.)

have contributed something to Hegel's stock of information, but it is scarcely likely that he had any effect on his ideas or interests.[1] G. C. Storr was certainly the most notable and the most influential of all Hegel's teachers at Tübingen, and his influence on Hegel was in fact considerable, though almost entirely negative. His 'biblical supernaturalism' provided something for Hegel and Hölderlin to react against. He summed up for them everything they were opposed to, the spirit of the visible Church in general, and of the *Tübinger Stift* in particular. As a theologian he was remarkable in two main respects. In the first place he was an extreme conservative in a liberal era. Against all the critical-historical tendencies of the Enlightenment, which had hitherto dominated Hegel's intellectual formation virtually unchallenged, Storr maintained the traditional Lutheran conception of the Bible as the inspired word of God, a single indivisible revelation of God's will and purpose in the creation of man. Thus for him dogmatic theology coincided with New Testament exegesis, and every passage in the Bible had to be viewed in the context of the total message. Storr used the weapons of historical research, just as he did those of philosophical criticism, entirely for apologetic purposes. He was, to use his own term, a 'realist'. Thus in defending the book of Revelation, which was the obvious weak point in the New Testament canon the integrity of which he wished, above all, to defend, he sought first to put the case for its authenticity as a work of the apostle John as strongly as possible, and secondly to show that the book was in itself credible as prophecy because the prophecies contained in it were being fulfilled in actual historical fact. From the 'realistic' interpretation of Revelation (1783) he passed naturally enough to the study of the most contentious epistles and then in 1793 he published the *Doctrinae Christianae pars theoretica e sacris litteris repetita* which more or less immediately became the official textbook of dogmatics in Württemberg. By that time Hegel had left the *Stift*, of course, but there can be no doubt that the contents of the new compendium were in large part declaimed at him from the lectern,[2] for it was the systematic expression of Storr's

---

[1] Betzendörfer, pp. 53–4, and Lacorte, p. 139.

[2] In the *Tübingerfragment* and even more explicitly in the early Berne fragments Hegel pours scorn on the professor who thinks that the publication (or the reading) of his new compendium will change the moral situation of the world (see below, Chapter III, section 2).

interpretation of the New Testament as a single body of positive doctrine.

In Storr's work all argument and exposition of doctrine begins from a direct appeal to the sacred text. As Lacorte puts it: 'The doctrine that is established in this way cannot be subjected to testing by any other measure that pretends to prove its validity.'[1] The second remarkable thing about Storr's work was the way in which he used the weapons of the new philosophy to show that, contrary to the deepest conviction of the Enlightenment, human reason itself can provide no yardstick for such a test. Pfleiderer's account of Storr and of the relation between the 'older' and the 'later' Tübingen school is in this respect both accurate and revealing:

We may notice as a curiosity that many theologians, both Protestant and Catholic, beheld in Kant's distinction between phenomena and noumena and his limitation of knowledge of the former, the means of rescuing the orthodox system from the onslaughts of neological doubt. Though in the world of phenomena three persons are not equal to one person, and one person cannot have two natures, still, they argued, the possibility of this cannot be disputed in the case of the Divine Persons, since they belong to the noumena, of which we know nothing except that in this realm everything is in all respects different from what prevails in the case of phenomena. A similar position was held by Storr and his colleagues and disciples, the so-called older Tübingen school, who exercised greater freedom with regard to ecclesiastical dogmas, but held all the more strictly to Biblical supernaturalism, which they rested upon the traditional theory of inspiration. They maintained their Biblical system against all the objections and doubts of the Aufklärung by an appeal to the Kantian philosophy; since, according to the critical philosophy, reason itself admits its inability to know anything of the supersensible, it has logically no right to protest against what has been made known to us concerning supersensible things by historical revelation; with regard to the practical reason, Kant himself allows that it demands a requiting Deity for the satisfaction of our desire for happiness, and is therefore in its own interest called upon to receive upon authority the historical revelation concerning God and his government of the world. Hence the truth of the Biblical doctrines stands higher than the critique of the speculative reason which confesses its own incompetence, and accords with the demands of the practical reason; it has

---

[1] Lacorte, p. 156. The present discussion of Storr's theology is heavily indebted to the summaries given by Lacorte (pp. 139–41, 154–61, 166–72). See also the Bibliographical Index.

therefore nothing to fear and nothing to expect from philosophy, but rests entirely upon the positive authority of a supernatural revelation, which has only to be first historically proved and then reduced to a system. Storr did this by putting together a dogmatic system, in the fashion of a mosaic, from detached Biblical texts, without caring for any other proof of his propositions, either by appealing to the philosophy or to the religious consciousness. We cannot but recognise the strength of this position, which meets all rationalistic objections by a sceptical depreciation of reason; in all periods this standpoint of faith, founded purely upon authority, has been popular, but especially in those when philosophic thought was at a low ebb owing to the overweening flights of previous speculation. Its weak point is the unhistorical arbitrariness with which individual passages of Scripture, torn from their context, are used in proof of a system which is foreign to them, because unknown to any of the Biblical writers. This method of using the Scriptures as one uniform code of doctrine quite ignores the peculiarities and variety of the religious habit of thought of the Biblical authors, so different in point of time, place and character. Hence this Biblical dogmatism could not survive a really historical examination of the Scriptures, such as was undertaken by the later Tübingen school. History had been the sole basis of the system of the older Tübingen school, and by means of history it was overthrown by the younger Tübingen school. Profound thinkers, like the youthful Schelling, had, indeed, before this clearly perceived how little this application of the Kantian philosophy to the service of theological dogmatism accorded with its real meaning and spirit. His ridicule of these pseudo-Kantians was not undeserved; and dislike of this movement may well have been one of the motives which soon began to lead Schelling himself to subordinate, and this too absolutely, the critical to the speculative side of Kant's system.[1]

One would have thought that the effect of 'these pseudo-Kantians' (i.e. Storr and J. F. Flatt) on the 'youthful Schelling' (and of course on the 'old man' Hegel as well), and hence on the subsequent development of post-Kantian idealism as a 'speculative' philosophy, was sufficiently important to make their interpretation of Kant rather more than a 'curiosity'. Certainly it was more than that to Hegel himself, though he responded to Schelling's bitter jibes at the local 'Kantians', and his paeans in praise of Kant, by remarking that 'philosophy at Tübingen consisted of saying "yes, yes, quite so!" when faced with something contrary to one's convictions, and then getting up in the morning, drinking

---

[1] Pfleiderer, pp. 85–7. The claim that Storr's dogmatics was an unhistorical mosaic was in fact first put forward by F. C. Bauer.

one's coffee and going about one's business as if nothing had happened'.[1] We shall see when we come to examine some of the fragments of the Berne period that Hegel knew very well that the Kant-interpretation of Storr and Flatt could not simply be dismissed with a sociological explanation as a 'System des Schlendrians'.[2]

In Storr's system the purpose of historical research was to remove sceptical doubts concerning the authenticity of the canon, and the purpose of philosophical research was to raise sceptical doubts to a rational certainty of reason's incapacity to investigate the supernatural, while at the same time exhibiting the moral necessity of supernatural knowledge. Thus the mind would be prepared to accept the authority of a supernatural revelation signalized by miraculous events. The *positive* facts of the Christian revelation are what endow it with an *authority* superior to any reason. The 'spirit' revealed thus in positivity and authority is for Hegel the spirit of despotism,[3] the spirit to which he remained always unalterably opposed. But in Storr's doctrine of the authority of faith, the ultimate foundation is provided by the personality of Christ himself. In his rejection of the rationalizing tendencies of the preceding generation, the tendency to view Christianity as continuous with 'natural religion' or with the operation of reason, Storr turned again to the fundamental appeal of the Pietists—the appeal to the inner witness of the moral conscience: 'We ought to believe in his [Jesus'] word, because of the sort of man he was in thought and act.'[4]

The view that the 'wonders' in the historical record prove the divinity of Jesus certainly never had any force in the minds of Hegel and Hölderlin, any more than in that of Schelling. Storr's 'realism', his emphasis on the scripture as literal fact, distinguished him sharply from all forms of pietism and mysticism—and of course, as Pfleiderer says, the development of his methods was

---

[1] *Briefe*, i. 16; cf. Kaufmann, i. 302 (Anchor edn.)

[2] Henrich claims that Storr's interpretation can be derived quite consistently from Kant's moral philosophy in its earlier critical phases. (See 'Carl Immanuel Diez' in *Hegel-Studien*, iii. 281, and 'Some historical presuppositions of Hegel's system' in D. Christensen (ed.), *Hegel and the Philosophy of Religion* (The Hague, 1970). Hegel himself analysed out the basic fallacy involved—without explicitly acknowledging that *Kant* had been guilty of it—in *Ein positiver Glauben* (Nohl, pp. 233–9; end of 1795.)

[3] *Briefe*, i. 31.

[4] Betzendörfer, p. 55.

bound to reveal the untenability of his assumptions. But in his appeal to the witness of the spirit through the moral personality of Jesus he was striking a chord which re-echoed sympathetically in the minds of his most 'enlightened' hearers. Hölderlin retailed this part of Storr's argument to the assembled *Stiftler* in one of the midday sermons with which they customarily regaled one another as they ate.[1] Of course we are not bound to admit that Hölderlin believed all he said on this occasion. But the way in which he reported the sermon to his mother as the conclusion of a year-long progress of his knowledge ('der Gang meiner Erkenntnisse') of divinity would seem to guarantee at least that, of all the arguments that he heard in the lecture hall, this was the one that seemed to him to have most substance, the one that he could most easily bring himself to repeat without that consciousness of cowardice or hypocrisy in which Hegel said later the whole spirit of Württemburg was founded.[2]

Hegel, like Hölderlin, was far more impressed by the moral argument for the existence of a personal God than Schelling ever was.[3] Hence he would have followed the Tübingen interpretation of the first two critiques willingly enough, up to the point at which the appeal to revelation as a supra-rational authority was introduced. The conception of a positive authority superior to reason offended against everything in him, against his reason, his instincts, his education, call it what you will—how one speaks of this revulsion on his part will necessarily depend upon one's own attitude toward the conception that provoked it. There were two ways in which he could make Storr's appeal to conscience acceptable and he tried them each in turn. On the one hand he could claim that Jesus possessed authority indeed but that there was nothing *positive* about it, since he was nothing but the mouthpiece of practical reason. This was the way which he tried first; it harmonizes neatly with the rationalism of the Enlightenment and represents an extreme reaction against Storr's conception of

---

[1] Letter 41 (probable date 14 Feb. 1791): *GSA*, vi. 63–4 and 578–81. There is no reason to distrust any of the facts that Hölderlin gives in this letter, though some of his attitudes, e.g. towards the study of Spinoza, have probably been disguised a little in order not to hurt his mother's feelings. We must assume therefore that Storr's argument really did have considerable force in his mind, though not quite the literal force that he allows it to appear to have.

[2] *Briefe*, i. 31 (Letter 14, to Schelling, 30 Aug. 1795).

[3] Cf. *Briefe*, i. 18 (Letter 8, to Schelling, Jan. 1795).

revelation as a matter of concrete historical facts and particular events. But it was not consistent with Hegel's own 'spiritual empiricism', the concern with human nature as an integral whole that drew him to the Greeks, and *in primis* to the Greek poets, not to the philosophers. Hence he was bound, in the end, to try the other way, admitting that the gospel of Jesus had something positive about it, that a knowledge of his historic personality and destiny was essentially bound up in it, but arguing that 'authority' was not a word that properly applied to it.[1]

I do not want to suggest that Storr's influence was in any sense, even negatively, decisive for Hegel's subsequent development. The tension between eternal reason and historical development, between the abstract and the concrete universal was present in Hegel's mind from the beginning. It was almost bound to come to a head when he was confronted by Kant's ethics; between Kant and the Greeks the course of his development could hardly have been other than it was. But, because of Storr, the pull of Kant was more powerful than it would otherwise have been, and both the intensity and the extent of Hegel's experienced awareness of his heritage of enlightenment rationalism was correspondingly increased. The zeal in defence of Kant which Storr provoked, in turn increased Hegel's feeling for and comprehension of the historical aspects of experience. Thus, by setting historical experience and critical intelligence, the two things which Hegel always meant to reconcile and unify, into glaring contrast with one another, Storr did not change Hegel's aims or attitudes or the course of his development. But he gave to that development a depth and a poignancy that it might never otherwise have achieved; and no one who sympathizes with Hegel's initial aims and truly values the results that he achieved in pursuit of them would wish to underestimate the importance of that fact.

4. *The theory of the ἕν καὶ πᾶν*

But all of this constructive activity lies in the future. Hegel's immediate reaction was one of withdrawal, almost of flight. Even before the examination he was probably thinking of transferring

---

[1] I am not saying that Hegel came to believe in a 'good' kind of *positivity*. Rather, I think he came to see that the whole opposition of *rational* and *positive* authority, the very framing of the question in terms of authority at all, was a mistake.

to the study of law. Being obliged—at the insistence of his father—
to proceed, he fell victim almost immediately to a lingering
sickness, which while it was clearly genuine enough, was equally
clearly exploited to the limit as a justification for absence from
the *Stift*. At the half-term report of 20 January 1791, just before
this merciful release sent him home to meditate upon the structure
of plants and the fate of Oedipus and Antigone, he was sentenced
to two hours 'Karzer'; and his conduct report for this term is
'poor' (*mores languidi*).[1] This was the term before the great 'ball';
he was probably fencing this winter, and drinking the baker's
wine while talking of his love for the Professor's daughter.[2] It
was also the period when enthusiastic interest in the progress of
events in France was at its height among the *Stiftler*. One of the
accidents of history had endowed Württemberg with a small
slice of French territory, and Hegel was particularly friendly
with at least two of the students in the *Stift* who came from
there—Billing and Fallot. The album leaves that his friends
presented to him when he left the *Stift* to go home in February
were filled with appropriate expressions of devotion to liberty, and
of undying fraternity.

Hölderlin's contribution on this occasion was a quotation from
Goethe: 'Lust und Liebe sind / die Fittige zu großen Täten.'
To this someone, perhaps Hegel himself, perhaps Hölderlin,
added at a later date the 'Symbolum' ἐν καὶ πᾶν.[3] Whoever added

[1] Klaiber in *Briefe*, iv. 165; cf. *Briefe*, iv. 77 and 79 for the semester report and
permission to go home. The incarceration was actually brought about by the
escapade reported by Rosenkranz in which Hegel, Fink, and Fallot rode out,
without permission, to a village at some distance, and were unable to get back
before the *Stift* gate closed because Fallot became ill (cf. Rosenkranz, p. 31:
Dok., p. 432).   [2] See above, pp. 67–8 and 68 n. 1.

[3] *Briefe*, iv. 48. The words 'S. ἐν καὶ παν' are written with a different pen
and ink. Hegel himself added dates and notes about the later destiny of the writer
to several entries, but there is no other case of his adding a *symbolum* (there is
also, however, no other case in which, from all that we know, he would have any
reason or incentive to do this).

The collection of leaves made by his friends between 12 and 15 Feb. 1791
(twenty-two in all) formed the first nucleus of his *Stammbuch*. One of his
friends (Fallot) wrote a postscript on the back of his sheet that same autumn,
and Hegel himself wrote a postscript to his entry in Fink's *Stammbuch* of the year
before. Fink himself made, at this time, his first contribution to Hegel's
Stammbuch as we have it, though it seems incredible that he should not have
supplied a leaf in February—unless perchance he was himself away at the time.
My own guess would be that Hölderlin himself added the *Symbolum* in the
autumn. (All of them, it may be noted, habitually wrote their Greek without
accents.)

it, there is no doubt that it was added because Hölderlin had adopted the words as a motto which somehow typified his attitude to the world. Nor does it greatly matter when the addition was made, for we know where he got the motto from and, at least roughly, when he found it. The letter to his mother of February 1791 gives a history of his studies in divinity from which we can readily gather that some time in the previous autumn, probably, he read writings 'about and by Spinoza'.[1] It is also certain that among the very first 'writings about Spinoza' that came to his hand were Jacobi's *Letters on the Teaching of Spinoza* (1785; 2nd edn., which Hölderlin may have possessed, 1789). Rosenkranz says that 'according to reliable reports' Hegel, Hölderlin, Fink, Renz and other friends 'read together and discussed Plato . . . Kant, Jacobi's *Woldemar* and *Allwill*, the *Letters on Spinoza* and Hippel's *Lebensläufe nach aufsteigender Linie*'.[2] The 'reading together' (and making of translations) from Plato may well have been confined to Hegel and Hölderlin; but a larger group could study the German authors together with profit, and they would have had reason to do it, if they were all enrolled in Flatt's course on 'Metaphysics and Natural Theology' in the summer term of 1790.[3]

[1] Letter 41, *GSA*, vi. 63–4, lines 24–50. (In November 1790 Hölderlin reported to Neuffer that for some days he had been entirely occupied with 'Leibniz and my Hymn to Truth . . . the former influences the latter': Letter 35, lines 19–21, *GSA*, vi. 56. Hölderlin's Spinoza studies were probably over by then; he has almost certainly simplified the course of his reflections about God in his account for his mother.)

[2] Rosenkranz, p. 40. (The 'reliable reporter' is, in all likelihood, Fink.) The novels of Jacobi and Hippel may very probably (as Beck suggests in *GSA*, vii. 1, 454) be the non-metaphysical works that Leutwein vaguely remembers in connection with Hegel's study of Rousseau. Hegel refers to *Woldemar* in (a) *Unter objektiver Religion* (Nohl, p. 49; see pp. 508–9 below).

[3] This reading group may also have been the beginning of the group which seem to have drawn together to defend an enlightened rationalist interpretation of Kant and his followers against the 'theologisch-Kantianischer Gang' of Storr and Flatt. At any rate the formation of this group during Flatt's course in summer 1790 would have provided fertile ground for the activities of the 'kantischer enragé', Diez, who returned to the *Stift* as *Repetent* in 1790 and remained until he transferred to medicine in 1792. From his recently discovered letters and manuscripts which are soon to be published we know that he developed a radically sceptical interpretation of the Critical Philosophy as applied to religion. His conclusions were too radical even for most of his friends, but he argued with equal cogency and fervour, and his interpretation of Kant was generally accepted until the publication of [Fichte's] *Kritik aller Offenbarung*. The comfort which this last work offered to the orthodox—and specifically to Diez's close friend, the *Repetent* F. G. Süskind—caused the young radicals (including Hegel and Hölderlin) to view it with considerable reserve. Diez was the author of many of

In any case it was about that time that Hölderlin acquired his 'symbol'. For he made an excerpt from Jacobi, beginning with the account of a conversation between Jacobi and Lessing, in which the latter used the formula to express his own agreement with Spinoza:

1. Lessing was a Spinozist. *page 2*. The orthodox concepts of the Divinity were not for him. He could get no nourishment from them. Ἐν καὶ Πᾶν: He knew no other.[1]

Jacobi's book was addressed to Moses Mendelssohn; and his avowed aim was to show that the enlightened rationalism of men like Lessing and Mendelssohn must logically issue in pantheism or deism of a fatalistic kind. His attack led to the famous 'Pantheismusstreit', for Mendelssohn refused to accept the characterization of his dead friend as a deist. There was, he insisted, a higher, 'purer' Spinozism (*geläuterte Spinozismus*) perfectly reconcilable with theism and with rational moral principles. The progressive development of enlightenment certainly did not and could not culminate in the acceptance of fatalism.[2]

Hegel must, without doubt, have been extremely interested in this controversy, for Lessing and Mendelssohn were old heroes of his. Nor can there be any question that he sided with Mendelssohn in the controversy. His own concern, like that of Lessing himself, was with the 'education of the human race';[3] 'Reason and

the watchwords of the 'invisible Church' at Tübingen. But we can, I think, take Leutwein's word for it that Hegel was not very much involved in the Kant controversy while Diez was actually present in the *Stift*; and for my part I am inclined to believe that the prominence of J. F. Maerklin in the Kant group was a contributory cause of Hegel's holding aloof from it. (This would provide a plausible basis for the view of Hegel's later career formulated by Leutwein, a defeated and embittered but still faithful member of the 'invisible Church'.) See the following sources: Betzendörfer, pp. 19, 24; *Hegel-Studien*, iii. 56, lines 114–15, 136–8; on C. I. Diez see the articles of D. Henrich and J. L. Doderlein in *Hegel-Studien*, iii. 276–87.   [1] *GSA*, iv. 207.

[2] *An die Freunde Lessings* (Berlin, 1786). Mendelssohn himself died before this reply was published, but this did not prevent Jacobi from retorting further with a violently personal attack. The main documents of the *Pantheismusstreit* are collected in H. Scholz, *Die Hauptschriften zum Pantheismusstreit*, Berlin, 1916. The passages Hölderlin excerpted from Jacobi will be found in Scholz, pp. 67 and 77–90. The retort of Mendelssohn cited in the text is on page 295.

[3] If Hegel had not already read *Die Erziehung des Menschengeschlechts* (1780) at Stuttgart (as I feel sure he had) he certainly read it in his first years at Tübingen; and he certainly took it in hand again in 1793, when he began to write out his views on the religion of Greece. It is a reasonable guess, too, that he read Lessing's *Leben des Sophocles* (1790) while he rested at home in 1791.

Freedom' were his watchwords, as he said to Schelling, and he would scarcely have taken kindly to the suggestion that the full development of Reason as he understood it, must lead to the denial of Freedom.[1] Schelling, who only came into the picture later, and whose own background was formed much more by Kant, Jacobi, and Fichte, could cheerfully accept Jacobi's view of the case, at least as far as belief in a personal God was concerned, without sharing Jacobi's feelings—indeed Schelling positively glorified in his 'Promethean' defiance of traditional theism.[2] He was therefore surprised to find that a 'Vertrauter Lessings' like Hegel was still dallying with the moral argument for the existence of Jacobi's 'verständige persönliche Ursache der Welt' in 1795.[3] But he would not have been surprised had he been like Hegel a 'Vertrauter Lessings'. In 1791 neither Hegel nor Hölderlin took the ἓν καὶ πᾶν of Lessing to involve any surrender of personal identity either for themselves or for God. Rather than pantheists, they were, in the modern phrase, panentheists. The sense of union without loss of individuality, of rationality without loss of spontaneity, the sense of joyful community, of freedom in friendship or brotherhood; this was the ideal to which they were devoted. If Hölderlin chose ἓν καὶ πᾶν as his symbol it was because he found in Lessing's conception of the All 'nach der Analogie eines organischen Körpers'[4] an appropriate expression for his poet's sense of joyful communion with all life. The 'union of the mind with the whole of nature' was for him a matter of feeling not of intellect, of 'Lust und Liebe' as his Goethe quotation has it, or of *Freude* and *Liebe* in the Schillerian terminology that he generally adopted. It is possible

---

[1] Cf. the formula in *Briefe*, i. 18, discussed below..

[2] Cf. *Briefe*, i. 21–2. The statement Jacobi ascribes to Lessing, 'Die orthodoxen Begriffe von der Gottheit sind nich mehr für mich', which Schelling there echoes, was supposedly made as a comment on Goethe's Prometheus Ode (see Scholz, pp. 75–6).

[3] Cf. *Briefe*, i. 18. The phrase of Jacobi is from the *Letters on Spinoza* (see Scholz, p. 80); the denial Hegel found worrying in Schelling was of an 'individuelle persönliche Wesen'.

[4] Jacobi, *Letters* (Scholz, pp. 92–3): 'Wenn sich Lessing *eine persönliche Gottheit vorstellen wollte*, so dachte er sie als die Seele des Alls; und das Ganze, nach der Analogie eines organischen Körpers' (the italics are mine). Jacobi could quite fairly object that this was not a normal concept of a personal God; and certainly it was not *orthodox* because 'Lessing glaubt keine von der Welt *unterschiedene* Ursache der Dinge' (ibid., p. 102). But except for that it is easily reconciled with such orthodox notions as 'the body of Christ' or the God 'in whom we live and move and have our being'.

that Kant's critique of the traditional proofs of the existence of
God, along with Jacobi's attack on Spinozism, did leave Hölderlin
momentarily bewildered, having no definite object on which to
focus his essentially religious emotions until Storr presented him
with the argument that the moral personality of Jesus was an
evident sensible proof of his divinity. At least, that is how Hölderlin
presents the matter to his mother. In that case it must have been
some little time before he adopted the Spinozistic *symbolum* as his
own. But it is more likely, I think, that, like Hegel, he took
Mendelssohn's view of the matter, and that Storr's Jesus simply
fell into place as the perfect model of a citizen of the Kingdom of
God, the 'Son of Man' who 'lived and moved and had his being'
with a perfect consciousness of being the 'Son of God'. I do not
mean to imply that Hegel was in any important sense Hölderlin's
philosophical 'genius' or 'mentor' about the controversy—for I do
not believe that either of them looked to the other as a leader in
that way—but Hegel was an acknowledged expert on Lessing, and
we know that he had begun to think of the Christian 'Kingdom of
God' in this way before he was sixteen years old.[1]

The general tendency, since Haering's great work appeared,
has been to emphasize that ἐν καὶ πᾶν was Hölderlin's symbol, not
Hegel's, and to argue that in so far as it possessed a meaning for
Hegel at all its significance was strictly human and social. But
this view is rather in conflict with the few fairly solid facts that
we possess about the interests of the two friends in 1791 and 1792.[2]
This was the period when we know that Hölderlin became
interested in astronomy, while Hegel for his part was certainly

---

[1] Hölderlin's remarks about Hegel being his 'mentor' or 'genius' (*Briefe*, i.
9 and 45) refer mainly to a moral dependence—compare what he says to Neuffer
about Hegel in Letter 136: 'I love calm *Verstandesmenschen*, because one can
orient oneself so well by them, when one does not rightly know in what case one
is with oneself and the world' (*GSA*, vi. 236, lines 42–5). The intellectual
relationship between the two friends is aptly summed up in his comment to
Hegel himself in Jan. 1795: 'I have long been mulling over the ideal of a
Volkserziehung, and since you are concerned precisely with religion, which is
one aspect of that same ideal, perhaps I may avail myself of your image and your
friendship as a *conductor* of my thoughts into the external world (*die äußere
Sinnenwelt*) and write what I might perhaps have written later (for the public)
to you beforehand in letters which you must criticize and correct' (*Briefe*, i. 20).
(For Hegel's early encounters with 'enlightened Christianity' see *Dok.*, pp. 87–
100, and Chapter I above, pp. 23–6.)

[2] The researches of Henrich on Leutwein have shown that the symbolism
of the ἐν καὶ πᾶν did *not* belong exclusively to Hölderlin. Leutwein—and
probably others too—accepted it as the expression of a shared ideal; and

studying botany in the summers and may quite possibly have taken his anatomy course in the winter of 1791–2.[1] It would scarcely be possible for one who had been reading Kant and Jacobi to turn to the study of astronomy without remembering the closing paragraphs of the *Critique of Practical Reason*. When we reflect further that this same student has been reading Plato with enthusiasm for some time[2] it seems entirely plausible that he should conceive of God as 'die Seele des Welt-alls', without ceasing thereby to regard him both as the creative architect and as the supreme monarch whom we find in Leibniz. The only serious conflict between a Platonic conception of the deity in which the conceptions of the Demiourgos and the World-Soul have been conflated together, and the Leibnizian conception inherited by Kant, is that the World-Soul of Plato is more directly involved in the moral struggle to maintain order in the realm of becoming. It is in this struggle, rather than in the ideal realm, that he has his being, and the task of men is to collaborate with him in it. Whereas the God of Leibniz and of Kant's practical reason has the role of

Leutwein certainly felt, in old age, that he had personally remained faithful to a youthful ideal which Hegel had abandoned for the sake of worldly success (see *Hegel-Studien*, iii. 43–50).

[1] On Hölderlin's interest in astronomy see Letter 47 (dated by Hölderlin himself 28 Nov. 1791) which expressed regret that he had not come to astronomy sooner and the fixed intention to make it his particular concern in the coming winter. Hegel's interest in botany is fairly decisively dated by Betzendörfer's report that he borrowed Linnaeus from the *Stift* library in the summers of 1791 and 1792 and by the entry of Sartorius in his *Stammbuch*, 7 Sept. 1791. His course in anatomy cannot be dated from documentary evidence more precisely than to the period of the theology course as a whole (Rosenkranz, p. 25). I think the winter of 1791–2 is a plausible guess because it would fit so neatly with his botanical interest, but nothing really hangs on this dating.

[2] The only definite indications we have about Hölderlin's Plato reading are for Sept. 1792 (when he borrowed volumes from the *Stift* Library which probably contained the *political* dialogues—*Republic, Statesman, Minos*—Betzendörfer, pp. 30 and 128) and July 1793 (Letter 60 to Neuffer contains explicit references to the *Phaedrus, Timaeus, Phaedo*, and *Symposium: GSA*, vi. 86). But the references in the letter of 1793 are meant as a general characterization of his interest in Plato and it is surely reasonable to assume that the *Pantheismusstreit* would have led him to study the *Timaeus* if he had not already done so. The *Phaedo* he would certainly have been familiar with much earlier and it is reasonable to assume that he would have studied the *Symposium* earlier also. The volumes borrowed from the library do not prove anything either, except that there was some dialogue in them that he did not himself own but wished to read. He may for instance have had to restore a borrowed copy of the *Republic* to its owner, or he may have wished to go on from the *Republic* to study the other dialogues on government.

supreme judge as an essential function, and hence he has his being and his abode necesarily in the courts of the eternal. He is above the struggle. It is perfectly appropriate to use the personal pronoun to refer to either of them, and to conceive either of them as the object of a personal encounter. One does not have to agree with Goethe that the Earth-Spirit is too strange and alien for human converse—indeed the possibility of a real sense of fellowship with God is more obvious if one takes the process of life itself as a continuation and extension of the original work of creation.

It is more than probable I think that Hegel shared this Platonic conception of the World-Soul, and that both he and Hölderlin saw in the study of astronomy not just a confirmation of the operation of practical reason in the world, but evidence of the divine life itself. Thus, it may well be that the incorporation of Hegel's interests in mathematics and physics into his philosophical concerns began just at the time when he no longer had external occasion and incentive to pursue them for their own sake. But his own attention was focused at this period and for some years to come on the more limited problem of the nature of life in the sublunary sphere. The contrast between comprehending the living unity of an organism, and dissecting a corpse in order to understand its anatomical structure so as to be able to take it to pieces and put it together again, is one that frequently recurs in his mature works; so also does the contrast between living nature as an organic whole, stable and self-subsistent in spite of all tensions, and the individual living organism, with its essential instability, its need of another in order to overcome in the continuity of the species its own inevitable mortality. The ἐν και παν undoubtedly meant for Hegel even in 1791 primarily this living unity of all organic life, this immortal equilibrium of unstable, mortal elements, sustained by the universal power of life.

Jacobi's interpretation of Lessing's Spinozism would have appeared to Hegel as a typical example of 'bad' abstraction, i.e. of determining the meaning of words by reference to how they function in relation to other words rather than by reference to actual experience; whereas his own studies in botany and anatomy gave meaning to the concept of the ἐν και παν in the proper, natural way. But aside from these two kinds of 'meaning' the concept possessed also a 'use': he would not have devoted his time to the giving of proper or concrete meaning to such a high-level abstraction as the notion of 'life' if it had not been 'useful'.[1] The 'use' of a clear and concrete concept of 'life' (which is what the ἐν καὶ πᾶν represented for Hegel in my view) lies in the fact that we can derive from it a proper conception of the vocation of man. Concepts in general, and this one in particular, are 'useful' in Hegel's sense in so far as they aid us to 'become men'—to employ a phrase that recurs several times in Hölderlin's letters at this time[2]—or show us how to establish the 'Kingdom of God' on earth.[3]

It was from the study of Greek culture that Hegel and Hölderlin derived their model of the ideal society in which every individual expresses his humanity fully, freely, and with natural spontaneity. The transition from the notion of the ἐν καὶ πᾶν to the ideal vision of the humanity of the future in a world of universal liberty, equality, and fraternity,[4] is made through the Platonic con-

---

[1] Hegel explicitly refers to the criterion of 'usefulness' only in his letters to Schelling some years later (1795, Briefe, i. 16), where he says that he wants to 'learn to apply' Kant's results, whereas he can afford to neglect the work of Reinhold because it represents an advance 'only from the point of view of theoretical reason' and does not have 'greater applicability to concepts of more general usefulness'. But this insistence on the *applicability* of theories and the *usefulness* of concepts is a direct development of the attitude toward theoretical philosophy that he displays from 1787 onwards. In the Stift, as Leutwein tells us, he hoped to 'get free from his fetters' through the study of Rousseau, (*Hegel-Studien*, iii. 56, lines 124–30). The comment on Reinhold in this letter is another sign of Hegel's relative aloofness from the Diez group—Diez was the first champion of Reinhold in the Stift.

[2] The most important expressions of this ideal in Hölderlin's letters are in letters 86 and 103. But a long list of passages can be cited in which the ideal expounded in these two letters of 1794 and 1795 is fairly clearly alluded to. See, for example, the following (all in GSA vi): Letter 36, line 231 (Nov. 1790); Letter 43, lines 26–7 (Mar.–Apr. 1791); Letter 49, line 25 (Feb.–Mar. 1792); Letter 76, lines 5 and 53 (Mar. 1794).

[3] Briefe, i. 9 (Hölderlin to Hegel, 10 July 1794): 'Ich bin gewiß, daß Du indessen zuweilen meiner gedachtest, seit wir mit der Losung "Reich Gottes" voneinander schieden. An dieser Losung würden wir uns nach jeder Metamorphose, wie ich glaube, wiedererkennen.' Briefe, i. 18 (Hegel to Schelling, Letter 8, Jan. 1795): 'Das Reich Gottes komme, und unsre Hände seien nicht müßig im Schoße.'

[4] Cf. Hölderlin's letter to his younger half-brother in September 1793 (Letter 65): 'I love the race of the coming centuries. For this is my most sacred hope, the faith, which keeps me strong and active, that our descendants will be better than we, that freedom must sometimes come to pass, and that virtue will flourish better in the holy light and warmth of freedom, than it does in the ice cold region of despotism. We are living in a period when everything works together toward better days. These seeds of enlightenment, these silent wishes and strivings of

ception of love. The discourse of Diotima in the *Symposium* establishes a continuum between the Aristophanic conception of sexual desire as the primitive expression of life itself, 'the desire and pursuit of the whole', and the rational passion of the philosopher king who aims to establish on earth a copy of that 'city in the heavens' which the scientific study of astronomy reveals. In this way the lowly aspect of the ἐν καὶ πᾶν with which Hegel was concerned in his botanizing is linked to the moral exaltation of Hölderlin's study of 'the starry heavens', and the relevance of both to the coming of the Kingdom is made clear.[1] But why, when their inspiration came from classical Greece on the one hand, and from the rationalist enlightenment on the other, did they choose to employ Christian language for the 'application' of their fundamental conception? The language of 1789 would seem to have been more natural for their purposes than that of St. John or the council of Nicaea.

One might be tempted to think that their choice was the accidental result of circumstances. They were after all theology students who were professionally obliged to concern themselves for much of their time with the language and concepts of Christian theology; and the 'application' of Platonic philosophy for this purpose was already a revered tradition. In some part, no doubt, their choice of terms was governed by their particular circumstances. This is particularly evident in the use of the expression 'the invisible Church' as the rallying point for all who were working for the coming of the Kingdom.[2] But in the main their use of

individuals towards the formation of the human race [*Bildung des Menschengeschlechts*] will spread and grow stronger, and bear noble fruits.' The whole context of this passage must be considered, for Hölderlin's emphasis on his own devotion to the human race as a 'universal' throws light on *his* adoption of the symbol ἐν καὶ πᾶν (*GSA*, vi. 92–3).

[1] *Sym.* 205 d–212 a; *Rep.* 529–30, 592 b. (Hölderlin studied botany at some time before 1796—see Letter 116, *GSA*, vi. 202; and Hegel was interested in astronomy from his school years onwards.)

[2] *Briefe*, i. 18 (Hegel to Schelling, Letter 8, Jan. 1795): 'Reason and Freedom remain our Watchword, and our rallying point the invisible Church.' It seems to me virtually certain that for Hegel, at any rate, the 'invisible Church' originally referred to the cosmopolitan ideal of Freemasonry as envisaged by Lessing in *Ernst und Falk*. Rohrmoser ('Zur Vorgeschichte der Jugendschriften Hegels', p. 194) has found an interesting comparison of the 'fraternity of liberty and the rights of man' to an 'invisible Church' in one of the political pamphlets of F. K. von Moser. It is more than likely that one of the *Stiftler* discovered this and brought it to general notice. But I agree with D'Hondt (*Hegel secret*, pp. 328–9) that if Hegel knew of it he would be more apt to see in it 'un décalque de la Maçonnerie "à la Lessing"' than a development of pietism.

traditional Christian concepts was part of a deliberate policy of religious enlightenment which they adopted as the best way to achieve their end, because of the crucial role which religion has to play in their ideal society. Had they not believed that religion is the natural and proper expression of the ἐν καὶ πᾶν at the human level, the language of the Revolution, which was the ordinary currency of their secret political club, and of the 'invisible Church' in general, would have appealed to them precisely because in using it they could make a clean break with the 'old sourdough' of the theology school and the pulpit. 'Reason and Freedom' was what they meant by their talk of 'Kingdom Come'.[1] But because their aim was the transformation of society, and of the quality of individual life and individual experience itself, the proper *use* or *application* of their theory was to the 'enlightening' of fundamental theological concepts in order to get rid of the old 'sourdough'.[2]

[1] Compare the remark quoted in the preceding note with the passages cited above, p. 104 n. 3. It does not seem likely that the *Stiftler* spoke of the 'Kingdom' and the 'invisible Church' much at the secret political club. The 'Watchword' and 'rallying-point' were not regarded as private personal concerns, of course, but they were more appropriate topics for sermons and doubtless also for study groups. The 'Watchword' 'Reason and Freedom' on the other hand did occur in ordinary conversation. 'Liberté raisonnée' was the 'Symbolum' chosen by Andre Billing for his entry in Hegel's *Stammbuch* (5 Oct. 1795: *Briefe*, iv. 44). Compare also the 'patriotic' entries in the *Stammbücher* of L. von Seckendorff and C. F. Hiller given by Beck in Hölderlin, *GSA*, vii. 1, 431–2. In the same way Hölderlin does not write to his brother of the 'invisible Church' though he clearly hopes to make him a member of it, but of 'enlightenment' and 'freedom' (p. 104 n. 4 above). Schelling does not himself use any of the theological watchwords so far mentioned (see the following note); but in reply to Hegel's letter (cited on p. 105 n. 2 above) he says: 'The Alpha and Omega of all philosophy is Freedom' (*Briefe*, i. 22).

[2] These expressions are applied by Hegel to Schelling's earliest published essays—the *Magisterdissertation* and *Über Mythen* (Briefe i. 11). The name *Sauerteig* may have been given to the traditional theology by Schelling (cf. Letter 10, 4 Feb. 1795, *Briefe*, i. 20); his earliest surviving manuscripts are 'enlightened' commentaries on some of the Pauline Epistles. But Schelling abandoned the programme of theological enlightenment even before he left the *Stift*. He became increasingly impatient with classical and theological studies as he advanced toward mastery of the contemporary disputes in philosophy. It was through philosophy that he expected the new world to be born; and when Hegel protested that his interests were too purely theoretical, he retorted that Hegel's practical urgency was premature: 'Certainly my friend, the revolution that will be produced by philosophy is still far off' (Letter 13: *Briefe*, i. 28); cf. Letter 7 (*Briefe*, i. 14). Hegel, of course, 'expected a revolution in Germany' from the perfecting of the Kantian system (Letter 11: *Briefe*, i. 23), but even in the letter in which he says so, it is clear that he is preoccupied by the problem of making people *feel* the truth of what Kant has *shown* (ibid., p. 24).

Almost everything that we know about this programme of theological enlightenment comes from the letters that Hegel exchanged with Hölderlin and Schelling after he had left Tübingen. By that time he was himself caught up in the enthusiasm of the other two for the Kantian philosophy. Leutwein tells us, and there is no reason to doubt the accuracy of his report, that Hegel was not much interested in the prevalent discussions of the critical philosophy in 1791 and 1792.[1] Leutwein himself did not believe that

[1] *Hegel-Studien*, iii. 56–7, lines 138–51. The dating is based on a comparison of the career dates of the students he there mentions. Most of them were in the *Stift* together only during those two years, viz.

K. I. Diez	*Stiftler* 1783–8; *Repetent* 1790–2
J. C. F. Hauff	178(?)–90
J. F. Duttenhofer	1785–90 (*Repetent* 1793–8)
C. P. F. Leutwein	1787–92
J. F. Maerklin	1788–93
K. W. F. Breyer	1789–94
K. C. Flatt (brother of Prof. J. F. Flatt)	1789–94
F. W. J. Schelling	1790–5
C. F. Hauber	1791–6

There are several points worth noticing about this list:

(a) The inclusion of the names of Hauff and Duttenhofer, who had left the *Stift* before most of the others achieved the dignity of *Magister* and did not, like Diez, return as *Repetenten* in Hegel's time. Henrich's hypothesis that the memory of the ageing Leutwein was influenced by Hauff's subsequent successful career in academic life is possible but to my mind unconvincing. It harmonizes well enough with his forgetting G. C. Rapp (*Repetent* 1790–3; died 1794) but not with certain other omissions. Hauff's later career was as a professor of mathematics and physics; and if Leutwein's memory was influenced by later eminence of that sort why did he not mention either Niethammer, who passed his theological examination in the autumn of 1788 but remained in the *Stift* for a further six months for the specific purpose of studying Reinhold under J. F. Flatt (*Hegel-Studien*, iii. 284), or that *assiduus cultor philosophiae Kantianae* Hölderlin? And in any case the mention of Duttenhofer remains unaccounted for. The most probable hypothesis I think is this: that there was a sort of 'Kantian tradition' in the *Stift* from 1785 (when Diez became a *magister*) onwards; that the tiny minority who carried on this tradition typically became involved in it through attendance at J. F. Flatt's 'private' classes in their second year; that this is what happened to Leutwein in the winter of 1788 or the spring of 1789; that he then began to look on Hauff and Duttenhofer as his 'mentors' so to speak; and when they departed and Diez returned, he assumed their role.

(b) This hypothesis provides a natural explanation for the second oddity in the list: the fact that only Maerklin is named from Hegel's own year (and not, for example, Hölderlin). I assume that Leutwein knew very well who was in the 'apostolic succession', so to speak, and who was not. Everyone with brains enough was talking about Kant by this time—except Hegel—but Maerklin was the 'Erz Metaphysiker und Kantianer' of this class.

(c) With the return of Diez the situation changed. But the first class to be

Hegel would have changed much in this respect in his last year. But all the evidence we have shows that Hegel did in fact become deeply interested in the practical and religious philosophy of Kant and Fichte in 1792–3; and in the following years his interest gradually extended even to their more theoretical treatises.

Kant's essay 'On the Radical Evil in Human Nature' appeared in the *Berlinische Monatsschrift* in February 1792, and the publication of the complete text of his *Religion* at Easter 1793 was soon followed by Storr's Latin commentary (*Annotationes quaedam*). At this point certainly, if not much sooner, Hegel's interest was aroused. Similarly the visit of Fichte to Tübingen in June 1793 no doubt aroused general interest among the students in the *Critique of All Revelation*, published at Easter 1792 and acknowledged by Fichte in the autumn. Examination of Hegel's Tübingen fragments reveals that he had certainly read Fichte's book and Kant's first essay before he left the *Stift*. It is of course quite possible, though not demonstrable, that he had read the whole text of the *Religion*.[1]

5. *The sermons*

The very title of Kant's first essay must have had an alarming ring for the young revolutionaries at the *Stift*; and there is reason to believe that on first reading the *Critique of All Revelation* Hegel, Hölderlin, and Schelling all agreed that Fichte's work exhibited certain reactionary tendencies.[2] But the appearance of these

noticeably affected was the class of 1789 (the second-year class of 1790). I assume that this class provided Diez with his first real converts; and Leutwein did not foresee how much the situation would change again in 1793. Thus he does not mention F. G. Süskind (*Stiftler* 1783–8) who returned as *Repetent* in 1791—either because he did not count as a 'true' Kantian or because Süskind made no memorable impression on Leutwein before he left the *Stift* in Sept. 1792. With the departure of Diez and the publication of the *Kritik aller Offenbarung* and of Kant's essay on 'Radical Evil' a completely new situation came into being by the end of 1792, and Süskind had a major part to play in it. (F. G. Süskind should not be confused with his younger brother J. G. Süskind, who was in Schelling's class and is mentioned several times in the correspondence between Schelling and Hegel.)

[1] See pp. 142–4 (and particularly p. 142 n. 1 below). The watchword 'Reich Gottes' was probably derived from the reading of Kant. For 'das Reich Gottes' see *Kritik der praktischen Vernunft, Akad.*, v. 127–8, 136–7, etc., and *Religion, Akad.*, vi. 93, 95, 101, 115, 131, 134, 136, 151, 152, etc. The 'unsichtbare Kirche' also occurs in Kant's *Religion* (ibid. 101, 122, 131, 135, 152–3), but for this watchword see p. 105 n. 2 above.

[2] See Letter 8 (Hegel to Schelling, Jan. 1795); Letter 9 (Hölderlin to Hegel,

books served as a sort of signal of battle between the radical disciples of the Critical Philosophy in the *Stift* and the moderates who wished to use it in support of Lutheran orthodoxy; and the extent to which Hegel himself became involved in the struggle can be seen by examining the texts of the four sermons that remain to us from his last two years in Tübingen.

On 10 January 1792 he preached on the justice of God in reward and punishment (with Isaiah 61: 7–8 as his text). Some effort toward 'enlightenment' is apparent, and Hegel probably went as far in 'putting aside the old sourdough' as the censoring eye of his *Repetent* would allow. But his whole performance, at least in the outline that we have, was mechanical in the extreme, and shows little sign of being part of a struggle for the coming of the King-dom.[1] Like the Savoyard vicar he regards the voice of conscience as the voice of God revealing himself to every man. But the voice of reason alone is insufficient to control the passions—especially in a state of nature—hence the need for revealed religion, the message of which agrees exactly with the voice of conscience itself.[2]

The sermons of 1793 are much less perfunctory.[3] On the feast of St. Philip and St. James (1 May) Hegel preached on the topic of faith in Christ. The topic was obviously suggested by the story in St. John's Gospel[4] of how Philip interrupted Jesus'

---

26 Jan. 1795); Letter 10 (Schelling to Hegel, 4 Feb. 1795): *Briefe*, i. 18–21. The evidence contained in these passages is discussed below in Chapter III, pp. 187–9.

[1] *Dok.*, pp. 175–9. This would have been a weekday sermon delivered during the midday meal. Hegel speaks of the natural penalties of wrong-doing, and of how fear of punishment 'in the future' acts as a sanction against wrongdoing. But he avoids any explicit assertion that there is punishment in a future life at all, and what he does say makes it clear that the idea of eternal damnation is inconsistent with the ascription of justice to God. He is obviously more at ease when he turns to the topic of reward, and although he makes the appropriate gestures regarding God's grace in sending his Son and so freeing us from the fear of punishment, he emphasizes that we are rewarded for 'faithful exercise of virtues'. In closing, he envisages the future life as 'a transition to the further development of man's faculties and to greater joys'.

[2] This view of revealed religion is supported by the Savoyard Vicar (Rousseau, *Émile* (Everyman edn.), pp. 276–7), by Hegel's own Stuttgart essay (*Dok.*, p. 47), and by his Berne essays. Hence I think we must take it that he is not here speaking tongue-in-cheek (cf. also Lessing, 'Education of the Human Race', § 7).

[3] This may be very largely because of the new regulations governing the delivery of sermons which came into effect that spring. See Betzendörfer, p. 57, and p. 111 n. 1 below.

[4] John 15: 6–9. For the sermon outline see *Dok.*, pp. 182–4.

discourse—'I am the way, the truth, and the life: no man cometh
unto the Father but by me'—with a request to be shown the
Father, and was told emphatically that Jesus was in the Father,
and the Father in him. This passage was clearly a foundation-
stone for Storr's Christology, and Hegel's argument seems to have
followed the lines of Storr's exegesis fairly faithfully. The failure
of the disciples to understand that Jesus was truly the 'Son of God'
is put down to the fact that they had not yet experienced the
Resurrection, 'the keystone of Christian belief'.

'Why do we call ourselves Christians?' Hegel asks; and he
answers the question first by citing the claim in Ephesians, 'For
through him [Christ] we both have access by one Spirit to the
Father',[1] and then claiming (as Storr did) that Jesus must have
'known best whence he came and who it was that sent him'. But
we do not have to rely only on his word, for we have his works
and the 'witness of the Father himself' in the miracles of Jesus'
birth, the descent of the Spirit at his baptism, and above all his
Resurrection and Ascension. Our faith however is not simply a
matter of wonder and amazement at things we cannot understand.
The disciples failed to cure the lunatic boy of whom Matthew
tells us because they lacked faith, they had not the right attitude
and thought only of making a sensation.[2] The true object of
faith is the Spirit, and the true fruit of faith is likewise the possession
of the inward spirit—as is shown by the story of the widow's
mites.[3]

In all of this there is still no outward sign of 'enlightenment'.
Hegel simply repeats the sort of thing that Storr doubtless said
himself in lectures. But one cannot help suspecting that the choice
of topic is significant. The passage 'I am the way, the truth, and the
life', the indwelling of the Father in the Son and of the Spirit in
us, are topics to which Hegel recurs in his own independent
attempts at 'enlightened' exegesis in Berne. And his closing on
this occasion strongly hints that the programme of enlightened
exegesis associated with the slogans 'Reich Gottes' and 'die

[1] Ephesians 2: 18.
[2] Matthew 17: 14–21. All the 'enlightened' *Stiftler* must have suffered from
a self-disgust like that of Renz when they were obliged to talk like this.
[3] Luke 21: 1–4. Anyone who feels it is legitimate to look as far ahead as 1798
can find in 'The Spirit of Christianity' (Nohl, pp. 337–9; Knox, pp. 295–8),
good evidence that this doctrine of the object of faith is meant as an implicit
critique of the preceding appeal to miracles.

unsichtbare Kirche' is already in his mind. For his outline ends with the words: 'that we may become perfect, as Christ was perfect—friendship, freedom, and children of God'.

The suspicion that 'the setting aside of the old sourdough' has already begun is further confirmed by Hegel's next appearance in the pulpit on the third Sunday after Trinity (16 June).[1] For now he discourses publicly on the Sermon on the Mount, which became the foundation for his picture of the enlightened Jesus in *Das Leben Jesu* and 'Die Positivität der christlichen Religion'. His subject now is explicitly the Kingdom of God, and what it means to be a member of it. He announces that he will show first that the Kingdom is an inward, not an outward reality, and secondly that Christ has opened the way to it for us. These claims are orthodox enough, but by concentrating on 'The Kingdom of God is within you' and 'Thy Kingdom come . . . on earth' one can quite quickly arrive at the point where the Kingdom of *Heaven* is almost irrelevant.

The Kingdom is not a 'worldly State'; for, as Christ said to Pilate, 'My Kingdom is not of this world'. Nor does membership in the 'visible Church' make one a member of God's Kingdom; for 'Not everyone that saith unto me "Lord! Lord!", but he that doeth the will of my Father, shall enter into the Kingdom'. The Kingdom does not show itself in outward ceremonies: churchgoing, baptism, participation in the communion service, the confessions of our lips, do not make us children of God. The letter killeth but the spirit giveth life. The spirit of Christ must dwell in us, and we must be born again through the grace of God.

At this point Hegel cited a whole string of texts. After John 3 : 3 and 1 Peter 1 : 22–3 came Ephesians 4 : 22–4, about which he specifically notes 'Putting off of the old man and putting on of the new'. His own nickname was 'the Old Man', and if he read out with full ceremony 'That ye put off concerning the former conversation the old man, which is corrupt according to the deceitful lusts' he must have known perfectly well that all of his fellow students would be inwardly consumed with mirth. Surely he meant them to

---

[1] Outline in *Dok.*, pp. 179–82. Under the old regulations the theology students preached in turn each day, and each could expect the duty to fall upon him about once every six weeks (cf. Betzendörfer, p. 57). But these two sermons were probably delivered under the new regulations of 1793, according to which five candidates preached one after another for two and half hours in the afternoon on Sundays and feast days.

laugh at his 'former conversation' about the doctrine of grace?
For in the account of the 'new man' which follows the saving
grace is provided by Kantian morality: 'If we are thus born of
God, if we become new men, i.e. if we die unto sin and become
masters of our sensibility, if our hearts are transformed by the love
of God and Christ so that we obey His commandments freely and
joyfully, then we are citizens of His kingdom, then the Kingdom
of God is come, and then also we are certain of our future blessedness.'[1]

The orthodoxy of this conception of the Kingdom is un-
impeachable, but the slighting references to the 'visible Church'
and to the outward ceremonies of 'divine service' in a seminary
where great emphasis was laid on regular attendance at public
worship, and the students had to wear cassock and surplice every
time they went beyond the gates, were well calculated to suggest
to all who had ears to hear that the hosts of the orthodox were not
the true followers of Christ.

In the second part of the sermon Hegel begins by saying all the
appropriate things about our weakness and sinfulness, our need
of grace in order to be saved, and how we have received this
grace through Christ who 'freed us from the bondage of the Mosaic
law'. But soon the emphasis on our own efforts, on good works as
the fruits of faith, creeps back, and we can hardly be in doubt
about the esoteric significance which the following passage had for
Hegel himself and at least some of his hearers:

If we [have] a faith of this sort, then we are children of *light*, i.e. we
hate the works of *darkness*, of evil which has to hide itself, we love the
truth, which can let itself be seen *publicly and freely by anyone* . . . then
we are citizens of the kingdom of God—i.e. citizens and members of
that kingdom where God as highest lawgiver and ruler, is worshipped
by us in spirit and in truth—not by crying Lord! Lord! but by imitating
Him within the limits of our human weakness—by being earnest in
good works, and letting His light shine forth among men, and offering
to Him the most acceptable service of our own goodness and righteousness . . .[2]

---

[1] *Dok.*, p. 180. The Kantian inspiration of this passage can hardly be doubted—
even the reference to our 'future blessedness' is easily interpreted in terms of
Kant's postulate of immortality, which Hegel probably accepted at this time,
just as he accepted the postulates of God and freedom.

[2] *Dok.*, p. 183 (my italics). The sermon closes, as students' sermons often did,
with a verse from the Württemberg Songbook—concerned with the grace of

There was a special poignancy about this passage in Hegel's June sermon because, during the interval which had elapsed since the feast of St. Philip and St. James, a report of the revolutionary fervour of the students in the *Stift* had reached the Duke's ears in Stuttgart. On 13 May 1793 he came on a state visit for the official inauguration of the 'new constitution' for the *Stift*—a project on which Schnurrer had laboured since 1789—but he also took the occasion to inquire into such scandalous matters as the reading of French newspapers and the singing of revolutionary songs.[1] The focus of open scandal, so it would seem, was a public concert organized by a classmate and friend of Schelling's named August Wetzel, at which 'the Marseillaise' was sung in German. Wetzel ran off from the *Stift* shortly before the Duke's visit—quite probably at the instance and with the connivance of the Ephor, Schnurrer. Most of the blame for the corruption of his fellow

'being born again'. And it may be significant that his quotation ends with the words 'How blessed is / Thy Child, Thine Own one, / The true Christian', for the word 'true' was inserted by Hegel himself and is not in the original text of the hymn. (The sermon on forgiveness ended in the same way. It seems the students were taught to lead their congregations directly from the conclusion of the sermon into the singing of the hymn that was appointed to follow it.)

[1] For Schnurrer's 'public' account of the visit, and of the earlier labours for the reform of the *Stift*, see Hölderlin, *GSA*, vii. 1, 404 ff. (Lebensdokumente (LD.) 66). For his private opinions and feelings—as expressed in letters to a former pupil—see LD. 67, 74, 80, 95. It is worth noting that in LD. 95b (*GSA*, vii. 1, 436), which is an excerpt from a letter to Scholl of 10 Mar. 1793, Schnurrer expresses the fear that 'the new statutes' will now be too late: 'Unsre junge Leute sind großentheils von dem FreyheitsSchwindel angestekt, und das allzulange Zögern mit der neuen Einrichtung hat viel dazu geholfen.' We have here I think a veiled reference to the problem posed by Wetzel and his Club (as well as to the *Unsinnskollegium* that Klüpfel tells us about—see further, p. 114 n. 2 below).

I cannot see any reason to set aside the report in Rosenkranz (p. 33) that the Club was betrayed to the Duke 'durch einen Apotheker'. The likely source of this report I take to have been Fink—whose memory for vocations and avocations was better apparently than his memory for names, since he also recalls Wetzel as a notable musician. The view that the Duke came to the *Stift* without suspicions and only began inquiries when he heard of Wetzel's flight leaves the flight itself unaccounted for. Rosenkranz is of course wrong in supposing that the Duke came *in order* to make inquiries. But by the same token he is right in saying that 'the Duke was wise enough not to make too much of the matter'. The Duke's 'wisdom' consisted first in waiting to inquire until he had another occasion to visit the *Stift*; for the rest it was, no doubt, a matter of paying heed to the advice of Schnurrer. (It appears likely that, as Fuhrmans suggests, the traitorous 'Apotheker' was S. J. Kob, the student of medicine, himself a Strasbourger, who wrote 'Vive la liberté' in Hegel's *Stammbuch* in Dec. 1792: Fuhrmans, i. 17 n; *Briefe*, iv. 35.)

students could be laid on his head, since he had already run away once before. In April 1792 he had gone off to join a Jacobin club in Strasbourg. In all probability he brought the text of the 'Marseillaise' with him when he returned to the *Stift* in August 1792;[1] I think myself it is quite probable that he brought the idea of founding a 'political club' back with him into the *Stift* as well.[2]

[1] The 'Marseillaise' was in fact written in Strasbourg by Rouget de Lisle at about this time. It says a great deal for Schnurrer's moral courage as well as his liberality of mind that Wetzel was readmitted—even allowing for the fact that C. F. Rösler was his uncle and probably spoke for him. The two professors must have faced some stinging rebukes from the Duke in May 1793—far worse than anything endured by Schelling, who on account of his youth would appear as an innocent misled by an older schoolfellow. (He and Wetzel had been together at Maulbronn for two years before they entered the *Stift*.)
    Klüpfel's account of the revolutionary fervour in the *Stift* offers a very plausible reason for Wetzel's earlier escapade (see *Briefe*, iv. 166). He says that some of the French-speaking students began corresponding with General Custine's forces in the Mainz campaign of 1792. What he reports about Schelling's involvement and the Duke's inquiry may perhaps involve some confusion between the events of 1792 and those of 1793; but the Duke certainly visited the *Stift* often enough and would not fail to inquire into the matter if any rumours reached him. I should think that we can take it for granted that Wetzel was involved in this correspondence. Unlike most of his fellows he properly deserved the name of *Jacobin* (Hegel and Hölderlin—and probably most of the club members—sympathized with the Girondins against Robespierre and the Mountain). Wetzel went straight to France in 1793, joined the army of the Revolution, and remained in France for the rest of his life.

[2] There is no reason to believe the fairy tale that Schwegler puts into Leutwein's mouth to the effect that Hegel was 'the most inspired orator for freedom and equality' in the *Stift*. (Schwegler actually does not mention the club because he knew nothing about it.) But this is *not* in itself a reason to doubt the existence of the Club (as Beck seems inclined to do: Hölderlin, *GSA*, vii. 1, 450). Even if my hypothesis that Rosenkranz's authority was Fink (see p. 113 n. 1) is not accepted, there is too much indirect evidence (bonds of 'patriotic' sympathy between *Stiftler* and non-*Stiftler* such as Hiller, Kob, Sinclair, von Seckendorff, and so on) for us to doubt the essential truth of this report. There is also Hegel's reference in *Eleusis* to 'the *Bund* that no oath sealed / For the free truth alone to live, peace with the established order that dictates opinions and feelings never never to conclude' (*Briefe*, i. 38, lines 19–21). This, like the watchword of the 'invisible Church', suggests a brotherhood inspired by the ideals of freemasonry but without formal organization.
    Perhaps the only organization that had a formal existence was the *Unsinnskollegium* which Klüpfel records (see *Briefe*, iv. 166–7). This looks like a normal reaction of undergraduate high spirits against authority and decorum. But much political protest could conveniently be disguised as 'ragging'. I cannot help suspecting that the 'Club' used the *Unsinnskollegium* as a front; and further that both the *Repetenten* and the Ephor knew this was so, and used the cover themselves in their official reports. This seems to me particularly evident in the scandals of the last months of 1793 (cf. p. 115 n. 2 below).

It was Schelling, himself, however who apparently had to take the blame for translating the words of the 'Marseillaise' into German verse; and so the Duke had now to rebuke the young man whom he had earlier caused to be promoted to the position of *Primus* in his class.[1] It is only reasonable to suppose that all of the club members, including Hegel, were very anxious in this crisis, and that the polite exchanges that Schnurrer recorded for the public view were the outward mask of some very uncomfortable hours for everyone concerned.[2]

Immediately after the oldest villain followed the newest hero. In June 1793 Fichte passed through Tübingen for the first time. Hegel and his friends were reading the *Kritik aller Offenbarung* and one of the *Repetenten*, F. G. Süskind, was writing a commentary to bring it in line with Storr's interpretation of Kant. It seems likely

[1] Schelling was placed second in his class at the time of entry and promoted to first subsequently as the result of a public oration before the Duke (Plitt, i. 29). There is a difficulty about the report that Schelling was rebuked for translating the 'Marseillaise'. Sinclair wrote to Jung on 29 Oct. 1793 that J. J. Griesinger was the translator of the 'Marseillaise' (*GSA*, vii. 1, 471). But the problem is easily resolved since, in all the circumstances, the translation is likely to have been the work of more than one hand. It was Griesinger's remarkable control of French which—along with his 'patriotism'—drew Sinclair's attention to him. If he was the acknowledged French expert and Schelling the principal German versifier in a common undertaking then both of them could legitimately claim to have 'translated the "Marseillaise"'.

[2] There was another scandalous report to the Duke in August—this time to the effect that the execution of Louis XVI had been publicly defended in the *Stift*. By now Hegel was back home in Stuttgart, but the affair is of interest to us nevertheless, because it provides a plausible explanation and a final quietus for the famous myth of the 'Freedom tree'. This story came to Rosenkranz's notice through Schwegler—who had nothing but *Stift* rumours of forty years later to rely on—and to Klüpfel and Schwab from better-informed, but still misinformed or misreported sources. Both of the latter say the tree was 'set up in the market-place' and Klüpfel adds that Hegel and Hölderlin were personally involved; Schwegler mentions Hegel and Schelling and places the event 'nearby' Tübingen on a fine Sunday in springtime. (See *G.S.A.* vii, 448, *Briefe*, iv. 166, and *Hegel-Studien*, iii. 61.) Schnurrer says: 'A few months ago someone wrote to me from Ulm that it was generally said and believed in those parts that the students in the *Stift* had set up the Freedom Tree right before my very eyes.' He wants to convince the Duke and his advisers that they should not believe reports about the *Stift* from distant sources (the August accusation came from Freiburg); and whatever may have happened on 14 July 1793 it is safe to assume that it did not occur in a public place. But we can also assume that the report from Ulm was retailed with great glee by the 'patriots' in the *Stift*, who would be delighted at this evidence of the sort of reputation they enjoyed in the world outside. Nor is it hard to understand how the story of an accusation could reach Klüpfel (or Schwab) as the account of a fact. (Hegel was quite probably at home in Stuttgart on 14 July 1793—see p. 116 n. 4 below.)

that both Schelling and Hegel met Fichte on this occasion, or at least saw him, for when Schelling mentioned Fichte's second visit (May 1794) in his first letter to Hegel (5 January 1795), he did not bother to give any description of the 'new hero' whom he 'greeted in the land of the truth'.[1] Certainly at the end of the month Hegel met the poets Stäudlin and Matthisson when they visited Hölderlin; both of them wrote leaves for his *Stammbuch* on this occasion, and Stäudlin, who was shortly to be banished by the Duke for his revolutionary sympathies, doubtless summed up the feelings of his young friends and admirers in the *Stift* very aptly at that moment by recalling the cry of Ulrich von Hutten, 'In tyrannos'.[2]

If we are to believe Schnurrer's perhaps exaggerated comment that Hegel spent almost all of the summer of 1793 at home, this visit of the two poets must have come virtually at the end of his studies at Tübingen. In June, along with eight other candidates, he defended a thesis of Chancellor Lebret's *De ecclesiae Württembergicae renascentis calamitatibus*.[3] It was probably early in July when he went home to Stuttgart to read Kant and Fichte, meditate on the Kingdom of God, and elaborate his conception of *Volksreligion*, as his own contribution toward the coming of the Kingdom.[4] His ideal was mainly Hellenic in its inspiration, though both the Gospel record and Lessing's *Nathan* made important contributions. The influence of his readings in the new religious

---

[1] Letter 7, *Briefe*, i. 14–15. What Hegel and Hölderlin call the 'Kingdom of God' is for Schelling 'the land of the truth': cf. p. 106 nn. 1 and 2 above.

[2] *Briefe*, iv. 55. Entry 61, by Stäudlin, is not dated, but Matthisson's quotation from Horace is dated 27 June 1793, and the visit of the two poets is confirmed and dated both by Hölderlin's letters and by Matthisson's diary. The diary further records for 24 June 'Besuch bei Mamsel Hegel', which seems to show that Matthisson was already (like Stäudlin) a family friend (see *GSA*, vi. 88 and Beck's note at 626). (Hegel was very likely present when Hölderlin read his 'Hymnus an die Kühnheit' to the two poets: cf. Letter 94, lines 22–4, *GSA*, vi. 154 and 723.)

[3] Rosenkranz, p. 39; *Dok.*, p. 438. The other eight students were Hölderlin, Klüpfel, Mohr, Mögling, Weiss, Schweickard, J. W. Maerklin, Rothacker (see *GSA*, ii. 973). The order is according to their *Lokation*. Rothacker was bottom of the class—and J. W. Maerklin is *not* to be confused with the J. F. Maerklin who was placed above Hegel.

[4] His own *Stammbuch* shows that Hegel was in Tübingen on 2 July (entry 37); and his entry in Ehemann's *Stammbuch* shows that he was back again on 23 Sept. (the period of the annual examination). He was away when Schnurrer wrote to Scholl on 10 Sept. and we must suppose that he had then been away for some considerable time (*Briefe*, iv. 50 and 66; Haering, i. 114).

and moral philosophy of Kant and Fichte is also apparent, but it is noteworthy that amid all the revolutionary excitements of his last year Hegel remained true to the programme of using classical sources to enlighten the study of the Judaic tradition, which he announced at the outset of his university studies.

Before we can pass on to deal with these private concerns, however, one other sermon remains to be discussed. There is no date at the head of the manuscript to indicate when it was delivered—a fact which is all the more surprising because, unlike the other sermons, the text of the discourse is fully written out in the style of a 'fair copy'.[1] The content of the sermon presents an even greater paradox, for it is concerned with the Christian doctrine of forgiveness, a topic which had already assumed a central importance in Hegel's speculations about religion, and one about which his ideas were scarcely orthodox; yet the sermon itself is so rigidly orthodox that it might have been written by the most conscientious disciple of Storr in the *Stift*. The capacity to forgive is treated as one of the essential marks of true faith, and several varieties of false forgiveness, behind which the will to vengeance is still concealed, are distinguished and denounced. Christian forgiveness is further distinguished from the type of moral laziness that offers indulgence in return for indulgence, and the essentially strenuous character of Christian love is affirmed. But there is no hint in the text of any attempt to interpret forgiveness in terms of Kantian ethics, and although what Hegel says is consistent with the conception of Christian love as the consciousness of union or harmony with the universal spirit of all life, which he expressed in his Frankfurt essays, nothing of this sort is explicit in the text. All that is plain is that forgiveness was a topic in Christian ethics where no strain was created in Hegel's mind between his own ideals and the requirements of orthodoxy.

Although this sermon is not dated, there is an explicit reference in the text to 'the gospel for the day' from which it is clear that it was written for the twenty-second Sunday after Trinity. In 1793 this fell on 27 October, by which time Hegel had already gone to

[1] Cf. the description by Gisela Schüler in *Hegel-Studien*, ii. 136–7. On the basis of the handwriting alone Miss Schüler hazards the guess that this sermon was somehow bound up with the final examination of the theology candidates before the Stuttgart consistory. This confirms the hypothesis which I had already arrived at from analysis of the text as printed by Hoffmeister (*Dok.*, pp. 184–92).

Berne.[1] Setting aside the hypothesis that it was delivered in 1792 (4 November) which is improbable on all counts, we are left with two possibilities. Either Hegel prepared a sermon for the twenty-second Sunday after Trinity as an exercise for one of Flatt's private classes in homiletics in the summer of 1793, or he prepared it for his final examinations at Tübingen (in the week following 20 September 1793) or before the Consistory at Stuttgart. The Consistorial examinations regularly took place in December,[2] but Hegel was allowed to take his examination early at the same time as he was granted permission to take a position as house-tutor in the family of Hauptmann von Steiger at Berne. He was summoned on 13 September to appear at 8 a.m. on the nineteenth, and his successful completion of the examination together with the permission to take up his post abroad was recorded on the twentieth. Permission was granted 'on condition that he exercises himself diligently in preaching, wherein he is still very weak'.[3] The extreme caution that is evident in the sermon that we are considering is easily explicable if it was prepared for the eyes and ears of the examining committee of the Consistory, which was a very conservative body, and one that Hegel had to satisfy at all costs, in order to escape from its authority as he did by going to Berne. It is less easy to understand why he should be so cautious in a sermon prepared for Flatt or for an examining committee at Tübingen. Indeed the absence of explicit references to Kant's moral philosophy are almost inexplicable on that hypothesis. The Tübingen records show that Hegel was called on to explicate 1 *Corinthians* 11: 14 at his *Consistorialprüfung* on 20 September, and that he did not do it very well.[4] He would never have chosen this text, which is part of Paul's discourse on the duty of women to cover their heads in church, of his own free will; whereas Christian

---

[1] For the intended occasion of the sermon see Miss Schüler's data (loc. cit.); for his letters to von Rütte and the dating of Hegel's journey to Berne compare the entries for 8 and 9 Oct. 1793 in his *Stammbuch* (27, 28, 47a, 53, and 22): *Briefe*, i. 4–6 and iv. 45, 47, 53, 55.

[2] Hölderlin was summoned on 26 Nov. 1793 to appear before the consistory on 5 Dec. (see Beck's notes in *GSA* vi. 640, and the summons itself in *GSA*, vii. 1, 477–8).

[3] *Briefe*, iv. 83.

[4] *Briefe*, iv. 87: 'Textum I Cor. 11, 14, non plene explicavit, nec justo ordine orationem S. [i.e. satis?] decenter tamen recitavit.' Anyone who looks at the remarks about religious practices and ceremonies which Hegel was writing just about this time (Nohl, pp. 24–6) will know how he must have felt about the 'explication' of this text.

forgiveness was a topic on which he could discourse in a perfectly orthodox way without hypocrisy or an unbearable sense of constraint. If he was, or expected to be, allowed to preach on a topic of his own choice, as well as upon one assigned by the examiners, he may well have prepared the sermon that we have for the occasion.[1]

6. *The function of a folk-religion*

If not absolutely certain, it is at least highly probable that what has often been called the 'Tübingen fragment'—the first of the fragments published by Nohl under the general heading *Folk-Religion and Christianity* with its associated 'Entwürfe'—was in fact written in Stuttgart between July and September 1793. There are a number of signs in the text that Hegel was consciously embarking on a fairly large-scale project, which indicates that he expected to have sufficient leisure to proceed without serious interference; and the explicit reference to Fichte's *Kritik aller Offenbarung* in one of the earliest preparatory outlines proves fairly conclusively that he did not begin even to put his plans on paper before May or June of 1793.[2]

The explicit object of his studies is, as he says,

not to investigate what religious doctrines are most appealing to the heart, ⟨or⟩ most apt to elevate and give comfort to the soul—nor [is it to investigate] how the doctrines of a religion should be constituted in order to make a people better and happier—but rather what arrangements are requisite in order that the doctrines and the force of religion should enter into the web of human feelings, become associated with human impulses to action and prove living and active in them—in order [that is] that religion should become wholly subjective . . .[3]

It is important to remember this declaration at the outset, because the achievement of a completely *subjective* religion does turn out

---

[1] Only further information about the general character of the *Consistorialprüfung* will really settle this question. There are also other points that need to be cleared up. Why, for instance, was he summoned for 8 a.m. on the 19th if the examination took place on the 20th? Was it then that he was instructed to prepare a discourse on 1 Corinthians 11 : 14 to be delivered on the following day?

[2] Nohl, p. 355. The first edition of the *Versuch einer Kritik aller Offenbarung* to bear Fichte's name as author appeared in Oct. 1792. The rumour that Kant himself had written it was not denied till August. But there is no reason to suppose that Hegel was interested in the religious philosophy of either Kant or Fichte before the publication of Kant's *Religion* and Storr's *Annotationes* in 1793. I think it is quite probable that his interest in Fichte was first aroused by the visit in June 1793 (cf. above, pp. 108 and 115–16).

[3] Nohl, p. 8 (italics mine).

to require the discovery of the doctrines that most appeal to the heart, and are best calculated to make the 'people' (hereafter used regularly to express Hegel's *das Volk*) better and happier; and when Hegel begins to speak of this ideal, which he found instantiated in the Greece of the fifth century B.C.,[1] he loses his analytical objectivity and is carried away by his enthusiasm, like Machiavelli in the last chapter of *The Prince*.[2] The fact that this happens has led to several mistaken estimates of what Hegel is attempting to do.

Of course what we have before us is only an unrevised first draft written by a young man whose mind was a ferment of ideas, which he needed to write down partly in order just to get them sorted out. So we must expect to find that his aims and purposes change and develop even while he is writing, and we must not put absolute faith in the infallibility of his initial pronouncements about them. But this only makes it all the more essential to study the actual sequence of his reflections. Certainly we must not allow ourselves to be carried away just because the author gets carried away and gives up writing at the point where he can see that what he is about to embark on will not answer to his purpose and must be radically recast. That, I think, is what happens at the end of the fragment *Religion ist eine*.[3]

[1] There are two main grounds for dating Hegel's Hellenic ideal to the fifth century: (*a*) the remark that from its father Chronos the Greek spirit inherited 'trust in its good fortune and pride in its deeds' (Nohl, p. 28), which appears to be a plain reference to the fortunes of Greece in the Persian War and to the proud claims of Pericles in the Funeral Oration; (*b*) the fact that so much of what Hegel says, and even the way he says it, is inspired by Plato. The very account of the Greek spirit as a child of Chronos and Politeia, referred to above, is an example of this, for it is transparently modelled on Plato's myth of love as the child of Poros and Penia in the *Symposium*.

[2] Hölderlin was recommending Machiavelli's *Prince* to his brother in Aug. 1793 (Letter 62, *GSA*, v. 189): 'Seine ganze Schrift beschäftigt sich mit dem Problem, wie ein Volk am leichtesten zu unterjochen sei.' It may well be that Hegel had this model in mind in setting himself the opposite problem of how a people can most easily cast off their fetters.

[3] I can see no convincing reason for speaking of 'das Nohlschen Anordnung der Fragmente' (in the plural) as Haering does (i. 63), followed by Peperzak, p. 11, and Lacorte, pp. 302–3; for a cautious doubt on my own part see p. 132 n. 1 below. The question would be easier to settle if we knew more precisely where the transitions from sheet to sheet occur in our printed text, and which, if any, of the sheets were not completely filled by Hegel's manuscript. (For an explanation of the way in which the opening phrase of *incipit* is used in referring to Hegel's manuscripts and fragments from mid 1793 onwards see the Note on References at the beginning of this volume (p. xiii). The Chronological Index to Hegel's early writings (pp. 517–26) will enable the reader to discover exactly what text is referred to by each *incipit*.)

This is not the only reason, however, why a properly sequential analysis of the text is imperative. Another reason is provided by the set of extremely complex relations that exist between the series of concepts employed in, and in part uncovered by, Hegel's analysis of religion as a psychological and social phenomenon. All the attempts hitherto made to disentangle the 'themes' of his discussion have resulted in at least a partial falsification or confusion of his meaning and purpose precisely for this reason. Several critics have correctly remarked, for example, that the title *Folk-Religion and Christianity* is misleading. But the grounds which have usually been given for this assertion are just as misleading or misguided as Nohl's editorial attempt to characterize the fragments, and often more so. The chief reason for objecting to Nohl's title is that the concepts 'folk-religion' and 'Christianity' are not of the same type or on the same level. 'Christianity' is an extremely complex historical phenomenon embracing at least two 'folk-religions' (Protestantism, Catholicism) and perhaps a third (Primitive Christianity, if Hegel was willing to count it as a folk-religion in the full sense) as well as various systems of theological dogma and private piety which are not folk-religions. If we confine ourselves to the Protestant Christianity of Germany in the eighteenth century, this is a particular folk-religion, as well as a 'public' religion, a 'private' religion, a rational religion, and a 'fetish-faith' or system of superstition. As such it can be compared with other folk-religions such as that of Periclean Greece or the biblical people of Israel, which also have all of these other aspects.[1] 'Folk-religion' on the other hand is a pure concept, which we can arrive at either concretely by considering our own social experience, or the experience of the Jews or the Greeks, so far as we can reconstruct and relive it on the basis of the fragmentary records of their culture that have come down to us; or else abstractly by studying the different meanings and uses of the general terms 'religious' and 'religion' and of religious language generally both in our ordinary and in our learned vocabulary.[2]

[1] For practical reasons (and not only from excessive enthusiasm) Hegel sometimes wrote as if the religion of the Greeks was free from the aspects of 'privacy' and 'fetishism'. But I believe it can be shown that he knew better and would readily have admitted the presence of the darker side in Greek religion as soon as he was sure that his audience understood his reasons for concentrating on the bright side.

[2] I think it is possible, and, provided that we do not lose sight of the ambivalent

Hegel's discussion ranges backwards and forwards over the field of historical actuality, and both types of abstraction. One of his primary concerns is to show that the theoretical, or viciously abstract, study of religion is useless for practical purposes. His aim, as he says, is to discover how religion becomes an active social force. This leads him inevitably to the Greek experience as the natural, fully-developed, perfect exemplar of religion as a social force. But he is not just theoretically interested in discovering how religion functions in society; he wants to use the power of religion to reshape his own society. This has two consequences which mutually reinforce each other in the production of false impressions. On the one hand he is very cautious and restrained in what he says—or at least in what he allows to stand when he sees it on the paper before him—about the religion of his own society, except when he is dealing with the viciously abstract study of religion as practised therein. On the other hand, when he sees religion functioning properly to produce a society which is concretely rational he cannot restrain his enthusiasm, although his own principles require him to do so if his own work is to have the desired effect of advancing concrete rationality in his own society.

In the opening paragraphs of *Religion ist eine* he describes as briefly as possible the total parabola of religious experience from the first religious *act* of the child (joining his hands in prayer) to the highest religious *ideas* of the philosopher with a long and full life to reflect upon (the 'sublime requirement of Reason'). Religious practice enters into our lives from our earliest years: it punctuates our daily lives and sanctifies the critical turning

character of *all* our concepts it may be helpful, to distinguish—*abstractly* as the young Hegel would have said—between the vocabularies that typify the 'concrete' and the 'abstract' approaches to the concept of 'folk-religion'. Roughly speaking, when we are approaching the concept *concretely* we find it (in Hegel's usage) in the company of other *concrete* concepts such as 'reason', 'superstition', 'freedom', 'servitude', 'spirit', 'letter'. This is the origin or root of the conceptual framework that Hegel developed in the Frankfurt period. The name of God (or the names of the Gods) will certainly figure in our inquiry; but the name of our religion (Christianity, Protestantism, etc.) will not occur except in an accidental and peripheral way. When we approach the concept *abstractly*, on the other hand, the discussion moves in a cloud of metalinguistic terms such as the words 'concrete' and 'abstract' themselves and others like 'subjective', 'objective', 'theology', 'dogma'. Here the names of religions and the *concept*, rather than the *name*, 'God' will occur. Of course, there is a mass of terms—particularly ethical and psychological terms—which will occur in both types of inquiry, and even the ones I have listed are not by any means rigidly confined to the types of inquiry which I believe they nevertheless typify.

points of our existence such as birth, marriage, and death.[1] But
the theoretical development of religious experience also begins
early. As children we do not only learn the act and habit of prayer;
we also learn a lot of theoretical formulas by heart, although
genuine reflection upon the meaning of the formulas and the
practices is a function of adult reason:

> Human nature is so disposed that the practical aspects of the doctrine
> of God, the aspects that can become mainsprings of action, sources of
> the knowledge of our duties and sources of solace, quickly present them-
> selves to the uncorrupted mind [*Menschensinne*]—and the instruction
> that we are given about this from youth up, the concepts [*Begriffe*], and
> all the external [trappings] pertaining to it which make an impression
> on us, is of such a kind that it can be grafted on to a natural need of the
> human spirit—often immediately, but all too frequently alas, it is
> attached only by means of bonds rooted in arbitrariness, and not in the
> nature of the soul, or in truths engendered and developed from the
> concepts themselves.[2]

At this point four pages of Hegel's manuscript are missing.
But it is apparent that he means to discover how this arbitrariness
can be eliminated, and how a proper grafting of religion on to the
human spirit, one which is both sensibly harmonious with the
nature of the soul and rationally coherent with the structure of
the religious concepts can be achieved.

The text recommences with the tantalizing words 'to set the
. . . of human life in motion'. It is fairly clear that Hegel wanted
to set the 'whole' of life in motion, but it would be nice to know for
certain what the subject of the sentence was. It seems likely in the
light of what follows that he was saying that pure reason alone is
not able to set the whole of life in motion. For he goes on to declare
that the 'sublime demand' (*erhabene Forderung*) that reason makes
of mankind 'whose legitimacy we so often recognize with our whole
heart' ought never to master us to the point that we 'expect to
find many [guiltless or wise men] in the actual world, or believe
that somewhere we shall see and touch this beautiful chimera'.
Again we cannot tell precisely what the 'sublime demand' or the
'beautiful chimera' are but there are some distinctly Kantian

---

[1] Originally Hegel mentioned sickness also, but then he struck it out, probably
because the comforting of the sick, in Protestant Christianity at least, is a
private rather than a public function of religion and he wished to emphasize the
publicly recognized functions of religion.

[2] Nohl, pp. 3–4.

overtones in Hegel's language, and Kant is almost certainly his main target here. For he alludes immediately to the difficulty of deciding whether the 'Bestimmungsgrund' of the will is mere 'Klugheit' or 'wirkliche Moralität', and points out that 'satisfaction of the impulse to happiness as the highest goal of life' would produce the same outward pattern of behaviour 'as if the law of reason determines our will'.

This is an example of the strictly pragmatic attitude towards theoretical disputes in philosophy which Hegel advocated consistently from the essay of 1787 onwards. We can see in this case how his faith that pragmatic reconciliation of the differing views of serious thinkers is always possible, is related to his conception of life as an organic whole. For no matter what abstract moral principle one adopts, one has the same problem of applying it to a life which is both sensitive and rational, and any principle which adequately expresses the requirements of one side of our nature will be found to be pragmatically consistent with a principle that expresses the needs of the other side as long as they are not interpreted with an abstract rigorism that simply ignores the compound character of human nature. Thus the apostle of practical reason has to accept the fact that 'sensibility is the principal factor in all the action and striving of men'; and the seeker after happiness has to be able to 'calculate properly' what will really produce it.

Hegel lays much more emphasis throughout his discussion on the danger of rationalist rigorism in ethics than on the opposite excesses of hedonism. But it is fairly clear that although he wants to defend the claims of human feeling, and particularly of such social emotions as love and sympathy—which Kant dismissed as 'pathological motives'—against the rigorism of pure 'respect for the law', he is not really seeking to defend the rational endaemonism of Wolff and of the many minor moralists of the Enlightenment. These were, in his eyes, thinkers who did not help us to 'reckon well' what happiness consists in. The moral philosopher whom he really admires and follows is Aristotle—though the shadow of Rousseau looms over much of his discussion also.

Human nature, in Hegel's view, was a mass of sensible impulses, natural needs, and blind instincts, somehow 'pregnant [geschwängert] with the Ideas of reason'. The 'ideas of reason enliven the whole web of [man's] feelings' like light penetrating everywhere, affecting everything, playing a vital part in the life of plants without being itself a substance.[1] 'They show themselves seldom in their essence', says Hegel, who does not want to deny that the ideal of completely rational action can be achieved. He rejects the Cartesian conception of reason as something quite separate from sensibility, with the associated view of soul and body as distinct 'substances'; but he accepts the other view of reason as the terminus of a social process of education and development of the human race as a whole which was prevalent in the later Enlightenment. Haering tends to treat Hegel's attitude towards Enlightenment rationalism as rather more simply and directly negative than it was. Years later, when he was about to embark at last on his career as a professional philosopher, he wrote to Schelling that his philosophical development had begun with a concern for the 'lower' side of man's nature. But he never at any time felt the slightest inclination to reject 'die erhabene Forderung der Vernunft and die Menschheit', and when he calls it 'dies schöne Luftbild' he is being quite sincere and not at all satirical as Haering supposes.[2]

The development of religious consciousness, and, as we shall see, of political consciousness at the same time, is the natural course by which the 'ideas of reason' are brought from pregnancy to birth. These 'ideas' are essentially two: God as creator of the order of nature, and legislator of the laws of morality; and the immortality of the soul.[3] But there is more to religion than the mere knowledge of these ideas, and we may come to this knowledge either through pure reason or in some other way.[4] Religious

---

[1] Hegel was here developing Plato's simile of the sun (*Republic*, vi) on lines suggested by his own study of botany.

[2] Nohl, p. 4; cf. also p. 357; *Briefe*, i. 59; Haering, i. 82 (cf. also 63). Haering wavers somewhat in his account of Hegel's 'realism' in relation to the Enlightenment background. He is generally very fair and balanced on particular issues and parallels—as for instance when he calls Hegel's notion of human sensibility as pregnant with reason 'Leibnizian—evolutionary' (i. 65). But he does not distinguish carefully enough between the abstract rationalism that Hegel rejected (e.g. Campe's *Theophron*) and the concrete 'Ideen der Vernunft' which he accepted.

[3] Hegel does not here say that these two conceptions are the 'Ideen der Vernunft' with which our nature is 'geschwängert'. But the phrase 'Ideen der Vernunft' has a Kantian ring which makes the identification natural, and it is confirmed by everything that Hegel says later. If my account of the transition in his thought here is accepted we cannot doubt that Hegel has thought fairly hard about the way in which Kant's 'Ideas of pure reason' become 'postulates of practical reason'.

[4] It is not clear what other way there is besides revelation and reason. But Hegel regards these principles as depending ultimately not on any philosopher's

consciousness reinforces the sense of duty and strengthens us against the temptations of impulse; but it does so only because 'for men who live at the level of sense-impulse, religion also has sensible form'.[1]

Hegel is now finally able to introduce the twin conceptions of 'public' religion and 'folk' religion, which together form the central topic of his discussion:

If we speak of public religion—then we mean to include thereunder the concepts of God and immortality and all that goes with them [was darunter Beziehung hat], so far as they make up the conviction of a people, so far as they influence the actions and mode of thought of a people—to public religion belong also, furthermore, the means by which these ideas are partly taught to the people, and partly enabled to penetrate their hearts—in this effect [i.e. the understanding and emotional assimilation of these two conceptions] is included not merely the immediate ⟨consequence⟩ that I do not steal because God has forbidden it—the more distant ⟨consequences⟩ should particularly be taken into consideration and have often to be accorded the most weight. These are, above all the elevation, the ennobling, of the spirit of a nation— that the so often slumbering sense of its dignity comes to be awakened in its soul, that the people does not degrade [i.e. subject] itself and does not allow itself to be degraded, that it does [i.e. the citizens do] not merely feel itself [themselves] men, but that gentler tints of humanity and goodness are also brought into the picture.[2]

In this definition three rather disparate influences are definitely present. There is first the Kantian–Fichtean ideal of religion within the bounds of reason. This provides the essential core of the idea. This core Hegel 'applies to', or interprets in terms of, two historical cases: a minimum case, the Jews, and a maximum case, the Greeks. The Jews received the Law at the hands of Moses—Hegel chooses the example 'Thou shalt not steal', first because it is in the Decalogue, and secondly because regulation of property rights is,

reasoning but on the universal 'good sense' of mankind (cf. Nohl, p. 13); and his confidence of this rested partly on his knowledge that different philosophers —such as Plato and Leibniz (Wolff), to take two with whom he was well acquain- ted—had defended them by very different lines of argument from that followed by Kant. Plato's *Timaeus* is certainly 'another way' if 'durch bloßen Vernunft' is taken in *any* of the senses it has for Kant. There is also of course the 'feeling' to which Rousseau's Savoyard Vicar appeals.

[1] 'Bei sinnlichen Menschen ist auch die Religion sinnlich.' This was a necessity that Hegel recognized already in 1787 (cf. *Dok.*, p. 47, discussed above in Chapter I, pp. 31–4).

[2] Nohl, p. 5. I have made the translation as literal as I could.

in his view, a minimal condition for the formation of a human society[1]—but it did not suffice for them: they 'degraded' themselves by demanding a king.[2] The Greeks, on the other hand, once their lawgivers had done their work, would not suffer tyrants and developed high ideals of patriotic loyalty and heroic humanity which they summed up for themselves in their conception of the gods.[3]

But what, we may ask, has the philosophical core to do with these historical examples? What have God and immortality, as postulates of practical reason, to do with the relative failure of the Jews and the outstanding success of the Greeks? The Jewish people were not monotheists in a philosophical sense, as is evident both from the words of the Commandment 'Thou shalt have none other gods *before* me', and from their continual backslidings in respect of it; and in the case of the Greeks the formation of a pantheon round Father Zeus, and even the exaltation of human heroes to a place in it, is clearly viewed by Hegel as one of the grounds of their superiority.[4] As for belief in immortality, he must surely have known that it played no part in the public or 'folk' religion of the Greeks, or of the Jews either—at least in the period before their 'degradation'.[5]

The answer to this problem is quickly given. Rational reflection is the final stage in the development of religious consciousness both for the individual and for the people. It is the mark of full maturity; and hence, as any botanist or any student of Aristotle knows, it is the defining characteristic of the species. A folk-religion has only come to proper maturity when these philosophical

[1] The same consideration governs his choice of an example when he complains in the *Phenomenology* that pure reason alone cannot tell us how to regulate property rights. More is contained in the law of Moses than in the law of Kant, and the contrary only appears to be the case because the organization of an actual society is presupposed by the latter: cf. *Inwiefern ist Religion* (Nohl, p. 356).

[2] This is, I think, a reasonable inference from the remarks in *Inwiefern ist Religion* (Nohl, p. 355).

[3] Cf. *Man lehrt unsre Kinder* (Nohl, p. 359) and *Religion ist eine* (Nohl, p. 28; see p. 507 below).

[4] Compare the later discussion of the requirement that the doctrines of a folk-religion must be rational—especially Nohl, p. 23; pp. 501–2 below—and the remark about deification of folk-heroes, Nohl, pp. 26–7; p. 505 below.

[5] Pericles' Funeral Oration I take as a decisive document for Hegel's conception of the public religion of the Greeks. I have no knowledge of how Mosaic religion was expounded at Tübingen, but if I am wrong in thinking that Hegel saw the need to distinguish the religion of Moses from that of the Psalmist and the Prophets, this only accentuates the paradoxical fact that the Jewish religion was more 'rational' than that of the Greeks.

insights are proclaimed in the form that is appropriate to it—by Plato, by the prophets, and by Jesus,[1] or for Protestant Germany by Kant and Fichte.

One further point needs to be made about the definition. Hegel seems here to identify 'folk-religion' with the 'public religion' that he is explicitly defining. The two conceptions are not however identical, for 'public' religion is something opposed to or contrasted with 'private' religion, whereas 'folk-religion' is a more inclusive concept, ultimately indeed an all-inclusive concept. All the phenomena of 'private' religion—phenomena which arise either in private consciousness or in group activities which are consciously distinguished from the politico-legal structure and the traditions and *mores* of a 'people'—can also form part of, or have their analogues in, any fully developed, naturally perfect folk-religion. Hegel approaches 'folk-religion' through the conception of public religion, because a folk-religion is *minimally* a system of publicly recognized and publicly shared religious observances.

In framing his initial definition Hegel deliberately leaves Christianity out of account, for a reason which he goes on to indicate by saying that, although the doctrines have remained the same since its inception,[2] attention and emphasis have been focused on different aspects at different times. As a result, although he does not explicitly say so, Christianity cannot be regarded as a single folk-religion at all. Even in the history of Germany, which is all that concerns him, we can see from his notes that Hegel distinguished sharply between the Catholicism of the medieval feudal society and the Protestantism of his own time.[3]

---

[1] Jesus is a transitional figure. There is not much evidence in the Tübingen fragments that Hegel has begun to ponder the relation of Jesus to the Jews. At this stage he seems to think of him only as the founder of primitive Christianity, which is, I think, the model case of a 'private religion' in his mind, rather than a distinct folk-religion in its own right. But the evidence of the manuscripts is not decisive on this point.

[2] We may well wonder whether he really believed this; and the answer probably depends on how much is included in 'die Hauptlehren'. Of course if only the 'Ideen der Vernunft' are meant, the assertion is almost trivially true. But all of Hegel's explicit references to Christianity have to be interpreted with caution in the light of his practical aims. Only in the preparatory notes intended for his own eyes alone does he say exactly what he thinks about the religion of his own *Volk*—even his references to the Judaic tradition are somewhat guarded for the same reason. We must always remember that he meant ultimately to publish his work as a contribution to the coming of the 'Kingdom of God'.

[3] See especially *Die Formen der andern Bilder* (Nohl, pp. 358–9). It is not clear how far he regarded Protestantism and Catholicism as distinct folk-

In any case he felt that his own society had grown old and was now in decay. The sign of this was that religion had now become an instrument of political oppression, rather than a fount of patriotic freedom, and religious observance was now a matter of gloomy talk rather than joyful activity.[1]

With this comment Hegel's introductory section ends. The next section is concerned with a philosophical analysis of religious experience in which the central aim is to distinguish practical, living, concrete religious experience from theoretical, dead, abstract, theological knowledge. The categories that he employs for this purpose are 'subjective' and 'objective' religion. He notes that his distinction is closely analogous to the distinction made by Fichte in the *Kritik aller Offenbarung* between 'religion' and 'theology'; but the way that he does so strongly suggests that he had arrived at his own distinction and terminology independently before he ever read Fichte.[2] For the moment the Greeks and the Jews are forgotten and Hegel's interest is focused on the religious life of his own time.

The fact that the basic dichotomy he wants to make comes so close to being a direct opposition between theoretical reflection and practical activity—though it is not really as simple as that— has caused some misunderstanding on the part of students who have not paid sufficient attention to the relation between religious practice and religious reflection established in his opening pages.

'Objective religion' is primarily the content of the faith, the dogmas of a religion, the creed, but also the ceremonial forms

religions in contemporary Germany. He may well have felt unable to decide this question and the wish he expressed in 1800 to live in a Catholic city may perhaps have been conditioned by his uncertainty about it.

[1] Nohl, p. 6; p. 483–4 below. For the reasons stated on p. 128 n. 2 Hegel leaves the reader to shade in the darkest patches for himself. He speaks of attachment to tradition and of 'dragging fetters', but explicit reference to the alliance of religion and despotism is confined to his Berne notes (Nohl, p. 360) and of course it is explicit in his correspondence with Schelling two years later (*Briefe*, i. 24). Nor does he actually *say* that Christian sermons are gloomy—he leaves his radiant picture of Greek festivals to make the point by implication.

[2] Nohl, p. 355; cf. also Nohl, p. 9; p. 487 below. The distinctions are not in fact identical, for objective religion would include practices and observances carried out mechanically or under duress, whereas theology is a cognitive or theoretical domain only. The difference here points up one of the main contrasts between Hegel on the one side and Kant and Fichte on the other. Whereas they thought of religious experience as a form of individual cognition which led, or ought to lead, to social action, he thought of it as a form of social action which led, or ought to lead, to individual cognition.

and procedures one must learn and be trained to perform in order to take part in public worship. It is a matter of *Verstand* (which we might perhaps translate here as 'technical understanding')[1] and *Gedächtnis* (memory). It is something that can be taught verbally, whereas subjective religion is a matter of direct experience in feeling and action. Thus subjective religion is essentially personal and individual, whereas objective religion is essentially abstract and common. The community of subjective religion is like the order of living nature, where every creature lives its own life and has its own purposes, but they all nevertheless depend on one another; whereas the abstract system of objective religion (expressed in a handbook of faith and practice) is like the cabinet of the naturalist, where everything is killed and then pinned into its place in a logical order that answers the singular, purely theoretical purpose of the investigator.

Hegel does not explicitly say that any religion *must* have an objective content that can be communicated and ordered in this way. But he appears to take this for granted.[2] He is more interested in the fact that the objective content of any folk-religion is a small and relatively unimportant part of it. He says, indeed, that a single objective religion might even be shared by the whole world, whereas it is not at all certain that he regarded a universal folk-religion as possible.[3] The subjective meaning

[1] I cannot agree with Peperzak's claim (p. 41) that *Vernunft* and *Verstand* are used synonymously in the Tübingen fragment. Indeed I do not think he really means what he says (although I am not sure what else he means), for his list of instances is entirely confined to the word *Vernunft*. Perhaps he means that Hegel uses *Vernunft* to refer indifferently to both of the faculties that *Kant* distinguished. But his list of instances does not prove *that* by any means (the one example that looks as if it might do so (Nohl, p. 5) turns out to be inaccurately cited). In general Hegel uses *Vernunft* and especially *bloße Vernunft* to mean what Kant calls *praktische Vernunft*, although in one or two places it may have the richer meaning that he later gave it himself (and first accorded to it in his notes from Garve's *Prüfung der Fähigkeiten* in 1787: see above, Chapter I, pp. 36–9). He is in difficulty now, because in 1787 he only wanted to contrast verbal knowledge with real experience, whereas now he wants to distinguish *two* types of real experience—one where *Vernunft* is alienated from sensibility and one where it is not. Again, even if not alienated, it may be linked with sensibility in the wrong way, as when one is 'deaf to the voice of conscience' (cf. Nohl, p. 7, though Hegel does not use the word *Vernunft* there).

[2] It seems to me to follow logically from his definition of 'public' religion and folk-religion in terms of one another that *any folk-religion must have an objective content*.

[3] All folk-religion terminates in rational religion. If everyone were to arrive at this terminus together, we should have the Kingdom of God realized or the

and force of the religion will differ for each individual, and individuals at different stages of human development will be impressed by different aspects of the objective doctrine and practice. Some cannot be reached by sensible appeals to the higher gentler emotions, but only by stimuli that arouse awe and fear. Some are deaf to the voice of conscience and heedful only of arguments that appeal to self-interest.

'Man is an entity [*Wesen*] compounded of sensibility and reason', as Hegel noted in one of his preparatory outlines. 'But the main body, the stuff from which everything in him is formed is sensibility.'[1] Hence it is natural that, here and elsewhere, he regularly considers the practical impact of religion on the emotions *before* its influence on the reason, though that too is of practical importance. And because instruction about the objective content of religion is an intellectual process, he is naturally very conscious of the danger of suffocating religious feeling and thereby preventing the proper development of reason by placing too much emphasis upon it. His own 'tenacious memory' had been stuffed with catechisms and explanations of doctrine for many long years, and he had himself come to the point where much that he was required to do and say had lost its proper significance for him.

The right development of *Vernunft* begins not with religious instruction, but with the development of the 'moral feelings' of which the seeds are innate in human nature. There is no need here to invoke the name of Shaftesbury and the philosophy of the moral sense, although the idea may well have reached Hegel, directly or indirectly, from that source. His own text shows clearly enough that he is thinking of the 'sensibility for the gentler images of love' (*Sinn für die sanftern Vorstellungen von Liebe*) which he mentioned a little earlier.[2] For right development these feelings

invisible Church made visible. This consummation is definitely not a real possibility, however, but an ideal of reason, for if a man sins he ceases to be a member of the invisible Church, but not of his folk-religion (Nohl, p. 357). Now any folk-religion is distinguished from others by virtue of its distinct history and traditions. So a universal folk-religion *could* be conceived if we are willing to postulate some new and greater Theseus who is able to unite all of our folk-religions into a new pantheon. Something like this was certainly envisaged by Mazzini when he founded 'Young Europe'. Hölderlin, at least, seems to have dreamed of something of this sort (Beck, Letter 65: *GSA*, vi. 92–3), and it is possible that Hegel did too when he wrote (Letter 8, *Briefe*, i. 18): 'Das Reich Gottes komme.'

[1] *Aber die Hauptmasse*, Nohl, p. 357.

[2] Nohl, pp. 7–8. See Nohl, p. 51 for a passage (written in 1794 at Berne) in

need to be guided by, and linked with, the two postulates of practical reason which form the rational core of all subjective religion. This rational core is to be looked for in the doctrines of divine providence associated with each religion. Apart from this, all systems of religious ideas are simply 'theology' (in Fichte's sense) and are a product of *Verstand*, not of *Vernunft*.

At this point the second section of Hegel's discussion ends with his declaration (cited earlier) that what he is concerned with is the question of *how* religion becomes subjective. Accordingly he gives to the next section the title 'Subjective religion'. It seems that at first he intended to go on employing Fichte's distinction between 'religion' and 'theology'. For as we saw he has just dismissed all 'scientific or rather metaphysical knowledge of God' as 'theology, not religion'; and he originally gave to his new section the heading 'The way religion acts: (*a*) how the mind [*Gemüt*] must be constituted in order that it may gain entry, (*b*) once it has gained entry, how does it act?' It is clear enough, I think, that he abandoned this complex title because he found it necessary to recur quite soon to the topic of *Verstand*—which is excluded from *Religion* in Fichte's usage.[1]

The opening of the third section is largely a repetition and expansion of the ideas about subjective religion already set forth. But the conception of superstition (*Aberglauben*) is now for the

which Hegel himself invokes the name of Shaftesbury. But the most probable source of most of his opinions about human sensibility, and particularly about the emotions of love, sympathy, and friendship is, in my view, Rousseau.

[1] In the opening paragraphs of the section the terminology is Fichte's. Hegel's own distinction (between 'subjective' and 'objective' religion) recurs at the beginning of the fourth paragraph. At the end of the section the argument shifts to the opposition of *Verstand* and *Herz* and Hegel needs a more inclusive conception of religious experience within which this contrast can be situated.

Just here however, there is either a lacuna of eight pages caused by the loss of sheet *e*, or else, as I am inclined to believe, Hegel made a slip in the marking of his sheets. (This is a section where it would be very useful to know just where in our text the transitions from sheet to sheet are. It does rather look as if this section with the corrected heading 'Subjektive Religion' might be an originally independent fragment incorporated into his manuscript by Hegel himself.)

Against the view that no sheet marked *e* has been lost, it must be mentioned that Rosenkranz inserted in the excerpts from this manuscript that he printed, a sentence which is not to be found in the manuscripts we have (see Nohl, p. 20). Nohl suggests that it may have come from sheet *e* (presumably because he felt it would fit in with the trend of the argument at the end of sheet *d*). But if my analysis of Hegel's introductory section is right it may just as well have come from the unquestionably missing inside pages of sheet *a*. (We should remember also the missing inside pages of *Inwiefern ist Religion*.)

first time introduced. Religion is declared to be *superstition* in two cases where it provides what Hegel regards as the wrong sort of foundation for action. First when it governs our behaviour in matters where we ought to be governed by ordinary prudence (*Klugheit*). One supposes that dietary regulations may well be a case that Hegel had in mind here. Secondly when we allow ourselves to be governed by prudence in a religious context: i.e. when we seek to turn away the wrath of God by actions which are supposed to placate him. But this superstitious image of God as behaving like a man, and subject to the limits of our sensibility is, as Hegel has already said and now repeats once more, the one that properly belongs to a certain stage in human development; and though there may not be much morality in it at its crudest, it can be increasingly moralized through the development of the sentiments of gratitude to God and reliance upon him in all undertakings. In other words Hegel concedes that fear is not a moral motive, and that anthropomorphism is superstition; but he holds firmly to his view that faith in God's providence and justice is an essential element in rational religion, which is primitively expressed in these erroneous forms.

He supports his claim that the subjective religion of all good men is in essence identical, whatever their objective religion may be, by citing Nathan's remark to the Friar: 'What to you makes me a Christian, makes you to me a Jew.'[1] This makes explicit what was previously only implied—the view that folk-religions are only distinguishable from each other on their objective side; and already we can see looming over the ideal of the living folk-religion that problem of 'positivity', of being unavoidably tied to a particular set of historical traditions and customs, which contain the seeds of its decay and death.

Hitherto Hegel has considered the destructive power of *Verstand* only as stifling the development of the individual. But now it appears for the first time as a *socially* divisive power which sets men against one another, each side being convinced of the superior truth and value of its own verbal formulas. Hegel points the contrast between the freezing power of *Verstand* and the warmth of sympathy and natural feeling which the spectacle of devotion to God, under any of his names, arouses in the heart of any subjectively religious person. His first impulse at this point was to invoke the

---

[1] Lessing, *Nathan the Wise*, Act IV, Scene 7 (Everyman edn., p. 197).

example of creative rationality set by Theseus in uniting the different tribes into a single city, Athens, by establishing a pantheon of their Gods; but he struck out Theseus' name and substituted the examples of Coriolanus and Gustavus Adolphus, a Roman and a modern Protestant leader who typified for him the primitive piety of true feeling. The implied connection between true religion and devotion to the principles of political freedom is especially noteworthy here.

Having offered a Roman and a Protestant man of action to exemplify the essential identity of religious feelings, Hegel offers us a Greek and an early Christian Father, Socrates and Tertullian, as examples of contrasting types of religious men of thought. Tertullian takes Socrates as an atheist, who made an offering to the son of Apollo only because the oracle had recognized his wisdom. But Hegel now offers his own definitive interpretation of 'Socrates' Cock'—about which as we know he had been collecting divergent opinions for some years—as a thank-offering to the god of healing for the gift of death which Socrates considered as a healing of mortality.[1]

The dialectic of his next paragraph, the last of this section as we have it, is more subtle than most commentators have perceived. For his initial text is that 'the heart must speak more loudly than the *Verstand*'. In support he cites the story of the woman whom tradition identifies as Mary Magdalen, and of how Jesus justified her impulsive act in anointing him, against the objections of the disciples, who quite correctly said that the ointment she had used might have been sold for charitable ends. He clearly implies that the disciples were rationalizing their own failure of sympathy, and that this is what we are always doing if we stop to think it over whenever we have a generous impulse. Then he turns quite suddenly

---

[1] Nohl, p. 11; cf. *Dok.*, pp. 10 and 86–7, and Chapter I, pp. 14–16 above. When we compare this paragraph about Socrates with Hegel's reflections about the Greek attitude toward atheism in the fragmentary *Aber die Hauptmasse* we can see that there was an unresolved problem in Hegel's 'Hellenic ideal'. In the light of those notes, furthermore, Hegel's switch here, from the example of Theseus at the beginning of the Athenian experience to that of Socrates at the end of it, seems to indicate that he has already begun to wrestle with the tragic destiny of the Greek religion of beauty. It was, after all, not the Romans or the Christians who put Socrates to death and threatened Aristotle, but those same Athenians who laughed at the gods with Aristophanes at their great festivals (cf. Nohl, p. 357). Even when he penned his first eulogy of the Greek spirit, Hegel had already recognized that it was self-doomed.

to a rather different contrast involving *Verstand*: Gellert's claim that a Christian child knows more of God than the wisest of pagan sages. This, Hegel says, is just like Tertullian's remark that a Christian artisan easily understands all the things about the creator of the world, which Plato says are so difficult to discover and even more difficult to tell about. It is easy to see that both authors could defend their claim by reference to a text which we might think Hegel would find rather embarrassing in the present context: 'Suffer little children to come unto me, for of such is the Kingdom of God' etc. But Hegel is armoured against this retort also, for he says that even the heart of Frederick II is worth more than a manual of morality, which one can ,if one chooses, use to wrap stinking cheese in; and he then justifies the equation of Gellert's child and Tertullian's workman with the manual on the grounds that like the book their minds contain nothing but the verbal formulas—they lack the experience, which the sinners Frederick II and Mary Magdalen had, which alone provides concrete consciousness of what the words mean.[1] Thus Hegel's doctrine is that the impulse of the heart must be heeded first— and not inhibited by reflective criticism—but that it is not sufficient or authoritative by itself. We must express it and experience it in order to arrive at moral consciousness and eventually reach philosophical wisdom. Gellert's child must experience life to the full— like Frederick II, not like Tertullian's *opifex christianus*—in order to achieve the moral consciousness of the repentant Magdalen,[2] and finally the philosophical insight of the 'wisest of the pagans', Plato.

At this point we pass from sheet *d* of the manuscript to sheet *f*. It may be that in sheet *e* Hegel went on to develop his doctrine of 'experience', and to set it in still sharper contrast with the life that is effectively insulated against real experience by a cloud of verbal doctrines fabricated by the understanding. The sentence that

---

[1] There is here, I think, an implicit analogy between the stuffing of simple minds with 'the theological sourdough and the catechism' and tearing the pages out of a book of moral philosophy to wrap stinking cheese (Nohl, p. 11; p. 489 below. Hegel's references are to Gellert's poem 'Der Christ', and to Tertullian, *Apologeticum* 46.)

[2] Whereas Frederick had a 'zuweilen ungerechte Herz'—i.e. he was partially governed by the cold calculations of selfish prudence—the woman of the Gospel was 'ill-famed' but certainly open to 'the gentler images of love' (cf. Nohl, p. 7). The seeds of Hegel's Frankfurt doctrine of reconciliation with life through love are quite apparent here.

Rosenkranz inserted in his excerpt from a later section can be fitted in very naturally here, upon this hypothesis: 'Men, early immersed in the dead sea of moral verbiage, emerge certainly invulnerable like Achilles; but their human power is also drowned in it.' But it is also possible that this sentence comes from the lost centre leaf of sheet *a*, and that there never was any sheet *e* because in marking his sheets Hegel omitted the letter *e* by accident; for the transition here to the next section on 'Enlightenment—the intent to work through *Verstand*', is natural enough.

As we already know, *Verstand* serves only for the elaboration of objective religion. But in identifying it as the principle of the *Aufklärung* Hegel does not mean to underestimate or misprize either of them. An index of this is the fact that he names Lessing's *Nathan* as one of the fruits of *Verstand*, and he has already explicitly indicated how much his own conception of the union of feeling and reason in subjective religion owes to that work. We should remember in dealing with his subsequent strictures against *Verstand* that since, or in so far as, they apply to *Nathan*, they apply also to his own work and he is quite aware of it.

Verstand has no practical direction in itself. All it can do is to provide the plausible semblance of rational justification for the impulses of self-love; genuinely rational principles are only given practical effect by the higher impulses of altruism. Enlightenment of understanding might bring us to accept the utilitarian principle that we cannot be happy without virtue; but this calculation is too subtle and too cold to be an effective motive at the moment of decision or in the general conduct of life.[1]

Thus learning the best manual of moral philosophy by heart and trying to apply it will only result in the making of bad decisions or no decisions. This is not what the writers of manuals want students to do, but it is all that one can do with a manual. The idea that enlightenment of the understanding can prevent the development of evil impulses is a mistake, and the use of a manual of enlightened morality as a censoring authority is in conflict with the

---

[1] Nohl, p. 12. There is certainly a flaw in Hegel's reasoning here. It has always been rightly urged against any moral calculus that we cannot apply it in the particular circumstances of most moral decisions. But a calculus obviously can be, and is, applied in making long-term plans; and Hegel generally recognizes this. His real argument against this 'Einfluß aufs Leben überhaupt' is that it is always pernicious, because it produces an impoverished existence by stifling and denying the impulses of our nature even before we are aware of them.

fundamental principle of all enlightenment—that a man must act
and decide for himself, not let others act for him.[1]

The 'enlightening of a people' is a more appropriate object of
intellectual endeavour. What is involved here is a programme of
removing religious prejudices, which like the enlightenment that
replaces them are products of *Verstand*. These prejudices are of
two different types: false beliefs on the one hand, and true beliefs
the grounds of which are not understood, on the other. Prejudices
of both kinds can be removed by a clearer understanding of causal
relations, for in general they are based on mistaken concepts of
causality suggested by sense experience, and imaginative extra-
polation.[2] But we must not, of course, suppose that intellectual
analyses can remove the selfish practical impulses that hide behind
the prejudices.

The enlightenment of the understanding, proceeding as it does
by argument and discussion, is an essentially endless process which
cannot produce final results. No mortal man therefore can finally
declare what is true on this level. This does not mean, however,
that we cannot recognize the universal validity of the practical
principles on which all human society is founded. These principles
are evident to 'healthy human understanding' (*dem gesunden
Menschenverstande einleuchten*) on the one hand, and they lie at the
foundation of 'every religion worthy of the name' on the other.
It is certain that there are not many of these principles, since they
are necessarily very abstract, and indeed 'when they are expressed
in their pure form as reason [*Vernunft*] requires' they conflict with
experience and sensible appearance. 'They are not a rule for it,
but are only consistent with an opposite order of things.' Hence

[1] Nohl, p. 12. This is the first of two explicit references by Hegel to Campe's
Theophron, 'the experienced adviser to inexperienced youth', which he acquired
in the fall of 1785 (*Dok.*, p. 24). He may well have tried to learn it by heart when
he was fifteen, for he tells us, a little further on, what the subjective consequences
of such an experiment would be. Here he is only concerned with objective results.
There is also, I think, an implicit reference to Kant's 'What is Enlightenment'
(1784) in this passage. My analysis makes this hypothetical allusion rather more
explicit.

[2] It should be noted that most religious prejudices are by Hegel's canons a
mixture of true belief with false. To take the example that seems to be implicitly
referred to in his text, belief in miracles is a mere superstition (false belief) in so
far as we hold that the ordinary course of nature can somehow or other be
suspended. But it is a true belief (or so Hegel would argue) in so far as it is the
expression of a calm trust in divine providence which does not look for any
miraculous interventions on its own behalf.

they do not easily get 'living recognition' from the people and when learned by heart 'they still make no part of the spiritual and desirous system of man'.[1]

Hegel is now face to face with the difficulty created by the yoking, in his original definition, of the immortal horse of Kantian practical reason with the mortal one of religious mythology, to borrow a Platonic image that he would find appropriate. The rational principles are found at the basis of every religion 'worthy of the name'. But the fact that this qualification is needed destroys most, if not all of the evidential value of the historical record of human religious experience as a support for the principles. This does not matter much, since Hegel is concerned not with the adoption of a theoretical belief on the basis of evidence, but with the clarification of a practical faith that one already has. But the unavoidable necessity of an experienced content in that faith, the impossibility that a folk-religion, a *positive* religion, as Hegel now for the first time calls it, should ever be confined within 'the bounds of reason alone', or should ever do more than *point towards* the ideals of practical reason on which it is 'founded', was a focus for anxious meditation on his part for several years to come. Rational religion is a terminus at which only a tiny minority of dedicated and highly gifted men will ever arrive. The moral virtue of ordinary citizens must rest on the practice of a folk-religion that has been handed down to us. Enlightened criticism of this religious practice should not go beyond the setting of it in its right light as a technique for the development of the sentiment of *devotion*.

At this point Hegel cannot help asking himself whether enlightened criticism can even do this—as he clearly holds that it must and will do, and indeed already has done in the Reformation —without destroying the living force of religious devotion.[2] He

---

[1] Nohl, pp. 13–14; pp. 491 f. below. The reference here is of course to the doctrine of practical reason in Kant and Fichte, and we have a very clear instance of Hegel's difficulty over terminology. For he is dealing with something that is proper to *reason* in his sense—the *Grundsätze* of 'menschlichen Wissen *in concreto*'. But what is provided by Kant and Fichte is only technical understanding (*Verstand*) in his sense of the term.

By a slip Hegel left out the verb that expresses the relation of the intelligible to the sensible world. Nohl supplies *widersprechen*, which is very plausible in the light of Kant's doctrine of the antinomies. But I have deliberately tried to be as neutral as possible—both here and in my translation—and not to supply more than is absolutely required by the context.

[2] To suppose—as Haering and other pious critics do—that when Hegel asks, as he does here, how far abstract reasoning can enter into religion without

knew perfectly well from his own personal experience that long reflection about the origins and social use of religious practices or the history of dogma destroyed their 'halo of sanctity'. If one knows that 'divine service' is really a matter of one's daily life, the knowledge certainly changes one's attitude toward church-going. But it does not in itself enable one to live any better. Wisdom is not acquired by the mathematical method any more than it was earlier by syllogisms. Of course understanding and its science does not cause one to live any worse either.[1] It has always its own proper instrumental value, but that is quite incommensurable with such higher (moral) values as goodness and purity of heart.

Thus the implicit answer to the question how far abstract reasoning can enter into religion without destroying it is the one given at the end of the preceding section. *Verstand* should not be allowed to inhibit or strangle the natural expression of the higher emotions. Just how it may do this is illustrated by considering more closely the subjective experience of a youth who, in his innocence, sets himself to learn Campe's *Theophron* by heart and to guide his own conduct by it. Real moral knowledge is a product of long experience, whereas our youth will be quite sick of his experiment in a week. He will be indecisive and worried about everything, which will make him intensely irritating to others; too timid to enjoy anything properly; always willing to give way from a sense of his own imperfection. The breaking-point, at least in Hegel's picture—which may perhaps be autobiographical—is the nervous strain imposed by shyness in his relations with the opposite sex.[2]

destroying it (Nohl, p. 14; cf. also p. 355), he means to defend religion against its attack, is to ignore the process of his development and the sources of his own thought. He was anxious only that we should not throw away the baby with the bath-water, and take abstract reasoning as a substitute for the actual experience that we reason about. We must reason fearlessly, whatever perishes as a result. Hegel was never one to cry over spilt milk. Even in his eulogy of the Greeks, where he seems momentarily close to fruitless lamentation, it is obvious that he never felt any inclination to side with the people against Socrates. Nor did he at any time sympathize with Jacobi's appeal to religious feeling against the rationalist criticism of his contemporaries.

[1] This is a point which the critics overlook, although the very paragraph after the sarcastic comments about mathematical method and syllogism emphasizes that 'Aufklärung bleibt . . . ein schöner Vorzug'. Hegel's view is that *Verstand* is morally neutral. Of course, in its capacity as a flattering courtier of self-love *Verstand* is always liable to make us worse; but it is equally at the disposition of the higher kind of love if that has been allowed to develop properly.

[2] The experiment, if it took place, occurred when he was fifteen or sixteen

At this point, when we might think the topic exhausted, it emerges that Hegel really wants to distinguish two types of enlightenment—or rather two types of men among those who are called enlightened. This should not surprise us, for we saw in his earliest meditations on the subject a tendency to distinguish genuine spiritual enlightenment from the vainglorious superiority of the *Buchstabenmensch*. The concept of the 'man of the letter' was actually coined by Moses Mendelssohn, from whom Hegel copied his first notes on *Aufklärung*; the first reference to the concept itself in his papers is in a quotation from Lessing's *Nathan*. It is amusing to see how with an obvious bow towards these two earliest masters of his, he makes a little bonfire of all the *Buchstaben* of the Enlightenment to which he had himself become addicted at Stuttgart and Tübingen: *Aufklärung, Menschenkenntnis, Geschichte der Menschheit, Glückseligkeit, Volkommenheit,* all of them are dismissed almost like the *theologische Sauerteig*, as a 'sapless phlegm that cripples free movement in every limb'. But of course he would not be interested in the death-dealing power of these 'letters' if he did not believe that beneath them flows the life-giving power of the spirit.[1]

By clarifying the theological sourdough, the enlightened understanding erects the imposing theoretical structures of rational theology. But this is still only objective religion. It is a palace of the intellect in which mere men cannot dwell. Every man must build his own little home for himself in the world—or in other words he must think for himself and make his own decisions.[2]

(see above, p. 137 n. 1). Hegel had already arrived at his conception of the relation of *Vernunft* and *Verstand* by Mar. 1787 when he wrote his notes on Garve. If we suppose that he took his own Latin eloquence seriously, we could argue that he was in the right state of mind for the enactment of this solemn farce in March 1786 (*Dok.,* pp. 28–31). But perhaps nothing much more than a *Gedankenexperiment* occurred even at that time.

[1] Nohl, pp. 16–17 (see pp. 493–5 below). Theword that Hegel uses first is again Lessing's expression *Buchgelehrsamkeit,* for which cf. *Dok.,* pp. 49 and 169. *Buchstabenmensch* occurs on the next page, and there are several references to Mendelssohn's *Jerusalem* in *Inwiefern ist Religion* which was probably the earliest of Hegel's outlines for the Tübingen fragment (Nohl, pp. 355–7).

[2] Nohl, pp. 17 (see pp. 494–5 below). Actually Hegel uses two not quite consistent metaphors in successive paragraphs here in a way which reveals that he is not clear in his own mind what point he wishes to make. First he contrasts living in a place where one does not even know all the rooms, with living in a small house one has made for oneself, turning over every stone and personally laying it in place. Then he contrasts the castle-dweller (the castle being the *new* one at Versailles) with the *paterfamilias* living in his ancestral home (which, obviously,

The question how far religion can aid us in this brings us back to our main topic of folk-religion—now contrasted with private religion.

The transition from objective to subjective religion, from the realm of the letter to that of the spirit, is marked not only by reference to Lessing's *Nathan* again but by the use of the term *Vernunft* instead of *Verstand*. The religion of Nathan is exactly what Hegel describes under the heading *reiner Vernunftreligion*; and there can be no doubt that in Nathan himself it is completely 'subjective'. He is the model case of the wise man who at the end of a long life of devotion really exemplifies pure reason in its practical exercise. When compared with his active rational piety, the traditional forms of piety appear as mere superstition. But even Nathan recognizes in his parable of the three rings and in other utterances that 'a universal spiritual church is a mere ideal of reason', existing only in the realm of the spirit and forever bound to remain invisible.[1] The highest achievable ideal in a visible church, a public folk-religion, is that of minimizing as far as possible the occasions for literalism and fetishism, and maximizing as far as possible the acceptance of *Vernunftreligion*.

Since he accepts not only the conception of obedience to practical reason as the consummation of ethics, but also the postulate of

he cannot have built for himself). The first metaphor remains within the context of Hegel's Enlightenment heritage. It expresses Nathan's contrast between *personal knowledge* and *book learning*. The second is more distinctively Hegelian, since the contrast here is between membership in *two types of community*, one that is constitutive of one's 'ethical substance' (the family and the *Volk*) and one that is not (the world of *Verstand*).

Each of the metaphors says something which Hegel regarded as important and true. But clearly the second one is more fundamental and the implications or intimations of the first are false so far as they conflict with it. The 'bourgeois' overtones of the metaphor(s) have been remarked on by other critics; and there are clear indications in Hegel's notes that he was quite aware that he was here invoking a value that was peculiar to his own society and which was not without its dark side. See *Die Formen der andern Bilder*, where he contrasts the old feudal hall in which everyone ate and slept together with the modern private chamber, in a way which is by no means to the advantage of the latter. The pattern of life in the Greek city is, of course, exalted above both (Nohl, pp. 358–9). (It is one of the quaintest ironies of intellectual history that Kierkegaard should have employed the same metaphor in one of his most celebrated diatribes against 'the System'.)

[1] Compare Nohl, pp. 17 and 357 (first paragraph), with Kant *Religion, Akad.*, vi. 101. There is no explicit reference to *Nathan* in this paragraph of Hegel's text but the question he is answering is framed in terms derived from that source and the parallels are, I think, obvious.

immortality, Hegel has to accommodate the Kantian ideal of holiness in his scheme:

> When the ideal [*Idee*] of holiness is set up in moral philosophy as the ultimate apex of ethical conduct [*Sittlichkeit*] and the ultimate limit of all striving, the objections of those who say that such an ideal is not attainable by man (which our moralists themselves grant anyway) but that, apart from pure respect for the law, he needs other motives, motives which affect his sensibility—these objections do not so much go to show that man ought not to strive to come ever closer to that ideal even for all eternity, but only that in savagery [*Roheit*] and when there is a powerful propensity toward sensibility [*Hang zur Sinnlichkeit*]—in most men ⟨we⟩ frequently have to be content with the production of legality . . .[1]

The rather embarrassed and indirect way in which Hegel refers to his own aims and endeavours here, arises probably from his consciousness that as far as life in this world is concerned there is a quite dramatic difference between his attitude and that of Kant, in spite of his acceptance of the regulative ideal of holiness. He can afford to concede that holiness is the 'letzte Punkt des Bestrebens' only because that limit is the terminus of an infinite process. But in reality his conception of the 'letzte Höhe der Sittlichkeit' for man is a concrete ideal that can actually be realized, for he believes that the Greeks realized it; and whatever may be true in eternity it is quite clear that in this life the regulative ideal of holiness has only an instrumental role in the achievement of 'the holy, delicate web of human sensations'.[2] Hegel allows it to appear that the converse is the case, that the moralization of the lower impulses

---

[1] Nohl, pp. 17–18. Peperzak (p. 40 n.) has drawn attention to the connection between this passage and a passage in Kant's essay 'On the radical evil in human nature' (*Berlinische Monatschrift*, Apr. 1792: see *Religion, Akad.*, vi., pp. 28–30).

[2] It is almost certainly no accident that Hegel calls the web of sensations 'holy' immediately before discussing the Kantian ideal (see Nohl, p. 16). The necessary bridge is provided by his account of how the 'moral feeling' has to send out its 'delicate tendrils' over the 'whole web' of the empirical character. Of course, once he gave up the Kantian postulates, as a result of the fuller development of his own postulate of 'Providence', which in the present work appears alongside of them, the whole Kantian conception of the 'supersensible world' at once took on the character of an illusory looking-glass land in which all relations are inverted. But he always continued to hold that the 'inverted world' is a *necessary* illusion at a certain stage of rational development, and in the realm of practical reason at least, we can already see why he thought so. (The metaphor of the web and of weaving, which plays such a large role in his discussion, is derived, I think, from Plato's *Politicus*.)

is a stage in the infinite process of approximation to rational holiness, because this belief does no practical harm, and it would therefore be almost immoral, by the standards of Lessing's *Nathan*, to provoke a theoretical quarrel. It does no harm because it is quite true that, in order to find the way in which all human needs and feelings are to be harmonized and all human capacities fully expressed and enjoyed we must fix our gaze on the 'letzte Punkt alles Strebens', the abstract ideal of holiness. But this self-discipline that produces virtue is distinct from the experience of virtue itself. Once the web of human sensations is properly woven we can enjoy life and its activities for its own sake.

 Because our natural impulses require to be developed under rational control, Hegel can even assimilate Kant's doctrine that 'respect for the law' is the only moral motive in the same instrumental way. Thus he admits in one sentence that 'compassion, benevolence, friendship' are *not* moral motives, because they do not spring from respect for the law. But in the next he asserts that 'the moral sense [*das moralische Gefühl*] must send its delicate threads out through the whole web' of the empirical character, to which it thus belongs (whatever Kant may say). The bridge between the 'good tendencies' of nature and the 'moral feeling' is provided by the concept of love which is the *Grundprinzip* of the empirical character. For love is analogous to reason in that

just as love finds itself in other men, or rather forgetting itself—puts itself outside of its own existence, and, so to speak, lives, feels, and acts in others—so likewise reason, as the principle of universally valid laws, knows itself again in every rational being, recognizing itself as fellow citizen of an intelligible world. The empirical character of man is certainly affected by desire and aversion [*Lust and Unlust*], ⟨—⟩ love, even if it is a pathological principle of action, is disinterested [*uneigen-nützig*], it does not do good actions because it has calculated that ⟨the⟩ joys that arise from its actions will be less mixed and longer lasting than those of sensibility or those that spring from the satisfaction of any passion—thus it is not the principle of refined self-love, where the ego is in the end always the ultimate goal.[1]

Here Hegel is, as it were, driven into a corner, and is forced to point out that although what Kant says about love is not exactly wrong, he has none the less overlooked something which is of fundamental importance—the great contrast that exists between

[1] Nohl, p. 18.

selfish and unselfish love. What is not clear in Hegel's own account is the relation between these two. It is only by taking them together that he is able to assert plausibly that love is the *Grundprinzip* of the empirical character, and his whole positive ideal of the 'holy web of human feeling' depends on this principle, so that for him as for Origen, even the Devil himself must in the end be saved.[1] As far as we can see from his text his view is that love only becomes selfish through the premature intervention of reflection (*Verstand*); but he probably held (already in 1793, as he certainly did in 1797) that man's natural needs force upon the spontaneous sense of life a distinction between self and other that is originally foreign to it.

Principles can only be derived from rational ideals. But in any case the question of how to bring men closer to these ideals can only be settled by considering the situation they are actually in and the capacities for good that they actually have, says Hegel. With this he says farewell to the regulative ideals of pure reason, and begins to develop his own account of folk-religion as the means by which the concrete ideal is achieved. Folk-religion must satisfy the demands of pure reason in the end; but first it must meet the needs of the imagination and the heart. It must stimulate the sense of beauty and the emotion of love, and it must do so in such a way as to arouse in what Plato called the 'spirited' part of the soul, the twin sensations of self-respect and patriotism.

It is because the task of folk-religion is essentially to create a *free* society that Hegel has to distinguish between folk-religion and private religion. The personal virtues of daily life depend upon private religion for their maintenance. Hegel distinguishes three tasks that typically belong to it: resolving conflicts of duty, developing private virtues, and bringing comfort in distress. But by the time he has finished dealing with them, private religion has virtually disappeared back into folk-religion. Thus he settles the problem about conflicts of duty by saying that we must either 'take the advice of upright and experienced men' or decide for ourselves what is right on the basis of the conviction implanted in us by public religion 'that duty *and virtue* are the supreme

---

[1] This is I think the best way to express Hegel's rejection of Kant's doctrine of the 'radical evil in human nature'. To speak as even a careful critic like Lacorte does of the 'Hegelian denial of the reality of evil' is grievously unjust to a thinker who even as a schoolboy was maintaining that 'every good has its bad side' (cf. Lacorte, pp. 90, 92).

principle'—and this of course is the principle that the 'upright and experienced man' (Aristotle's man of practical wisdom enlightened by Kant) would use if we went to him for advice.

The techniques for 'teaching virtue' are all—as we have already seen—more harmful than helpful. Even public instruction about moral philosophy involves an attempt to inject into us from outside something that can only properly be developed from within; and the only real comfort in distress is faith in providence (which is, as we have seen, an essential part of public folk-religion).

In practice, therefore, the distinction between private and public religion—or private and public virtue and duty—falls *within* the concept of folk-religion; and the two questions that have to be settled—objectively, at the verbal level of *Verstand*, which is the level that Kant's discourse, Hegel's discourse, and even Lessing's *Nathan* exists on—about folk-religion arise from the two regulative canons mentioned earlier: maximizing rationality (the vitality of the spirit) and minimizing fetishism (the mortality of the letter).

Concrete rationality has three levels—which appear to be in descending order but are actually in ascending order as counsels of 'perfection'.

1. Minimally the requirements of practical reason must be met (the Jewish religion meets this requirement).
2. 'Fancy, heart, and sensibility must not on this account go empty away' (the Christian religion—especially Catholicism—meets this requirement).[1]
3. 'All the needs of life, and the public activities of the state, must be tied in with it' (only the religion of the Greeks has ever yet met this most exhaustive standard properly).

Hegel discusses each canon in turn. Much of what he says merely repeats and sums up what we have already learned, but he makes some interesting new points. Thus the first requirement of rational universality opens the way to theoretical discussion and argument about the doctrines, and hence the doctrines themselves

---

[1] For the satisfaction of *Phantasie* in Christianity, see Nohl, p. 24; p. 502 below. Cf. also *Aber die Hauptmasse* (Nohl, p. 358); and—with particular reference to Catholicism—*Die Formen der andern Bilder* (Nohl, p. 359). For the satisfaction of *Herz und Sinnlichkeit* cf. Hegel's defence of love against Kant (Nohl, p. 18; p. 496 below).

become the focus of intolerance and heresy hunting. So that *any* religious creed, as an object of *Verstand*, remains always 'unnatural' in relation to 'the true needs and requirements of *Vernunft*'.[1] For this reason the formulations of doctrine must be kept as simple as possible—and they must be expressed as *humanly* as possible.

This requirement of *Menschlichkeit* is not easy to interpret. It really means, I think, that we have always to consider the first canon as an abstraction from the second—and ultimately from the third. Hegel uses it as if it were equivalent to the pragmatic principle that we must deal with men as they are and as we find them, and not as abstract 'rational beings'. As an example he takes faith in divine providence. Only the few exceptional wise men arrive at a fully rational conception of providence; the faith of the populace is shaken by a storm at the wrong moment.

The postulate of providence, which is Hegel's own addition to the Kantian postulates of God and immortality, is obviously chosen because it is sufficiently prominent in Greek religion—or at least in Hegel's image of it—to enable him to draw a parallel and point to a contrast between Greek religion and Christianity. Earlier, as we saw, he remarked that the only real consolation in distress is that which arises from faith in providence. But he regards the appeal to Providence in private religion, which is typical of Christian culture, as thoroughly degenerate. In view of the comforts of our religion we might as well be sorry that we have not a mother or father to lose every week, he says acidly.

---

[1] This may be one answer to the problem of the condemnation of Socrates which clearly exercised Hegel's mind at this time. Bigotry was certainly one element involved. But when he goes on to explain the requirement of *Menschlichkeit*, he may, by the same token, mean to suggest that Socrates brought his fate on himself by not conforming to the proper role of the wise man in society (as Plato did). I am assuming that he has Socrates in his mind here because the Greeks are very much in his mind throughout his discussion of the three canons—and we know that he was much struck by the contrast between the treatment accorded to Aristophanes by the Athenians and the fate of Socrates (see *Aber die Hauptmasse*, Nohl, p. 357). For the contrast between Socrates and Plato see Hegel's excerpt from a review of Tennemann (*Dok.*, p. 174: this excerpt was probably made in 1794, however; cf. Nohl, p. 35). The reason for holding that the excerpt expressed Hegel's own view is that he was quite obviously modelling himself on Plato as described by Tennemann: 'He had the education of the human race in general, the perfecting of morals as a science, and the laying of foundations for a philosophical system of law and political constitution as his aim.'

When *Verstand* begins to work on the premiss that God sees the fall of every sparrow it brings the very foundation of religious faith into disrepute.[1]

The Greeks on the other hand believed in the benevolence and the justice of the Gods, but were never tempted to view misfortune as a blessing in disguise. Fate for them was a blind, ineluctable power. 'This faith . . . seems humanly appropriate both to the sublimity of the Godhead, and to the weakness, the dependence on nature, and the limited vision of man.'

Hegel makes one final point about religion as rational faith, which is that the doctrines of religion should never interfere with civic justice or be used as the basis for a moral censorship in private life. Hence, the power of the priests in a rational religion will be limited. His point about intervention in civic justice is obviously that there can be no foundation for separate ecclesiastical courts or for 'benefit of clergy'. Nor can there be any justification for a peculiarly religious judicial institution like the Holy Office, though the trial of Socrates for impiety, since it took place in the context of civic justice, is left on a very ambiguous border line. The point about censorship is a more subtle one. Moral censorship—as distinct from public justice—is wrong because it involves inhibition of the natural growth of the personality and spontaneous expression of the feelings by *Verstand*. Like verbal indoctrination it stifles the only process by which real learning can occur.[2]

We turn now to the second canon. The truths of rational religion must be embodied for the popular imagination in myths. The historical foundation of Christianity provides scope for the imagination, but not scope for its *joyful* use: 'The beautiful colours of sensibility are excluded by the spirit of our religion—and we are

---

[1] Nohl, p. 22; pp. 500–1 below. This is the beginning of a long process of critical reflection on the right interpretation of the principle 'Virtue deserves happiness' which was clearly sparked by Storr's *Notes on Kant's Religion*.

[2] The most portentous philosophical shadows have been detected behind Hegel's obvious animus against the *ancien régime* here. Peperzak affects to see in this passage 'a preference for the State when there is conflict between it and religion', though he admits it is only embryonic (Peperzak, p. 26). This embryo was never conceived, and certainly never came to birth. Hegel's conception of the relation between the State and religion remained all his life rather like that of Dante—although his conception of the terms was quite different. Religion cannot 'interfere' because it is on a higher plane altogether. Certainly Hegel does not 'prefer' the State where there is conflict. *If* there is conflict, the State is already on the point of death, since religion is its foundation.

in general too much men of reason [*Vernunft*] and of words [i.e. *Verstand*] to love beautiful pictures.'[1]

Apart from the presentation of doctrine in pictorial and dramatic modes there is scope for the imagination and the heart in the ceremonial forms of religious action. Hegel distinguishes three elements in religion: concepts, essential practices, and ceremonial. But the distinction between 'essential' practice and ceremony immediately turns out to depend on the point of view of the worshipper. For an enlightened worshipper, as we know, the 'essential practice' of his religion is 'walking acceptably in the sight of God' and all else, baptism, the eucharist, and 'divine service' generally, is ceremonial which helps both to stimulate his sentiments of devotion and to express them for experience and enjoyment. For someone who is less enlightened this experience itself has the character of an 'extraordinary benefit' or gift of grace and hence for him ceremonies become essential practices.

The particular case that Hegel chooses to consider in detail is that of *sacrifice*. Probably his choice was dictated by a desire to defend the 'heathen' practice of the Greeks against the arrogant misunderstandings of 'enlightened' and unenlightened Christian critics. But in any case we can see how easy it was for him to come to the conclusion, once he began to think about it, that sacrifice is *the* essential practice of all folk-religion, just as divine providence is *the* fundamental doctrine.[2]

Sacrifice, he says, can be viewed in two ways: it can be thought of as an act of expiation for sin, a prayer for pardon, and remission of punishment. Viewed in this light it is intellectually absurd, and morally perverse. Nowhere—except perhaps in the Christian Church—has the rite of sacrifice been so crassly conceived.[3]

---

[1] Nohl, p. 24; p. 502 below. Hegel is here referring to German Protestantism; he recognizes that his criticism applies less to Catholicism because of its Graeco-Roman heritage (cf. *Die Formen der andern Bilder*, Nohl, p. 359).

[2] The Christian eucharist as at present practised is a ceremony essential to private religion but not to folk-religion, Hegel remarks (Nohl, p. 26; p. 504 below). Presumably he means that it makes us feel a private union with God but does not give us any sense of belonging to a national community of free, self-determining citizens (cf. the sarcastic comment a little further on about the Catholic practice of communion in one kind: Nohl, p. 27; p. 505 below).

[3] Nohl, pp. 24–5; p. 503 below. Here Hegel is almost certainly thinking of the *indulgences* that Luther protested so vigorously against. But how any one who had studied the second book of the *Republic* could seriously maintain that 'outside the Christian Church the sinner's conscience . . . was not set at rest' by this kind of sacrifice (Nohl, p. 25 n.) passes my comprehension.

Even so, we ought not to overlook its value as a stimulus of the higher religious emotions. The practice of pilgrimage in particular, ridiculous though its objects may appear to the enlightened intellect, does not deserve our scorn, since it involves devoting one's actual life to the service of God.

On the other hand we can view sacrifice, as Hegel believes the Greeks did, as an act of love and gratitude by which the aid and protection of the gods is invoked or their provident help acknowledged. Here the ideas of placation and penitent reparation are absent. This is 'probably the basic and universal type [*Gestalt*] of sacrifice'.

When we come to the final requirement Hegel's enthusiasm for his Greek ideal overflows all bounds and puts him for a moment into that posture of yearning that we associate rather with Hölderlin. Any gap between the doctrine and the way of life must rouse the suspicion, he says, that there is something wrong with the 'form of the religion': either it is too subtle in theory, or too ascetic in practice, or both. Religion ought not to make us ashamed; rather all the joys of life should be sanctified by it, as in the great Greek festivals. Whereas our religion makes us solemn and alienates us from all human feelings in order to make us citizens of heaven.

Folk-religion goes hand in hand with political freedom because it arouses and nourishes the noble emotions (*große Gesinnungen*) that sustain a free constitution. The religion, the historical tradition, and the political constitution of a people together constitute the *Volksgeist*. This political connection causes Hegel to distinguish once more between folk-religion and private religion, although, as we saw, the distinction is scarcely tenable in his vision of the ideal, and is only useful in contrasting that ideal with the Christianity of his own society.

To express the relation of the three terms in the Greek *Volksgeist* Hegel wrote a little Platonic myth in which Chronos (historical tradition) appears as father, Politeia (the constitution) as the mother, and Religion as the nurse of the infant spirit of Greece. Subsequently he crossed it out. I do not think that he cancelled it immediately, in spite of the fact that his next paragraph contains a less elaborate analogy which was obviously conceived as an alternative version. For he made use of his myth in the rest of his discussion and he had just embarked on a parallel allegory about the spirit of Germany when he stopped and struck that out. Almost certainly he cancelled the first myth at the same time but without modifying the subsequent references to it.

In the simpler version of his allegory which Hegel allowed to stand, the Greek spirit is said to be a 'child of fortune [*Glück*] and freedom . . . fettered [like other *Volksgeister*] to Mother Earth by the brazen bond of his needs, but he has so worked over it, refined it, and beautified it, with feeling and fancy, twining it with roses by the aid of the Graces, that he takes delight in his fetters as in his own work, as in a part of himself.'[1] From his father (i.e. Chronos—also called here 'a darling of fortune and son of force') he inherited 'faith in his fortune and pride in his deeds'. I take this to be a fairly transparent reference to Periclean Athens, with the memory of Marathon and Salamis to look back on. His gentle mother (i.e. the Constitution) entrusted him to the education of nature. That is, no censorship of *Verstand* was imposed on his discovery of his natural powers—the education of 'nature' is that which Rousseau's Émile received. His nurse (i.e. Religion) did not terrify him with the rod and the bogyman (has Hegel *forgotten* the Furies and the Gorgons, or does he feel perhaps that even they, in their total context, are somehow beautiful and *menschlich*?), or feed him the 'sour-sweet sugar-bread of mysticism that weakens the stomach'. This remark is surely a reference to the inversion of natural values in Christianity—the doctrines that the last shall be first, that the meek and the persecuted are blessed, etc., are hardly calculated to arouse the noble sentiments of patriotism and free- dom. Nor did the nurse 'keep him in the leading-reins of words which would have held him in eternal infancy'. Here Hegel has connected his metaphor with Kant's definition of enlightenment, which may have suggested it. Enlightenment, said Kant, is 'coming of age', not needing a nurse or a tutor. But Hegel does not want to imply that folk-religion can ever be dispensed with, so he goes on to say that the nurse remained as an intimate companion in the

---

[1] Nohl, p. 28. In this alternative version the separation and opposition between soul and body (Plato) or Reason and sensibility (Kant) is fairly clearly maintained. The *als* of the final clause is an *als ob*. In the cancelled paragraph the imagery is more strikingly reminiscent of Plato (and of Hölderlin) but *human nature* is conceived as an organic unity. The 'leichtes Band' that ties the 'ätherisches Wesen' to the Earth 'durch einen magischen Zauber allen Versuchen es zu zerreißen widersteht, *denn es ist ganz in sein Wesen verschlungen*' (see below, pp. 506-7, for a full translation of both passages in context).

family circle as long as the Greek spirit lived. She brought the child up on the fresh milk of pure feelings (*Empfindungen*) and adorned the 'impenetrable veil that hides the Godhead from our gaze with the blossoms of free and beautiful fancy' so that the child saw it as peopled with 'living pictures from which he carried forward the great ideals of his own heart with all the power [*Fülle*] of his higher and more beautiful feelings'. She never lost her authority over her young friend because it was founded on love, 'and his own conscience punished any slighting of her dignity'. Probably it is the fall of Alcibiades rather than the trial of Socrates that Hegel has in mind here, for he did not himself hold Socrates guilty of slighting the dignity of the Gods.

This genius, he concludes sadly, is known to us now only in fragments and by hearsay:

We are permitted to gaze in love and wonder at the surviving copies of his form which awake in us only a sorrowful longing for the original —He is the beautiful youth, whom we love even in his caprice, followed by the whole company of the graces, and with them the balsam-breath of nature, the soul, inspired by them ⟨—⟩ he sucked every flower and is fled from the world.

I find it hard to understand how anyone who has studied the pages that close with these words can say, as critics frequently do, that the young Hegel shows few signs of real aesthetic sensibility. This claim is usually supported by pointing out that his youthful attempts at poetry are all very weak, and his Alpine diary of 1796 is very pedestrian; as if no one could rightfully lay claim to a sense of beauty unless he was either a capable versifier, or was prepared to say, like Elizabeth Bennet: 'What are men, to rocks and mountains!'—a sentiment which Hegel would certainly never have been tempted to express, and which Jane Austen's heroine was no longer inclined to endorse when she stood in the park at Pemberley. To me, at least, Hegel's prose carries the unmistakable impression of an ideal vision that was less intellectual than Schiller's, even if it was not as full-bloodedly human as Goethe's.

Furthermore, although it is highly idealized and extremely one-sided—the 'brazen fetters' of Mother Earth are so beautified that slavery goes unmentioned, and no trace of the chthonic underworld of Greek culture is visible—Hegel's vision rests on a sound critical intuition with respect to his historical sources. His ideal is the ideal of Athens in the golden age, the Athens of the *Pentekontaetia* and of Pericles. The original features (*nur einige Züge*) of his picture come from Herodotus, Thucydides, and Plato; and Hegel is well aware that all else is only 'hearsay' and 'copies', even if his inspiration comes also in part from later authors like Theocritus.[1] He does not deserve therefore to have quoted against him the ponderous verdict of Wilamowitz upon Goethe's tastes in classical art, for he seems already to have an intuitive awareness that his ideal perished with Socrates.[2]

On his last page Hegel began to pen a very embittered portrait of the very different 'Genius of the nations' which the West has bred:

> His form is aged—beautiful he never was—but some slight touches of manliness remain still faintly traceable in him—his father [i.e. the historical tradition behind present society] is bowed—he dares neither to look with joy at the world around him—nor to straighten himself from a sense of his own life (*Gefühl seiner Selbst*)—he is short sighted and can see only little things one at a time ⟨—⟩ without courage, without confidence in his own strength he hazards no bold throw, iron fetters raw and

Here he broke off and struck out what he had written. There is an indication in his manuscript that he had this contrast of 'the young genius of a people—and that which is ageing' in mind from the beginning. But he was right not to develop it here, for he has in all essentials fulfilled the task that he set himself at the beginning.[3] Between the spirit of youth with which his inquiry properly terminates and the ageing spirit of his own time there lay a career of nearly two thousand years that had first to be investigated before the contrast between them could be rightly understood and the moral correctly drawn, the way to rejuvenation found.

[1] According to Rosenkranz (p. 11) Hegel wrote 'eine sehr ausführliche Präparation zum Theokrit' which was undated, but belonged probably to the Tübingen period.

[2] Cf. Peperzak, pp. 5, 22. Peperzak seems to want (correctly) to deny that Hegel was guilty of Goethe's errors of taste; and at the same time—again correctly—to admit his enormous debt to some authorities—Winckelmann for example—whom Wilamowitz condemned. The lectures on the *Philosophy of Art* bear witness, years later, both to Hegel's careful study of Winckelman, and to his profound awareness of the gulf between fifth-century Athens and the Hellenistic age.

[3] See Nohl, p. 6, for the original contrast, and the passage already quoted on p. 119 above for his declared aims. Both passages are translated in context on pp. 483-6 below.

My conclusion therefore is that Hegel stopped because his immediate task was complete. The 'Tübingen fragment' is improperly called a fragment, even though it may well be composed of fragmentary discussions rather crudely stitched together. It is the very rough first draft of a complete essay, with one obvious lacuna of four pages in the manuscript as we have it, and possibly, but not quite certainly, another one that may be of any length up to eight pages. In any case nothing essential is lost, and when the essay is considered in its organic integrity, it reveals itself as a work of quite striking originality and depth. It is not the work of a mere eclectic but of one who, as Hegel's leaving-testimonial from the University quite certainly said, *Philosophiae multam operam impendit.*[1]

---

[1] *Briefe*, iv. 87. If there is anyone who still takes the reading *nullam* seriously he should heed first the witness of the biography in the Brockhaus *Lexicon* of 1827 which I take to depend on information supplied by Hegel himself (see *Dok.*, p. 395). If he desires further evidence he should then consider Betzendörfer's report that there is no parallel for the *nullam* reading in other *testimonia* (Betzendörfer, p. 128 n. 63). Hegel's own *testimonium* shows that when the authorities were somewhat less than happy about a student's performance, they indicated the fact in his testimonial by using a double negative. For about his performance in theology—which we know left much to be desired—we read: 'Studia theologica *non neglexit*. Orationem sacram *non sine studio* elaboravit, in recitanda *non magnus* orator visus.' Indeed, although I am scarcely ever tempted to say with Richard Bentley, *ratio atque res ipsa centum codicibus potior*, I believe this is a case where the dictum applies. I do not think that the authorities of the *Stift* were fools, which is what in the light of the evidence we should have to think if we accepted the reading *nullam*.

III. BERNE 1793-1796

Reason and Freedom

1. *The background of Hegel's life in Berne*

EARLY in October 1793 with several album leaves freshly inscribed by his friends with suitably revolutionary sentiments, Hegel set out for the 'land of divine freedom' where, like many of the great figures of German literature and culture in his time, he was to begin his career as a private tutor.[1] He had heard in August through the landlord of the 'Golden Ox' at Stuttgart, of an opening in the household of Hauptmann von Steiger at Berne, and he wrote promptly on the 24th to Herr von Rütte in Berne from whom the news had come, saying that he hoped to be able to take the post and would write again when he was able to make a definite commitment. His twenty-third birthday passed as he waited, perhaps a little anxiously, for official permission to take a post abroad, but on 11 September he wrote again that he could take the post as soon as his examinations were over if Hauptmann von Steiger would send a letter for him to deliver to the Consistory at Stuttgart.[2]

---

[1] It would seem that he left Stuttgart on 10 Oct. 1793 (if I am right in assuming that entries 22, 24a, 47a and 48 in his *Stammbuch* were all written at a farewell party on 9 Oct.: see *Briefe*, iv. 45, 46, and 53). For the local tradition of a 'Hofmeisterzeit' in Switzerland see Hoffmeister's note in *Briefe*, i. 433, or *Dok.*, p. 447; cf. also Rosenkranz, p. 42.

[2] It is certain that at some point in the summer Hegel was asked if he would like to have the post which Hölderlin subsequently took with the von Kalbs in Waltershausen. But it is not clear that he ever really had a choice between this position and the position in Berne. Charlotte von Kalb asked for Schiller's help as early as 28 May 1793 (*GSA*, vii. 440). Schiller presumably sought first for a suitable candidate in Jena; and not finding one, asked the advice of Stäudlin. Stäudlin probably recommended Hegel first (Hölderlin had still to persuade his mother to let him follow a career outside the Church). But Hölderlin himself told Stäudlin that Hegel was committed to the von Steigers; and on 20 Sept. 1793 Stäudlin informed Schiller of this, and recommended Hölderlin (*GSA*, vii.

Hegel was glad enough, no doubt, to escape from the clutches of the 'visible Church' in Württemberg at last—though the Consistory made it a condition of his going 'that he exercise himself diligently in preaching, in which he is very deficient'. He was also obligated to return if called upon, and 'not to neglect the study of theology', reporting the progress of his studies to the Consistory from time to time.[1] Until he received this formal release from his obligations as a stipendiary of the *Stift*, he probably suffered like Hölderlin from the nightmarish fear that the Consistory would make him a curate somewhere under the stern eye of an older minister.[2] But he was not too sanguine about the post with the von Steigers even before he took it—in his very first letter he complained politely but firmly that the salary was too low[3]—and his three years in Switzerland were not destined to be happy ones.

The account of Hegel's life in Switzerland that has become traditional is rather overdrawn in some respects, however. The von Steigers were an old patrician family of Berne, with a country estate at Tschugg near Erlach, where they lived during the summer. The young bourgeois scholar lived with them on terms that were rather easier and more familiar than one might have expected. But loneliness was an inevitable occupational curse of the *Hofmeister*, typically a young man fresh from the company of his peers at the University, finding himself suddenly without peers, since his education set him apart from the other servants and his position was never quite that of a member of the family. Even Hölderlin, who had certainly no grounds for complaint about his treatment at the hands of the von Kalbs, and whose letters are full of their praises, remarks rather wryly in the middle of an enthusiastic description of his situation for the benefit of his grandmother: 'I live indeed pretty much alone, but I find this quite favourable for the development [*Bildung*] of the spirit and the heart.'[4]

467). Hölderlin does write later as if Hegel might have chosen the von Kalbs (see *Briefe*, i. 9); but since both of them seem to have believed at the time that the post was in the 'Jena region' I find this hard to credit. (For Hegel's letters to von Rütte see *Briefe*, i. 4–6.)

[1] *Briefe*, iv. 83 (Consistory records for 20 Sept. 1793).

[2] See Hölderlin's letter to his mother about the end of Aug. 1793 (Beck, Letter 64, *GSA*, vi. 91); compare also his letters to Neuffer and Ebel in 1795: *GSA*, vi. 183 and 186–7.

[3] *Briefe*, i. 5: cf. the report of v. Rütte to v. Steiger quoted by Hoffmeister, ibid. p. 433.

[4] Beck, Letter 74, *GSA*, vi. 107. For the necessary revision of the traditional

In Hegel's letters we hear almost nothing of his personal circumstances, though I suppose we should know more about them if his letters to his sister had survived, as so many of Hölderlin's to his mother and sister have. The duties of a *Hofmeister* were not enormously onerous, and we cannot doubt that as a keen student of Rousseau's *Émile* Hegel approached his task with a certain enthusiasm. For the balance of his time he was free to do as he would, but there was not very much that he could do, except read, think, and write, so it was fortunate that, on the whole, these occupations pleased him.[1] He chafed against his life and was dissatisfied with himself, however, especially when he received letters from Schelling about his first publications, and from Hölderlin after the latter went to Jena, where Fichte was lecturing (along with Schiller) and the whole culture of Germany had for the moment a living and visible focus. Hegel complained in his replies that he could not do anything serious because his time was so broken up and he needed books.[2] Actually he had the use of quite a good library and one which suited him very well, even if it did not contain the current works that Schelling and Hölderlin were excited about; and he was quite astonishingly busy about his own concerns. Even he could not pretend that he was idle; and if he seemed to himself, as he obviously did, to be getting nowhere in comparison with his friends, that was perhaps more because his aims were so ambitious that he often despaired of their achievement, than because his other commitments stood in the way. He followed events in France with close attention and interest, and it must have seemed to him often, that while everyone and everything in the world was on the move, he was merely dreaming the time away in his quiet backwater. His dreams were important enough,

picture of Hegel's relations with the family of von Steiger see Hans Strahm, 'Aus Hegels Berner Zeit', *Archiv. für Geschichte der Philosophie*, xli (1932), 514-33.

[1] Hegel was too sociable a creature to remain for ever in his study, however. Thus we hear of one family circle in Berne, where he was a welcome guest for cards and music in the evenings. They kept up a correspondence with him for a time after he went to Frankfurt, and they used to sing Schiller's 'Ode to Joy' in his memory (Rosenkranz, p. 43; *Briefe*, i. 57). (This association, like all of Hegel's subsequent connections in Frankfurt—as far as these can be traced—has strong overtones of Freemasonry. See D'Hondt, p. 241.)

[2] *Briefe*, i. 11, 17; it is worth remembering that the letters discovered by Strahm which show that Hegel was on a friendly, nearly familial footing with the von Steigers, also provide some evidence to bear out his complaint that his time was much broken in upon (Letter 12, 9 July 1795: *Briefe*, i. 26).

at least in his own eyes, but he felt he ought to be contributing something more concrete to what Schelling spoke of as the 'revolution that will be made by philosophy'.[1]

A note of political urgency is evident even in the earliest fragments of the Berne period. In part the change of emphasis is a result of circumstances. In Hegel's fundamentally Hellenic ideal of a *Volksleben* in which all human capacities were fully, freely, and harmoniously expressed, artistic and religious spontaneity always went hand in hand with political freedom. In Berne he was in a position to study a different type of 'constitution' and he took full advantage of it. But the natural development of his reflections on religion also led him to ponder the problems of political revolution and the destruction of class distinctions. His fundamental concern, we must remember, was not metaphysical but moral. He was not concerned with the nature of God, but with the nature of man. Religion was for him, as for Lessing, the great instrument of Providence by which human nature is rightly developed and truly revealed. Thus Haering's perfectly correct insistence that he was a *Volkserzieher* does not really conflict with Lukács's portrait of him as a kind of proto-Marx. It is in and through political action that man realizes and displays the power of *Vernunft* which it is the providential function of religion to develop. In Greece Hegel saw the ideal union of constitution and religion for the achievement of reason and freedom; in his own society he saw rather an unnatural alliance of throne and altar for the maintenance of despotic authority. He had to understand, and ultimately to make others understand, how this corrupt state of things had come about, in order to discover the way toward a better condition of life as a whole.

The library at Tschugg contained a number of books that were admirably adapted to Hegel's interests.[2] He found there Gibbon,

---

[1] *Briefe*, i. 21; cf. ibid. 23, 28. Hegel's sarcastic comment in later years that Schelling had conducted his own education in public (Rosenkranz, p. 45) may partially reflect a feeling that he actually had at this time. But if this was the case we must view the remark as a backlash from his own feelings of inferiority and frustration. It should not lead us to believe that Hegel consciously regarded all of his undertakings in this period as being merely part of a programme of self-education. He knew very well how much he had to learn and to master if he was to fulfil his self-appointed task—he had known since he was fifteen (*Dok.*, p. 37). But he certainly aimed to set the results and products of his own education before the public as soon as possible. He did not preserve his manuscripts only as a kind of philosophical journal. [2] See Hans Strahm, pp. 526–32.

Hume's *History of England*, Montesquieu, Raynal's *Histoire des deux Indes* and Schiller's newly published *History of the Thirty Years' War*; a fair number of the extracts from various historical studies printed by Rosenkranz most probably belong, as Rosenkranz himself believed, to the Berne period.[1] Hegel also studied the constitution and finances of the canton of Berne itself and observed the political processes of the 'land of divine freedom' with a rather sardonic, and perhaps not quite unprejudiced eye. To Schelling in April 1795 he wrote:

My delay in answering is due partly to my having much to do, partly to the distractions occasioned by the political festivals that have been celebrated here. Every 10 years the 'sovereign' council is reconstituted and about 90 members retire. How humanely [*menschlich*] it is all done, how all the intrigues of cousinage and nepotism in princely courts are as nothing to the combinations that are formed here, I just cannot describe to you. The father names his son or the son-in-law who made the best marriage settlement and so on. To gain a real understanding of an aristocratic constitution, one must have spent a winter like this one here, before the Easter when the council is reconstituted.[2]

The results of his studies and observations, Hegel largely incorporated in the introduction and notes to a translation of J. J. Cart's *Lettres confidentielles*, which he published a year after he moved to Frankfurt, and which was thus his first actual venture into print. The book was published anonymously, and the author was wrongly stated to be already dead on the title-page in 1798. Also, for a mixture of reasons including fear of the censor's eye, some letters were omitted from this protest against the tyrannical oppression by the Berne aristocracy of part of the 'pays de Vaud' which fell within their domain. Some notion of the polemical

[1] Rosenkranz's dating of Hegel's manuscripts is not to be relied on, except where he indicates that Hegel himself put the date on the sheet. He has a general tendency to date things too early. This may be the reason why Hoffmeister chose to put these fragments in the Frankfurt period (*Dok.*, pp. 257–77). It seems likely in the light of their content that many of them may belong to the last year of Hegel's residence in Berne, but it would be foolish to put too much weight on this argument. In reconstructing the genesis of Hegel's thought we must rely first on the manuscripts that we still possess and can date by objective criteria. Only after this has been done can we hope to place these fragments in the most plausible context—and we must always recognize that the most plausible context may still, in fact, not be the right one. (See further, p. 232 nn. 3 and 4; p. 271 n. 2; p. 417 n. 3; and p. 418 nn. 1 and 2.)

[2] *Briefe*, i. 23.

tone of the book can be gathered from the title-page itself, which reads: *Confidential Letters | concerning the former Constitutional | Relation of the Wadtland (Pays de Vaud) | to the State of Berne. | A complete Exposition of the earlier Oligarchy of the Berne Nobility* [des Standes Berne] | *Translated from the French of a deceased Swiss author | and supplied with Notes.*[1] The fundamental claim, of course, was that the constitutional freedom which had earlier existed had now been destroyed. Doubtless Hegel felt that this was an apt verdict on the government of Berne itself. It probably gave him no little pleasure to prepare his little bombshell for the press, when he had at last escaped to the bourgeois society of Frankfurt, and found himself again in the company of Hölderlin.

Even the Swiss landscape failed to move him as he expected that it would. We hear of two journeys in this period. In May 1795 he went to Geneva, but we have no record of his impressions of the birthplace of his 'hero' Jean-Jacques. Then in July 1796 he set out on a walking-tour in the Alps with three Saxons, all of them tutors like himself, for company.[2] On this tour he kept a very detailed journal—the writing of which must sometimes have kept him out of bed when he was very weary from a hard day's walking that usually began at sunrise. As a boy he had read Meiners's *Journeys in Switzerland* with considerable enthusiasm, and he was obviously delighted to be seeing the sights that Meiners had described, and even meeting the very guides who had accompanied him. So he had some very definite notions about what to see and what sensations to expect; but generally speaking the sights did not come up to his expectations and the sensations did not materialize. The Jungfrau was just a mountain, and the glaciers were only muddy masses of ice. He found it more interesting to learn from the peasants about cheese-making and to make

[1] *Vertrauliche Briefe über das Vormalige staatsrechtliche Verhältnis des Wadtlandes (Pays de Vaud) zur Stadt Bern* (Frankfurt, 1798). The translation was published anonymously and is only known to be the work of Hegel because it was listed under his name in Meusel's *Lexicon* of German Writers in 1805. It remained unknown to Rosenkranz and was only rediscovered by H. Falkenheim in 1909. (See *Dok.*, pp. 247–57 and 457–65, for the text of Hegel's introduction and notes, and p. 529 below for further details. Hegel's aims and attitudes in this, his first publication, are discussed below in Chapter V, pp. 418–27.)

[2] Hegel's journal for this later journey was printed by Rosenkranz (pp. 470–90) and reprinted by Hoffmeister (*Dok.*, pp. 221–44); the manuscript is lost. The 'pass' through which we know of the earlier journey was first printed by Hoffmeister (*Dok.*, p. 447) and is now most readily found in *Briefe*, iv. 88.

notes on German-Swiss dialects. Only the mountain streams and
waterfalls really stirred his emotions. Like Heracleitus, he found in
their restless permanence an appropriate symbol of the ἑν και παν:

> Through a narrow rock-cleft the water is forced from above, then it
> falls straight downwards in spreading waves; waves which draw the
> gaze of the spectator ever downward but which he still cannot fix or
> follow, for their shape and form breaks up at every instant, it is forced
> into a new one at every moment, and *in this fall it always looks the same,
> and yet at the same time one sees that it is not the same.*[1]

Hegel insisted however that this natural image of life was
beyond the compass of human art, whether verbal or graphic:
'Even in the best pictures the most fascinating, the most essential
thing in a spectacle [*Schauspiel*] of this sort is lacking: *the eternal
life, the powerful mobility in it.*'[2] Art, and the aesthetic sense
generally, was for Hegel an avenue through which we are able to
explore the whole range of *human* experience. Thus there was
nothing in the 'formless masses' of a mountain landscape that
appealed to his eye or his imagination; and for *Vernunft* the
permanence of the mountains in their 'eternal death' offered only
the idea of ineluctable fact: 'It is so.' But he could readily appreciate,
and enter into the consciousness of, those who lived against this
changeless background. He sets the stoical fatalism of those who
live at the mercy of flood and avalanche in sharp contrast with the
self-complacent optimism of the rational theologians, the town
dwellers who tried to make out that everything in nature was
somehow fitted and designed for man's use and enjoyment, and
believed that if anyone denied this he was somehow robbing God
of his honour. The blind might and the indifferent endurance
of natural forces should not be thus disguised to flatter our vanity—
the *Stolz* 'that is characteristic of our age'; but neither is it properly
an occasion for feelings of sublime awe and exultation.[3]

---

[1] *Dok.*, p. 231. If we may trust Rosenkranz's editing the underlining both in
this and in the following passage comes from Hegel's own manuscript.

[2] Ibid., pp. 231–2. He also remarks (p. 231): 'eine Beschreibung kann so
wenig als ein Gemälde nur einigermassen die Selbstansicht ersetzen'.

[3] Ibid., pp. 234–5. I do not think it is fair to accuse Hegel of being without
aesthetic sensibility because his philosophical commitments caused him to set
a low value on certain sensations whose existence he nevertheless recognized.
It would certainly have been difficult, if not impossible, for him to develop the
kind of sensibility associated with an aesthetics of 'significant form'. At this
level the only art that he really appreciated was music—because here the form
is overtly dynamic. Art was only 'significant' for him as an expression of *human*

The one thing which, by reason of its human associations, Hegel was doubtless prepared to be exalted by, was Tell's Chapel. But it proved to be a disappointment too: 'It seemed to be fresh-painted, and had not, as I expected, anything worthy of reverence about it by reason of its age and simplicity.'[1] In short nothing was right in Switzerland; the 'Devil's Bridge', over another of the torrents that he found so impressive, provoked him to the comment that where one might have expected the 'Kindersinn dieser Hirtenvölker' to have produced a genuine myth, the 'Christian imagination' had produced 'as always' only an 'absurd legend'.[2]

2. *In search of a way forward*

Before he left home, Hegel had managed to put on paper a description of the ideal toward which men ought to aim as rational and social beings, and at the same time to demonstrate that the ideal was no mere utopian dream, since the Greeks had actually realized it. The problem that offered itself for his reflections when he arrived in Berne was thus obvious enough. He had to find some way in which his own society could regain possession of the ideal or at least come closer to it. It was clear to him, as we shall soon see, that there could be no simple return to the Greek situation. Modern man could not go 'back to Nature'. He must somehow go forward from the situation of civilized corruption that he was now in; and to this end it was necessary to understand how the corruption had come about.

Precisely because the ideal was not a utopian fancy but a historic actuality, it was difficult to see how it could be 'regained', or applied to the situation of another people in another time. Every

nature, and the *meaning* was always more important than the *form* for Hegel, even though he stressed the indissoluble unity of form and content (compare his remarks about Tell's chapel below). The insistence on *meaning* is a limit on Hegel's aesthetic sensibility certainly—but it is a flaw to which one whose aesthetics is primarily directed towards the appreciation of *poetic* communication is typically liable. It is no more serious surely than the opposite excess of pure formalism, to which theorists of *graphic* and visual art are peculiarly liable. To say that it is *less* serious, would perhaps only be to exhibit my own bias. The inescapable fact is that all or almost all of us suffer from limitations of sensibility in one direction or the other. To say *this* is by no means the same as to say that someone has no aesthetic sensibility at all (or very little).

[1] Ibid., p. 242.
[2] Ibid., pp. 241–2. Hegel actually makes this remark about an isolated crag (*ein isoliertes ungeheures Felsenstück*) in the immediate neighbourhood; but he applies it to the *Teufelsbrücke* at the same time.

people has its own individual way of life which has been determined for it by its own historical tradition, political constitution,
and religious experience. The educational system and methods of
a society necessarily reflect the total pattern of the way of life of
which they are a part; and no would-be *Volkserzieher* can afford
to disregard the accepted conception of the teacher's place in his
society.

But then if a society has become corrupt, and in the process
the conception of education itself has been falsified and the very
means and prerequisites of natural education themselves destroyed,
how can an educational reformer go to work? This is the focal
problem around which all of the early Berne fragments revolve,
and the *Life of Jesus* represents Hegel's first decided attempt at a
solution to the problem. Once we recognize this focus point it is
easy to understand the 'shift of emphasis' that is apparent in these
fragments as compared with the so-called 'Tübingen fragment'.
In the earlier essay it is whole patterns of social life and organization that are contrasted, whereas now it is the typical individual
teachers of the society who occupy the limelight—Socrates, Jesus,
and Professor G. C. Storr[1]—and the fundamental topic is the
relation between doctrine and life, theory and practice in different
societies.

In what is quite possibly the earliest of the fragments written
at Berne—the little piece beginning *Außer dem mündlichen Unterricht* which has attracted attention hitherto only because of a quite
pointed contrast of Jesus with Socrates that was added some time
later[2]—the essential problem is put squarely before us. The only

[1] The author of the new *compendium*, whose publication is at last going to put
contemporary society on the right track, remains anonymous in Hegel's manuscripts (e.g. Nohl, pp. 60, 360) but I do not think I have mistaken his identity.
Storr's *Doctrinae Christianae pars theoretica e sacris litteris repetita* was published
in 1793. Hegel doubtless heard a great deal about the blessings that would
descend upon the world with its arrival in the lectures that he attended between
1790 and 1792. (But we should not forget that the compendium Hegel had
himself used and studied most was that of Sartorius. Sandberger has argued
convincingly that one of his earliest comments on compendia—the comparison
between what is emphasized in 'all the compendia' and what is 'taught nowadays', Nohl, p. 356, compare also pp. 43–4—is based on the contrast between
the book of Sartorius and the teaching of Storr. See Brecht and Sandberger,
p. 73. Wherever Hegel refers to 'compendia' in the plural he is probably thinking
primarily of Sartorius.)

[2] The order in which a particular set of short fragments were written is not
usually of any particular importance as long as we are able, as we are here, to
arrange them in groups that are fairly closely contemporary. But we must take

method of folk-education available to a contemporary reformer is the writing of a book. This is like mounting an invisible pulpit, and the invisibility increases the element of distance and impersonality that is already implicit in the relation of the pulpit orator to his congregation. The invisible preacher is tempted to say things about man in general or society in general, things that he would never want to say to his neighbour or about his face-to-face society; and people are willing to hear things said about 'men' which they would never suffer to be said about themselves or their friends personally. Even in the case of the visible pulpit, the typical institution of the Judaic tradition, this corruption of consciousness has already begun, and no teacher in the society can altogether escape it; even Jesus, who taught, like Socrates, by personal example and face-to-face communication, spoke of his people as a 'generation of vipers'—a locution which was unthinkable in the everyday converse of citizens that Socrates engaged in.

Recognizing the corruption of his society Jesus sought to separate himself and his followers from it. Thus he became consciously and deliberately a *private* teacher. Even in this, however, he had to conform to the spirit of the wider society: his isolated group had to know themselves as the Twelve, the 'chosen' from among the Chosen People. While Socrates, on the other hand,

care to keep fragments which are objectively distinguishable distinct, or we may find ourselves making invalid assumptions. Thus in an article which explicitly sets out to refine upon the pioneer work of Nohl by the application of statistical canons, Dr. Schüler classifies *Man lehrt unsrer Kinder* (Nohl, pp. 359–60) as the earliest of the Berne fragments on the grounds, already noted by Nohl, that the first eleven lines (as printed) are written in Hegel's earlier script. Next after this she places *Außer dem mündlichen Unterricht* (Nohl, pp. 30–5). This will not do because it conceals several problems and may lead to mistakes.

The fragment *properly* referred to as *Man lehrt unsrer Kinder* is just the first eleven lines indicated by Nohl. There is no continuous argument linking this with *Nicht zu leugnen sind* which Hegel added later. And again, what is referred to as *Außer dem mündlichen Unterricht* is really *two* fragments, of which the second—which begins *Christus hatte zwölf Apostel* (Nohl, pp. 32–5)—may have been written quite some time after the first.

I do not mean that a properly critical editor must treat every distinguishable fresh beginning as a new fragment—though it would be valuable if clearly distinguishable breaks in the continuity of the writing were indicated. Where it is clear that Hegel himself meant to continue from the point where he left off, so to speak, it would be foolish to treat his train of thought as a collection of fragmentary reflections. But smaller fragments which have not yet definitely received their place in a larger design (such as *Religion ist eine*) must be kept distinct.

did *not* separate himself in any way from the life and affairs of his
time and his pupils were of all kinds and gave up nothing in order
to become his followers. All that he did for them was to help them
to develop themselves as distinct individuals, everyone with his
own gifts, purposes, and duties, all quite different both from
one another and from Socrates himself, and all engaged to the
full in the active life of their society.

   In Greek society a parallel to Jesus is offered not by Socrates
but by Diogenes,[1] and Hegel admits that by ascetically establishing his independence of all normal social ties and relations Diogenes
'earned a kind of right to be called a great man'. But the contrast,
which he does not himself draw, is an obvious one. Diogenes is
properly just a limiting case in the Greek pattern; asceticism is
simply one way, his way, of establishing his autonomous individuality. Eccentrics of this kind exist everywhere—whereas the
rebellion of Jesus was a justified rebellion against a society that was
really corrupt.

   At this point Hegel for the first time comments on Roman
society as a distinct entity.[2] Rome had no teachers of human
rational autonomy. In Rome there were only citizens, not men.
The subjectivity of virtue was ignored and the only standard
recognized was the standard of public law. Already here we can
see the shadow of Hegel's mature conception of the Roman empire
as a society of pure legal right and authority.[3]

_____

   [1] It is not true, as Haering claims (i. 132), that Hegel offers *Socrates* and Jesus
as examples of individuals who set themselves apart from their society. One of
the main contrasts between Socrates and Jesus and between their societies lies
in the fact that Socrates did *not* set himself apart from his society because he did
not have to do so (as Diogenes felt he had to) in order to be an autonomous
individual.
   [2] There is one reference to Roman society in his notes at Tübingen—in
Inwiefern ist Religion where he remarks on 'Piety among the Greeks and
Romans—Romans and Greeks in their fatherland, Cato embraced his fatherland wholly and his fatherland fulfilled his whole soul'. In other words Romans
and Greeks alike recognized their city as what Hegel later called their 'ethical
substance'. This passage is quite consistent with the present one, though the
distinction here made between Rome and Athens must be taken to imply that the
society of Cato had not developed to 'perfection' like that of Socrates. Probably
Hegel thought of Lycurgan Sparta in much the same way.
   [3] By the time he wrote *Jetzt braucht die Menge*, less than a year later, Hegel
had come very close to his mature conception. Even in the earlier passage mentioned in the preceding note there are signs that he already clearly distinguished
Republican Rome (as an 'ethical substance') from the universal society of the
Empire. For his remark about Cato is flanked on one side by a reference to

Thus the proposition is proved, 'the mode of instruction must always be directed in accordance with the spirit [*Genie*] and tone that is established among the people'; and the problem is thereby raised of how one can reform a society where the established spirit and tone is corrupt. To exhibit the corruption in accordance with its own spirit is easy. Just as Jesus could cry out against the 'generation of vipers', so Hegel could preach sermons against sermons and preachers, and write a compendium against compendiums. But he recognized that it was not just useless to do this; it was positively harmful. The corruption of moral consciousness and the useless emptiness of moral education are themes that run through all of the fragments of this period; but having once said that it was wrong to declaim abstractly against human vices, Hegel could see the folly of declaiming abstractly against *that* vice. We can be quite sure that, just as he struck out the last lines of *Religion ist eine*, so he would never have published any of his diatribes against the Church and the seminaries unless he could find a context in which they served some positive purpose.

Quite clearly it was necessary for a corrupt society to understand the state that it was in, and the reasons and stages through which it had come to be in that state. All societies, Hegel believed, pass through a cycle of development like that of the individual in which the stages of childhood, maturity, and old age are distinguishable; and just as a mature man or an old one bears with him always some traces of his childhood, so also a society bears always traces of its childhood, particularly in the sphere of religious experience—for religion is peculiarly associated with the 'childhood' of a people. The mature society, like the mature man, is governed by *Vernunft*, which makes the moral character and purpose of religion ever more explicit, but at the same time destroys its power over our imagination. We feel this loss in a sentimental way but it remains inevitable. If peculiar responsibility for religion has been given to a particular class of the people, however, this necessary development cannot take place normally. Religion becomes then an instrument by which the governing class strives to keep the mass of the people in a state of childish dependence. Thus the establishment of the

Mendelssohn's *Jerusalem* ('According to the teachings of the Rabbis, all punishments, in so far as they were purely national, must cease to be just with the destruction of the Temple'), and on the other by the comment: 'Cosmopolitanism is only for separate individuals [*einzelne*].'

priesthood as a public *authority* is the point at which things go wrong and corruption sets in.[1]

In this whole process as it took place in the history of Germany, the spiritual content and purposes of Christianity were irrelevant. Christianity originated in a private rebellion against an authoritarian society, but even in its origin it could not avoid being contaminated by the spirit of authority. The original relation of the Twelve to the Master was necessarily perpetuated in the spreading of the faith, and became fundamental in the structure of Christianity as a public religion; it gave rise to heresy-hunting, crusades, and finally to a situation where the ministers of the Son of Man and the Prince of Peace serve as chaplains with armies and on slave ships. The original message of Jesus concerning a kingdom that is 'not of this world' had to be taken to refer to another life in a quite different world; for the doctrines of absolute community and perfect humility or charity ('selling one's goods' and 'turning the other cheek', etc.) are quite inconsistent with such fundamental principles of civil life as the rights of private ownership and self defence.[2]

The Protestant Reformation coincided, it would seem, with the passage of the German *Volk* from childhood to maturity.[3] The Reformers recognized the ideals of *Vernunft* in Christianity. But they could not break from the fundamental conception of priestly authority. They established a moral police force, and thereby all of their true insights were corrupted. The realities of religious experience—penitence, conversion, betterment—were reduced to words and outward forms; and religious knowledge became a game of *Verstand* with verbal counters, while in practical life hypocritical humility and spiritual conceit usurped the places of energy, self-confidence, and self-respect.[4]

---

[1] This paragraph summarizes the main line of thought in *Die Staatsverfassungen* (Nohl, pp. 36-9). But other contemporary fragments could also be adduced in support, and I am passing over much that is not new in this fragment. My aim is to present a sort of logical skeleton of the thought progression that underlies the fragments, taking them as far as possible in the order in which they were written.

[2] Cf. *Wie wenig die objektive Religion* (Nohl, pp. 39-42) in which much of the thought of *Nicht zu leugnen sind* (Nohl, pp. 359-360) reappears, but the passionate violence of the earlier fragment is somewhat tempered. (In following Nohl's order here I do not mean to commit myself to the view he appears to have held that these fragments are the remains of what was originally a continuous manuscript.)

[3] Cf. Nohl, p. 38 where the *Ritterzeit* is clearly identified as the *kindliche Geist* of contemporary Germany.   [4] See *öffentliche Gewalt* (Nohl, pp. 42-4).

Thus Hegel arrived again at the problem from which he started: the contrast between moral education in fifth-century Athens and eighteenth-century Germany. But now the contrast had its place as part of the objective diagnosis of a diseased society compared with a healthy one. The fundamental premiss of the Christian religion is that this life is only a preparation for life in another world. Yet we have only to compare the description of Socrates' last day in the *Phaedo* with the deathbed of a respectable Lutheran burgher to see how our alienation from all natural enjoyment of life in this world has destroyed our ability to face death, and made death itself the spectral skeleton of an empty life instead of a friendly spirit.[1] Whereas Socrates, as Hegel pointed out earlier,

spoke with his disciples before his death about the immortality of the soul, as a Greek speaks to reason [*Vernunft*] and to fancy [both to-gether]—he spoke so vividly [*lebendig*], he brought this hope so close, so convincingly before them in its whole essence, ⟨and⟩ they had been assembling the premisses for this postulate in their whole lives. That so much should be given to us as to raise this hope to a certainty contradicts human nature and the capacity of man's spirit—but he enlivened it to such a point—as the human spirit forgetting its mortal companion [i.e. the body] can become exalted—even if it should come to pass that he rose as a spirit from his grave, and brought us greeting from the Avenging Goddess [the reference is to Schiller's ode 'Resigna-tion', 64–5, but Hegel is not sure whether he wants to use it, for he proceeds to write down several alternative continuations for his sentence] —that he should give us more to hear than the tables of Moses and the oracles of the prophets which we have in our hearts—that even if this were to have been against the laws of human nature—he would not have thought it necessary to confirm it through resurrection—only in poor spirits, who have not the premisses of this hope alive in themselves, i.e. the ideal [*Idee*] of virtue and of the supreme good, is the hope of immortality itself also weak.[2]

In discussing the development of societies Hegel remarked explicitly that the gradual growth of *Vernunft* involved the loss of many feelings and sensations associated with the *kindlich* stage

---

[1] *So kann in einem Staate* (Nohl, pp. 44–5) and *Über den Unterschied der Szene des Todes* (Nohl, pp. 45–7), which was probably a quite independent meditation rather than the next stage in a continuous essay.

[2] *Christus hatte zwölf Apostel*, Nohl, p. 34. The complexities of the last sentence arise from Hegel's wish to bring together the three religions and their contrasting moulds or sources—Greek myth, Hebrew Law, and Christian miracle—all at once.

of culture, and said further that this was not something to be
lamented. In another place, discussing methods of education, he
comments that just as children learn more by example than from
correction, so a people coming to manhood will not endure a
religion that keeps them in leading-reins. Children, he goes on,
are led by means of love and fear, while grown men are led by
Vernunft. Putting these two passages together,[1] we can successfully construe a note which is otherwise hard to reconcile with his
general conception of religion as the main educational instrument
in the history of mankind. In *Nicht zu leugnen sind* he waxes very
bitter about the claim that Christianity was the real agency of the
moral improvement produced by the Enlightenment:

> The arts, the Enlightenment have bettered our morality, ⟨and⟩
> afterwards they say the Christian religion would have done this even if
> philosophy had not discovered its fundamental principles for it.
> . . . Where has a fortunate change in the pattern of scientific culture
> ever been seen to be preceded by a change in religious concepts which
> would then operate to produce it—has not rather the advance of the
> sciences—the spirit of proof in the sciences always first drawn after it
> enlightenment of theological concepts, and only indeed over the
> strongest possible opposition of the supporters of these concepts?[2]

The answers 'Nowhere' and 'Yes', which are rhetorically demanded
here, seem at first sight to be irreconcilable either with the role of
'Nurse' that was explicitly assigned to Greek religion in the
preceding Stuttgart essay, or with the important place which, in
spite of trenchant criticism, Hegel plainly allots to the Reformation in the immediately subsequent Berne fragments. We might
evade the problem by simply saying that Hegel obviously did not
have Greek religion in mind, or anything in mind except the
contrast between the claims of the Tübingen theology professors
and the actual behaviour of Lutheran pastors; and that in writing
his rough notes he allowed himself to be carried away into a rather
wild generalization which he would never have wished to maintain
in more sober moments.

But reflection on the passages I have just referred to, and on the
relation asserted to exist between religion and *Vernunft* even in
ideal conditions, leads us rather to the view that the general

---

[1] *Die Staatsverfassungen* (Nohl, p. 37) and *So kann in einem Staat* (Nohl,
p. 45).
[2] Nohl, p. 360.

principle laid down in this emotional outburst really is one that Hegel fervently believed in, and that his conviction is what lies behind his indignation. Religion as such has nothing to do with clarification of concepts. Ideally its proper task is to reconcile man's active nature with his reason, to keep all of his needs, feelings, desires, and emotions in harmony with *Vernunft* and so to supply the concrete experience out of which genuine *Begriffe* are abstracted. The abstraction itself, the uncovering of the rational (moral) essence of religion, is the work of mature *Vernunft*, the privilege and responsibility of a tiny minority of sages. Even in the ideal society they are opposed, as Socrates was, by defenders of religion; the death of such a one is, so to speak, the final proof required in his science. A healthy religion will always be favourable to the advance of the sciences, for it aims at the enrichment of experience in all directions. But theological *concepts* will be the last things upon which the advance of reason takes effect. The Reformation was an attempt to restore the *spirit* of religion to health which failed because it accepted the principle of authority. The *concepts* came afterwards and they were all falsified into a verbal mechanism, a product of *Verstand*. In this situation religion was no longer favourable to the advance of science at all: but *also* the only hope of salvation now lay in the development of *Vernunft* through that advance.

Despite the breakdown of society into classes, and the consequent corruption both of politics and religion by a principle of social authority other than that of *Vernunft* itself—or alternatively despite the breakdown of society which *resulted from* that corruption—mankind had achieved maturity and enlightenment. In France reason was laying claim to its rights in practice; in Germany Lessing, Mendelssohn, Kant, and Fichte had rediscovered the rational grounds and ends of religion itself.[1] This then was the gospel to be preached. Mature men can be guided by reason, even

---

[1] Fichte's *Kritik aller Offenbarung* (1792) and Mendelssohn's *Jerusalem* (1783) are explicitly mentioned in Hegel's earliest sketches (see *Inwiefern ist Religion*, Nohl, p. 355). The influence of Lessing's *Nathan* and Kant's essay 'On the radical evil in human nature' (1792) is visible in *Religion ist eine* (see above, Chapter II, pp. 141–3). Hegel may not have studied the rest of Kant's *Religion* until after he had embarked upon his project—the first clearly identifiable references are in *Es sollte eine schwere Aufgabe* (Nohl, pp. 51–2—for the parallels see Peperzak, p. 50 n). Finally, Allison (p. 193 n. 1) has pointed out the close affinity between Hegel's 'Positivity' essay and Lessing's fragment on 'The Religion of Christ'.

though no one, not even a perfectly reasonable man, can escape the contagion of his society. Nothing can restore to us the simple faith of uncorrupted natural feelings, but reason *can* purify our religious experience.[1]

Hegel's reflections on religion and society had now reached a point where he felt able to make a plan in which all of his fragmentary essays could be incorporated, and by which his further efforts could be guided.[2] In this short piece α) *Unter objektiver Religion*, which has tremendous significance for the development of his thought over the next five years, Hegel uses the concept of 'objective religion' as his starting-point. By identifying this with the practical aspect of 'theology', he manages to reaffirm his Socratic heritage and commitments while at the same time plainly accepting the modern quite un-Socratic position of the teacher in society. The most important concern of the State is 'to make objective religion subjective' (where 'subjective' religion means the active presence and power of this theory as an ideal in men's lives and actions). This is exactly the task assigned to the *Church* by Moses Mendelssohn in his *Jerusalem*; and Hegel agrees at least that in modern society it must be the function of 'religious institutions'.[3]

But because of his Hellenic ideal of an organic community life as the substantial bearer and sustainer of freedom and rationality Hegel could not accept Mendelssohn's distinction of 'Church' and 'State' and of the doctrine of 'separation of Church and State'

---

[1] That is the reason why, once the ideal has been described and the malady of his society diagnosed, Hegel's thought and language become 'more solid, less vague and pseudo-poetic' (Peperzak, p. 57 n.). It is not that he has only now begun upon 'more properly philosophical studies'; rather it is because these studies are now relevant. As Peperzak himself notes, Hegel does not cease to use the older vocabulary whenever he has occasion to recur to the description of his ideal. The thought and language that Peperzak calls 'plus solides', Hegel would probably have called 'Mehr abstrakt'.

[2] The plan, (α) *Unter objektiver Religion* (Nohl, pp. 48–50), is the last of the first series of fragments. A complete translation will be found in the Appendix to this volume (pp. 508–10 below).

[3] Hegel himself uses Mendelssohn's word *Anstalt*. Mendelssohn's *Jerusalem*, which appeared in 1783, is cited in Hegel's earliest notes for his project: see *Inwiefern ist Religion*, Nohl, pp. 355–6. (The collocation of the excerpt from Tennemann on the back of the sheet containing *Christus hatte zwölf Apostel* is interesting. It indicates that as a result of his reflections about the *types* of *Volkserzieher* Hegel has come to feel that the whole notion of *Volkserziehung* by direct individual action is a mistake. The essential vehicle of *Volkserziehung* is the State and all of its institutions; and the would-be *Volkserzieher* must be first and foremost a political theorist as Plato was. In this respect Socrates was just as mistaken as Jesus.)

that was consequent upon the sharp distinction that Mendelssohn drew between them. He recognized that if social institutions are to be distinguished as Mendelssohn distinguished Church and State, in terms both of function and of method, then the guardianship of morality as a whole, not just of this highest level where it merges into rational religion, must rest with the 'Church'; the 'State', as the focus of external authority and force, could have only legality, not morality as its aim and concern. But for Hegel the political community was essentially a moral, not just a legal, entity.[1] Like the Greeks he regarded all the institutions of life as subordinate organs of the political community—the πόλις in antiquity, the 'State' in the more complex world of civil relations at the end of the eighteenth century. 'To make objective religion subjective, must be the great concern of *the State*', therefore—and religious freedom, freedom of conscience, must be seen as the essential and fundamental expression of political freedom, the living evidence of the moral character of society itself.

Here, however, I have anticipated the point that Hegel makes in the fourth section of the plan. In the intervening third section a contrast is drawn between the true moral spirit of religion, and the false spirit of authoritarian or sectarian religion with its insistence on formalities of personal allegiance and formal membership. By making this distinction Hegel could remove all such formal considerations from the moral purview of the State, and so provide quite different grounds for just that freedom of religion, and equality of all citizens before the law, which Mendelssohn's doctrine of separation was designed to secure.

The common concern of both Church and State—or rather of Religion and the Constitution—with the moral development of the people forms the topic of section five. Religious education through teaching and ceremonial is paralleled by political education through the constitution and the 'spirit of the government [*Geist der Regierung*]'.

---

[1] This essential contrast between Hegel and Mendelssohn is well drawn by Haering (i. 146 ff.). But there is an equally essential agreement between them regarding the fundamental character of rational freedom, which we must never forget. Hegel did not just take over Mendelssohn's words and reject his spirit—he reintegrated that spirit with its Hellenic sources. To put the point another way, Hegel's ideal is related to that of the enlightened Jew Mendelssohn in very much the same way that it is related to the ideal of the enlightened Jew Jesus, and to Christianity as a 'private' religion.

Thus far the argument is stated only in the broadest outline. If Hegel wrote anything, subsequently, that was specifically designed to develop it in detail, the manuscript has been lost. The probability, however—which amounts in my mind at least to a virtual certainty—is that he did not. He was only summing up the position he had already reached. He may have intended for a time to recast what he had already written, to suit this new sequence of argument: but there are indications that he soon abandoned, or at least greatly simplified, this plan.[1] The following section, the sixth or *zeta* in Hegel's numeration, is what he was most immediately concerned about.

The plan for this section is worked out in detail, with subsections and sub-subsections to the point where Hegel began to have trouble in finding index letters that would indicate co-ordination and subordination unambiguously.[2] The main topic is how far the Christian religion is qualified to perform the function of developing morality in society. In its origin it was a private religion, suited to a particular community at a particular time, but it has since been modified considerably by the social needs of men and by their prejudices. With respect to doctrine, however, it meets the standards of practical reason fairly well, and it has the outstanding advantage that its essential moral message is

---

[1] The margin of this 'schema' (see Nohl, p. 48 n.) contains a much simpler schema as follows: 'A. Introduction. B. (*a*) Doctrines; (*b*) Traditions; (*c*) Ceremonies; (*d*) Public Religion.' Nohl suggests plausibly enough that the 'A. 1' at the head of the first sheets of *Religion ist eine* may refer to this plan. The subdivisions of 'B' correspond fairly well with the more complex articulation of section 6 (*zeta*) in the full schema, and also with the plan announced in the introduction to *Wenn man von der Christlichen Religion* (Nohl, p. 62). The natural hypothesis therefore is that after writing *Es sollte eine schwere Aufgabe* Hegel went back to his original schema and substituted a simpler plan in which the first five sections were collapsed into one.

[2] For some reason he avoids numerals, both Arabic and Roman, altogether. His main sections are indicated by Greek letters. So when he wished to subdivide section *zeta* he turned naturally to the Latin alphabet. But then he found it necessary to subdivide subsection (*a*) so he turned to the Greek alphabet again. After using (*a*) and (*β*) however, he apparently began to worry about the confusion of sub-heads with main heads, for he suddenly turned to the Hebrew alphabet for his third subdivision. Then he was able to pass on at last to subsection (*b*), and when the problem of subheadings arose once more under subsection (*c*) he needed only two, so he simply used (*a*) and (*b*) over again.

Thus, using numerals for his principal use of the Greek alphabet and capitals for his principal use of the Latin alphabet, the formal organization of the schema is as follows: Sections 1, 2, 3, 4, 5, 6, with section 6 subdivided as follows: A, *a*, *β*, [*γ*]; B; C, *a*, *b*.

enshrined in concrete examples of virtuous action. But the great *theoretical* statements of Christian morality—such as the Sermon on the Mount—are peculiarly subject to misunderstanding and have in fact been misunderstood.

The fact that Christianity is founded on a historical tradition is a notable *dis*advantage. For the miraculous elements in the historical account are bound to arouse some scepticism; and while this does no harm in a private religion where adherence is entirely voluntary, the inevitable existence of 'unbelievers' poses a serious problem for a public religion. Also it is not properly adapted to the needs of the imagination, as Greek religion was, being altogether too melancholy and alien. This was a point already made in his earlier essay, and Hegel probably meant to incorporate some of that discussion here.

There is virtually nothing good to be said for Christian cere-monial. In the original 'private' religion of the primitive church, the Eucharist was both an expression and an appropriate symbol of the true spirit of love and brotherhood. But now it is only a shibboleth for sectarian bigotry.

Finally Hegel makes two points, one very general, one specific, about the 'other commands concerning the way of life'. First he remarks on the withdrawal from public life which makes Christianity *essentially* a private religion. Secondly he notes that the communism of the primitive Church, which is not feasible in a political community, has been replaced by the giving of alms but in the process, the original spirit of almsgiving as an act of private piety has been completely corrupted. Presumably he meant to treat the degeneration of Christian communism into the formality of the Sunday collection plate as somehow summing up all those aspects of Christian moral doctrine that made it unsuitable as a foundation for the folk-religion of a bourgeois society. The point that the ideal of Christian communism is quite inconsistent with the fundamental assumptions of *bürgerliche Gesellschaft* is one that he had made in earlier fragments.[1] But he continued to meditate about this aspect of primitive Christianity for some time, probably because he was not sure how to reconcile the obvious egoistic tendencies of 'civil society' with his ideal of the State as a moral organism.

Having made this plan, Hegel seems to have delayed some time

---

[1] See *Nicht zu leugnen sind* (Nohl, p. 360); the examples of Nathanael and Diogenes in *Außer dem mündlichen Unterricht* (Nohl, p. 31); and, most explicitly, *Wie wenig die objektive Religion* (Nohl, p. 41).

before proceeding with it. Apparently he began at about this time to work over all of the notes that he had by him concerning psychology and to read, or at least study reviews of, various works on the subject which had appeared since he took Flatt's course at Tübingen.[1] A plausible explanation for Hegel's voluntary postponement of further work on his new-made plan is provided by two related hypotheses which are to some extent directly supported by the evidence. On the one hand Hegel probably felt unequal to the task which he had now clearly defined for himself in his plan, and was in the mood to procrastinate about it;[2] and on the other hand he may very well have felt that he must get clear about individual psychology before he could solve his problem of religious and social reformation. He remarks in one of his earlier Berne fragments that the corruption of the spirit of Christianity by the principle of authority had resulted in the replacing of genuine religious experience by a kind of routine for the production of certain states of mind and the substitution of psychology for real theology in religious education.[3]

[1] Almost certainly Hegel had been reading and making excerpts on philosophical psychology since he took Flatt's course in 1789. It is reasonable to assume that almost all of the reading and studying of which the Psychologie of 1794 is a record was done in the Stift between 1790 and 1793. But there is no question that the manuscript as we have it was written in 1794 (and after Unter objektiver Religion)—see Miss Schüler's categorical assertion in Hegel-Studien ii. 141. The evidence for holding that the material was assembled in Tübingen is given in the following notes.

[2] Hegel was much troubled in his first year at Berne by an inability to settle firmly to work at anything—see especially his first letter to Schelling, 24 Dec. 1794, Briefe, i. 11). In his last year at Tübingen he had become involved in the controversy in the Stift about the interpretation of the Critical Philosophy. At Berne he pined for those discussions and bewailed his lack of the latest philosophical literature (see Briefe, i. 11, 17). That he should have turned back to work over his old notes and excerpts was natural enough in the circumstances; but it was also a distraction from the long-pondered project on which he had begun to work so earnestly as soon as he left Tübingen. I assume that his attention wandered intermittently from the Psychologie back to his religious concerns, and that Es sollte eine schwere Aufgabe was written in this same period. If so, he had good reason for remarking to Schelling that his activity was 'too heterogeneous'. (The affinity between the reflections in the short essay on Lessing's correspondence with his wife (Ich las neulich Lessings Briefwechsel, Jub. xx. 451–5), and Hegel's general concern about the relation between abstract principles and concrete behaviour in 1793 and 1794, seems to me to make 1794—the year of 'heterogeneous' activities—the most probable time for its composition. That it belongs somewhere in the Tübingen or the Berne period can hardly be doubted; and the influence of Lessing during the early years at Berne was probably not confined to the 'exoteric' Nathan—see p. 169 n. above.)

[3] See öffentliche Gewalt, Nohl, pp. 43–4.

This reflection upon the education that he had himself received would have provided Hegel with strong grounds for studying psychology. But even without taking it into consideration we can easily see why anyone faced with Hegel's problem about the relation of an educational reformer to his time, and to its assumptions and methods, should feel that he ought to understand as clearly as possible what was known or believed by the best qualified of his contemporaries about human nature. It would seem that this was all that Hegel meant to achieve in his *Psychologie*—which was to all intents and purposes his first venture in purely theoretical philosophy. There is no sign anywhere in his manuscripts at this period that he meant to incorporate a systematic account of his theory of human nature into an essay intended for publication. The compilation that he made, which Hoffmeister published under the imposing title 'Materials for a Philosophy of Subjective Spirit', should rather be described more neutrally as 'Notes on Psychology'.[1] There is no sign in it of the urgency of personal conviction that we find in Hegel's sketches and fragments on social topics.

Flatt's course at Tübingen in 1789 or 1790—together with the notes he made from his reading during the Tübingen period—provided an organized body of notes from which he began.[2] But he had been reading and excerpting from books on the subject since he was a schoolboy of fifteen, and Hoffmeister has provided an impressive list of parallels with the works of authors such as Abel, Meiners, Zimmerman, and Feder whom we know he studied in those early days. Some of the most obvious and explicit parallels or references are to works that appeared after 1789—notably to Kant's *Critique of Judgement* (1790) and Reinhold's *Versuch einer neuen Theorie des Vorstellungsvermögens* (1791).[3] What we have

[1] Reprinted in *Dok.*, pp. 195–217. The lines of the text are numbered consecutively in the margin, which considerably facilitates exact reference.

[2] Henrich had discovered some sets of students' notes from one of Flatt's courses (he does not say definitely which one) on the basis of which he assures us that Hegel's *Psychologie* is 'in its middle section an excerpt from Flatt's class' (*Hegel-Studien*, iii. 70–1 n.). See Chapter II, pp. 83–4 above.

[3] For the *Critique of Judgement* see lines 696–703; for Reinhold's *Versuch*, lines 58–60 with Hoffmeister's notes (*Dok.*, pp. 452–3). *Repetent* Diez was an early champion of Reinhold in the *Stift*, so Hegel may have studied the *Versuch* at Tübingen. (But at line 397 Hegel refers explicitly to a review of the *Versuch* which appeared in 1793, and which he probably excerpted at Berne). Hegel probably read J. Schulze's *Erläuterungen über Kants Kritik* (1784) at Tübingen— though it is conceivable that he had excerpted it as early as 1787 or 1788 (for

before us must therefore be thought of as a mosaic composed by Hegel himself from his excerpt collection.[1]

Regarding the doctrines set forth in the *Psychologie* there is perhaps only one point that deserves particular mention. The basic articulation of the manuscript is in terms of mental faculties: *Empfindung* and *Phantasie* are treated as the 'lower' cognitive capacities, and *Verstand* and *Vernunft* as the 'higher' ones. The influence of Kant upon the account of *Empfindung* is evident from the basic division into 'outer' and 'inner' sense. The discussion of *Phantasie* is quite un-Kantian, being filled with empirical observations and details. But the account of *Verstand* and *Vernunft* and of the intermediate *Vermögen zu urteilen* is entirely Kantian and is full of explicit references to the *Critique of Pure Reason*. *Vernunft* is treated as a power that goes beyond sense experience altogether, and not as a power by which all experience is integrated. This Kantian opposition between *Vernunft* and sense experience has appeared explicitly in some passages in the fragments already examined. But in spite of it Hegel has always tended to regard *Vernunft* as a faculty that only operates properly as a function of completed integrated experience. There is no sign of a discussion of this integrative power in the notes. Indeed *Vernunft* is not even allotted a separate heading, but is discussed under the general heading *Verstand*.[2]

the influence of this book see Hoffmeister's notes, *Dok.*, p. 451); and he was almost certainly familiar with I. D. Mauchardt's *Allgemeine Repertorium für empirische Psychologie* (Nürnberg, vol. i, 1792) from the moment it began to appear—if not sooner—since Mauchardt was a *Repetent* in the *Stift* until 1793 (Hegel asked Schelling to get J. G. Süskind to send him a review of this work at Christmas 1794—*Briefe*, i. 13).

On the other hand, Hegel probably made the excerpt from a review (which appeared in 1792) of C. C. E. Schmid's *Empirische Psychologie* (1791), at Berne in 1794. Hoffmeister prints it as a Tübingen excerpt (*Dok.*, pp. 172–4), but he is almost certainly wrong (as he is in the case of the excerpt from Tennemann which was written on the back of *Christus hatte zwölf Apostel*). No doubt his dating was influenced by his view that the *Psychologie* was written at Tübingen. Actually it is another example of Hegel's conning the reviews while he yearned for access to the books themselves.

[1] It is even conceivable that Hegel's notes from Flatt's course were themselves an 'excerpt' from the notes of Schelling or Hölderlin on the Kant course of 1791. (Schelling is the only one of the three friends who can be conclusively shown to have attended Flatt's lectures on the Critical Philosophy—see Fuhrmans, i. 20 n.)

[2] But the heading *Verstand* at line 539 should probably be regarded as shorthand for *Verstand ⟨und Vernunft⟩* in view of the way these two are linked both in the introductory analysis (line 67, 'III Verstand und Vernunft: oberes

The next group of three fragments which comes at the end of Nohl's first section on 'Folk-religion and Christianity' seems, in terms of handwriting, to have been contemporary with the last pages of the *Psychologie* and with Hegel's first letters to Schelling (24 December 1794 and late January 1795). The two longer ones are plainly successive attempts to carry out the programme laid down in the sixth section of the schema *Unter objektiver Religion*. The sheets were originally numbered in separate series (1, 2, 3, 4 and α, β, γ, respectively) and the later version contains two references back to parts of the earlier one, which Hegel presumably meant to incorporate in any eventual fair copy. In the end, however, he simply linked the second essay to the first by renumbering the sheets 5, 6, 7, and laid them both aside. The third fragment is briefer and more literally fragmentary, being apparently the second of another series of sheets. In order of composition it may very probably have fallen between the other two, though there is scarcely enough of it to make a secure judgement upon this point possible. I shall here deal with it after the other two, partly for obvious reasons of convenience, and partly for reasons which will appear in the course of the exposition.

The two essays *Es sollte eine schwere Aufgabe* and *Wenn man von der christlichen Religion* are both essentially critical examinations of the fundamental *doctrines* of Christianity with a view to deciding how far it meets the requirements of a healthy folk-religion.[1] *Es sollte eine schwere Aufgabe* is written strictly from the point of view of *Vernunftreligion*. At the very beginning the influence of Mendelssohn is apparent, as it was in the schema; as the discussion proceeds the echoes of themes and doctrines in Kant's *Religion* become plainer. In *Wenn man von der christlichen Religion*, the influence of Mendelssohn and Kant is still strong, but it has been digested, as it were, and Hegel is more typically himself. Probably he went back to his schema and noted how it could be summarized and simplified before he began this second

⟨Erkenntnisvermogen⟩') and in the first sentence of the section (line 540–1, 'Die Gesetze des Verstandes und der Vernunft sind Gegenstände der Logik'). In the body of the following discussion the main division is between the *Vermögen der Begriffe* (line 543) and the *Vermögen zu urteilen* (line 597); *Verstand, Reflektie-*⟨*rende Urteilskraft*⟩, and ⟨*Vernunft*⟩ appear as particular faculties under the latter heading.

[1] Nohl, pp. 50–69. In spite of his insistence that he has tried to distil the essence of Christian tradition (Nohl, p. 61), Hegel's image of orthodox doctrine probably derives largely from the compendium of Sartorius.

version. For it opens with a brief introduction at the end of which the four heads of the main discussion are announced as (a) Doctrines, (b) Traditions, (c) Ceremonies, (d) The Relation of Religion to the State, or its 'public' character.[1] Once more, however, he did not get beyond the first topic in the body of the essay.

In both versions Christianity is fairly severely handled, and in both Hegel's primary concern is to distinguish the message of the man Jesus from the Gospel of the God Christ. But in the first essay he seeks to focus attention on the message of Jesus, while in the second he concentrates on the concept of 'faith in Christ'. The two discussions do not overlap a great deal, and Hegel probably meant to conflate them eventually. I shall therefore attempt to do so here, following the hints in his discussion as far as I can and picking up any loose ends afterwards.

The introduction to *Wenn man von der christlichen Religion* emphasizes the need to identify the 'aim and essence' of Christianity correctly, not in terms of what some learned professor says, because at that level there is always controversy, but by reference to what is generally believed and universally taught. We must not 'fall into the error of those who give others the itch in order to have the pleasure of scratching them', says Hegel, using for the first time an image from Butler's *Hudibras* which obviously delighted him very much, and which he himself had found, most probably, in Lessing's *Letters on Recent Literature* (1759).[2] The proper rational purpose of religion, of course, is the strengthening of *Sittlichkeit* by establishing the *Idee* of God as giver of the moral law and guarantor of the highest good (i.e. the harmony of virtue and happiness postulated by Kant). From this point of view a human statesman or lawgiver can concern himself with the religion of his society, though the most he can do usually is to see that the traditional folk-religion is directed towards this truth and does not decay into superstition. In societies where the constitution is monarchic and there is a hierarchy of classes, however, there is a danger that the traditional religion may become a reactionary force, employed by the powerful to maintain their power. Then proper development is arrested for centuries; and even the revo-

---

[1] Nohl, p. 62; cf. also p. 48 n.
[2] Nohl, p. 61; on the origin of the expression and Hegel's three subsequent uses of it see Wolfgang Ritzel, 'Zur Herkunft eines Hegelschen Ausdrucks', *Hegel-Studien*, ii. 278–81.

lutionary upheaval when it comes is likely to subside again without getting to the root of the evil. The new insights are corrupted through their being established with all the old authority.[1]

With this fairly broad hint of his views about the present state of the Christian religion Hegel proceeds to his analysis. The fundamental doctrine of Christianity, he says, is that the hope of eternal blessedness is more important than anything else. Christians therefore seek to 'please God' as the giver of eternal blessedness. The *Idee* of blessedness agrees 'well enough in its material aspect' with what *Vernunft* establishes;[2] but the rational conception of what is chiefly pleasing to God is quite different from that of orthodox religion. Christianity demands 'faith in Christ', while what Reason requires is 'adaptation [*Angemessenheit*] of the disposition [*Gesinnung*] to the moral law'. This difference has led to all the horrors of bigotry and intolerance typified by the proverbial dismissal of the virtues of the pagans as 'splendid vices', and to the allied doctrine that men cannot do anything for themselves but must depend on God's grace and mercy in absolute humility of spirit. There is a fundamental conflict here between Christian doctrine and the universal principle of practical reason that 'virtue deserves happiness'; and when the doctrine of human helplessness is backed by the dogma of original sin, the very freedom which is the condition of all moral responsibility is denied.[3]

In his earlier version Hegel attacked the fundamental contention that certain 'mysteries' of the faith are 'above' reason, arguing that even if, perhaps, they were not *contrary* to reason, still it is contrary to reason to believe in them, for only our reason can tell us what is essential to moral salvation. Thus the conception of reward and punishment according to desert is rationally bound up with the postulate of immortality, but the unsoundness of the

[1] In his earlier version Hegel stresses rather his optimistic conviction that reason will eventually overthrow all such authoritarian class structures—but he also mentions the Kingdom of Naples and the Papal States as examples of how far the corruption of human society can go and yet be maintained by the instinctive goodness of man's nature (Nohl, p. 52).

[2] Nohl, p. 62. A remark in the earlier version (Nohl, pp. 50–1) makes it clear that Hegel is fully conscious of the gulf between 'acting from respect for the law' and 'acting for the sake of obtaining blessedness'. This *may* therefore be part of what is implied by the qualifying phrase 'in Ansehung der Materie' here.

[3] Nohl, pp. 62–4; see also pp. 52–3 for a not quite parallel discussion of 'pleasing God' and the 'means of grace' in the earlier version.

Christian doctrine of salvation or damnation in the other world is evidenced by the excesses of arrogance and anxiety which these conceptions induce among believers in this world.[1]

To say that moral freedom itself requires 'faith in Christ' is irrational, because the acquiring of faith is contingent upon historical testimony, and is not simply a matter of developing the universally available capacities of *Vernunft* itself; and since it conflicts with rational equity to suppose that some men have been arbitrarily chosen as the 'elect', we cannot maintain that 'faith in Christ' is the *exclusive* condition for the achievement of blessedness.[2]

This is not the most serious weakness that arises from the historical character of the Christian faith, however. For even a non-historical faith may be irrational in this way. What is still worse is that since a historical tradition of foreign origin cannot by its very nature be a popular possession, the establishment of a priestly class with its own peculiar authority is unavoidable in a public religion founded on such a basis. Furthermore the historical trappings of the faith make it, if not less subject to rational criticism, at least less liable to stimulate and arouse it, since special preparation and training is requisite for intelligent criticism of a body of historical evidence. Thus the ordinary man is inevitably obliged to depend on the *Verstand* of experts instead of being spurred to use and rely on his own *Vernunft*. This dependence destroys the proper character of religious faith itself, the very thing that gives religion its practical value and importance. For it ought to be a 'stretching of the soul' (*Spannung der Seele*), not a 'function of the memory' (*Sache des Gedächtnisses*).[3]

Awareness of the peculiar problems that arise from the historical character of Christianity grew upon Hegel only after he had written his first version, or perhaps while he was writing it. In his first draft the conviction that *Vernunft* both could and would cast off everything in a folk-tradition that conflicted with its requirements remains more or less unclouded and unqualified. He still holds to this faith in his second draft, but he recognizes that the rational criticism of a historical religion presents special difficulties.[4]

He also holds to the conviction expressed both in his schema

---

[1] Nohl, pp. 54–6.   [2] Nohl, pp. 64–5.   [3] Nohl, pp. 65–6.
[4] Nohl, pp. 66–7; cf. also pp. 50–1.

and in the first draft, that the historical reality of Jesus is the main source of strength in the Christian tradition. His final version contains at this point a laconic note 'Faith in Christ is faith in a personified ideal' with a reference to his discussion of this thesis in the first draft.[1] This topic must therefore be incorporated here.

In his initial schematic estimate of Christianity, Hegel remarks, 'its practical doctrines are pure and have the advantage of being mainly set forth in examples';[2] and the practical example of Jesus is the real kernel of positive value which all the negative criticism in his first draft is designed to strip bare. For at the beginning of it he remarks that many moral philosophers—'Spinoza, Shaftesbury, Rousseau, Kant'—having developed their own sensibilities to the point where their own heart served as a mirror for the beauty of the *Idee* of morality, have reverenced the moral teaching of Jesus the more, the higher their contempt for everything else in the Christian faith became.[3] Having demonstrated the justice of that contempt, as it were, he turns to the justification of the reverence. Jesus, he says, differs from a teacher like Socrates, in that for the believer he is not just a model case of the virtuous man, he is *virtue itself personified*. How this can be the case may be a headache for the understanding, but the imagination (*Phantasie*) is fired by the visible presence of its ideal, for, as Plato said, if virtue were to come before us in visible form all mortals must love it.[4]

This conception of the significance of the Incarnation was one which Hegel retained and deepened as the years went on. But no one who has read his eulogy of Socrates as portrayed in the *Phaedo*—the man whose arguments had such force that a return from the grave would not strengthen them—would expect this view of Jesus to have for him in 1794 the meaning and value that it came to have later. 'Why should the supernatural power by which Christ healed the sick concern us?' he asks. 'Why should the lives and deaths of Socrates and Jesus not serve as exemplars of Virtue arousing in us the urge to imitate and emulate them?' The

[1] Nohl, p. 67; cf. also pp. 56–8.

[2] Nohl, p. 49. Hegel is presumably thinking of the parables as well as the acts of Jesus (many of which were themselves intended as parables, of course). But he explicitly excludes such discourses as the Sermon on the Mount.

[3] Nohl, p. 51; cf. also pp. 58–9 where the agreement between Christian ethics and Kantian ethics is emphasized.

[4] Nohl, pp. 56–7.

answer is found in the whole Christian doctrine of atonement and grace, which has caused the *name* of Christ to become more important to the Christians than his living example, as Lessing's Nathan complained.[1]

This is the reason why the second draft is focused entirely upon the concept of 'faith in Christ'—and what was originally seen as the great strength of Christianity is now seen to be *also* its great weakness. It is only because we are so corrupted and degraded by that sense of our own helplessness which Christian doctrine is calculated to induce and to reinforce, that we feel the need of the God–Man Jesus, and cannot clasp the hand of the human sage, Socrates. In the virtuous hero we can recognize flesh of our flesh and bone of our bone, but not spirit of our spirit and power of our power. For we have lost our power, it comes to us as an alien thing, a gift of grace from on high, and only a visible divinity can bring it to us. But even so, concludes Hegel, the divinity that we recognize in him is still just our own uncorrupted moral nature and rational power. Jesus is still virtue personified and it is as such that he must be worshipped, not as the second person of a mystic trinity, who was 'begotten before all worlds'. As long as we remember this we shall not fall into the error of exalting the name of Jesus at the expense of his essential message.[2]

Of course Christianity itself did not originally create the climate that led to its acceptance. This is the subject of *Jetzt braucht die Menge*, which can plausibly be regarded as the second sheet of an essay on 'Traditions'.[3] Not much hangs on the question whether it was written before or after the second draft of the essay on 'Doctrines', but if, as the handwriting seems to indicate, it was written before, then the sequence of Hegel's thoughts was something like this. He began with the normal 'enlightened' idea of exalting the 'spirit' of Jesus himself, as opposed to the 'letter' of the gospel preached in his 'name'.[4] But when he came to consider the personal impact of Jesus as compared with that of Socrates, he realized that the authoritative character of his

---

[1] Nohl, pp. 59–60.

[2] Nohl, pp. 67–9. Here Hegel makes his second backward reference indicating that his earlier discussion of this point is to be integrated with his closing attack on the mystery of the Atonement in the second draft (compare Nohl, pp. 59–60).

[3] Nohl, pp. 70–1. That it is the second sheet of *some* series is indicated by its being marked with the letter *b*.

[4] Cf. *Unter objektiver Religion*, section Gamma (Nohl, p. 49); *Es sollte eine schwere Aufgabe* (Nohl, pp. 51, 60).

teaching and example, together with all the shibboleths on which he had remarked earlier as evidence of the influence of the national tradition upon any teacher, were connected with quite a different conception of the nature and power of Jesus from that which the followers of Socrates had of their master. Socrates was the shining example of how to live life to the full as a citizen of Athens; while Jesus was the personification of an ideal that is 'not of this world'. He is the ideal of humanity appearing in a world where life has lost every vestige of joy and beauty, the morally autonomous individual existing in a society where men have lost all faith in their power to exert moral freedom. Hence he can only appear as a God, and the recovery by his followers of their human status is necessarily seen as the result of his saving power, and hence as conditional upon faith in him. This was the condition of the Jews in bondage to their law and their priesthood as individuals, and to the Romans as a nation; as the Empire began to decay it became the condition of the whole world. Thus the spirit which vanished from the world when the Greek cities passed under a conqueror's yoke, appeared now, not in its proper guise, but as an individual who brought news of its existence in another world. But the people of this world would only finally be redeemed by 'faith' in him, when they recognized the alien power as their own, the life and joys of the other world as the proper expression of man's social nature in this world. When this happens, however, the political quietism of Christianity and its associated ethics of humility will disappear, and 'constitutions which only guarantee life and property will never be thought the best'.

This is the burden of Hegel's reflections in *Jetzt braucht die Menge*, which offers us the first sketch of what appears in the *Phenomenology* as the 'Unhappy consciousness'. It is entirely plausible to suppose that after writing it he felt moved to turn back and write a new meditation upon the ambiguity of the concept 'faith in Christ'.[1]

---

[1] On the other hand the insight which first came to Hegel at the end of *Es sollte eine schwere Aufgabe* is so much more trenchantly stated in *Jetzt braucht die Menge* than in *Wenn man von der christlichen Religion* that it would not be surprising to find that *Jetzt braucht die Menge* was the last of the series. (In that event it may be linked with Hegel's reading of Gibbon and Forster, which certainly reinforced his own views about the degeneration of ancient republican virtues under the Empire. See *Unkunde der Geschichte*—for the correction of Nohl's *incipit* see p. 196 n. below—and *In einer Republik*, Nohl, pp. 363–4, 365, 366.)

Peperzak has rightly drawn attention to the community of thought and feeling that is evident in *Jetzt braucht die Menge* on the one side, and Hegel's third letter to Schelling on the other.[1] This letter was written on 16 April 1795, when Hegel's mind must already have been set upon *The Life of Jesus* which he began to write three weeks later. It shows that his sense of the disastrous political and social consequences of the promulgation of Christianity had become even keener as time went on; and so likewise had his conviction that the time had finally arrived when the real message of Jesus could be received and understood correctly. His own *Life of Jesus* thus emerges as an attempt to undo the evil consequences of the gospel of salvation through faith, by restating the gospel of salvation through reason. For he writes:

I believe there is no better sign of the times than this, that humanity is set forth to itself as so worthy of respect; a proof is that the halo round the heads of the oppressors and gods of the earth is disappearing. The philosophers are proving this worthiness, the peoples will come to feel it and not simply ask for their rights which are now brought low in the dust, but take them back themselves—repossess themselves [*sich aneignen*]. Religion and politics have played *the same* hidden game together [*haben unter einer Decke gespielt*], the former has taught, what despotism willed, the dishonouring of the human race, its inability to achieve any good, or to amount to anything on its own. With the spread of the ideals [*der Ideen*] of how things *ought* to be, the apathetic tendency of the solid citizens [*die Indolenz der gesetzten Leute*] to accept everything always just as it is, will disappear. This enlivening power of ideals —even though they have always still some limitations—like that of the fatherland, of its constitution, etc.—will raise men's hearts [*Gemüter*] and they will learn to sacrifice themselves, whereas at present the spirit of the constitutions has made a pact with personal advantage [*Eigennutz*] and has based its rule upon that. I exhort myself always in the words of the *Lebensläufe*: 'Strive toward the sun my friends, that the salvation of the human race may soon come to fruition! What use are the hindering leaves? or the branches? Cleave through them to the sunlight, and strive till ye be weary!' 'Tis good so, for so shall ye sleep the better!'[2]

[1] Peperzak, pp. 56–7.

[2] *Briefe*, i. 24–5. The italics represent Hegel's own underlining. The quotation is from Th .G. von Hippel, *Lebensläufe nach aufsteigender Linie* (1778–81), a semi-autobiographical novel, full of philosophical reflections, which Hegel and a group of friends read together at the *Stift* (see Rosenkranz, p. 40). In Hippel's *Collected Works* (Berlin, 1827–39) the passage can be found in Volume III at page 137. Hoffmeister gives the reference for the first edition as Teil III, 1, p. 200. Hegel's citation is not quite word perfect.

We might sum up the progress of Hegel's reflections during the eighteen months between his arrival in Berne and the writing of this letter, in terms of the contrast between Jesus and Socrates which gradually developed in his mind. He saw both of them initially simply as great moral teachers who sought to enlighten the ethical and religious convictions of their own society. The principal contrast between them arose from the contrast between those societies. The 'care for the soul' which Socrates preached to his fellow Athenians did not involve any severing of their social, political, and economic ties, but if anything a strengthening of them; whereas the call of Jesus involved forsaking the world. Thus Socrates was a *public* teacher, while Jesus was essentially a *private* one, not only in the obvious sense, but in the etymological sense that his teaching had a *privative* effect. By cutting his followers off from the world he made it impossible for them to achieve independence and personal individuality in it. He became for them a model in a sense in which Socrates was never a model for his followers. To 'follow the example' of Socrates was only to be 'like' him in the sense of being unique, and hence as much different from him as from anyone else. Whereas to follow Jesus was to become absolutely dependent on him, and on the little group of the 'brethren'. Out of this dependence arose another far greater contrast between the roles of Socrates and Jesus in history. The death of Jesus conferred a halo of divinity upon him, whereas the death of Socrates merely set the seal upon his perfect humanity.

As Hegel reflected he came to see *this* contrast as the crucial one, and even to hold that the initial contrast of public and private teaching was partially mistaken. Not Socrates but Plato, was the public educator of the Greeks.[1] Both Socrates and Jesus were private teachers who sought to develop particular individuals rather than to improve society as a whole. Only the contrast between their attitudes to society, integrative and privative respectively, was really correctly drawn, and it was from this that the greater

---

[1] See the excerpt from the review of Tennemann which Hegel wrote on the back of *Christus hatte zwölf Apostel* (*Dok.*, p. 174; cf. Nohl, p. 35 n. and p. 170 n. 3 above). This distinction between Socrates and Plato was relevant for the justification of Hegel's own activity (which was modelled on that of Plato rather than that of Socrates). But it did not affect Hegel's choice of Socrates (not Plato) as the exemplar of the spirit of popular enlightenment among the Greeks. Cf. *Unkunde der Geschichte* (Nohl, p. 363, early 1795) where Socrates, Jesus, and Kant are compared from this point of view.

contrast in their historical destinies arose. For the health of modern society it was vital that this false contrast should be abolished. The halo must be stripped from the head of the god Christ in order that the message of the man Jesus might be rightly understood. First the conception of original sin must be shown to be an illusion, produced by the historical circumstances that made his followers so absolutely dependent on him. But then too, and partly as a means to the destruction of the illusion, the human truth behind it must be revealed. Thus we see how it was that Hegel could pen his most violent attack on the evil alliance of throne and altar at the very moment when he was about to embark on his *Life of Jesus*.[1]

3. *The God of Reason and his gospel*

The correspondence between Hegel and Schelling had so far been mainly dominated by the interests of the latter, which were already more purely philosophical than Hegel's. The spur, or perhaps only the pretext, for Hegel's first letter was provided by the appearance of Schelling's first published essay *Über Mythen*. Hegel wrote on Christmas Eve 1794 that from the notice he had just seen, he could recognize that Schelling was 'on his old track' seeking 'to enlighten important theological concepts and bit by bit to set aside the old sourdough'. About his own efforts in the same direction he spoke rather slightingly, wishing that he might obtain a place somewhere—'not in Tübingen'—where he could 'harvest what he had formerly neglected'.[2]

Schelling's answer, which came fairly promptly (6 January 1795), can scarcely have fallen kindly upon Hegel's ears. For Schelling was full of the latest developments in philosophy, and bubbling with enthusiasm for Fichte; and he reported that his mythological concerns had been only a marginal interest for 'nearly a year'.

Who [he asks scathingly] can bury himself in the dust of ancient times, when *his own* time is in motion every instant sweeping him along with it ⟨?⟩. I live and move presently in philosophy. Philosophy is not yet finished. Kant has given the results; the premisses are still lacking. And who can understand results without premisses?[3]

---

[1] The violence of his feelings on this topic was no doubt intensified by his reading of Gibbon at about this time—see *Unkunde der Geschichte*, Nohl, pp. 365–6.   [2] Letter 6, *Briefe*, i. 11.

[3] Letter 7, *Briefe*, i. 14. Contempt for those who mistake the *Staub* of historical

This must have made harsh reading for poor Hegel, buried as he was in the dust of ancient times still, and trying desperately to concentrate his efforts and sustain his industry enough to produce something fit for publication. Schelling did not even bother to send a copy of his own latest essay 'On the possibility of a form of philosophy in general' (1794), so Hegel had to ask for it explicitly in his reply, a few weeks later. Since Kant's *Vernunftreligion* touched so closely on his own concerns he was happy to join in Schelling's condemnation of the Tübingen interpretation of Kant. But for him Kant's philosophy provided not theoretical results for which 'premisses' had still to be found, but theoretical results which still need to be applied to practical problems, and can so be made to yield practical premisses, as it were. In what Hegel says about Fichte there are signs of a mischievous desire to give Schelling a nasty pill to swallow in his turn. For he suggests that Fichte is not wholly innocent of responsibility in the matter of making the new criticism fit in with the traditional dogmatism:

If his principles are taken as fixed once and for all, no limit or barrier can be set up against the theological logic. He deduces from the holiness of God what He must do on account of His purely moral nature etc., and thereby he has reintroduced the old technique of proof in dogmatics; it is perhaps worth the effort to clarify this point.—If I had time, I would try to determine more precisely how far—after the establishment of moral faith ⟨—⟩ we may employ the legitimated idea of God backwards, e.g. in the clarification of teleology [*die Zweckbeziehung*] etc., how far we may take it back with us from ethical theology to physical theology and still exercise control with it there. This seems to me to be in general the road people take with the idea of providence—and equally with miracles and, in Fichte's case, with revelation.[1]

This complaint that Fichte was returning to the old Leibnizian tradition of reasoning out the way the world *must* be, if it is the work of an absolutely perfect being, seems, whether justified or not, to reflect a very definite impression which both Hegel and Hölderlin gained from their first encounter with the *Critique of all Revelation*.[2] This is indirectly confirmed by the letter which

research for the living truth is frequently expressed by Lessing (see especially *Ernst und Falk*, Dialogue IV). No doubt Schelling had heard Hegel, that *Vertrauter Lessings*, expressing similar sentiments—as he does later again in *Eleusis* (lines 57–63). [1] *Briefe*, i. 17.

[2] If, as I suspect, Hölderlin read the book first, he may have passed on his impressions before Hegel ever began to read it.

Hölderlin wrote to Hegel from Jena just at this time—a letter
filled with all the literary excitement of life in Jena and Weimar.
Hölderlin devotes the second half of this letter to his impressions
of Fichte—recommending the *Grundlage der gesamten Wissenschaftslehre* and the lectures on the *Vocation of the Scholar* to
Hegel's notice, but also acknowledging: 'To begin with I held him
very much in contempt for dogmatism; he seems, if I may make a
guess, to have actually stood at the crossroads or to be still standing
there . . .'[1]

Schelling may have suspected that his first letter had hurt
Hegel's feelings a little, for in his reply to Hegel's second letter
(4 February 1795) he echoes Hegel's original opening about 'Dein
alt Weg' and the 'alt Sauerteig': 'we find ourselves on the old tracks
together . . . we both want to prevent the great things that our age
has produced from being lumped together with the stale sourdough of times past . . .'[2] In the body of the letter he bends over
backwards in his efforts to agree with Hegel wherever possible.
He had probably shared the unfavourable initial impression of the
Critique of all Revelation—and of course he knew that *Repetent*
Süskind had added an appendix giving the Tübingen interpretation of it to his German translation of Storr's *Notes on the
Kantian Philosophy of Religion* (1794). He now suggests apologeti-
cally that its dogmatic tendencies were due either to 'accommoda-

---

[1] Letter 9, 26 Jan. 1795, *Briefe*, i. 19; Beck thinks that 'Im Anfange' refers to
the impression Hölderlin formed while reading the first sheets of the *Grundlage*
at Walterhausen the previous summer: cf. *Briefe*, i. 20. But it is more likely, I
think, that he is referring to the impression of Fichte that he had *before* he began
to read the latest work at all. This is all the more probable if, as Beck thinks
possible, Hölderlin's letter came as a reply to one from Hegel asking his opinion
of the *Grundlage* which Schelling was urging Hegel to read (*Briefe*, i. 15). If
Hegel knew that Hölderlin had shared his opinion of the *Kritik aller Offenbarung*
this would be a natural thing for him to do (see Hölderlin, *GSA*, vi. 723–4, for
Beck's notes on this passage).

(This letter provides also the earliest definite evidence, so far as I know, that
Hegel read Herder at Tübingen. For in describing his first meeting with
Herder, Hölderlin says: 'He spoke often in a wholly allegorical way, just as you
know him already [*wie auch Du ihn kennst*].')

[2] Letter 10, *Briefe*, i. 20. It may be fanciful to suggest that Schelling is trying
to smooth Hegel's ruffled feathers here, but it is quite certain that he was extremely
anxious that they should not become 'alienated' (*fremd*). 'We have not' or 'We
must not' or 'We shall not become strangers', he reiterates in every letter. Hegel
himself chants the same refrain, but the string of Tübingen watchwords at the
end of his January letter ('Reich Gottes', 'Vernunft und Freiheit', 'die unsichtbare Kirche') would certainly have made Schelling realize he must tread
softly in the ancient dust that was the stuff of his old comrade's dreams.

tion' or to deliberate irony on Fichte's part. He had himself thought, he says, of satirizing the theological logic, but had been put off by the knowledge that some people were sure to take him seriously.

One thing he confesses had surprised him in Hegel's letter. In his own first letter he had given as a particularly laughable example of theological logic, the use of Kant's moral proof to demonstrate the existence of 'the personal individual being who reigns above in Heaven'.[1] This disturbed Hegel, who accepted the moral proof, and had never thought of taking it in any other way. So he asked Schelling to explain. At this, it was Schelling's turn to be puzzled; for he knew Hegel to be a convinced follower of Lessing (*Vertrauter Lessings*) and it had never occured to *him* that Lessing's Spinozism could be taken in any way except the way Jacobi took it. He himself had moved a step further from Spinoza's Absolute Substance to Fichte's Absolute Subject, and he now explains to Hegel why it is a mistake to conceive of Fichte's transcendental Ego as a conscious individual or person:

For me the highest principle of all philosophy is the pure, absolute Ego, i.e. the Ego in so far as it is simply [*bloß*] Ego, not yet conditioned by objects, but posited through *freedom*. The Alpha and Omega of all philosophy is Freedom.—The absolute Ego embraces an infinite sphere of absolute being, ⟨and⟩ in this *finite* spheres form themselves, which arise through the limiting of the infinite sphere by an object (spheres of *existence*—theoretical philosophy). In these there is strict causal dependence [*lauter Bedingtheit*] and the unconditioned [*das Unbedingte*] leads to contradictions.—But we *ought* to break through these limits, i.e. we ought to emerge out of the finite spheres into the infinite one (practical philosophy). Thus this [practical philosophy] requires the destruction of finiteness and leads us thereby into the supersensible world. 'What theoretical reason was incapable of, whereas it was weakened *by the object*, that practical reason achieves.' But in it [the supersensible world] we can find nothing but our absolute Ego, since only this [the absolute Ego] has described the infinite sphere. There is no supersensible world for us except that of the absolute Ego.— *God* is nothing but the absolute Ego, the Ego inasmuch as it has annihilated everything theoretical [i.e. all limits], is thus equal to zero in *theoretical* philosophy. Personality arises through the unity of consciousness. But consciousness is not possible without ⟨an⟩ object; but for God, i.e., for the absolute Ego⟨,⟩ there is *no* object *at all*, since thereby

[1] Letter 7, *Briefe*, i. 14.

[i.e. if there were one] it would cease to be absolute,—hence
there is no personal God and our highest striving is for the destruction of our personality, ⟨and a⟩ passing over into the absolute sphere
of being, which however is not *possible* in all eternity;—hence ⟨there
is⟩ only ⟨a⟩ *practical* approaching toward the absolute, and hence—
Immortality.[1]

With this letter came Schelling's essay 'On the possibility of
a form of philosophy in general', which expounded this same
doctrine at greater length. Hegel made some attempt to study the
essay, and he probably absorbed and adopted the conception of
God as the impersonal moral order of the world, which Fichte had
put in the place of Spinoza's impersonal natural order. But the
whole form of the discussion was too abstract for his taste, and the
idea of 'striving to destroy our personality' was utterly repugnant
to his own ideal of integral humanism. So when he at length replied, over two months later, in April, he avoided detailed discussion of Schelling's essay, pleading, rather weakly, that he had
not had time to study it properly, but that, as far as he could
understand it, he saw in it a 'completing of science which will yield
us the most fruitful results';[2] and then going on, as we saw
earlier, to enthuse over the political implications of the new moral
philosophy.

Evidence of Hegel's efforts to come to grips with this strange
world of the Ego and the non-Ego, and to relate it to the more
concrete terms of the traditional moral psychology that he was
himself accustomed to use, is supplied by a sheet of notes that
he wrote at about this time concerning the proper use of the
method of moral proof in general, and of the principle 'virtue
deserves happiness' in particular.[3]

Even if speculative reason could prove the 'reality and existence'
of a transcendent God, he argues, we would achieve no knowledge
of his properties except through the concept of a final aim or

[1] Letter 10, *Briefe*, i. 22. I have preserved Schelling's punctuation and underlining, and translated as literally as I could. For the way in which he relates
Fichte's Ego to Spinoza's substance cf. Hölderlin (Letter 9), ibid., pp. 19-20.
[2] Letter 11, *Briefe*, i. 23. This acknowledgement is one ground for thinking that
Hegel accepted Schelling's interpretation of the moral proof. Another is that
the conception of God as the moral order agrees with his own conception of
'spirit' as a supra-personal power that unites a community of free individual
persons.
[3] *Die transzendente Idee von Gott*, Nohl, pp. 361-2. The key to a right understanding of these notes was found by Haering (i. 198-206).

purpose in nature. Since this concept fails to help us in any morally relevant way, only practical reason can ground belief in God.[1]

Practical reason produces the moral law, which is a fact experienced as the form of the higher desirous faculty. This Kantian formula which he has modified to suit himself, Hegel promptly translates into the Schelling–Fichte terminology as the determination of the finite Ego by the absolute Ego and the consequent overcoming (*Aufhebung*) of the non-Ego. Similarly he equates the sensible impulse of the lower desires with determination of the Ego by the non-Ego, and identifies Fichte's *Willkür* both in Kantian terms and in the language of Schelling.

Having thus satisfied himself, so to speak, that he knows the translation rules for his basic terms, Hegel begins to deal in his own terms with the question that really interests him. The sensible impulses when they are ordered by *Vernunft*, or controlled by the ethical law ('bestimmt durchs Sittengesetz'), are 'lawful' (*gesetzmäßig*); they are not 'lawlike' (*gesetzlich*). They are 'morally possible' (i.e. permissible or hypothetically imperative) but not 'morally actual' (i.e. compulsory or categorically imperative). An impulse would only have 'lawlike' status, it would only have categorical force, if it 'governed the whole world of appearances' (i.e. if the whole of our experience were conformable to it, or if everyone could have whatever they wanted in the world). Since conformity to the requirements of practical reason is presupposed throughout we have here a reformulation of the conditions for Kant's 'highest good' (the harmony of virtue and happiness) which does not have the paradoxical appearance that it assumes in Kant's own discussion, because Hegel begins explicitly from the premiss that there *ought* not to be (and hence *a priori* there need not be) a conflict between desire and the law, rather than from the experience of a conflict as revealing our freedom.

For Hegel it is not the fact that our natural desires are not 'lawful', but rather the fact that our 'lawful' desires are not 'lawlike' which reveals our freedom. This idea is the foundation for a doctrine of reconciliation with our fate in this world, which will ultimately make any transcendent conception of God, or of

---

[1] The influence of the *Critique of Judgement* is plainest here, but the mention of 'reality and existence' is perhaps an echo of Schelling's distinction between the infinite sphere of *Sein* that belongs to the absolute Ego and the finite spheres of *Dasein* that belong to limited egos.

immortal existence in a supersensible world, unnecessary. Hegel
has certainly not yet seen all of the implications of his view for
the Kantian postulates, but he is moving inexorably toward their
destruction. The problem that he raises is: 'Can the ethical law
take back all the rights it has granted?' and his answer, of course,
is 'No'. If we sacrifice something in doing our duty, the voluntary
abandonment of our right is just what constitutes the sacrifice,
and to suppose that we have only postponed the satisfaction destroys
the fundamental moral dignity of our free act.[1] But if on the
other hand our 'lawful' desires and purposes are frustrated by
natural forces, or by the unlawful acts of others, our right to
satisfaction remains. It is on this aspect of our experience in this
life that Hegel apparently wants to ground the rational postulates
of God and immortality at this stage in his reflections.

Hegel is, I think, only trying to follow what he regards as the
valid argument in Kant's work—avoiding on the one hand all talk
of a 'radical evil' in human nature, and on the other hand the
theological logic' which asked for a 'recompense' for every moral
sacrifice made in this life. He has probably not yet seen that if
we ground the knowledge of freedom in the experience of *sacrifice*,
rather than as Kant did in the experience of *temptation*, the principle 'virtue deserves happiness' takes on a somewhat curious
aspect as far as free individuals are concerned. Like Schelling (and
of course Kant also) he was ready to affirm that 'the Alpha and
Omega of all philosophy is freedom'. Hence he could see that the
realization of a 'lawlike' state, where every desire was satisfied,
was not a task that human reason could lay upon *itself*. But it is
certainly not clear that he also saw that free rational beings cannot
demand it from 'another being' either. His Hellenic ideal of a
society that was happy, because its members were free, and hence
prepared to sacrifice their own happiness whenever the *Sittengesetz* required it, would certainly incline him to this view; but on
the other hand he did not want to give up the postulate of immortality for which Socrates had died. In view of the fact that
Schelling had just offered him an impersonal conception of God
as identical with the moral realm in which all free individuals

---

[1] Hegel actually makes this point about the patriotic sacrifice of life by citizens
of ancient republics in *Jetzt braucht die Menge*. The concept of Elysium or
Valhalla is there invoked to avoid contradiction of the postulate of immortality,
but the element of *recompense* involved in passing from one life to another is too
obvious for the inconsistency to be glossed over for very long.

immortally exist, it is possible that he did now reject the postulate of God as 'another being'. But his text is ambiguous:

Reason [*die Vernunft*] posits as ultimate aim of the world the highest good, ethical life [*Sittlichkeit*] and in proportion therewith happiness—but it does ⟨not?⟩ posit this ultimate aim itself—it requires the realization of the aim, therefore from another Being [*von einem andern Wesen*], but certainly not from man, or from the causality of reason, so long as it is limited by sensibility.

Haering thinks the whole tendency of the argument is critical of Kant's *Vernunftreligion*; and it is tempting, in the light of *Jetzt braucht die Menge*, to agree with him that the underlying thought is: 'As man is, so is his God; the ruptured [*zerrissene*] man has a God separated from the world, standing over against him as a stranger [*Fremd*].'[1] But Hegel has not, so far, shown any inclination to view *Vernunftreligion* in this way. Quite probably he does not see himself as criticizing Kant at all, but only as saving him from his orthodox 'friendly critics' at Tübingen. This whole sheet of notes *could* be taken as tracing the reason why 'another being' *must* be postulated. The most plausible view of all, I think, is that Hegel has not yet made up his mind just what the moral proof *does* demonstrate. He was quite content to have made the terms of the problem, and the method for its settlement, clear to himself. His notes conclude:

D. The Godhead—the power to follow through, to make effective, the rights that reason has granted ⟨—⟩ by this criterion [*Bestimmung*] must the knowledge of all its other properties be determined [*bestimmt*].[2]

This criterion for the nature of God is exactly the one that forms

---

[1] Haering, i. 206. Haering seems to read 'But does it posit this ultimate aim itself⟨?⟩' in the passage cited (Nohl, p. 362) instead of postulating the accidental omission of a negative as I have suggested. The answer to the question is 'No' as the following explanation shows. So in any case the sense of the passage is clear.

[2] Nohl, p. 362. Uncertainty about God's existence as an independent *agency* seems to be implicit in his notes from the *Theological Journal* of Hanlein and Ammon (*Unkunde der Geschichte*, Nohl, p. 364). In what appears to be a personal reflection of his own, he asks how divine omniscience is consistent with freedom, and answers that on his own (Kantian) principles God may control the *Lauf der Natur* as long as the *Gesetze* remain unchanged. His concern is always focused upon Divine Providence, rather than upon the existence of a Divine Lawgiver. (His Kantian criterion for ascription of properties to God is reaffirmed in the same place in a passage which he crossed out, presumably because he realized it was superfluous.)

the basic premiss of the life of Jesus which Hegel began on 8 May 1795 and finished on 24 July.[1] God is there identified at the beginning as 'unlimited Reason'; and in the light of everything said about Him in what follows it seems most natural to conclude that Hegel has accepted from Schelling the identification of God with the Kingdom of God, or of the 'absolute Ego' with the 'supersensible world'. He has given up altogether the idea of 'another being' who governs and judges in that realm, because it conflicts with the autonomy of reason everywhere, the autonomy on which man's dignity (*Würde*) is founded.[2]

The seemingly rigid Kantian orthodoxy of *The Life of Jesus* has occasioned much discussion. On the one side there are students who believe that Hegel underwent a sort of Kantian 'conversion' beginning about now and lasting for some years; on the other are those who follow Haering in regarding the *Life of Jesus* as a *Gedankenexperiment* to which Hegel was only provisionally committed, and which represented at most only one aspect of his integral view.

Neither of these extreme hypotheses appears to me to be necessary. There is an element of truth in both views, and it is, by and large, the same element. There are a few places where Hegel is so carried away by Kant's *strenuous* doctrine of practical reason and virtue, that he almost loses hold of his Greek ideal of life as characterized properly by grace and spontaneity and an *absence of strain*. But this is partly because a strenuous life of self-sacrificing virtue appears to him to be the only road *back* to the golden age of Greek humanism; and partly because the influence of Kant and Fichte is a new one which he has not as yet fully digested.

If we survey the progress of Hegel's reflections from the moment when he escaped from Tübingen—which coincides

---

[1] *Die reine aller Schranken*, Nohl, pp. 75–136. Hegel gave no title to the manuscript, but it has always been known as *The Life of Jesus*. The sub-title 'Harmony of the Gospels according to his own translation' is certainly more accurate, and may just possibly have some claim to authenticity, since Rosenkranz could conceivably have found it in the 'schemata' for this project which he mentions (Rosenkranz, p. 51). (But see p. 196 n. 3 for what is, to my mind, a more probable hypothesis.)

[2] Peperzak (p. 72 n. 5), points out that *Würde* is not properly a Kantian ideal. Haering (i. 185) suggests, rightly as I think, that Hegel's adoption of it as a name for his absolute value derives from Schiller. I shall regularly use 'dignity' as a translation for it.

pretty closely with the moment when he first began to feel the influence of Fichte and Kant—the writing of *The Life of Jesus* becomes a perfectly comprehensible undertaking, and its character largely predictable and not at all surprising. Before he moved to Berne Hegel had formulated his own ideal of life as it should be. In his first eighteen months at Berne he was preoccupied with the analysis of how life had come to be the way it was, in order to discover how the ideal could best be restored. He had found that the only hope lay in the reintegrative powers of *Vernunft*, and that the original root of our falling away from the Greek ideal lay in the acceptance of a non-rational principle of authority in religion and society. The first essential for the redemption of man's dignity as a rational being, therefore, was the re-establishment of religion on its rational foundation.

It is necessary to remind oneself continually that Hegel believed that all well-established systems of religious belief and practice have a common rational foundation. This foundation rises to consciousness as the postulates of immortality and divine justice (or 'providence'). It is inevitably articulated in different ways in the religious and philosophical traditions of different societies, but it is always the same in substance, and is easily recognized and identified by any rational man; for it is a matter of *Vernunft*, which is an innate human capacity, not of *Verstand*, which is a culturally conditioned skill. In the Germany of 1795 the clearest, articulation of it was to be found in the *Critique of Practical Reason* —with which Hegel was 'repeatedly occupied in Switzerland' (Rosenkranz). Hence the project of rewriting the record of the Gospels in the language of Kantian moral psychology was almost a mandatory one for anyone who wished to distinguish its rational content, or eternal message, from the incidental forms in which it was originally couched—which were those appropriate to a very different cultural tradition.

In Hegel's mind this did not involve any falsification of the historical record, and we can safely assume that he is not consciously or deliberately guilty of any falsification. Rather he is seeking to undo a certain 'falsification of the record' which is inherent in its existence as a 'historical' record at all. His account is not meant to take the place of the historical record, or even to be read independently of it, but rather to throw light on it. He obviously believes that in many places the *literal sense* of the words

he puts into the mouth of Jesus is in fact closer to the literal sense
of what Jesus actually said, than is the language ascribed to him in
the Gospel account that has come down to us; but there are other
places where he explicitly acknowledges that the record itself is
correct, but nevertheless still stands in need of his gloss.[1] He is
not primarily interested in the question how far the record is an
accurate account of what Jesus *said*, but rather in the question of
how far it is a safe guide to a right understanding of what Jesus
did or tried to do (including the effects he hoped to achieve by
saying what he said). Hegel seeks with quite dedicated intentness
to give *the most literal account possible of what Jesus meant*.[2]

Rosenkranz tells us that in preparation for his essay Hegel made
'Schemata for the unification of the facts which are partly scattered,
and partly told differently in the separate gospels'.[3] We can see
from the finished product[4] that one purpose of these schemata

[1] See, for example, his remark about the 'rather strong' expressions that Jesus
employed against the Pharisees (Nohl, p. 104; Luke 11 : 42–54; cf. Peperzak,
p. 67). Hegel was quite ready to point out examples of provable historical
ignorance on the part of the Evangelists: consider, for example, the laconic
opening, 'Unkunde der Geschichte bei Lk. 2: 3; 3 : 1' in the notes from the
Theological Journal (Nohl, p. 362—Nohl's reading *Urkunde* is a mistake—cf.
Schüler, p. 141 n. 70). But he was not really interested in attacking dogmatic
theology with the weapons of the higher criticism (compare Nohl, p. 363). His
purpose was to 'fulfil' (πληρῶσαι) the Gospel of Jesus in the sense in which Jesus
himself had 'fulfilled' the law.

[2] Peperzak quite correctly says that 'Hegel has caused not only religion but
even its poetry to disappear from the four gospels' (p. 66). But he does not seem
to realize that this was Hegel's set intent. He takes it rather as another evidence
of Hegel's essentially prosaic cast of mind (p. 68). Whatever one thinks about
that, we can be certain that Hegel would never have passed over the paradox and
dialectic that is often to be found in the sayings of Jesus, without remark, unless
his deliberate purpose imposed a discipline of silence upon him. Whatever
limitations of aesthetic sensibility he may have suffered under—and it might be
held that they were less serious than those of most of his critics—he was certainly
never deficient in his appreciation of verbal wit (for an example see p. 205 n. 1
below).

[3] Rosenkranz, p. 51. The most probable hypothesis, I think, is that Rosenkranz
had nothing more before him, in this connection, than we do. What he took to be
'schemata' for *The Life of Jesus* may very well have been some of the later notes
for the 'Spirit of Christianity'. (The fragment *B. Moral. Bergpredigt* could
easily be mistaken for part of such a schema; so could the separate sheets of
Zu der Zeit da Jesus.)

[4] Among Hegel's early manuscripts *The Life of Jesus* is the only thing that is
quite definitely finished and complete in the form in which it has come down to
us. The first editor, Paul Roques, printed four words of a new unfinished
sentence at the end of one paragraph and marked a lacuna in the manuscript.
But if there is a lacuna at that point (Nohl, p. 83, line 17) it is plainly no more
than a line or two; and the probability is that, as Nohl seems to have assumed,

(if Hegel really did make them) was to establish if possible a plausible sequence of events in the fragmentary accounts of Jesus' ministry. But, except in so far as he was able to trace the gradual growth of antipathy between Jesus and the Pharisees, and to make this conflict one of the mainsprings of the story, this was not an important concern for Hegel. He was content to follow for long stretches the order of topics as he found it in Luke or Matthew,[1] without wanting to make a historical sequence of it at all. His main aim in comparing parallel passages and integrating divergent accounts was to discover the rational content which lay behind the tradition. Sometimes the rational content was directly recoverable through close attention to the common core of the accounts; and sometimes it could be reconstructed by postulation and then justified by showing how a plausible explanation of the divergence of the actual record from it could be provided.

Hegel supplies a more or less complete key to his sources at each stage of his discussion, and, if we study his text in the light of the original texts cited, a number of his fundamental convictions, both about matters of principle and about matters of fact, become plainly evident, although they are nowhere explicitly stated or even referred to in his manuscript. 'I think', he wrote to Schelling at Christmas 1794, 'the time has come when men should speak more freely, and in part they already can and do.'[2] But

Hegel cancelled or at least meant to cancel his abortive continuation. (Compare Roques, p. 11 with Nohl, p. 83: after 'aber dem Geiste des Gesetzes nach ist er so strafwürdig als jener' Roques prints a semicolon and continues 'Wer aber aus Menschenverachtung (*Lucke der Handschrift*)'; Nohl simply begins a new paragraph with 'So ist est euch befohlen' etc.)

[1] Of the four Gospels that of John was certainly the most important to Hegel; but in his present undertaking he seems to have depended most on Luke. He had a low opinion of Mark, which he appeals to only occasionally for corroboration or for some additional detail. (For a hypothesis which would account for Hegel's attitudes and policies in dealing with the four Gospels see p. 367 n. 1 below.)

[2] It was not even strictly necessary to Hegel's purpose that Jesus should lose his halo, although that halo had been both a source and a shield for so many evils. Hence he preserves silence about almost all of the supernatural elements in the Gospel story. It would have amused him, doubtless, that a university professor at Tübingen should be the one to take advantage of the licence thereby conceded to simple faith, and argue that he is only analysing the *ethical* aspect of religion, and that what he is silent about is *meant* to be integrated into what he says (Haering, i. 187–9). The question which he surely expected the university professor to ask was rather how such integration is possible at all, once the notion of a *personal authority possessed by Jesus* (which is the principal object of his attack) is given up. But it was a Catholic priest who took this point (see Peperzak, pp. 62–3).

aside from the obvious political restrictions on freedom of speech, which were so dramatically illustrated by Kant's difficulties with the censorship over the *Religion*, Hegel had sound reasons of principle for expressing himself cautiously in his present undertaking. He certainly accepted Kant's view that full freedom of expression is essential for scholarly research and intercourse. But one does not write a *Life of Jesus* for scholars. For them one does what Kant had already done, one writes an essay on the principles and criteria of rational religion, and leaves the scholars to apply it to the texts for themselves. When one is setting out, as Hegel is here, to provide a model of how the principles can and should be applied, one assumes all the responsibilities of a public teacher, who must take care not to do or say anything calculated to disturb the peace. Hegel's whole conception of public religion required that he should not wilfully undermine the faith of the devout. His purpose was rather to see that their devotion was properly directed. As long as they understood that the only effective way of 'pleasing God' was the living of a virtuous life, it was not vital for them to have completely enlightened ideas about such matters as prayer, fasting, and miracles.[1] But for those with eyes to see and ears to hear Hegel made sure the truth was there to be found.

There is only one brief statement of principle in the essay. It is contained in the opening paragraph and it is meant to provide us with a ready principle of explanation for all the divergences of Hegel's account from the sources that he indicates throughout:

Reason [*Vernunft*] pure and exceeding all limits is the Godhead itself—According to Reason therefore is the plan of the world in general ordered (John 1); Reason it is which teaches man to recognize his vocation [*Bestimmung*], an unconditional purpose of his life; often indeed it is obscured but never wholly quenched, even in the darkness he has always retained a faint glimmer of it—

Among the Jews it was John who made men conscious again of this their dignity—which ought not to be something foreign to them, but which is to be sought for in itself, in their true self, not in their lineage, and not in the urge towards happiness. It is not to be sought in being servants of a man greatly revered [Moses, explicitly, but by implication Jesus himself also], but in the development of the divine spark which has been allotted to them, which bears witness to them, that in a

---

[1] The simple faith embodied in hallowed practices and stories withers by itself as reason advances—and this is not an unmixed blessing—compare *Die Staatsverfassungen*, Nohl, p. 37.

sublime sense they are the children of God [rather than of Abraham]—
The development of Reason is the unique source of truth and peace of
mind, which John perchance did not proclaim as belonging exclusively
or exceptionally to him but which on the contrary all men could open
up in themselves.[1]

Even this opening is clearly marked as an interpretation of the
first verses of the Gospel according to Saint John. But the gap
between the original and the gloss is nowhere wider, and it is wise
to treat it at first as a principle of explanation for what follows and
only return at the end to trace the correspondence which does
exist between it and John 1: 1–18.

Jesus and John the Baptist appear throughout Hegel's account
as teachers and exemplars of the gospel of *Vernunft*, John being
more ascetic, and Jesus presenting the less rigorous, more reconciliatory and joyful ideal of a rational harmony of all human
capacities and feelings. The witness of both is identical in essentials;
and the witness of John is necessarily presupposed by that of Jesus,
for otherwise Jesus would have no ready answer to complaints about
his free and easy attitude toward both the pleasures and the conventions of ordinary life. Jesus did *not* set himself apart from the
ordinary life of his time in any way. He did *not* seek to establish any
status which could be the foundation of a special authority. All
of the elements that had earlier led Hegel to draw a sharp contrast
between the attitudes of Socrates and Jesus to social life and social
ties as such ('Let the dead bury their dead' etc.) are now either
silently eliminated as distortions of Jesus' views or explained in a
way that makes them consistent with a positive commitment to
social life.[2]

Jesus did *not*, therefore, do miracles. The text of the Gospels
affords Hegel two opportunities to make this point, and the general
enlightenment of his own times made it possible for him to be fairly
explicit about at least two types of miracle stories, the working of
physical wonders and the 'casting-out of devils'.

His first opportunity comes with the biblical account of the
Temptation. Jesus, he says, considered and rejected the possibility
of fulfilling his vocation by studying nature in order to gain

---

[1] Nohl, p. 75. The page of comment which Roques prints before this opening
is actually a series of excerpts derived from Hegel's studies in the theological
journals.

[2] Compare, for instance, Hegel's gloss on Luke 14: 26: Nohl, p. 109.

mastery over it, 'perhaps through alliance with higher spirits'.[1] By turning stones into bread he would certainly be solving the main problem of man's animal existence, but that is not the true human vocation. Our daily bread has nothing to do with the development of *Vernunft*, which involves the fixing of our attention upon the super-sensible world.[2] And the achievement of *physical* independence of nature—symbolized in the original by the temptation of Jesus to cast himself from the pinnacle of the temple—would be an utter degradation of the moral autonomy that is man's true goal. We can be sure, therefore, though Hegel says nothing further on this topic, that Jesus did not calm the tempest or walk on the waters.

The authority of the wonder-worker, like political authority generally—the object of the third and most serious temptation, which Hegel deals with separately—is rejected as inconsistent with the preservation of human dignity, above all, one's own dignity.[3] For not even the most benevolent of despots can be morally autonomous while he has to concern himself about the maintenance of his power. So Jesus rebukes James and John when they suggest that they should call down fire on the Samaritan village by saying 'Ye know not what manner of spirit ye are of'; and all that Hegel adds by way of a gloss is a clause which transparently implies that the 'forces of nature' do not 'stand at the command' either of the disciples or of Jesus himself.[4]

[1] Nohl, p. 77. See also in this connection the comment on Luke 4: 4 given in Roques, p. 1. This is not of course the orthodox definition of a miracle. But Hegel shows in his notes at this time why the orthodox definition is completely unusable on (Kantian) theoretical grounds and absolutely illegitimate on practical grounds (Nohl, p. 365). The Faustian conception of a wonder-worker is the only one that can be made consistent with the basic tenets of the *Critique of Pure Reason*.

[2] It ought not to surpise us therefore to find that the reference to 'our daily bread' has disappeared from Hegel's 'translation' of the Lord's Prayer: Nohl, p. 85.

[3] Peperzak complains: 'Hegel does not justify his rationalist reading of the gospels. . . . Nowhere . . . does Hegel justif yhis translation of certain words which receive thereby the opposite sense to that which they have in the Gospel' (p. 63). This is an unfair comment because Hegel's explicit interpretation of the temptation to fall down and worship the devil as a temptation to *seek* personal authority (i.e. his identification of the temptation with the reward) is surely a sufficiently clear justification for the policy of direct inversion which he adopts towards all passages in which Jesus is represented as claiming peculiar authority or as urging men to have faith in him. Actually, as we shall see, Hegel *does* give an explicit justification for his reading of the Gospels in *man mag die widersprechendsten Betrachtungen* (the main text of the 'Positivity' essay).

[4] Nohl, pp. 101–2; Luke 9: 55–6. The words of the rebuke do not, it seems

In Hegel's account of the Temptation the figure of Satan as an independent character disappears altogether—which is itself a clear enough indication that his reference to a possible 'alliance with higher spirits' was made with tongue in cheek. He felt sure, obviously, that most of his audience would agree with him that Satan and his angels regarded as demonic personalities were simply figments of superstitious imagination.[1] Because of this he felt able to indicate quite openly what he regarded as the correct interpretation of the stories in the Gospels about 'casting out devils'. Thus, where St. Luke writes:

> Then he [i.e. Jesus] called the twelve together and gave them power and authority over all devils, and to cure diseases. And he sent them forth to preach the Kingdom of God and to heal the sick;

Hegel provides the following gloss:

> Jesus sent forth his twelve apostles about this time, to strive, as he did, against the prejudices of the Jews, who took pride in their name and lineage, which was a greater glory in their eyes, and which they prized more highly than the unique worth which ethical life [*Sittlichkeit*] confers on man.[2]

Here $\pi\acute{a}\nu\tau a$ $\tau\grave{a}$ $\delta a\iota\mu\acute{o}\nu\iota a$ is explicitly identified with moral prejudice generally and specifically with racial pride. And since the power of healing is also implicitly included in the explanation, this passage together with the account of the Temptation effectively disposes of virtually all the miracles credited to Jesus. All the stories about miracles of healing are taken to refer to experiences of spiritual conversion and rational illumination. For example, although I do not think Hegel actually *says* this anywhere, stories of the restoration of sight and hearing refer to the same experience as Jesus' injunction: 'He that hath ears to hear, let him hear.' And finally the forgiving of sins is merely the recognition by Jesus that someone has found for himself the courage to begin a new life.[3]

rest on good authority, and they were consigned to the margin in the English Revised Version of 1881. But doubtless Hegel would have invented something rather like them if he had not been fortunate enough to find them in his text.

[1] In his own private notes Hegel turns the dogma of original sin against itself, saying, in the language of Lutheran orthodoxy, that the externalization of evil in the figures of Satan the tempter and Adam ⟨and Eve⟩ the sinners, has been the source of a 'universal bankruptcy of humanity' (*Unkunde der Geschichte*, Nohl, p. 362).   [2] Nohl, p. 94; Luke 9: 1 ff.

[3] This last point is made explicit by Hegel's analysis of the story of the woman who anointed Jesus at the house of Simon the Pharisee (Nohl, p. 92; Luke 7:

Once we grasp his principles of interpretation, some of Hegel's silences speak volumes. Thus immediately before his identification of devil possession with moral prejudice there occurs a passage where (as Rosenkranz put it) 'scattered facts' are brought together and 'divergent accounts' reconciled. Luke records that on a certain day, for no given reason, Jesus decided to cross the Sea of Tiberias. After stilling a tempest on the way he reached the Gadarene (or Gerasene) shore, where he cleansed a man of a legion of devils, sending them into a herd of swine which were drowned in the lake as a direct result. Matthew on the other hand, tells us how when Jesus heard of the death of John the Baptist he went away by boat to a desert place; but a multitude of about five thousand followed him, and he fed them all with five loaves and a few small fishes. From these two sources Hegel produces the following abrupt paragraph: 'On the news of the murder of John, he [Jesus] had himself taken over to the eastern shore of the sea of Tiberias— but he spent only a short time among the Gadarenes and then came back again to Galilee.'[1]

We might think there is nothing here except the operation of what Hegel called *Verstand*—the use of one story to provide the motivating reason that is not given in the other and the purging of fantastic elements from both. But it is only really the stilling of the storm that is simply purged. We know from Hegel's acount of the Temptation story that Jesus could not arbitrarily create food and we know also by the light of reason that he would not arbitrarily destroy it as he is made to do in the story of the Gadarene swine. These two certainties, allied with a certain coincidence of multitudes (the legion of men and the legion of devils) strongly suggest that Hegel had pedagogic grounds for

37–50). In his notes about polemical attacks on dogma (Roques, p. 1) Hegel speaks of 'disturbing those who slumber in the death-sleep of self-satisfaction untroubled by *Vernunft*'. Presumably this was one meaning that he attached to stories of the 'raising of the dead'. But moral despair over one's sinfulness and corruption is rather more obviously the kind of death from which one could be 'reborn' through hearing the Gospel (compare Hegel's reading of the conversation between Jesus and Nicodemus, Nohl, pp. 79–80). Thus 'raising the dead' is a metaphor for 'forgiving sins', which is in turn a metaphor for awakening in someone the faith in his own power as a rational being to begin again. To be 'born again' is to recognize one's essential freedom.

[1] Nohl, p. 94. Hegel himself provides the references Luke 8: 22; Matthew 14: 3; and—for the shortness of the visit—a specific reference to (Luke 8) verse 37 is added. (The real purpose of this last reference, I think, is to draw attention to the presence of a *multitude of people* in both accounts.)

bringing together the two accounts as he does. If we think about the stories together we shall realize, he hopes, that what Jesus did was to 'feed the multitude' by casting out the prejudices existing in a legion of minds against the eating of pork![1]

About the central miracle of the Christian faith, the Resurrection itself, Hegel preserves silence. The pointlessness of it is implied by the parable of Dives and Lazarus, which he records quite straightforwardly, though he does not call the place of Dives' punishment 'hell', and does not mention any 'great gulf fixed' between Dives and Abraham.[2] His account of the Passion ends with the burial of Jesus, and the only hint of an explanation for all that follows in the Gospel accounts is to be found in his emphasis on the haste with which the body had to be removed and buried at night because of the onset of the Passover festival, 'during which it was not permitted to have to do with dead bodies'.[3] This deliberately flat and prosaic ending could be taken as offering a reason why there was a mystery in the popular mind about the disappearance of the dead body. And this disappearance, in conjunction with some rather gnomic remarks about the building of a new temple in three days—which Hegel takes to refer to the fact that the rational God does not need a temple at all[4]—would then become the basis for a Resurrection myth. But the most natural explanation for Hegel's silence on this topic seems, at this point at least, to be that he felt we ought not to trouble our heads over the explanation of the Resurrection story, because there is no moral lesson to be derived from it.

When we turn from the interpretation of Jesus' deeds to that of his words the path, both of Hegel and of his readers, is easier and more direct. Jesus never said anything that was *meant* to create a peculiar faith in him or a belief in the authority of his 'name'. Hence we have to read between the lines of the assertions on which this faith and authority have been grounded. With this one *caveat*, most of the recorded teaching, especially the parables, can be

[1] It would be reasonable enough to pray 'Give us this day our daily bread' if all we meant was 'Free us from moral prejudice against wholesome food'; so there is nothing inconsistent in crediting Jesus with *this* miracle!

[2] Nohl, pp. 111–12 (Luke 16: 19–31). 'Moses and the prophets' becomes the 'law of Reason' of course. In general Hegel eliminates 'the prophets' altogether. Where he cannot simply ignore references to them he calls them 'teachers' (cf. for example the translation of Matthew 7: 15: Nohl, p. 87).

[3] Nohl, p. 136.

[4] Cf. the note on John 2: 19 in Roques, p. 1.

accepted as it stands. Examination of Hegel's treatment of the sources in detail would therefore be as superfluous here as it would be tedious. The Pharisees followed the letter of the law, while Jesus taught and acted in its spirit, gradually arousing their enmity until they conspired successfully to have him executed. This is the basic plot of Hegel's story. But I shall deal briefly with one sample passage—the Sermon on the Mount—because Hegel offers alternative exegeses of it in his later essays.[1]

Hegel's version follows the fuller account given in Matthew with an eye always on the parallel text in Luke. He translates the Beatitudes literally except that the pure in heart are not *promised* the sight of God but are said to be actually drawing near to him ('sie nähern sich dem Heiligen').[2] 'Heaven and earth shall pass away, but not the requirements of the ethical law'; the law of Moses is a 'dead skeleton' which Jesus came to 'fulfil' by breathing a new spirit into it.[3]

The spirit of the law is viewed by Hegel as an absolute precondition of the harmony of natural feelings and spontaneous action that characterized his Greek ideal. His Jesus does not go in for such picturesque metaphors as the plucking out of eyes or the cutting off of hands—metaphor is something he avoids because it breeds misunderstanding; but he tells us firmly to 'do violence to the most natural, the dearest inclination' rather than let it 'run beyond the line of what is right and bit by bit undermine your maxims'.

---

[1] Nohl, pp. 82–8 (Matthew 5–7; Luke 6: 20–49). From the beginning Hegel regarded the Sermon on the Mount as the most basic expression of Jesus' ethical message (see *Unter objektiver Religion*, Nohl, p. 49). He returns to it in the 'Spirit of Christianity'. This later interpretation deserves to be compared with the present account fairly carefully (see Nohl, pp. 266–75, Knox, pp. 212–24, and the discussion below, Chapter IV, pp. 337–46).

[2] In his letter to Schelling of 30 Aug. 1795 (i.e. five weeks after he finished the 'Life of Jesus') Hegel says: 'I once had the notion of making clear to myself in an essay, what it might mean to draw near to God [*was es heißen könne, sich Gott zu nähern*] and thought therein to find the satisfaction of the postulate that practical reason governs the world of appearances, and of the other postulates' (*Briefe*, i. 29). It looks very much as if this was the plan behind *Die transzendente Idee von Gott* (Nohl, pp. 361–2); but Hegel abandoned it in favour of the more direct *application* of the Kantian ideal which he makes in *The Life of Jesus*.

[3] The concept of the spirit of reason as a *pleroma* of the established custom is the most fundamental and lasting heritage that Hegel retained throughout his life from his early studies of the New Testament. Compare *Unkunde der Geschichte* (Nohl, p. 363). Hegel's essentially reconciliatory cast of mind is very appropriately summed up in the concept of πλήρωσις.

Regarding the relation of the new precept 'love your enemies' to the old law, Hegel is more accurate and more just than the Evangelist. The principle 'Thou shalt love thy neighbour as thyself' is, of course, expressly contained in Leviticus 19: 18. But it is there interpreted by reference to 'the children of thy people'. So that, as Hegel's Jesus says, 'Love of your friends and your nation is *commanded*, but at the same time hatred of your enemies and of foreigners is *allowed*—I say to you on the other hand: Respect humanity even in your enemies, wish well to them that curse you, do good to them that hate you' etc. Almsgiving is a virtue only if done in a virtuous spirit. It is not to be 'announced from pulpits or in the newspapers', says Hegel, seeking an appropriate contemporary equivalent for the 'sounding of a trumpet'. Nothing, least of all prayer, should be done for show, since then it is fruitless. The real fruit of virtue is precisely the consciousness of having acted rightly.[1] We should pray in solitude, either in or out of doors, and the only proper object of prayer is the coming of the Kingdom of Ends as defined by Kant.

The injunctions about fasting Hegel omits altogether, probably because, on the basis of a number of other passages, he was convinced that Jesus did not accept or in any way encourage fasting.[2] Instead Hegel offers 'participation in brotherly love' as the index of moral perfection and fitness for forgiveness; and makes in this way a natural transition from the Lord's Prayer to the injunctions about laying up treasure in heaven, 'a treasure of morality which alone can be called your own property in the full sense of the word since it belongs to your inmost self'. *Vernunft* is to the soul what the eye is to the body; if it is darkened, every impulse and every inclination goes astray. One cannot serve two masters:

[1] 'Wahrlich ihr Gebet ist ohne Frucht' (Nohl, p. 84) translates the acid irony of 'Verily I say unto you they *have* their reward' (Matt. 6: 2 and 4). We can measure the disciplined sacrifice involved in Hegel's self-imposed policy of prosaic flatness by reflecting that he himself wanted to maintain that those who act and pray in the right spirit *also* have their reward because their charity is fruitful—But only the contrast in objective results ('fruitless' or 'fruitful') is the concern of *Vernunft*. The fact that 'virtue is its own reward' in two quite opposite senses is a matter for the free play of *Phantasie*.

[2] Cf. Nohl, p. 84. Of course arbitrary self-denial was contrary to his Greek ideal, and in that sense contrary to reason. Doubtless he would have argued that if Jesus *did* say anything about fasting, here or on other occasions, he was only applying the ideal of reason as far as possible to the traditions and circumstances of his time. So he would presumably read Matthew 6: 16 thus: '(It is best not to fast at all, but if you feel you must do it then) be not as the hypocrites' etc.

reason and sense. Therefore the important thing is to understand man's spiritual vocation. Seek ye first the Kingdom of God (and of *Sittlichkeit*) and all these things will be added unto you. We may note, in passing, that the declaration that reason is the eye of the soul shows that, although the Kantian influence is very much the dominant one, Hegel has by no means given up his Greek ideal of reconciling and harmonizing all natural impulses.[1]

The rather conflicting injunctions 'Cast not pearls before swine' and, on the other hand, 'Knock and it shall be opened' seem to be reconciled in the Gospel by being referred to our dealings with men and God respectively. Hegel has no recourse but to take them as referring to dealings with bad and good men. Teachers must choose their pupils wisely, but, on the other hand, if one really seeks for a way of approach to a man's heart one can find it. Every door will open if you can only find the right knock.

The so-called Golden Rule obviously caused Hegel much heart-searching. His treatment of it provides the one clear instance of his tampering with his texts in a way for which the texts themselves provide no shadow of excuse. Kant had taught him to think of the principle 'Do unto others as you would they would do unto you' as the essential principle of prudential action; thus it epitomized for him the rational egoism, the pursuit of personal comfort, that he found so abhorrent in his own society. At first therefore he translated the Gospel text as 'the rule of prudence' and contrasted it with the first formulation of the Categorical Imperative: 'What you can will, that it should be valid as a universal law among men, against yourselves also, act ye upon such a maxim' as the ethical law that Jesus came to preach. Almost immediately he struck out his own reference to the Gospel altogether, leaving the reader with a bare opposition between the two texts, that of the Bible and that of Kant. His cancellation of the earlier version seems to show that

---

[1] Hegel was not unconscious of a conflict between his Greek ideal and the moral rigorism of Kant. He strove continually to reconcile the Platonic-Aristotelian conception of φρόνησις with the Kantian *Vernunft*; and whenever he encountered arguments tending to show that by the standards of Kantian morality the virtues of the ancients were really only splendid vices, he rejected the conclusion quite decisively, even though he did not *explicitly* renounce any of the premisses. See for example his comments on a Kantian criticism of the suicide of defeated political leaders in the ancient world (*Unkunde der Geschichte*, Nohl, p. 362). Apparently he does not think that the conclusion validly follows from the premisses. Suicide in the appropriate circumstances is *not* inconsistent with respect for oneself as a rational being.

reflection convinced him that one could not here plausibly suppose that the historical record had been distorted. The historical Jesus was simply wrong and Kant was right. In reality it was surely the view of the Golden Rule that Kant had imposed on him that was mistaken, being inconsistent with the Hellenic, life-enhancing emphasis in his own attitude to social intercourse. In the end the simplest and oldest formula, 'Love thy neighbour as thyself' (of which the Golden Rule is only an expanded form), triumphed over Kant's abstract rationalism in his mind.[1]

4. The evils born of authority

The man who came so close to anticipating the Categorical Imperative, the teacher who taught that men should have faith in themselves and strive to develop their own reason, rather than look for a Messiah, the moral hero who lived and died for rational autonomy and freedom, telling his followers that it was expedient for them that he should go away, precisely in order that they might cease to be followers[2]—this was the man on whom the halo of supra-rational (and hence demonic rather than divine) authority descended. Why had this happened? This was a problem with which Hegel had been wrestling for almost a year when he finished *The Life of Jesus* in July 1795, and he now had his answer ready. It seems quite probable that he conceived the essay on 'The Positivity of Christianity'[3] at the same time as *The Life of Jesus* and as co-ordinate with it. The two essays together answer the question raised in the plan of 1794: 'How far is the Christian Religion qualified (for the furthering of morality)?'[4] And much that remains of necessity only implicit in *The Life of Jesus*, because of its direct linkage with the Gospel text, is stated or explained explicitly in the later essay. Furthermore we can

[1] Nohl, p. 87 (cf. p. 206 n. 1 above). Hobbes had already pointed out long before that the only reliable principle of prudence is the more cautious formula 'Do *not* unto others what you would *not* that they should do unto you' (*Leviathan*, Chapter 13). The Golden Rule could scarcely function in a prudential calculus at all; it is only really intelligible as applying to the spirit in which one should act. (For Kant's strictures on it see the *Grundlegung*, *Akad.* iv. 430 n.)

[2] Nohl, pp. 125–7.

[3] *man mag die widersprechendsten Betrachtungen* (Nohl, pp. 152–313). The first page of the manuscript is missing. All save the concluding two pages (added in Apr. 1796) was written before the end of Nov. 1795 (cf. the date in the margin of the text, Nohl, p. 204). The essay has been translated by Knox in *Early Theological Writings*, pp. 67–145.

[4] *Unter objektiver Religion*, Nohl, p. 49.

see from the notes that Hegel made from readings in Ammon's *Theological Journal* and in Gibbon that his mind was already full of ideas for the 'Positivity' essay before he began *The Life of Jesus*.[1]

It seems probable, nevertheless, that Hegel did not begin to write the 'Positivity' essay immediately after completing *The Life of Jesus*. At some point during the next few months he certainly considered doing for the Pauline Epistles what he had already done for the Gospels; and he almost certainly contemplated abandoning his whole undertaking in despair. This much emerges from Hölderlin's letter of 25 November 1795, for Hölderlin tells Hegel that 'a paraphrase of the Pauline Epistles in accordance with your view [*nach Deiner Idee*]' would certainly be worth the effort, and urges him 'not to lay your literary concerns aside'.[2]

It is clear from the opening of Hölderlin's letter that he felt guilty about his long silence. It is possible, though not in my opinion likely, that he was prompted to write at the end of November by an appeal he had just received from Hegel himself. For Hegel certainly laid the 'Positivity' manuscript aside early in November, and this would have been a natural moment for him to have begun thinking about the Epistles. But Hegel's correspondence with Schelling strongly suggests that there was a hiatus in his work between the finishing of *The Life of Jesus* and the beginning of the 'Positivity' essay. Schelling wrote to him on July 21. Hegel delayed for about a month before replying on August 30; and when he comes to speak of the state of his own work in this letter he says it is 'not worth talking about; perhaps I will send you in a little while the plan of something that I am thinking of working up, a project in which I would particularly like to ask for your friendly assistance in matters of Church History, an area in which I am very weak and in which I can get the best possible advice from you.'[3] This was written some five weeks after the completion of *The Life of Jesus* (24 July 1795). And Hegel certainly had good reason to be shy in talking about an undertaking of this sort to Schelling, who heartily despised the whole field of Church History

---

[1] *Unkunde der Geschichte* (Nohl, pp. 363, 364, 365, 366). The probability is that these notes are slightly earlier than *Die reine aller Schranken* (Schüler, p. 142).

[2] Letter 15, *Briefe*, i. 34. See further, p. 209 n. 2 below.

[3] Letter 14, *Briefe*, i. 33.

in which his school record was 'outstandingly good'.[1] But for Hegel to speak of his 'Positivity' essay as a 'plan' if he had already written almost a third of it—as we might expect if he had begun it as soon as he completed *The Life of Jesus*—is rather odd, to say the least. My own conclusion therefore is that he was at this time making new 'plans' and had not yet seriously embarked on the next step in their fulfilment.[2] Unfortunately, because of the loss of the first page of the 'Positivity' manuscript, which was probably headed like *The Life of Jesus* with a date, the question cannot be decisively settled.[3]

Schelling was certainly as depressed as Hegel could possibly have been when he wrote on 21 July. He was badly downcast both about the reception of his first philosophical essay and about the prospects of his hero Fichte, who had turned the whole student body against himself at Jena by trying to interfere with the running of their clubs. For a time Fichte had had to withdraw from the University altogether. By this time he had returned again, but all the forces of reaction were now aroused against him; both he and his youthful disciple were severely handled in reviews, and even Schiller was criticized for associating with him. The shadow of the *Atheismusstreit*, which eventually drove him from Jena altogether, already loomed on the horizon. Schelling, at twenty, was volatile enough to be deeply depressed. He had been accustomed ever since he was ten or eleven years old to see everything that he did greeted with adult admiration and amazement; and this was

[1] See Fuhrmans, i. 43–4. Of the three reports preserved for this subject, the first (winter 1793/4) is 'auszeichnend gut', the other two (summer 1794, winter 1794/5) 'sehr gut'.

[2] The 'plans' of the 'Old Man' were a byword among his friends at Tübingen (cf. Chapter II, p. 71 above). I believe that while he was still writing *The Life of Jesus* Hegel wrote to Hölderlin about his plans for the Epistles and his desire to find a new position; and then he wrote again in November in a very disheartened vein, complaining of Hölderlin's silence, asking his advice about a return to Tübingen and saying that he was going to lay aside—or had laid aside—all of his 'literary concerns'. This appeal Hölderlin answered fairly promptly in the letter that we have. (Cf. further, p. 244 nn. 1 and 3 below.)

[3] If it bore a date then it was certainly lost before Rosenkranz came to examine the manuscript (see his rather misleading description on p. 54, where the rewriting of the introduction in 1800 is not distinguished from the original). The probability is, I think, that Hegel himself removed the first page, and perhaps destroyed it, when he made his revision in 1800. The later stages of the revision were made directly in the margin of the original manuscript: cf. Nohl, p. 139 n. (Hegel habitually began by folding his sheets down the centre. He then wrote on the right side of each page leaving the left half blank for his revisions and additions.)

probably the first time he had experienced a serious check in his career as a *Wunderkind*. Hence when he tells Hegel: 'Certainly, my friend, the revolution that is to be produced through philosophy is still far off',[1] we must not mistake the accents of Chicken Little for the sober voice of mature reflection as many critics have done. He sent both his thesis (*De Marcione*) and his second philosophical essay *Vom Ich als Prinzip der Philosophie* for Hegel's inspection and comment.

Hegel's reply (30 August 1795) makes clear that he did now fully accept the impersonal conception of God as the Absolute Ego. He does not say any more about its belonging to the 'esoteric' philosophy of the time,[2] but rather stresses that if Schelling's discussion of the 'moral proof' does not make the Tübingen 'Kantians' see the error of their ways, nothing will.[3] He realized that Schelling's pessimism was largely due to his personal disappointment, and he did all he could to raise his friend's spirits, telling him that the unfavourable reception of his ideas was a result of his being ahead of his time.[4]

[1] *Briefe* i. 28. Schelling's three-months' silence is quite sufficiently accounted for in the letter itself, without any necessity to suppose (as Haering does, i. 210) that he found Hegel's letters boring, misguided, or otherwise unsatisfactory. He was in his last semester at Tübingen and had enjoyed the onerous privilege of writing his own thesis for defence in the final examination. The pressure on him was such that when he finished it he was ill and had to go home for a time. He was clearly very happy to be able at last to think about things that were closer to his heart, and to write just what he thought and felt without the nagging consciousness of Storr's overseeing eye. There is, if anything, a tone of comfortable confidence in this letter which was not present earlier—this is the first letter in which he does not say anxiously that they must not become *fremd*.

The longer silence between Hegel's letter in August and Schelling's next in January is likewise to be accounted for by the pressure of Schelling's other interests and occupations, not by supposing that he thought the correspondence was not worth the trouble—even if he is a little ironic about the failure of any of Hegel's 'plans' to bear any *published* fruit. Of course in this period he was free from the boredom of the *Stift*, so he felt less need to write to Hegel. But he does still regard him as a potentially important ally. He tells Hegel that he may find the 'Letters on Dogmatism and Criticism' relevant to his interests; and in June he duly thanks Hegel for his comments on them (*Briefe*, i. 36–7).

[2] As he had done in April (*Briefe*, i. 24).

[3] *Briefe*, i. 30. 'Page 103' of Schelling's essay which Hegel there refers to is to be found in *Sämtliche Werke* (1856), i. 201.

[4] He adds the testimony of a Tübingen *Repetent* to the same effect! About Fichte's adventures he remarks with the sage prudence of a professional *Volkserzieher* that 'perhaps he would have accomplished more if he had left them their savagery [*Roheit*] and only set himself to bind a quiet, well chosen little group to him' (*Briefe*, i. 32–3). Fichte ought to have behaved more like Hegel's Jesus in fact!

He excused himself from the task of criticizing Schelling's essay on the sensible ground that he was 'only a learner' in these matters. This was quite obviously true; and it was also true that Hegel's interests were more strictly practical than Schelling's. But we must be careful not to overstate the contrast between them. They shared a common enemy in the Tübingen School of theology, and Schelling's reasons for opposing it were just as political and moral as Hegel's—in fact they were identical. While Hegel, on the other hand, was increasingly convinced that the rational theology, and even the purely theoretical philosophy of Kant and Fichte, was the great hope of the future. The one criticism that he ventured concerns Schelling's application of the concept of substance to the Absolute Ego. He objected on grounds of elementary Kantian theory that the concept is inapplicable at this noumenal level. It is clear, at least, that Hegel understood both the relation and the contrast between Spinoza and Fichte as Fichte himself expressed it and as Schelling had expressed it in an earlier letter.[1] Behind his present complaint lies the conviction that even the *theory* of the Absolute as Ego must remain true to its essentially practical origins, and not fall back into the use of the old dogmatic categories. The contrast between the Absolute as Substance and the Absolute as Subject is not yet clear in Hegel's mind, because he has surrendered the idea of a *personal* God without as yet finding anything very definite to put in its place; but the firm grasp of Kant's distinction between the theoretical and the practical use of reason, which is here evident, is the origin of this later distinction.[2]

---

[1] *Briefe*, i. 22; cf. *Briefe*, i. 19–20 for the same point in a letter of Hölderlin's.

[2] There is a sense in which the older view, now generally discredited, that there is a sequence of thought from Kant through Fichte and Schelling to Hegel is correct. Each of them drew more rigorously than his predecessor the consequences of Kant's restriction of the speculative use of reason to the practical realm, and each was consciously correcting the 'mistakes' of the thinker before him.

It is hard to decide, at least without more detailed study than I have been able to give to the question, how far Hegel actually misunderstood Schelling—as Haering claims (i. 208–9). I do not think that in the circumstances of this letter we should take seriously his implied doubt whether Schelling is speaking of the Absolute Ego or not; in fact I do not think any doubt *is* implied. The reference to the empirical ego as 'uniting the highest thesis and antithesis' I take to be a slip of the pen—either something has been left out, or Hegel just got lost in his own syntax.

Finally, Hegel's use of *Nicht-Ich* when he comforts Schelling against adversity by telling him that the basic trouble is that 'people absolutely will not give up their non-Ego' is certainly peculiar. But if Schelling did not see why Hegel used

Schelling's thesis *De Marcione* prompted Hegel to one comment that is interesting in the light of his current preoccupations:

I have found in it especially confirmation for one suspicion, which I had already harboured for a long time, that it would perhaps have turned out more honourably for us and for mankind, if one or other (and no matter which) of the heresies damned by Councils and Symbols had developed into the public system of belief, instead of the orthodox system maintaining the upper hand.[1]

Hegel's own essay which was 'not worth talking about' in the letter to Schelling begins, like *Wenn man von der christlichen Religion*, by alluding to the difficulty of establishing what the term 'Christian religion' properly refers to. Hegel now assumes that the Christian religion was *not* originally a doctrine of salvation through faith in Christ, that there was *not* originally a contrast between Christian salvation and salvation through reason, and seeks to account for the contrast between them which now so obviously exists. Probably he announced this presupposition and the resulting problem at the outset, for in the manuscript as we have it he declares that in the eyes of the orthodox—those 'sustained by the tradition of centuries and by the public power'—*his* inquiry is more suspect even than the rational critique of religion offered by the leaders of the Enlightenment. He goes on immediately to accept the general principles of enlightened criticism himself, so we must assume that he had already said *something* which distinguished his undertaking from the work of Kant and Fichte on the one side, or that of Montesquieu and Gibbon on the other.[2]

the term in this way, he had only to look at the context of the passage in his own essay referred to later: 'Gott in theoretischer Bedeutung ist Ich=Nicht-Ich, in praktischer *absolutes* Ich, das alles Nicht-Ich zernichtet', etc. (*Sämtliche Werke* (1856), i, 201). Since Hegel referred to this page one can hardly suppose that he *misunderstood* the concept of the *Nicht-Ich*, no matter how curiously he chose to apply it.

[1] *Briefe*, i. 32. Schelling's thesis dealt with the problem of whether Marcion had falsified the text of the Pauline epistles. The reading of it must almost certainly have had some effect on Hegel's nascent plan to do for the Pauline epistles what he had already done for the Gospels. But we cannot guess what the effect was.

[2] I take it that he has Kant and Fichte in mind when he speaks of those who take reason and morality as a basis for testing it [the Christian religion]' and Montesquieu and Gibbon when he speaks of 'drawing on the spirit of nations and epochs for help in explaining it'. Of course there are many others who may have been in his mind also. His own undertaking involves both of these approaches, as we shall see, but the distinctive assumption that all true religion

As in all of his later works, Hegel found it impossible to write the sort of preface that was expected, and his introductory remarks constitute the first sketch for a critical attack on the writing of prefaces, which appeared full blown in the Preface to the *Phenomenology*. One ought not, he felt, to begin with a statement of faith or a description of one's own peculiar point of view, since if all one had to offer was a personal opinion one's statement could have no public or universal significance, while if what one wished to say did have rational foundations, this could only be made clear in the body of the work and not in the preface. He began therefore with a statement of rational principle:

Wholly and entirely in reference to the topic itself, let it here be said that in general the basic principle to be laid down as a foundation for all judgements on the varying modifications, forms, and spirit of the Christian religion is this—that the aim and essence of all true religion, our religion included, is human morality, and that all the more specific doctrines of Christianity, all means of propagating them, all duties to believe and to perform actions that are otherwise in themselves arbitrary, are to be appraised for worth and sanctity according to their closer or more distant connection with that aim.[1]

Hegel's fundamental thesis is that this was the principle by which Jesus himself was guided in his attempt to 'raise religion and virtue to morality'. Jesus did not advance any new moral doctrines but sought to restore and develop the moral substance and meaning of existing usage and tradition.[2] Even in his life-time Jesus was misunderstood by those closest to him, says Hegel, referring to two cases which he had already examined in *The Life of Jesus*: the

---

is essentially rational (moral) makes Hegel closer in spirit to Rousseau's 'Creed of a Savoyard Vicar' and Lessing's 'Education of the Human Race' than to any of the other strands in the Enlightenment.

[1] Nohl, p. 153; cf. Knox, p. 68.

[2] Hegel provides a list of Old Testament references to support this claim (Nohl, p. 154; Knox, pp. 69–70). Knox finds the inclusion of Leviticus 18: 5 in this list puzzling. But it is easy enough to understand once we grasp the principle by which the series is articulated. First Hegel indicates the source of the two great Commandments (Matthew 22: 37⟨–39⟩) in Deuteronomy 6: 5 and Leviticus 19: 18. Then he compares Leviticus 18: 5 ('Ye shall therefore keep my statutes, and my judgements: which if a man do, he shall live in them: I am the Lord') with Matthew 5: 48 ('Be ye therefore perfect, even as your Father which is in heaven is perfect'). Thus Hegel identifies the idea of *living in* the law, of gaining life *from* it in some way, instead of subjecting life to it, as what is meant by the command 'Be ye perfect'. Finally he gives reasons for rejecting the Golden Rule as a summary of the moral law.

request of Zebedee's wife and the betrayal by Judas, and one
other which was there eliminated, the question 'Lord, wilt thou
at this time restore again the kingdom to Israel', directed to Jesus
just before the Ascension.[1] From the ambiguous relation of Jesus
to his tradition a new religion of authority has sprung; but all the
same, it is clear that Hegel thinks Jesus' policy of giving every
established usage its maximum value by relating it as closely as
possible to the moral end of man is the right one, and the only
one that a rational man can follow when he believes that the
forces of moral corruption are at work in his own society.

Because of this reintegrative attitude Jesus was not the founder
of a *philosophical* sect which rises superior to custom and tradition
without condemning it (except of course where it leads to immoral
actions), nor yet of a *positive* sect which makes a moral fetish out of
replacing the existing custom by some new (but equally *positive*)
pattern of behaviour.[2] Because Jesus did not simply set aside the
customs and traditions of his people as irrelevant, contemporary
philosophical sectarians (Kant) can deny that Christianity is a
virtue religion, and contemporary positive sectarians (the Tübingen
School) can exalt it as a revelation superior to reason. Against the
common assumption of both, that the teaching of Jesus was originally positive, Hegel urges the evident fact that as a system of

[1] Nohl, pp. 154-5. See Matthew 20: 20 and Acts 1: 6. Hegel gives no
specific reference for the case of Judas, but from *The Life of Jesus* we can see
that he followed the versions of Matthew 26 and John 13 (for the parallel
passages in the earlier work see Nohl, pp. 114-15, 123-5).

[2] Hegel's concept of a 'sect', and of the different types of 'sect', is not easy to
disentangle. I think that Haering (i. 227-8) has the basic doctrine right, although
his view that Hegel means to assert the existence of a good kind of *positivity* is
misleading. In any pattern of social life there are two elements, one which is
moral (*Sittlichkeit*) and one which is simply customary. Thus two kinds of sects
are possible: *philosophical* sects whose members hold special views about
morality and (hence about God as the pure fount of moral reason) and *positive*
sects who reject the established customs and substitute others, because they
wrongly believe God to be something other than 'pure Reason incapable of
limitations', and so strive to please him in non-rational ways. Established customs,
rooted in the imagination of the people, are not in themselves good, though they
may certainly be susceptible of some good use, and are to be appraised accordingly. In themselves, all such customs are morally indifferent. When someone
believes that a set of customs is good as such, he gives to it an authority that it
ought not to have, he sets up a positive authority, a *heteronomous* system in the
Kantian sense. Thus any *positive authority* is *ipso facto* evil, and though there is
a use of the word 'positive' which is morally neutral, there is no sense in which
positivity is ever 'good'. It is only one's attitude to it that can be good, and the
good attitude is most aptly described as 'making the best of it'.

positive doctrine Christianity as we have it is the result of a long process of historical development. Since much has been added, the hypothesis that Christianity was originally a virtue religion, in Hegel's own sense—that is to say a re-evaluation of a positive tradition by the standard of rational virtue—cannot be ruled out without investigation. In any case this hypothesis 'will be recognized by all parties of the Christian communion as correct, though it will also be pronounced very incomplete'.[1]

For the Jews the law of Moses was the direct deliverance of God himself, so that anyone seeking to reinterpret it, had of necessity to claim like authority. To appeal simply to reason would be like 'preaching to fish' because the Jews had lost the awareness of reason as an autonomous faculty.[2] Jesus therefore had to demand faith in his own person as a step towards the recovery of that autonomy. Thus one mystery of *The Life of Jesus* is resolved. Where St. John makes Jesus say 'He that believeth on me, believeth not on me, but on him that sent me', Hegel takes this, with what follows—'If any man hear my words and believe me not, I judge him not . . . the word that I have spoken, the same shall judge him in the last day. For I have not spoken of myself' etc.—as the clearest indication Jesus could give that he was *not* asking for

---

[1] Nohl, pp. 156–7 (Knox, pp. 72–3). As we have seen, this hypothesis is really a matter of principle for Hegel. To rule it out is to admit that Christianity is not a 'virtue' religion (i.e. a 'true' religion) at all. As a ground for rewriting the plain text of the Gospels in an inverse sense this may not satisfy Father Peperzak (see above, p. 200 n. 3), but it did have some force in the eyes of the Tübingen theologians, since their argument was that positive revelation was needed precisely because practical reason is unable to solve all the problems with which we are inevitably faced in moral experience. In particular, they emphasized the omnipresence of sin which made the postulate of gratuitous forgiveness (which reason cannot justify) necessary. This problem troubled Kant himself gravely. Hegel alludes to it but, of course, he cannot allow that raising the problem itself to the rank of a 'postulate' is any solution. His own solution came later in the Frankfurt essay 'The spirit of Christianity'. (From his own point of view the concessive allusion to the 'incompleteness' of his hypothesis in the 'Positivity' essay is very probably an anticipatory reference to the task that he had still to perform in that later essay.)

[2] Nohl, pp. 159; Knox, p. 76. This metaphor echoes the earlier reference to the pious behaviour of St. Antony of Padua (Nohl, p. 157; Knox, p. 73) in a way that can hardly be accidental. In the earlier passage it is argued that if we suppose that Jesus made a positive revelation we must suppose that human beings are endowed with a faculty to receive it. Here it is argued that one cannot appeal directly to *Vernunft* if men have lost the consciousness that they possess it. Hegel is obviously trying to show how *Vernunft* itself comes to appear as if it were, and to be appealed to as if it were, a faculty for receiving divine revelation.

reverence or faith in his own person, but rather for faith in the power of reason by which his word was apprehended. Taken in this way the passage provided Hegel with a warrant for reinterpreting the many statements about 'believing on me' in John and elsewhere, without having to assert, or meaning to imply, that they were wrongly reported.[1]

Those who accepted the words of Jesus as authoritative were bound, in the circumstances of Jewish culture, to believe or suspect that he was the Messiah. Jesus himself could not contradict this belief without denying the Messianic hope itself, which would have been contrary to his whole method of procedure, and would also have prevented him from obtaining an effective hearing at all. He strove therefore to bring out the spiritual meaning of the Messianic hope by referring the kingdom and the glory of the Messiah to another life and another world. The persecution and death of such a one was bound to make a tremendous impression on his followers, says Hegel. He still does not allude to the Resurrection directly, but goes on to discuss the miracles of healing in a way which, very discreetly, casts doubt upon the literal interpretation of the record;[2] and he specifically says that the miracles did more than anything else to make the religion of Jesus positive. We can infer, I think, that Hegel believed that the Resurrection story grew out of Jesus' attempts to give the Messianic hope a higher meaning; and certainly it was this story *in conjunction with* the account of the Passion which 'fettered the imagination' to him.[3]

Turning now from the *sources* of faith in Jesus as a positive authority or saving power, to its *consequences*, Hegel comments that belief in the miracles of Jesus would be all very well if, as

[1] John 12: 23–50; Nohl, p. 119. It is odd that Peperzak should have chosen this passage to make an issue over Hegel's falsification of the record, for it is the one passage in John that seems most plausibly taken in Hegel's sense, and it is the key to his frankly Pickwickian interpretation of all the others (cf. Peperzak, p. 63 n.).

[2] He points out that the Scribes and Pharisees were not impressed by miracles of healing which reportedly took place in their presence, but only by the violation of the Sabbath where that was involved; and that the curing of demoniacs is ascribed to others in the Gospels themselves.

[3] Nohl, pp. 160–1; Knox, pp. 77–9. Just as there is here (I think) a tacit allusion to the Ressurrection, so also the remark about 'insignificant traits which pass unnoticed [*gleichgültig sind*] when told of an ordinary man' is a tacit dismissal of the Nativity story. For the significance of the word *fesseln* in Hegel's personal vocabulary, see the reminiscences of Leutwein (*Hegel-Studien*, iii. 56, line 130).

Storr and the Tübingen theologians held, it really led men to follow his moral example. But in fact this 'round-about way' (*Umweg*) to morality has the effect, first of distracting attention from morality as the real destination of the journey, and secondly of making us too humble to believe in our own capacity to be moral —so that in fact it cannot really lead us to the destination at all, and according to the principle announced at the outset it ought to be discarded altogether as mere superstition.[1]

Hegel clearly wants to maintain that the establishment of a positive sect was not the deliberate act of Jesus himself. Both in *The Life of Jesus* and in the 'Positivity' essay he tries as far as possible to explain away all evidence to the contrary. His treatment of the relations between Jesus and the disciples shows this very clearly, especially when we compare it with the sharp contrast drawn between Socrates and Jesus in the fragments of 1794.[2] This contrast is still present: the disciples of Jesus were not, like those of Socrates, men who had their own aims and purposes, and a firm consciousness of their own capacities. They had given up their private lives to follow Jesus and they had no share in public life; and twelve of them were finally singled out. But in *The Life of Jesus* three stages are distinguished in the calling of the apostles, so that the eventual fixing of their number at twelve is seen as entirely accidental. Jesus simply chose the best available pupils for more direct and personal instruction, and it was only after his death that their number became significant because they assumed in the infant community the authority of a college of magistrates.[3]

---

[1] Nohl, pp. 161–2; Knox, pp. 79–80. This point was first made in *Es sollte eine schwere Aufgabe* (Nohl, p. 59).

[2] See especially *Christus hatte zwölf Apostel*, Nohl, pp. 32–4.

[3] Cf. Nohl, pp. 78, 90; and Nohl, pp. 163–4 (Knox, pp. 82–3). It is quite plain—as Knox indicates in his footnote on p. 84—that Hegel will not allow Jesus to be held responsible for anything that is credited to the Risen Lord. His conviction that Jesus certainly never promised that 'He that believeth and is baptized shall be saved; but he that believeth not shall be damned' explains the antipathy to the Gospel of Mark, which we noted earlier (see p. 197 n. 1 above). Hegel points out that Mark 16: 15–18 is inconsistent with the last discourse of the living Jesus as recorded in John, and seems to be expressly contradicted at the end of the Sermon on the Mount (Matthew 7: 21–3). In *The Life of Jesus* these two discourses are regarded as the basic accounts of Jesus' own doctrine. This contrast between the teaching of the living Jesus and the command of the Risen Christ struck him even before he began to study the Gospels in the light of his principle of πληρῶσις (see *Christus hatte zwölf Apostel*, Nohl, pp. 32–3). But it does not seem to have occurred to him in 1794 that the Risen Christ need not be identified with the man Jesus.

The recorded action of Jesus himself in sending the Twelve forth to preach did provide a basis for their authoritative position. As Hegel says, this method of procedure is only suited to the spreading of positive religion, not to the advance of virtue. In attempting to account for the story he seems to have wavered. In *The Life of Jesus* it is presented as an experiment which Jesus tried without any very high hopes, and which he immediately recognized as a failure so that he never attempted to repeat it. In the 'Positivity' essay Hegel seems more inclined to the view that the story is simply false, for he sandwiches it into his account of the authority and the command given to the Twelve after the Resurrection, and about this he is quite overtly sceptical.[1]

In any case, whether or not Jesus himself tried any mistaken experiments, the real degeneration of his mission into the founding of a positive sect began with the preaching of the Gospel in the name of the Risen Lord.[2] This involved the transformation of Jesus' message into a contradictory conception—a *positive* doctrine of *virtue*: the earliest Christian community was a sect that took a *positive* attitude toward *philosophical* tenets. But it was also a 'positive' sect in the ordinary sense of Hegel's definition, for it regarded the established law and custom as sinful and had distinctive positive ordinances of its own. As long as it was a small community whose membership was entirely voluntary there was nothing pernicious in any of this. But as soon as it grew to embrace whole societies, leaving individuals without the opportunity for that employment of free choice from which alone the con-

---

[1] On the first view the later 'sending of the seventy' had to be explained away—and Hegel accounted for it by assuming that it arose from a misunderstanding of the obviously sensible habit of sending two disciples ahead whenever Jesus was journeying with the whole company. In the 'Positivity' essay, however, he alludes to both stories quite neutrally. It is easy to see why he may have been in some doubt about what line to take. For to admit the sending of the seventy seemed on the one hand to involve casting a grave slur on Jesus' intelligence; but on the other hand, it could be used to show that the twelve had no peculiar privilege or authority in his eyes. See Nohl, pp. 102 and 164 (Knox, p. 83). (Hegel discusses these stories again in his notes for 'The Spirit of Christianity': see Nohl, pp. 396, 400–1; and in that essay he does not distinguish between them but treats both stories together as evidence of the dream-like character of Jesus' faith: Nohl, pp. 325–6; Knox, pp. 282–3.)

[2] This point was first made in *Wenn man von der christlichen Religion* (Nohl, p. 59): 'John's call to the people was: "Repent"; Christ's: "Repent and believe in the Gospel"; that of the Apostles was: "Believe in Christ".'

sciousness of moral autonomy can spring, its positive character became the root of evil.[1]

When this happened, both the distinctive institutions (community of goods etc.) and the distinctive quality of life (brotherhood and family feeling generally) characteristic of the early Church disappeared, and purely symbolic observances replaced them. Thus, for instance, at the Last Supper Jesus enjoined the disciples to think of him whenever they were eating together; the early Church made this into a religious rite, and a substitute for pagan sacrificial feasts; and finally the fraternal character of the observance has disappeared almost entirely and the private, mystical aspect of it has been exalted above all else.

But the establishment of Christianity as a 'public' religion had its good as well as its bad side. Any positive sect is naturally bound to be zealous in the making of converts, since salvation depends on adherence to its distinctive (positive) doctrines.[2] While, on the other hand, any virtuous member of a philosophical sect will always respect virtue even if it appears to him to be allied with illogic. Hence if such a one encounters a Christian who has chosen to cleave to the rational rather than to the purely positive aspect of his faith, he will be led 'to marvel at the invincible might of the Ego which triumphs over an intellect [*Verstand*] full of morally destructive convictions and a memory packed with learned phrases'; and really virtuous members of different sects will recognize one another as brothers, just as Nathan and the Lay Brother do in Lessing's play. But this 'triumph of the Ego' is not likely to occur until the anxieties of positive faith have been allayed by the comforting presence of a multitude of like-minded believers.[3]

---

[1] This point was first made in *öffentliche Gewalt* (Nohl, pp. 42, 44) and in *So kann in einem Staate* (Nohl, pp. 44–5).

[2] Hegel asserts this as if it was a necessary truth about all positive sects. But, in fact, the beliefs of the sect may be such as to make all proselytizing activity appear somewhat anomalous—as was the case, for example, with Biblical Judaism, founded as it was on the covenant of God with his Chosen People, and on the expectation of a Messiah who would 'restore the kingdom to Israel'. What Hegel says is, however, necessarily true about a 'positive doctrine of virtue'.

[3] Nohl, pp. 169–73; Knox, pp. 91–5. The missionary impulse is itself rooted in an urge to escape from the burden of rational freedom; when we try to convert someone 'our secret reason is often our resentment that another should be free from fetters [*Fesseln*] which we ourselves bear and which we have not the strength to cast off'. The establishment of the *consensus gentium* relieves

At this point we might say that the diagnosis of the problem is complete, and Hegel begins to make recommendations for its solution.[1] The decline of zeal in missionary work, and the allied growth of interest in missionary reports as a source of anthropological and other scientific information, marks the point at which we can at last recover the true sense of the Gospel that was to be preached to all nations. The absolute Ego of Schelling—Hegel's 'reine, aller Schranken unfähige, Vernunft'—can now exhibit its 'invincible might'. The gospel of Jesus must now be 'fulfilled', as he 'fulfilled' the law of Moses. In other words the positive aspects of religious faith must be deprived of their authority, for only then will the adherents of the various religions be able to recognize the paramount authority of reason—the moral law—in all of them. Hence the Churches must give up all coercive power, and become what they originally were, entirely voluntary associations. There must be complete separation of Church and State because the establishment of morality, the ultimate goal which they have in common, cannot be achieved by legal coercion; and in any alliance between the two of them the Church inevitably requires the State to exercise coercive force on its behalf.

Hegel's discussion of Church–State relations is heavily indebted to Mendelssohn's *Jerusalem*, in which a doctrine of the rigid separation of Church and State is based on the view that while the aim of the State is to secure legality by coercive sanctions, the aim of the Church is to secure morality by voluntary conviction. Hegel himself says explicitly at one point:

Since an ideal of moral perfection could not in principle [*überhaupt*] be the object of civil codes of law and least of all could the ideal of the

us of the duty and responsibility for rational investigation so to speak; and, as Hegel remarks, against the terrors of hell we have at least the comfort that a lot of other people will be there with us. But in gaining this comfort we have exhausted the missionary impulse, and so finally the power of reason is able to reassert itself.

[1] Outwardly his discourse continues to have the form of a diagnosis of the process by which throne and altar became allied, but from here on (Nohl, p. 173; Knox, p. 95) his fundamental concern is the proper relation of Church and State; his primary authority for Church History is Mosheim, and his inspiration comes mainly from Mendelssohn's *Jerusalem*. I shall treat this part of his discussion rather cursorily, because the text is readily available and quite easy to follow. (The stages of 'positivity' involved are well analysed by Hočevar, pp. 77–87.)

Christians be an objective for Jewish and heathen governments, the Christian sect attempted to influence the disposition [*Gesinnung*] and take that as the standard for determining men's worth and the rewards or punishments they deserve.[1]

The highly ironical context in which this passage occurs—Hegel has just said that both from its methods and its heroes we can see that the 'holiness' of Christianity is just 'what really pious men have in common with vagrants, lunatics, and scoundrels, unified in a single concept'—tends if anything to make Hegel's acceptance of the principle here stated more certain. The methods of the Christian Church are condemned precisely because they attempted to import the methods of civil justice into the moral realm where the concepts of reward and punishment have no place. But, for all that, we must not fall into the error of thinking that Hegel agrees with Mendelssohn's separation of Church and State in terms of aims and methods. The State, in his view, must have a monopoly in the use of legal coercion; but it does not thereby cease to be a moral organism with essentially moral aims. The State is above both the *bürgerliche Gesetzgebung* and the *religiösen Anstalten*, as Hegel indicated in *Unter objektiver Religion*. The principle of distinction between these subordinate agencies was first stated in the second paragraph of that sketch and the whole of his present discussion is a development of the fourth:

To make objective religion subjective must be the great concern of the State, the institutions must be consistent with the freedom of individual dispositions, so as not to do violence to conscience and to freedom, but to work indirectly on the determining grounds of the will —how much can the State do? How much must be left to each individual man?[2]

The Church is essentially a voluntary society within the State,

[1] Nohl, p. 178; Knox, p. 101.

[2] Nohl, p. 49. I think it likely that *Unter objektiver Religion* is the 'Skizze' referred to in the deleted heading near the beginning of the 'Positivity' essay. At least the cancelled heading (Nohl, p. 153) 'comparison with the articulation of a State Constitution (see Outline)' fits in very well with the parallel in paragraph five of *Unter objektiver Religion* between Religion and the State as agencies for advancing morality, just as the present discussion fits paragraphs two and four. (A hint of what Hegel may have meant to say under the cancelled heading can be gained from the remarks about the Sermon on the Mount further on (Nohl, p. 176; Knox, p. 99); and, for that matter, it is not too hard to see how the parallel applies to the 'state of the Jewish Religion' which Hegel actually goes on to analyse at that point in his text.)

and hence the rights a citizen concedes to his Church can never be
such as to result in any infringement of his civil duties.[1] The State
needs the Church—or rather, as we shall see, it needs the Churches
—because it cannot do anything that will directly cause its citizens
to behave morally. A church which men join freely will aid the
development of morality in so far as it appeals to moral motives;
but it may actually impede the development of morality if it sets
out to terrorize the imagination. A 'State-Church' is *bound* to
impede the development of morality if civil penalties are appointed
for those who refuse to join it or seek to withdraw from it. Any
society, from the State downwards, has the right to exclude from
its members those who refuse to obey its rules; but just for this
reason ecclesiastical regulations must never be given the force of
State laws.

The main area of difficulty, as Hegel recognizes, is education.
For it is here that the State's moral concern is most apparent, and
also the dangers of sectarian prejudice. A *man*, he argues, who
disagrees with the political organization of his society, has at least
the freedom to emigrate (if there is any freedom in his society at
all). But a child educated by an authoritarian church may never
become a free man at all; he may grow up in a kind of slavery—
either the mental slavery of one who does not know *how* to think
for himself, or the psychological slavery of one whose imagination
is so terrorized that he does not *dare* to do so. Yet to bring up a
child without a positive faith would be to deprive both the state
and the individual of the aid of the imagination in the formation
of the moral character; and although Hegel's echoing of the
shocked sentiments of the Patriarch in *Nathan* on this point is
transparently ironical, he certainly does not mean to take this way
out.[2]

His hope lies rather in the development of what he takes to be
the essential spirit of Protestantism. No child can enjoy freedom
of choice while he is being educated; any freedom secured by law,
or even by the 'law of nature' (i.e. by *Vernunft*), can only be
exercised on his behalf by his parents. But steps can be taken to

---

[1] Nohl, p. 174 (Knox, p. 97). In the following paragraph (Nohl, p. 175) Hegel
draws an explicit distinction between *der Staat als Staat* (Mendelssohn's State)
and *der Staat als moralische Wesen* (his own conception based on the Greek
ideal of the πόλις).

[2] Nohl, pp. 188–90; Knox, pp. 114–16. The two occurrences of *Fesseln*
(verb and noun) indicate Hegel's own attitude.

see that his education is not such that his reason is 'fettered' (*gefesselt*) by it. Hegel's own proposal to remove every vestige of hierarchic authority from the structure of the Church and make every form of religious observance entirely voluntary and absolutely democratic would certainly ensure this. He does not propose to restore the communism of the early Church, but he does propose that the Church should once more be dominated by the spirit of absolute equality and brotherhood.

To this end he sets himself to show that there cannot be such a thing as an authoritative declaration of the faith, or an authoritative interpretation of a commonly accepted symbolic formula or creed. This is because one cannot, in the nature of things, bind oneself to *believe* something. There cannot be a social contract in matters of faith. One cannot subject one's own opinion to the General Will.[1] A Council of the Church can, if it is properly representative, i.e. if it is democratically elected, declare what the general faith of the congregation *is*; but no one can lay down authoritatively, even for himself, what the faith ought to be. Everyone, always, must retain the liberty to think again, because this is the precondition of thinking better, and so of becoming better. Hence, a civil contract to 'defend the faith' or to 'respect another's faith' can *only* be a recognition of the civil obligation to defend and respect universal freedom in matters of faith. Toleration, which is a necessary evil for believers, because they are rationally obliged to recognize that no man can be saved by force, is a rational duty for citizens and for the political authority.

In discussing religious education, therefore, Hegel does not appeal to freedom of thought and of conscience, since they are matters of civil right, but to the quality of religious faith itself. A cloistered faith, a faith that must be protected against all outside influence is not a genuine personal conviction at all. It is not, in his earlier terminology, 'subjective', but only 'objective' or, as he says

[1] It is noteworthy that Hegel at twenty-five is enough of a revolutionary democrat to accept the identification of the General Will with the majority vote, without apparently troubling his head over all the difficulties that this identification entails: see Nohl, p. 191 (Knox, p. 118). Of course we should remember that he is speaking only of the Church Assembly regarded as an ideal democracy (which would satisfy Rousseau's conditions perhaps better than any actual political community ever could) and the whole theory is only postulated as an Aunt Sally to be knocked down. Also, we should note that the civil contract is defined as a contract for the maintenance of *individual* rights. Clearly Hegel's study of *Du contrat social* was by no means cavalier or superficial.

here, it is 'a faith that can be pocketed in the brain, like money'.[1]
He ends his essay with a long diatribe against this objective conception of faith and morals as something that can be learned from
compendia. Only legality can be produced in this way, and the long
history of proliferating sects which have sprung from the original
Christian heresy within Judaism is the inevitable result of the
assumption that the spontaneity of moral reason can be confined
within the verbal strait jacket of the understanding.[2]

Hegel's attack on the disciplinary conception of morality, and on
asceticism generally, is based on the premiss that feelings can no
more be produced or changed at will than opinions can. The
result of all attempts to constrain feelings is either *Angst* (on the
part of those who recognize their failure) or hypocritical com-
placency (on the part of those who falsely believe they have succeeded). Religious life must rest on the feelings we actually have
and not on those which we are theoretically supposed to have.[3]

5. *A polemical interlude*

Having arrived at this point Hegel laid his manuscript essay aside
for five months or more. In April 1796 he returned to it and added
a brief conclusion which we shall consider in its due place below.
All the available evidence indicates that for the time being (in
November 1795) Hegel turned away from his historical studies to
write the fragment *Ein positiver Glauben*.[4]

[1] Nohl, p. 204; Knox, p. 134 (the metaphor comes from Lessing's *Nathan*).
[2] Nohl, pp. 205-11; Knox, pp. 135-43. (The concluding pages which follow
this passage were added some five months later.)
[3] Hegel first advanced this argument explicitly in the fragments of 1794—
öffentliche Gewalt and *So kann in einem Staate*—but behind it lies his Greek
ideal of a natural spontaneous harmony of thought and feeling, and his revision
of the Kantian idea of holiness in this direction in the essay of 1793; see Nohl,
pp. 17-18, 42-5, and 206-10 (Knox, pp. 136-42). Compare also the discussions above (Chapter II, pp. 142-4 and Chapter III, pp. 191 ff.). The
Pietists are singled out for their emphasis on the discipline of feelings, and the
Calvinists are praised for getting the emphasis in the right place. This is illuminating in a slightly paradoxical way, for though one can see the resemblance
between Calvinism and Kant's rational rigorism, the only affinities between
Geneva and the Greek cities seem to be with Sparta rather than with Athens.
Hegel had visited Geneva a few months earlier (in May 1795); and I suppose
we must always remember the influence of Rousseau's ideal picture on his mind.
[4] Nohl, pp. 233-9. For the dating see Schüler, p. 144. Nohl thinks this fragment is connected with the idea Hegel once had of writing an essay on 'What it
may mean "to draw near to God"' (*Briefe*, i. 29, 30 Aug. 1795); and there is in
fact a thematic connection between it and *Die transzendente Idee von Gott* (which
represents, in my view, all that Hegel ever did about *that* project).

Both the thought and the handwriting of this fragment are closely linked to that of the section on 'The form morality must acquire in a Church', which was written on and after 2 November 1795. Because of these affinities Miss Schüler has suggested that *Ein positiver Glauben* may have been intended as a new introduction for the 'Positivity' essay. This is at first sight a plausible hypothesis, but in actual fact the fragment is ill suited for insertion at the beginning of that essay because of its rather aggressive and polemical tone. If Hegel began it with that idea in mind, he must soon have realized that the whole essay would have to be recast to fit it. I am more inclined to the view that, having completed the most conciliatory defence of his views that he could contrive, he felt ready to move on to the attack. In other words, this fragment should be viewed as an attempt to continue his plan rather than as a revision of part of it. In the end, however, he set it aside, wrote a new ending to the 'Positivity' essay, and began working on a different, more positive, kind of continuation for it, in which his conception of Christianity is brought into direct relation with his Greek ideal.

Ein positiver Glauben purports to set forth the essential nature of a faith grounded upon pure authority, and examines the arguments of the Tübingen School in defence of such a faith.[1] A 'positive' faith is defined as a system of religious propositions accepted as true upon the command of an authority whom we cannot refuse to believe.[2] The propositions are 'objective' truths (i.e. they are true in the abstract, regardless of whether we believe them or not) and our duty of belief is the duty to make them into 'subjective' maxims (i.e. principles that guide our actions). This duty of belief upon authority is quite different from belief upon authority generally (for example acceptance of historical testimony), because ordinary belief of this kind is grounded upon a prior estimate of trustworthiness, whereas positive faith can only rest initially on recognition of the absolute power of the commanding

[1] There are signs that the essay may have been occasioned by Süskind's essay on Fichte's *Kritik aller Offenbarung* which formed the appendix to his German translation of Storr's *Notes on Kant* (*Bemerkungen* usw., 1794). Cf. Asveld, p. 109.

[2] Hegel sometimes uses the word 'positive' in a quite neutral, descriptive way. But in connection with 'religion' or 'faith' it always retains something of the force that it has in legal theory ('positive law' is that which is established and maintained by a sovereign authority). As such, 'positive faith' and 'positive religion' are always regarded by Hegel as evils.

authority. As we take the first steps toward wisdom we become aware of God's beneficence and of his being the source of truth, but only the fear of the Lord can be there in the beginning. About this 'fear of the Lord' Hegel says something very interesting, which reflects his study both of Greek tragedy and of the book of Job at Tübingen. *Everyone* must recognize the supreme might of 'Nature, Fate, or Providence' over his natural desires; but anyone who allows this supremacy to extend to his spiritual concerns will not be able to escape from a 'positive faith'. Thus the choice, for Hegel, lies between finding a purely 'spiritual' interpretation of the postulates of practical reason, or else allowing 'revealed' or 'positive' truths to have the status of postulates. The problem of showing that there is no *Übermacht* in the world of the spirit is the problem of showing that *Vernunft* is somehow self-sufficient at this level. Thus we come back to the problem of how Kant's postulates are to be interpreted, and in the present essay Hegel carries through the programme of *Die transzendente Idee von Gott*.

That *Vernunft* has an essential tendency to postulate whatever will satisfy its requirements is common ground for both rational and positive faith; and *Vernunft* is accepted on both sides as the criterion of religious truth. This represents, as Hegel notes, a considerable shift on the part of the Tübingen School from the older tradition of theological exegesis according to which it is natural to find that 'the thoughts of God are not comprehensible by human reason'.[1] Since the defenders of positive religion do not deny that Reason is able to provide a complete system of moral principles ('because they cannot deny what happens before their eyes') all belief or unbelief in a positive faith turns upon the admission of a power before which Reason is itself helpless. The content of the positive faith is admitted to be contrary to the laws of 'a moderately experienced understanding'—for Storr and his school laid great stress on the miraculous as a sure index of revelation itself. The imagination can picture what is asserted, but *Verstand* forbids us to believe it. *Verstand* now is overruled by

---

[1] Nohl, p. 235. Herein lies the justice of Asveld's comment (from the point of view of the whole tradition of Christian orthodoxy) that 'without doubt Storr and Süskind think that the essential truths of Christianity, just as they were then presented by their church, answer to a universal practical requirement; but in admitting the primacy of practical reason, in sacrificing to the anthropocentrism of the *Aufklärung*, we hold that they introduced a principle of dissolution into Christianity' Asveld, p. 74).

Vernunft, which recognizes in the duty of belief the means of satisfying the almighty power and obtaining the fulfilment of its own requirements.

The fault in this chain of argument lies in the assumption that Reason actually requires something lying within the domain of 'Nature, Fate, or Providence'. The confusion of sensible needs and satisfactions with rational requirements leads to a misunderstanding of the fundamental postulate of self-sufficiency. The principle that 'virtue deserves happiness' is made the basis of demands for the satisfaction of sensible desires (which are at the mercy of fate), because where the moral will exists in a mind dominated by sensible desires, its command is interpreted as the condition of *sensible* happiness. Where reason itself attains its full and proper mastery over the mind a man may sacrifice his whole sensible existence (his life) for an ideal of honour or patriotism—'and only in our times have men been able to say "That man was worthy of a better fate".'[1]

Reduced thus to a powerless arbiter of sensible satisfactions for which men are dependent on the alien power, reason can only lead us to the duty of faith. But 'faith' here is only 'lack of consciousness that reason is absolute and sufficient to itself'. A citizen of a free republic fighting for his country has an aim in which his own private happiness, conceived in terms of these sensible satisfactions, plays no part. He has *voluntarily* renounced his right in these areas, and so in this case reason cannot 'take back' its rights.

Having thus disposed of Heaven, Hegel turned to consider the fear of Hell. This brought him face to face with the problem of the forgiveness of sins. On the one hand a direct remission of sins appears to be contrary to every rational principle of equity, and on the other it is obvious that no human being is quite without sin. This problem was a very serious one for all the theologians of pure reason, and the Tübingen view that the Christian promise answered to a need of reason was therefore very attractive. It is unfortunate, therefore, but perhaps not altogether surprising, that Hegel broke off at this point. We can see from the way he interprets 'forgiveness of sins' in *The Life of Jesus* that the first step in his answer would have been provided by his interpretation of Kant's postulate of freedom as the power of reason to wipe the slate clean and make a new beginning. Probably this was all that he had to offer at this

[1] Nohl, p. 238.

time; but probably, too, he was dissatisfied with it because it is too negative—the *integrative* aspect of reason is lacking. In the case of the renunciation by reason of its rights in the sensible world, Hegel's interpretation of Kant is reconcilable with his Greek ideal because, for instance, the 'free republican' dies in order that his society may continue to live a completely integrated, rationally controlled life.[1] Nothing corresponds to this redemption of sacrifice in the case of sin.

My own belief is that Hegel's polemical undertaking foundered upon this difficulty. He eventually found a solution for it in the doctrine of reconciliation with fate set forth in the 'Spirit of Christianity'. But that solution was achieved at the cost of a considerable revolution in his own attitude to Kant's ethics and theology. He never for a moment accepted the Tübingen interpretation of Kant, but he did eventually come to hold that Kant's rational religion shared some of the basic weaknesses of Storr's positive religion.[2] He was certainly *not* thinking along these lines in the early months of 1796, however. For in April he returned to the 'Positivity' manuscript and added a conclusion which was explicitly designed to reconcile Kantian terminology with his own (as far as possible) and the Kantian conception of *Vernunft* with his Greek ideal.

Kant has shown us, he says, what the domains of reason and understanding are. The Church had confused the 'subjective' principles of *Vernunft* with the 'objective' principles of *Verstand*. It is true that Kant calls the moral laws of Reason 'objective', but this objectivity is not like the objectivity of the rules of the understanding. This seems to be an implicit acknowledgement that Kant's usage is different from his own, but Hegel does not stop to investigate the difference. The problem as he sees it is in any

---

[1] Hegel is not consciously concerned about this reconciliation with his earlier ideal here—or at least there is no sign that he is. He is only concerned about the question of what kind of happiness the virtuous *individual* is 'entitled' to. For this purpose only an appeal to the Greek concept of Fate is relevant.

Nor does the postulate of immortality (on which, as we saw, Fichte and Schelling laid great emphasis) enter into the question; that postulate cannot have anything to do with a doctrine of future recompense for present sacrifices in the sensible realm, because (for instance) in the Kingdom of Heaven there is neither marrying nor giving in marriage: 'the immortal souls who have entered into the society of pure spirits will lay aside needs of this sort along with the body' (*The Life of Jesus*, Nohl, p. 120).

[2] See Chapter IV, Section 4, pp. 310–22 below.

case to make the 'objective' laws (objective both in Kant's sense and in his own sense) 'subjective', i.e. 'to make them into maxims, to find motives for them'. Hegel's use of the plural 'motives' here strictly implies that his use of 'subjective' is different from Kant's also, since there is only one possible motive for a *moral* maxim in Kant's view—pure 'respect'. Hegel is quite well aware of this difference too, but he chooses to ignore it, because there is no way in which *both* usages can be justified in this case, and he does not want to say outright that Kant is wrong. In his own view, of course, all of the 'higher feelings', all altruistic impulses, are good 'subjective' grounds for a maxim, even though he verbally concedes that 'respect for the moral law' is 'the sole *moral* motive'. His notion of *autonomy* is thus broader than Kant's, as it must be, since he wishes to replace Kant's legalistic rigor with the Hellenic conception of reason as an organizing, harmonizing, and reconciling power. The Greeks, he says, had a naturally correct feeling for the distinction between morality and legality, between reason and understanding in practice, even though Kant was the first to draw the distinction correctly 'for science' (i.e. in theory). The very conception of a positive Church, a body organized on the model of the social contract, with its own 'legal system', or 'moral code', violates this distinction and reduces moral reason to a type of technical understanding, a very complex art, or a special skill which can be (and of course has to be) learned or developed, with a due and proper reliance on expert advice and guidance. Hence: 'The whole authority [*Gewalt*] of the church is unlawful; and no man can renounce the right to legislate for himself, and be responsible to himself alone for the administration of his own law, for by the alienation [*Veräußerung*] of it he would cease to be a man altogether.'[1]

[1] Nohl, p. 212 (Knox, p. 145). In this account of the concluding summary of the 'Positivity' essay I have deliberately sought to elucidate Hegel's clearly enunciated doctrine, without reference to the textual crux on page 211 (Knox, p. 143). I do not think we can possibly accept Nohl's emendations for this passage, since one cannot plausibly suppose that Hegel would have made such a systematic series of substitutions through any ordinary inadvertence or momentary confusion. We must therefore re-examine the original text as reported from the manuscript.

Setting aside, for the moment, our knowledge of Hegel's argument in the rest of the essay and elsewhere, the only difficulty in construing the text arises from the phrase 'von der christlichen Kirche *hingegen*' in the final clause of the sentence. This phrase is odd because the first half of the sentence also refers to the 'christliche Kirche', and it says the same thing as the last half, so an opposition

The final paragraph of the new conclusion provides a clue to
what Hegel had been doing since he laid the 'Positivity' essay
aside—and probably since he had abandoned his projected attack
on the Tübingen theologians. In all probability he turned at this
time to the study of German medieval mysticism and made the
excerpts from Eckhart and Tauler of which Rosenkranz tells us.
For in his closing lines Hegel appeals to the rise of all the Christian
sects in the Middle Ages and in modern times 'as evidence of the
right of *Vernunft*'; and the one excerpt on this topic that remains
to us was taken from Mosheim's *Institutiones historiae ecclesiasticae*,
which was available to him in the library at Tschugg.[1] The doctrine

between them is scarcely conceivable. A slight change of punctuation however
is enough to make the whole passage quite intelligible, though it remains
pleonastic. This is the insertion of a bar or a period in place of the comma after
the first *aufgestellt*. I propose therefore that the sentence be read as follows:
'Die moralischen Gebote der Vernunft werden nämlich in der christlichen
Kirche sowie in jeder, deren Prinzip reine Moral ist, gerade wie Regeln des
Verstandes behandelt, und aufgestellt ⟨—⟩ jene sind subjektiv, diese objektiv;
von der christlichen Kirche hingegen wird das subjektive der Vernunft wie
etwas objektives als Regel aufgestellt.'

To *understand* the text (now that it is self-consistent), in a way consistent with
Hegel's general argument, all we have to remember is the difference between a
religion and a *Church*. Hegel speaks of the Christian *religion*, of the Christian
Church, and of the Greek *religion*; but never of the Greek *Church*, because
there was no such thing, and, if his conception of Greek religion was correct,
there *could not* be such a thing. (That is why, although it is conceivable that
he might write 'the *Christian* religion' when he meant to say 'the Greek religion',
it is almost unthinkable that he should have written, as Nohl supposes him to
have done, 'the Christian *Church*' instead of 'the Greek religion').

Any true religion has morality as its object (e.g. the Greek religion, the
Jewish religion, the Christian religion); so any true religion that is organized
into a *Church* (an assembly with a legal structure and a constituted authority,
whether democratic, aristocratic, or monarchic) commits the fallacy of confus-
ing the moral law with legal rules. Haering seems to have grasped the right
interpretation of the passage—but his reading of it is so complicated both by his
preconceptions about Hegel's view of the relation between religion and morality,
and also by the desire to connect Hegel's use of the terms 'subjective' and 'objective' with Kant's, that the meaning of the sentence is hard to disentangle in his
account (i. 245–6).

[1] Rosenkranz, p. 102; for the presence of the Mosheim volume in the library
at Tschugg, see Hans Strahm, p. 530; the excerpt is in Nohl, p. 367. This
excerpt cannot possibly have been, as some critics have suggested or implied,
the only one that Rosenkranz had before him. For in the first place Eckhart's
authorship is not mentioned in the excerpt at all; in the second place, Rosenkranz
specifically mentioned Tauler as well as Eckhart; and in the third place he says
the excerpts were from *Literaturzeitungen*. It is true he did speak rather loosely,
and generalize a trifle rashly at times, but how could he possibly invent so many
concrete details on the basis of an excerpt for which Hegel indicates the actual
source with great exactness? (See Rosenkranz, p. 102.)

of *The Life of Jesus*, and even the very idea of reinterpreting the Gospel record in accordance with the dictates of our own reason is clearly expressed in this one short excerpt about the 'Brethren of the Free Spirit', and it seems certain that Hegel's conviction that the needs of reason itself lay behind the genesis of sects derives from this source.[1]

6. *The road to Eleusis*

Hegel never for a moment forgot or abandoned his view that the ideal of human existence was the life achieved in the Greek cities, and especially in Periclean Athens. The influence of Kant's moral philosophy, which was dominant in his mind throughout 1795, sprang, as we have seen, from his conviction that the self-conscious awareness of the powers and rights of reason which was the most notable achievement of the Enlightenment, was the principal instrument and main resource for the regeneration and reintegration of life in accordance with that ideal. He knew that it was through the work of his older contemporaries, Rousseau, Lessing, Mendelssohn, Kant, Fichte, and Schiller that he had been placed in a position to appreciate the Greek achievement as he did; and he believed that through the right 'application' of their theories the wholeness of life could be restored. This was the motive behind his Kantian reinterpretation of the Gospel. When he first asked himself the question 'How far is Christianity qualified to serve as a folk-religion?' he was mainly impressed by the extent to which its rational doctrines had been corrupted by the fundamental principle of 'faith'—i.e. passive acceptance of a positive authority. The attempt made by the defenders of positive faith at Tübingen to

---

[1] Mosheim reports that the rescript against the Brethren charged them with holding that: 'Multa sunt poetica in Evangelio, quae non sunt vera, et homines credere magis debent conceptibus ex anima sua Deo juncta profectis, quam Evangelio . . .' This remarkable coincidence with Hegel's doctrine raises the question whether perhaps it was the reading of Mosheim that first inspired Hegel to write his Kantian *Life of Jesus*. We cannot, of course, say when he *began* to read Mosheim, but he used him as an authority on Church History in writing the 'Positivity' essay (Nohl, p. 193; Knox, p. 120) and he quotes him again at the end of Apr. 1796 (Nohl, p. 210; Knox, p. 142). But the crucial excerpt *Der gute Minsch* was almost certainly made in the early months of 1796, since the last excerpt on the same sheet was taken from the *Allgemeine Literaturzeitung* for Feb. 1796. So it seems best to assume that Rosenkranz's date for the Eckhart and Tauler excerpts ('at the end of the Swiss period') is correct. (K. I. Diez, the 'Kantian *enragé*', is a somewhat more probable source for the inspiration of *The Life of Jesus*.)

absorb even the latest achievements of reason into their system
of revealed truths, spurred him into a contrary attempt to exhibit
the subordination of religion to reason. Although his fundamental
concern continued always to be with the quality of life as lived
in this world, his attention was thus temporarily, and partially,
deflected on to the problem of the relation between life in this
world and life in the world beyond.[1] He never meant, certainly, to
commit himself to any position that was inconsistent with his
Hellenic ideal,[2] but some problems and tensions remained hidden
and hence unresolved until his thoughts turned again, specifically,
to the Greeks, as they did early in 1796.[3]

After writing his brief conclusion to the 'Positivity' essay, in
which he adverts to the Greeks explicitly for the first time in some
fifteen months, Hegel began to work on an essay of which the
central topic is the question 'How did Christianity conquer
paganism?'[4] In this new essay he returns first to ideas put forward

[1] Of course what we may call his 'political' concern (using the term in its
widest Greek sense) was never far from the limelight. This can be seen by
considering the relation between the first part of 'the Positivity of the Christian
Religion' (dealing with the Gospels and the Apostolic Church) and the second part
(dealing with the relations of Church and State).   [2] Cf. p. 206 n. 1 above.

[3] If the Thucydides translation mentioned by Rosenkranz (p. 60) does indeed
belong to the Berne period as he thought, then it is most reasonable to suppose
that it was made in spring or summer 1796; and some of the 'Fragmente
historischer Studien' can plausibly be assigned to the same period on account
of their affinities either with *Jedes Volk hat ihm eigene Gegenstände* or with the
study of Thucydides—see especially Fragments 3, 4, 5, 6, 7, 8, 9, 11, 17, and
compare the following note and p. 271 n. 2.

It must be emphasized that any attempt to date these fragments is beset with
ambiguities, because of many affinities with the dated manuscripts of the
Frankfurt and even of the Jena period; and it is peculiarly infuriating not to
know how many distinct manuscripts Rosenkranz took the fragments from.
But if we suppose that the Thucydides fragments in particular came from a
sheet headed by some definite date in 1796, we can thereby explain why Rosenkranz thought the undated translation of Thucydides *in all probability* belongs
to the period when Hegel lived in Berne' (Rosenkranz, p. 12).

[4] The reference to the Greeks in the conclusion of the 'Positivity' essay
(written 29 Apr. 1796) will be found at Nohl, p. 211. For reasons which will
appear, I am inclined to think that when Hegel wrote it, he already had (at
least) fairly definite plans for *Jedes Volk hat ihm eigene Gegenstände*, which is the
subsequent essay referred to here (Nohl, pp. 214–31).

Comparison of the last sentence of the Apr. 1796 addendum to the 'Positivity'
essay with the undated 'historical fragment' 9, *Die ungezügelte Einbildungskraft*
(*Dok.*, p. 267), further suggests that Hegel may have tried to write an essay
contrasting the Golden Age of Greece with the Age of Chivalry in this period.
(Fragment 8, *Was ein gebildeter Geschmack*, would also fit neatly into the context
of such an essay. But see the caution in n. 3 above.)

in the so-called 'Tübingen fragment' of 1793 (or in the plans and outlines associated with it) and then to theses expressed in the early Berne fragments of 1794 (especially *Jetzt braucht die Menge*). There is an obvious continuity with the 'Positivity' essay, in that the polemic against 'positive Christianity' is maintained, but the 'religion of *Jesus*' which was the central focus of his attention in 1795 drops out of sight altogether, and he returns to the attack on 'faith in *Christ*' which he mounted in 1794. It comes as a surprise therefore, and at first sight it seems almost a paradox, that the pagination of the new manuscript links it to the 'Positivity' essay in a way which indicates that Hegel regarded it as being somehow a continuation of the same project.

If we do not fall into the error of regarding the 'Kantian' essays of 1795 as a sort of hiatus in Hegel's development, but rather ask as I have done just how they fit into the programme of work that he hammered out in 1794, the appearance of paradox is soon dissipated, and the surprise is seen to be unjustified. Before he ever went to Berne Hegel had established the canons by which a 'folk-religion' was to be judged; he went to Berne with the problem of how the requisite organic unity of life was to be re-established in his own society; and after nearly a year spent in diagnosing the problem he finally focused it in the form 'How far is the Christian religion qualified [to serve as a folk-religion]?'.[1] All of his subsequent labours in 1795 and early 1796 were directed towards answering this question.[2]

The connection between the first canon ('Its doctrines must be founded upon universal reason') and the fragmentary essays, *Es sollte eine schwere Aufgabe* and *Wenn man von der Christlichen Religion*, is explicit. The polemical tone of these preliminary efforts obscures the connection between the first canon and *The*

[1] See *Religion ist eine* (Nohl, pp. 20–1) for the first formulation of the canons; and *Unter objektiver Religion* (Nohl, p. 49) for the statement of the problem (with repetition of the canons). I have already argued that the relation between *Unter objektiver Religion* and *man mag die widersprechendsten Betrachtungen* (the 'Positivity' essay) is close enough to suggest that the former may be the 'Skizze' that Hegel referred to in a cancelled heading of the latter (Nohl, p. 153 n.). Even if this suggestion is set aside, I do not think the focal importance of the question about the potentialities of Christianity as a folk-religion can be doubted.

[2] That is to say all of the labours that can be dated. We do not know when he made his studies of the public financial system of Berne, or when he began to work on his translation of Cart's *Vertrauliche Briefe*. But if, as it seems plausible to suppose, these two enterprises were linked, it is most probable that they lobeng to his last months in Berne.

Life of Jesus. But if we consider *The Life of Jesus* in the light of the summary verdict on Christianity in *Unter objektiver Religion*: 'its practical doctrines are pure . . .', the relevance of *The Life of Jesus* to the basic problem becomes clear. Finally, in the 'Positivity' essay, the negative and the reconstructive approaches are combined, and an outline of Christianity re-formed into a folk-religion is sketched.

With the writing of the 'Positivity' essay the application of the first canon has now been completed and it is time for Hegel to move on to the second: 'Fancy, heart and sensibility must not go away empty.' This is the phase of his task that he seeks to develop in *Jedes Volk hat ihm eigene Gegenstände*, and his first approach to the problem is again negative. In respect of the second canon, Hegel's initial assumption was that not very much could possibly be said on the constructive side, as a glance at the relevant sections of the plan will confirm. This was where the Greek ideal was particularly powerful in his mind. Greek religion did not in fact satisfy the canon of rationality very explicitly, and he knew that it did not. Only in Socrates, and particularly in the argument of the *Phaedo*, did it reach the level of self-conscious *Vernunft*. But the execution of Socrates posed a problem, and instead of alluding to Socrates in *Religion ist eine* Hegel simply adopted the Kantian postulates of practical reason as the fundamental doctrines of all true folk-religion, without offering any explanation. Throughout his application of the first canon to Christianity, he continued to use Kant's moral philosophy as his yardstick, though it is true that in the process he reinterprets the postulates of practical reason in accordance with a criterion of *rational self-sufficiency* which is essentially Greek in its inspiration. Thus the origins of his 'Kantian phase' are quite explicitly present in the initial formulation of his Greek ideal, though an explanation of its presence is not to be found there. The missing explanation is offered only now, as we turn to the canon which is entirely Greek in origin and inspiration, and for which Greece remained the exemplar in Hegel's eyes as long as he lived. The Greeks had a 'sure feel' for what was rational in practice, but they had not reasoned it out. Only at the point where the feeling began to go wrong did anyone grasp the truth consciously.[1]

[1] Nowhere in the fragments of Tübingen or Berne does Hegel actually say that anything had gone wrong in the Athens of Socrates; but he does remark very

The new essay begins with several points with which we have long been familiar. Every nation has its own stock of imagery, expressed in stories about Gods and demons (religious tradition) or about founding fathers and heroic leaders (political tradition).[1] But Christianity has emptied the Valhalla of the German *Volk*, and, save perhaps for Luther, whose achievement is celebrated by a dreary annual reading of the Augsburg Confession and a still more boring sermon, the Germans have now no heroes.[2] Their traditions survive only as superstitions among the people, and the attempts to raise them to the level of art and literature have no popular appeal or resonance; whereas even an Athenian who had to sell himself into slavery knew the stories, watched the great dramas, and worshipped before the great statues.[3] Shakespeare has made the history of England live for its people, but Klopstock cannot do this for the Germans, because their great drama is a story not of political freedom but of subjection to an alien religion.[4]

early that the Greeks would not give to philosophers the critical licence which they accorded to poets (*Aber die Hauptmasse*, Nohl, p. 357); and his comment on Cato's recourse to the *Phaedo* at the last (Nohl, p. 222; Knox, p. 155; discussed below) certainly bears out the view here maintained.

[1] Nohl, p. 214; Knox, p. 145. The more carefully we compare this passage with the cancelled myth (in *Religion ist eine*) about the *Geist* who is the child of Chronos and Politeia and the nursling of Religion, the better we can understand both that myth and the inadequacies that caused Hegel to cancel it (cf. Nohl, pp. 27–8, text and footnote). Both the religious and the political tradition are a product of time, but the constitution is something which abides unchanged through time, and religious myths are properly distinct from historical tradition because they have a *permanent* spatial location or association, rather than a *definite* temporal one (cf. Nohl, p. 217; Knox, p. 149).

[2] Nohl, p. 215, Knox, pp. 146–7; cf. *Man lehrt unsre Kinder* (1793) (Nohl, p. 359), *Die Staatsverfassungen* (Nohl, pp. 38–9), *So kann in einem Staate* (Nohl, pp. 46–7).

[3] It is interesting that in recurring here to the very first form in which the contrast between the integrity of ancient society and the divided, alienated condition of modern society struck him (see *Über einige charakteristische Unterschiede der alten Dichter* (1788), *Dok.*, pp. 48–9), Hegel also makes his first explicit allusion to ancient slavery. Even the slaves in a free society, he seems to be hinting, had more real spiritual freedom than the self-seeking individuals who remained when the free republics perished.

[4] This contrast is not absolutely explicit in Hegel's text, but I think there cannot be much doubt that it was present in his mind—cf. the comment about the poetic ideals which are seen on a closer look at be 'cut out of the Catechism'. It is not really the *foreign* character of Christianity that troubles him either, so much as its authoritarian character and its emphasis on human helplessness. His attitude both to the native tradition and to the German hero Luther was ambiguous to the point of despair, because on the one hand Luther personified the spirit of joylessness and authority which made religion essentially private; and

Finally Hegel comes to a point which, as far as I can recollect, he has not made explicitly before, although it explains certain comments and notes that he made earlier: that the imagery of a free people must be linked with *places* rather than with *dates*. He praises the Catholic Church in this respect, for the reverence accorded everywhere to local patron saints.[1] But by emphasizing the *historical* character of what should properly be only a myth round which religious observances can be built, Christianity has generated a theoretical problem about the historical status of miracles, and a practical problem of intolerance toward all who do not accept the overriding moral authority of the historical record. Even when we put aside the 'positive faith' which it is our 'duty' to believe, even when we try to view our Scriptures as the Greeks viewed their myths, we are faced with these problems arising from their supposedly historical character. It seems that either we must say: 'It all happened, just as it is described' (which violates the first canon because Storr is wrong in holding that *Vernunft* requires us to override our own *Verstand*); or else we must say: 'Of course it did not happen'—for example Moses did not see God in the burning bush, because, on the one hand, God is *never* a visible object in that way, and on the other hand (as Lessing makes Recha say), 'Wherever Moses stood it was before his God'. This solution violates the second canon by sending imagination away empty. In Hegel's view Moses really was directly and immediately aware of being in the presence of God at some times

yet on the other hand, in making the break with the past which made the earlier tradition 'as strange as the imagery of Ossian or of India', he was advancing the cause of reason, for the ideals of the Age of Chivalry were quite irrational (cf. Fragments 8 and 9 in *Dok.*, pp. 266–8).

Again, Luther and the Teutonic knights represented different ways in which Christianity had corrupted the native tradition. But Hegel's own hope lay in a foreign tradition which was not corrupt. At the very least he wanted the 'Teutons' to reinterpret the traditions of their fatherland in the spirit of Achaea *rather* than that of Judaea.

(It should be noted that there *may* be a lacuna in the text between the paragraph on the attempt to revive the old German traditions and the paragraph on the adoption of the Greek traditions by the educated. The fact that the same points about the alienation of the educated from the vulgar, and of both from the old German imagery, are made in both paragraphs seems to me, however, to make it more probable that there is no break. (Cf. Nohl, p. 217 (Knox, p. 148), and Nohl's footnote on p. 214.)

[1] Nohl, pp. 217–18 (Knox, pp. 149–50); for an earlier attempt to account for the imaginative superiority of Catholicism see *Die Formen der andern Bilder* (Nohl, p. 359).

and in some places, and not at other times or in other places. At such moments of awareness God was present in a way in which he is not usually present. Being a sensible feeling, the awareness must have an objective aspect (for example, the burning bush, the light on the road to Damascus, or any other perceptual experience sufficiently dramatic to express its intensity) which is of no *positive* significance, but which somehow satisfies the imagination, and helps Moses (or Paul) to hold on to the experience, and communicate something of its enormous significance to others.[1]

Hegel now poses the contrast between myth and history as a basis for religion in an even more extreme form, as the next topic for discussion. His new heading reads: 'Difference between Greek Imaginative and Christian Positive Religion.' But what he actually discusses is how the former could ever have given way to the latter, and his immediate problem is: 'What must life be like in order for men to feel the need of a divine authority over their existence as a whole, so that they are ready and eager to accept the fancies of the imagination as historical facts?' His answer, in a nutshell, is that when the political freedom of a society is destroyed, its members lose all confidence in, and even awareness of, their own moral autonomy, their control over destiny at the spiritual level. For what after all can they *do* that is not subject to immediate nullification by external force? The old myths expressed vividly the power of natural forces, including of course the forces of man's

---

[1] Nohl, pp. 217–19 (Knox, pp. 149–51). Hegel specifically refers us to Herder's views on this topic. In interpreting what he says I have drawn freely on the critique of the Tübingen doctrine of the miraculous which he first made (as far as we know) in *Ein positiver Glauben*. He repeats the doctrine at the end of the present essay (Nohl, pp. 230–1; Knox, pp. 165–7), and again in an undated fragment first printed by Rosenkranz, which may have been the earliest of the three or may have been written some time later. Nohl adds the Rosenkranz fragment, *Der Streit über die Möglichkeit*, as a footnote (pp. 231–2), but it can hardly have been part of the present essay because it repeats the argument too closely. All we can be sure of, I think, is that it was not written before *Unkunde der Geschichte* (early 1795), because there Hegel is obviously still feeling his way toward a theory of the miraculous. I am inclined to think that it was the latest of the three discussions, precisely because Hegel speaks with such incisive authority in it. In any case, we should note that once again he refers us to Herder's views on the subject. Herder's views on the Old Testament would have come to his notice by 1792 at the latest, through Schelling's concern with them: cf. the latter's master's thesis, and Hegel's familiarity with the announced topics of 'Über Mythen' (*Briefe*, i. 11). Herder may well be the ultimate source of Hegel's second canon; and the failure of Lessing's *Nathan* with respect to the second canon explains why it is designated as a product of *Verstand* in *Religion ist eine* (Nohl, p. 12.)

own nature, but men knew these divine powers could be resisted, for they came into visible conflict with one another. They had to be respected, but no one supposed that they could compel obedience. Even reason itself claimed no such right, says Hegel, anticipating his eventual quarrel with Kant: 'Good men acknowledged, in their own case, the duty of being good, yet at the same time they respected the freedom of others not to be, and hence they did not set up either a divine moral code or one which they had made or abstracted themselves to be exacted from others.'[1]

The sense of moral autonomy is essentially linked with political and economic democracy. For as soon as economic classes are established the rich must bear heavier political burdens and responsibilities; and where this is the case an unresolvable moral conflict is created. The poorer voters cannot assert their right to make an independent decision, by turning out their leaders, without accusations of treachery and ingratitude being made. There is thus a conflict between the two essential constituents of republican 'virtue': the sense of loyalty or solidarity and the spirit of free independence. In this situation there is faction, a state where force is the only arbiter and the will of the stronger must prevail. Thus the free citizen becomes either a minister of the sovereign or a private person with no right to meddle in political matters at all. In the Hellenistic age 'the picture of the State as a product of his own activity disappeared from the soul of the citizen'.[2] Man

---

[1] Nohl, p. 222 (Knox, p. 155); cf. *Verachtung der Menschen* (Fragment 10) in *Dok.*, p. 268. We should compare here the earliest formulation of Hegel's Greek ideal (1788; *Dok.*, pp. 49–50). It is fairly certain that this is one feature of his ideal for which the source is Hellenistic, not Periclean: see Epictetus, *Enchiridion* 42.

It is clear here that Hegel has not abandoned his earliest conception of *Vernunft* as the power by which we make original or genuine abstractions from experience. These abstractions *cannot* be universalizable in the sense in which Kant is generally assumed to have claimed that they must be. For to apply them to anyone else's experience or situation is to turn them into *bad* abstractions, and to accord the status of *Vernunft* to *Verstand*. My reflection upon experience does not even have *authority* over my own actions unless I stop reflecting at some point. But as soon as I do that and begin *imposing* some previously reached conclusion upon myself, *Verstand* has usurped the place of *Vernunft*. It is from this usurpation by *Verstand* that all *authority* is born. *Verstand* is properly only a technical ability to calculate with one's verbal counters; it must always submit to the test of actual experience, rather than dictating to us how we ought to feel and to act.

[2] Nohl, p. 223 (Knox, p. 156). The text of the preceding paragraph cannot be construed, and I do not think Knox's suggestions for its revision are at all

became a cog in a machine, and all that he could sensibly do was to look after himself. His own mortality became an awful thing to him because there was now nothing beyond himself to live and die for. Military service became a mercenary matter—and in order to collect one's pay one has to stay alive.[1] Whereas 'for the republican the Republic survived him, and there hovered before him the thought that it [the Republic which was] his soul was something immortal'. 'Cato turned to Plato's *Phaedo* only when his world, his republic, hitherto the highest order of things in his eyes, had been destroyed; only then did he take flight to a higher order still.'[2]

The way Hegel speaks about immortality here, raises the question whether he has now decisively abandoned his own belief in the validity of this 'flight to a higher order'. Certainly he believed in it two years earlier when he wrote so enthusiastically about the *Phaedo* himself; and certainly he held later that Socrates had been a tremendously destructive force in Athenian society, but that his influence had been both necessary and salutary. But at this moment he does not seem to be thinking of Socrates as a critical social force at all, and the substitution of the immortality of the rational soul for the immortality of the Republic is obviously not one that affords him much pleasure. I have suggested above that he knew that Greek culture satisfied his second canon better than the first, and deliberately adopted Kant's philosophy as his 'rational' standard. But we have already seen how he transformed the rational postulate of God in the process; and one may wonder if he has already recognized that the postulate of immortality was similarly in need of transformation. On the whole, I think that this is not the most plausible hypothesis. I think he felt Cato was right to turn to the *Phaedo*, and that the destruction of the Roman Republic—as a direct result of its own destruction of freedom elsewhere[3]—was necessary in order to make clear to all

plausible. But there is no real problem about Hegel's meaning; cf. also *In Italien, wo die politische Freiheit* (Fragment 12) in *Dok.*, pp. 269–70. On the evils of political and economic classes, cf. *Die Staatsverfassungen* (Nohl, p. 38).

[1] Cf. Nohl, pp. 229–30 (Knox, pp. 164–5). Hegel connects this point with the Christian doctrine of pacifism (which is obviously unacceptable as a constituent in a folk-religion).

[2] Nohl, pp. 222–3 (Knox, pp. 155–7).

[3] Nohl, p. 221 (Knox, p. 154); it is the destruction of the Greek cities, not the death of the Republic, that Hegel really regrets. The way he assimilates the Romans to the Greeks in the present passage contradicts his own earlier contrast

men the difference between the realm of nature which is subject to
fate and the realm of the spirit which is not.

Cato was right, then, to turn to Socrates; but those who turned
rather to the promise of the God–Man, Christ, were wrong. The
Jews, it seems, were in Hegel's opinion wiser. It was only in their
weakness that they cherished the Messianic hope; when they were
offered a Messiah who cared nothing for national independence,
they chose to die fighting for it themselves.[1] To have the courage
of despair was better than to wait passively upon God to satisfy
the demands which *Vernunft* by its nature could never surrender.
But the degradation of human nature in Christianity went further,
for even this ability to wait passively was treated as the 'gift of
faith'. The 'free world of the spirit'[2] was surrendered not to God
alone but to the Devil also. As Hegel remarks with caustic irony:
'While the Manichaeans appeared to concede to the evil principle
an undivided dominion in the realm of nature, the orthodox
church vindicated God's majesty against this dishonour by granting
His mastery of most of nature; but at the same time it compensated the evil principle for this loss by granting it a certain power
in the realm of freedom.'[3]

This absolute corruption of man's moral nature through the
doctrine of original sin was still not the limit of degradation, however. With the acceptance of Christianity as the official religion of
the Empire, even God was corrupted. The moral perfection of the

between the individuality of the latter and the insistence of the former on
adherence to the common norm (*Außer dem mundlichen Unterricht* (1794),
Nohl, pp. 31–2). 'In Rome there were only Romans, not men' and it certainly
would scarcely occur to Romans as Romans to demand a personal immortality
distinct from that of the *Urbs*. Equally certainly one who found in Socrates the
example of a *Mensch* was bound 'für sein Individuum Fortdauer oder ewiges
Leben zu verlangen'. Hence even if Hegel's enthusiasm for ancient 'virtue' and
his distaste for the Christian 'virtues' did here carry him away for a moment
and make him feel that the 'higher order' was *only* an illusion born of weakness,
I do not think he would have maintained this seriously, once he began to think
about Socrates and Cato, rather than about Cato and St. Ambrose.

[1] Nohl, pp. 224–25 (Knox, pp. 158–9). It is easy to see that the young Hegel
would have applauded the refounding of Israel, and the resolution with which
the young nation has defended its right to life. His criticism of Judaism is anti-
racist and anti-clerical, not anti-semitic.

[2] Nohl, p. 226. It is a pity I think that Knox, whose Hegel translations are so
much better than anything previously done in English, should here have fallen
into the bad old habit of translating *Geist* as 'mind' (Knox, p. 160).

[3] Ibid. There is probably an echo here of Hegel's remark to Schelling that the
triumph of almost any of the ancient heresies might have proved better 'for
mankind' than the triumph of orthodoxy (Letter 14, *Briefe*, i. 32).

Saviour was forgotten. The Church became a hierarchy which mirrored the mechanical system of social classes, and God became an object of theoretical contemplation, rather than an ideal of the will. The practical import of Hegel's doctrine is clear enough here, I think, but the passage in which he describes this transition is replete with metaphysical implications which have engendered a lot of discussion:

The mirror showed no more than the picture of its own time, the picture of nature put to a purpose that was lent to it at discretion by the pride and passion of men—'nature' because we see every interest of knowledge and faith shifted on to the metaphysical or transcendental side of the idea of God. We see ⟨men, moreover,⟩ occupied less with dynamical concepts of the understanding [*dynamischen Verstandsbegriffen*] which theoretical reason is capable of stretching to the infinite, than with numerical concepts [*Zahlenbegriffe*], with the concepts of reflection [*Reflexionsbegriffe*] such as difference [*Verschiedenheit*] and so on, yes even with the application to its infinite Object of mere ideas of perception [*Wahrnehmungsvorstellungen*] such as origin, creation and begetting, and with deriving the characteristics of that Object from events in its nature.[1]

Remembering Hegel's fundamentally moral concern it seems to me the right approach to this passage is the simplest and most obvious one. Hegel is not interested in developing any theories of his own, he is simply trying to describe a transformation that occurred in early Christian speculation about God, and at the same time to contrast it with a further transformation that had occurred in the recent past. Because he speaks in a way which clearly implies that 'dynamic' categories are somehow more adequate than the ones which the early councils employed in hammering out the creeds, some scholars have been led to the mistaken view that he was moving toward a speculative theology of his own conceived in 'dynamic' terms. This is certainly not the case—or at least the present passage cannot possibly provide any evidence for such a view—since the whole conception of God as an 'object' of con-templative knowledge is, in Hegel's view, a horrible error.

The 'dynamic concepts of the understanding' to which Hegel refers in this passage are the concepts of post-Cartesian rational dogmatism. And if the consequence of the original perversion of *human* nature from its proper end (of self-fulfilment) to the arbi-trary service of pride and the lust for power, was a world in which

[1] Nohl, pp. 226-7 (Knox, p. 161).

men slew one another for the sake of the iota which made the Son of 'like' substance with the Father rather than of the 'same' substance, the consequence of the further perversion of *all* nature from its proper end (in the 'natural' theology of the rationalist metaphysicians) was a complacent quietism in which men no longer felt they had to act in the interest of reason at all, because everything in the world had been designed by Providence for their peculiar convenience and 'everything was for the best in the best of all possible worlds'. The 'finely painted Providence-and-comfort-theory of our day'—the eudaemonism of Wolff, and more immediately of the Tübingen school—represented in Hegel's eyes not a higher theology (even though it was certainly a more 'enlightened' one) but the *absolute* limit in the corruption of reason (and hence of God and man alike).[1]

The regeneration of reason began with Kant, who exposed the hopelessness of any attempt by 'theoretical reason' to extend the 'concepts of the understanding' so as to embrace the infinite, before going on to restore speculative reason to its proper throne of dominion in the practical sphere. The distinction between the 'mathematical' and 'dynamical' categories of the understanding is one that Kant appeals to several times, and it is one that has a special relevance to Hegel's second canon. For the 'mathematical' categories (unity, plurality, totality, reality, negation, limitation) are, as Kant says in several places, 'constitutive' with respect to intuition. Thus the theology of the mathematical categories still deals with a God who can satisfy the needs of the imagination. But the 'dynamical' categories are only 'regulative' principles of intuitition: hence the God of 'natural' or 'rational' theology eludes the imagination altogether. Thus the point of ultimate corruption is the point at which religion becomes purely a matter of *Verstand*, a tissue of verbal subtleties.[2]

---

[1] The two stages of theological speculation and their counterpart societies are distinguished in the text immediately after the passage quoted. The relevance of Hegel's description of the early persecutions and wars over heretical doctrines is obvious. But Hegel's aside: 'It was still not yet time for the finely painted Providence-and-comfort-theory of our day which constitutes the keystone of our eudaemonism' (Nohl, p. 227; cf. Knox, p. 162) parallels his earlier glancing reference to the pretensions of theoretical reason, stretching its 'dynamic' concepts to embrace the infinite.

[2] The index to Kemp Smith's translation will enable the English reader to track down all of Kant's remarks about the mathematical/dynamical distinction in the *Critique of Pure Reason*. All of them are worth examining in connection

We should notice that when Hegel was applying the first canon, the point of absolute breakdown came much sooner. The first canon requires that God should never be made an object of purely theoretical study and cognition at all. For *Vernunft* there is 'objective religion' (theology, or the abstract theory of moral values), but not, as here, an 'objective God' (part of the system of nature or of the world of facts). The absolute Lord of nature, secret and invisible, but all-seeing and ineluctable, is the God of positive religion in its pure form. Thus Hegel's original title for this part of his discussion—'Difference between Greek Imaginative and Christian Positive Religion'—is seen at the end to be justified. The question of 'how Christianity conquered paganism' is revealed as having only an instrumental function; and Hegel's essay ends by contrasting the Christian concepts of 'piety' and 'sin' (definable only in terms of obedience to the will of the Lord) with the nearest available Greek and Latin equivalents:

> *Pietas* and *impietas* express holy human feelings, and the dispositions or acts which correspond or conflict with those feelings; they [the Greeks and Romans] also called them divine commands likewise, but not in a positive sense, and if the question 'How would you prove the divine origin of a command or prohibition?' could have occurred to anyone, he could not have appealed to any historical fact, but only to the feeling of his own heart and the agreement of all good men.[1]

There are not many hints in this essay, certainly, of how Hegel proposed to redeem the Christian tradition for the free imagination.[2] He saw clearly that the 'authority' of Scripture rested on its claim to be a true historical record of God's dealings with men. To admit this claim was to open the doors to 'positive' religion; but to deny it would be to deprive the Scriptures of religious significance altogether, and so cheat the imagination out of its rights. Hegel had in fact found a way between the horns of this awkward

with the present passage, but the one that was probably uppermost in Hegel's mind is A 528-32 (B 556-60). For the constitutive/regulative distinction as it applies to the two groups of categories see A 664 (B 692).

[1] Nohl, p. 229 (Knox, p. 164). The short notes on military service and miracles which follow are fairly obviously illustrations or developments of points mentioned earlier in the essay which Hegel intended to work into the body of the essay when he came to revise it (Nohl, pp. 229-31; Knox, pp. 164-7; cf. above, p. 237 n. 1 and p. 239 n. 1).

[2] All that I can find are the admiring comments about Herder's work on the imagery of the Old Testament and the remarks about the Catholic conception of patron saints (cf. above, p. 236 n. 1 and p. 237 n. 1).

dilemma in the works of Herder. It is possible, however, that he could not see how to go on at this point, but felt rather disheartened and turned for a while to other things.[1] His work on the public finances of Berne and perhaps the translation of the *Confidential Letters* of J. J. Cart can very plausibly be assigned to this summer, the last that he spent in Berne. No doubt he went on struggling with the problems of the Christian imagination—but every comparison turned to the advantage of the Greeks.[2]

Viewed against this background, the poem *Eleusis* forms a very appropriate ending to Hegel's Swiss period. He wrote it in August 1796, when he knew that Hölderlin was actively seeking a post for him in Frankfurt and that the prospects of his success were good.[3] The poem is addressed to Hölderlin, but I do not think this should be taken to mean that it was conceived as a letter.[4] The

[1] Just possibly discouragement with his own project contributed to the *Unentschlossenheit* and *Niedergeschlagenheit* which Schelling strove to spur him out of in the letter of 20 June 1796. When Hegel wrote to Schelling he must have been feeling very hopeless about his own job prospects (see n. 3 below). But Schelling already knew when he replied that Hegel would probably be getting the post in Frankfurt. So it seems likely that depression on that score was not all that was involved (*Briefe*, i. 36-7).

[2] Cf. Fragments 5, 6, 8, and 9 in *Dok.*, p. 263–7. See also the suggestions made on p. 232 nn. 3 and 4 above and p. 271 n. 2 below.

[3] Already in Sept. 1795, Hölderlin was seeking a post for Hegel as well as for himself (Letter 103, lines 132–7, *GSA*, vi. 180). He told Hegel in November there was 'still no news to give either in your affair or in my own'. But actually there was bad news and he gave it—the child in the family his friend Ebel had thought of for Hegel was four years old. Then 'early in the summer' (i.e. early June 1796; cf. n. 1 above) he wrote with news of the post with the Gogel family. Hegel no doubt answered quickly, and waited anxiously for further news. But the French invasion disrupted communications and sent Hölderlin to Cassel with the Gontards. Only when things were settled down again and they were all back in Frankfurt was Hölderlin able to write definitely offering the post with the Gogels. Then (Oct. 1796) he said explicitly: 'If we ever come to the point where we must cut wood or do valet's work [*mit Steifelwachs und Pomade zu handeln*], *then* let us ask whether perhaps it would not be better to become a *Repetent* in Tübingen' (*Briefe*, i. 41–2; cf. ibid., 33–4).

[4] Jacques D'Hondt has recently pointed out (*Hegel secret*, pp. 227–81) that the Gogel family were well-known Masons and that the whole poem is full of the sort of imagery that freemasons habitually employed. He also argues very plausibly that Hegel's conception of the reverent silence of those initiated in the Mysteries derives from Lessing's 'Dialogues for Freemasons' *Ernst und Falk*. He underestimates Hegel's own historical concern with Greek religion; but his arguments and interpretations deserve careful study in themselves, and they provide a plausible reason for Hegel's sending of the poem to Hölderlin as part of his indirect correspondence with the Gogels. What was sent, if anything, was a revised fair copy, which Hölderlin or the Gogels did not preserve. What we have is an early rough draft.

dedication was intended by Hegel as a recognition of the fact that Hölderlin shared his ideals and attitudes, both with respect to Greece and with respect to contemporary Germany. For the inspiration of the poem we must look to Hegel's own current pre-occupations, and particularly to *Jedes Volk hat ihm eigene Gegenstände*, rather than to anything that Hölderlin himself had written.[1]

This does not mean that we should expect to find Hegel's own philosophical views expressed directly in the poem. In fact, as we shall see, he deliberately tried to keep philosophy out of it. What he tried to put into the poem was the truth as he believed the Greeks themselves had grasped it, the truth as intuitively felt and imaginatively expressed. This, rather than any conscious borrowing from Hölderlin, explains the 'mystical' tone of *Eleusis*.

The poem falls into two parts: first there is a proem, in which Hegel, alone at Tschugg by the shore of Lake Bienne,[2] feels himself set free by the darkness and silence of the night, freed from the limitations of time and space, so that he can speak directly to Hölderlin, and recall immediately the days when they were together at Tübingen. This section culminates when the future too is conquered, and Hegel anticipates their reunion in imagination. As this moment fades, and the real world breaks in once more, the main poem begins. Originally Hegel tried at this point to explain how the imagination achieves the union of finite and infinite spirit which reflective thought breaks down. But later, he wisely cancelled these lines, not because he was dissatisfied with his doctrine but because he had found the proper way to express it imaginatively in the body of the poem.

As a result of this cancellation the transition to the main poem is

---

[1] The poem can be found in Haering immediately after the title page of volume i. This was the first properly critical edition made from the manuscript, and Haering supplied also a photo-facsimile of the first half of the manuscript (in which, among other things, the cancellation of lines 30–8 is plainly visible). Haering's text was used (but not exactly followed) by Hoffmeister, first in *Dok.*, pp. 380–3, and finally in *Briefe*, i. 38–40. The text has now been re-edited by Beck in *GSA*, vii. 1, 233–41. Beck's is the most exact edition, but I normally refer to Hoffmeister's edition in the *Briefe* because it is most generally available. There are French translations by Asveld (pp. 112–17) and D'Hondt (see p. 244 n. 4 above). Asveld's translation is in some places rather free—for instance he uses 'esprit' to translate *Sinn* as well as *Geist*. An English translation can be found in Mueller, pp. 60–2.

[2] D'Hondt has rightly emphasized the intimate associations of Lake Bienne with Rousseau (see *Hegel secret*, pp. 231–6).

made directly from the moment of reunion with Hölderlin to the greater moment of reunion with the Athenian people in their worship at Eleusis. As the real world breaks in upon his reverie Hegel recognizes in the night stars the Gods of Olympus. His address to Ceres and his evocation of the Mysteries is couched at first in terms of longing for what is no longer possible, but the poem ends triumphantly. Night drowns not only the time and distance that separate Hegel from Hölderlin and from their bond of fellowship in the old time and in future time; it also brings Hegel into the presence of the Goddess who abides unconquered, even when her whole world is lost.

There are two intimately connected key ideas in the poem, and both are stated at the point of transition from Tschugg to Eleusis. First, at the end of the cancelled passage Hegel says 'Fancy brings the eternal nigh to sense, / and marries it with form' (lines 37–8). Realizing—perhaps immediately, but more probably only later when his thoughts completed their circle and reached once more the point at which *Phantasie* must give place to *Vernunft*—that this was his proper starting-point, he cancelled the preceding lines which already anticipate that consummation.[1] By the power of *Phantasie* he was able in Tschugg in the year 1796 to speak his welcome to the 'high shades' of the Greek gods, and to have confidence in his other key idea: 'It is the ether of my homeland too / the solemnity [*Ernst*], the splendour that surrounds you' (lines 41–2). He could wish that the gates of the temple might open again, secure in the knowledge that he could play his part, and understand the symbols and the mysteries. But all that, the actual words and ceremonial, is irretrievably lost, and the scholars who think the wisdom of the Goddess, the high secrets of the Mysteries, could be penetrated if only the formulas could be dug up out of the dust, have missed the significance of the 'mystery' completely. Their curiosity dishonours the goddess, whose secret lies in the depth of an actual felt experience, not in any outward sign. Reflection (*der Gedanke*) cannot grasp the experience of a soul which drowns and forgets itself in the 'presentiment' (*Ahnung*) of the Infinite beyond space and time, and then awakes to consciousness again. One who speaks of this must speak with the 'tongues of angels', and he must speak only to those who are as aware as he is of the in-

---

[1] The fact that this starting-point is itself included in the cancellation is what suggests to me that Hegel crossed the lines out later rather than at once.

adequacy of language to express what he has lived through. Only to the initiates, therefore, can he speak. To speak of it is to fall short and so to sin against it. It is not something for Sophists to play verbal games with in the market-place; nor is it something to be put into a creed or a catechism and learned by heart. In that way the natural vitality of the child, which alone makes the experience possible, is stifled and destroyed. The real initiate does not speak of the Goddess with his mouth, because he worships her in the holy of holies of his own breast. His own life is the outward expression of this worship. This true worship is still possible, even though the whole world of the Greeks has perished; the spirit of the Goddess abides, and she reveals herself to her true worshipper, Hegel, in the historical record that remains.

Noting that the word-play of the Sophists is assimilated to the catechetic method of religious instruction,[1] Asveld has drawn attention to the animus against 'historical Christianity' that is evidenced in the last twenty lines of the poem. Even more significant, and no less obvious if one is prepared to see them, are the echoes of Hegel's own interpretation of the Gospels.[2] Hegel's Jesus condemns the hypocritical showing of religious feeling, and urges men to worship God in their hearts and their lives; and it is implicit in what Hegel says that the secrets of the Goddess lie open to a still unspoiled child, as does the message of the Gospel. The secret that becomes at last so empty that it has 'the roots of its life only in the echoes of alien tongues' (lines 89–90) is the Gospel message itself; and the implication is that before it fell prey to the 'rhetorical hypocrite' it was itself a holy mystery like that of Eleusis. Unlike the mystery of Eleusis it can be recovered from the echoes of alien tongues, and Hegel believes he has recovered it. But how is he to 'bring the eternal nigh to sense'? The fundamental conviction expressed in the poem is that the particular forms to which the eternal truth was 'married' in Greek religion

---

[1] Lines 81–90. The parallel is meant to extend, I think, even to the making of a profit out of what is holy—cf. Hegel's remarks in his letter to Schelling of Jan. 1795 (*Briefe*, i. 16), and the general tenor of his proto-Marxist thesis that in an authoritarian society the profit motive is universally dominant (*Jedes Volk hat ihm Gegenstände*, Nohl, p. 223; Knox, p. 156–7).

[2] Asveld, p. 116 n.; cf. Peperzak, p. 126 n. There is actually a direct parallel in *The Life of Jesus* for the passage that caught Peperzak's eye: 'Thy sons, O Goddess, do not parade thine honour about street and market place, but guard it in the inner sanctum of their breast': compare Hegel's interpretation of Matthew 6: 1–5: Nohl, p. 84 (analysed on p. 205 above).

are not necessary for the reopening of the temple gates. Both the splendour and the moral substance (*Ernst*) of that ideal belong to human life everywhere where men cleave firmly to the spirit of the 'old covenant' between Hegel and Hölderlin: 'For the free truth alone to live, peace with the statute [*Satzung*] / That ordains thoughts and feelings, never to conclude' (lines 20–1).

Peperzak seems to me to be right, therefore, to dispose of all the supposedly 'pantheistic' implications of the poem by saying that Hegel identifies God with 'the human absolute of the free heart'.[1] The Goddess here is the great Earth–Mother, and the mystic union the worshipper experiences is the union of his finite life with the infinite life of nature as a whole. But that is all a figure for the *Phantasie*. Hegel has already told us as plainly as he could what the Godhead is for a rational man at the beginning of *The Life of Jesus*. He deliberately adopts in that essay the most flatfootedly prosaic style that he can manage, avoiding both the subtleties of the intellect, represented for him by the Fichte–Schelling theory of the Absolute Ego,[2] and the ambiguities of metaphor which appeal strongly to imagination, but are the commonest source of misunderstanding among ordinary men. But what is there said so plainly that no literate man of good will can misunderstand it, is *ipso facto* deprived of its moving power. The imagination and the heart go empty away. We can see from the poem that Hegel believed that the religion of free reason could be brought to life. One is left wondering just how soon the parallel between the mysteries of Eleusis and the miracle of Easter struck him. That parallel, surely, was the required key to the problem of how to apply his second canon to Christianity in a *constructive* way?

[1] Peperzak, p. 126.
[2] We have here another reason for the cancellation of lines 30–8 in *Eleusis*: If the philosophical use of the term 'ego' was too recherché for *The Life of Jesus*, then the line 'was mein ich nannte schwindet' could hardly be allowed to stand in a poem.

APPENDIX

THE 'EARLIEST SYSTEM-PROGRAMME OF GERMAN IDEALISM'

According to Miss Schüler's ordering of the surviving manuscripts the last theoretical essay that Hegel wrote at Berne was the so-called 'earliest system-programme of German idealism'.[1] It was for a long time generally held that this essay was written by Schelling, or by Schelling and Hölderlin together, and sent to Hegel (presumably in a letter that is now lost), who copied it out, either wholly or in part, because he found it interesting.

I suppose that the missing letter might still turn up—or the original manuscript of the essay written in the hand of Schelling or Hölderlin might be found. But until something of this sort occurs I think it can be shown that all hypotheses about Hegel's copying the fragment that we actually have from another author are gratuitous.[2] It is not even necessary to depart from the chronology proposed by Miss Schüler— but since the fragment is a fairly short one we cannot absolutely insist that those scholars who wish to account for the supposed influence of Hölderlin upon it by transferring it from 1796 to 1797 are wrong.

The third paragraph of *eine Ethik* begins with the words 'From Nature I come to the *work of man*'. It was presumably this sentence that suggested the title 'system-programme'. But the previous two paragraphs are part of a theory of practical reason, and of rational faith in the Kantian sense, not of a 'philosophy of nature' of the kind that Schelling was shortly to begin writing. They remind one immediately of Hegel's remark to Schelling in January 1795 that 'if he had time' he would try to see how far one could go back from the field of moral theology to that of 'physical theology'. What he was proposing to do at the outset of the present manuscript was not quite that, for he does not begin here from a moral faith in the existence of God but from the

[1] *eine Ethik, Dok.*, p. 219–21. (The reader should note that Hoffmeister has silently filled out the abbreviations in the manuscript. For a letter-perfect transcription see Fuhrmans, i. 69–71).

[2] This view has been argued very cogently by Otto Pöggeler ('Hegel, der Verfasser des ältesten Systemprogramms des deutschen Iealismus', *Hegel-Studien*, Beiheft 4 (1969), 17–32); until I read Pöggeler's article I had not thought of reclaiming the fragment for Hegel. Thus the whole of my reconstruction of Hegel's early development was completed without reference to it. The fact that the fragment *eine Ethik* fits neatly into its place in my account is—I hope—an argument for the essential soundness both of my views and of Pöggeler's thesis. But if the missing letter or rough draft were to turn up and the sceptics were to be vindicated, nothing in my general account of Hegel's development would be affected in the slightest.

ideal of the free self-conscious Ego—'the *Vorstellung* of *myself* as an
absolutely free being'. This, not the existence of God, is now for him
the first premiss (*erste Idee*) of metaphysics; and since the first complete
sentence of the fragment that we have roundly asserts that 'the whole
of metaphysics falls for the future in the area of moral philosophy' I do
not see how we can escape the conclusion that, in spite of the topical
division between 'nature' and 'the work of man', the whole essay was
concerned with ethical theory.

'Kant with his pair of practical postulates has only given an *example*'
of the new moral metaphysics; he has not produced the 'complete
system of all Ideas, or, what is the same thing, the system of all practical
postulates'.[1] This is what the new Ethics—the metaphysical testament
of the new age, as the *Ethics* of Spinoza was that of the older one—will
provide. A whole world comes into being out of nothing along with
self-conscious freedom; and this is the only 'creation out of nothing'
that is really conceivable.

Thus far we are promised only a rational reinterpretation of a traditional theological dogma. But now Hegel tells us how he proposes to
make the transition from *Ethikotheologie* to *Physikotheologie*. He will
'give wings' to Physics and endow it with the freedom of the new
creative spirit by starting from the right question: 'How must a world
be constituted for a moral being?' This moral salvation of Physics is a
curious project, and we might be pardoned for wanting to believe that
it was Schelling's, not Hegel's, if we did not know that Hegel had
conceived it when he first began to study Fichte. He probably made a
serious attempt to carry it out in the 'System' manuscript of 1800.
Until then he seems to have been preoccupied with the problem of
applying his new Ethics to 'the work of man'.

The 'Idee der Menschheit', says Hegel, cannot provide us with an
Idea of the 'State' because the 'State' is something mechanical and
Menschheit is a living organic ideal. There cannot be an *Idee* of the
machine at all because only an objective (*Gegenstand*) of freedom can be
an *Idee*. So we must 'go beyond the State', which can only treat free
men as cogs. In dealing with this topic Hegel promises that he will
'lay down the principles for a History of Mankind and strip to the skin
the whole wretched human structure [*Menschenwerk*] of State, constitution, government, code of law'.

---

[1] Kant enumerates his practical postulates differently in different places; but
it is clear that in his canonical doctrine, so to speak, there are three 'postulates
of pure practical reason': Freedom, God, and Immortality. Only God and
Immortality receive distinct treatment as postulates in the second *Critique*,
however—and presumably these two are 'seinen beiden praktischen Postulaten'.
This is confirmed by the prominence given to these two *Ideen* later in the fragment.

This proposed treatment of human politics and its history is the most surprising novelty in *eine Ethik*. For this is the first time as far as we know, that Hegel has ever written as if he might be prepared to give up his essentially Hellenic conception of the political community as a self-sufficient—and hence necessarily an ethical—community. We saw him come to grips with the mechanical-instrumental theory of the State for the first time in Mendelssohn, and we know why he was ready enough to make use of it. He could see how neatly it applied to modern society, and how it could be appealed to in defence of such liberal values as freedom of conscience. But he has never before accepted it as a complete account of the political community, which is what he appears to be doing here. Nor does he accept it later, as we shall see, in any of the drafts for his essay on the German constitution.

This seeming inconsistency can be made to look quite glaring. The political problem that stood in the forefront of Hegel's mind from 1795 onwards was that of the relation between State and Church. 'To make objective religion subjective, must be the great concern of the State, its institutions must be concordant with freedom of conscience . . .', he wrote in his plan of 1794; and he recognized then that this involved distinguishing between the legal system of the State and the moral life of its citizens.[1] But then the 'Positivity' essay provided good grounds for thinking of the political community, rather than the religious community, as the guardian of moral freedom. Only the State can be a proper focus of authority, and only the enlightened State can keep the churches from setting themselves up as authorities. So it is no surprise to find that some years later, in his commentary on Kant's *Rechtslehre*, Hegel maintained that 'the principle of the State is a perfect whole'. If this was his position in August 1795 and August 1798 why should he have said, in August 1796 or shortly thereafter, that 'die Idee der Menschheit . . . keine Idee vom Staat gibt'?

The problem is less serious than it looks, however. All that we have to do is to find a plausible reason why Hegel should momentarily and for his present purpose have accepted the 'machine State' as the State *sic et simpliciter*. And such a reason is not far to seek. For we know that the 'machine State' which he attacks in the German Constitution manuscripts is the State of Fichte in theory and of Prussia in practice. Fichte's *Grundlage des Naturrechts* appeared at Easter 1796.[2] If Hegel

---

[1] See (a) *Unter objektiver Religion* (Nohl, pp. 48–50) and the discussion on pp. 170–1 above.

[2] Only the first part of Fichte's *Grundlage des Naturrechts* appeared in March 1796; and one might be tempted to object that the remarks in *eine Ethik* about 'the whole wretched human construction of State, constitution, government and legal system' presuppose a reading of the second part (Sept. 1797) if they allude to Fichte at all. But Fichte gives notice in his introduction to the

read it just after he wrote *Jedes Volk hat ihm eigene Gegenstände*—not to speak of working on the budgetary structure of the Canton of Berne in connection with his Cart translation—there would be nothing wonderful in his setting himself to show that the whole structure of contemporary political thought must be discarded.[1] Fichte seems, more than any other writer, to have had the power to irritate Hegel into plans for theoretical reconstruction.

The rest of the fragment provides support for this view. For, at this time, as we have suggested, Hegel probably felt himself to be at an impasse in his programme of practical religious reform, and it would be natural enough for him to turn his attention to theoretical reading and the reformulation of his own ideas. This had already happened once in 1794, when he temporarily set aside his blueprint for the rehabilitation of Christianity as a *Volksreligion* in order to straighten out his own ideas about psychology. But that was a bypath, and did not produce any startling results, whereas here we are faced with a major theoretical development, together with its practical corollary (or 'application'). It is no wonder, therefore, if the excitement of his new discovery combined with his critical reaction to Fichte and his jaundiced observation of the political scene to upset his intellectual balance a little, and cause him to say things that were valid only within a conceptual scheme which he could not finally accept.

It is clear that he does not really accept it even here. For he says that the treatment of free men as cogs must cease; and some kind of political life will exist even when we have 'gone beyond the State' and stripped the 'whole wretched human structure of State, constitution, government, and code of law' naked. But Hegel is not interested, for the moment, in what the 'absolute freedom of all spirits' will be like on the political level. He has found in the 'Idea of beauty, taken in its higher

first part of what is to come in the second part; and the final chapter of the first part contains a 'deduction of the concept of a Republic' that is quite detailed enough to account for Hegel's reaction. Also we must remember that Fichte had already delivered the whole treatise from the lectern, and students' reports (including some that were trenchantly critical) were already current. See Fichte, *Werke*, i. 3, 322, and 432–60; and compare the editors' introduction, ibid., 305–6.

[1] A remark of Hölderlin's in his letter of 20 Nov. 1796 makes it clear that Hegel must have said he was currently occupied with the problem of State and Church either in the private letter that he certainly sent earlier that same month along with Letter 20 (which was intended for the eyes of the Gogel family) or else in a slightly earlier letter that is now lost: 'Mit den Jungen wirst Du, so sehr der erste Unterricht unsern Geist oft drücken muß, Dich dennoch lieber beschäftigen als mit Staat und Kirche, wie sie gegenwärtig sind' (*Briefe*, i. 45). This odd antithesis only seems natural to me upon the hypothesis that Hegel had not merely spoken of his interest in the problem, but had further suggested that the *Repetentstelle* at Tübingen would be a good position in which to pursue it.

Platonic sense', the supreme moral ideal under which every other *Idee* in his Ethics must be subsumed; and he wants to apply it at once to the problem of reforming Christianity which was always his most immediate concern.

'I am now convinced that the highest act of *Vernunft* . . . is an aesthetic act, and that *truth and goodness only become sisters in beauty*—the philosopher must have as much aesthetic power as the poet. The men without aesthetic sense are our *Buchstaben*-philosophers.' This recognition that 'the highest act of *Vernunft* is an aesthetic act' is a major advance in Hegel's theory of human nature, for it involves a revolution in his conception of the relation between *Vernunft* and *Phantasie*. We already know that without aesthetic sense one cannot be a *Volkserzieher*; but the discovery that without it one cannot be a philosopher either, means that as *Volkserzieher* Hegel must begin to be his own philosopher; he cannot lean on others, and particularly on Kant, as he has done in the past.

Is he now leaning not on a philosopher, but on a poet? Did he get this new insight not from Kant and Schiller but from Hölderlin? It is possible—especially if this piece was written in 1797—but it is by no means certain, or even highly probable, and the answer to the question is far less important than some scholars seem to think. Hölderlin certainly had the idea first, and in view of its focal importance in the development of German thought after Kant, we could make a strong claim for him as the 'real founder' of absolute idealism. But Hölderlin's inspiration came from the *Critique of Judgement* and from Schiller's *Aesthetic Letters*; and anyone who shared his aims and ideals, as Hegel did, could have arrived at the idea by the very same route.[1] We know how much impressed Hegel was with the *Aesthetic Letters* when he read the first instalments in 1795. Considering the problems that he was himself concerned with, it would have been natural enough for him to re-read the whole series in the summer of 1796.[2]

[1] Hölderlin first put forward the thesis that the absolute 'union of subject and object' was aesthetic in a letter to Schiller (Letter 104, 4 Sept. 1795, *GSA*, vi. 181), and the source of his inspiration is clear enough when he tells Niethammer that he is going to put his views into a series of 'New Letters on the Aesthetic Education of Man' (Letter 117, 24 Feb. 1796, ibid., p. 203).

[2] Hegel wrote to Schelling in Apr. 1795 (*Briefe*, i. 25) that Schiller's Letters were a 'masterpiece'. But he got the title confused with Lessing's 'Education of the Human Race' and he had not yet read the whole series since the third part (Letters xvii–xxvii) did not appear until June. Hegel refers to 'the first *two* numbers' of *Die Horen* (i.e. Jan. and Feb. 1795). The first appearance of the idea which I take to have been crucial for the leap that Hölderlin and Hegel made, although Schiller did not—the idea of beauty as the 'consummation of humanity'—is in Letter xv. 5, which was in the February number. But Letter xxi. 6 and Letter xxii. 1 are much more suggestive (see Wilkinson and Willoughby, pp. 102–3 and 146–51).

'Poetry thus acquires a higher dignity, it becomes once again at the end what it was at the beginning—the *teacher of mankind*; for no philosophy or history remains at last, the bardic art [*die Dichtkunst*] will alone survive all other arts and sciences.' This first practical consequence or 'application' that Hegel derives from his new discovery is the particular element in *eine Ethik* that reminds us most forcibly of Hölderlin. But there is not the slightest reason for thinking that Hegel could not have come to this conclusion by himself in Berne without any very direct intervention by his friend. From his earliest years he was impressed by the role of the poet as a teacher in Greek society, and by the achievement of Shakespeare in making the history of England a living heritage for his fellow countrymen. Among German poets Klopstock is the one to whom he refers most explicitly; but Klopstock is, of course, the poet who failed the supreme test in the eyes of Hegel as a schoolboy, or the poet of the dying age, as he would say now. The poetic impulse of the new age is rather to be looked for in Schiller. Schiller is the modern poet who exemplifies what Hegel means by claiming that poetry 'survives' philosophy, just as Shakespeare shows us how poetry 'survives' history.[1]

Poetry 'survives' in fact as a necessary element in religion; and thus this fragment heralds the most fundamental development of the Frankfurt period: the claim that religion is somehow the ultimate or highest form of experience, and belongs to a different plane altogether from that occupied by reflective reason. From the beginning Hegel had embraced the view—held even by the most radical foes of 'superstition' in the Enlightenment—that the masses need a religion that appeals to their senses, to set them, or keep them, on the path of morality. But now he tells us that 'not only the great mob but also the philosopher' needs a religion of this sort. This is a radical departure from the conception of *rational* religion as the goal of human progress which dominates all his work from the Tübingen fragment of 1793 to the concluding paragraphs of the 'Positivity' essay written in April 1796. But it is a natural outgrowth of his reflections on the aesthetic and imaginative aspects of Greek religion, and of his renewed study of Herder, both of which are clearly documented in *Jedes Volk hat ihm eigene Gegenstände*. The first section of that essay clearly demonstrates that the superiority of Greek religion over Christianity arose largely from its *mythical* character. A

---

[1] For Hegel's schoolboy reflections on the Greek poets and Klopstock see *Dok.*, pp. 48–51; for the contrast between Klopstock and Shakespeare see the first section of *Jedes Volk hat ihm eigene Gegenstände*, Nohl, pp. 214–19 (Knox, pp. 145–51). The contrast between the status of mythology in Greek religion and culture and its status in Christianity and modern culture, which is the central topic of this section, provides us with the context for a proper understanding and appreciation of Hegel's proposal that 'we must have a new mythology'.

'historical' religion, such as Christianity, is bound to be hostile to myths; and a religion cannot reconcile and unify peoples if it is hostile to their myths. So Hegel's final promise in this fragment is that he will explain something which, as he proudly says, no one has thought of before: that 'we must have a new mythology, which stands at the service of the *Ideen* [i.e. of our new Ethics], it must be mythology of Reason'.[1]

The last paragraph of the plan might *almost* have come straight out of the Tübingen fragment (*Religion ist eine*):

> Until we express the *Ideen* aesthetically, i.e. mythologically, they have no interest for the *people*, and conversely until mythology is rational the philosopher must be ashamed of it. Thus in the end enlightened and unenlightened must clasp hands, mythology must become philosophical ⟨in order to⟩[2] make the people rational, and philosophy must become mythological in order to make the philosophers sensible [sinnl⟨ich⟩]. Then reigns eternal unity among us. No more the look of scorn [of the enlightened philosopher looking down on the mob], no more the blind trembling of the people before its wise men and priests. Then first awaits us *equal* development of *all* powers, of what is peculiar to each and what is common to all. No power shall any longer be suppressed, for universal freedom and equality of spirits will reign!—A higher spirit sent from heaven must found this new religion among us, it will be the last ⟨and⟩ greatest work of mankind.

Almost, but not quite. For the 'subjective' religion that makes reason palpable to the senses in *Religion ist eine* is only a handmaid of *Vernunft*, a childhood governess who remains as an old friend in the house of the grown man who is governed by his own reason; whereas this 'mythological philosophy' does away with all 'governors', even—by implication —with the authority of reason. Religion now is neither a governess nor an old friend, but a 'new spirit' of equality and freedom.

The fragment *eine Ethik* fits with perfect logic into the exact sequence of Hegel's manuscripts that is suggested by graphic analysis. For on the

---

[1] The idea of reforming mythology in the service of reason might very well have occurred to Schelling in 1794; but even allowing for his well-known volatility it hardly seems plausible to ascribe it to him in 1796. For this reason alone it seems to me that any claim that Schelling was the original or the main author of this piece must be set aside. If Hegel *did* transcribe it from a manuscript by someone else, the only plausible hypothesis is that it is part of one of Hölderlin's plans for the 'New Aesthetic Letters'. (Cf. Letter 117, line 38: 'And I shall advance [in the 'Letters'] from philosophy to poetry and religion.') The way that *eine Ethik* begins with the moral philosophy of physics tells rather strongly against *this* hypothesis however.

[2] Here I have ventured to read *um* in place of the *und* that appears in our printed texts. I assume (for reasons of syntactical balance that will I hope be obvious) that *und* is simply a *lapsus calami*. In the rest of the fragment the form *und* occurs only three times; the abbreviation *u.* is used nine times.

one side the essay *Jedes Volk hat ihm eigene Gegenstände* helps us more than anything else to understand why Hegel wrote it, and how he came to conceive the project of a 'mythology of reason'; and on the other side *eine Ethik* helps more than anything else to explain why Hegel went on to write *Eleusis*. In the light of the doctrine that the highest act of *Vernunft* is aesthetic, and that even rational religion must be *sinnlich*, Hegel's invocation of the Great Mother appears no longer as a mere 'aside'. It is a contribution to rational mythology, an expression— however lisping and imperfect—of the new spirit of freedom and equality. The poetic form is not chosen simply because it is historically appropriate, but because it is only in the poetry that 'survives' them that history and philosophy are finally consummated.

There is, in fact, no other point in the sequence of datable manuscripts where this fragment could be inserted at all comfortably. We have already noticed that the political doctrine of *eine Ethik* is essentially transitional between that which we find in the 'Positivity' essay, and the views reported by Rosenkranz from Hegel's Kant studies of 1798 and worked out in the *Verfassungsschrift*.[1] Something similar can be said about the theory of religion put forward here. The problem of how a religion is founded holds the centre of the stage in the Frankfurt manuscripts. Hegel discuses this problem theoretically and studies the founding of two religions, Judaism and Christianity, in considerable detail. He is concerned with comparative mythology in his earliest studies of Judaism; but after that the place of myth in religion is alluded to only in the most marginal way. Instead the fundamental thesis is that 'Religion ist eins mit der Liebe': all religion, Hellenic as well as Judaeo-Christian, is analysed as an aesthetic consciousness of love and of an absolute love-object. Only when this analysis is completed does Hegel turn from the principle of *Herz* back to the principle of *Phantasie* which was in the forefront of his mind in his last months in Berne.[2] There are signs that in the great manuscript, of which the so-called *Systemfragment* is all that we have, Hegel did attempt finally to provide at least some elements of a new mythology.[3] But this attempt was made in the total context of a conception of religion that is both broader and deeper than the one sketched in *eine Ethik*.

---

[1] For a summary account of the evolution of Hegel's *political* ideas—without reference to the doctrines of *eine Ethik*—see the first two sections of Chapter V below.

[2] Even the extremely prosaic Alpine diary bears witness to this concern; see the remarks about the *Teufelsbrücke* and the neighbouring crag cited on p. 161 above.

[3] See Chapter IV, Section 10 below, pp. 391–7. Of course if we possessed, and could date, all of the manuscripts from which Rosenkranz took the *Fragmente historischer Studien* the picture might look rather different. It is at least possible that these 'studies' included an essay on 'comparative mythology'.

My conclusion therefore is that the fragment *eine Ethik* is indeed a piece of Hegel's own work, and not something that he copied; and that he wrote it in Berne—or more precisely at Tschugg—in the summer of 1796. There is, however, one fact about the manuscript which might seem to give cause for serious doubt about the authorship, and which still remains to be dealt with. The plan is presented as a series of intentional statements in the first person singular, and the last paragraph rises to a pitch of prophetic enthusiasm that is without parallel in Hegel's other 'plans'. Hegel did not in any other instance write out a plan in the first person singular; and when one is making a plan in this mode it is more natural to write 'Here I *must* do this' or 'Here I *should* do this' than 'Here I *shall* do this'. This latter mode of expression —like the little note of self-congratulation about the 'idea which as far as I know has never yet occurred to anyone else'—is only appropriate when one is setting forth one's plans for the information of someone else. Hegel did at least once promise to do this in his correspondence with Schelling; and we know by inference that he must actually have done it at least once in his correspondence with Hölderlin. Hölderlin would have been by far the most natural recipient for this statement of intentions, and perhaps it is legitimate to explain the tone of the last paragraph by supposing that the 'calm *Verstandesmensch*' Hegel caught a little of Hölderlin's prophetic enthusiasm from the very act of writing to him about something that he knew would be close to Hölderlin's heart.

IV. FRANKFURT 1797-1800

Phantasie und Herz

1. *The 'crisis of Frankfurt' and the supposed 'revolution in Hegel's thinking'*

CHRISTIANE HEGEL remembered, many years later, that her brother returned from Switzerland 'very withdrawn, and only happy in his circle of close friends'.[1] He was not at all the boy pictured in her memories of Tübingen; and we may infer from the general tone of Hölderlin's last two letters to him in Switzerland (October and November 1796)—especially from the assurance: 'You'll be the "Old Man" again next spring'—that Hegel had remarked on and openly bewailed the change in himself.[2] From the correspondence with Hölderlin it is clear at least that Hegel suffered a sort of crisis of confidence during his last year in Switzerland. His faith in himself, and in his own capacity to carry out the task of *Volkserzieher* that he had laid upon himself, wavered. He seriously contemplated applying for the position of a *Repetent* at Tübingen; and he must have said something quite uncharacteristic about accepting Hölderlin's guidance and leadership in the future, for Hölderlin (who regarded the project of a return to Tübingen as a folly which only the direst economic necessity could justify) commented thus: 'What you write about guidance and leadership, my dearest friend, has made me very sad. You have so often been my mentor when my low spirits made me into a young fool, and you'll often have to be so again.'[3]

---

[1] 'Kam in sich gekehrt zurück, nur in traulichen Zirkel fidel' (*Dok.*, p. 394). Christiane's recollections were recorded by Hegel's widow for the use of Rosenkranz.

[2] Letter 21 in *Briefe*, i. 45 (20 Nov. 1796).

[3] Ibid. We should note also Hölderlin's open amazement that Hegel should be asking *him* for advice about the Tübingen plan in the first instance (Letter 15, *Briefe*, i. 34). (It is clear from the passage quoted in the text that Letter 20 represents only the *public* part of Hegel's reply to Letter 19. It contains nothing

It has been the view of some scholars that Hölderlin's confidence in Hegel's powers of recovery was somewhat misplaced, and that Hegel's depression actually continued for some time after his move to Frankfurt. This hypothesis—for it is certainly no more than that—is generally advanced as one important element in the explanation of a supposed 'revolution' which occurred in Hegel's thinking at Frankfurt. The view—which is developed and defended at some length and with considerable skill by Lukács—is expressed in its barest essentials by T. M. Knox:

> The revolution in Hegel's thinking came about because, during his first two years in 'unhappy Frankfurt', in order to cure himself of melancholia, he worked with all his energies at Greek literature and philosophy, as well as at history and politics, and then brought the result of these studies to bear anew on the reinterpretation of the life and message of Jesus.[1]

Inasmuch as there was in fact no 'revolution' in Hegel's thought, which develops with such steady and organic continuity that we might never have suspected a crisis of self-doubt if it were not externally documented, the hypothesis of a long period of 'melancholia' is quite gratuitous; and as soon as we take a careful look at the evidence, the alleged fact of Hegel's unhappiness in Frankfurt dissolves. Hegel's own reference to 'unhappy Frankfurt' occurs in the draft of a letter to Sinclair written in October 1810; when it is read in its context by one who knows something of Hegel's relations with the intended recipient, and with the other people there referred to, it is easily recognized as a transparent allusion to the emotional crisis that *Hölderlin* passed through in the household of the Gontards—the crisis that culminated in the first onset of his insanity.

Hölderlin always emphasized Sinclair's respect for Hegel. But Sinclair was essentially Hölderlin's friend rather than Hegel's, being like Hölderlin a poet, and an admirer of Schiller; and philosophically his enthusiasm for Fichte linked him with Hölderlin (and with Schelling who was born like Sinclair in 1775) rather than with Hegel. It can hardly be doubted that it was

that could have made Hölderlin 'sad' in this way, and is obviously just the letter which Hölderlin advised him to write to be shown to Herr Gogel (Letter 19, *Briefe*, i. 42); with it Hegel doubtless enclosed a more personal and confidential sheet which has been lost.)

[1] 'Hegel's attitude to Kant's ethics', *Kant-Studien*, 49 (1957–8), 73 (cf. Lukács, Chapter 2, section 1).

through his friendship with Hölderlin that Sinclair was first drawn into the circle of Hegel's friends, and it was the memory of their common friendship with Hölderlin that formed their closest bond in later years.

They corresponded for a time in 1806 and 1807, mainly about Sinclair's literary efforts (two tragic dramas); but each of them at that time displayed also a willingness to help the other as far as he could in practical difficulties.[1] In particular Sinclair wished to help Hegel find a secure position after the disastrous interruption which the campaigns of Napoleon caused in his career at Jena.

Three years later, when Hegel was comfortably settled as Rector of the Gymnasium at Nüremberg, Sinclair did at last hear of something in his own neighbourhood which he thought would suit Hegel. When he made inquiries into Hegel's whereabouts in order to write to him, he realized that Hegel would almost certainly not want to move, but by way of renewing their earlier friendship he wrote Hegel a long letter about the position, and about the old friends in Frankfurt who still remembered and wished to see him. Hegel had no interest in moving, but he appreciated and reciprocated the friendly memories which had prompted Sinclair's letter, and suggested that since Sinclair was better able to leave Homburg for a time than he was to leave Nüremberg, Sinclair should come to visit him. He sent Sinclair a copy of the *Phenomenology*, though it is probable that after reading Sinclair's comment on 'the charlatanry of Schelling' he scarcely expected that 'stubborn Fichtean' to approve of it.

The closing paragraph of Hegel's draft, which he made some seven or eight weeks after receiving Sinclair's letter, deals with Sinclair's messages from or about old friends. About the death at Wagram of Zwilling, a young friend of Sinclair and Hölderlin whom Hegel first met when he arrived in Frankfurt, he wrote in 1810 just what he might well have said in 1797—that it was a 'hero's death' which had 'greatly moved him'.[2] The kind remembrances of Sinclair's mother he acknowledges with sincere good

---

[1] When Sinclair was finally cleared of the charges of treason and conspiracy against Württemberg, Hegel apparently expressed the intention of inserting an announcement about it in the *Bamberger Zeitung* (Letter 91, *Briefe*, i. 163). Sinclair for his part had earlier done what he could to forward Hegel's plan to obtain a post in the nascent University of Berlin (Letter 60, *Briefe*, i. 107).

[2] Letter 167, *Briefe*, i. 332; compare his comment about death in battle in *Ein positiver Glauben* (1796), Nohl, p. 238.

feeling. The mention of another old acquaintance, Molitor, he responds to by recalling an essay on the philosophy of history which Molitor had sent him in the Bamberg days. Only one of Sinclair's messages is left without an explicit acknowledgement. Sinclair writes: 'About the unfortunate [*unglücklichen*] Hölderlin I have heard nothing, but his condition has probably not changed in the meantime; please do tell me what you know of him.' Hegel, since in all probability he has had no news of Hölderlin for even longer than Sinclair, does not reply directly. Instead he recalls the *happy* days which they had passed together at Homburg when he lived in the city made *unhappy* for them by the misfortunes of their friend: 'Give my greetings also to the high Feldberg and Altkönig, towards which I raised my eyes so often and with so much pleasure from unhappy [*unglückseligen*] Frankfurt, when I knew you at their feet. Farewell, don't hold my dilatoriness against me and let me hear from you again soon.'[1] Hegel was, I believe, scrupulously honest in his letters. But his honesty always went hand in hand with a tact which sprang from a remarkable sensibility for the feelings and concerns of his correspondents. To suppose that he would answer a letter written with such evident goodwill to urge upon him the advantages of a move to Frankfurt, by saying that he had been miserable there, is to credit him with an indifference to other people's feelings so absolute as to constitute a kind of moral blindness. If he had in fact been *personally* unhappy in Frankfurt he would *never* have closed his letter thus. The fact that he wrote as he did clearly indicates that he knew with absolute certainty that Sinclair would not for a moment be tempted to take his words in that sense. Thus, the letter tends to show—so far as it shows anything—that Hegel himself was at least outwardly quite happy in Frankfurt.[2]

The plain truth is that we do not have *much* evidence about Hegel's state of mind or his outward disposition while he was in

[1] Ibid., p. 333.

[2] Sinclair's next letter (Letter 179, *Briefe*, i. 354–5) reached Hegel on 7 May 1811. It came with his three-volume work on *Truth and Certainty* (Frankfurt, 1811) and was mainly devoted to an explanation of the method employed therein. He thanked Hegel for sending the *Phenomenology*, but made no comments on it until Feb. 1812 (Letter 199, *Briefe*, i. 394–6) after he had received Hegel's verdict on his own work. Then in Oct. 1812 he wrote to announce an impending visit to Nüremberg. He there speaks again of remembering 'our days with Hölderlin and Zwilling, which will always remain unforgettable for me' (Letter 210, *Briefe*, i. 416).

Frankfurt. His letters to his sister are lost, and he was not now driven by loneliness to commune with other old friends by letter as he had been at Berne. But all the evidence we have goes to show that he recovered his spirits rapidly and completely when he went to live there, and was perfectly satisfied with his general situation. When he first arrived in Frankfurt he still felt that the mission which he had laid upon himself was too much for him, and that since in his day and age the human race had become degraded to the level of a wolf pack the only sensible thing to do was to learn to howl along with them. St. Antony of Padua did more good by preaching to the fish, he wrote to Nanette Endel in February 1797 when he had been in Frankfurt for only a week or two, than anyone would do here by trying to set an example like that of St. Alexis.[1] But even this earliest letter from Frankfurt is written more in a spirit of humorous irony than of genuine despair, and in the one that follows six weeks later Hegel introduces his notes about visits to the Opera (*The Magic Flute, Don Giovanni*) and to the theatre with the remark: 'I am becoming here in Frankfurt more equal to the world again.'[2] On 17 July (the feast of St. Alexis), Hegel was quite willing to call that remarkable ascetic his patron saint once more, though he denies the title *Magister*.[3] In November he is again reporting: 'I go more often to the theatre [*die Komödie*] here than in Stuttgart. Music and some actors are very good'; and he hopes that Nanette will forgive the habit of running over into 'general reflections' in one 'who was once a *Magister* and drags himself along with this title among his belongings like an angel of Satan that buffets him with its fists'.[4] Finally in May 1798, in

---

[1] Letter 22, *Briefe*, i. 49. According to the legend, St. Alexis (fifth-century Roman, feast day 17 July) returned the betrothal ring of his espoused bride, and went as a pilgrim to Edessa in Syria, where he lived for seventeen years as a beggar. After this he returned to Rome, where his betrothed had remained faithful to him; but he did not reveal himself to her or to his parents, and lived there as a beggar for a further seventeen years. He then died at the moment when his sanctity was revealed to Pope and Emperor by an oracular voice from Heaven. (It is clear from their letters that Nanette Endel and Hegel himself had between them decided that Alexis was a most fitting patron saint for him.)

[2] Letter 23, *Briefe*, i. 52.

[3] Letter 24, *Briefe*, i. 54–5. After Hegel's signature there follows the post-script '(Nur immer Magister in der Addresse)'.

[4] Letter 25, *Briefe*, i. 56. Cf. 2 Corinthians 12: 7: 'And lest I should be exalted above measure through the abundance of the revelations, there was given to me a thorn in the flesh, the messenger of Satan to buffet me, lest I should be exalted above measure.'

what seems to have been the last letter of this rather touching little interlude, he inquires: 'Have you had no balls in Memmingen? I am very good at balls; they are the jolliest thing left to us in our gloomy times.'[1]

These letters to Nanette Endel, which are virtually all that we have from the Frankfurt period save the epistle to Schelling with which it ends, are mainly interesting for what they reveal about Hegel's state of mind during his short stay in Stuttgart after the return from Berne. For it was only during that period of a few weeks at most that he really knew the young Catholic girl who was living in the house with his father and sister when he came home. To say that he fell in love with her in that short time would probably be to overstate the case, but he was interested enough in her to play with the idea of visiting her 'in a year or two', if they should chance to be close enough to be within the compass of a twenty-four-hours' journey.[2] The difference of religion put a barrier between them which Hegel in all likelihood never seriously thought of crossing.[3] From the beginning Nanette rallied 'Magister' Hegel about 'the abundance of his revelations' and about his high hopes of bringing enlightenment to mankind, and he retorted by poking gentle fun at the confessional, the rosary, and the saints. He compared himself to St. Antony preaching to the fish, and she gave him St. Alexis (who fled to Edessa on the day of his marriage and lived there as a hermit) as a patron and model. When Hegel compares his title of *Magister* to St. Paul's 'thorn in the flesh, the messenger of Satan to buffet me lest I should be exalted above measure through the abundance of the revelations', we may, I think, legitimately infer that Nanette had pointed to the contrast between the full, free, spontaneous, and joyous life of Hegel's 'revelation', and his own actual withdrawn and introverted condition. He recognized that Nanette was a more 'natural' being than

---

[1] Letter 27, *Briefe*, i. 58. This was the passage which particularly amused D. F. Strauss when he first discovered these letters. Probably (since Rosenkranz's biography had not appeared) Strauss knew nothing of *La belle Augustine* and the ball at Tübingen, or of Hegel's early love of dancing in general; but he would not have needed Christiane's notes to tell him that the Herr Professor was never very good at it. For Strauss the letters had 'almost a comic interest only' (see Hoffmeister's note on Letter 22, *Briefe*, i. 442).

[2] See Letter 24, *Briefe*, i. 53.

[3] But it might also be argued that their conversation and correspondence revolved so much around the religious barrier because they really did seriously consider breaking through it (cf. further, p. 266 n. 1 below).

he was, but he wanted her to understand that the figure of magisterial gloom and despair who had appeared before her in Stuttgart was not his real self; and the self who emerges in the letters from Frankfurt is indeed very different, even if he does tend to run on into 'general reflections' all the time.[1]

Hegel had felt at Tschugg, and had sought to express in *Eleusis*, that communion with the Earth Mother was a healing power against the ills of civilization. It was a pleasure still in Frankfurt, where there were operas, concerts, plays, and other delights which were almost wholly lacking in Berne, to escape to the country. But the reasons now were different. As he told Nanette in July:

> The memory of those days spent in the country [i.e. at Tschugg] continually drives me out of Frankfurt, and as there I sought to be reconciled with myself and with other men in the arms of Nature, so here I often fly to this true mother, to separate myself again from other men in her company, and to protect myself from their influence under her aegis, and to prevent any covenant with them.[2]

In Berne Hegel felt isolated and cut off from the real life of his time; he sought to reconcile himself with his lot through his solitary communing with Nature; but in Frankfurt it was rather the pleasures and temptations of social life that he had to escape from. It is not true, therefore, that Hegel's 'psychological' pre-

---

[1] Letter 25, (13 Nov. 1797), *Briefe*, i. 56. The tendency to moralize too much was a fault which Hegel never lost. The forty-year old professor had to apologize for it to his twenty-year old bride in 1811 (see Letter 187, *Briefe*, i. 369).

[2] Letter 24, *Briefe*, i. 53. Because of the weight placed on this passage by Lukács I give here the original text of the entire paragraph:

'So viel ich mich aus der Geschichte Ihrer bisherigen Schicksale erinnere, haben Sie noch nicht aus eigner Erfahrung das Landleben kennen gelernt; und ich zweifle nicht, daß es bei Ihnen nicht erst einer Angewöhnung bedurfte, um sich darin zu gefallen, sondern daß Sie gleich von Anfang sich selbst ohne Mißton darin fänden, ohne daß die Stimmung, in die uns eine freie schöne Natur versetzt, einen Widerstand in Ihnen gefunden hätte; — ich muß gestehen, bei mir brauchte es einige Zeit, ehe ich mich von den Schlacken, die die Gesellschaft, das Stadtleben, die daraus entspringende Zerstreuungssucht in uns einmischt, von der Sehnsucht darnach, die sich durch Langeweile äußert, — ein wenig reinigen konnte Aus Frankfurt treibt mich jetzt immer das Andenken an jene auf dem Lande verlebte⟨n⟩ Tage, und so wie ich dort mich im Arme der Natur immer mit mir selbst, mit den Menschen mich aussöhnte, so flüchte ich mich hier oft zu dieser treuen Mutter, um bei ihr mich mit den Menschen, mit denen ich in Frieden lebe, wieder zu entzweien und mich unter ihrer Aegide von ihrem Einflusse zu bewahren und einen Bund mit ihnen zu hintertreiben.'

occupations at Frankfurt are the reflection of a crisis in his personal life, as Rosenweig and Lukács have maintained.

The principal evidence for this rather strained hypothesis is found in a letter of May 1810, where Hegel speaks of a certain 'hypochondria' which he has himself experienced 'for a couple of years' and which he believes to be an essential element in human development; later still in his lectures on the philosophy of spirit he marked out the decade 'from the twenty-seventh to the thirty-sixth year' (with particular emphasis on the twenty-seventh year) as the time of transition from youth to manhood when man has 'to conquer a certain hypochondria'. It can scarcely be accidental that he should have singled out the decade bounded in his own life by his return from Berne and the writing of the *Phenomenology*.[1] But the 'hypochondria' of which he speaks in the letter of 1810 is a peculiarly intellectual experience, rather than a psychological condition in any ordinary sense. It is the feeling—which has certainly afflicted every author if not every man—that although one knows where one wants to go, one does not quite know how to get there:

I know from my own experience this state of mind or rather of the reason [*diese Stimmung des Gemuts oder vielmehr der Vernunft*] where one has once got oneself through one's interest and the intimations that go with it into a chaos of phenomena, and where one is inwardly certain of the goal but not thoroughly ⟨in possession of it⟩, one has not yet achieved a clear articulation of the whole in detail. I have suffered from this hypochondria for a couple of years to the point of losing my grip altogether [*bis zur Entkräftung*]; [I am] every man, surely, has in general such a turning point in his life, the nocturnal point of contraction of his being, a narrow strait through which he forces his way, emerging confirmed and certain of his secure self-possession, of the security of ordinary everyday life, or, if he has already rendered himself incapable of fulfilment in that way, with the security of a nobler inner life.[2]

[1] For a citation of the manuscript lecture notes see Rosenzweig, i. 101; Rosenzweig's note thereto (i. 236) informs us that the original '*in* the twenty-seventh year' was subsequently modified to '*about* the twenty-seventh year'. The next note cites Gabler's record that Hegel spoke of suffering from 'hypochondria' again in 1805. We should remember, however, that Hegel is not speaking autobiographically. He was probably thinking of the experience of Hölderlin at least as much as of any experience of his own—a glance at his remarks in their context will speedily confirm this.

[2] Letter 158, *Briefe*, i. 314. According to Rosenzweig, i. 236, Hegel originally wrote and cancelled the words 'Ich bin' where I have inserted '[I am]'; he

This passage—whether or not it actually refers to this period rather than, say, to the gestation of the *Phenomenology*—describes very well what I believe to have been Hegel's state of mind during his last summer at Berne and his first spring in Frankfurt. He knew where he wanted to go—this 'inward certainty of the goal' is perfectly, if not beautifully, expressed in *Eleusis*—but he did not know how to get there. But his bewilderment—which may well have combined with his loneliness to produce a veritable agony of self-doubt—was in actual fact almost, if not quite, irrelevant to the objective progress of Hegel's reflections; and all the temptations of 'ordinary everyday' happiness which acquaintance with Nanette Endel may have introduced into the mind of this modern votary of St. Alexis, were equally irrelevant in this respect.[1] His psychological condition is so far from determining the direction or providing the explanation of his reflections in the Frankfurt period, that it would not make any notable difference to us in seeking to interpret his manuscripts if the letters to Nanette had perished, if he had never written as he did to Windischmann, if his notes on the typical pattern of human psychological development had not contained those suggestive numbers, and if his widow had not recorded his sister's recollections about his return from Berne. The likelihood of a check in the progress of his thought after *Jedes Volk hat ihm eigene Gegenstände* can already be foreseen in his plan of 1794 (*Unter objektiver Religion*); the presence

thinks Hegel originally meant to make 'the personal reference stronger'. But it is more likely, I think, that he simply began to write 'I am ⟨convinced, or something similar, that⟩ every man' etc. and then decided to express his conviction as a general categorical proposition. In other words we have here a good example of his natural tendency to fall into 'general reflections'.

[1] If the reference in the letter to Windischmann really is to the period of Hegel's acquaintance with Nanette Endel, it may be that I, like other interpreters have treated their relationship rather too lightly. Perhaps Hegel seriously thought of marriage ('the security of everyday life') and deliberately renounced it at this time. One could, I think, read the evidence that we have as indicating that Nanette tried to get Hegel to the sticking-point of matrimony, but that Hegel's own inclination gradually hardened into a firm refusal. (Cf. especially Letter 27— there is also the poem which Nanette sent to Christiane for Hegel's fifty-seventh birthday, mentioned in Hoffmeister's note, *Briefe*, i. 447—and the suggestive fact that Nanette kept Hegel's letters, whereas that instinctive hoarder of documents seems not to have kept hers. For the poem see Nicolin, pp. 28-9.)

It is also just possible that Hegel's relations with Nanette Endel contributed to his analysis of sexual love in *welchem Zwecke denn alles Übrige dient* (Nohl, pp. 378-82; Knox, pp. 302-8). But in any case his experience affected only the degree of concreteness with which he was able to work out his thought, not the direction or the structure of the thought itself.

of all the elements of his eventual solution of the difficulty can similarly be demonstrated in the fragments of that period—particularly in the 'Tübingen fragment' (*Religion ist eine*) and in *Es sollte eine schwere Aufgabe*; finally his secure hold on the clue that eventually led him to the solution can be proved by analysis of *Jedes Volk hat ihm eigene Gegenstände* itself.

The presence of his eventual solution in the manuscripts of 1793–4 is quite dramatically revealed by the remarkable aberrations which it has produced in the work of two students of the early manuscripts—one of whom has made what will certainly remain the most monumentally exhaustive analysis of them. Theodor Haering was so struck by the resemblance between the way in which the 'Zusatz des Göttlichen bei Jesus' is described in *Es sollte eine schwere Aufgabe* and the eventual analysis of the divinity of Christ in 'The Spirit of Christianity', that he could not really understand why Hegel wrote *The Life of Jesus* at all, and his interpretation of everything else that Hegel wrote in 1795 and 1796 was seriously warped.[1] While Sofia Vanni-Rovighi has even gone so far as to suggest, on the basis of an *obiter dictum* of Nohl himself about the resemblance between Hegel's handwriting in its 'first' and 'third' stages, that the 'Tübingen fragment' which Nohl places before *The Life of Jesus* really belongs after the 'Positivity' essay.[2]

Haering's blindness is illuminating, because it is an exact counterpart of Hegel's own. What Haering does *not* see was all that Hegel himself in 1794 could see. The 'Zusatz des Göttlichen

---

[1] Nohl, p. 57 (cf. also Nohl, p. 67 for the phrase 'personifiziertes Ideal' so much beloved of Haering); Haering, i. 173, and *passim*, i. 454 ff., i. 514 ff.

[2] 'Osservazioni sulla cronologia dei primi scritti di Hegel', *Il Pensiero*, 5, 1960, 157–75; compare Nohl's note on 'The Chronology of the Manuscripts' (page 402). Gisela Schüler has dealt faithfully with this suggestion in her much fuller account of the development of Hegel's handwriting and the chronology of his manuscripts (*Hegel-Studien*, ii. 111–59—see especially 139 n.). But I do not think any careful student of the available printed materials would agree with her that Professor Vanni-Rovighi could legitimately 'stand by this interpretation until a counter-proof is brought forward'. One has only to compare Roques's edition of the manuscripts with that of Nohl to recognize that anyone who could bring order out of such a chaos would not be likely to make such an error. In particular, anyone who could restore the revised version of 'The Spirit of Christianity' to intelligible sequence, as Nohl did, would not have overlooked the links that exist between it and the Tübingen fragment. Even one who has not seen the manuscripts themselves can fully share Miss Schüler's wonder over Nohl's 'Scharfsinn' and his 'sure eye for connections' (op. cit., p. 116).

bei Jesus' was for Hegel at that time only the halo of authority which—thanks be to Kant, Lessing and the other heroes of the Enlightenment!—had at last begun to fall 'from the heads of the oppressors and the gods of the earth'.[1] The resurrection of Jesus, his apotheosis as the Christ, is condemned by Hegel from various angles, but in very similar terms at the end of 1793 (*Christus hatte zwölf Apostel*), the end of 1794 (*Jetzt braucht die Menge*), and the beginning of 1796 (*Jedes Volk hat ihm eigene Gegenstände*).[2] As one who had believed from his youth up that 'every good has its bad side' Hegel had no difficulty in identifying the historical aspect of Christianity as its 'bad side'. But the 'good side' of Christianity—the rationality of its doctrines—had a 'bad side' all of its own in that it could not satisfy 'imagination and the heart'. It was quite some time before the young dialectician realized that the healing of this weakness could be achieved by converting the maxim of his schooldays and reading 'Every evil has its good side'. In several places in the early essays and notes, Hegel recognizes that the historical character of Christianity does in a way answer to the needs of the imagination, but he always remarks how inadequate it is for this purpose. It is because this point was made so trenchantly in his plan of 1794 (*Unter objektiver Religion*), that I said earlier that the check in the progress of his reflections is already there foreshadowed.[3] But he had already begun to find

---

[1] Letter 11 (to Schelling, 16 Apr. 1795) *Briefe*, i. 24; cf. the notes from Gibbon in *Unkunde der Geschichte* (Nohl, pp. 365–6).

[2] Nohl, p. 34; pp. 70–1; p. 226 (Knox, p. 160). In the last two cases the resurrection is not specifically mentioned, but the reference to the resurrected Christ seems to me to be quite clear.

[3] Nohl, p. 49, section zeta, subsection (*a*). On the good side: '(*a*) its practical doctrines are pure and have the advantage of being mostly exhibited in examples.' On the bad side: '(*β*) the historical truths on which it is founded—therein the miraculous is always subject to unbelief' and secondly it is 'not designed for the *Phantasie*—as with the Greeks—it is sad and melancholy—oriental, not native to our soil, it cannot be assimilated therewith'. (See the full translation in the Appendix to this volume, pp. 508–10 below.)

For the direct opposition of *Vernunft* and *historische Traditionen* (which rests ultimately on Hegel's rejection of Storr's doctrine of the miraculous) see *Unkunde der Geschichte*, Nohl, p. 365: 'It must seem incredible that the primacy of *Vernunft* should be so far misunderstood that historical traditions are placed beside it, yes even exalted above it.'

For critical comments on the imaginative aspect of Christianity, see: *Aber die Hauptmasse*, Nohl, p. 358; *Die Staatsverfassungen*, Nohl, p. 39; *Unkunde des Geschichte*, Nohl, pp. 363 and 364; and finally of course *Jedes Volk hat ihm eigene Gegenstände*, *passim* (Nohl, pp. 214–29; Knox, pp. 145–64). The first origin of Hegel's criticism in this respect was his early sense of the alienation of

his way out of the difficulty before he left Switzerland. In *Jedes Volk hat ihm eigene Gegenstände* (1797) he offers an interpretation of the miraculous element in the historical record of Christianity which meets the worst difficulty mentioned in his plan.[1] This clue alone would probably have sufficed in the end to bring him through his 'narrow strait', for by its aid he could bridge the gulf between the mythical mystery of Eleusis and the historical mystery of Easter. In fact he had also a second clue at his disposal, for he had rejected at the very beginning the Kantian opposition between reason and the emotions;[2] and as soon as he began to think of Christianity, not from the viewpoint of *Phantasie* but from that of *Herz*, he was bound to reflect that St. John does not only say that God is Reason ('In the beginning was the *Logos* . . . and the *Logos* was God') but also, even more explicitly, that 'God is Love'. Thus from the point of view of *Herz*, the 'sad and melancholy' character of Christianity with its 'heroes in suffering' (all of which is repellent to a healthy *Phantasie*) is quite rapidly and naturally transformable into a joyous sense of communion.

There is only one important respect in which Hegel's 'psychological crisis' may have contributed, and indeed probably did contribute, to the advance of his thought. His loneliness at Berne, his sense of the utter futility of his efforts, his doubting—perhaps— of his own powers, and—even more hypothetically—his feeling that he was sacrificing worldly happiness for a will-o-the-wisp, may very well have given him an insight into and a sympathy with the alienation of Jesus from the society of his time, which he (Hegel) certainly did not have when he wrote *Außer dem mundlichen Unterricht* and *Christus hatte zwölf Apostel* shortly after he arrived in Switzerland. In saying this I do not mean to suggest for a moment that Hegel's crisis was of such a magnitude as to be

the literate classes (and consequently of literary artists) from the mass of the people. In other words it antedates his critical concern with the religion of his own time altogether (see 'Über einige charakteristische Unterschiede der alten Dichter', *Dok.*, pp. 48–9).

[1] Nohl, p. 218 (Knox, pp. 150–1).

[2] See *Religion ist eine* (Nohl, p. 18); the analysis of love there given could hardly have been absent from Hegel's mind when he paraphrased John 13: 34–5 in *The Life of Jesus* (see Nohl, p. 125). The first hint of 'The Spirit of Christianity' can perhaps be found when he reaches John 15: 17 ('These things I *command* you, that ye love one another') and turns it into 'since now the spirit of love, the power that inspires [*begeistert*] you and me, is one and the same' (Nohl, p. 126).

directly comparable with the Agony in the Garden. Hölderlin, who would certainly have regarded a return to Tübingen as tantamount to crucifixion, would perhaps have considered such a comparison valid; and for someone like Hölderlin an experience of this sort really would have been a crisis of that order of magnitude. But for Hegel it was not. He simply needed to be in contact with others who shared his interests. The measure of his 'crisis' is that, whereas after fifteen months in Switzerland he wrote: 'I deeply long for a place—not in Tübingen' etc., after another nine months there his longing was great enough to make him consider even a place in Tübingen;[1] and though we may well be glad that he did not have to go back there, we can hardly doubt that, whatever Hölderlin may have thought, it would have been for Hegel a less 'unbearable trial' than remaining in isolation.[2] Hegel suffered certainly, and he had fits of black depression; but he was always, probably, as much the master of himself as any man can reasonably hope to be— a fact which Hölderlin recognized when he called him a *'ruhig Verstandesmensch'* and spoke of his 'ever cheerful attitude'.[3] It was just because feelings and emotions, spiritual experiences generally, never went to extremes or rose to the highest pitch of violence in Hegel's consciousness, that he was able to make them the object of rational observation and analysis. The sureness of his intuitive appreciation, even of the extremes of human experience, was a function not of direct acquaintance with these extremes, but of his capacity for imaginative empathy, which was greater perhaps than that of any other philosopher. This is just as true in respect of Hegel's analysis of suffering as it is in respect of the other human passions.

2. *The spirit of Judaism*

I do not quite know what evidence Knox is relying on when he says that 'during his first two years in "unhappy Frankfurt", in order to cure himself of melancholia, [Hegel] worked with all his energies

[1] Letter 6 (to Schelling, 24 Dec. 1794) *Briefe*, i. 11; the first that we hear of the Tübingen project is in Letter 15 (from Hölderlin, 25 Nov. 1795), *Briefe*, i. 34. But Hegel may have mentioned it as early as July: see p. 209 n. 2.

[2] 'Seriously, my dear fellow, you ought not so wantonly to put your spirit to such an unbearable trial', wrote Hölderlin in Oct. 1796, when he had found the post with the Gogels for Hegel; but he had earlier admitted that Renz would make good company at the *Repetententisch* at Tübingen (see *Briefe*, i. 34 and 42).

[3] Letter 136, line 42, *GSA*, vi. 236 (to Neuffer, 16 Feb. 1797); and Letter 128, lines 39–40, ibid., p. 222 (*Briefe*, i. 45).

at Greek literature and philosophy as well as at history and politics'.[1] It is true that some, perhaps most, of the 'fragments of historical studies' published by Rosenkranz probably belong to this period. But there is not really a lot, even in them, that can fairly be said to indicate a serious and continuous study of 'Greek literature and philosophy'—even if, as I expect Knox would wish, we count Thucydides in that category rather than under 'history and politics'.[2] Most of the manuscripts that can be firmly dated to 1797 and 1798 are concerned with the Judaic tradition from the Flood to the birth of Jesus. Plato's *Phaedrus* and Shakespeare's *Romeo and Juliet* certainly played a part in Hegel's reflections about love in this period.[3] But until he took up Kant's *Metaphysik der Sitten* in August 1798, I suspect that the Old Testament, Josephus, and Herder[4] occupied more of his attention than any works of

---

[1] 'Hegel's attitude to Kant's Ethics', *Kant-Studien*, 49 (1957-8), 73.

[2] Fragments 2, 3, 4, 5, 6, 7, 8, 9, 11, 13, 14, and 17 are concerned to a significant degree with classical themes (though I should say that the historical-political interest predominates over the literary-philosophical one). The concern with *Phantasie* which is evident in almost all of these fragments strengthens my conviction that they belong to the last year at Berne and the first year at Frankfurt. On the whole I am inclined to suspect that most of the more distinctively Hellenic fragments belong to the last summer in Berne (when Hegel wrote *Jedes Volk hat ihm eigene Gegenstände* and *Eleusis*) rather than to the first year in Frankfurt (where most of the datable manuscripts are concerned with the history of the Jews). It seems certain that Fragments 1 and 7 belong to Frankfurt; so I should guess do 13 and 17.

[3] The *Phaedrus* is quoted in *so wie mehrere Gattungen* (summer 1797) and *Romeo and Juliet* in *welchem Zwecke denn alles Übrige dient* (about Nov. 1797; revised a year or more later); see Nohl, pp. 378 and 380 (Knox, p. 307).

[4] Of all the major influences on the young Hegel, Herder's is the hardest to estimate reliably, but I suspect that it was great. From a remark of Hölderlin's we know that Hegel must have read some of Herder's work at Tübingen (Letter 9, 26 Jan. 1795, *Briefe*, i. 19). It may well be that they read *Gott* together in connection with their study of the *Pantheismusstreit*.

The influence of Herder's theory of culture upon Hegel's own study of the Old Testament is certified by what he says in *Jedes Volk hat ihm eigene Gegenstände* (Nohl, p. 218; Knox, p. 150). This only takes us back to 1796. But Hegel's remark in his first letter to Schelling about 'meeting you on your old track' shows that he was quite familiar with the latter's Master's Thesis (*De prima malorum humanorum origine*); and this essay would quite certainly have made him conscious of the relevance of Herder's works on the general philosophy of culture to his own concerns. I myself think that he needed no prompting in this respect even as early as 1793. I am strongly inclined to believe that his concept of a *Volk* and of a *Volksreligion* owes a great deal to Herder's *Ideen*, and that the essay *Religion ist eine* (the 'Tübingen fragment') is already a more or less conscious attempt to mediate the disagreement between Herder and Kant. Only a close comparison of all the relevant texts (and a conscientious considera- tion of the equally plausible parallels that can be drawn with *alternative* sources)

literature or philosophy in the ordinary sense, either classical or modern.

The earliest of Hegel's sketches of Jewish history, *Die Geschichte der Juden lehrt*, may quite possibly have been written in his last month or two at Berne. It is primarily concerned with the condition and attitude of the Jewish people at the time of the Exodus, and already expounds the conception of Moses and the Exodus which Hegel set forth in the final version of his essay on 'The Spirit of Judaism' about two years later (*Abraham in Chaldäa geboren hatte schon*).[1] In his subsequent sketches Abraham gradually came to occupy a key position comparable to that of Moses. Hegel tried for a time to push his inquiry back to the Flood, but eventually decided that the true beginning of Jewish history was to be found in the story of Abraham:

With Abraham, the true progenitor of the Jews, the history of this people begins, i.e. his spirit is the unity, the soul that governs the whole fate of his posterity; it appears in a different guise after every battle against different forces, or whenever it has defiled itself by adopting an alien nature [*Wesen*] after giving way to force or to temptation. Thus it appears in a distinct form of the appeal to arms and conflict, or of the way in which it endures the fetters of the stronger; this form is called 'fate'.[2]

We meet here for the first time (somewhere around August 1798) the conjunction of 'spirit' and 'fate' which was crucial for the development of Hegel's thought in the Frankfurt period. In order to understand properly both the preliminary notes and drafts from which this conjunction gradually emerged and the great essay on 'The Spirit of Christianity' for which it provided the basis, we

offers any prospect of confirmation (or the reverse) here; and quite probably we must resign ourselves, in the end, to uncertainty and ignorance. Herder's own views are capable of a considerable variety of interpretations, so the initial belief of the investigator is bound to prejudice any inquiry into his influence on Hegel.

[1] Nohl, pp. 370–1 and 245–60 (Knox, pp. 185–205). For the dating, cf. Gisela Schüler, *Hegel-Studien*, ii. 146. Unambiguous reference to the final version (itself a revision of a first draft) is made difficult by the fact that between *Die Geschichte der Juden lehrt* and it lie two short sketches which both begin *Abraham in Chaldäa*—Nohl prints these as 'Entwurf II' and 'Entwurf IV', so I shall refer to them as *II. Abraham in Chaldäa* and *IV. Abraham in Chaldäa* respectively, and to the final version as *Abraham in Chaldäa geboren hatte schon*.

[2] *Mit Abraham dem wahren Stammvater*, Nohl, p. 243 (Knox, p. 182). On the relation of this piece to Hegel's essays on 'the Spirit of Judaism' and 'the Spirit of Christianity' see p. 280 n. 3, p. 330 n. 2, and p. 332 n. 2, below.

must get a firm grip on the underlying theory of human culture, which Hegel never articulated fully anywhere,[1] but which can be reconstructed from his hints and *obiter dicta* if we consider his development in a sufficiently broad perspective.

In the so-called 'Tübingen fragment' the concept of 'spirit', as the operative form in which a community is conscious of its unity, is already central. But in that essay Hegel was concerned about the Greek 'spirit' as an achieved ideal. We can see that a process of achievement was involved, and we know that the hero of this process was Theseus, who reconciled a number of *natural* communities (tribal or blood-clans) into a *city*. But Hegel does not dwell on this process, probably because he could not yet see any obvious lessons to be learned from it for the reintegration of life in his own society, which was his ultimate goal.

The concept of 'fate' also appears in the Tübingen fragment. But it is not a 'fate' that belongs to the Greek spirit or to any other determinate spirit; it is simply the impersonal might before which all things mortal and immortal must yield. *This* power, against which not even the Gods can contend, is the natural necessity that is the correlate of rational freedom generally, not the 'fate' which is the correlate of 'spirit' in the Frankfurt manuscripts.

However, the Greek spirit as Hegel presents it to us in the 'Tübingen fragment' was certainly distinguished by its particular attitude towards this *absolute* fate. The Greek never conceived of the possibility of a 'mastery of fate'. He accepted fate and was reconciled with it as far as possible. This was the right or rational attitude. *Positive* religion, the religion of an absolute Lord, who was master of all things, even of *Ananke*, seeks to justify itself by making moral claims on behalf of reason against the power of fate. But the justification is spurious because the demands are illegitimate.

When Hegel's reflections reached this point—in the fragment *Ein positiver Glauben* written at the end of 1795—he was in a position to say, as soon as he turned his mind to the problem, that the essential difference between the spirit of the Hellenes and that of the Jews was expressed in the contrasting attitudes to the might of nature revealed in their respective myths about the Flood. But he could not yet have said why the history of the Jews begins with Abraham rather than with Noah, or the history of the Greeks with

---

[1] Unless, perhaps, he did so in the lost manuscript of which the so-called *Systemfragment* of 1800 is all that remains to us. (See further pp. 379–82 below.)

Theseus and Lycurgus rather than with Deucalion. We have, so far, found reason to speak of distinctive attitudes to fate, but not of distinct fates. We have identified, perhaps, the beginning of universal history in the breach of the 'State of nature' produced by some cataclysmic manifestation of the might of nature herself,[1] but not the beginning of any particular history.

We can regard the original breach with the state of nature as a 'beginning of history' in some sense, because although the breach is, *ex hypothesi*, quite involuntary, the attitude that men adopt towards it is not. But the genuine spiritual self-awareness of a 'people' (*Volk*) does not begin with their spontaneous reaction to this breach. It begins only when they deliberately adopt towards other *peoples* the attitude which they have reactively adopted towards the revealed might of universal fate. Thus the involuntary breach (which usually produces what Hegel calls a state of 'need' (*Not*)) generates the possibility of a voluntary breach (which is what Hegel generally uses the word *Trennung* to refer to); and the character and manner of that voluntary breach, if it occurs, determines a 'fate' that is peculiar to the spirit that makes the breach.

'Fate' in this new sense is quite distinct from the universal might of fate over all things. Abraham made explicit in history the breach between God and Nature which is implicit in the myth of Noah, and basic to faith in God's promise that mankind would not again be threatened with extinction by natural catastrophe. Through Abraham's conscious decision the people of the promise were separated from all others, as the Lord of creation is separated from His creatures. In an analogous way the work of Theseus expressed historically the religious attitude symbolized by that confident trust in Mother Earth that is symbolically represented in the myth of Deucalion and Pyrrha.

'Fate' now—the fate that arises in the context of a voluntary

[1] Hegel is very shy about the aboriginal state that exists before the primitive breach that makes men aware of *Not*. The analogy of the Garden of Eden story with Greek myths of the Golden Age and with Rousseau's 'State of Nature' is obvious enough. In *Mit Abraham dem wahren Stammvater* (Nohl, pp. 243–4, Knox, p. 182) Hegel speaks of the 'loss of the state of nature' as if it was distinct from the cataclysmic breach with which history begins. But in another place he acknowledges that this breach need not be cataclysmic (see the remark about the ancient Germans in *Joseph. jüd. Alterth*, Nohl, p. 368). In that case I do not see how we can distinguish it from 'the loss of the state of nature'. (See further, p. 281 n. 4 below.)

Trennung between man and his fellows, and hence within human nature itself—is something very different from the almighty impersonal power of *Ananke* that is acknowledged in Greek religion. It is the 'Nemesis' of Greek drama; it is 'poetic justice'.[1] The action of fate is 'poetic' because the individual or community that is subject to it is also the agent who brings it about; and 'just' because it is retribution exacted for the violence done to human nature in its integrity. This Fate always appears as *involuntary*, because the agent is not conscious of doing violence to himself. He does conscious violence only to others, or to some aspect of his own being which he does not regard as part of his true nature, but as evil or alien. But it is always a voluntary rupture within the self that causes this fate to arise, and when the rupture is voluntarily healed, the fate disappears or at least ceases to appear as hostile.

We can see how gradual the full emergence of the doctrine of 'spirit' and 'fate' was, if we compare Hegel's first sketches and notes about Judaism with his mature treatment of the same topics a year or so later. As we have said, the earliest sketch already expresses his considered view of Moses and the Exodus. But he does not yet think of the fate of the Jews as something that they made for themselves. He insists rather that their political development was *not* spontaneous, or independent of the influence of other nations, and indeed it was not voluntary at all. The transition from a pastoral patriarchal society to a political constitution (*vom Hirtenleben zum Staate*) was forced on them by the domination of the Egyptians. They were on the whole content that this should be so, and Moses (who had been educated by the Egyptian priests in isolation from his people, and so felt the inadequacy of this slavish mode of existence) could only rouse in them a vague aspiration toward the free life of their forefathers. They were passively willing to believe in his divine mission, and through this belief, he was able to bring about the Exodus. But he could not bring them to an imaginative grasp of his own vision of free

[1] 'Nemesis' appears in the Tübingen fragment as a form of fate which is clearly distinguished as *moral* rather than a *natural* necessity. It is clear enough, I think, that Hegel's developed concept of *Schicksal* arose from the application to the Jewish tradition of the idea of Nemesis as 'law of moral equilibrium' (Nohl, pp. 25–6; see p. 504 below) which he got from Sophocles. But there is no sign that this development had begun at Tübingen. Of the two occurrences of *Schicksal* that I have noted in *Religion ist eine*, one seems to refer primarily to *natural* necessity, though it may very probably be meant to cover Nemesis as well (Nohl, p. 29; see p. 507 below. See also Nohl, p. 6; p. 484 below).

political existence; and because of this failure they bore the sufferings of the forty years in the wilderness very grudgingly and with frequent backsliding. This fact dictated the positive, authoritarian character of much of the Mosaic Law. In place of the genuine republican equality of free citizens, the Jews enjoyed an 'equality of insignificance'.[1] Only with the establishment of the monarchy did they come to recognize, through the explicit establishment of inequality, that individual men could really count for something.

In his final account of the bondage of Israel in Egypt, on the other hand (*Abraham in Chaldäa geboren hatte schon*), Hegel treats Joseph as the architect of the Egyptian constitution under which the Jews became for the first time a settled nation. Thus their transition *vom Hirtenleben zum Staate* is shown up as a spontaneous or natural expression of their native genius, even though it was still something passively endured by the people as a whole; for Joseph's work as a statesman expressed the Judaic conception of the relation between 'the Lord' and his 'servants'.[2] The account of Moses' work is in all essentials unchanged.[3]

The period of Israel's existence as an independent nation, before and after the Babylonian captivity, receives only the most cursory notice, either in Hegel's preparatory sketches or in the final essay. As we have just noted, Hegel took the establishment of the monarchy to be the only possible means by which the Jews could come to an appreciation of true human dignity and freedom. The work of the prophets during and after the Captivity in Babylon he alludes to only indirectly in his first sketch, and all that is added in his later essay is an explanation of why he takes it to be irrelevant to the 'fate' of the Jews, though relevant to the birth of Christianity. This explanation, however, illustrates once more how greatly the perspective has changed in the final account:

Inspired men [*Begeisterte*] had tried from time to time to cleave to

---

[1] Nohl, p. 370; cf. *Abraham in Chaldäa geboren hatte schon*, Nohl, p. 255 (Knox, p. 198).

[2] Nohl, p. 248 (Knox, pp. 188–9).

[3] In the final version Hegel emphasizes Moses' use of conjuring and wonderworking as a means of maintaining his authority (Nohl, p. 249; Knox, pp. 180–90). He first remarked on this in the unpublished part of *Fortschreiten der Gesetzgebung* (about a year after his initial sketch). Another point that seems to be quite new in the final version is the comparison of the 'Spoiling of the Egyptians' to the behaviour of the robber bands during the plague of 1720 at Marseilles—on the origin and import of this comparison see D'Hondt, pp. 184–203.

the old genius of their nation and to revivify it in its death throes; but when the genius of a nation has fled, inspiration cannot conjure it back, it cannot turn away the fate of a people by its spell, though it may call forth a new spirit from the depths of life if it be pure and living. But the Jewish prophets kindled their flame from the torch of a flagging daemon; they tried to restore its old vigour, and, by destroying the many-sided interests of the time, its old dread sublime unity. Thus they could become only cold fanatics, circumscribed and ineffective when they were involved in policies and statecraft; they could only bring back the memory of bygone ages, and thereby add to the confusion of the present, without resurrecting the past. The mixture of passions could never again turn into uniform passivity; on the contrary, arising from passive hearts they were bound to rage all the more terribly.[1]

In the first sketch the prophets were not thus saddled with partial responsibility for the civil strife and patriotic wars of the Maccabees, and the fanaticism of the Jews in defence of their religion was blamed at least partly on the intolerance of their 'masters or enemies'. In the final version the view that fanaticism was a late development is abandoned, and the story of the vengeance of the sons of Jacob for the ravishing of their sister Dinah is cited as evidence of the primitive Jewish hostility to life. Hostility to life, first in the form of outward aggression and later, when their independence is taken from them, in the form of internal faction and sectarianism, was the only way in which the conscious-ness of freedom, once it had been awakened, could be harmonized with the Jewish sense of passive belonging to their God. The whole 'fate' of the Jewish nation as Hegel analyses it in the final version is contained in this destructive tension.

This tension did not become actively destructive, it did not reveal its whole nature, until the twelve tribes began to come into close contact with other settled nations. But Hegel finds the explanation for the tension, and hence for the subsequent fate of the children of Abraham, in the story of Abraham himself. Abraham represents the pure 'spirit' of the Jewish people, while the history of the twelve tribes is the 'fate' of that spirit when it seeks to express itself in the world, a fate which is 'inevitable' in the sense of being self-wrought, or explicable directly by examination of the contrast between the goal which Abraham set for his own life and the natural tendencies or propensities of human life itself.

[1] Nohl, p. 259 (Knox, p. 203).

Let us now observe just how Hegel reached this conclusion. Beginning, as he did, with the work of Moses, it was not easy for him at first to see how the 'fate' of the Jews could be self-wrought in any but a negative sense (i.e. they voluntarily *accepted* the sufferings and trials that befell them as sent by God). In this perspective their backsliding appeared only as a form of passivity, and their zeal as a late (and fundamentally irrelevant) development. But as he thought about Abraham, Isaac, and Jacob Hegel realized more and more how complex the 'spirit' behind the passivity of the Jews was, how little of it could be captured by an intellectual analysis of what he would have called their 'objective theology'. This growing awareness explains why his reflections—which ranged over the whole tradition from Noah to Joseph and his brethren—focused quite soon upon the figure of Abraham, though they reached their final form only after much drafting and re-drafting.[1]

The way in which Hegel's thoughts ranged before he had definitely located the beginning of Jewish history, is evidenced by the first fragment that can be definitely assigned to the Frankfurt period. This is a sheet of notes (*Joseph. jüd. Alterth.*) about the patriarchal tradition, which were worked up in subsequent sketches. The first notes are about Nimrod, the tower of Babel, and the 'breach with Nature' created by the Flood. Then follows a paragraph about the blessing that Isaac mistakenly bestowed on Jacob, and finally some reflections about Moses and Abraham—not, as Nohl reports, about Abraham alone—which were incorporated almost verbatim in later sketches.[2]

---

[1] Unluckily for us Nohl felt that two of Hegel's four meditations upon Abraham (prior to his final statement in *Abraham in Chaldäa geboren hatte schon*) could be omitted as repetitive. He eliminated the first of the four (contained in *Joseph. jüd. Alterth.*, Nohl, p. 368, spring 1797) and the fourth (*Zu Abrahams Zeiten* which preceded the notes *Fortschreiten der Gesetzgebung* on the same sheet—written in spring 1798?). The two he has given us both begin with the same sentence: *II. Abraham in Chaldäa* (Nohl, pp. 368–70) was written immediately after the notes *Joseph. jüd. Alterth.*, and *IV. Abraham in Chaldäa* (Nohl, pp. 371–3) a few months later; Miss Schüler dates it 'before July 1797'.

[2] Nohl, p. 368. Nohl did not print the reflections on Nimrod, or those on Moses and Abraham. He quotes only a single sentence: 'The Spirit of the Greeks is beauty; the spirit of the Orientals sublimity and greatness'. This occurs as an isolated reflection after two paragraphs about Moses (mostly repeated in Nohl, p. 249, Knox, pp. 189–90), and before the concluding paragraph on Abraham. No doubt this is the reason for Nohl's oversight when he says 'what follows about Abraham is omitted'.

The most interesting point in Hegel's first notes on the 'breach with nature' is his aside about the Germans. A breach (*Entzweiung*) is necessary, he claims, if human political existence is to begin, but it may come about in a variety of ways. For the Israelites it resulted from the Flood, and for the ancient Germans 'perhaps by acquaintance with the products of a milder climate'. The effect of two such disparate events would obviously be very different; and since the intervention of another human cultural group would almost certainly be involved in the second case, the two events cannot properly be assimilated to one another in Hegel's own conceptual scheme as they are here. But the German tribes are very much in Hegel's mind, because he is always thinking of the 'application' of his results; and he must have felt that the differences were of less practical importance than the analogy.

Everything that Hegel noted about Nimrod and the tower of Babel in the spring of 1797, he incorporated into *Mit Abraham dem wahren Stammvater* which he wrote about eighteen months later. But he built his notes into the larger structure of a contrast between Nimrod, Noah, and Deucalion and Pyrrha. Nimrod responded to the hostility of Nature, as revealed in the Flood, by seeking to establish *human* mastery over Nature. He sought the 'supreme unity of mastery' in something *actual*. Noah on the other hand found the 'supreme unity of mastery' in something that he conceived in his own mind—his God. Noah's God granted to him a legal authority over the animal creation, saving only the life principle itself (contained in the blood which Noah was forbidden to eat). This was the beginning of the legal covenant relationship to God and the world, which was the essential expression of the Jewish spirit.[1] Nimrod on the other hand defied Nature and its Lord, becoming a hunter and seeking to build the Tower of Babel as a defence against all natural perils. But Nimrod's call to men to trust in their own strength and assert a *de facto* mastery of their world only issued in the founding of a despotism. In the Greek myth on the other hand the idea of mastery simply does not occur. Deucalion and Pyrrha are reconciled with nature after the flood. They 'made a peace of love, were the progenitors of more beautiful

---

[1] Cf. the note in *Fortschreiten der Gesetzgebung* (early 1798 and hence intermediate between *Joseph. jüd. Alterth.* and *Mit Abraham dem wahren Stammvater*), Nohl, p. 373.

nations, and made their age the mother of a new-born nature which maintained its bloom of youth'.[1]

Both the Judaic and the Greek myth are regarded by Hegel as 'different ways of returning from the barbarism [*Roheit*] which followed the loss of the state of nature to the union [*Vereinigung*] which had been destroyed'.[2] We shall have to discuss the meaning of the term *Vereinigung* later. For the moment I simply want to point out that in this sentence Hegel has, by implication, pushed his inquiry back to the very beginnings of the Hebraic tradition, and is putting the story of the Garden of Eden alongside the Greek myths of the Golden Age. But, as he says in this same place, 'only a few dim traces of this important period have been preserved for us'. By the time he wrote *Mit Abraham dem wahren Stammvater* he had decided, as the opening sentence tells us, that the real beginning of Jewish history was with Abraham. His object in this piece was to pull together his reflections upon Jewish prehistory; but he seems to have decided after trying it that this was not the right approach to his problem. All available indications point to the conclusion that he was minded, in the end, to set aside his reflections on the first eleven chapters of Genesis altogether.[3]

Next in order after Nimrod in his first sheet of notes, Hegel offers us a reflection upon the blessing which Isaac mistakenly bestowed on Jacob. He does not seem to have made use of this

---

[1] Nohl, pp. 244–5 (Knox, pp. 182–4). We may note that Noah and Nimrod seem to prefigure the Church and the Empire respectively; but it is not clear that Hegel meant to draw this parallel.

[2] Nohl, p. 243 (Knox, p. 182).

[3] The fragment *Mit Abraham, dem wahren Stammvater* (Nohl, pp. 243–5) is printed by Nohl as if *Abraham in Chaldäa geboren hatte schon* were a direct continuation of it. But it is not in fact part of the continuous manuscript, and was certainly never included by Hegel in his revision of it. This is shown by Hegel's note about the length of his continuous manuscript and by the fact that there is another (unpublished) sketch—*Die schönen ihrer Natur nach*—on the last page of the sheet that contains *Mit Abraham dem wahren Stammvater*. (Nohl sought to evade the former difficulty through the hypothesis that *Mit Abraham dem wahren Stammvater* was written later than the continuous manuscript. But in the light of Miss Schüler's re-examination of the handwriting it seems that we can safely reject this suggestion. The piece was almost certainly written a few months earlier (Schüler, p. 151). That Hegel intended at the time of writing it to incorporate it in a continuous study of the development of Jewish religious law and custom is fairly clearly indicated by the sheet of notes on the topic written shortly before it (*Fortschreiten der Gesetzgebung*, partially published as 'Entwurf V' in Nohl, pp. 373–4. But those notes also reveal the difficulties involved in this plan.)

subsequently,[1] but it is interesting because it reveals what an enormous change of perspective is involved when we turn from the requirements of *Vernunft* to those of *Phantasie*. It must seem strange, Hegel says, that anyone could think of a blessing or a curse as irrevocable, since blessing and cursing are essentially linked with subjective feelings, and are consciously voluntary acts. From the point of view of *Vernunft*, therefore, they can have no validity as mere outward forms. But the story of how Jacob obtained the blessing reveals 'the sublimity [*das Höhe*] of a purely subjective thing'. It is clear that Hegel has fastened on this treating of the verbal act as inviolable as a typical expression of the legalistic spirit of the Jews. Noah's God (and Abraham's) as Hegel later describes him is similarly only 'an ideal produced by thought and made into an existing object'.[2] Already we can see why Hegel's reflections on the history of the Jews went hand in hand with further meditation about the nature of God in positive religion generally.

As we have already said, the final paragraphs of this sheet of notes were incorporated almost *verbatim* in Hegel's later sketches. The remarks about Abraham in particular were repeated in the immediately following sketch *II. Abraham in Chaldäa*[3] (spring 1797), to which we shall now turn.

Abraham grew up, says Hegel, in a state of undisturbed peace with nature, symbolized by his worship of the nature gods of his own people; but he ruptured this stable relation by his own choice, and became a wanderer, first in the plains of Mesopotamia and then in Canaan.[4] He wanted to have no ties. He was the supreme

---

[1] A reference back to it in *Zu Abrahams Zeiten* shows that Hegel did at least consider making some use of it at one point subsequently.

[2] Nohl, p. 244 (Knox, p. 183), for the God of Noah; the point is also made specifically about Abraham's God in *Zu Abrahams Zeiten* (which Nohl did not print). [3] Nohl, pp. 368–70.

[4] It is obvious that Hegel would have found it difficult to reconcile this account of Abraham's rupture with nature with his interpretation of the Flood as an *involuntary* rupture which determined the form of the Jewish state. Noah is a prototype of Moses, but Abraham, who stands between them in the tradition, is logically prior to them both. This becomes apparent when Hegel declares that Abraham's original stable relation to nature was one of enjoyment, and that when he ruptured that relation by his own act, he only changed the form of the enjoyment. This point—which becomes explicit only at the end of *II. Abraham in Chaldäa*—is introduced at the beginning of *IV. Abraham in Chaldäa*; and that is where we find it again in the final version *Abraham in Chaldäa geboren hatte schon* (Nohl, pp. 245–6; Knox, p. 185). The Biblical authority for Hegel's account is Joshua 24: 2–3. (On the comparative situations of Noah and Abraham see further, p. 283 n. 1 below.)

egoist, for whom his own existence was the ultimate concern. His God was for him not a friend bringing gifts (like the Greek gods), but the protector and guarantor of his existence. The promise of progeny was part of that existence, but Abraham had none the less to be sure of his own ability to sacrifice Isaac in order to establish his fidelity to his ideal of freedom from all the bonds of natural existence and natural love.

The crucial difference between Abraham and his descendants is that for Abraham nothing appeared as *fate*. He was at one with his God, so that in everything that happened, whether joyful or painful, he saw the hand of Providence. The division (*Trennung*) in his consciousness was between the natural world (which he had left behind) on the one side, and himself and his God on the other. Both the word *Trennung* and its correlate *Vereinigung* already appear in Hegel's first continuous draft.[1] In the second draft Abraham's God is simply 'the Union (*Vereinigung*) of all that he did, or was, or enjoyed, envisaged as one great whole or object'.[2] By thus projecting (to use the Freudian term) the image of his own happiness into an external being Abraham was able to rupture all of his natural links with the world without giving up his enjoyment of it. The world owed him a happy existence, but he owed it nothing and he was resolved never to owe it anything. In his relations with outsiders he was studiously careful to pay his debts, and he avoided all permanent connections of feeling or of blood.[3]

---

[1] The first occurrence of *Vereinigung* is interesting: 'His [Abraham's] *Einheit* was security, his manifold was the circumstances conflicting with it, his Supreme [Being or Value] the *Vereinigung* of both. The *Trennung* had not yet become so complete in him as to make him set himself and *Schicksal* in opposition to one another; the particular *Vereinigungen* that the Greeks had the courage to make with fate were their Gods' (*II. Abraham in Chaldäa*, Nohl, p. 369). It is not quite clear here whether *Schicksal* is being used in the new sense. But it seems certain that the new concept is at least on the point of birth, and probable that it is not yet quite born (by spring 1797).

[2] *IV. Abraham in Chaldäa*, Nohl, p. 371. In the final version Hegel employs the Kantian term *Ideal* for Abraham's God. The passage cited from Kant by Knox (p. 187 n.) highlights the reason behind this transition very neatly. Abraham's God is his life *idealized*.

[3] Nohl, pp. 246–7 (Knox, pp. 186–7). In the first draft of *Abraham in Chaldäa geboren hatte schon* Hegel inserted here a reference to the driving forth of Hagar and Ishmael. But in the revision he cancelled it, probably because it was a blemish upon the *Einheit* which he wanted Abraham to represent. He wished to make the contrast between Abraham's untroubled isolation and the 'satanic atrocity' of the sons of Jacob as sharp as possible. (He does however refer to the story of how Abraham smote the five kings in order to rescue his brother Lot: Genesis 14: 13–16.)

In place of union with nature he could claim union with nature's Lord.

But his descendants served the Lord without enjoying an equal certainty of their union with him. They felt the pressure of natural necessity, and they had to obey God's law—neither of which weighed upon Abraham.[1] As they grew in numbers, they had to serve God with whole heart as individuals, but they could only enjoy his favour as a group, and the needs of the group became more various. Thus the *Trennung* with nature became for the children of Abraham what it had never been in Abraham's simple existence as a wandering stranger, a barrier to enjoyment. For the first time they became subject to fate. Joseph's brothers cast him into the pit, and avenged 'with satanic atrocity' the violation of their sister Dinah; the recompense of marriage offered by Shechem would, of course, have involved the re-establishment of the most fundamental of those natural ties that Abraham had broken. These two examples show forth the need of the children of Abraham for laws to regulate their relations both with one another and with other peoples. Thus, although the acceptance of a settled abode was contrary to the spirit of the herdsman Jacob, the subjection of his sons to Pharaoh in Egypt was unavoidable;[2] and by reorganizing Egypt as an absolute despotism in which Pharaoh played the role of Abraham's God, Joseph made the state of political subjection acceptable to them.[3]

[1] The point about Abraham not being under the pressure of natural necessity is made most explicitly in the passage which Nohl omits from *IV. Abraham in Chaldäa* because it is largely repeated in *Abraham in Chaldäa geboren hatte schon:* cf. Nohl, pp. 371 and 246 (Knox, pp. 185–6).

We have here at least part of the explanation of the reciprocal relation between *Trennung* and *Not* established in *Fortschreiten der Gesetzgebung* (Nohl, p. 373). The more one is able to break natural ties the less one is subject to the pressure of natural necessity; and where one is not under this pressure there is no need for divine prohibition. Thus Noah, who is under the most violent pressure of need, receives laws from God. Moses receives more laws. But Abraham does not need them. He lives a simple life in virtual isolation against a relatively stable natural background. The development of culture (as Hegel goes on to notice in the same place) disturbs the simple reciprocal relation that he lays down.

[2] Jacob like Abraham is the patriarch of a single tribe of wanderers. But in the history of his sons we behold the breach of one tribe into twelve. This is the point at which the spirit of Judaism brings its own fate upon itself; and on the other hand, the salvation of the Greek spirit from fate is first revealed when Theseus reconciles the warring tribes of Attica without recourse to despotic authority or enslavement.

[3] The general point about the difference between God's relation to Abraham as an individual and his relation to Abraham's descendants as a group is made in

The ambiguity of the terms *Trennung* and *Vereinigung* which seem to refer sometimes to man's relations to God, sometimes to the satisfaction of his natural desires, and sometimes to both together, has seriously impeded the understanding of Hegel's text. The important thing to realize is that where the *Trennung* between man and nature is consciously voluntary and absolute, there is no *Trennung* between man and God, and hence no *actual* sacrifice of material happiness. But wherever the *Trennung* between man and nature appears as involuntary and burdensome, a *Trennung* between man and God appears, in the shape of the commandment of the Lord, and the worshipper himself is threatened by God's jealous wrath. Moses, like Abraham, felt no barrier between himself and God. But he could not raise the enslaved Jews to the sense of a *Vereinigung* with God. So he had first to convince them by signs and wonders that he was sent from God, and then to give them the law and threaten them with God's wrath. The religion of Abraham was the faith of a happy or fortunate people, the religion of Moses is the religion of an unhappy, unfortunate one. The Jews who trembled before the might of Pharaoh, and groaned over the hardships of life in the wilderness, could be aware of God only as an awful commanding and punishing presence. Thus Mosaic Judaism is the perfect type of a positive religion in which every aspect of life is directly subjected to the authoritative command of God.[1]

Abraham's original covenant with God expresses the spirit of Judaism; in the law of Moses we are presented with its fate. Everything that happens to the Jews thereafter is a 'consequence or development' of that fate, says Hegel in his final version.

IV. Abraham in Chaldäa (Nohl, p. 372). The detailed development is all given in *Abraham in Chaldäa hatte schon* (Nohl, p. 248; Knox, pp. 188–9) except for the mention of Joseph's being cast into the pit, which is my own addition.

[1] *IV. Abraham in Chaldäa* (Nohl, p. 372). Hegel here dissents explicitly from Mendelssohn's view that Judaism is not a positive religion because moral principles are not transformed into authoritative commands in it. Mendelssohn distinguishes between the (moral) Jewish *religion* and the Judaic *Law* which applied only to Israel as a political community. Hegel had been pondering on this distinction—with evident scepticism—since 1793 (see *Inwiefern ist Religion*, Nohl, p. 356). See further Nohl, pp. 253–4 (Knox, pp. 195–6).

The analysis of Mosaic religion here given is based on *IV. Abraham in Chaldäa* (Nohl, p. 372), *Zu Abrahams Zeiten, Fortschreiten der Gesetzgebung* (Nohl, pp. 373–4), and *Abraham in Chaldäa hatte schon* (Nohl, pp. 249–56; Knox, 189–99). Since this last is readily available in English, I have passed over the mass of illustrative detail and elaboration which it contains.

Initially, as we saw earlier, he held that the establishment of the monarchy was an event of some considerable significance; and, as we have already remarked, he repeats in his final account more or less everything about the later history of Israel that was continued in his earliest sketch; he even elaborates upon it somewhat.[1] But when it is all placed in the context of his final discussion it sinks into relative insignificance. The successors of Moses and Aaron in Hegel's developed vision are not the kings but the priests. Israel is not so much a monarchy as a theocratic tyranny. Hegel spares an unkind word for the 'very oppressive glory' of Solomon;[2] but it was the hierarchy of the sons of Levi that maintained the unity of the people through all their misfortunes. The high priests, the Pharisees, and the Sadducees were the direct heirs of Moses, and even in his preliminary sketches (after the first) Hegel tends to move directly from Moses to them.[3] We have already quoted what he says about the prophetic tradition; we are now in a position to identify the 'flagging daemon' that the prophets sought to revive as the simple life of the wandering herdsmen Abraham, Isaac, and Jacob. It was Hegel's view that Abraham's decision in favour of a life of this sort was a regressive or reactionary one in the first place.[4] To revive it in the circumstances of a settled community was quite impossible. But from this hopeless endeavour the Messianic hope itself was born (and hence ultimately the new spirit of Christianity). Hegel regarded the Essenes and John the Baptist as the first stirrings of the new spirit that was born with Jesus:

> In a period of this sort, when upon one who thirsts after inward life (with the objects around him he cannot be united, he has to be a slave to them and live in contradiction with the better part of himself, he is treated by them only as an enemy, and he treats them in the same

[1] One of the intervening drafts contains a point that is not brought out again in the final version. In *Zu Abrahams Zeiten* Hegel sums up the history of the Jewish nation after Moses as an alternation of foreign slavery and native independence, and remarks that in the latter state the Jews were 'either disunited among themselves or in prosperity they served alien Gods; prosperity [*das Glück*] silenced hatred and union with other peoples resulted. These unions appeared as Gods.'

[2] Nohl, p. 258 bottom; Knox, p. 202.

[3] Cf. *IV. Abraham in Chaldäa* (Nohl, pp. 372–3).

[4] *Zu Abrahams Zeiten* begins by suggesting that even in Abraham's time the adoption of a nomadic existence was a reactionary or regressive move in a world where there was no longer any place for it.

way—), when upon one who seeks something better in which he might live, a cold privileged dead command is laid, and he is told moreover 'This is life itself'. In a period of this sort the Essenes, or a man like John or Jesus, brought life to birth in themselves and rose up in battle against the eternally dead.[1]

Abraham's spirit was the spirit of enjoyment, of mastery, and of independence; the fate of his people was to become slaves both of their law and of the world that Abraham left behind him—to become persecuted, needy, and despised. Throughout his final connected account Hegel draws contrasts and parallels with the Greeks: Abraham's departure from his homeland is contrasted with Greek colonization myths, and the wrath of Jehovah is compared with the petrifying power of Medusa; the secret emptiness of the Holy of Holies is contrasted with the shared experience of the Eleusinian mysteries; the property regulations of Moses are compared with those of Solon and Lycurgus, and the civic equality of the Greeks is contrasted with the equal serfdom of the Jews.[2] But for the Jewish fate the best parallel he can find is not a Greek tragedy but a modern one: 'The fate of the Jewish people is the fate of Macbeth who stepped out of nature itself, clung to alien beings [*Wesen*], and so in their service had to trample and slay everything holy in human nature, had at last to be forsaken by his gods (for they were objects and he their slave) and be dashed to pieces on his faith itself.'[3]

[1] *Die Geschichte der Juden lehrt* (Nohl, p. 371); compare the remark about the Essenes at the end of *Abraham in Chaldäa geboren hatte schon* (Nohl, pp. 259–60; Knox, pp. 203–4) and the opening of the revised version of 'The Spirit of Christianity' (*Jesus trat nicht lange*, Nohl, p. 261; Knox, pp. 205–6). It may perhaps be worth pointing out that all of these passages written between the end of 1796 and the end of 1799 are only echoing a passage in the 'Positivity' essay that was probably written in Aug. or Sept. 1795 (Nohl, p. 153; Knox, p. 69).

[2] Nohl, pp. 246, 248, 251, 254, 255 (Knox, pp. 185, 188, 193, 197, 198). Sometimes the contrast or comparison is obvious but tacit, as, for instance, in the comment about Abraham's attitude to the groves where he sometimes encountered his God (Nohl, p. 246; Knox, p. 186). (Hegel's use of the 'sacred grove' as a symbol of Greece does not derive from Hölderlin's poetry as Peperzak seems to think (p. 138 n. 3); both Hegel and Hölderlin got it from Klopstock's ode 'Der Hügel und der Hain'. No doubt Klopstock's contrast is in Hegel's mind here.)

Another of these tacit examples is the ironic contrast between the 'truth' of Hebrew monotheism and the 'beauty' of Greek polytheism (which is not directly mentioned): Nohl, pp. 253–4 (Knox, pp. 195–6).

[3] Nohl, p. 260 (Knox, pp. 204–5). There is of course an implicit Greek parallel here too, since Macbeth's 'weird sisters' are fairly obviously the three Fates.

3. *Authority and love*

As Hegel studied Josephus and the five books of Moses his thoughts recurred continually to the fundamental contrast between an objective 'positive' religious faith and a subjective 'living' faith. The history of Judaism is the story of the decline and fall of a living folk-religion to the status of a system of positive law; and in this story the crucial step is the step from Abraham to Moses. It is not surprising, therefore, that as Hegel began to formulate his view of these two folk-heroes, he was moved to record also his general conclusions about positive religion and living religion as such. We must always remember that Hegel was not concerned with the criticism of Judaism for its own sake. He was more interested in the errors of G. C. Storr than in those of Moses Mendelssohn let, alone those of the author of the Pentateuch. Doubtless he would have argued that his extremely selective emphasis on some elements in the Judaic tradition, some parts of the Old Testament, at the expense of others, was justified because it enabled him to account for the historic fate of the Jews. But the continual contrast that he draws between the Jews and the Greeks takes no account of the historic fate of the latter. The fate of Israel had for him an exemplary significance, while that of Athens had none—at least, as yet. It was the spirit, not the fate, of Hellas that interested Hegel, for he wished to see his own society enlivened by a Periclean spirit, and so preserved, or rather rescued, from a Mosaic fate.

For Hegel himself, the fruit of his labours on the Pentateuch was the validation of his theoretical analysis and critique of 'positive faith'; and similarly, by comparing Israel with Greece he sought to establish his fundamental contention that 'Religion is identical with love.'[1] Certainly the drawing of the contrast between Greece and Israel rather than, as previously, between Greece and Protestant Germany, helped him in his revaluation of the New Testament. But here again we must realize that Hegel was not so much concerned with the faith and fate of Jesus, as with the actual establishment of a religion of love in his own society; and just as the fragments *Positiv wird ein Glauben genannt* and *Glauben ist die Art* show us what he thought to gain from the study of the Old Testament, so the fragment on love (*welchem*

---

[1] *so wie mehrere Gattungen* (summer 1797), Nohl, p. 377.

Zwecke denn alles Übrige dient) illustrates what he was hoping for as he turned back again to the New Testament. These more theoretical excursions certainly appear very slight when compared with the imposing mass of his historical studies. But it is possible that if we possessed the whole of the manuscript to which the so-called 'fragment of a system' (*absolute Entgegensetzung gilt*) belonged, we should find that Hegel actually wove his more theoretical reflections into a fabric as impressive as the essay on 'The Spirit of Christianity'.[1]

The division between historical interpretation and theoretical construction in the surviving manuscripts is not, of course, a clear and sharp one, precisely because Hegel's ultimate objective was always in his mind. Much of his technical vocabulary occurs in contexts of both kinds, and has to be interpreted with this fact in mind. In fact, it is fortunate for us that we can usually locate the abstract terms in a historical context, since the theoretical pronouncements are often extremely enigmatic because of their fragmentary character and their extreme brevity. Hegel derived his technical terms from various sources—he flirted with Schelling's language at Berne, and in Frankfurt he seems to have adopted Hölderlin's terminology wholesale—but he seems to have felt that the problem of discovering what the terms meant was identical with the problem of 'applying' them to his historical cases, and it is therefore clear that if we want to understand what *he* meant we must study his own 'applications'.

To take one example which we have already followed through several stages, the terms 'object' and 'objective' play an important role both in the historical and in the theoretical fragments of this period. In the notes on Judaism these terms are applied variously to God as conceived by Abraham and by Moses;[2] but the most revealing comment is contained in a single terse note: 'Objektivität Gottes Ex⟨odus⟩ 20';[3] for the twentieth chapter of Exodus contains the most familiar statement of the Decalogue. The notion of

---

[1] For the fragments mentioned see Nohl, pp. 374–7, 378–85, and 345–51. *welchem Zwecke denn alles Übrige dient* has been translated by T. M. Knox and *absolute Entgegensetzung gilt* by R. Kroner in Knox, pp. 302–19.

[2] For Abraham's God as 'Objekt' see *II. Abraham in Chaldäa*, and *IV. Abraham in Chaldäa* (Nohl, pp. 369, 371–2); *Abraham in Chaldäa geboren hatte schon* (Nohl, p. 246; Knox, p. 186). For the God of Moses see *IV. Abraham in Chaldäa* (Nohl, p. 373), *Fortschreiten der Gesetzgebung* (in a passage which Nohl omits), *Abraham in Chaldäa geboren hatte schon* (Nohl, p. 250; Knox, p. 191).

[3] *Zu Abrahams Zeiten* (not printed by Nohl).

God as the 'infinite Object' is inseparable from the conception of him as a commanding authority. Once we are in possession of this clue we soon realize that *Objekt* in Hegel's usage at this time generally denotes an external compulsive power or authoritative purpose. But there still remain a few difficult cases—as for instance when Hegel says that 'in misfortune there is separation and we are aware of ourselves as objects' (*im Unglück ist die Trennung vorhanden, da fühlen wir uns als Objekte*);[1] and when he sums up the legislation of Moses in his final draft (i.e. when he comes to explain the laconic memorandum quoted above) we find him using the term *Objekt* in two explicitly different senses:

The principle of the entire legislation was the spirit inherited from his forefathers—the infinite Object, the sum [*Inbegriff*] of all truth and all relations, and hence strictly the sole infinite subject—for it can only be called 'object' inasmuch as man with the life given him is presupposed and taken as the living or the absolute subject—⟨it is⟩ so to speak the sole synthesis and the antitheses are the Jewish nation on the one hand, and the whole remainder of the human race and the world itself on the other. These antitheses are the true, or pure objects [*die wahren, reinen Objekte*], that is what they are as against an existent infinite outside of them, empty and without import, without life, not even dead but nothing—they only are something, in so far as the infinite object makes them something, ⟨and then they are only⟩ something made, not something with an existence of its own [*kein Seiendes*], or life, or rights, or a love of its own. A universal hostility leaves only physical dependence, an animal existence which can only be assured at the expense of the rest, and which the Jews received as their fief.[2]

It is apparent from this passage that the 'infinite object' is properly speaking just as much subject as object, and can only be viewed as object simply, if the viewing intelligence assumes the role of subject. But when we adopt this posture everything else except the object loses all value and significance. 'God', the name by which we mean to denominate the source of all our practical and moral values, ought not to be thus objectified, for when he is, the existence that remains to us is reduced to the level of blind natural impulse. If we try to formulate the conception of God as an 'object', the net result is that we reduce ourselves to mere objects, in what is for Hegel the proper sense of the word—i.e. we

---

[1] *Fortschreiten der Gesetzgebung* (Nohl, p. 373).

[2] Nohl, 250 (Knox, p. 191). This passage represents a working up of some unpublished notes in *Fortschreiten der Gesetzgebung*.

become simply part of the order of nature, and our 'absolute object' is simply the inevitability of the natural law itself. When we feel the pinch of some natural necessity, then 'we are aware of ourselves as objects'; if we reduce everything to this level, then the avoidance of this sensation, union with the absolute object, the harmony of the course of nature itself with our own finite natural impulses is the highest ideal we can conceive; and the inevitable conclusion is that Nature will be concordant with our desires, if we for our part are obedient to Nature's Lord. This is the moral reasoning of a being who is in conflict with the world. For in a world where natural needs and impulses appear as the bondage of necessity, freedom can only appear as mastery, and the moral law has to be thought of as the will of a master.

The injection of the idea of mastery into our relations with other people, and the world in general, is a fundamental moral error which comes about naturally enough when our 'animal existence' is seriously threatened (as for instance by a major natural disaster like the Flood). If we react as Nimrod did, however, the error will be less serious in its effects than if we react as Noah did, for any human tyrant must die, whereas the Lord God abides forever. Thus, when Noah, or Abraham, or Moses, projected the theoretically rational 'ideal' of the harmony of nature into the postulate of an 'ideal' divine creator and governor of the world,[1] the original fall of man (the sin of hostility which natural needs and necessities continually urge upon us) became an irrevocable fact. The very possibility of moral action was made dependent on the existence of the divine Lord, since moral action was defined in terms of obedience to his will; and the absolute duty of obedience entailed the maintenance of at least a potential hostility towards everything else. The sacrifice of Isaac is an apt symbol for the absolute mastery, the absolute authority, of God. When that which is absolutely subjective, essentially practical, is conceived theoretically as an absolute object, we find ourselves faced with the ultimate moral horror.[2]

---

[1] Hegel employs the Kantian term 'ideal' more or less synonymously with absolute object'. It is first used in connection with Moses in *Die Geschichte der Juden lehrt* (Nohl, p. 370); applied to Noah's God in *Mit Abraham dem wahren Stammvater* (Nohl, p. 244; Knox, p. 183); and to the God of Abraham and of the sons of Jacob in *Abraham in Chaldäa geboren hatte schon* (Nohl, pp. 247, 248; Knox, pp. 187, 188).

[2] Hegel's treatment of the sacrifice of Isaac in his final version (Nohl, p. 247;

Hegel's doctrine of God as the 'sole synthesis', the absolute object who is at the same time the absolute subject, is expressed in language that was probably borrowed from Hölderlin; but it seems, at the same time, to be a direct 'application' on his part of Schelling's theory of the Ego. For Schelling writes, in a passage which we know Hegel had studied carefully: 'God in the theoretical sense is Ego = Non-ego, and in the practical sense *absolute* Ego which annihilates all non-Ego.'[1] This hypothesis is certainly supported by the first section of *Positiv wird ein Glauben genannt* which is a rather threadbare restatement of part of the argument of *Ein positiver Glauben* (Berne, early 1796) in the Ego/Non-ego terminology:

A faith is called positive, [Hegel begins] in which what is practical is present in theoretical form—the originally subjective only as something objective, a religion which offers representations of something objective which cannot become subjective as the principle of life and of action. ... Moral concepts do not have objects in the sense in which theoretical concepts have them. The object of the former is always the Ego, and of the latter the Non-ego.—The object of the moral concept is a certain determination of the Ego. ... A concept is a reflected activity. A moral concept which does not arise in this way, a concept without the activity is a positive concept; yet it has at the same time to be practical; it is only something recognized, a datum, something objective which gets its force and power, its effectiveness, only through an object that awakens reverence or fear ...[2]

Knox, p. 187) evolved gradually through the whole sequence of drafts (*II. Abraham in Chaldäa, IV. Abraham in Chaldäa*, Nohl, pp. 369, 372); the parallel reference to Hagar and Ishmael appeared in *Zu Abrahams Zeiten* and in the first draft of *Abraham in Chaldäa geboren hatte schon* but was deleted in the final revision (see p. 282 n. 3 above). No doubt Abraham's relations with his sons were in the forefront of Hegel's mind when he wrote the pungent comments on family relations in Mosaic law which are contained in the hitherto unpublished fragment *Die schönen, ihrer Natur nach*. That fragment begins: 'Nothing is more opposed to the beautiful relations which are naturally grounded in love than lordship and bondage.'

[1] *Vom Ich als Prinzip der Philosophie* (1795), *Werke* (1856–64), i. 201; compare Hegel's remarks in *Briefe*, i. 30, and the discussion above, Chapter III, pp. 210–11. All of Hölderlin's philosophical reflections in 1796 and the following years were focused on the *Vereinigung* and *Trennung* of *Subjekt* and *Objekt*: see especially Letter 117, lines 29–39 (to Niethammer, 24 Feb. 1796), *GSA*, vi. 203. He also made use of the concepts of *Not* and *Schicksal* in a way that Hegel may have found suggestive (see for instance Letter 147, lines 23–32, *GSA*, vi. 254).

[2] Nohl, pp. 374–5.

He goes on to say that a positive concept can lose its positive character if it can derive its active force from within itself (i.e. if we can autonomously impose it upon ourselves), but that what is ordinarily called 'positive' is essentially something objective (i.e. imposed by external agency). While on the other hand a moral concept can be objectified for theoretical study; but from that point of view it has no practical force, although we are aware of, or can always restore, its practical force as an expression of our free reflective activity. 'In the ordinary sense "moral" and "objective" are exact opposites.'

Even for theoretical cognition, the ways in which the infinite object acts are 'positive', i.e. they are imposed arbitrarily and not in accordance with the laws of our understanding. The operative cause of divine manifestations such as miracles, revelations, visions is not related to its effects as cause and effect are normally related in our experience. Because its actions are theoretically incomprehensible we cannot regard it either as an Ego (whose moral action is theoretically comprehensible as part of the order of nature, although it belongs to the realm of freedom) or as a mere non-Ego (something that belongs simply to the order of Nature). Yet we assign to it a moral purpose, which means that however incomprehensible it may be on the theoretical side, we suppose that its action is rational on the practical side at least.

Thus far Hegel seems to be simply repeating his critique of Storr. But now he begins to look at the problem constructively for the first time. Under the heading 'Religion, ⟨and the⟩ founding of a religion' he examines the whole question of how a synthesis of subjective (practical) and objective (theoretical) elements can give rise to the sense of divinity.[1]

At the opposite extreme from 'positive' religion, the fear of an external power, lies the religion of pure reason in which 'righteousness' (*Rechtschaffenheit*) is all that counts and there is no 'objective' content at all. From some remarks in *Jedes Volk hat ihm eigene Gegenstände* we know that the paradigm case of this extreme in Hegel's mind was the education that Nathan gave to his adopted daughter Recha in Lessing's play; and what he means here when he speaks of 'fearing objects, flying from them, fear of union

---

[1] For reasons given below, p. 294 n. 2, Henrich thinks that this heading indicates the beginning of a new meditation, which should be treated as a separate fragment.

[*Vereinigung*], supreme subjectivity' is beautifully illustrated by the passage which he there cites:

> Templar: What? Whether it is true
> That still the self-same spot is to be seen
> Where Moses stood with God, when . . .
> Recha: No, not that
> Where'er he stood, 'twas before God; whereof
> All that I need, I know.—[1]

This 'enlightened' attitude is less pernicious in practice than the naïve faith of a positive believer, but it is nevertheless wrong for an analogous reason. The positive believer is mastered *by* the object; the enlightened rationalist insists on mastering it. 'Begreifen ist beherrschen'—'to comprehend is to master'—says Hegel succinctly but enigmatically. He is probably thinking of Kant's doctrine that in cognitive experience the mind gives laws to objects, for he goes on to draw a contrast between viewing the flow of a brook as the result of the operation of the law of gravity, and 'enlivening' it, 'making it a God' by imaginatively endowing it with an indwelling spirit.[2] The spirit of a brook cannot be more than a demigod, however, because the brook itself remains a natural phenomenon spatio-temporally located and subject to natural law. The divine is only really present where Subject and Object (which Hegel now explicitly identifies as Freedom and Nature respectively) are thought of as so inseparably united that 'Nature *is* freedom . . . such an ideal is the object of every religion.'

How is such a synthesis possible? It cannot be 'theoretical' (i.e. it cannot be an *a priori* synthesis of intuition and concept by means of the categories of pure reason) for a theoretical synthesis is

---

[1] *Nathan the Wise*, Act III, Scene ii (Everyman edn., p. 158); Nohl, p. 218; Knox, pp. 150-1. Although the interval between the writing of these two passages is not less than a year, and may be as much as eighteen months, I think that it is legitimate to bring them together in this way for two reasons. In the first place Moses' receipt of the Law on Mount Sinai can hardly have been absent from Hegel's mind when he wrote his new heading in *Positiv wird ein Glauben genannt*; and secondly there is an evident continuity in the doctrine of the imagination contained in the two fragments.

[2] Running water as a symbol of the divine (the power of life) exercised a great fascination for Hegel (cf. his Alpine diary of July 1796: *Dok.*, p. 224). It was significant in his mind that Abraham drew his water laboriously from deep wells, so that it was for him always still, and not a thing that 'plays' or should be played with (cf. *Abraham in Chaldäa geboren hatte schon*, Nohl, p. 246; Knox, p. 186: the point that it 'was not to be played with' is made in the passage that Nohl omits from *IV. Abraham in Chaldäa*).

'wholly objective' (i.e. it is absolutely 'necessary' and leaves no room for freedom). On the other hand 'practical activity annihilates the object and is wholly subjective'. We can understand this remarkable dictum from the religious point of view if we remember Recha's claim that *'Wherever* Moses stood, 'twas before God'; in its literal sense I take it to be an allusion to the endlessness of the striving for moral perfection; in moral action the finite Ego has always to overcome some limitation: duty (the absolute Ego) must triumph over inclination (the non-Ego, the Object). Putting the doctrine in more familiar terms, the aim of moral action is always somehow or other to exercise mastery over nature.[1]

The principle of union (*Vereinigung*) that is superior both to reason (the principle of mastery) and to positive authority (the principle of slavery) is love:

Only in love are we at one with the object, it does not assert mastery [as in positive faith] and it is not mastered [as it is by pure reason].— This love made by the imagination into the *Wesen* is the Godhead. The sundered [*getrennte*] man stands then in dread or awe of it—the love that is whole in itself [*in sich einige*]; his bad conscience—his awareness of dismemberment [*Zerteilung*]—makes him afraid before it.[2]

[1] The sacrifice of Isaac and the 'satanic atrocity' of the revenge that the sons of Jacob took on the men of Shechem illustrate how 'Practical activity annihilates the object' when the fanatics of a positive religion presume to act for the absolute subject (Nohl, p. 248; Knox, p. 188: the original draft for this passage was in *Zu Abrahams Zeiten*).

[2] Nohl, p. 376. Henrich argues that the sudden appearance of this doctrine of love here does constitute something like a 'revolution' in Hegel's thought; and he further claims that the revolution was produced by Hegel's discussions with Hölderlin and Sinclair concerning a criticism of Fichte put forward by Hölderlin and systematically developed by Sinclair. After studying Hölderlin's little piece 'Über Urtheil und Seyn' (written about Apr. 1795), which I had completely overlooked, I feel certain that he was indeed a catalyst for Hegel's reflections (and that he provided the new conceptual framework for them). But I do not agree that any sudden transformation is involved. I think that the demonstration I have given of the continuity of development in Hegel's reflections, especially during the last six months at Berne, when he probably felt that his programme for religious reform had reached an impasse, is sufficient to indicate clearly that he was prepared to be influenced by Hölderlin's critique of Fichte before he heard of it. Of course, if my hypothesis that the 'revolutionary' concept of love has its origins in the theory of the ἓν καὶ πᾶν as formulated in 1791 is correct, then the question of priority or influence in this development of their shared ideal is of relatively minor importance. The evidence of *Eleusis* alone— read in the context of *Jedes Volk hat ihm eigene Gegenstände* and against the background provided by *Religion ist eine*—is enough to convince me that Hegel did not absolutely *need* any inspiration or conceptual assistance that he may have got from Hölderlin. (The nature of the 'revolution' that does occur is discussed

Love is the uniting of subject and object, freedom and nature, on a basis of equality, of likeness, and of reciprocity.[1] The myths of 'the old days' when God or the gods walked among men, symbolize this state of nature from which we have become so far removed (*entfernt*) that now we can be united with God only by force.

It is wiser not to speculate too much about what the word 'love' means for Hegel at this point; the picture will be rather clearer when we have more material before us. At the same time, it is obviously important to approach the interpretation of our material with the right preconceptions, or at least without any radically mistaken ones. Since Hegel is not primarily thinking of any relationship between persons (unless we want to call the image of the divinity created by the worshippers' imagination a person) we must be wary both about the ordinary usage of the term, and about its traditional use in Christian theology. Both the ordinary canons of human sex relations and the Christian ideal of charity contribute in an important way to Hegel's conception of *die Liebe*, but it is best not to anticipate what he himself will tell us on those topics. The safest starting-points for an understanding of his doctrine are to be found in Plato's *Symposium* and *Phaedrus*, and in the romantic Spinozism of his own time. As we shall shortly see, Hegel himself refers us to the *Phaedrus*; and the whole tenor of his discussion strongly suggests that his own guiding light was the contrast between *natura naturans* and *natura naturata* as reinterpreted (for instance) in Herder's *Gott*.[2] Religion is the experience of *natura naturans*, the universal power of life, the ἕν καὶ πᾶν; whereas reason, whether theoretical or practical, deals with the world as a system of determinable objects, with *natura naturata*.

In this perspective, for example, the assertion 'Religion ist eins mit der Liebe', which makes no sense on any ordinary view of

below on pages 322–30.) For an outline of Henrich's views see *Hölderlin-Jahrbuch*, xiv (1965/6), 73–96, and 'Some historical presuppositions of Hegel's philosophy' in *Hegel and the Philosophy of Religion* (ed. D. Christensen, The Hague, 1970).

[1] 'Love can only take place towards our equal, the mirror, the echo of our being', says Hegel in his last sentence. It is important to realise that he is not here thinking primarily of the relation between the sexes (where equality would be a principle of reason) but of the general relation between God and man, reason and nature, duty and inclination, man and his organic environment.

[2] The terms *natura naturans* and *natura naturata* do not occur in Herder's first edition (1787). But the reference to the distinction in the second conversation (Suphan xvi. pp. 457–8) is plain enough. Herder made it explicit only in the second edition of 1800 (compare Burkhardt, pp. 107–8 and 196).

love, becomes intelligible. The form of words was no doubt suggested by the Christian doctrine that 'God is love', but from the context it is plain that Hegel is not thinking primarily of anything described in the New Testament. The remark occurs in the brief fragment *so wie sie mehrere Gattungen*, which was part of a manuscript written perhaps a month or two after *Positiv wird ein Glauben genannt*.[1]

It is not easy to decide whether this fragment was part of one of Hegel's meditations on Judaism, or of his more theoretical reflections on religion in general. The contrast between Hellenic religion and Judaism is in the forefront of his consciousness, and some of the points he makes were developed later in *Fortschreiten der Gesetzgebung* and incorporated in *Abraham in Chaldäa geboren hatte schon*. But the concluding quotation from the *Phaedrus*, together with the proposition that we have just quoted, suggests that it was not really the religion of the Jews (or of the Greeks for that matter) but religion as such which is the principal focus of Hegel's interest here.

The first page of the fragment is lost. At the beginning of what remains Hegel is discussing the formation of a Pantheon (like that of Athens). When two tribes come together in amity, they accept one another's gods and say: 'Your god shall be ours also.' On the other hand, 'a people which despises all foreign gods, must carry in its breast hatred for the whole human race'.[2] It is difficult, though not impossible, for a people to maintain this attitude of universal hostility in a time of prosperity.[3] Only a God who was worshipped

[1] Nohl, pp. 377-8 (about July 1797). Probably only the first page is missing, as what we have appears to be the inner half of a quarto sheet (eight sides). There is no definite evidence of incompleteness at the end, and I am inclined to suspect that the fragment printed by Nohl did not fill four sides in Hegel's script. But we must keep in mind that it may well have been one of a loose sequence of fragments (like the notes and sketches on Judaism) which were eventually taken up into the manuscript of which the *Systemfragment* is all that now remains: *welchem Zwecke denn alles Übrige dient* (written about Nov. 1797 and revised roughly a year later) was almost certainly part of such a sequence.

[2] Nohl, p. 377; compare *Abraham in Chaldäa geboren hatte schon*, Nohl, pp. 247-8, 252-3 (Knox, pp. 188, 194-5).

[3] Hegel seems to waver a little on this point. In *Zu Abrahams Zeiten* he says explicitly: 'Good fortune silenced hatred and produced union with other peoples.' A few months later in *Abraham in Chaldäa geboren hatte schon* he firmly rejects this proto-Marxist view, declaring that 'what unites men is their spirit and nothing else, and what now separated the Jews from the Canaanites was their spirit alone' (Nohl, p. 253, Knox, p. 194). But since the spirit of hatred is itself a perversion of the human spirit as a result of misfortune, it was never

in fear could inspire his people to maintain it. In other words, hostility is an attitude that belongs essentially to a positive faith, and originates in the experience of misfortune. Where the misfortune is serious enough to contribute what Hegel calls 'sorrow' (*Schmerz*) men postulate a God who is angry or hostile; but if they have the memory of happier days to look back on they do not think of their God as being essentially hostile, but rather as punishing them for sin. The idea of kissing the rod of a divine master will not occur, however, to men who know (as Job knew) that they have not sinned, and who are strong enough to endure extreme misfortune. They will postulate an inscrutable divine power but will not seek to be reconciled with it through the acceptance of servitude.[1]

Where this strength of mind is lacking, a positive religion is born. 'When what is eternally sundered by nature, when that which cannot be united is united, we have positivity. This unity, this ideal is then Object, and there is something in it which is not Subject.' The interpretation of this passage poses severe problems. For how can there be 'eternal *Trennung* in nature', how can there be elements that are *unvereinbar*, if the divinity itself is properly the union of nature itself with freedom? It is plain from a passage which Hegel cancelled in revising his first draft that he was thinking primarily of the *Trennung* between 'the world' and 'the Kingdom of Heaven'; and if we take the notions of 'virtue as obedience' and 'happiness as reward' as examples of 'positivity' we can soon see what he means by speaking of the uniting of what is sundered by nature. Virtue and happiness, far from being sundered, are in Hegel's view inseparable; but the virtuous obedience that springs from fear is not happy, and the heavenly bliss that rewards it is not virtuous (no moral activity is involved). These 'positive' states occur in experience, for example in the tribulation of Israel in the wilderness, followed by entry into the land flowing with milk and honey, but they are 'eternally sundered' in the sense that their true character is destroyed by the way they are related (or 'united'). The virtue is not genuine virtue and the happiness is not *human* happiness. The ideal of positive Christianity (Heaven)

wholly dominant, and could in fact be 'silenced' by good fortune. Hegel's real view seems to be that the spirit produces union, but that material causes may produce division by perverting it (or rather by occasioning its perversion).

[1] Both versions of this passage are translated below, p. 498 n 2.

belongs to another world, it is an enjoyment which does not arise directly from our own rational activity.

The true ideal is rational enjoyment of union with nature, which is both within us and without. This is the union of love, and hence 'Religion is identical with love'. In the experience of love we find ourselves in another being which is not opposed to us but merged in our being; and yet it remains other than we are—'a miracle, which we cannot grasp'.

To express his doctrine of the identity of religion with love, Hegel takes over a passage from the *Phaedrus* about how the initial awe of the lover before the beloved passes over into an attitude of worship like that of one sacrificing to a god.[1] The real point of the analogy here is the implication that the relation between a man and the divine being whom he worships must in a certain sense be a relation between equals. As Hegel wrote in *Positiv wird ein Glauben genannt*, 'Love can only take place towards an equal, the mirror, the echo of our own being.' This explains why the Greeks were naturally led to represent their gods as human beings of ideal beauty.

Ordinary human love falls short of this level of religious experience but it does, nevertheless, provide Hegel with his paradigm for the 'miracle, which we cannot grasp'. The extremely difficult fragment *welchem Zwecke denn alles Übrige dient* offers us an analysis of sexual love in this same context of the contrast between 'positive union' and 'real union'.[2] The manuscript (at least half of which is

---

[1] Hegel knew of course that Plato was speaking of a homosexual relationship, and his own account of heterosexual relations does not terminate in a religious experience. It is worth while to examine the citation (*Phaedrus* 251 a) in its context, for this will enable us to see, among other things, how far Hegel's doctrine of love is from Plato's:

'Now he whose vision of the mystery is long past, or whose purity has been sullied, cannot pass swiftly hence to see Beauty's self yonder, when he beholds that which is called beautiful here; wherefore he looks upon it with no reverence, and surrendering to pleasure he essays to go after the fashion of a four-footed beast, and to beget offspring of the flesh; or consorting with wantonness he has no fear or shame in running after unnatural pleasure. *But when one who is fresh from the mystery, and saw much of the vision, beholds a godlike face or bodily form that truly expresses beauty, first there comes upon him a shuddering and a measure of that awe which the vision inspired, and then reverence as at the sight of a god; and but for fear of being deemed a very madman he would offer sacrifice to his beloved, as to a holy image of deity.*'

Hegel cites only the passage in italics. He had no sympathy with Plato's sharp separation of the love of the spirit from the love of the flesh.

[2] Nohl, pp. 378–82. There is an English translation of the manuscript in its second (revised) state in Knox, pp. 302–8. The text of the first draft cannot be

lost) was written about November 1797 and radically revised about
a year later, when Hegel was writing, or had just written, the first
draft of 'The Spirit of Christianity' (i.e. the fragment ⟨*leben*⟩*digen
Modifikation*).[1]

At the beginning of the sheet that remains Hegel is speaking of
the relation between a certain kind of community and its God—
the absolute purpose of its existence:

> . . . to which end everything else is subordinate, nothing can contend
> with this, or is of equal status with it; as, for example, Abraham set
> himself and his family and afterwards his people up as the ultimate end,
> or Christianity as a whole sets itself up—But the more widely this whole
> extends, the more it is transposed into an equality of dependence—
> ⟨to the point⟩ where the [Stoic] citizen of the world comprehends the
> whole human race in his whole—and so much the less of the lordship
> over objects and of the favour of the Ruling Being falls to the lot of any
> one individual; every individual loses that much more of his worth, his
> pretensions, and his independence; for his worth was his share in lord-
> ship; without the pride of being the centre of things, the end of the
> collective whole is for him supreme, and he despises himself for being
> as small a part of that as any other individual.

The interpretation of this opening paragraph is, of necessity,
slightly conjectural. But the historical context is clearly the whole
parabola from Abraham's sense of being uniquely chosen by

reconstructed with certainty from Nohl's edition—though Miss Schüler has
told us that the two phases can be perfectly separated in the manuscript—first
because Nohl did not print all of the cancelled passages, and secondly because
he does not tell us where the revisions and additions in his printed text end.
(Ocular evidence of the difficulties and uncertainties involved on both scores is
provided by a comparison of Roques, p. 105, with Nohl, p. 381. No doubt Nohl's
text is in general more reliable. But it is hard to have perfect confidence in his
separation of the two versions.)

In the following discussion I shall indicate what, to the best of my belief,
belongs to the first stage, what to the second, and what is common to both. But
I do not feel very sanguine about the reliability of my own judgement at some
points and my one comfort is that I believe we shall find that nothing very
crucial hangs upon it.

[1] See Nohl, p. 261. The first state of this manuscript cannot now be reconstructed with certainty (see discussion below). The handwriting resembles that
of the revisions in *welchem Zwecke denn alles Übrige dient* (Schüler, pp. 147, 152).
Miss Schüler is inclined to guess that the revision of *welchem Zwecke* is later;
and it is a plausible hypothesis that Hegel was led to rethink and hence revise
the earlier fragment while writing the later essay. The state of the manuscript
⟨*leben*⟩*digen Modifikation* is such as to suggest that it was not originally a continuous discussion but a collection of related fragments. Hegel may quite possibly
have regarded his revised draft of *welchem Zwecke* as one of these.

God to the absolute humiliation of the individual in the Roman Empire at the time of the final triumph of Christianity; and if we read the passage in the light of *Fortschreiten der Gesetzgebung* and *Positiv wird ein Glauben genannt* it can be quite easily and plausibly construed. To begin with, we learn from *Fortschreiten der Gesetzgebung* that 'Need [*die Not*] has *Zwecke* and acts on the basis of *Zwecke*, but Joy does not, nor does Sorrow, nor yet Love'; but 'the legal system of Israel, like every other, only served to help out need'.[1] And we know from *Positiv wird ein Glauben genannt* that in a positive faith there is an absolute authority of which we stand in awe. We are in a state of absolute dependence upon a power which does not in any way need or depend upon us. Our very existence is evidence of God's loving grace and favour toward us.[2] That any created things should exist at all is an inscrutable mystery, but being what we are, i.e. creatures possessing moral reason, we cannot avoid presuming to have some insight into God's purpose with respect to ourselves (the '*Zweck* to which everything else is subordinate'.) As Hegel put it a few months before this: 'In assigning a moral purpose to the providence of the Divinity, we do not reflect on the divine nature [*Wesen*] which is otherwise unknown to us, but we judge at this point, that his activity is in this respect the activity of an Ego.'[3] Once the basic premiss of positive faith is granted, that 'the Lord is our God', the only moral purpose that can possibly be assigned to Divine Providence is 'the helping out of need'. For we have no power of ourselves to help ourselves. We must be obedient to the will of the Almighty Power, so as to receive in return the lordship over nature which will enable us to satisfy all of our natural needs and desires.

The *first* commandment of all positive faith therefore is 'Thou

[1] *Fortschreiten der Gesetzgebung* (last paragraph), Nohl, p. 374.

[2] Compare the following remark from the unpublished notes in *Fortschreiten der Gesetzgebung*: 'Wenn das unendliche Objekt alles ist, so ist der Mensch nichts; was er noch ist, ist er durch jenes Gnade.'

[3] *Positiv wird ein Glauben genannt*, Nohl, p. 375. It should be noted that the same interpretation of the *Zweck* mentioned in the opening phrase will force itself upon us, if we follow the obvious path suggested by Hegel's first example (Abraham's conception of his family and people as 'chosen'), and turn both back and forward from the present fragment to what Hegel says elsewhere about Abraham's relations with his God (see especially *II. Abraham in Chaldäa* (Nohl, p. 369, bottom) and *IV. Abraham in Chaldäa* (Nohl, p. 372, middle)). But the connection between Abraham's folk-hedonism and universal cosmopolitanism still has to be made via the generalized theory of *Ein positiver Glauben* and *Positiv wird ein Glauben genannt*.

shalt *love* the Lord thy God', etc.; and the ground for it is 'that it may be well with thee, and that ye may increase, mightily, as the Lord God of thy fathers hath promised thee, in the land that floweth with milk and honey'.[1] But the character of the duty enjoined will vary considerably according to our conception of the nature of the reward promised. Not only is it the case that we must limit God by ascribing some moral purpose to him, but also the particular purpose that we ascribe to him is bound to be a mirror image of our own moral horizon. Abraham's God differed from other family gods because Abraham recognized no moral ties save the family tie between himself and his descendants. The grace and favour of the Lord was extended to him and his seed uniquely, and the reward of obedience was conceived as a *de jure*, and ultimately a *de facto*, mastery over all the rest of the Lord's creatures.[2] The highest object of Abraham's love was his own existence and the multiplication of his seed after him; for this and this alone could he love God with heart and soul and mind and strength. The outward sign of the covenant—circumcision—became in the vengeance of the sons of Jacob upon the men of Shechem, merely an instrument of the wrath of their God against those who sought to defile the honour and the blood of the tribe.[3]

This is the ultimate extreme of positive faith, 'where there is universal hostility' and 'nothing left save . . . an animal existence

---

[1] Deuteronomy 6. The duty of obedience even to this law of love rests on the fear of the Lord: 'That thou mightest *fear* the Lord thy God, to keep all his statutes and commandments etc.' I have chosen to refer to Deuteronomy 6 rather than to Exodus 20 (which we know Hegel was more preoccupied with at this time: cf. p. 288 above), partly because of the explicit reference to love, which makes this formulation of the law more appropriate to the present context in any case, but mainly because the law is here formulated in terms which apply to all the forms of positive faith, to Abraham with his family, to Moses and Israel, to the 'preaching of the Gospel', and to a positive interpretation of the 'rational postulate' that 'virtue deserves happiness'. In all cases 'love' is synonymous with 'gratitude' for rewards and favours either already received ('I am the Lord thy God which have brought thee out of the land of Egypt, out of the house of bondage. Thou shalt have no other Gods before me', Exodus 20: 2–3) or promised and covenanted for.

[2] In *Zu Abrahams Zeiten* Hegel accuses Abraham of dreaming of a world dominion for his descendants: 'sollte in seiner Familie herrschen über alles; aber sein Gedanke war der Wirklichkeit entgegen, denn in dieser war er beschränkt und wand sich mit Noth überall durch; also die Herrschaft seiner Ideal, in diesem alles vereinigt durch Unterdrükkung—Abraham Tyrann in Gedanken.'

[3] Cf. *IV. Abraham in Chaldäa* (Nohl, p. 372 top); *Abraham in Chaldäa geboren hatte schon* (Nohl, pp. 247–8, Knox, pp. 187–8).

which can be assured only at the expense of all other existence'.[1] But where man is conscious of himself as a rational being, not merely as an animal, the reward is envisaged as a spiritual salvation offered alike to all men if they will only accept the faith. At this level the external sign becomes a thing of crucial importance, because it really does mark off those who are included in the covenant from those who are not. Hence the highest aim of the Christian, the purpose to which all else is subordinate, is 'that all the world may be baptized'. When the irrationality of a special revelation is finally recognized, and dependence on an outward sign is discarded, we finally reach the opposite extreme of enlightened optimism or stoic cosmopolitanism, where the positive (authoritarian) element is reduced to the minimum assumption of the 'Author of Nature', who is a supremely just Judge and Monarch in his own kingdom of the spirit. As this transformation of positive faith occurs, the dominion which the positive believer originally hoped to receive over the rest of the created world, diminishes to the vanishing point. For, in order not to be secured at the expense of other rational beings, the reward has to be projected into a future life, where we are face to face with the Lord and hence absolutely conscious always of his Lordship and our own dependence. In a positive faith like that of the crusaders, the believer still exercises mastery on behalf of his Lord over the heathen, but in the positive faith of reason itself the authority of the Divinity becomes at all times direct and absolute. The absolute powerlessness of man is now revealed, and, since power is the measure of reality in all positive faith, the individual despises himself.[2]

In all the forms of positive faith the *love* of man for God is 'love for the sake of a dead thing'. Since the second paragraph begins without further ado to speak of '*this* love' we can safely infer that

---

[1] *Abraham in Chaldäa geboren hatte schon*, Nohl, p. 250 (Knox, p. 191). (The fullest discussion is in *Zu Abrahams Zeiten*.)

[2] This conclusion points to the Stoic sage as the *Kosmopolit* of whom Hegel is thinking. The problem is really how we are to take 'ohne den Stolz der Mittelpunkt der Dinge zu sein'. On the one hand this was Abraham's pride—and to be rid of it in that sense was an advance; on the other hand it is also Kant's—and to regain it in that sense is the key to a final overcoming of positive faith. One who does not have it (in either sense) can only interpret Kant's moral philosophy in the way Hegel analyses it in *Ein positiver Glauben*, where he is clearly thinking of the 'theological Kantians' at Tübingen. The following context of the fragment shows that Hegel has them in mind also, so it is best to take the *Stolz* both ways.

the context of the fragmentary first paragraph and so of the fragment as a whole is a discussion of the kinds of love relationship that need to be distinguished in human experience. The special attitude that marks off all forms of authoritarian religion is one of *gratitude for happiness received or promised as a reward for obedience.* The paradoxical thing is that this love is demonstrated only through indifference to the happiness that is looked for as a reward.

The world in which the positive believer lives is just a complex of 'dead' matter, and he proves his love for God by showing his indifference towards it. Being on the side of God he is 'set against it' (*entgegengesetzt*). He knows that by the grace of God he is independent of it:—that is his reward. From the way that Hegel describes the content and structure of positive faith in this paragraph we can see that he is thinking mainly of the Tübingen School. The fundamental article of faith is that

man is in his inmost nature an opposite [*ein Entgegengesetztes*], an independent being [*Selbständiges*], everything is for him an outside world, which is thus just as eternal as himself, the objects of his experience change, but they do not fail; as surely as he is, they are and his Divinity is; hence his tranquillity in loss and his sure confidence that his loss will be made up to him, since a substitute for it can be provided.[1]

Without the grace of God the positive believer could not have this confidence either in his own immortality or in the eternity of his world. For his experience of his own being is only a set of contingent experiences of the outside world; but if he did not exist the world would not exist for him. Consciousness and the material world are strictly correlative notions having no self-subsistent independence. The material world has absolute being

---

[1] In the unpublished section of *Fortschreiten der Gesetzgebung* Hegel asserts roundly that there is 'no immortality' in Mosaic Judaism, 'since it is independence of man'. In the final version *Abraham in Chaldäa geboren hatte schon* nothing is said about immortality; but actually there is no inherent difficulty involved in reconciling Hegel's thesis about positive faith generally with his account of Judaism in all its details. In positive faith generally the confidence of immortality is what the believer owes to the grace of God. It is not guaranteed by reason—in that sense there is 'no immortality', no 'independence of man' in any positive faith. On the other hand, a kind of immortality (the immortality of his seed) is what was promised to Abraham; and thus Abraham's religion satisfies the formula for positive faith as here laid down. (Indeed the remark about 'tranquillity in loss' and 'sure confidence that the loss will be made up, since a substitute can be provided' seems to refer to the sacrifice of Isaac just as plainly as the rest of the passage points to the Tübingen school.)

for consciousness, because the option of solipsism, though it is conceivable, is not bearable. Man has to 'think of himself outside of himself', that is to say he has to believe that the world of which he *is* the experience exists outside of him. But this absolute existence *for him* is not an absolute existence *in and for itself*. Only the absolute might of the Lord guarantees the reciprocally dependent existence of man and his world.[1]

The material world has absolute existence for the positive believer because he does not realize that what really lies 'outside' of his collection of limitations is 'the self-completed, eternal *Vereinigung*'. The true union of love has no place in this world of dead mechanism and opposed forces. Genuine love can only exist between living beings who are equal in power so that each is in all respects alive for the other, never dead. In the sight of the 'living God' of the Jews no man living can be justified; and the ways of the living God are not man's ways. Thus a man must either be aware of his own 'death' through sin, or else of God's 'death' through incomprehensibility. Here there is certainly no 'equality of power' —whatever that may mean as between man and God. It is clear at least that in order for two parties to count as 'entirely alive for one another', the kinds of things that they can do and feel must be commensurate enough to be imaginatively communicated. Being 'entirely alive' is not a matter of *Verstand*, which reduces the integral unity of our world to a complex equilibrium of opposed forces.[2] It is not even a matter of *Vernunft*, for both theoretical and practical reason legislate for phenomena, and practical reason preserves always the distinction between duty and inclination, the higher and the lower nature. Love gives no laws and recognizes none of these boundaries; it is a feeling.

[1] The key to an understanding of Hegel's argument in this paragraph (Nohl, p. 378, Knox, pp. 303–4) lies in giving full weight to the word *sein*. The question is about the kind of absolute self-subsistence that belongs to Spinoza's substance. If man *is*, then he is eternally—that he might *be* is conceivable, but to exist alone in the void is unbearable. On the other hand, what could guarantee the permanence of the world if consciousness itself were not permanent? It is as a guarantee of permanence for both of the 'opposites' equally, that God's existence is necessary. (The argument should be compared with that which we shall find a little later on in *Glauben ist die Art*. I suspect that it owes much to Hamann. See pp. 311–18 below.)

[2] 'It is not *Verstand* whose relations always leave the manifold as a manifold and whose unity itself ⟨the⟩ opposites are' (Nohl, p. 379). We can recognize here for the first time, I think, the world view which is analysed in the *Phenomenology* under the heading 'Kraft und Verstand'.

The explanation of this psychological term (*Gefühl*) gave Hegel some trouble. In his 1797 draft he thought it sufficient simply to say that he is not talking about a phenomenon at the level of *Verstand*. In the feeling of love we cannot distinguish the subject from the object, the activity of feeling from what it is that is felt. A year later he felt it necessary to be a bit more explicit. Love is not a *particular* feeling among a range of others, for in that sense a feeling is only a 'life-element' (*Teilleben*), whereas the feeling of love is the sense of life itself. To be alive is to experience a whole gamut of these transitory elements ebbing and flowing, but love is not to be thought of as the equilibrium of this manifold.

In the version of 1798 the word *Verstand* does not occur; the experience is concretely described instead of being abstractly characterized and labelled. Love is the sense of one's own life as doubled, and yet still one's own. Through love the original organic unity of the living thing (the life which is subject to analysis as an equilibrium of tensions) runs through a cycle of development to achieve in it maturity, a different kind of unity altogether.

Here again Hegel was dissatisfied with his first attempt at explanation, but his second try was certainly not clearer. In the higher union of love, he wrote in 1797, life is perfected, because here the requirements of reflection are satisfied (i.e. life is raised to self-consciousness). For the original organic unity, the possibility of reflection, of *Trennung* (i.e. of encountering another being in which it sees itself reflected, and which it recognizes as its 'like') is 'opposed' to it (i.e. such another being is by nature hostile, a competitor for the very things which the organism itself needs); while in the completed unity, the separation actually exists but the opposition is not absolute. '*Einigkeit* and *Trennung* are united' because each party is aware how the other feels; they experience their life as common to them both. 'Thus in love all problems, the self-destructive onesidedness of reflection, and the infinite opposition of the unconscious undeveloped unity, are resolved' (i.e. one does not lose one's individual identity in the universality of the species, and one does not lose the sense of the other's life in the blind hostility of natural instinct towards all obstacles).

The revised version of 1798 is again rather more concrete, but the basic doctrine has not changed. Not only 'the possibility of *Trennung*' but also 'the world' is now said to stand against the organism initially;[1] out of this opposition reflection produces in the course of life a whole series of oppositions (i.e. the organism becomes conscious of things which it *needs* and *obstacles* in its path) until the limit is reached when 'the whole of man' is set against the reflecting consciousness. (We may think here of Hobbes and the *bellum omnium contra omnes*, or of Hegel's later analysis of 'bondage' in the *Phenomenology*; but I suspect that Hegel himself has Abraham's discovery of God in mind. This was the supreme achievement of 'reflection' and it distinguishes both the warfare and the bondage of the Jews from the struggles and sufferings of other less 'reflective' peoples.) Finally 'love transcends [*aufhebt*] reflection in complete objectlessness' (if Abraham's God was in Hegel's mind before, it is safe to say that here we have the God of Jesus and the doctrine of 'pure life' which, if Miss Schüler's dating is right, Hegel has just finished writing about in the first draft of 'The Spirit of Christianity').[2]

Thus, in the second draft, if my interpretation is correct, the revision gives to this paragraph on *eigentliche Liebe* a religious dimension which was not present in the original version, but which was certainly required by the context of the discussion. As a result of this religious concern there is a very slight shift of emphasis in his attitude toward 'reflection'. The 1797 version culminates, like that of 1798, in the *Aufhebung* of reflection. But the word *aufheben* is not used till 1798; in the earlier version love is viewed more as the experience that *satisfies* the requirements of reflection than as the power that *does away* with them.

The difference is not very great, but it seems to have resulted in the transfer of one point from the third paragraph in the original version to the opening of the fourth paragraph in the second draft. The complete union of love is one that can only be broken by

---

[1] A reader who is dependent on the translation of Knox should eliminate all the explanatory phrases, derived mainly from Haering's commentary, which Knox has generally taken scrupulous care to put into square brackets. Most of these additions are singularly unfortunate because they employ the terminology of reflective opposition (subject/object etc.) which Hegel is explicitly trying to get away from. In one place Knox has been led by his dependence on Haering's interpretation to misrepresent Hegel's text. He writes: 'there still stood over against it the world and the possibility of a cleavage between itself and the world', where Hegel's text has simply: 'stand die Möglichkeit der Trennung und die Welt gegenüber'. The word-order is here vital to a correct understanding.

[2] Schüler, p. 147; see below, pp. 330–1.

death.[1] This is a point about ordinary love relations between one human being and another; and from here onwards Hegel is clearly thinking primarily of love between the sexes, and of how the 'complete' unity produces, in the child, a new 'undeveloped' unit. In the *thought* of their mortality the lovers are faced again with the 'possibility of *Trennung*', but it is not now (as it was for the isolated individual) the sort of possibility which becomes actual through the 'addition of being'.[2] If one of the parties were to die this would not produce an actual *Trennung* of living beings (a situation where each regards the other as 'dead', i.e. simply as an object to be manipulated) but rather the confrontation of a living being with something that actually is dead. The 'matter' of a living thing is simply its mortal aspect. So lovers, being wholly alive for each other, have in them no 'matter' (here the contrast is between real love and the positive relationship of gratitude for a material benefit). Love strives to overcome even the mortal aspect which gives rise to the thought of distinction. It seeks to immortalize the union of mortal beings.[3] In the original versions (inspired probably by the speech of Aristophanes in the *Symposium*),[4] Hegel referred

[1] 'Sie können sich nur in Ansehung des Sterblichen unterscheiden' (first draft; Nohl, p. 379 note *a*); 'so können Liebende sich nur insofern unterscheiden, als sie sterblich sind' (first sentence of next paragraph in second draft: Nohl, p. 379). It is clear, I think, that Hegel is speaking of how lovers *feel* about their destiny in the world. He is not saying that love itself cannot perish—the way he uses 'dead' in the preceding context shows that living organisms can be 'dead' to one another in this sense. But natural mortality is different in that it imposes a terminus on 'living' relationships from outside. One can fall out of love certainly; but this does not produce a separation *between lover and beloved*. The thought of *this* separation is what makes the awareness of mortality terrifying.

[2] There can be no doubt, I think, that Knox is right in suggesting that the allusion here is to Baumgarten's doctrine (originally Wolff's: see L. W. Beck, p. 453) that 'being is the complement of possibility'. No doubt it pleased Hegel to contrast this formula from the old metaphysics with his own doctrine of love as the complement of natural life, the πλήρωμα of the law and of reason (compare his explicit reference to the dictum in 'The Spirit of Christianity', Nohl, p. 268; Knox, p. 214). (I am assuming that the first sentence of the paragraph belongs to the *second* draft and that we return to the original version with 'An Liebenden ist keine Materie usw.'.)

[3] Compare here Diotima's comment that physical love is 'an immortal principle in the mortal creature' (*Symposium* 206 c–e). This dictum is a guiding principle for Hegel's whole discussion.

[4] *Symposium* 189 c–193 d. The definition of love as 'the desire and pursuit of the whole' (193 a) is another of Hegel's guiding principles; and although Diotima's sarcastic comment, 'I know it has been said that lovers are people who are looking for their other halves, but as I see it, Socrates, Love never longs for either the half or the whole of anything except the good' (205 d–e), is reflected

quite directly at this point to the physical act of copulation as an instinctive attempt to overcome (*aufheben*) the awareness of separateness at the level of sense experience (*Anschauung*). A year later he apparently replaced this brief comment with a much lengthier analysis of the emotions of shame and modesty as experienced by lovers who are prevented from coming together by social and moral taboos; in this context the reference to copulation becomes more delicate and slightly more indirect, but I think that the real force of the doctrine comes through more convincingly as a result.[1]

'The separable [das *Trennbare*], as long as it is still a private possession, before the consummated [*vollständigen*] union, is a cause of embarrassment for the lovers.' Out of this embarrassment arises shame. In conventional morality lovers are supposed to be held back by 'self-respect' from consummating their union before it has been publicly sanctioned and recorded; and girls, particularly, are taught to hold back from motives of prudence, out of a fear of being abandoned or 'let down' if the union has not been publicly acknowledged. But 'self-respect' and prudence of this sort can have no place in true love: the girl who will not sleep with her beloved till she has a wedding-ring is a paradigm case of *Liebe um des Toten willen*. Shame in true love is rather aroused by the desire to hold back: it is anger directed *at* one's own selfish desire to retain independence, or one's fear of being 'betrayed'. Only in the face of force does loving shame become self-defensive anger. If we do not distinguish between shame and self-defensive indignation, if we insist that a loving surrender of oneself is shameful, then we shall be forced to regard tyrants and prostitutes as models of self-respect, and to treat the coquette who wishes to 'make a conquest'

in Hegel's conception of the relation between human love and religious experience, the 'Aristophanic' element plays a far greater role in his over-all view than it does in Plato's.

[1] I am assuming here that virtually a whole page of Nohl's text, from p. 380 line 4 'Das Trennbare usw.' down to p. 381 line 2 '. . . der Aufhebung aller Unterscheidung', was inserted into the manuscript in 1798 in place of the single clause given by Nohl in his footnote on p. 380. My reason for this is not only that we have to read on this far in Nohl's text before we come to a restatement of the cancelled passage, but also that a comparison with Roques' edition (pp. 103–4) shows that the sequence of the manuscript is not clear between these points. I do not see how confusions as serious as those which Roques's transcription of the manuscript reveals could have arisen unless Hegel's revised version ran over on to the right-hand side of several following pages (or unless he inserted a loose page at this point).

without surrendering herself as an exemplar of modesty. Prostitutes and *femmes fatales* do not exhibit in their attitude a modest reluctance to 'lower' themselves to the animal level; rather they show how much importance they attach to their right of property in their own body (i.e. they make their own living unity into a dead thing, an object). This is the essence of *shamelessness* in Hegel's analysis.

True love is a gradual conquest of one's own mortal, prudent concerns, a conquest first of the fear that one's love will be rejected, then of the fear that it will be betrayed; and true shame is what one feels in this process: it is love which 'has no fear of its fear but is led by it to overcome separateness [*hebt die Trennungen auf*]'.[1] Copulation is, at it were, the ultimate expression of this sharing of experience at the physical limit: 'What is most private to oneself [*das Eigenste*] is united in mutual contact and shared feeling to the point of unconsciousness, of the transcending (*Aufhebung*) of all distinction.'

When the twain become one flesh, a child is conceived and the immortality of the life-cycle reveals itself: this is the joining of God which no man shall put asunder. The new life which now begins is a mere potentiality, an unconscious seed. It must develop its own consciousness, distinguishing itself and setting itself against the world and the rest of life in the process, till it arrives at the point where the circle is once more closed in love.[2] 'The united lovers separate, but in the child the union itself has become inseparable', says Hegel in his second draft; this is much plainer than the curious remark in the original version: 'The child is the parents themselves.' But the relation of the parents after their union is only properly discussed in the earlier version:

The separable returns to the state of separability; but the spirits are more united than before and what was still separated by finite consciousness [i.e. all former differences of opinion etc.] is all put aside. All the points at which one has impinged on the other, or been impinged upon, and hence has felt or thought alone, are equalized, the spirits are mutually exchanged.

---

[1] At this point (Nohl, p. 380; Knox, p. 307) Hegel quotes from the balcony scene in *Romeo and Juliet* to illustrate the enrichment of life which follows the free surrender of love. It is probable, I think, that this scene as a whole provided him with his model case for the analysis of shame as the conquest of external impediments to love, and of love's fearfulness.

[2] In the first version Hegel wrote simply: 'The seed becomes a plant, from the utmost unity it goes through the animal level to human life.'

This passage is eliminated in the second draft, not because Hegel ceased to believe it—it is easy to prove that he held to this ideal of marriage all his life—but probably because he wished in 1798 to emphasize the imperfection of ordinary love as against union with God in religious experience. This seems to be the underlying purpose of the concluding paragraph of the fragment, which is devoted to proving that two individuals cannot really have common property. Spiritual experience is such that each party is enriched by sharing; but material things can only be shared *out*. Ownership is essentially a relation of mastery and it is only an illusion to suppose that mastery can be shared in any sense other than that of alternation.[1] We shall see how important this limitation is when we come to study Hegel's analysis of the religion of Jesus.

4. *Faith and being*

The way of authority and the way of love are different approaches to religious experience—the discovery of 'being'. The analysis of 'life' in *welchem Zwecke denn alles Übrige dient* strongly suggests that all men are bound to begin with the way of authority, and certainly they *ought* finally to achieve the insight of love. We are bound to begin upon the way of authority, because the alternative that faces us as we mature into self-conscious reflective beings is: 'Is it the subject or the object that is ultimately real?' When the question is once posed in these terms it must normally be decided in favour of the object. We cannot speak of a 'right' and a 'wrong' answer here, but Hegel does seem to have held that there was a natural course of development leading from the 'normal' answer, through the experience of absolute opposition, to reconciliation.[2]

---

[1] Hegel rewrote virtually all of this paragraph (Nohl, pp. 381–2; Knox, p. 308) in 1798. But I cannot find any significant differences of meaning or intent in the two versions. The rather surprising transition to the question of property rights between lovers may well have been prompted by Hegel's desire to contrast his conception of the marriage relation with the orthodox Christian doctrine established by St. Paul: see 1 Corinthians 6: 15–7: 11.

[2] The 'normal' course of development is indicated fairly plainly in *welchem Zwecke denn alles Übrige dient* (Nohl, p. 379; Knox, p. 305). But Hegel's interpretation of the myth of Nimrod and his Tower shows that he believed that a spontaneous decision in favour of the subject could be given before human culture had arrived at the limit of philosophical reflection represented by the work of Fichte and the young Schelling. The example of Nimrod also serves to show, however, that no progress is possible from an initial claim to absolute

It is the question itself that is 'wrong'; the very attitude of 'reflection' which generates the exclusive alternatives is what has to
be overcome.

When he reached this conclusion it was natural, not to say
imperative, for Hegel to reconsider the rational religion of Kant
which represented for him the highest achievement of 'reflection'.
In all of his own reflections about theology hitherto there had been
a great gulf fixed between 'positive' and 'rational' religion; and it
is fairly plain that one of his prime objects was to save the Kantian
philosophy from perversion at the hands of the Tübingen school.
But he had now arrived at a standpoint from which the 'positive',
authoritarian character of Kant's own doctrine had to be acknowledged.

The acknowledgement is first made at the end of the extremely
difficult and abstract sketch *Glauben ist die Art*, written around the
beginning of 1798, shortly after the first draft of *welchem Zwecke
denn alles Übrige dient* and about the same time as the important
set of notes on the Judaic tradition, *Fortschreiten der Gesetzgebung*.[1]
In the main body of the piece Hegel developed the theory of
positive faith which he had already employed in *welchem Zwecke
denn alles Übrige dient*; but it is clear both from the terminology
employed and from the notes in the concluding paragraph that
his object in doing this was to prepare the ground for a demonstration that Kant's 'religion within the bounds of reason' is a form of

being on the part of the subject (*Mit Abraham dem wahren Stammvater*, Nohl,
pp. 244–5; Knox, p. 184).
  (That reflective alienation must reach the extreme of absolute hostility if the developed unity of 'religion' is to be achieved is shown by the way Hegel conceived of
the achievement of Theseus in reconciling the warring tribes of Athens.)
  [1] Nohl, pp. 382–5; a complete translation is given below. Miss Schüler groups
Zu Abrahams Zeiten, *Fortschreiten der Gesetzgebung*, and *Glauben ist die Art*
together as 'völlig gleich'. They are later than *welchem Zwecke denn alles Übrige
dient* (which Nohl places with letter 25, 13 Nov. 1797) and earlier, Miss Schüler
thinks, than *Daß die Magistrate* (Lasson, pp. 150–4), which was certainly
written before Aug. 1798.
  When I wrote the following analysis I did not realize that Hölderlin had
already developed a Spinozist theory of Being as the primordial Union of
Fichte's Ego and Non-ego three years earlier. (See the little piece 'Über Urtheil
und Seyn', *GSA*, iv. 216–17—translated in the Appendix below—and D.
Henrich in *Hölderlin-Jahrbuch*, xiv (1965/6), 73–96). If I had known this, my
task would have been easier. I have no doubt that in the present piece Hegel is
applying Hölderlin's insight in a Kantian context (but with critical side glances
at Fichte). The reader can see for himself by comparing the translations in the
Appendix, pp. 512–16 below.

positive faith. This demonstration he provided in due course in 'The Spirit of Christianity'.

Glauben ist die Art begins with a definition of *Glauben*: 'Faith [Belief] is the mode in which the unity, whereby an antinomy has been united, is presented in our *Vorstellung*. The union [*Vereinigung*] is the activity; this activity reflected as object [*Objekt*] is what is believed.' There is much that is unclear about this definition, but it does have the merit of situating the new concept *Vereinigung* fairly definitely in relation to the established terminology of the critical philosophy. In this context *Vereinigung* takes the place of Kant's conception of 'synthesis'. 'Synthesis', wrote Kant, 'is that which gathers the elements for knowledge, and unites [*vereinigt*] them into a definite content.'[1] At all levels this Kantian 'synthesis' results in a *Vorstellung*; and Hegel's basic complaint against religious faith, whether of the traditional positive kind, or of the new Kantian rational kind, is that it postulates a 'union' on the level of, or in the mode of, *Vorstellungen*; and this is somehow inadequate. Assuming, for the sake of argument only, that Hegel's reflections began with the dogma of the eventual 'union' of the 'saved' Christian with God in the Kingdom of Heaven, we can follow the explicit chain of reasoning in the present piece backwards, and suggest that it was reflection on the 'union' which faith is supposed to produce between the 'sundered' extremes of our life in this world and our destiny in the other world, which led Hegel to recognize the general problem of empirical belief in the existence of a world of 'independent' things as the ultimate root of difficulty, and the source of all the paralogisms by which 'faith' is exalted above 'reason'.[2]

---

[1] *Kritik der reinen Vernunft*, B 103; for the classification of the logical species of *Vorstellung* see B 376–7. (Henrich points out that the terms *Vereinigung* and *Trennung* are Platonic technical terms adapted for use in the interpretation of Spinoza by Hemsterhuis—*Hölderlin-Jahrbuch*, xiv (1965/6), 80. I suspect that we have here another link with those 'writings by and about Spinoza' that Hölderlin and Hegel read in the *Stift*.)

[2] In the context of the theological controversies of his own time it is not at all surprising that Hegel should have arrived at this conclusion. Hamann had already turned Hume's theory of belief to fideistic account in a celebrated passage of his *Socratic Memorabilia* which begins: 'Our own existence and the existence of all things outside us, must be believed and cannot be settled upon in any other way', and concludes: 'Faith is in no way the work of reason, and cannot therefore succumb to any attack by it; for *faith* arises just as little from rational grounds as *tasting* and *seeing* do.' (*Sokratische Denkwürdigkeiten*, *Sämtliche Werke* (ed. Nadler), ii. 73 lines 21–2 and 74 lines 2–5; translation by J. C. O'Flaherty

But in what way, precisely, does our ordinary perceptual experience involve the presence 'in our *Vorstellung*' of a 'unified antinomy'? I see my desk and the paper on which I write and I feel their solidity as I press against them with hand and pen. But there is an 'antinomy' between everything that I directly experience, and everything that I believe about the existence of the things experienced. This is because my experience is all of it a function, in a variety of ways, of my sensible and intellectual capacities; whereas the objects of my belief are things which must, if my belief is to be true, be self-subsistent beings quite independent of and sundered from all my modes of being aware of them. The 'union' of the antinomy is my actually believing at one and the same time that the awareness is all *mine*, and that it is *true*, i.e. that the things I am aware of do *exist* with all of the properties etc. of which I am aware. This set of existential propositions, the abstract content or object of my actual experience, is *das Geglaubte*. In the ordinary course of events we are not initially conscious of any 'antinomy'. 'Seeing is believing', as the proverb has it. The idea that our experience needs to be measured or tested against a 'standard' of some sort, before it can be warranted as veridical, only comes to birth when our naïvely accepted, untested beliefs prove to be mistaken. The resulting development of 'philosophical realism' out of 'naïve realism' is an intellectual elaboration, a recognition at the theoretical level of the felt conflict between that independent existence of things which is the standard of *truth*, and our contingent consciousness of them which is the condition of *belief*. We can prove that 'the real nature of things *must* be knowable', since the postulate that there is something real would otherwise be unintelligible. But this 'must' is a *sollen*; it does not follow from the proposition that 'the real nature of things is knowable' that anything really is or ever will be truly known. We cannot *prove* that we know anything without first knowing (without need of proof) what the canon of proof is to be; and this knowledge without proof is impossible if the reality to be known is opposed to our cognizing consciousness as a permanent independent being

(Baltimore, 1967), pp. 166–9. For Hamann's acknowledgement of his debt to Hume here, see the letter to Jacobi cited by O'Flaherty, pp. 41–2.)

We cannot be sure, of course, that this passage was in Hegel's mind when he wrote *Glauben ist die Art*. But it seems, to me at least, very likely; and upon that hypothesis Hegel's acceptance of Hamann's contention would go a long way to explain his lifelong antipathy toward empiricist theories of knowledge.

set against a contingent and dependent awareness. We must always begin from a belief; and this means that the supposedly independent term is really an 'opposite' which *ought* to be one of the dependent terms, and *would* be a dependent term if the inadequate 'pictured' union of belief were replaced by a real union of knowledge.

At this point in the argument (at the end of his first paragraph), Hegel makes a remark which is pregnant with implications for the future: 'what is independent in respect to these opposites, may certainly be in another respect a dependent term, an opposite in its turn; and then there has to be once more a progression to a new union which is now once more what is believed.' We shall have to defer our consideration of what Hegel meant by this until we have examined the rest of the argument, since the best clues to his meaning are to be found further on. But whatever it meant to Hegel in 1798, the most important fact about this sentence is that it contains the germ of the programme that he eventually carried through in the *Phenomenology of the Spirit*. The explicit object of that work, as stated in the *Einleitung*. is to arrive at absolute knowledge through the critical demolition of a sequence of fundamental beliefs about knowledge which succeed one another in a progression that is, in some sense, natural and necessary; and when Hegel referred to his completed programme in the *Vorrede* as a 'highway of despair' he was pointing up its moral and religious aspect. The *Phenomenology*, like *Glauben ist die Art*, is a practical critique of faith, not just a theoretical critique of cognitive belief.

The second paragraph of the sketch is extremely condensed and difficult. It begins with the assertion that 'Union and Being are synonymous'; and Hegel justifies this claim by pointing to the way in which the verb 'to be' functions as a copula to 'unite subject and predicate'. This argument, which might well be dismissed as a typically Wolffian sophism, actually serves to introduce Hegel's doctrine of the different 'modes of being'—specifically actual and possible being, or existence and conceivability. Actual being, independent existence, is something that can only be believed in. It is something that we have to accept because we stumble against it.[1] It is what it is whether we stumble upon it or not, but if we do not stumble on it, it can only enter our consciousness as a possibility. On the other hand, it is equally true that a logical possibility

[1] I suspect that we have here not only a conscious justification of Hamann's theory of belief, but also a glancing reference to Fichte's doctrine of the *Anstoß*.

remains a possibility whether it is actualized or not, and whether we think of it or not. So we have two 'sundered' modes of being, the actual and the possible; and just as we cannot help believing in the independent existence of actual being when we stumble over it, so also we cannot help believing in the merely dependent existence of all possible being as long as we are merely thinking of it. 'What is, is not bound to be believed, but what is believed must be [or else the belief would be false].'

The last sentence of the paragraph is again very hard to interpret. It can, perhaps, be most plausibly construed as a reference to the 'thought-ideal' which Abraham, like Noah before him, projected into an absolute reality as his God.[1] The mere conception of a self-subsistent almighty power is not 'an existent thing'. God must reveal himself before he can be believed in. But the revelation is really Noah's (or Abraham's or any subsequent worshipper's) actual thinking, and it is this that is the 'union' (of conception with actuality) in which faith finds its necessary basis.

This line of interpretation finds some support in what follows. For the 'distinct being in One Respect' which we meet in the next paragraph is very reminiscent of the 'thought-ideal' of Abraham and Noah. But we have now come to the point at which the influence of Hegel's study of the Spinoza controversy at Tübingen becomes apparent: 'The sundered thing finds its union only in One Being', i.e. in Spinoza's God as the living God, the God who is subject rather than substance. The expression *das Getrennte* now refers indifferently to both of the 'sundered' modes of being: to God as a pure possibillity still unrevealed, or to man as an existent consciousness seeking union with the whole. 'For a distinct being in One Respect'—i.e. something that from the point of view of actual consciousness is a pure thought-ideal, or something that from the point of view of reflective thought is an absolute (independent) existence—'presupposes a nature which would also not be nature.' The God of orthodox faith is in himself an *ens realissimum*; but for us he is a pure object of thought, a conceptual possibility. These two opposite 'modes of being' take the place of Spinoza's two attributes in Hegel's analysis of reflective consciousness; and their absolute separation results in a 'nature which is

---

[1] *Mit Abraham dem wahren Stammvater* (Nohl, p. 244; Knox, p. 183); *Abraham in Chaldäa geboren hatte schon* (Nohl, p. 247; Knox, p. 187): cf. pp. 281–2 above.

not nature', because there is no intelligible relation between *natura naturans*, the creative activity of God, and *natura naturata*, the system of created things. The 'union' of the mind with God, in a revelation which comes by faith, is at the same time no union, for it does not make God in any way intelligible; the *grace* of revelation only reveals the *mystery* of creation. Even the pure conception of a free creator turns out to be incomprehensible because, although we assert that God *is* pure activity, we also deny that he *needs* to create anything, or to reveal himself.[1]

Thus positive faith puts an incomprehensible mystery in the place of the genuine experience of the divine life which we enjoy in love. Love is the 'only possible union' and the 'only possible being' in which the two 'modes' sundered by reflection are properly reintegrated.[2] This has important implications for the

[1] The problem that Hegel is struggling with in this third paragraph is that of the relation between possible and actual being. From the standpoint of reflection it is natural to say with Wolff and Baumgarten—and ultimately with Leibniz —that 'Being is the complement of possibility'. And as soon as we say this we have to have recourse to a positive faith when we seek to explain why a particular set of possibilities—our world—has been 'complemented with being'. The 'creation of the world' must be thought of as the 'free' act of an almighty Lord and all free creative activity remains strictly within the Lord's prerogative. Thus the converse, or 'Spinozist', view of the relationship between possibility and actuality—that possibility is the complement of being—offers the only hope of preserving freedom and independence in the realm of human consciousness and action. The whole principle of *Entgegensetzung* is an illusion. Only the ἐν καὶ πᾶν is real; and the free spontaneity of life belongs to it just as much as the mechanical necessity of the 'laws of nature'. We shall not achieve the one and only genuine 'union of the mind with the whole of nature' until we discover how the terms of this antinomy can be reconciled. (I do not mean to assert positively that Hegel had the dictum of Wolff or Baumgarten in mind here; but see p. 307 n. 2 above. I do think, however, that the contrast produced by the converse of this dictum illuminates his 'Spinozism'.)

[2] This is quite conclusively shown by some passages in the other 'theoretical' fragments of this same period. Consider for example the following notes from *Positiv wird ein Glauben genannt*, which also bear out the contention that *Vereinigung* replaced the Kantian 'reflective' term *synthesis* in Hegel's new terminology:

'The theoretical syntheses are wholly objective, wholly opposed to the subject—Practical activity annihilates the object, and is wholly subjective— only in love alone are we at one with [*ist man eins mit*] the object, so that there is no mastery or being mastered—this love made by the imagination into the entity [*Wesen*] is the Godhead; the sundered man stands then in dread or awe of it—love in its oneness [*der in sich einige Liebe*]; his bad conscience— his awareness of dismemberment—makes him afraid before it.'

'That union we may call union of subject and object, of freedom and nature, of actual and possible' (Nohl, p. 376).

Or this from *so wie sie mehrere Gattungen*:

development of the concept. Hegel would not want to call his 'one and only possible union' a 'miracle that we cannot grasp'. Love is something that cannot be comprehended *by reflection* certainly; but it is also, as Hegel insisted in the first draft of *welchem Zwecke denn alles Übrige dient*, an experience that *comprehends* reflection. It is a self-conscious mode of experience in which the exigencies both of life and of reflection are for the first time really satisfied.[1]

Just what the 'incomplete' or 'imperfect' unions are, which are put in the place of love in positive religions, we shall find it easier to decide if we first consider what Hegel says in his next paragraph about the knowledge of God by faith. This paragraph certainly offers powerful evidence in support of the claim that Hegel's lifelong antipathy to empiricist theories of knowledge was directly rooted in his rejection of 'revelation by grace'. All the knowledge that comes by positive faith must have its origin in some sort of sense experience—it must be 'given' as sensible objects are. And so, although it is voluntary in a way in which ordinary empirical belief obviously is not, religious faith remains a theoretical mode of knowledge, in which the object is not 'brought to life', so that we are not united with it as we are with the other self of the beloved.[2] The God of positive faith is a 'living God', who stands opposed to the believer precisely in respect of the immortal life with which we endow him in thought; or he is a 'dead Saviour', opposed to us precisely in respect of his actual humanity which lies now in the tomb. The believer accepts an imperfect mode of knowledge or of being (Abraham's thought-ideal, Storr's dead Saviour) in lieu of one which is 'perfect' (i.e. not 'opposed' to the worshipper) in the respect in which it is supposed to be perfect. Examples of this 'perfect' union can be found wherever the

'If things that cannot be united are united we have positivity. This unified result, this ideal is thus [an] object, and there is something in it which is not subject.

'We cannot posit the ideal outside of ourselves, or it would be an object—nor yet merely within us, or it would be no ideal.

'Religion is one with love. The beloved is not opposed to us, he is one with our own essence [*Wesen*]; we see only ourselves in him—and yet also on the other hand he is not we—a miracle that we cannot grasp' (Nohl, p. 377).

[1] *welchem Zwecke denn alles Übrige dient* (Nohl, p. 379 n. [*b*]); cf. also *Jesus trat nicht lange* (Nohl, pp. 293–6; Knox, pp. 244–7).

[2] Cf. *Positiv wird ein Glauben genannt*: 'To conceptualize is to make oneself master. To bring objects to life is to make them into gods' (Nohl, p. 376).

worshipper is not deceived about the way in which the divine object of his love is present. The Greek, for example, recognized Apollo not in the stone but in the beauty which was the work of the artist; while the young Hegel and Hölderlin (probably) recognized the true conception of the ἐν και παν in the *Gott* of Herder.[1]

The discussion of the 'determining' and 'determined' factors in 'union' which follows, has its roots in Hegel's interpretation of the way in which the Kantian understanding 'gives laws to experience'. *Begreifen ist beherrschen*, he says trenchantly in *Positiv wird ein Glauben genannt*. In 'The Spirit of Christianity' he develops this view at length as a critique of the Kantian doctrine of practical reason, according to which the rational moral agent becomes a slave to himself, since his relation as a living being to the moral law of his own reason is that of a slave to a master. But the positive believer is in a still more curious position, which Hegel here interprets on the analogy of the Kantian doctrine of sense intuition.

The knowledge of God comes to the positive believer by faith; but faith itself is the gift of God—it comes by grace. In the same way the knowledge of God's will comes to the believer by faith; and even if the will to do what God wills somehow belongs to the believer himself, the power to do God's will is necessarily held by the believer to be the gift of grace. 'The determining factor is supposed, even so far as it determines to be determined.' The believing Christian, however, or the believing Jew, receives the will of God through the gospel of Jesus or the mouths of Moses and the prophets, who were real men in whom existence and thought were united. And in the former instance the Christian believer holds that Jesus did not simply have faith in God, he was at one with him. Thus in the case of Jesus, at least, 'the doing was active'. But the relation of the believing Christian, even of the disciples themselves, to Jesus is a 'lower form of union'. Peter, for example, could recognize Jesus as the Christ, but he did not realize that in grasping the relation of Jesus to God, he was also grasping his own relation to God. His was the relation of 'trust' which Hegel here defines as 'identity of person, of will, of ideal, with difference of accidental aspect'.

---

[1] For the Greek attitude to Apollo see *Jesus trat nicht lange* (Nohl, p. 300; Knox, p. 252); and there is surely an echo of Herder a little earlier on: 'To love God is to feel one's self in the "All" of life, with no restrictions, in the infinite' (Nohl, p. 296; Knox, p. 247).

The 'difference of accidental aspect' between Peter and Jesus ought not to be accorded any *essential* significance. But it is just this error of mistaking accident for essence which distinguishes 'trust' from the fully self-conscious state of 'love'. Thus, for Peter salvation depended on the presence of 'the Master'. 'The Master' was someone quite different from himself and it was only by 'following' him that Peter could be saved. Peter's faith and his following were his own act, but the 'form' of his activity was laid upon him by the 'command' of the 'Master'.[1]

For the believing Jew, on the other hand, the commandment he receives is laid not only upon him but also upon the human source from whom he receives it, so that all mankind becomes on his view 'an exclusively passive thing, an absolutely determined factor'. The insight into the universal fatherhood of God or the perfect union of 'pure life' which Peter might have achieved, though in fact he did not, is not even a possibility for the Pharisee in the parable. But, of course, even at the extreme of Mosaic Judaism men are assumed to be free agents with respect to the life of the senses. As Hegel wrote a few months later in his essay on 'The Spirit of Judaism': 'In this thoroughgoing passivity there remained to the Jews, apart from testifying to their servitude, nothing save the sheer empty need of maintaining their physical existence and securing it against necessity.'[2]

Positive faith is faith in a promise of salvation; it sunders experience into the actual world of here and now and that other merely possible world that is the object of faith. The positive believer holds that the future 'Kingdom of God' does indeed already exist, but elsewhere. He prays that God's will may be done on earth, 'as it *is* in Heaven'. This 'sundering of feeling' with respect to the will of God is analogous to the antinomy which arises when we formulate our sensible awareness of things as a belief in their 'absolute' or 'external' existence. The reference

---

[1] Cf. *Jesus trat nicht lange* (Nohl, pp. 313–14; Knox, pp. 267–8, 171).

[2] *Abraham in Chaldäa geboren hatte schon* (Nohl, p. 252; Knox, p. 194). I may be wrong in assuming that Hegel has Mosaic and Pharisaic Judaism specifically in mind at this point in *Glauben ist die Art*. The consequence of being 'an exclusively passive thing' applies even more clearly to some Christian traditions in which God's gift of grace is viewed by the believer as an act of predestination or election on his part. But this Christian doctrine of election has its origins in God's 'choice' of the Jews; and Hegel does explicitly reduce the free life of the Jewish believer to the minimum level of animal need and satisfaction (and meaningless ceremonial).

to the future contained in the promise of salvation—which would be the 'union' of our actual consciousness with the ideal formulated in our thought—corresponds to that knowledge of the 'truth' which is the ideal goal of ordinary empirical belief. But this 'union' is precisely what is formulated and presented, in both cases, only as a *Vorstellung*. The 'opposition' between our actual state of sin (or error) and our ideal of redemption (or knowledge) is what really exists in fact; but the 'union' is what really exists in thought (i.e. it is what we claim to believe in as the permanent and independent reality). This supposedly self-subsistent 'ideal' or standard is a 'union' because it can only be formulated by 'picturing' the reintegration of our actual consciousness out of its fallen state, or the coincidence of our belief with the truth of 'what is'.

The 'religion of reason' as formulated in Kant's Critical Philosophy is therefore exactly analogous to positive religion in respect of the fundamental reflective antinomy of 'possibility' and 'being'. 'Rational' faith does not, like 'positive' faith, involve any recourse to a miraculous source or a supernatural guarantee; but all the paradoxes of the reflective dichotomy between 'is' and 'ought' arise equally in both: 'Kant⟨ian⟩ philosophy—positive religion. (Divinity holy will, man absolute negation; in the *Vorstellung* it [this antinomy] is united, *Vorstellungen* are unified—*Vorstellung* is a thinking process, but the thing thought of is no existent being).'

'Divinity holy will, man absolute negation': this was the contrast that Hegel planned to dwell on when he was ready to develop the startling conclusion that he has here arrived at. Just two years earlier in *Ein positiver Glauben* (somewhere round Christmas 1795) he had tried without any visible success to face the problem posed for practical reason by the forgiveness of sins. He is ready now to concede Storr's claim that the upshot of rational theology is the recognition that we are absolutely dependent on God's grace. We cannot be certain that he broke off his discussion earlier because he could not find an answer to Storr that satisfied him at that time. But it is reasonable to suppose that the chain of reflection which leads through the assimilation of rational and positive faith in *Glauben ist die Art* to the treatment of crime and punishment in the 'Spirit of Christianity' had its origin in his continuing meditation upon the problem of forgiveness.

The assimilation of rational faith to positive faith and the consequent rejection of Kant's conception of practical reason is the most obvious and radical novelty in the present essay. The lesson here compressed into a few laconic notes is spelled out explicitly in the long discussion of slavery to the moral law, and of just retribution for breach of the law in 'The Spirit of Christianity'. But the analysis of the concept of 'belief' which underlies Hegel's attack on Kant here has a long-term significance that is far greater. The whole logical structure of the *Phenomenology of the Spirit* rests on the antinomy between the experience of belief and the ideal of knowledge that is first analysed here. It is true that the idea of a systematic progression towards absolute knowledge through the reflective criticism of the forms of belief which present themselves in a genetically necessary sequence—i.e. a sequence in which the breakdown of each form of consciousness leaves the germ of the next one as its natural residue—is not yet present in Hegel's mind. The mysterious sentence at the end of his first paragraph, to which we must now finally return, speaks of a 'progression' from one state of belief to another in search of a more complete 'union'. In the light of our analysis of the fragment as a whole it would seem that the simplest and most consistent interpretation of this sentence is to take it as a reference to the substitution of faith in an 'other-worldly' promise of salvation for faith in a promise of salvation in this world. Thus when Jesus died the object of the disciples' faith was shown to be 'in anderer Rücksicht (i.e. on the side of actuality) ein Abhängiges', and they had to progress from faith in 'the Master' to faith in the Risen Lord and the 'kingdom that is not of this world'. If this view is right there is no hint here of a conviction in Hegel's own mind that the progressive development of belief in this way leads to an eventual transcendence of belief altogether. Hegel seems at this stage to have held that the 'antinomy' of belief could only be overcome by a single great leap out of the 'sundered' condition of reflective consciousness into the 'union' of the mind with 'God or nature' that is experienced in love. But even in this supposedly 'mystical' phase of his thought the seeds of his later 'rationalism' are easy to detect. On the one hand we shall observe in 'The Spirit of Christianity' what is plainly meant to be a phenomenological progression from the positive religion of Moses through the rational religion of Kant to the religion of love as proclaimed by Jesus—and from that to the religion of the Greeks; and on the other hand, even in the experience of love the requirements of reflective reason are not simply abrogated. Love itself is a reflective condition, though it is not a 'sundered' one; and because it is not sundered the needs of reason can for the first time be satisfied or fulfilled. Just how Hegel believed that the demands of reason were met by the experience of love we are not yet in a position to say. But the fact that he never ceased to believe that its demands both can and should be met is a point that has not been properly noted by many critics.

5. *Prospect and retrospect: the 'Spirit of Christianity'*

A willingness to criticize Kant openly, and indeed an explicit rejection of Kant's conception of practical reason, is one of the most obvious and most remarkable novelties of the long series of manuscripts concerned with the spirit of Jesus and of the community that he founded. As a consequence of his demonstration of the mutually exclusive character of authority and love, Hegel can now explicitly declare what he had long believed, that is, that the conception of reason as an authority that gives laws to sensibility is fundamentally mistaken. From the beginning (in *Religion ist eine*) he was convinced that the enlightened ideal of critical rationality and autonomy must be so interpreted as to refer to a harmony of all the faculties, propensities, and needs of human nature; and because of this he rejected from the beginning the Kantian op-position of reason and sensibility. His own conception of rationality was always more Platonic than Kantian. His earliest comments about the function of love in human nature show this clearly in two ways. On the one hand, he replaces Kant's simple antithesis of reason and sensibility with a more complex hierarchy of human capacities, in which love is certainly placed below reason, but is not on that account deprived of all intrinsic moral significance. On the other hand, the distinct though cognate thesis that love is an 'analogue' of reason has no really plausible interpretation if we try to work out the analogy in terms of the critical philosophy; while its affinity with Plato's general view of the relation between love and reason is obvious.[1]

Plato, Kant, and Hegel were at one in affirming that only the

---

[1] *Religion ist eine*, Nohl, p. 18. That aesthetic sensibility is an *analogon rationis* was of course a Leibnizian doctrine, which Hegel would certainly have been familiar with in the works of Baumgarten.

completely rational man is really free, and that the freedom of rational autonomy is the ultimate goal of human practical activity. It seems that because of this basic agreement, Hegel initially felt that it would be a fairly simple matter to reintegrate the contemporary ideal of enlightened rationality back into the older Greek ideal of a rational harmony of life to which he was always drawn. It was natural enough that he should believe this, for Plato and Aristotle insisted just as firmly as Kant on the authority of reason, its natural right to rule the rest of man's capacities, even if they did not insist that reason was the only source of value, that only by the use of reason could man decide what is right. No doubt this was why Hegel placed the requirement that 'Its doctrines must be founded upon universal reason' first among his canons for a genuine folk-religion;[1] and it is clear that, when he had finished applying this canon to Christianity, he felt he had, among other things, vindicated both the Greeks and Kant. It was Kant's achievement to have provided a clear account in theory of what the Greeks had achieved in practice. The problem that remained was to find a way to make Kant's theory effective in practice once more; and in this respect—in his theory of human motivation—Kant was weak.[2]

But when Hegel turned to the problem of how this gulf between theory and practice, this 'Trennung zwischen Leben und Lehre',[3] was to be removed, he found that it could only be achieved by going altogether beyond the point of view of 'reflection'—the point of view which it was Kant's great achievement to have clarified. The whole conception of the authority of the 'higher' nature over the 'lower', common to Kant and to Plato and Aristotle, is fundamentally inadequate; and the idea of a complex hierarchy of human capacities—the idea found in Plato and Aristotle, through which Kant's simple reflective opposition between 'reason' and

---

[1] Nohl, p. 20.

[2] See the brief conclusion added to *man mag die widersprechendsten Betrachtungen* on 29 Apr. 1796 (Nohl, pp. 211–13; Knox, pp. 143–5).

[3] Cf. *Religion ist eine*, Nohl, p. 26: 'Sobald eine Scheidewand zwischen Leben und Lehre — oder nur Trennung und weite Entfernung beider voneinander ist — so entsteht der Verdacht, daß die Form der Religion einen Fehler habe . . .' This first appearance of the term *Trennung* in Hegel's manuscripts is very revealing. In his usage, it refers almost always, if I am not mistaken, to a separation of theoretical from practical consciousness; of thought (*Gedanken*) from sensation (*Empfindung*), of consciousness (*Bewußtsein*) from actual existence (*Wirklichkeit*), of desire (*Sehnen usw.*) from consummation (*Vollendung usw.*).

'sensibility' was to be healed—must not be conceived in terms of an abstract system of 'faculties', but rather in terms of a sequence of phases in the proper development of a mature human being in actual life.

How far this development—the need to move from the plane of 'reflection', with its hierarchy of faculties under the control of reason aided by love in a subordinate capacity, to the plane of 'life', with its succession of phases through which love develops to full self-consciousness—came as a surprise to Hegel himself we cannot be certain. Before we could decide the question definitely, we should have to know far more than we do about the nature and extent of his undergraduate studies in connection with the Spinoza controversy, and about his original conception of the ἑν και παν. I have suggested above that Hegel's whole formulation of the standpoint of 'reflection' has its origins in his study of Spinozism, and it seems unarguably obvious that his conception of 'life' is derived from the ideal of the ἑν και παν. On these grounds we might argue that even while he was arguing on the plane of reflection, he knew that it was destined ultimately to be *aufgehoben*.

This does seem, however, to be psychologically implausible. The contrast between theoretical abstraction and actual living experience was never absent from Hegel's mind, from the time that his own independent reflection began at about the age of sixteen. Hence the idea that the theoretical standpoint *ought* somehow to be surpassed would occur naturally to him, and may have been in his mind already when he wrote *Religion ist eine* in 1793. But it seems safe to assert that he did not then, or at any time before June 1796, have a clear idea of *how* the transformation was destined to take place. He gives no sign of believing in 1793 that love as an experience was on a different plane from *Vernunft* (i.e. *practical* reason) altogether. He thought of it rather as the essential complement of *Vernunft*, and as properly subordinate to the authority of reason from an abstract point of view. Love was an analogue of reason at a 'lower' (i.e. more primitive) level of development: it was a sensible appetite for the beautiful, as compared with the intellectual appetite for the good. Because of the essential identity between the beautiful and the good, reason itself must be guided by the ideals of beauty and harmony in all of its dealings with the sensible world; rational appreciation both of its own nature, and of the nature of things, would lead reason to be persuasive rather than imperious. But this did not affect the theoretical superiority of reason in the hierarchy of nature at all; its essential authority, its natural *right to command* remained intact. The idea that there was a level of experience where this *right* of reason (and the whole system of rights deriving from it) was altogether suspended did not at that time occur to Hegel at all.

The evidence of a check in the progress of Hegel's reflections during 1796, which has already been discussed at some length, provides some further support for this view. But that evidence is rather tenuous, and the main root of any psychological crisis that Hegel may have passed through was certainly not his theoretical difficulties. Much more solid grounds for holding that Hegel did not recognize a higher level of consciousness than rational reflection are provided by certain overt assertions of his own. First there are his remarks in April 1796 about 'the healthy separation (*Trennung*) of the domain of the powers of the human spirit which Kant has made for science', and about the 'ignoring of the rights of every faculty of the human spirit, *especially of the first among them, reason*'.[1] It is true that these assertions can be taken in a sense that is quite consistent with all that Hegel wrote in the next two years, and hence they cannot be held to imply unequivocally that he has not yet recognized a higher point of view. But, in the second place, there is one crucial passage in *The Life of Jesus* that does seem to point firmly to this conclusion. If Hegel believed in a higher level than that of moral right in 1795, then it is odd that he should have accepted Kant's view that the 'Golden Rule' is only the most general counsel of prudence, and hence far below the level of the categorical imperative; yet his first impulse was to make Jesus say exactly this.[2] By crossing out the reference to the Golden Rule altogether, he produced in the end a text that is completely consistent with his subsequent views. But the presence in the manuscript of those two cancelled lines makes the inference that he did *not* at that time believe in a higher level, and that his conception of the relation between love and reason was the Platonic one outlined in the preceding paragraph, almost inescapable. If that was indeed Hegel's position at the end of July 1795, then it is natural to interpret his remarks about Kant and about *der Vernunft* in April 1796

---

[1] *Der Grundfehler, der bei dem ganzen System*, Nohl, p. 211 (cf. Knox, p. 143). The italics are mine.

[2] *Die reine aller Schranken*, Nohl, p. 87.

in accordance with it. The earliest unassailable evidence that he has begun to have any qualms about the absoluteness of reason's rights, and the final supremacy of its laws, is to be found in *Positiv wird ein Glauben genannt*; and it is only when we come to *Glauben ist die Art* that we can say definitely that Hegel's doubts have crystallized into certainty.[1]

It would never have occurred to Hegel, however, to regard his discovery as involving a 'revolution' in his thought. Everything that he had already written retained its validity, and the new dimension that was now added to his reflections arose directly from the maturing of ideas and commitments that he had embraced at the beginning. I have been careful to speak of the 'plane of reflection' and the 'plane of life', because the antithesis between the 'standpoint of reason' and the 'standpoint of love', which is so frequent in the literature concerning the *Jugendschriften*, is one that is alien to Hegel's own attitudes and preoccupations, and results in a falsification of his beliefs. It is *not* the case that whereas in 1795 he believed in the supremacy of 'reason', in 1798 he came to believe in a mystical supremacy of 'love'. It is the case that from 1793 onwards he believed, like Plato and Kant, in the natural authority of reason, and he believed, like Plato, that love is itself the most important manifestation of reason as a living force (i.e. of *Vernunft*, as distinct from *Verstand*, the faculty for abstract calculation and 'reasoning'). But the word *Vernunft* had been pre-empted for the plane of reflection by Kant; and it was Kant's great achievement to have shown precisely why *Vernunft* was 'first' among man's faculties on that plane. When Hegel moved in 1798 to the quite different plane of 'life' he hesitated, at least for a time, to use the word *Vernunft* in any but a 'reflective' sense, precisely because on the plane of 'life' the notions of supremacy and

---

[1] If the contention that Hegel is the author of the 'earliest system-programme' is accepted (see Chapter III, Appendix), we can say fairly definitely that Hegel has begun to have doubts about the *authoritative* character of reason in 1796. The most plausible sequence (with dates) is as follows: *Jedes Volk hat ihm eigene Gegenstände* (May 1796) led Hegel to recognize that the 'highest act of *Vernunft*' is an aesthetic, not a legislative one (*eine Ethik* (? June 1796)). Continuing reflection on this aesthetic-religious act led to the conclusion that 'Religion ist eins mit der Liebe' (*Positiv wird ein Glauben genannt* (? June 1797), and *so wie sie mehrere Gattungen* (? July 1797)). After *Glauben ist die Art* (early 1798) Hegel breaks off for a period of political pamphleteering. Then in Aug. 1798 he returns to the criticism of Kant's ethics (commentary on the *Metaphysik der Sitten*) and makes his first attempt at 'The Spirit of Christianity'.

authority, of 'higher' and 'lower' faculties no longer make any sense. 'Life' goes through a cycle of development, in which we can distinguish 'higher', more developed phases from 'lower', more primitive ones; but the activity of distinction, and particularly the characterizing of what is distinguished as 'higher' and 'lower', is typical of just one of those phases, the phase of reflection. Reflective life develops out of, and is thus in a certain sense an *advance* from a level of unreflective consciousness which Hegel calls 'oneness' (*Einigkeit*); but to say that reflection is 'higher' than 'oneness' is, from the point of view of reflection itself, extremely Pickwickian, since the whole aim and purpose of all reflective life is to return to 'oneness'. Reflection attempts to re-establish 'oneness' through the establishment of a 'hierarchy of powers', but in the systems of reflective thought there is no 'living' union: the elements in the hierarchy retain their separate identities and are 'opposed' to one another; at the best there is only a relatively stable equilibrium of opposed 'forces'. The difference between such a balance and a living union is made apparent to reflection itself in the actual experience of a living union. The genuine, reflective, return to 'oneness' is love as a self-conscious experience. This return has two aspects (which Hegel generally refers to as 'consciousness' and 'actuality'), and it can vary in both respects. In either respect it is liable either to fall short or to exceed the mean which is the natural harmony of life, i.e. it may be either too reflective or not reflective enough, and either inclusive or exclusive in some inappropriate way. The expression of reflection's *ideal* of living union is 'religion'; and whenever the ideal of a religion departs in some way from the natural ideal of human life itself, man's actual existence becomes in some respect alienated from his consciousness and appears as 'fate'.

To take the most elementary example, which has been discussed in some detail already, Abraham's ideal of living union was just the primitive, undeveloped, unreflective consciousness of the living organism with its natural urge to perpetuate itself. The 'fate' of his love was therefore to find all other life hostile to it, and to be subjected in all things, save only for the saving of life itself, to a law emanating from an alien life. This is the situation where both consciousness and actuality are rendered to a minimum. At the opposite extreme stands Jesus. His love was absolutely self-conscious and all-inclusive, nothing was alien to him, except, as we shall see, the natural bounds of life itself—and his fate was to forfeit that life. Forfeiture of life is, in Hegel's view, the universal fate of Christian love, though the mode of forfeiture varies with the degree of self-consciousness and actual effectiveness of the love itself. Between these two extremes lies the false mean of reflective life itself—instantiated perfectly in Kant's religion of moral reason— and the true mean of Greek religion (in which the moral law is preserved but *aufgehoben*).[1]

It is clear enough from the sequence of the manuscripts that Hegel meant to move on from his first canon of true religion (which we can now call the canon of reflective criticism) to his second (which we can call the canon of living experience); and it is also clear from his first outline of his aims and ideals in *Religion ist eine* that when he did so the Greeks were bound to replace Kant and Lessing as his exemplars. What I have called the 'plane of life' is an analysis of human experience which satisfies the requirement that '*Phantasie, Herz*, and *Sinnlichkeit* must not be sent empty away'. On the plane of reflection (or abstract theory) it is legitimate, I think, to distinguish four levels in Hegel's hierarchy of the faculties. There is, first, a 'lower sensibility' (the 'desirous part' in Plato's terminology, except that in Hegel's view sexual desire certainly does not belong *simply* to this level); then there is the abstract understanding (*Verstand*), which has no practical function except that of prudence; above that (because of its potentially moral character) there is the 'higher sensibility', the part of the soul with which *Phantasie* and *Herz* are themselves associated (and, although Hegel never explicitly says so, everything that Plato assigns to the 'spirited part' probably belongs here);[2] finally, at the top, there is *Vernunft*. If each of these levels is imaginatively embodied and ensouled, if we try to envisage and to feel what it would be like to experience our life from each successive level in turn, we shall find we have pictured the four phases in the cycle of 'life'.

---

[1] The evidential basis for this summary must be looked for in the more detailed discussion of the texts themselves which follows.

[2] The main reason for believing this is Hegel's evident admiration for the public-spiritedness of the Greeks and Romans. The devotion of the spirited part to the cause of the city is, I take it, the 'courage' of Plato's auxiliaries. I do not think that this patriotic feeling can be plausibly identified with 'respect for the law', but it is quite certain that it belongs *at least* to the level of the 'gutartigen Neigungen' (Nohl, p. 18).

The only equivalence which is not perhaps immediately obvious is that of *Verstand*, the faculty of abstract reasoning and of prudence, with reflection itself, as a level of life. It would certainly have been a strange idea to Kant himself that the faculty which makes the theoretical distinction between *Verstand* and *Vernunft*, the faculty that produces the theoretical critique of *Vernunft* (both 'pure' and practical), is really *Verstand*. But even in 1793 Hegel was already saying explicitly that Lessing's *Nathan* is a fruit of *Verstand*, and fairly clearly implying the same about Fichte's *Critique of all Revelation*.[1] Even so, the claim that on the plane of life the prudential function of *Verstand* takes ideal shape as Kant's rational religion and ethics may well seem too paradoxical to be ascribed to a critic as serious and as consciously indebted to Kant as Hegel unquestionably was. Anyone who doubts that this was in fact Hegel's belief,[2] must suspend judgement until we have had time to examine his account of how *Verstand* does 'picture' the world (i.e. how it satisfies *Phantasie* and *Sinnlichkeit* if not *Herz*) and to compare it with the 'fate' of Kantian religion and morality.

It should be clear from what has already been said that there is a 'religion' for each phase of development. *Vernunft*, therefore, does not correspond on the plane of religion to any and every religion but to the perfect harmony of life exemplified in the Greek experience. Thus Greek religion was the absolute religion, the ideal of 'Religion' as a phase of life itself; the ultimate consummation of experience in which life and love, actuality and consciousness, are finally and completely united and satisfied, is exemplified neither in the *Vernunftreligion* of a German professor nor in the Sermon on the Mount, but in the discourse of Socrates in the *Phaedo*. It is important to realize this, because there are no more explicit comparisons between Jesus and Socrates in the manuscripts that we have now to examine. If the texts are attentively examined, Hegel's continuing belief in the superiority of the Greek ideal to that of Jesus does become apparent; but the fact that Jesus' religion of love is the highest phase of living experience that he actually

---

[1] See *Religion ist eine*, Nohl, p. 12.

[2] There have already been many hints of this in his various discussions of the principle 'virtue deserves happiness' (e.g. in *Ein positiver Glauben*). In the material that we have so far examined Hegel comes closest to an explicit avowal of this belief in *Glauben ist die Art* (Nohl, p. 385). The belief itself would seem less paradoxical (perhaps) if, like Hegel, we were always accustomed to think of Kant's ethics in context of his *Religion*.

discusses, together with the hardly less evident fact that his whole conception of 'love' owes more to the New Testament than to any other source, have combined with certain other less relevant factors—notably the Christian background and prejudices of many interpreters, and the knowledge shared by all of them that, for the mature Hegel, Christianity was the 'absolute' religion[1]—to obscure the essentially critical, dissatisfied attitude of the young Hegel towards both the early Church and its founder.

It will be best to delay further argument upon this point until we have examined the texts. The present attempt to sum up Hegel's conclusions in this anticipatory way is only justified because the extreme subtlety of the doctrine is almost matched by the confused state of the manuscripts. The long essay published by Nohl as 'The Spirit of Christianity and its Fate'[2] is really a series of essays with no absolutely determinate sequence. The essays themselves were put together by Hegel during 1799, or even perhaps early in 1800, by cutting up, revising, and making lengthy additions to, a set of meditations written in the last few months of 1798 and the first few months of 1799. The earlier version may have been no more than a series of fairly lengthy fragments gradually worked up from

---

[1] For the mature Hegel, Christianity is the 'absolute' religion; but religion itself is no longer 'absolute knowledge' as it was for Hegel in 1798. The reconciliation of all experience into final harmony belongs now to philosophy—and any reader of Hegel's *Lectures on the History of Philosophy* will know how highly he rated the achievement of the Greeks in that direction. One could plausibly argue that the 'ideal of his youth' never lost its pre-eminence in Hegel's mind.

[2] Nohl, pp. 243–342. The proper *incipit* of this complex is *Abraham in Chaldäa geboren hatte schon* (Nohl, p. 245; cf. p. 332 n. 2 below). The opening fragment *Mit Abraham, dem wahren Stammvater* belongs properly to the category of 'Entwürfe' (cf. p. 280 n. 3 above). But the section on Judaism (Nohl, pp. 245–60) was drafted earlier and has already been discussed; and the sequence of the subsequent sections was not definitely indicated by Hegel himself, but imposed by Nohl (on the basis of hints in Hegel's preparatory sketches). I do not generally use any *incipit* for Nohl, pp. 261–342 as a whole (referring to it as 'The Spirit of Christianity' where necessary); but I do cite the *incipits* of the various sections. Occasionally, where it seems advisable, I shall give the *incipits* of fragments which appear to be distinguishable within Nohl's sections. The reasons for doing this will vary in particular cases, and will be explained as the occasions arise. One general consideration that is relevant in this connection however is that the manuscript is a conflation of two separate drafts throughout—though it is generally not possible to separate them with certainty in Nohl's edition. Thus the *incipit* of the first draft of the first section in Nohl (so far as it survives) is ⟨leben⟩digen Modifikation, and I sometimes use this to refer to the first draft as a whole. The *incipit* in Nohl's edition *Jesus trat nicht lange* I sometimes use for the second draft as a whole, and sometimes to refer *only* to the new first page that Hegel wrote for his second draft (Nohl, p. 261).

notes and memoranda like those which we find intermingled with passages of continuous argument in the two surviving fragments which Nohl classes as 'Entwürfe'.[1] In any case the sequence of the manuscript in its original form cannot now be restored; all we can say with certainty is that the ordering of topics and arguments was in places very different from that of the second draft.

The sequence of composition cannot be restored either. We cannot tell which of his interwoven themes Hegel chose to disentangle first—if indeed he wrote about them in any definite order at all: morality and love, punishment and fate, virtue, the fate of Jesus, etc. The dating of the manuscripts is rendered exceptionally difficult in this period by two circumstances: first Hegel's handwriting was in a more stable condition than at any time hitherto—only the single letter z was now in process of evolution—and secondly there are very few securely dated exemplars of his handwriting during this period to provide standards for measuring such evolution as there was. All that can be certainly established is that a considerable interval occurred between the composition of the first draft and the subsequent revision and additions. This interval very probably began not later than February 1799. How long it lasted, just when the manuscript as we have it was begun and completed, it is impossible to say.[2]

In view of the almost astounding consistency of Hegel's development up to this time, which our investigation has already revealed, the impossibility of pursuing our inquiry in strict chronological sequence at this stage does not matter very much. It will be sufficient to study the text as Hegel finally left it, making use of any information available about its earlier states simply in order to throw light upon the meaning of the final version. Generally speaking, the final text is fuller and more explicit than any earlier version; but this is not universally the case, and even where it is so, we can sometimes get important clues from the earlier, more

---

[1] *Zu der Zeit, da Jesus*, Nohl, pp. 385–98 (the so-called *Grundkonzept*); and *B. Moral. Bergpredigt*, Nohl, pp. 398–402; no doubt these fragments belonged to a slightly earlier phase of the evolution of the manuscript. In view of the way in which the essay on Judaism (*Abraham in Chaldäa geboren hatte schon*) evolved, it seems likely that there were other sets of notes and brief fragments like these. Hegel also drew material, no doubt, from his notes on Kant's *Metaphysik der Sitten*; and his revision of *welchem Zwecke denn alles Übrige dient*, at about that time, indicates that he may have thought of this piece too as belonging to the same complex.

[2] See Schüler, pp. 151–3.

condensed statements, because the stimulus or occasion of Hegel's thought is more apparent in them than in the final version, where he is trying to put his case for an outside audience rather than to get his ideas clear for himself.

6. *Morality and love*

The earliest notes for 'The Spirit of Christianity' seem to indicate that Hegel had it in mind to deal with five topics in sequence.[1] There was first of all the spirit of 'positive faith' or legality, enshrined in the religion of Moses and represented in the time of Jesus by the Pharisees. This was dealt with in the first essay on 'The Spirit of Judaism', which we have already examined.[2]

[1] In *Zu der Zeit, da Jesus* the four levels *Positivität, Moral (Gesinnung), Liebe, Religion* are distinguished at the foot of Nohl, p. 389. See also pp. 393–4 where the first level appears as *Ceremonien*: the levels of *Liebe* and *Religion* are there run together under one heading (no title is given, but the one supplied by B. *Moral. Bergpredigt* is *Religion*). B. *Moral. Bergpredigt* also supplies the fifth heading D. *Geschichte* (Nohl, p. 400) which is thematically required in *Zu der Zeit, da Jesus* at the top of Nohl, p. 396. It is apparent that as his reflections developed Hegel found that he could not effectively separate the topics of *Moralität* and *Liebe* except on the negative side. Thus he decided to write an essay on the moral ideal of Jesus, and another on punishment and forgiveness; then one on the religion of love, and finally one on the 'fate' of that religion (in the 'history' of Jesus and the Church).

[2] There cannot be any doubt that Nohl is right to print *Abraham in Chaldäa geboren hatte schon* as the first section of the final version. The figure '5' added by Hegel to the note '24 Bogen' on the manuscript *must* refer to the essay on Judaism, since the preparatory notes for 'The Spirit of Christianity' total not five but six double sheets. Hegel himself indicates that B. *Moral. Bergpredigt* is a supplement to *Zu der Zeit, da Jesus*. Compare the cancelled heading 'Moral in der Bergpredigt Mt 5-7', Nohl, p. 393, with the *incipit* of the supplementary fragment; also the second heading in B. *Moral. Bergpredigt*: 'Zu C. Religion' (Nohl, p. 400), shows that the material there following was to be added to *Zu der Zeit, da Jesus* at the corresponding point 'C' (Nohl, p. 394).

Thus the ambiguity Miss Schüler suggests about the possible reference of the added numeral (*Hegel-Studien*, ii. 150) does not exist. The essay *Abraham in Chaldäa geboren hatte schon* occupies five sheets and Hegel marked it accordingly, in order to distinguish it from all the previous drafts and fragments—including *Mit Abraham, dem wahren Stammvater*. (As Miss Schüler has shown, Nohl is not simply mistaken in thinking this was added later, but mistaken in thinking that Hegel meant to include it at all.) On the other hand the preparatory notes for 'The Spirit of Christianity' occupied six sheets at least (there may possibly have been more) and if Hegel had felt concerned about keeping them together he would have marked them as six or more. He could not simply number them because the material is not in order on the sheets. But this did not matter in the case of the preliminary notes, whereas it was vital to keep his manuscript together; so he noted the extent of the two complexes which contained his final version, precisely in order to facilitate keeping them separate from everything else.

Secondly there was the spirit of rational faith or morality. Hegel had already written *The Life of Jesus* as a story of opposition between Jesus and the Pharisees, of the ideal of autonomy against the tradition of heteronomy. This opposition is still acknowledged in 'The Spirit of Christianity'.[1] But it is now viewed as part of Jesus' 'fate', being contrary to his deliberate intent. Jesus now appears as the protagonist of the higher spirit of love, which refuses to be 'opposed' to anything, and can therefore fairly be *said* to be 'opposed' to the whole spirit of opposition. In this sense Jesus 'opposes' the whole 'fate' of Judaism; but he also 'opposes' Kant in a different way. On the positive side the spirit of love 'fulfils' the spirit of morality; but it is 'opposed' to it in its relation to what morality itself is opposed to: it is opposed to morality as punishment. Thus, Hegel had to write two essays, one on love as the $\pi\lambda\eta\rho\omega\mu\alpha$ of the moral law, and another on the contrast between penal justice and forgiveness.

The ideal of perfect reconciliation takes us beyond love as a simple mode of consciousness to the level of religion as the perfect *self*-consciousness of reconciled life; but then, finally, actual experience—the history of Jesus and his Church—shows that the Christian ideal of perfect reconciliation, absolute fatelessness, is only a noble dream.

The first problem that now faced Hegel, therefore, was to characterize Christian love, for which I shall hereafter use the traditional term 'charity', as an 'actuality', to show how it appears in the world as a working relation between men. Charity is the spirit which is 'raised above fate', since by 'fate' we mean the reaction of some living power upon the consciousness that suppresses it, mutilates it, or regards it as alien. For charity there can be no fate, because nothing in life is alien to it. It stands therefore at the opposite pole from the life that regards all other life with hostility, and hence is everywhere subjected to external authority, or else to suffering and violence. The Jews had experienced the extremity of this fate when they lost their national independence. They looked now for a Messiah to save them from it, but since they could not recognize it as their own self-wrought fate, only death in battle (in the great revolt of A.D. 70) could overpower it. Jesus could bring the gospel of peace only to those who no longer had a

---

[1] Cf. *B. Moral. Bergpredigt*, Nohl, p. 401; *Mit dem Mute und dem Glauben*, Nohl, pp. 326–7 (Knox, p. 283).

share in 'fate', because they had given up the fight and had nothing left to uphold or defend, i.e. no 'spirit' to express.[1]

In this state of absolute subjection to authority, a fully self-conscious observer can perceive three distinct levels: religious law; moral law; civil law. An 'enlightened'—i.e. reflective—critic (Kant's rational man) will perceive only moral law and civil law, since for him the law of God must coincide with the law of reason. But for an unreflective man, who simply recognizes his own absolute subjection, there is simply 'the law', which is the condition of his self-preservation. This is, in Hegel's view, the condition of the law-abiding Jew before his God: '⟨Even relations which⟩ we might recognize as grounded in ⟨the liv⟩ing modification of human nature [i.e. in the conscious individual]—rights which he himself surrenders when he establishes dominions [*Gewalten*] over him— were positive throughout.'[2]

There really are only two levels of law and right: the moral level where the rational man preserves autonomy, and the civil level where all men, whether rational or not, recognize that they must surrender the right to judge and execute judgement to a constituted

---

[1] See *Jesus trat nicht lange* (Nohl, p. 261; Knox, pp. 205–6) and *Zu der Zeit, da Jesus* (Nohl, pp. 385–6). I assume that the latter gives us a fairly clear idea of the general tenor of Hegel's opening in the first version. In that event the main difference here between the first and the second version consisted in the elimination of much concrete detail in the latter (e.g. the reference to the attitudes of Pharisees, Sadducees, Essenes). In a continuous account this material belonged more naturally to the preceding section on the spirit of Judaism.

Knox is mistaken, I think, in taking 'keinen Anteil mehr an dem Schicksal' to refer specifically to the fate of the Jewish people. The Jews did not heed the Gospel precisely because they were preoccupied with their fate. The 'publicans and sinners' with whom Jesus himself consorted and the subjects of the Roman Empire who were later converted to the new religion had these two things in common: they were subjected to an absolute authority in this world, and they had 'no longer any share in fate' (of any kind) because they did not claim any right to live their own lives as they saw fit.

[2] This is a conservative reconstruction of the opening sentence of the first draft, ⟨leben⟩digen *Modifikation*, Nohl, p. 261. Cf. Knox, p. 206, for a translation of Haering's slightly more ambitious reconstruction. We should naturally assume that what is 'grounded in the living modification of human nature' is a complex of harmonious ties of affection and love. In that case Hegel *is* speaking, as Haering supposes, 'in the spirit of Jesus'; but the immediate introduction of the word 'Rechte' in apposition to whatever it is that is 'grounded etc.' brings us down to the level of practical reason. It *may* be, of course, that this use of 'Rechte' is only accidental, being imposed as it were by the contextual reference to the establishment of civil law. But the whole terminology of 'grounding' and 'surrendering' 'rights' suggests that the *Metaphysik der Sitten* is in Hegel's mind rather than St. John's Gospel.

authority, the sovereign power (*Gewalt*) that keeps us all in awe. But there is also a higher level—our relations with the divine—which is not properly a matter of laws and regulations at all. When we feel ourselves to be in the presence of the divine we act reverently because reverent action expresses what we feel, not because we have decided that we *ought* to act thus, still less because it has been decreed by God, or anyone else, that we *must* act thus. The pressure of natural necessity may destroy the feeling of reverence, or prevent its natural expression, as when David ate the shewbread. But when the need is slight, there is a stark contrast between the holiness of the object or command and the attitude expressed in its desecration.[1] Hence, when Jesus cited the example of David in justification of the plucking of the corn by his disciples on the Sabbath he was *not* simply saying that reverence for the Sabbath must be bounded by reason; he was implying that the most trivial and momentary impulses of life are more holy than the *command* that God gave to Moses.

In the case of moral laws (and of civil laws also in so far as they have a basis in moral reason and hence have the force of moral imperatives for the rational man)[2] we might have expected, says Hegel, that Jesus would concentrate upon revealing their rational character, and so do away with their merely positive aspect as part of the total complex of Jewish law. This is in fact what Hegel's Jesus does in *Das Leben Jesu*.[3] But a transformation of this sort is no longer sufficient. All moral laws, whether capable of civil enforcement or not, have a positive aspect that cannot be eliminated, inasmuch as they enforce the authority of reason over the rest of human nature. They are civilly enforceable when they govern relations between different individuals, whereas when they concern only the personal attitudes and conduct of the rational individual

[1] Nohl, p. 262 n. [*a*]. This was in the first version of the paragraph beginning on p. 207 of Knox's translation.

[2] According to Roques's edition (p. 90) the cancelled passage given by Nohl, p. 264 n. [*a*], continues as follows: 'Alle bürgerlichen Gesetze sind zugleich moralische, und sie unterscheiden sich von den rein moralischen, die nicht fähig sind, bürgerliche Gesetze zugleich zu werden, dadurch daß sie ihre Bed⟨ingungen?⟩ . . .'; the continuation is lost but at least it is clear that the sentence which Nohl does print has to be interpreted along the lines of my parenthesis here.

[3] The cancelled passage from the first draft given by Nohl, p. 265 n. [*a*], seems to have been specifically directed against Hegel's own earlier position. (It was probably cancelled and rewritten precisely for this reason.)

they are purely and simply moral laws. But the very fact that purely moral laws about private attitudes can be made positive, as they were in the Mosaic Law, by being thought of as the commands of God, the reflective consciousness 'from whom no secrets are hid', reveals the unresolved dualism that is implicit in a legalistic ethics: 'Since laws are unitings of opposed terms in a concept, which thus leaves the terms as opposites—and the concept itself exists in opposition to actuality, it follows that the concept expresses an *ought*.'[1]

In the case of laws which are not laws of reason, or in cases where we are not conscious of them as laws of reason—i.e. where we consider only the *content* of the law (as a *command*) rather than its form (as a *concept*)—the abiding opposition between the terms (sovereign and subject) is obvious enough and needs no dwelling upon. But even the laws of reason which 'express natural relations of men in the form of commands' retain their objective validity whether we obey them or not; and because they thus 'exist in opposition to actuality' the opposition between the actual element (inclination) and the conceptual element (duty) persists in them. It is always legitimate to distinguish the form from the content of a moral act, because they are not essentially united, they exist as elements in the quite distinct orders of freedom and nature, of reason and necessity, of moral and natural law. Thus Reason in virtue of its independent status becomes a kind of internal sovereign, and the man who prides himself on his enlightenment is really only a slave to himself, instead of being a slave to someone else.

The spirit of love is just as much 'opposed to opposition' in *this* form as it is opposed to the less subtle forms of hostility and bondage. It is 'raised above morality'. The law, so far as it is a requirement of human nature itself, must be fulfilled; it cannot be flouted in the interests of a momentary whim (as Jesus flouted the *positive* 'law of God': 'Remember the Sabbath day, to keep it holy'). But love must overcome the opposition between concept and actuality,

---

[1] Nohl, p. 264; Knox, p. 209. Knox's explanatory note on this passage begins to go wrong when he says that 'Law is *only* a concept, because it can be disobeyed, etc.'. If this point were crucial, we could create a problem for Hegel by retorting that 'Love is *only* an ideal because it can be sinned against etc.'. The point is that moral laws possess as 'concepts' an independent status which stands opposed to the actual situation, whether it is concordant with the law or not. Their validity is quite independent of our obedience. Whereas when love is sinned against, either love must perish, or the sin itself must be *aufgehoben* in forgiveness and reconciliation.

duty and inclination, in a union such that the terms no longer have independent status. Instead of being commanded to achieve something whose possibility has been rationally demonstrated, men must be made aware of the actual presence in themselves of a state of being. Living actuality is essentially prior to conceived possibility; only when this has been made manifest can the point of view of reflection be transcended.

It is easy enough to *say* this; but to make its truth or validity manifest is not easy, because language is the natural mode of reflection. The obvious and explicit opposition between what is and what is said makes it difficult for us to realize that a prophetic statement about the true character of human relations is not meant as an impossible command or as a paradox. The beatitudes with which Jesus begins the Sermon on the Mount, like the prophetic remarks and 'inadequate parables' with which it closes (Matthew 7: 6–29), are intended, Hegel thinks, to put us on our guard against this temptation. The 'commands' of the new law are not *concepts of a possible order of things*; they are *evocations of the potentialities for life* which are actually present in human nature.

As a starting-point, Hegel took from Kant himself the term *Gesinnung* to express the living union of reason with inclination. It is not clear how far he regarded his own use of the term as concordant with Kant's—and I do not, for my part, wish to express an opinion as to how far it *is* concordant—but it is probable at least that he deliberately decided that this was the best growing-point in Kant's theory. In the place of Kant's 'moral disposition' he put 'the disposition of *Menschenliebe*'.[1] In *Zu der Zeit, da Jesus* there is a formula which sums up his doctrine thus: '*Gesinnung* cancels (*aufhebt*) the positivity, objectivity of the command; Love ⟨cancels⟩ the limits of the *Gesinnung*, Religion the limits of love.'[2] A passage in the first version of 'The Spirit of Christianity' shows us how *Gesinnung* and *Tugend*, as the moral aspect of 'life', are distinguishable from *Liebe*, yet so intrinsically connected with it that the

---

[1] Nohl, p. 268 and the cancelled passage in n. [c] (cf. Knox, p. 215 and n. 40). 'Die Gesinnung der Menschenliebe' is not here explicitly accorded a status of equivalence in generality with 'die moralische Gesinnung'; but this passage, together with the discussion of how love reconciles the virtues (Nohl, pp. 293–6; Knox, pp. 244–7), makes the interpretation of the bare term 'die Gesinnung' in the axiom cited from *Zu der Zeit, da Jesus* fairly plain sailing.

[2] Nohl, p. 389. The first two clauses of this axiom are echoed in *Die Liebe versöhnt aber* (Nohl, p. 295; Knox, p. 246): 'Just as virtue is the complement of obedience to law, so love is the complement of the virtues.'

distinction can never constitute an opposition; and the subsequent revision of this passage shows how, once Hegel had clarified his attitude to Kant's ethics for himself, he began to remove all explicit indications of a direct relationship between his view and Kant's, in order to eliminate the danger of a 'reflective' interpretation of his view, and perhaps also in order to accentuate the contrast between his view and Kant's. In the first version Hegel wrote: 'Against complete subjection to the law of an alien lord, Jesus set, not a partial subjection to a law of one's own, the self-coercion of Kantian virtue, but the virtuous disposition—the expression "disposition" has the disadvantage, that it does not include a direct reference to the activity, the virtue in action.'[1] In the second draft he substituted 'virtues without lordship and without submission, modifications of love' for 'the virtuous disposition etc.'; and his remark about the inadequacy of the term 'disposition' explains the cancellation. We may well remember at this point that Aristotle gave much the same reason for refusing to identify 'happiness' with 'virtue'. Hegel's *Liebe*, like Aristotle's εὐδαιμονία, is 'activity of soul (the life principle) in accordance with virtue'. He decided to speak of the different virtuous activities as 'modifications of love' rather than as actualizations of different dispositions, because in that way the artificiality of all talk about

---

[1] *Die Liebe versöhnt aber*, Nohl, p. 293 with n. [*b*]; for the second version see Knox, p. 244. I prefer to regard the part of the manuscript beginning on Nohl, p. 289, *Daß auch Jesus den Zusammenhang*, as a series of discrete fragments, because it is clear from Nohl's note at that point that Hegel himself never quite decided what the sequence of his discussion should be. Nohl thinks it likely that he meant to pass on to *Im Geiste der Juden* (Nohl, p. 290). In Roques's edition (pp. 178–9) the paragraph *Kühnheit, die Zuversicht* (Nohl, p. 290) is printed immediately before *Die Liebe versöhnt aber* (Nohl, p. 293). The connection of *Die Liebe versöhnt aber* with the following discussion of the Last Supper, *Der Abschied, den Jesus* (Nohl, p. 297), is unquestionable, since the manuscript is here continuous. But I have decided to lift it out of this context nevertheless, because of its obvious relevance to the discussion of the ethics of Jesus as presented in the Sermon on the Mount.

Apparently Hegel thought of making the transition from his discussion of punishment and forgiveness to the level of religion by way of a new discussion of love as an achieved state of being. But this plan would really have required the incorporation of almost all of the earlier essay ⟨*leben*⟩*digen Modifikation* at this point.

When we take into account the cancelled passage (Nohl, p. 296 n. [*b*]) which trails off into notes as Hegel's first drafts so often do, it becomes quite clear that *Der Abschied, den Jesus*, even though it began on the same sheet (cf. Roques, p. 94 for the break between the sheets), is the beginning of a new meditation on Hegel's part.

'collisions' between the virtues or 'conflicts of duty' is most clearly revealed. From the beginning he felt that one of the most evident weaknesses of the Kantian approach to ethics was that it led to the raising of problems of this kind,[1] and his study of the *Metaphysik der Sitten* fully confirmed this opinion. He admitted that even upon Kant's view it was not really correct to speak of a collision of virtue with itself, but this is only true because in actual life Kant's assumptions are *aufgehoben*:

> We may indeed say that the virtuous disposition considered by itself and in general, i.e. abstracted from the virtues here posited [two different virtues of a virtuous man], does not come into collision, since the virtuous disposition is one and one only. But with that assertion the presupposition [of different virtues] is *aufgehoben*; and if both virtues *are* posited, then the exercise of one removes [*aufhebt*] the matter and thereby the possibility of exercising the other, which is just as absolute as the first, and the justified claim of the other is rejected.[2]

The best way to understand what Hegel is driving at here is to consider the way in which Kant discusses his 'casuistical questions' in the *Metaphysik der Sitten*. One case that must have made a most forcible impression upon Hegel, because Kant's attitude and approach is so far removed from his own, is the discussion of sexual love. But although Kant himself speaks of a 'collision of the determining grounds of morally-practical reason' in this connection, his view of sexual love is so low that we can hardly interpret this as a case of 'collision of virtues'.[3] So it will be both easier and

[1] Cf. *Religion ist eine*, Nohl, pp. 19–20 (pp. 497–8 below).
[2] Nohl, p. 294; Knox, pp. 244–5.
[3] 'Nature's purpose in the intercourse of the sexes is procreation, i.e. the preservation of the race. Hence one may not, at least, act contrary to that end. But is it permissible to use the sexual power *without regard for that end* (even within marriage)?

'For example, if the wife is pregnant or sterile (because of age or sickness), or if she feels no desire for intercourse, is not the use of the sexual power contrary to nature's purpose and so also contrary to duty to oneself as well, in one way or another—just as in unnatural lust? Or is there, in this case, a permissive law of morally-practical reason, which in the collision of its determining grounds makes permissible something that is in itself not permitted (indulgently, as it were), in order to prevent a still greater transgression? At what point can we call the limitation of a wide duty a purism (a pedantry in the observance of duty, so far as the wideness of the duty is concerned) and allow the animal inclinations a play-room, at the risk of abandoning the law of reason?

'Sexual inclination is also called "love" (in the narrowest sense of the term) and is, in fact, the strongest possible sensuous pleasure in an object. It is not

fairer to take the simpler example of conviviality (which both Kant and Hegel enjoyed). Kant writes:

Although a banquet is a formal invitation to intemperance in both food and drink, there is still something in it that aims at a moral end, beyond mere physical well-being: it keeps a lot of people together for a long time so that they may exchange their ideas. And yet the very number of the guests (if, as Chesterfield says, it exceeds the number of the Muses) permits only a limited exchange of ideas (between people sitting next to each other); and so the arrangement is at variance with that [moral] end, while the banquet remains a temptation to immorality —intemperance, which is a violation of duty to oneself. How far can we extend the moral title to accept these invitations to intemperance?[1]

Here we have a genuine 'collision of virtues'. The rational man must be temperate, but he must also do all that he can do to stimulate and advance the rational exchange of ideas. Conviviality on a large scale, as at a banquet, is unjustifiable, but there is clearly a sort of no-man's-land where, if we think of virtue in terms of rational obligation, we are always subject to the imputation of guilt with respect to one obligation precisely because we have chosen to fulfil the other. The very existence of a 'casuistical question', a

merely a *pleasure of the senses*, such as we experience in objects that are pleasing when we merely contemplate them (capacity for which pleasure is called taste). It is rather pleasure from the *use* of another person, which therefore belongs to the *appetitive* power and, indeed, to the appetitive power in its highest degree, passion. But it cannot be classed with either the love that is mere affection or the love of benevolence (for both of these stop short of carnal enjoyment). It is a unique kind of pleasure (*sui generis*), and sexual burning [*das Brunstig-sein*] really has nothing in common with moral love, though it can enter into close connection [*Verbindung*] with it under the limiting conditions of practical reason' (*Akad.*, vi. 426; Gregor, pp. 89–90).

It is evident that Kant, like St. Paul, thinks of marriage as a contract for the enjoyment of one another's body. The contract would be absolutely immoral, the reduction of humanity to the status of a mere means both in one's own person and in that of the other partner, if entered into simply for the sake of carnal pleasure. What justifies it, and makes sexual intercourse itself a duty for the rational man, is 'nature's purpose' in making men 'burn'—the preservation of the race. The 'collision' is not here a collision of virtues, but of reason and nature, the two 'determining grounds' of all duty; it is a collision of rational purpose with natural instinct. Kant's view appears to be that every rational person must decide how much 'play-room' his animal instincts need in order to remain healthy. But this 'play-room' is at best only tolerated by reason. The instinct itself has 'nothing in common' with rational love, although it can be 'closely bound up with it'. In this 'Verbindung' we have the 'Aufhebung' of Kant's assumptions to which Hegel refers; he analyses it in *welchem Zwecke denn alles Übrige dient.*

[1] Kant, *Akad.*, vi. 428; Gregor, pp. 91–2.

question which can only be solved in living experience, bears witness to the collision; and the intuitive decision of the virtuous man restores the unity of 'virtuous disposition' and overthrows the basic assumption of the casuistical approach: the assumption that there really are distinct obligations. If we recognize that the virtues are 'modifications of love' we are not tempted to approach them casuistically in the first place, for we realize that it is not a matter of making a hierarchy of creditors but of living in charity with one's neighbours and oneself. One does not reflect within oneself about the varying claims upon one, and strive to balance the rights of the claimants; rather one seeks to get all the claimants to reconcile their claims and join in amity.

As far as duties to oneself are concerned the difference between Hegel's attitude and Kantian casuistry is one of feeling. If Hegel ever suspected on one of those convivial evenings at the Sonnenscheins's in the dark days of his loneliness in Berne that he was on the verge of getting drunk, he was not restrained by the categorical imperative, or by the thought of a rational exchange of ideas as the moral justification for his indulgence, but by the feeling of friendship itself.[1]

But where duties to others are concerned, there is a difference not just in feeling, but in action; for one will not reason with oneself (as the casuist does) but rather try to establish community with the others involved, treating them as one's neighbours and seeking to make them neighbourly to one another. Only if that fails does one descend to the level of a weighing of obligations and balancing of rights. ' "Love has conquered" does not, like "Duty has conquered", mean that it has subdued its enemies, but that it has overcome enmity.'[2] Love cannot be commanded, it has to be spontaneous; but it is voluntary in its spontaneity, and it can evoke a voluntary response.

This was the 'righteousness greater than that of the scribes and Pharisees'[3] which Jesus sought to evoke in his hearers: 'an inclination to act as the laws would command, not the underpinning of

---

[1] See Rosenkranz, p. 43, for the evenings at the Sonnenscheins's. Compare also Leutwein's memories of Hegel's *Moralität* being better than his *Legalität* etc. (*Hegel-Studien*, iii. 54, lines 38–58).

[2] *Die Liebe versöhnt aber*, Nohl, p. 296 (Knox, p. 247).

[3] ⟨*leben*⟩*digen Modifikation*, Roques, p. 93; this is an explicit reference in the first version which was not printed by Nohl. The echo at the bottom of Nohl, p. 267 (Knox, p. 214) appears to be the revised version.

the moral disposition (*Gesinnung*) by inclination (*Neigung*) but a naturally inclined moral disposition (*eine geneigte moralische Gesinnung*), i.e. a moral disposition without conflict.'[1] Thus the law loses its form as law; for it is not right to speak of being obliged to do something when one is really doing it because one wants to.[2] The correspondence of *Neigung* with *Gesetz* in Hegel's *geneigte moralische Gesinnung* is the correspondence of 'actuality' with 'concept' in such a way that they cannot be separated without being destroyed. In place of the empty abstraction, 'Thou shalt not kill', Jesus sets a willingness to be reconciled for which the command is superfluous; and indeed the 'rending' of life by the attitude of reflective neutrality, which is all that the law requires, is the one thing which the new attitude excludes. Even anger, being an uprush of living impulse, the expression of a living sense of injustice, is not so opposed to the spirit of reconciliation as the reflective attitude that we adopt in declaring someone else to be a fool.[3]

Love 'requires the *Aufhebung* of right';[4] but when love fails, there is necessarily a return to the level of right. Hegel's interpretation of what Jesus says about adultery and divorce shows that not only the rational principle of 'equal rights', but also the positive principle of 'natural lordship' is present, though *aufgehoben* in his doctrine of love. The husband cannot put away a loving wife simply because he has ceased to love her; but on the other hand if the wife has given her love to another, the husband 'cannot remain

---

[1] ⟨leben⟩*digen Modifikation*, Nohl, p. 268 and n. [*a*]. The contrast between Kantian and Hegelian *Gesinnungen* is eliminated in the second draft.

[2] For Kant's extremely subtle analysis of the ways in which we can and cannot, should and should not, like to do what we ought, see *Kritik der praktischen Vernunft*, Part I, Chapter III (*Akad.*, v. 71–89). The best gloss on my remark in the text occurs on pp. 83–4: 'A law would not be needed if we already knew of ourselves what we ought to do and moreover were conscious of liking to do it. . . . To such a level of moral disposition no creature can ever attain. . . . Consequently, it is . . . always necessary to base the intention of the creature's maxims on moral constraint and not on ready willingness. . . . This would be true even if the mere love for the law (which would in this case cease to be a command, and morality, subjectively passing over into holiness, would cease to be virtue) were made the constant but unattainable goal of its striving' (Beck, pp. 86–7).

[3] The questionable accuracy of Hegel's biblical exegesis here (see Knox, p. 216 n.) is less interesting than the comparison of his doctrine with Kant's— which undoubtedly suggested it (see 'Metaphysische Anfangsgründe der Tugendlehre', § 39, *Akad.*, vi. 463–4; Gregor, pp. 132–4).

[4] ⟨leben⟩*digen Modifikation*, Nohl, p. 270 n. [*a*].

her bondsman [*Knecht*]'. Apparently there is a natural relation of subordination involved in loving relations between the sexes such that, although the duty of fidelity continues to hold good equally for both partners even where love fails, the right to declare the existence of a breach in the event of a betrayal of that duty is not reciprocal, but devolves upon the husband. Hegel's theory reveals at this point Aristotelian rather than Platonic affinities.[1]

All that needs to be noticed about Hegel's discussion of oaths and retributive justice—the next topics of the Sermon on the Mount in Matthew 5—is that he takes both oaths and the principle of reciprocity to be natural to the viewpoint of reflection. There is nothing superstitious about oath-taking, because for reflection the visible world is only the manifestation of invisible power and law; the idea of an oath is to guarantee the truth of an assertion by equating it with an element in the order of nature. The more clearly we understand the order of nature the more powerful does the oath become, and the more surely we invite and deserve retribution if we swear falsely. But love rises above the whole principle of mechanical reciprocity.[2]

The discussion of almsgiving provides us with an interesting example of the contrast between the standpoint of love and the standpoint of reflection. The precept 'Let not thy left hand know what thy right hand doeth' is now seen as a condemnation of the

---

[1] The notes in *B. Moral. Bergpredigt*, Nohl, p. 398, should be compared with Nohl, p. 270 (Knox, pp. 216–17). The worst difficulty in this passage is to decide just what Hegel means by saying that 'ceasing to love a wife, in whom love still is, makes love become untrue to itself and sin'. The point is, I think, that husband and wife form one 'whole'—the 'whole' against which 'one of man's many sides' (e.g. sexual instinct) may rise up and claim its 'rights' or its independence in the absence of love. The 'whole' of human nature is man and woman united in love. Knox misses this Aristophanic meaning of the 'whole' in his translation. (In his notes Hegel speaks of the marriage bond as one of 'friendship', which was Kant's term for the ideal of moral love and implies strict reciprocal equality: cf. Gregor, pp. 46–7, 140–5.)

[2] Since the explicit verdict on oath-taking remains exactly what it was in *The Life of Jesus* (that the principle violates the essential autonomy of the will), we must ask ourselves why Hegel bothers to prove that there is nothing superstitious in swearing 'by the hair of one's head' etc. The answer, probably, is that he wished to maintain a place for oaths in 'living' religion. We should remember that the Greeks were as ready with oaths by all manner of things as any follower of Moses. But the religion of love, like the reflective religion of reason, goes to an unhealthy extreme in this matter. Being bound to the exegesis of Jesus' text Hegel cannot say this explicitly, but it is implicit in his critique of the 'enlightened' attitude. (We should compare here what he says about Isaac's blessing in *Joseph. jüd. Alterth.*, Nohl, p. 368.)

reflective distinction between reason and inclination, not just as a metaphor for the absolute avoidance of ostentation (as in *The Life of Jesus*). Hegel connects the precept plausibly enough with the parable of the Pharisee and the Publican; and, by ascribing everything 'positive' in the Pharisee's attitude to his 'modesty', Hegel contrives to exhibit him as a paradigm case of Kant's virtuous man. The consciousness of righteousness, which Kant declares to be a duty to oneself, is to be condemned on two counts. First, and most immediately, on practical grounds, because it must inevitably sully the motive for the good action of which one is conscious; secondly, on theoretical grounds, because it involves the assumption that virtue is a sum or system of dispositions, and the analysis of virtue in these terms is inexhaustible in principle and self-defeating in practice. The number of the virtues is forever increasing and so is the complexity of the collisions between their competing claims.[1]

Prayer and fasting, which follow the giving of alms in the text of Jesus' discourse, are not of course moral duties in the Kantian sense at all. As ritual practices they are like Sabbath observance and the washing of hands; and as expressions of a felt need they belong to the higher level of religion and hence discussion must be postponed.[2]

[1] 'Impartiality in judging oneself in comparison with the law and sincerity in avowing to oneself one's inner moral worth or unworth are duties to oneself that follow immediately from that first command of self-knowledge' (Kant, 'Tugendlehre', § 15, *Akad.*, vi. 441–2; Gregor, p. 108). In connection with the Pharisee's 'modesty' compare Kant's definition of the 'duty of religion': 'the duty of recognizing all our duties as if [*instar*] they were divine commands' (ibid., § 18, *Akad.*, vi. 443; Gregor, p. 110). Even Hegel's use of 'modest' (*bescheiden*) here is not without Kantian overtones. Kant defines *Bescheidenheit* as 'the willing limitation of one man's self-love by the self-love of others' but from his subsequent definition of 'arrogance' we can see that his definition of 'modesty' in a moral context would be 'the willing limitation of one's claims to respect out of respect for others'. If we extend this to cover relations with God as our inner Judge (ibid., § 13, *Akad.*, vi. 439; Gregor, p. 105) we shall see how the close analogy between positive religion and the religion of reason enables Hegel to give the parable a Kantian interpretation in spite of the distinction Kant draws between 'duty to' beings other than men and 'duty with regard to' them (ibid., § 16, *Akad.*, vi. 442; Gregor, p. 108).

Of course Kant himself seems to regard 'that first command of self-knowledge' as one that we can only strive to fulfil (cf. ibid., § 21–2, *Akad.*, vi. 446–7; Gregor, pp. 113–14). But this *Aufhebung* of the reflective assumption only leads to the opposite extreme of perpetual *Angst* (the state of the Publican seen from a reflective point of view). Hegel will examine this side of Kant's doctrine in his next essay (*Der Positivität der Juden*, Nohl, pp. 276–80).

[2] Knox's note on 'moral duties' (p. 220), 'i.e. duties as they are conceived in what Hegel takes to be Kant's ethics', is unjust, I think, in the implicit suggestion

At this point we reach the essential limit of love as an expression of life: the world of material, non-living things, the world of property. Hegel has already argued in *welchem Zwecke denn alles Übrige dient* that the ideal community of perfect love is only an illusion when applied to property. This is a realm where reflective analysis in terms of rights and duties properly holds sway, and the collisions of the virtues, the conflicts of rights, cannot here be overcome by love. The act of virtue does not here create a community between the agent and his neighbour, it expresses no 'whole' in which they are organs; on the contrary, it involves always a fixing of the boundary between *meum* and *tuum*, and whichever way the decision goes as between justice and generosity it will be 'opposed' to one virtue so far as it satisfies the requirements of the other. Love can only express itself in this realm as absolute indifference, as contempt. Material property is an alien master and the ideal of justice as fairness belongs to an alien world.

This, as Hegel says, is 'a litany pardonable only in sermons and rhymes, for such a command is without truth for us'.[1] In large part, as we shall see, the fate both of the religion of love and of its founder is traceable in Hegel's view to the excess involved in this 'flight from the world'. From Hegel's point of view it was this weakness that rendered Christianity incapable of becoming in its original form a true folk-religion, since the public life of men as citizens was *ipso facto* excluded from its purview, and thus the third canon of a folk-religion was flouted.[2]

---

that 'what Hegel takes to be Kant's ethics' is not really Kant's view. Compare, as the probable source of Hegel's remark, 'Tugendlehre', § 16 (Gregor, pp. 108–9).

[1] ⟨*leben*⟩*digen Modifikation*, Nohl, p. 273 (Knox, p. 221).

[2] The third canon requires that 'it must be so constituted that all the needs of life—the public activities of the State are tied in with it—' (Nohl, p. 20). I am inclined to suspect that through haste and inadvertence Hegel did not quite complete his sentence here, and that what he meant to write was 'that all the needs of life—the public affairs of the State being tied in with it—⟨are satisfied by it⟩'. But there is no need to make an issue about the insertion, since the text as we have it can hardly bear any meaning but this in any case. In *Zu der Zeit, da Jesus* there is a mysterious reference to 'Montesquieus mit Robert in Mars' (Nohl, p. 389), which casts considerable light on Hegel's conception of the relation between love and property once the key to it is found. D'Hondt (*Hegel secret*, pp. 154–82) has shown that it refers to L.-S. Mercier's play *Montesquieu à Marseille*, in which the action turns upon Montesquieu's determination not to allow the merchant Robert or his family to discover that he is the anonymous benefactor who ransomed Robert from captivity by pirates. When he is discovered, his last recourse is flight to escape the banquet that Robert arranges in

We ourselves stand close to the opposite pole where reflection annihilates love, and strict justice (honesty) leaves no room for mercy (generosity). We see the folly of attempting to evade the fate of property; but we also suffer the tyranny of legal regulation over all living relations. The impulse behind our reflection upon our own actions and those of others may be the supremely moral one of mutual improvement. But one who sets out in the friend-liest way to show another man his error (the 'mote in his eye') falls right out of the realm of love ('ist unter das Reich der Liebe gesunken'), because he has to set up a standard whose validity is absolutely independent of actual human relations. His whole world, himself included, is made subject to the higher authority whose mouthpiece he claims to be. This was the weakness of John the Baptist; but his mission (symbolized by 'the baptism of water') was, none the less, a necessary preamble to that of Jesus ('the baptism of the spirit and of fire'), because having the will to righteousness in this sense, and actually experiencing its fate, are preconditions for achieving the higher goal of life reconciled with itself in love.[1]

7. Punishment and fate

The righteousness of John is the righteousness of Kant; this, even more than the righteousness of the Scribes and Pharisees—'the virtue of positive obedience'—is the target of Hegel's criticism in his second essay. The subject of this second essay is atonement for wrong, as it appears on the plane of reflection and on the plane of life respectively. Positive disobedience and actual criminal justice are really below the level of the discussion altogether; but the historical context forces Hegel to begin by distinguishing the

his honour. The way in which the 'beautiful soul' is forced to violate the reciprocity of feelings essential to 'love' in order to preserve its purity, and the fact that both Montesquieu's good deed and Robert's gratitude depend on the possession of property and on a canny regard for its preservation, reveal the inadequacy and one-sidedness of 'pure love' as a moral principle.

[1] I have here ventured to interpret the 'contrast' that Hegel makes between John and Jesus (Nohl, p. 275; Knox, pp. 223–4) in the light of his comments about the relation of *Moralität* and *Liebe* in *Zu der Zeit, da Jesus* (Nohl, p. 394). The justification for this is, first, the remark about John's relation to 'he that cometh after me'; secondly, what Hegel says elsewhere about the sacrament of baptism (Nohl, pp. 318–21; Knox, pp. 273–7); and thirdly the fact that Matthew 7: 13 ff. (the 'allgemeines Bild des vollendeten Menschen' (*B. Moral. Bergpredigt*, Nohl, p. 399)) begins with 'Enter ye in at the strait gate etc.'.

different ways in which virtue is opposed to positive obedience and to vice respectively. The man who 'obeys the law' is immoral in respect of what he omits to do (for no system of imposed duties can exhaust duty as such); but in respect of what he does he is simply non-moral (because he does what he has a duty to do but does it for the wrong reason). Thus 'the immorality of positivity refers to a different aspect of human relations from the positive obedience'[1] (always assuming of course that the positive law involved is capable of becoming a moral law).

Virtue is opposed to mere obedience therefore as something neutral; but it is opposed to vice (including the inevitable blind spots involved in mere obedience) as what is directly contrary to it. In a passage which clearly reveals his own underlying concern, Hegel goes on to argue that whereas the theoretical moralist should properly be concerned with the definition of virtue and the 'deduction' of a system of duties from it, the *Volkslehrer* must be concerned with the destruction of vice. The whole enterprise of the theorist takes place on an eternal plane where change and development is unthinkable. He can only either calculate with his concepts (dispassionately) or (passionately) denounce the whole realm of living men for failing to live up to his standards. The problem of how to bring life closer to the ideal belongs to the *Volkslehrer*, and his instrument is punishment, a 'necessary evil consequence' of transgression that is such as to turn men away from it.[2]

The only thing that is clear about this passage at first sight is Hegel's underlying concern with the difference between his own enterprise and that of Kant in the *Metaphysik der Sitten*. The characterization of the *Volkslehrer* does not seem to correspond at all with Hegel's portrait of Jesus; though it chimes in very well with certain aspects of Jesus' recorded teaching which he habitually passes over in silence.[3] Still less does it correspond with anything in Hegel's own work. But it is obviously written from the reflective point of view, and it serves appropriately enough to introduce the

---

[1] *Der Positivität der Juden*, Nohl, p. 276 and n. [*a*]; cf. Knox, p. 224.

[2] Nohl, p. 277 n. [*b*].

[3] For instance, the passage in the Sermon on the Mount summed up in Hegel's notes as an 'allgemeines Bild des vollendeten Menschen' and dismissed in his text as 'inadequate parables' contains the forthright assertion: 'Every tree that bringeth not forth good fruit is hewn down, and cast into the fire' (Matthew 7: 19). For the explanation of Hegel's silence see p. 348 n. 1.

topic of punishment at that level. This is the key to our problem in understanding it. Hegel wanted, first of all, to show that once the reflective point of view is adopted the *Volkslehrer*'s task becomes impossible. Then by expounding the ideal of 'reconciliation with fate'—in which the reciprocity of punishment is preserved though in a different form—he could show how the *Volkslehrer* does in fact perform his task.

Fate is not, like punishment, a concept; it is experience itself viewed in a certain way. By getting people to view their actual experience in this way the *Volkslehrer* does in fact show them the 'necessary evil consequence of transgression'; but also, in that very recognition, they find the path to reconciliation, so that the 'evil consequence' does have the good effect which is required by the concept of punishment. Thus the work of the *Volkslehrer* (whether Jesus or Hegel) does in fact correspond to the abstract definition provided by reflection, but the authority, the judicial dominion that appears to belong to him in the concept, does not pertain to him in actual life at all.[1]

When he came to revise his manuscript, Hegel decided, here as elsewhere, to eliminate the explicit contrast between his point of view and Kant's. He substituted instead a simple characterization of Kantian morality in practice (i.e. with the necessary πλήρωμα or complement that the virtues are 'modifications of love') and proceeded directly to the practical problem of retributive justice. Love can absorb moral law which is only 'formally' opposed to it (i.e. in its character as a command) just as moral law absorbs positive law which is formally opposed to it (in its character as an *alien* command). But how can it deal with transgression which is 'materially' opposed to them all alike?

At the conceptual level the transgressor *deserves* punishment. The right he has cancelled (*aufgehoben*) is cancelled for him. This is simply a matter of conceptual implication, of practical reason as a dispassionate calculative function. But the judge who calculates and assesses the penalty in practice is not simply 'justice ensouled', to use a phrase of Aristotle's. He is a living man. He may not be

---

[1] Thus the doctrine of 'fate' is Hegel's account of all the 'inadequate parables' in which Jesus appears to speak of punishment. He passes over these dicta, for the most part, because he wished to emphasize that not 'fate' but 'reconciliation with fate' was the real concern of Jesus. From this point of view only the 'sin against the Holy Spirit' posited by Jesus as being beyond the limit of reconcilability, required specific notice—which Hegel duly accorded to it.

able to execute judgement on the one hand; or he may choose to remit the penalty voluntarily, on the other. So that in actuality, retribution is not inevitable; it is not 'necessary', but only contingent. But the proposition 'Transgression deserves retribution' remains a necessary truth; and hence, although the burden of retribution can be remitted in fact, there is no way in which it can be transferred to, or assumed by, any one other than the transgressor. Thus no consistent account of the Atonement is possible in terms of the concepts of transgression and retribution.

Furthermore, once we move from the plane of positive law with its appointed penalties for transgression, to the plane of rational moral autonomy, not only does the possibility of evading punishment or being pardoned disappear, but even paying the penalty, though it may satisfy the law, cannot satisfy the conscience of the transgressor. The laws of freedom are different from the laws of nature in this, that the restoration of equilibrium never means a return to the previous situation. Even an immoral man, after being punished, has always the knowledge that the law is there, that any further transgression of his will once more bring the penalty upon him. One who is roused by the experience to moral awareness, realizes further that the punishment does not change his status in relation to the concept of rational humanity. He is forever a transgressor, and he must live always with the gnawing consciousness that what he *is*, does not, and cannot ever, correspond with what he *ought to be*. He may cry 'Lord have mercy on me, a sinner', but this 'dishonest wish' for mercy is simply a pollution of his own rational consciousness. Not even God can change the past; and so not even God can cancel his eternal status as a transgressor.[1] As we have already noticed, the prerogative of mercy is one of the things that creates the gulf between the actual and the ideal. There can be no place for it in a world where this gulf is supposed by reflective consciousness to be abolished.

The principle of retribution is an analogue at the level of freedom for the natural principle of reciprocity. Just as in physics 'for every action there is an equal and opposite reaction' so in ethics 'an eye for an eye'—the transgressor must suffer the effect of his

---

[1] From this point of view God is 'only the power of the highest thought, only the administrator of the law' (Nohl, p. 281; Knox, p. 230); compare Kant, 'Tugendlehre', § 13, *Akad.*, vi. 438–9, especially the footnote (Gregor, pp. 104–5).

own transgression.[1] And just as in nature it is the succession of action and reaction that is visible, whereas the abiding equilibrium is something discoverable only by the mind, so in penal justice it is the succession of transgression and retribution that is visible, the law itself remains a pure concept.

Fate, on the other hand, is the actual experience of reciprocal action and reaction in the abiding equilibrium of a living whole. There can be here no question of evasion or of pardon because no law is invoked. The Eumenides and the ghost of Banquo speak not for the law but for the life that Orestes and Macbeth destroyed. Transgression of law may be, as we saw in the case of the plucking of the ears of corn on the Sabbath, a rebellion against slavery, a return to life from a condition of death.[2] But transgression against life can never be this. Life is never wiped out; to destroy life, or to mutilate it, is only to sunder one's own life, to raise the ghost of the slain against oneself. There is only the one 'living' God, in whom we all 'live, move, and have our being'.[3] All that is destroyed by transgression against life is the harmony of life, its 'friendliness'; in place of the harmony of love, a balance of natural forces is set up, and reflective consciousness is able to discover the law that governs the equilibrium. But *this* law, the law of life, is plainly only a reflex of life itself. Life in its integrity is above the law which governs it in its disruption. Thus if a transgressor can be reconciled with the fate he has roused against himself, he will not be troubled afterwards by the mighty shadow of the law of reason.

Reconciliation with fate is possible because no pollution of something that is pure is involved; the transgressor need not cry to a just Judge to have mercy and thereby cease to be just. He does not appeal to an independent, self-sufficient 'power' existing on a different plane, the universal realm of pure thought. Rather he surrenders voluntarily to the vengeance of the life he has injured. He recognizes that the might of fate is not that of an alien master,

---

[1] *Der Positivität der Juden*, Nohl, pp. 279–80; Knox, p. 228. With this passage, and Knox's illuminating note 54, compare the remark about the *lex talionis* in *Jesus trat nicht lange* (Nohl, p. 271; Knox, p. 218). That this remark is almost certainly an addition made by Hegel in the process of revision can be inferred from the disorder apparent in Roques's edition, p. 186.

[2] *Der Positivität der Juden*, Nohl, p. 280.

[3] Compare: 'Es [das Leben] ist unsterblich . . . denn Leben ist vom Leben nicht verschieden, weil das Leben in der einigen Gottheit ist' (Nohl, p. 280; Knox, p. 229). This 'living' God should be contrasted with the God of reflection referred to above, p. 349 n. 1.

before whom he must at all costs preserve his dignity at least; it is only his own life made hostile to itself by his own act.

Transgression and retribution do not stand in a causal relation to one another. If they did there could be no breaking of the chain of vengeance, no transformation of the Furies, the Erinyes, into the Kindly Ones, the Eumenides, because the law would be absolute. But if one who has roused the law of life against himself voluntarily accepts his fate, the original harmony is restored. Earlier we pointed out that Kant's 'law of freedom' is *not* like the 'law of nature' in this respect. But the *experience* of freedom is like the operation of nature. The *law* of freedom cannot restore the *status quo* as the law of nature does, precisely because the law of freedom is *below* freedom, whereas the law of nature is *above* nature.[1]

In the first draft the expressions 'life' and 'self-consciousness' were used interchangeably, and the reconciliation of life with itself was referred to indifferently as 'love', as 'friendship', or as 'faith of consciousness in itself'. In his revised version Hegel settled fairly consistently on the terms 'life' and 'love' respectively, though most of the others still occur here and there.[2] The reason for this development is fairly plainly Hegel's desire to minimize the use of 'reflective' terms. He decided, as we shall shortly see, that the first chapter of John employs the most 'authentic' language available— while his own earlier terminology was all of it spoiled in some way. 'Friendship' (*Freundschaft*), the natural antonym of 'hostility' or 'enmity' (*Feindschaft*), had the disadvantage of being the term Kant had employed for an ideal which so far as it went was almost identical with Hegel's own, but which was sharply distinguished

---

[1] This seems to be the thought behind the cancelled passage, Nohl, p. 281 n. [a]. The student should perhaps be warned that a comparison of Nohl's edition with that of Roques reveals a state of confusion in Roques's text extending from about the middle of Nohl, p. 280, to the middle of Nohl, p. 288 (cf. Roques, pp. 150–9). The natural hypothesis is that Roques did not understand the relation between the first draft (on the left half of the page) and the revisions and additions (written mainly on the right half of the page). In that case the text as we have it is a patchwork of first draft with many later explanations and expansions. One can only guess which passages are earlier and which later, but it does not seem to matter because nothing more serious than a few variations in terminology appears to be involved. Even where Hegel cancelled his first draft (as here), only a change of direction, so to speak, not one of doctrine, is involved.

[2] For cancellations and changes which demonstrate the interchangeability of the terms, see especially Nohl, p. 283 n. [a] and *Reines Leben zu denken* (Nohl, p. 302 with nn. [b] and [c]).

by Kant from the more general term 'love'.[1] 'Consciousness' is, of course, only one side of the reflective duality united in 'love', and even the term 'self-consciousness' tends to obscure the fact that 'pure life' or 'love' is not just the harmony and spontaneous free expression of all the powers and faculties *of an individual* (who is only a *'modification* of life')[2] but also refers, usually quite directly, to his integration into a wider 'whole' (minimally, the marriage tie). 'Faith of consciousness in itself' is a direct development of the interpretation of rational moral autonomy given in *The Life of Jesus*, and thus we have in it another connecting link between that work and 'The Spirit of Christianity'.[3]

Of course, the favoured terms 'life' and 'love' are meant in any case to retain the 'reflective' connotations of 'consciousness' and 'self-consciousness' even though the oppositions of subject and object, self and other, are done away with in them. Love is self-conscious, it is 'the feeling of life which finds *itself* again',[4] and the cycle of 'life' from birth to new birth is a cycle of developing awareness in which we move from the situation of the new-born babe to that of the parents who have brought the birth about.

The principal reason why Hegel now gives such prominence to the term 'love' (which he managed very largely to avoid in *The Life of Jesus*) is exactly the reason why Kant distrusted it, and was obliged usually to add a qualifying adjective when he used it: it applies to such a wide range of experience. It applies at one extreme to the 'feeling of life which finds itself again' in the sexual

---

[1] Cf. 'Tugendlehre', §§ 46–7, *Akad.*, vi. 469–73; Gregor, pp. 140–5.

[2] If 'modification of life' means simply 'an individual man or woman' (the most basic 'modifications' appear to be the two sexes just as the most basic expression of 'love' is their union) we might expect to find that a 'modification of love' is not 'one of the virtues' but rather 'a man or woman inspired by love'. But Hegel explicitly identifies the virtues as 'modifications of love'. Of course, *one* of his purposes in speaking this way is to emphasize that what he is here calling a 'virtue' is an activity, not a disposition. But in order to appreciate the coherence of his usage we only need to recognize that 'modifications' of 'life' are living mortals (transient 'modes' of an immortal life-line which is an 'infinite mode' of the life of God, the one real 'substance': cf. p. 366 n. 3 below). 'Modifications' of 'love' on the other hand are different natural ties between living mortals: e.g. husband–wife, parent–child, etc. These felt relations 'fulfil' the reflective duties of men to one another (the 'virtues' of Kant).

[3] For the interpretation of Kantian moral autonomy see the discussion with Nicodemus (Nohl, pp. 79–80); the development into a doctrine of 'faith in oneself' is implicit in what Jesus there says of himself, but is best seen in his remarks to the repentant 'Magdalen' (Nohl, p. 92).

[4] *Der Positivität der Juden*, Nohl, p. 283 (Knox, p. 232).

act, and at the other to the cry of Jesus on the cross: 'Father forgive them for they know not what they do.' It covers the whole range of fate, for it can reconcile not only the guilty but also the innocent with their fate. The Crucifixion is for Hegel the type of 'the most exalted guilt, the guilt of innocence [*der Schuld der Unschuld*]'.[1] If someone suffers 'innocently' then he is guilty of injury to life even though he may be quite unwitting of it, or his conscience may be perfectly clear in respect to it. Jesus is the perfect model of the 'pure soul' who quite consciously does injury to life in order to maintain the supreme value (*das Höchste*).[2] Because pure love was his motive his honour is the greater; otherwise the fact that he perfectly understood what he was doing would make his transgression so much the worse.

In the case of a 'pure soul' and generally in other cases also,[3] fate *appears* to arise from an 'alien deed'. But in reality, no matter how life may treat us, our fate arises from the attitude that we adopt toward what happens. Whether we fight back, or simply grieve over the unfairness of our lot, we are reflecting on our life, judging it, and laying claim to our rights. But in fighting back we know that we are appealing to might, not simply to right, and we recognize that our might may be overcome; we accept the risk of failure and assume responsibility. Passive grief, on the other hand, is denial of responsibility, and deserves its fate for that reason. Again, those who appeal to arbitration give up even the reflective disrupted life of grief and 'surrender themselves dead', for they no longer insist on living their own lives in their own way. The 'beautiful soul', finally, preserves its freedom (as thus defined) and

[1] Ibid. Knox (p. 233 n.) is wrong in thinking that the reference here is primarily to the 'fate' of a Greek tragic hero such as Oedipus. No doubt Hegel's concept of reconciliation owes a great deal to the *Oedipus Coloneus*. But Oedipus killed a man and married a woman. One could not say of him therefore either that he was innocent of all offence, or that his fate 'appears to arise only through alien action [*fremde Tat*]'. The fate of Jesus does appear to arise this way for he seeks *not* to act (either with hostility—as in the killing of Laius—or by establishing *natural* ties of love—as in the marriage of Jocasta).

[2] Nohl, p. 284. The injury that Jesus did to life consisted in not living it properly (and in encouraging his disciples not to live it either). He did not, like Socrates, marry and beget children; and he even denied that he had any family ties. See further below, pp. 369–72.

[3] In order to understand the assertion that 'a fate appears to arise only through alien action' we have to take the Furies pursuing Orestes, or Banquo's Ghost appearing to Macbeth, as the objective presences which they appear to be in Aeschylus and Shakespeare. The 'alien deed' in the case of Oedipus must presumably be the pestilence that falls upon his city.

avoids the disruption of its consciousness into the world of 'right' (things as they ought to be) and the world of 'might' (things as they are), by voluntarily surrendering whatever is seized, and not grieving over it. But in so doing it is guilty of grievous injury to life, for it withdraws from all the relationships in and through which life itself is developed. Jesus both fights (but not against others) and grieves (but not over what others have done to him). Through absolute forgiveness he sets himself above fate; but in his willingness to go to any lengths to preserve his freedom, to keep himself unspotted from the world, he must in the end give up life itself. He *does* no injury to life, but he is *guilty* of supreme injury to it.[1]

The 'beautiful soul' is a topic that does not properly belong in this essay, however; the 'fate' of Jesus is something to which we must return later. It is only relevant here because through the forgiveness of others (the attitude of the beautiful soul) we receive forgiveness ourselves (and so heal the ugliness of our sinful souls) In forgiveness we rise above all claims about rights and all judgement of wrongs. But we are not thereby pardoned, or exempted from any penalties that may be due at that level; recognition of the 'justice' of fate is part of what it means to forgive others.

Wherever Jesus found this attitude—*Lebensfülle*, the 'fulness of life' that gives one a sympathetic understanding even of those who injure one—he could confirm the 'faith' of whoever had it by assuring him that his sins were indeed forgiven. 'Faith in Jesus' was the recognition of the 'fulness of life' in him on the part of those in whom the same fulness was only implicitly present. This recognition is the 'light', the conscious aspect of the experience of love. The man who 'believes in the light' is aware of the actuality of love in his relation with Jesus, but not yet aware that it is his own actuality as well as that of Jesus.[2] Jesus on the other hand was never in this condition of faith: the beautiful soul knows its own

---

[1] The 'relationships' (*Beziehungen*) whose surrender is mentioned in Nohl, p. 285, are not, as Knox thinks, property relations—or even relationships of ordinary friendship. They are the natural ties of life mentioned in Nohl, p. 286, in the citation from Luke 14: 26.

[2] *Daß auch Jesus den Zusammenhang*, Nohl, p. 289 (Knox, p. 239): 'Faith is a knowledge of spirit through spirit and only like spirits can know and understand one another.' 'Faith' is here the *conscious* aspect of love as distinct from its actuality. Thus it is a rather special case of the 'faith' analysed in *Glauben ist die Art*. To have 'faith' here is to be conscious of the actuality of love in another but not yet clearly aware that what one is conscious of is a 'whole' that includes oneself.

beauty, and thereby knows the whole range of human possibilities. For the being of a human spirit is nothing but its actual and possible relations with others, so that to say that Jesus 'knew' himself logically implies that he knew also whose sins were 'forgiven', i.e. who could be reconciled with him.[1] To a people who believed that righteousness was a matter of obedience, and mercy the prerogative of a superhuman external judge, one who went about telling his fellows that their sins were forgiven could only appear to be either a shameless blasphemer or a madman. They hoped to purchase forgiveness from their God by 'paying their debts'. The attitude of one who desires to be reconciled (typified by Mary Magdalen) is different, in that he offers what he has freely, without any thought of 'making up for' the wrongs he has done. There was nothing that Mary Magdalen could *say* in the company of those who are righteous according to the law, because any words she might use would introduce, at least by implication, such reflective concepts as 'duty' or 'recompense'. Hegel declares that what she did is the only really 'beautiful' action in the Gospel, and that when Jesus described it as a καλόν ἔργον he was using the term καλόν in its proper living sense, as one 'beautiful soul' naturally would in speaking of another.[2] On the other side, the comment of Simon the Pharisee shows what *Lebensfülle* looks like from the standpoint of positivity: 'If this man were a prophet he would know the woman is a sinner'; and the attitude of the disciples is that of reflective rationality: 'The *oil* could be sold and the *money* given to the poor.'

8. *The religion of love*

When Peter recognized the divinity of Jesus he showed that he had realized the essential priority and superiority of life in its integrity,

---

[1] I have offered here an interpretation which goes beyond the text of *Kühnheit, die Zuversicht*, Nohl, p. 290 (Knox, p. 240), and seeks to explain *why* 'a whole nature has in a moment penetrated another through and through and sensed its harmony or disharmony'. 'Wholeness', if I understand Hegel aright, never belongs to any individual in isolation. This explains why Jesus was bound to go about 'forgiving sins'.

[2] *Im Geiste der Juden*, Nohl, pp. 292–3 (Knox, pp. 242–4). Hegel knew, of course, that the ordinary use of the adjective in moral contexts had little connection with 'beauty'. In its ordinary use he even calls it 'meaningless' (i.e. it does not have its proper living meaning, but only a dead conventional one). Even Jesus uses it 'meaninglessly' in a discourse for a general audience: see the note on Matthew 26: 10, as compared with Matthew 26: 24, in *Zu der Zeit, da Jesus*, Nohl, p. 397.

over all the conceptions of reflective consciousness: law and obedience, justice and mercy, were no longer relevant in his relations with God. He knew that God and man were one in love— hence he too, like Jesus, could speak for God and say: 'Thy sins are forgiven.'[1] With this recognition, the need for Jesus as an individual focus of faith ceased; it became necessary, rather, that he should 'go away'.

The leave-taking of Jesus took its appropriate form as a love-feast, a sharing of life at its most primitive level, self-maintenance.[2] By symbolizing his own surrender of existence in the feast itself Jesus gave the last supper a quasi-religious significance. But Hegel is anxious that we should understand that in so far as it was a *love-feast*, it was *not* symbolic, it was an actual experience and expression of fellowship. Eating together with one's enemies is against all natural feeling, and the guest-relation in a Middle Eastern society is not a ceremonial matter in which the understanding *uses* the imagination to *symbolize* the establishment of friendship; it is, rather, the direct and appropriate imaginative *expression* of friendship. The solemn declaration 'This is my body, etc.', though it brought the experience of love to the verge of religion, did not really make the supper a religious act, precisely because the religious symbol was consumed in the experience. The twelve could experience their union, the ceremony made it a visible fact which they could imaginatively grasp. They drank from the same cup, and Jesus called the wine his 'blood', knowing well that for the Jews the blood was the life principle, the bearer of the spirit, which the Lord has forbidden them to touch in the first law that was ever given to them.[3] Thus in the feast they felt the whole range of their fellowship. But it was not a religious experience, because the *abiding* presence of God was nowhere represented in it. In a religious experience, objectivity must be overcome but not done away with altogether (as it is in eating and drinking). The abiding presence of a beautiful object—the statue of the God—achieves this end, because sensibility takes its pleasure, but the thing is not thereby consumed. The thing *can* of course be consumed (ground

---

[1] *Im Geiste der Juden*, Nohl, pp. 291–2 (Knox, p. 242).

[2] *Der Abschied, den Jesus*, Nohl, pp. 297–301 (Knox, pp. 248–53).

[3] Cf. *Fortschreiten der Gesetzgebung*, Nohl, p. 373 and *Mit Abraham, dem wahren Stammvater*, Nohl, p. 244 (Knox, p. 183). (When Hegel says: 'Not only is the wine blood, the blood is spirit' (Nohl, pp. 298–9), he must surely have Genesis 9: 4 in mind.)

into dust, for example), but then its divine aspect (its beauty) vanishes also.

In this consuming of the Godhead, this 'promise of something divine which melted away in the mouth', the inadequacy of the religion of love is revealed. For the attitude of love in its purest form, the material world is simply a limit, an unsurpassable barrier. The God of love reconciles all life, and vanquishes forever the need to slip back into the reflective attitude, which threatens the integrity of love at every moment in ordinary experience; but his kingdom is not of this world, and he cannot be adequately represented in this world.[1]

Given that we cannot *picture* the 'Father'—any more than a man could see the face of Moses' 'Lord' and live—how are we to *think* of him? We must abstract from everything that man does and suffers, from the whole material sensible world against which his life expresses itself, and fasten upon the pure character of human activity. We must leave aside everything temporal, what man was or will be, and grasp what he eternally *is*; we must somehow grasp life in its 'oneness' before it develops and becomes reflective. But we must retain the consciousness that it is *our* life—for if we think of ourselves as determined by the universal *power* of life, we shall be faced with the 'living God' of positive religion (the Absolute Lord), or with the 'dominant universal' (the God of reflective Reason). Above the iron order of Nature (*das All der Objekte*) there is only the awful presence of the Author of Nature and Nature's law ('die leere Einheit des Alls der Objekte als herrschendes Wesen über dieselben').[2] This totality of causal connection (*das Ganze der Bestimmtheiten*) is quite another thing from the wholeness of life, the one fount from which all separate lives, all spontaneous impulses, and all free actions spring. Jesus expressed this relation of *origin* by speaking of the 'Father', though he did not mean to refer to anything other than life as he himself knew and experienced it. He had to speak in this way because he was only a

[1] *Am interessantesten wird es sein*, Nohl, p. 302 (Knox, p. 253). This appears to be a loose page which Hegel lifted, perhaps, from the beginning of an early complex of notes on the religion of Jesus and inserted here in order to make a bridge between the earlier discussion and *Reines Leben zu denken*, which contains his reflections on the first chapter of John (cf. Roques, pp. 201–2 where it appears as an appendage to *Zu der Zeit, da Jesus*; and Nohl, p. 394 (at heading 'C') for the notes of which it is a developed form).

[2] *Reines Leben zu denken*, Nohl, pp. 302–3 and 303 n. [a]. The comment about *das All der Objekte* occurs in the cancelled passage.

mortal man, setting his own life against the 'infinity of lordship and subjection to a lord' in Jewish life. The wholeness of life is not really something above or external to the living man, although it must appear so to those who are aware of it as an ideal in which they have *faith*.

One who really *has* the experience is in a difficulty about how to communicate it to those who are in this condition of faith. The reflective distinction between the actual and the possible, and the conceptions of power and causal agency, are so deep-rooted in language that he must either speak falsely or speak in riddles. He can only use those elements and strata of the language which are normally used to refer to bonds of spontaneous feeling in which freedom is preserved. He cannot properly speak in the 'reciprocal' style of the understanding ('Virtue deserves happiness', 'With whatsoever measure ye mete, it shall be measured to you again', 'For every action there is an equal and opposite reaction') because to do so involves accepting the assumptions of 'right' and 'law' which belong to life in its sundered state. But in a society where the spirit of lordship and obedience has penetrated even into the most intimate living relations—that of 'son' to 'father', to take the most crucial example[1]—so that all loving activity is forced into the language of mercy, or of material benevolence, and appears as the capricious bounty or grace of a lord, even the *Wechselstil* (i.e. the language of the reflective understanding) may sound less harsh than the materialistic images that we find in the gospel of John. Hegel believed, apparently, that it was because the Jews could only conceive of a loving God as a bounteous provider of material gifts that Jesus spoke of *himself* as the bringer of salvation to men as a gift, and spoke of his gift in terms of material enjoyment; and because even a father was for the Jews a 'Lord' Jesus could not avoid speaking of the reintegration of life as a kingdom.[2]

'The beginning of St. John's Gospel contains a series of propositions about God and the divine expressed in more authentic language.' To say that the Logos '*was* in the beginning' and that it '*was* with God' and so on is to speak in reflective, temporal terms

---

[1] In this connection the unpublished fragment *Die schönen, ihrer Natur nach* is particularly significant (cf. p. 290 n. 2 above).

[2] *Reines Leben zu denken*, Nohl, pp. 305–6 (Knox, pp. 255–6); cf. *Das Wesen des Jesus*, Nohl, p. 321 (Knox, p. 278), and *Mit dem Mute und dem Glauben*, Nohl, p. 328 (Knox, p. 285). As Knox says, the meaning of *Wechselstil* is doubtful; I hope that my interpretation will be found persuasive.

about something which is a living experience. Two ways of interpreting John's assertions naturally suggest themselves—both of them equally one-sided. If we think of them as propositions about a matter of fact, the Logos becomes an individual thing; while if we think of them as asserting relations of ideas, the Logos is identifiable as reason. Hegel himself *seemed* in *The Life of Jesus* to interpret the text in the latter way. But it was clear that even there he was not talking of conceptual relations but of an actual living power in the world. Reason in *The Life of Jesus* is not an abstract aspect of the world, an *ens rationis*. It is the *life* of the world itself: and the world as a living whole is God; or, as Hegel expresses it now, 'God is the matter in the form of the Logos'. God and Logos are *reflectively* distinguishable as matter and form; but in the primitive stage of 'oneness' ('before the creation', to use the theological metaphor) they are not distinct but identical ('the Logos was with God, the Logos was God'). The creation is the work of the Logos: that is to say life only achieves full expression through conscious development in a multiplicity of instances. In each instance the distinction of God and Logos appears as that between 'life' and 'light'. The 'light' is in every living man, but only in Jesus was this conscious side of his being developed to the perfect awareness of his own life. To others who are aware of the human order (the cosmos into which every man comes), the light appears as an ideal of what life ought to be: something to which, like John the Baptist, they 'bear witness' (as rational beings). The 'light' in fact *is* in the human order (i.e. it is the natural harmonious expression of human life itself) but those who 'bear witness' to it think of it as coming from elsewhere. Life and light in harmony produce the whole human order, but the members of that order do not realize this, and think of them as opposed (as the life of man and the law of the Lord, the living God whose glory no man may behold and live).[1] Moses and other great leaders and transformers

[1] 'He (i.e., according to Hegel, every man as he comes into the world lighted by the true light) was in the cosmos and the cosmos was made by him and the cosmos knew him not. He came unto his own and his own received him not' (i.e. men reached the point of development where they perceived the ideal of rational existence but they did not 'receive' that ideal into their own order of existence: compare, for instance, the inspiration of Moses).

This interpretation assumes that Hegel is serious when he says that until verse 14 the Evangelist speaks of 'truth' and 'man' in universal terms. But even as he says this he notes that the Logos has revealed itself already as an individual in the ἄνθρωπον ἐρχόμενον εἰς τὸν κόσμον to which he refers αὐτόν in verse 10.

of human society have been lighted by the true light, and have felt
the kinship between man and God; but only in Jesus did life
achieve perfect self-consciousness. Thus his name is the name
of the Logos, of the light itself; and through him men can learn
that they are not lighted by the light that comes from God above
them, but by the light of the life itself that is in them.

This whole discussion of the difficulty of expressing the true
relation between man and God for Jewish ears, with the accom-
panying exegesis of the first chapter of John, was inserted by
Hegel in his second draft. Having made this major insertion he
proceeded to fill out somewhat the rather spare outline of the
discussion of Jesus as 'Son of God' and 'Son of man', which was
all that he had originally written down. 'Father and son' is not a
relation of 'likeness', discoverable by reflective abstraction (the
'conceptual oneness' of things which are of the same type); it is a
'living relation of living beings, likeness of life'. Father and son are
'modifications of the same life', not separate substances. The substance that is modified in these ways is the life of the tribe or clan;
and the relation of a clan to its members is not that of whole to
part, for the whole nature of the clan, the community of blood, is
expressed in each clan member. This character of living relations—
that the 'whole' is present in every 'part' if it is a properly isolated
part—may seem to the eyes of enlightened Europeans to be an
oriental fancy, but it is evident enough in the most primitive form
of life, the life of plants. Jesus himself used the analogy of the vine
and the branches. Hegel takes this up, and pushes it further, in
what appears to be a reference to the Christian doctrine of the
Trinity:

A tree which has three branches makes up together with them One

I do not see how Hegel could say that 'thus far we have heard only of
truth itself and man in universal terms', unless he held that the human world
is the work of the true light in every individual man. But the point of his comment on verse 14 probably is that when we reach it, we realise that only *one* man
has actually come into the world lighted perfectly by the true light. So the
reference to πάντα ἄνθρωπον now becomes singular. Jesus is 'everyman', he
is the Logos itself in the shape of an individual, because the absolute 'power'
of light (consciousness), already present in each and every man, is in his case
exactly equal to the impulse of life. Each and every man can thus receive from
'everyman' not a new power, but a new direction of the light that he has.
Instead of being lighted from outside by the eternal holiness of the Lord 'in
whose sight shall no man living be justified', he can recognize that the light is in
him, that he is a 'son of God'.

tree; but every son of the tree, every branch (also its other children, leaves and blossoms) is itself a tree; the fibres bringing sap to the branch from the trunk, are of the same nature as the roots; a tree stuck upside down in the earth will put forth leaves from the roots spread in the air, and the boughs will root themselves in the earth—and it is just as true that there is only One tree here, as that there are three trees.[1]

I do not know whether there is in fact any plant in which all of these properties are in fact combined; but this is Hegel's version of that will-o'-the-wisp of Goethe's, the *Ur-Pflanze*. We have here three triads, two of them naturally given, and one stipulated by Hegel himself; and all are essential for the expression of his meaning. In the first place there is the stipulated triad of branches. Jesus himself said: 'I am the vine and you are the branches.' Thus ordinary men are related to Jesus, the 'light of the world', as the branches are to the trunk from which they receive the life-giving sap; and Jesus, 'the Son', is related to God, 'the Father', as the trunk is to the roots (there ought, I suppose, to be three of them too, for perfect symmetry when the tree is replanted upside down). Thus Hegel's supposition that if the tree were turned upside down or the branches were cut off and planted separately life would go on in the one tree or the three trees just as before, carries the implication that 'the Father', 'the Son', and 'those that believe on his Name', are only accidentally distinguishable. A branch can become a root or a trunk (but the root we may note must become a branch before it can become a trunk: the 'word' must be 'made flesh' if it is to be the 'true light').

This is not all, however. The natural triad of root, trunk, and branch is not the only reason why Hegel himself stipulated three branches. We have to consider also his reference to the 'other children' of the tree, the leaves and the blossoms.[2] Branches, leaves, and blossoms are the three moments of the process of development through which the propagation of the tree takes place in the ordinary way. The dividing or overturning of the tree is not, after all, a natural occurrence. But in the normal course of nature we do have the seasonal cycle of bare branches (oneness—the Father), bud and leaf (reflective consciousness—the Son), and pollination of blossoms (love—the Spirit), to produce the seed

[1] *Reines Leben zu denken*, Nohl, p. 309 (Knox, p. 261).
[2] The original nucleus of Hegel's analogy was the relation of the trunk to 'boughs, foliage, and fruit': see the passage quoted below, p. 362 n.

through which the cycle of new life is generated. Hegel's tree has three branches because the three Persons of the Trinity express the three phases in the development of human life towards the 'true light'. The 'One Substance' of this tree is the life, which in the shape of the sap goes up and down from root to branches no matter which way the tree is set. This movement of the sap is the 'proceeding of the Spirit' from the 'Father' to all of the 'sons'. For although the Spirit is on the one hand only one of the 'Persons' —one phase of life—yet that phase is the moment of perfect development (the tree in blossom), and if we ask what God is, or what life is, or what the One Substance is of which we and everything else are 'modifications', the only correct answer is 'Spirit'.

The clear statement of this doctrine presupposes a full understanding of the nature of freedom, which was only achieved at the theoretical level by Kant. Jesus could only utter paradoxes which seemed blasphemous to the 'positive' consciousness of the Jews, and are taken by enlightened reflection to be mere metaphors. Now, some metaphors really are only plays of intellect. But metaphor and imagery are the natural mode in which life and living relations express themselves; and if these expressions are regarded as mere play, forms whose truth content is entirely translatable into terms of the abstract concepts of *Verstand*, their real meaning may be lost. The name 'Son of God', for example, which appears to the enlightened man to be a 'mere' metaphor, really expresses the essential nature of Jesus as 'everyman'; while the name 'Son of man', which appears quite obviously applicable to him and to the rest of us, really does represent only an intellectual conceit. For no one can be the son of the abstract universal 'Manhood', and the expression 'Son of man' is only a picturesque way of saying 'a man'. The 'Son of man' is a member of the abstract class of men, as distinct from a member in the 'brotherhood of man' which is the brotherhood of sons of God.

For the enlightened man—for Kant—it is a 'holy mystery' that the 'Son of God' should also be 'Son of man', that the rational ideal of manhood should be an actual man. But this is only a mystery for reflective thought which takes its abstract definitions to have an absolute status. The function of judgement is assigned to the 'Son of man', not, as Kant thinks,[1] because it is only from a

[1] *Reines Leben zu denken*, Nohl, pp. 309–10 (Knox, p. 262). The context of the

human point of view that there can be a 'judgement of merit' (as against a 'judgement of guilt' pronounced in conscience by the Holy Spirit), but because it is only from the *abstractly* human point of view that there can be judgement at all. God the Father does not judge anyone because there is no one standing over against Him to be judged; and the function of the Son of God is not to condemn but to save (precisely in the sense of rescuing men from the abstract point of view under which they are bound in conscience to condemn themselves). It is, however, only as Son of God that the Son of man can have divine authority to judge; for only in the consciousness of being a son of God does one have the proper criterion by which men must be judged (the 'true light'). By this criterion those who are condemned are precisely the men who judge by the criteria of abstract reflection and are incapable of recognizing any other. This is the 'sin against the Spirit for which there can be no forgiveness'.[1]

In ordinary judgement, exemplified in the justice meted out in 'clear cases' where no discretionary power or prerogative of mercy is invoked, the judge is first (on the material side) invested with *positive* authority: he has the power to execute judgement, that is to say he can compel the accused to stand trial before him, and in the event of condemnation to suffer punishment according to his sentence. But secondly (on the formal side) he is only able to use this power because he has *rational* authority, he knows the law and can compare the actual deed of the accused with the conceptual ideal contained in the law. Where they are 'sundered' he condemns, where they are 'bound together' he acquits.

whole discussion of the dogmas of the Trinity and of the Last Judgement is provided by Kant's comments on these matters in the 'General Remark' to his *Religion* (cf. *Akad.* vi. 137-47; Greene and Hudson, pp. 129-38). As Nohl says, the point about the 'holy mystery' is plainer in the first version (given on p. 304, footnote, [b]):

'The connection [*Zusammenhang*] of the infinite with the finite is of course a holy mystery, because it is life, and hence the secret of life; once we begin to speak of a twofold nature, the divine and the human, no joining [*Verbindung*] is to be found, because in every joining they still remain two if both have been posited as absolutely distinct. This relation [*Verhältnis*] of a man to God, his being the son of God, as a trunk is father of the boughs, the foliage and the fruit was bound to shock the Jews to the depths, since they had placed an unbridgeable gulf between human and divine being [*Wesen*] and granted to our nature no share in the divine.'

[1] Cf. here *Reines Leben zu denken*, Nohl, pp. 310-11 (Knox, pp. 262-4); first draft of same, Nohl, p. 304 n.; and *Das Wesen des Jesus*, Nohl, pp. 316 (Knox, p. 270) and 318 (Knox, pp. 272-3).

Divine judgement is very different. First the aspect of material dominance is altogether lacking. The 'Son of God' has authority but no power. He does not *need* power, for his judgement as 'Son of man' is only the rational recognition of the cleavage existing between those who are 'sons of God' and those who are 'sons of men'. What he has to decide as Son of man is whether the particular 'son of man' before him still has the capacity to become a 'son of God' or not. The question then is: 'Does this man himself judge and condemn by ordinary reflective standards, and if so can he be brought, by the fate that befalls those who do this, to surrender his rational authority and adopt the ideal of reconciliation through forgiveness?' If he can, then the Son of God in his 'saving' capacity can say: 'Thy sins be forgiven thee.' If he cannot, then by his own unchangeable standards he is condemned already. No judgement is declared by the Son of God as such; but speaking on the finite human level, which is the only one on which communication is here possible, he *must* say 'Depart from me', for he cannot live with those who are simply 'sons of men'. The world of ordinary human judgement is one from which the Son of God must sunder himself by flight.

If we try to think of divinity and humanity as 'two natures' combined in the person of the particular individual Jesus then we 'posit the understanding', that is to say we operate on the assumption that 'everything is what it is and not another thing', and at the very same time we 'destroy' it, for we contradict the assumption by supposing that the two natures are united in one individual.[1] This suicide of the intellect shows, first, that the relation of Jesus to God cannot be grasped as an item of reflective knowledge (*Erkenntnis*); but in the readiness for such a suicide the practical experience of faith is already present, at least in so far as the superiority of love to all reflective canons of judgement is granted. In spite of the absolute inequality between God and man, we find in Jesus thus paradoxically conceived a ground for hoping that God may feel real 'compassion' (*Mitleiden*) toward us—a bond very different from that between a rich lord and a poor servant on whom he bestows largesse.[2]

---

[1] *Reines Leben zu denken*, Nohl, p. 311 (Knox, p. 264).
[2] *Wenn Jesus so sprach*, Nohl, p. 312 (Knox, p. 265). I take this to be a bridge fragment written to link the second version of *Reines Leben zu denken* to *Das Wesen des Jesus*. In the first version it appears that Hegel wrote only a brief

Religious faith differs from ordinary belief—and from Kant's rational faith—in being directed towards a *Gegenstand* which can never be an *Objekt*. God is not a distinct entity belonging to the actual order of things—even if we include here a 'supersensible' order. God is spirit and can only be known in spirit, that is by discovering the presence of the divine in oneself, and at the same time discovering that it overflows the boundaries of one's finite self. This overflowing of the self, the discovery that some 'other' is involved in the 'whole' which is one's real self, is what is meant by 'spirit'. But at first the identity of self and other (or in the most nearly analogous reflective terms, their reciprocal dependence, their complementary character) is not recognized. Only the dependence of oneself on the other is felt. This is precisely the state of faith (which Hegel identifies as the mean condition between ignorance and knowledge, and—like Plato—as love in its unfulfilled condition).[1] When Peter declared Jesus to be the 'Son of God', Jesus took his recognition as the sign that he had achieved 'knowledge', but as soon as he tested this by speaking of his own death Peter's condition was revealed as still only one of faith. Peter did not realize that his faith in Jesus sprang from the same presence of God in himself that he recognized in Jesus. In fact Jesus had to

essay, *Reines Leben zu denken*, which gave only the barest outline of his argument and tailed off finally into mere notes (Nohl, pp. 302–3 with nn. [a] and [b]). Then he went on directly to write the first version of *Mit dem Mute und dem Glauben* (Nohl, pp. 324–6, 326 n. [a], 331, 333–5). When he came to revise what he had written he realized that considerable development was required. So he first wrote *Das Wesen des Jesus* (four numbered sheets, Nohl, pp. 312–24) and marked the point at which it was to be inserted (see Nohl's note on p. 304). Then he cancelled his original discussion of Kant's 'General Remark' to Part III of the *Religion* and wrote his exegesis of John 1: 1–15 and a discussion of the titles 'Son of God' and 'Son of man'. Only the much less perfunctory discussion of this last title (Nohl, pp. 309–11) directly corresponds to the passage crossed out (if the cancellation had been correctly indicated by Roques, pp. 189–90), but by this time Hegel found he could discard some other parts of his first draft. He had to move *Das Wesen des Jesus* (which had originally been marked for insertion in the middle of the cancelled passage), so he rewrote his original 'lead-in passage' in expanded form on a separate sheet (see Roques, p. 202). In doing so he was struck by the fact that the 'two natures' view is itself a bridge or half-way house between the 'rational faith' of Kant and the 'living faith' with which *Das Wesen des Jesus* begins. (That *Das Wesen des Jesus* is part of the revision, not of the first draft, is certified by Schüler, p. 152, note 99. But we could, very plausibly, have inferred this from the absence of subsequent corrections, except 'einem' for 'dem' on Nohl, p. 314.)

[1] *Das Wesen des Jesus*, Nohl, p. 313 (Knox, p. 266). The name of Plato is not here mentioned, but his influence is obvious, and it is soon to receive explicit recognition (Nohl, p. 316; Knox, p. 270).

die before the disciples could become properly conscious of God in the spirit.[1]

Against the God who said 'I am', Jesus set his own Ego: 'I am the way, the truth, and the life.' But *his* God does not say 'I', and Jesus continually tries to make clear to his disciples that his own existence as a separate individual is of no special significance. Wherever two or three are gathered in his spirit he will be. Knowledge of one's union with God is a self-conscious return of life in its fully developed form to the 'oneness' from which it began. Jesus said that we must become as little children because 'in heaven their angels do always behold the face of my father which is in heaven' (Matthew 18: 10). Hegel expounds this passage in the light of his own interpretation of Plato's myth about the condition of the soul before birth.[2] Both the 'angels' and the pre-natal existence of the soul represent the conscious aspect of 'pure life' individualized (hence distinct from God), but not yet 'restricted' by the physical limits of life on earth (hence 'in the sight of God'). The 'angel' simply *is* the immediate vision of God (i.e. the consciousness of pure life). As we 'grow up' the 'angel' of each one of us must cease to be in the sight of God, because the world is too much with us and we are forced to reflect upon a life that is alien to us. To become as a little child is to be reconciled with this alien life, and so come again into the 'sight of God', but bringing with us now our whole world of developed relations, so that the 'vision of God' is not now simple but infinitely complex. If I have understood Hegel rightly this is the only *real* 'vision of God'. The child at the moment of birth (or perhaps only at conception) *is* pure life, but he is not the consciousness of it.[3] His consciousness

[1] This theme is directly taken up at this point (Nohl, pp. 313–14; Knox, pp. 267–8) but it is further developed when Hegel comes back once more to Peter's avowal a bit further on (Nohl, pp. 317–18; Knox, p. 272). He recurs often to the passages in which Jesus speaks of his own death, because it is in these passages that the Holy Spirit makes its first appearance.

[2] *Das Wesen des Jesus*, Nohl, pp. 315–16 (Knox, pp. 269–70). Compare also the first version of this passage in *B. Moral. Bergpredigt*, Nohl, p. 400; and the remark about the cycle of development from childhood to the descent of the Spirit a little further on (Nohl, p. 318; Knox, p. 273).

[3] Knox (p. 270 n. 92) is quite mistaken in thinking that Hegel is actually referring to the 'angels', not the children, when he says that 'unconsciousness, undeveloped oneness, being and life in God, are here severed from God because it is to be represented as a modification of divinity in the existing children'. The 'angels' *represent* 'being and life in God' as 'severed from God', because the children (whose angels they are) are *in fact* 'modifications' severed from God

is an 'angel', something that is not here but 'yonder' in the other world (or at another time). One who has 'become as a child' knows that the vision is eternally there, and so must speak of it, as Plato and Jesus do, as something which the existing children have lost by being born; or at least as something that they do not now have and must find again (actually for the first time). The 'angels in the sight of God' are immediately identical with him. Their only distinct significance lies in their plurality: that they are *all*, in their simple multiplicity, identical with God, shows forth the crucial fact that God the Father is not an individual ego. Even the 'Son of God' can only truthfully say 'I am' when he knows that it means 'We are'. 'Pure life' is actually the 'Spirit', although, in order to 'think' it (as Hegel sets out to do in this present essay), we must begin with the 'Father'.

The relation of the 'sons of men' to the Father, Son, and Holy Spirit, is the Gospel which the glorified Jesus commands the disciples to preach.[1] Their teaching is to be combined with baptism. This 'baptism' refers in Hegel's view to the 'baptism of fire and the Spirit' that John the Baptist foretold. It is related to John's own practice of baptism by immersion in the way in which the gospel of love is related to John's preaching of repentance and duty. For both John and Jesus baptism by immersion was an appropriate *Vorstellung* for the beginning of a new life, 'the entire

(though they do not know it yet, because they do not know anything, they are 'das Bewußtlose', their awareness is directly identical with the spark of life in them).

[1] *Das Wesen des Jesus*, Nohl, pp. 318–21. The comparative remarks about the synoptic Gospels are quite revealing. It is noticeable that whereas *The Life of Jesus* leans most heavily on Luke, 'The Spirit of Christianity' depends more upon Matthew. If it were not for the present passage we might think that the concentration on Matthew in *Zu der Zeit, da Jesus* and *B. Moral. Bergpredigt*, merely reflected the fact that Hegel already had a sufficiency of notes about Luke at hand in *The Life of Jesus*. But Hegel's discussion of the last words of Jesus definitely suggests that his choice may have been guided by the conviction that Mark is the 'positive' Gospel, Luke the 'rational' Gospel, and Matthew the Gospel of 'life'; he does of course specifically assert that John is the 'religious' Gospel (see Nohl, p. 304; Knox, p. 255). No doubt his estimate of the Synoptics was mainly determined by their respective treatments of the Sermon on the Mount. But it is notable that Matthew as the Gospel of 'life' begins with the life-stem of Jesus; in Luke the Gospel of Reason, the genealogy, like his baptism, is presented only as a symbolic apanage of his coming-of-age. From Hegel's point of view it is right that there is no genealogy at all in Mark, but we ought to find the Virgin Birth there instead of in Luke. (No doubt Hegel's low estimate of Mark was influenced by Storr's high estimate of it. Storr recognized the historical priority of Mark among the synoptic Gospels.)

consecration of spirit and character', but whereas for John it showed forth the cleansing force of repentance and the new life of rational autonomy, for Jesus it meant more than this. Hegel describes it in terms which come so close to a 'return to the womb' that (in view of the remark of Jesus to Nicodemus about being 'born again') it is surprising that he does not call it that. Of course, he is only speaking of John's baptism of Jesus, not of something done by Jesus himself; and it is only a 'symbol', an outward ceremony, for which Hegel therefore selects the version of Mark, the 'positive' Gospel.[1] The important thing about it is the descent of the Spirit, which was what distinguished the baptism of Jesus from the others performed by John. Jesus was inspired by a new spirit; he had returned to the 'oneness' of the child, and he withdrew to the wilderness in order that his new life should not be corrupted by the temptations and pressures of the world. But of course his conscious ties with the world went with him even into the wilderness: he had to be sure he had conquered them and put them aside before he returned to the world.

The 'baptism of the spirit' which is outwardly symbolized in the ceremony of immersion, makes the 'sons of men' into 'sons of God', members of the Kingdom of God.[2] This kingdom is the developed consciousness of the harmony of life as it exists in the 'oneness' of childhood; but as a self-conscious, developed whole it is only possible in a free society of perfect friendship, for which 'kingdom' is a most unfortunate and misleading title. The best term for it, Hegel thinks, is *Gemeine*, a communion. The members of the communion live 'in God', i.e. in charity with one another. They are aware of one another as individuals, as *different* modifications of life; but they know that it is the same life in all of them and they want that life to be as rich and varied as possible without becoming the private or personal possession of anyone. Their

---

[1] The event is recorded, together with the descent of the Spirit and the following period of temptation in the wilderness, by Matthew (3: 13–4: 17) and by Luke (3: 21–2 and 4: 1–13). In Luke the emphasis falls on the descent of the Spirit, baptism itself being almost an incidental circumstance; and only preaching of repentance and remission of sins in his name (not baptism) is commanded by the risen Jesus. But why should Hegel discuss the record of Mark rather than that of Matthew, whom he generally relies on in 'The Spirit of Christianity'? It can scarcely be accidental. The clue is provided by what he says about the 'characteristic tone' of Mark (Nohl, pp. 320–1; Knox, p. 277).

[2] *Das Wesen des Jesus*, Nohl, pp. 321–3 (Knox, pp. 277–81). Compare the earlier version in Nohl's footnote on p. 305.

consciousness is to be communal, however variously modified their existence may become. For this reason they must share the activities of life as far as possible and the tools of life absolutely. The limit of this communion would be community of wives, where even the most primitive and restricted, but also for that reason the most intense, form of love is resolved into charity (with which according to the canon of reflection it has nothing in common). Hence the scandals alleged against the early Church by reflective critics were founded at least on a correct understanding of the ideal of love. The resolution of the natural bonds of instinctive life (life in its unselfconscious 'oneness') into a self-conscious universal harmony of charity is what the Kingdom of God, as the final escape from the toils of fate, actually requires. From the Christian point of view there was no shame in the accusation therefore. Perfect love casts out fear. The shame lay rather in their failure to deserve the accusation; it was here in the sphere of family relations that the alienation of Christian love from actual life began. Here at last love was overtaken by fate.

9. *The fate of love*

The ideal of love is to be 'fateless' in the sense of being perfectly reconciled to life. Jesus achieved this goal. But we can also think of fate in another sense. We can ask whether the reconciliation is a 'happy' or an 'unhappy' one.[1] Jesus was reconciled with his enemies, but they were not reconciled with him; his life therefore was bound to be unhappy. Only in the πλήρωσις of love provided by his religion could he find comfort. His religion was a vision of forgiveness reciprocated and love fulfilled in the happy harmony of natural life:

This ideal of a Kingdom of God completes and comprises the whole of religion as Jesus founded it, and we have still to consider whether it completely satisfies nature, or what need drove his disciples to something beyond it. . . . Is there a more beautiful idea than that of a nation [*Volk*] of men who are related to one another by love? Or one more uplifting than that of belonging to a whole, which as a whole, as one,

---

[1] Compare here the cancelled remark in the first draft of *Am interessantesten wird es sein* (Nohl, p. 302; Knox, p. 253 n. 71): 'But love itself is still nature unperfected [*unvollständige Natur*]; *it may be happy or unhappy.*' I take it that in all his uses of 'unvollständig', 'unvollständigkeit', etc. Hegel intends a reference *both* to the theological doctrine that 'grace perfects nature' and to Aristotle's doctrine that 'happiness' must be 'complete'.

is the spirit of God—and whose members are the sons of God? Was
there still to be an imperfection [*Unvollständigkeit*] in this idea, so that
a fate would have power over it? Or would this fate be the Nemesis
raging against a too beautiful endeavour, against an overleaping of
nature?[1]

With these words Hegel introduces, at the end of *Das Wesen des
Jesus*, the final topic of his study, the fate of Jesus and his communion as revealed in their history. He had already written down
in the first draft of *Mit dem Mute und dem Glauben* his views about
the fate of Jesus himself. The closing pages of *Das Wesen des Jesus*
provide a summary account of the nemesis that raged against the
overleaping of nature in the early Church. When he came to revise
Mit dem Mute und dem Glauben he decided to combine both topics
in a fuller treatment. But he did not in this case manage to inter-
weave the old and the new material into one continuous argument
very well; and Nohl has managed to make a bad job worse by
presuming, on the one hand, to finish what Hegel himself may
possibly have abandoned in despair, and by attempting, on the
other hand, to divide the two topics that Hegel wanted to bring
together.[2] I shall do my best to keep the successive drafts separate
in my discussion; but my primary concern will be to indicate the
complementary relation existing between the fate of Jesus and that
of his communion, which was what led Hegel to try to treat them
antiphonally.

In *The Life of Jesus* the fate of Jesus is brought upon him by the
leaders of the established 'positive' order, especially the Pharisees.
In that essay he was the voice of reason, though of a reason which
reconciles and harmonizes impulses rather than judging and curb-
ing them; if he was optimistic it was with a confidence that could
be understood, even if not shared, by all rational observers. But now
he is the prophet of a new life, something that exists only as a
dream, and cannot be explained to the understanding of anybody.
In this perspective the Pharisees can hardly appear culpable, as
they did before, for their opposition to him. Their opposition is
something Jesus expects and discounts.[3] He hopes to win the

[1] Nohl, pp. 321–2 (Knox, p. 278).
[2] See Nohl's note at the end of p. 326 n. [a]; and the notes to pp. 330 and 331.
[3] 'Never once does he treat them with faith in the possibility of their conversion'
(Nohl, p. 327; Knox, p. 283). This (like the following remarks about the Jewish
people and the mission of the disciples) was an addition in the second draft. But
these additions are only expansions of the passage from the first draft which was

people with his call to a life of natural harmony, and Hegel thinks that, had the capacity for spontaneous living not been completely corrupted and dead in them, the Jews would certainly have responded to him. After the failure of the mission of the Twelve[1] Jesus gave up hope of a national rebirth, and devoted himself to the salvation of a small group. This was where the fate of his communion became linked with his own. Jesus was perfectly reconciled with fate, but only at the cost of a life 'undeveloped and unenjoyed'. 'In the Kingdom of God there can be no relation save that which proceeds from the most disinterested love and so from the highest freedom, that which acquires from beauty alone the form of its appearance and its link with the world.'[2]

Because of this ideal, the world of property relations must be surrendered to Mammon; and in a society where *all* civic relations were reduced to that level it seemed necessary to surrender the whole political sphere. All the legal structures of the State are of course below the level of love and beauty. But there are many 'beautiful' relations involved in political life (bonds of voluntary community, of friendship, and of loyalty, which the parties enter into on a basis of equality) which have to be surrendered by a love that seeks to be 'pure'; and this surrender means, moreover, that the Kingdom of God is always and necessarily faced by an Earthly City. In Jewish life the authority of the law reached into *every* human relation. Hence Jesus could not enter into any natural relation at all. He had to accept the paradoxical role of a prophet who proclaimed a gospel of living equality, but lived in a relation

---

allowed to stand (Nohl, p. 326). Cf. the notes in *Zu der Zeit, da Jesus* (Nohl, p. 396) and in *B. Moral. Bergpredigt* (Nohl, pp. 400 bottom–401 top).

[1] Hegel continued to waver about the interpretation of this episode. He notes in *Zu der Zeit, da Jesus* (Nohl, p. 396) that the Twelve were *not* sent 'to reconcile men, and make the human race friends'. It is true enough that Matthew (10: 1), Mark (9: 6), and Luke (9: 1) all give first place to authority over unclean spirits; after that comes healing the sick; preaching the coming of the Kingdom is mentioned third by Matthew and Luke; Mark merely says: 'And they went out and preached that men should repent.' But if one takes Hegel's earlier view about 'unclean spirits' and 'healing the sick' it is hard to defend the claim that the Twelve were not sent 'to reconcile men'. We have here, I think, a clear instance of how Hegel's interpretation of the 'spirit' of Christianity grew; for in his subsequent notes (*B. Moral. Bergpredigt*, Nohl, pp. 400–1) on the instruction of the Twelve, the announcing of the Kingdom is given prominence—as it is in his final text (Nohl, p. 325, Knox, p. 282). By then he has come to see that 'authority over unclean spirits', 'healing the sick', and 'preaching the kingdom' are all the same thing.

[2] *Mit dem Mute und dem Glauben*, Nohl, p. 328 (Knox, p. 285).

of equality with no one; even to those who loved him he was 'the Master', though the Kingdom that he preached was one in which there were no masters. He had to fly from the world, and live his own life in a dream. But at the same time his proclaiming of the Kingdom in this world, his acceptance of the role of 'Master', was a fight against the world, in which his 'mastery' was set against the established order. He knew that for this opposition he must perish. From the point of view of the 'sons of men' he merely risked the potential fate of all who try to be 'master'; but from his own point of view the risk became a certainty, the sacrifice of life a necessity. His vision required that his enemies should have their will in order that his 'mastery' might perish.[1]

Jesus foresaw the full horror of the opposition between the Kingdom of God and the life of this world. He required of those who followed him that they should abandon all the natural ties of love in doing so. He believed that even a small group would suffice for the establishment of the Kingdom. In this faith he died willingly, though he did not seek death, and found it hard to leave the stage where his dream was to come to pass.[2]

After his death his disciples were at first like sheep without a shepherd. With the death of Jesus, their faith in the new life died. But with the Resurrection it was reborn. Hegel's interpretation of the Resurrection is not in all respects as explicit as we might like, but it is at least plain that he does not regard it as a historical event, a return to life of the man Jesus. In his first draft he took note of the fact that it occurred two days after the Crucifixion.[3] Subsequently he cancelled this passage, probably because any time reference seemed to him inappropriate here. With the passing of time the immortality of the spirit would have made itself felt in any case; but the individual 'modification of life' would then, in the ordinary course of events, be remembered as closed, finished,

[1] This last point Hegel does not make in his discussions of the fate of Jesus, though he has made it previously (e.g. Nohl, p. 317). The discussion thus far and in the following paragraph is based on the first draft (and on some passages in the second draft which are expansions of the first: see Nohl, pp. 325–6, 326 n. [a], 331, with pp. 327–9, which are an expansion of p. 326 n. [a]).

[2] *Mit dem Mute und dem Glauben*, Nohl, p. 326 n. [a] with the revised version, Nohl, p. 329; and Nohl, p. 331 (Knox, pp. 286–7, with the footnote to pp. 288–9).

[3] *Nach dem Tode Jesu*, Nohl, p. 333 n. [b]; Knox, p. 291 n. 107. Instead of this brief remark Hegel later wrote *Es ist nicht die Knechtsgestalt* (Nohl, pp. 335–6; Knox, pp. 293–5).

and complete. The memory of the man as dead would persist along with the growing consciousness of the real significance of his life. Thus love would not possess its object. It would still be mere love, not religion; a state of longing, not of fulfilment.

Religion is distinct from love in that the immediate living of life does not predominate over the conscious appreciation of it. In all love there is the self-conscious aspect; where this aspect is completely overborne we have not love, but what Hegel calls 'need' (*Not*), the blind instinctual drive of hunger, thirst, and presumably sex.[1] On the other hand, where the 'actuality' of love (the harmony of desires achieving satisfaction in the normal course of life) is in perfect balance with its 'consciousness' love passes over into religion. This perfect balance can be achieved only in religious experience, because all other forms of experience are infected, even at their best, by the consciousness of mortality. The image of Jesus as 'Risen' differs from the memory of the crucified 'Master' because it is the image of a man *alive*. The image of the God, the element that was lacking at the Last Supper, is present at the love-feast of the Christian communion in the shape of the risen Lord.

Now even among the Greek gods there were human heroes who had undergone apotheosis. But they were not, like Jesus, deified for their simple humanity. The god who arose from the funeral pyre of Hercules, for instance, was just the spirit of Valour personified.[2] There was in his case no 'monstrous combination' (*ungeheure Verbindung*)[3] of the tortured man with the risen God. The particular circumstances of the Greek hero's life and death were only a shroud burned away on the pyre or left behind in the tomb (as they should have been in the case of Jesus).

---

[1] This is the Platonic triad. What Hegel says about David and the shewbread (Nohl, p. 262; Knox, p. 208) makes it clear that he admitted that hunger and thirst can rise to the pitch of 'supreme need'. I do not remember any passage where he is clearly committed to the same view about sex. But what he says about the state of *Not* should in general be read in the light of Plato's doctrine of the 'necessary desires'.

[2] *Nach dem Tode Jesu*, Nohl, p. 335 (Knox, p. 293). Hercules is mentioned because, like Jesus, he rose 'only through the funeral pyre'. Theseus presents a more interesting parallel in other respects. He was not reverenced simply for one-sided virtue but for political leadership. But just because he led a *politically* active life he could only be the hero of Athens (as opposed to other cities).

[3] *Nach dem Tode Jesu*, Nohl, p. 335 (Knox, p. 293). The explanatory remarks at the beginning of *Es ist nicht die Knechtsgestalt* (ibid.) make it clear that the intended meaning of 'ungeheuer' here is 'monstrous' or 'outrageous' rather than 'tremendous' as Knox thinks.

The offering of prayer and worship to the individual who suffered and died on the cross is the index of Jesus' failure. Jesus certainly did not die in the hope that men would make an absolute value out of suffering itself. For him the continual sacrifice of natural ties and impulses and the culminating sacrifice of life itself was acceptable because he was 'one with the Father', he had the vision of life in its undisrupted state. But the purpose of his sacrifice was to enable those who had faith in him to begin living a reconciled life. If they could have succeeded in doing that, they would never have been tempted to think that it was the 'Son of God' who died on the cross, but only the 'son of man'. But in fact they needed an image of divine suffering, because their love could only show itself in the sacrifice of life, in suffering.

The fate of the Christian community has two sides, negative and positive.[1] On the negative side, they sundered themselves, as Jesus had done, from the actual life of the world, the Kingdom of Mammon: they abolished private property. This constitutes in Hegel's view a *negative* bond, because *common* ownership is not possible—they were united with one another in *not owning anything* rather than in *owning things together*. But the whole world of property, legal rights, and political organizations stood over against their common life, continually encroaching upon it and threatening it with corruption. Their flight from it was thus infected with fear, and their fighting against it with a fanaticism which was really hostility masquerading under the false cloak of benevolence. Instead of achieving a genuine life of reconciliation in the world, they went from the Jewish promise of a land flowing with milk and honey as the reward for obedience to the law, to the opposite extreme of a love so pure that it could only despise all material things.

On the positive side their own actual life was informed by the spirit of love. But what living activities were there in which this spirit could express itself? Apart from the minimal ones of eating and drinking in order to maintain life, there was only the religious

[1] For the 'negative side' see *Mit dem Mute und dem Glauben*, Nohl, p. 330 (Knox, pp. 287–8); for the 'positive side' see *Der negativen Seite*, Nohl, pp. 332–3 (Knox, pp. 289–90). These two sections were (as in Knox) a single continuous development in the second draft. Compare also *Das Wesen des Jesus*, Nohl, pp. 322–4 (Knox, pp. 278–81). 'Positive' does not, of course, have in this context the legal sense that it generally has in Hegel's writings in this period.

act of contemplating their ideal, and the common task of spreading
the Gospel. The members of the group could not engage in joint
activity outside of this narrow range, without in the process setting
themselves against the common life that was their ideal, and being
false to the love that bound them together. Two lovers can share
life as a whole; more than two can share it wholly only by im-
poverishing it, by eliminating whatever is not a matter of interest
to all of them. The community, like Jesus himself, had to lose its
life in order to preserve its consciousness of love; and the main
reason for this was its surrender of the political realm to the
dominion of Mammon.

Judaism was the religious consciousness of law, and of *pure*
legal right. Christianity is at the opposite extreme. It is the religious
consciousness of *pure* life, of the highest love and the most perfect
freedom. On both sides the emphasis on purity destroys the actual
enjoyment of life, because life remains obstinately impure: the
intensity and vividness of living experience is always proportionate
to its exclusiveness, except in the shared activities of religion itself.
In place of 'der Herr, der unsichtbare Herr' Jesus set 'Schicksal-
losigkeit'.[1] But the fate of 'fatelessness' was to find itself postponed to another world and another life. Religion remained
separate from the actual experience of life. 'Christ risen' belongs
to another world; only 'Christ crucified' belongs to this one.

Jesus died in vain, he proved after all to be only a dreamer,
because his followers could not give up the image of the dead man
in their memory. They needed him still as they had done in his
lifetime, as a model of how to live, because they could not live the
life of which the risen Christ is the image. The more widely the
gospel of love was accepted, the deeper and more absolute this
cleavage between religion and life became. The necessity of life
in the world being accepted with the success of their preaching,
their religious consciousness became less and less a matter of living
experience, more and more a matter of hope.

The early Church stands condemned for perpetuating its
founder's flight from the world. Like the Jews they 'rigidified the
modifications of nature, the relations of life into brute facts
[*Wirklichkeiten*]' but they regarded them with the shame and
humiliation of the slave, rather than the pride of the master. The
ties of this world were all in one way or another exclusive or

[1] The phrases occur in *Zu der Zeit, da Jesus* (Nohl, p. 386).

selective. Hence they were bound either to live always with the humiliating consciousness of betraying their ideal of 'pure' love, or else not to live in any real sense at all but rather to practise the mortification of the flesh. They could not unite the 'unlimited' aspect of living harmony (freedom, 'pure life', 'the Father') with the 'limit' (inclination, 'love', 'the Son') in the stable equilibrium or 'mean' of beauty as the Greeks had done.[1]

Only the glorified Jesus, not the 'form of the servant', is really divine; and the glorified Jesus is the spirit that unites the community of Christians. This community is the proper embodiment of divinity. Jesus as an individual had no alternative save to sacrifice real existence, remaining in a state of undeveloped 'oneness'. But he died in the faith that, through his sacrifice, the Spirit would descend and the Kingdom would come. When a whole community 'lived in God' the *development* of life in its perfect form would be possible. Instead of this his own undeveloped life, the very negation of divinity, was exalted to divine status.

The divinity of the man Jesus was supposed to be attested by the miraculous stories of his birth and transfiguration.[2] But in the glare of this supernatural light his humanity only appears the more degraded; and when he is himself pictured as doing supernatural deeds, the conflict between the two natures that are supposed to be united in him is even more violent. The miraculous deed is done on the level of physical causality—which is the sphere of *Verstand*. But the causal agent is supposed to be quite outside of that sphere. That there is a spiritual realm outside that sphere is

---

[1] Compare *Mit dem Mute und dem Glauben* (second draft), Nohl, p. 330 (Knox, p. 288) with the remark about how Jesus was for his followers 'ihr lebendiges Band und das geoffenbarte, gestaltete Göttliche, in ihm war ihnen Gott auch erschienen, sein Individuum vereinigte ihnen das Unbestimmte der Harmonie und das Bestimmte in einem Lebendigen' (*Nach dem Tode Jesu*, Nohl, p. 334; Knox, p. 291). I have tried in the text both to indicate what 'das Unbestimmte' and 'das Bestimmte' are, and to bring out the Platonic and Aristotelian associations that were operating, I think, in Hegel's mind.

[2] *Es ist nicht die Knechtgestalt*, Nohl, p. 337. Hegel does not here tell us very explicitly what we are to make of the miraculous deeds ascribed to Jesus himself. But what he says about 'how a god acts [*wirkt*]' makes it clear that, as far as stories of healing and casting out evil spirits are concerned, the rationalizations implied in *The Life of Jesus* only need to be lifted from the plane of reflection to the plane of life in order to provide adequate explanations. In Hegel's view Jesus had ἐξουσία ('authority') but not δύναμις ('power') over evil spirits. See *Reines Leben zu denken*, Nohl, p. 311 (Knox, pp. 263–4); and Roques, p. 130, where explicit reference to the Greek terms represented by *Macht* and *Gewalt* is made.

true. But it is absolutely contrary to the nature of spirit for it to operate as if it were itself a body capable of exerting force. Spirit and body are 'absolute opposites', they have 'nothing in common', that is to say they cannot operate on one another causally or be 'linked' (*verknüpft*). They can, indeed, be 'united' (*vereinigt*) in a living body which is a 'configured spirit' (*gestaltete Geist*); but the condition of the union is that each preserves its own nature.

The conjoining of the two natures, their fusion to the point where their mode of causal operation is not distinguished, is a play of the imagination which is harmless enough as long as it is taken in the higher, subjective (spiritual) sense. But it becomes pernicious when it is taken in the lower, objective (physical) sense. The modern enlightened outlook is the extreme of reflection, in which everything, and particularly the imagination, is subjected to the scientific intellect. The oriental outlook, including that of the Jews and the early Church, is the extreme of 'oneness' in which the standpoint of the imagination and that of the intellect have not even been distinguished. Thus, for the enlightened intellect, the immortality of the soul is a 'postulate of pure practical reason', and the soul itself is only conceivable as belonging to a 'supersensible world'. For the oriental fancy, on the other hand, immortality means the resurrection of the body. Between these two extremes there lies the truth perceived by the Greeks: 'While for the Greeks body and soul persist in one living shape, in both extremes on the other hand, death is a sundering of body and soul; and in one case the body of the soul exists no longer, whereas in the other it also persists through without life.'[1]

Inasmuch as our whole philosophical tradition about the immortality of the soul, and the conception of death as a sundering of soul and body, goes back to Plato, it is rather puzzling that Hegel should say that for the Greeks 'body and soul persist [*bleiben*] in one living shape', since he is apparently using *bleiben* to mean 'remain [after death]'. But the 'Greek' view here is the view of Aristotle, for whom the soul was the 'form' of the body, and that form is the species that persists in 'one living shape' throughout the cycle of life from birth to death, and remains identical in the unending succession of the generations. In Hegel's first draft there is a passage which indicates fairly clearly how he wove together this Aristotelian theory of 'life' with the Platonic theory of 'love'

---

[1] *Es ist nicht die Knechtgestalt*, Nohl, p. 339 (Knox, p. 298).

to produce a synthesis which he could legitimately regard as 'the Greek view'. 'Miracle', he wrote, 'is the exposition of the undivine, of mastery over the dead; not a free marriage of beings that are kin, and the begetting of new ones, but the lordship of the spirit.'[1]

Hegel's doctrine of immortality is a doctrine of the 'marriage of beings that are kin, and the begetting of new ones'. The Platonic strand in this doctrine is to be found in Diotima's exposition of sexual love as 'an immortal principle in the mortal creature'. The soul is immortal because it immortalizes the body by generating new life to replace that which dies. But it does also inhabit a 'super-sensible' realm of its own, the realm of the 'spirit'. This realm is precisely the actual world of human social intercourse, in so far as that intercourse is 'spiritual' rather than 'material'. The world of the spirit is the world of goods that can be common possessions, things that can be shared without being 'shared out'. Thus the 'immortality of the soul' has nothing 'personal' about it. The doctrine does require that some individual life-lines should be immortal, in order that the body may 'persist' in its living union with the spirit. But from the point of view of the spirit itself, it does not matter which life-lines are maintained—though it does of course matter that they should be strong and healthy.

With this resolution of the last surviving 'postulate of practical reason' into the impersonality of 'life' on the side of existence and the inter-personality of 'communion' on the side of consciousness Hegel's essay reaches its culmination. Before summing up the fate of Christianity for the third time,[2] he discusses the difference between the intellectual truth of history and the imaginative truth of prophecy. But nothing that he says raises any new difficulty, and since he does not discuss the Greek mean between the extremes in this instance we do not need to concern ourselves with it for its own sake. All that needs to be said about it has already been said in connection with Jesus' own 'prophecy' of the Kingdom. Doubt-less Hegel only discussed the relation of Jesus to prior prophecy

[1] *Es ist nicht die Knechtgestalt*, Nohl, p. 338 n. [a]. My remarks above about how body and spirit can be so opposed as to have 'nothing in common' and yet be 'united' are largely based on this cancelled passage.

[2] If the last paragraph of the essay belongs (as I feel fairly certain that it does) to the second draft, then Nohl is wrong in saying that the material in *Die lebenverachtende Schwärmerei* (Nohl, p. 331; Knox, pp. 288–9 n.) was never incorporated in the second version. For the other summing-up (which also belongs, fairly certainly, to the second draft) see the end of *Das Wesen des Jesus* (Nohl, pp. 323–4; Knox, pp. 280–1.)

here, because miracle and prophecy were the two main props of Storr's historical argument for Christianity as a positive revelation. It is noticeable, however, that at this stage in the exposition of his views he is concerned at least as much to defend the attitude of the early Christians against their enlightened critics as to expose the mistakes of their fundamentalist interpreters.

10. *Religion and philosophy*

We must now turn from the most unfinished to what may well have been the most finished of all Hegel's early manuscripts—the longest sustained argument of his early years, and the only one which has come down to us so badly mutilated that we are obliged to guess even at its general outline and purpose. There is only one of Hegel's early essays (*The Life of Jesus*) of which we possess every word. In all of the others a page or several pages are missing here and there. But in the case of this essay we have only two widely separated sheets from the second half of a manuscript that may well have been about twice as long as the revised version of 'The Spirit of Christianity'—less than one-twentieth of the whole.[1]

We can get some clues as to the probable aim and purpose of this lost essay in two ways. On one side there is the analogy of Hegel's procedure in the past; and on the other there are some remarks that he makes in the new introduction to the 'Positivity' essay which he wrote immediately after finishing the lost essay. These later remarks we shall have to consider in more detail in their appropriate place. What they indicate, briefly, is that Hegel may, very probably, have come to view the first part of the

---

[1] The two fragments *absolute Entgegensetzung gilt* and *ein objektiver Mittelpunkt* are quarto sheets marked 'hh' and 'yy' respectively. The second one is definitely the conclusion of the whole (see p. 391 n. 3 below). Nohl reasons therefore that the manuscript may have consisted of forty-seven sheets. As far as I can see from the notes of Nohl and Miss Schüler, Hegel's utilization of the letters of the alphabet after 't' for the purposes of numeration is so erratic that this manuscript may have consisted of anything from forty-five to forty-nine sheets—which means that it would have filled anything from 150 to 180 pages of Nohl's text. (All the indications available suggest that a full sheet—eight sides—of Hegel's manuscript constitutes on the average slightly under three and a half pages of printed text in Nohl's edition. The best guide is provided by *Das Leben Jesu* and the main text of the 'Positivity' essay (*man mag die widersprechendsten Betrachtungen*), which consist of nineteen sheets each and fill sixty-two pages each. 'The Spirit of Christianity' itself is an unsafe guide, because both the extent of the manuscript and the volume of the text are hard to estimate reliably.)

'Positivity' essay as an inquiry into the 'death' of the religion of Jesus, designed to stand alongside two others: first an inquiry into its 'life' ('The Spirit of Christianity') and secondly a 'metaphysical treatise on the relation of the finite to the infinite' (including the answers to a whole series of 'special' questions about religion in general and the Christian religion in particular). The first surviving fragment of our manuscript would fit very well into the context of such a 'metaphysical treatise'; and the second fragment is directly relevant to the 'special' problems about religion which Hegel enumerates.[1]

Support for the hypothesis that Hegel had written a treatise of this sort, and was not simply talking in his revised introduction about things that *ought* to be done (which was never a habit of his), can be derived from an analysis of the structural relations that are discernible in his earlier work, and from reflection upon certain general facts that we know about the nature and origin of his guiding principles.

Let us consider, to begin with, *The Life of Jesus*. This essay provides a concrete, individualized ideal for rational contemplation. But when we compare it with the Gospel record we discover that it contains a number of implicit assumptions which are quite paradoxical. An explanation and justification of these assumptions is provided in the first part of the 'Positivity' essay, which plainly presupposes *The Life of Jesus*. In the 'Positivity' essay as a whole, Hegel first traces the causes of the deformation of his rational ideal, and then seeks to draw practical lessons from its restoration. The whole inquiry is carried out on the plane of reflective rationality, but there is no conflict or opposition between reason and feeling. We are on the level of what Hegel calls, in the first version of 'The Spirit of Christianity', *Gesinnung*. At this level (rational morality informed by the spirit of love) the Gospel record was virtually self-sufficient. Save for the introduction of the categorical imperative it needed no supplement from outside; and by 1799 Hegel would probably have admitted that he was mistaken in making that one emendation.[2]

But Hegel knew from the beginning that when he moved on to

___

[1] The passages here referred to (*Der Begriff der Positivität*, Nohl, pp. 143 and 146–7; Knox, pp. 172 and 176) are quoted and discussed below, pp. 405–7.

[2] Cf. Nohl, p. 87 and the discussions of this passage above, Chapter III, pp. 206–7 and Chapter IV, p. 325.

consider the needs of *Phantasie und Herz*, Christianity would no longer be adequate. It is not like the religion of the Greeks, a happy religion.[1] Just as *The Life of Jesus* exhibits a rational ideal, so 'The Spirit of Christianity' exhibits once more a concretely individualized imaginative ideal—the ideal of the 'beautiful soul'. But it is a 'too beautiful effort' which 'overleaps nature'.[2] Unlike the ideal rational society, therefore, the ideal society of 'beautiful souls' cannot simply be reconstructed and used directly for the drawing of practical conclusions. The fault in the ideal itself must first be corrected and a proper ideal constructed. In order to exhibit the fault, the whole theory of 'life' in its four phases must be expounded; and the construction of an adequate ideal must then follow as the culmination or application of the theory. These two tasks were, I assume, completed in the lost manuscript, which would thus have been parallel to the 'Positivity' essay as 'The Spirit of Christianity' is parallel to *The Life of Jesus*. But in place of the earlier sequence, 'Ideal defeated by circumstances, redis-covered, and restored', we have this time the sequence 'Ideal encountering its fate (i.e. self-defeated), fate comprehended, adequate ideal formulated'.

Thus far my hypothesis is, I think, *directly* supported by the evidence of the surviving fragments *absolute Entgegensetzung gilt* and *ein objektiven Mittelpunkt*, as well as by all the indications of the hidden presence of the higher Greek ideal against which the religion of Jesus as well as that of Abraham and Moses is measured and found wanting in 'The Spirit of Christianity'. I shall now offer some further surmises, which cannot in the nature of things be more than guesses, since they rest on indirect and external analogies and indications.

First, the analogy of the 'Positivity' essay strongly suggests that the first half of the new essay would have been constituted by a historical analysis of the fate of Christianity. In other words, some parts of the final revision of 'The Spirit of Christianity' were built into it. If this was the case, then the two essays (the 'Positivity'

---

[1] See particularly his original plan in *Unter objektiver Religion* (section zeta, part *a*, subsection Gimel), Nohl, p. 49 (translated on p. 509 below).

[2] Nohl, p. 322 (Knox, p. 278). Hegel actually uses these expressions about the social ideal of Jesus (The Kingdom of God) which was what he needed to restore for purposes of 'application'. But what he says about the 'guilt of inno-cence' (Nohl, p. 283; Knox, pp. 232–3) shows that he regarded the fate of the individualized ideal as the work of the same 'Nemesis'.

essay and the one that is lost) together formed a systematic statement of Hegel's philosophy of religion and of his programme for religious reform.

But in the second place we can be fairly sure, from what Hegel says in the revised introduction of the 'Positivity' essay, that he meant to work up 'The Spirit of Christianity' manuscript into a separate account of Christianity as a 'living' religion. I think it probable therefore that his programme embraced four parts—two concerned with the religion of Jesus, and two concerned with the historic fate of that religion and the regeneration of religious life in Hegel's Germany. Each topic was dealt with first on the plane of rational reflection and then on the plane of 'life'.[1]

It is time, however, to leave these general speculations and hypotheses, and to turn to the analysis of the text that remains to us. The first fragment opens with the words 'absolute Entgegensetzung gilt', which form the tail end of a sentence. In what follows Hegel discusses the 'multiplicity (*Vielheit*) of living beings' as a type of *Entgegensetzung* which is clearly not 'absolute'. Hence, the hypothesis that comes most immediately to mind is that Hegel has just been discussing opposition in the inorganic sphere, and that, as Kroner surmises, he has just said that '*Absolute* opposition holds good ⟨in the realm of the dead⟩'.[2] If we look back to 'The Spirit of Christianity', however, we shall find that Hegel has actually said more than once that there is an absolute opposition between spirit and body, that is, *between* the realm of the living and

---

[1] This hypothesis has the advantage that it avoids two slight objections that might be raised against the more radical view that Hegel's programme was completely contained in *two* essays. First there is the fact that Hegel speaks of the historic rehabilitation of the Christian religion in one place and of the 'metaphysical treatise' in another (the references are given above, p. 380 n. 1). Secondly, there is the fact that he preserved the confused mass of incompletely revised manuscripts for 'The Spirit of Christianity', which might be taken to indicate that there were at least some parts of it which he never did work up as he had hoped to do. I am not sure whether the further fact that there is a place for *The Life of Jesus* in the more moderate hypothesis can be claimed as an advantage. Perhaps the fact that Hegel obviously told Hölderlin about it, and even spoke of a similar treatment of the Epistles, should tip the balance in favour of the view that he did regard it as integral to his design, even when he had written most of the 'Positivity' essay (which might well be held to incorporate everything of philosophical importance in it).

[2] Kroner's translation of the two fragments (Nohl, pp. 345–8 and 349–51 respectively) are given in Knox, pp. 309–19. The reference here is to his conjectural reconstruction on page 309.

the realm of the dead, rather than *within* either one of them. It is best to leave the opening words alone and admit that we cannot reconstruct the sentence at all with enough verisimilitude for it to be either convincing or useful.[1]

The proper key to the discussion of 'living opposition' that follows, was pointed out by Haering.[2] Hegel wants to show how both 'joining' (*Verbindung*) and 'opposition' (*Entgegensetzung*) are involved in the concept of a human being as an 'individual life'. He is concerned both with the living organism as an entity that maintains itself *against* the flux of the inorganic environment, although it is made up of the same inorganic elements, and with the conscious individual prepared to maintain his own life *against* (and if necessary at the cost of) other living things, whether conscious or not. Hence much, but not all, of what he says can be applied to living things in general—even to plants, in which as we know he was greatly interested. But the only safe course is always to think first of life at the human level.

Whenever we consider any conscious living being 'the multiplicity of life becomes opposed'. On one side there is the conscious individual, who is 'himself an infinite multiplicity since he is alive': in other words, we have to think not of the mortal individual but of the immortal life-line that maintains itself through him. Abraham, the paradigm case of the human individual set against the world, is set against it on behalf of his 'seed'.[3] On the other side is the

---

[1] See *Es ist nicht die Knechtgestalt*, Nohl, p. 338; inasmuch as the assertion 'Geist und Körper . . . sind absolut Entgegengesetzte' is taken straight from the first version (p. 338 n. [*a*]) into the second, which Hegel had finished or abandoned only a few months before, it seems to me most likely that this is the 'absolute Entgegensetzung' referred to in the present passage. But, of course, we cannot be certain of this. Hegel *may* have been discussing inorganic opposites; or he may even have been saying something about 'the war of all against all'. If we had four words from this sentence and the first were *als* the hopeless ambiguity of the situation would be apparent. Luckily, nothing much hangs on the question—unless there is someone who still believes that the lost manuscript contained the first outline of a 'philosophy of nature'.

[2] Haering, i. 539. The terrifying ambiguities that have arisen as a result of Hegel's decision to use 'living being' in place of the traditional (and specifically Kantian) expression 'rational being', 'life' for 'self-consciousness', and so on, are graphically illustrated in the different interpretations which Asveld and Peperzak (for instance) have given of this fragment.

[3] The clue to the meaning of Hegel's assertion that 'this part is itself an infinite multiplicity since it is alive'—which seems to have escaped most of his interpreters—is provided by the example of the tree in *Reines Leben zu denken* (Nohl, p. 309; Knox, p. 261). In the divisibility of the one tree into three the multiplicity of life is spatially presented; at the human level it appears only in

world of which the individual is conscious, a world made up of things which maintain themselves as 'separate' from him, not (like his seed) 'simply in relation [*Beziehung*]' or 'only as union [*Vereinigung*]' with himself. It is 'self-evident', says Hegel, that the individualized life whose manifoldness is considered only in relation, whose being *is* this relation, 'can also be regarded as differentiated into a mere multiplicity'. This is in fact the ordinary way of looking at things. We do not think of Isaac, Jacob, and the twelve tribes as being somehow united in Abraham, but of the succeeding generations and the mortal individuals as distinct entities. But when we think of them in this way we are certainly not considering them as 'living beings'; for Abraham, Isaac, and Jacob are long dead. The point that is vital for Hegel is that Abraham, Isaac, and Jacob are not, like Bohun, Mowbray, Mortimer, and Plantagenet, in the famous phrase of Chief Justice Crewe 'entombed in the urns and sepulchres of mortality'. They live still in the twelve tribes; and just as it is essential to the concept of an individual as living to remember the descendants that he can have (and the forbears that he must have had) so also is it essential to the concept of life itself that there should always be some individuals who do in fact have living descendants. Life exists only in the form of determinate individuals who are the mortal sustainers of immortal family-lines. That is what Hegel means by saying that the 'relation [of this life whose manifoldness is considered only in relation] is not more absolute than the separation of this related [manifoldness]'. The immortality of life is not more essential than its mortality.

But of course, the individual does not produce his successors unaided. In order to achieve the 'separation of this related manifold' he must enter into a living relation (*Beziehung*) with at least part of the world that is initially excluded from him. Hence the world of a living consciousness cannot simply be an inorganic

the form of temporal mortality, and the succession of generations which is essentially characteristic of all life, not merely (like divisibility) a *Vorstellung* offered only by its lower forms.

Of course, in the case of the tribe member who is 'a son of the stem of Koresh' (Nohl, p. 308; Knox, p. 260) the 'related life' is both temporally and spatially presented. But in one who feels his identity with a tribal stem the 'multiplicity of life' has not yet 'become opposed'. Unless the tribe is exogamous, for example, mating will not have for the tribe member the aspect of 'relation with the excluded' that Hegel describes. The model that we need is Abraham, the individual who has broken from his tribe in order to become a tribal-father in his own right.

manifold, something made up of parts that are 'absolutely manifold' (i.e. indefinitely divisible); it has to contain another living individual (*in sich in Beziehung stehend*) with whom the first is so 'joined' that in the juncture (*Verbindung*) both of them 'lose their individuality'.

This 'loss of individuality' is what was described in *welchem Zwecke denn alles Übrige dient*; Hegel even speaks at this point as if the lover really could find his *whole* world in the beloved, just as the lover hopes to do in that earlier fragment. For Hegel does not say that the excluded manifold must be so constituted that it contains another living being. He says that it must *be* another living being: it must be 'posited on the one hand, not as absolutely manifold in and for itself, but as in itself related, and on the other hand joined with the living being excluded from it'. Influenced, no doubt, by the way Hegel has spoken of the excluded manifold up to this point and by the fact that in the definition that follows the inorganic as well as the organic environment of the living individual is explicitly mentioned, Nohl tried to avoid the paradox of this sentence by assuming that Hegel meant to write 'teils, nicht ⟨nur⟩ usw.': 'on the one hand not *simply* as absolutely manifold etc.' This, however, is a mistake. Hegel is tracing the development of 'opposition' in consciousness. First, the individual is conscious of himself as set against a world which is all of it equally 'dead' for him. But as he becomes more sharply aware of the life in him his whole 'world' is focused upon his mate, and in the moment when he loses his individuality in *Verbindung* (in the act of coition) his whole world *is* this excluded, self-related being with whom he is joined. *After* the act (in which, if it is successful, a new individual life is conceived) his experience becomes once more reflective, and now for the first time he can fully appreciate and express what it is to be a living individual.[1]

The concept of individuality includes opposition to infinite manifoldness and juncture with it; a man is an individual life, inasmuch as he is distinct from [*ein anderes ist*] all elements, and from the infinity of individual lives external to him, but he is only an individual life inasmuch as he is one with all elements, with all the infinity of lives external to him; *he* is only inasmuch as the totality [*das All*] of life is divided, he being one part and everything else the other part; he *is* only inasmuch as he is no part, and nothing is sundered from him.[1]

---

[1] *absolute Entgegensetzung gilt*, Nohl, p. 346 (Knox, p. 310).

Except for our ignorance of what Hegel meant by 'all elements' we should now be able to understand this definition. The differential emphasis on 'he' and 'is' which I have introduced will be enough, I hope, to make the meaning plain. A man is, first of all, a complex physical organism involving all the elements (whatever they are) but distinct from them in that he is alive; secondly, he is a singular individual distinct from all others, yet containing an infinity of lives in himself (his ancestors and descendants). But in this infinite aspect (his immortal being, as distinct from his mortal individuality) as life incarnate, he is not sundered either from the inorganic environment or from the other existing living things. Life depends for its maintenance on the total physical environment and more particularly on the conjunction of the sexes. The living individual (the man conscious of this dependence) is aware, therefore, both that he is a 'part' set against the whole world of which he is conscious, and that he is 'no part', that everything of which he is conscious is essential to him and not really sundered from him.

For reflection there are two ways of viewing this situation. We can think of life as 'undivided', as the abiding, immortal, substance which 'manifests' itself equally in Abraham, Sarah, Isaac, and so on *ad infinitum*, but which *cannot* manifest itself adequately in any finite chain, although each mortal link is fixed by reflection as a 'stable, subsistent, fixed point', an individual. Or we can think of it from our own point of view as 'stable, subsistent, fixed points'. When we do this what is revealed is not the immortality of 'life' in time, but the infinity of 'nature' in space. Here it is not just the manifestations of life, but life itself, in its infinite aspect, that is 'posited' or 'fixed' by reflection. 'Nature' is the concept in which the reflective intellect freezes 'life'; all of the essential aspects of 'life' are involved, but the emphasis falls upon the finite, mortal aspect of things, whereas in the other view the emphasis is upon immortality. Hence the living spectator of 'nature' feels the one-sidedness of his attitude and corrects it by turning from the contemplation of an infinity of finite elements back to the awareness of an infinity of living beings. This infinity of life he calls God.

Each of these points of view, the one in which we stand in the presence of the living God and the one in which we discover the infinity of nature, is one-sided. In our total conception of life in the world they are always united somehow. Our whole attitude toward our own lives will be determined by the way in which this union is consummated. The problem is always to overcome the 'fixing' of life by the reflective intellect. Finite life (the reflective individual) must raise itself to the infinite life of God. God is spirit,

for spirit is the living oneness [*Einigkeit*] of the manifold in contrast with the manifold as its embodiment [*Gestalt*], not in contrast with it as separated, dead, bare multiplicity; for in that case it would be the bare unity [*blosse Einheit*] which is called 'law', which is merely something thought of, not something alive [*ein bloß Gedachtes, Unlebendiges*]. Spirit is an enlivening law in union with the manifold which is then itself enlivened.[1]

Any student of 'The Spirit of Christianity' will be prepared for the contrast drawn here between the abstract 'law' of 'nature' and the actual 'spirit' of life. But it is a surprise to find—after his trenchant critique of both the Mosaic law and the Kantian moral law from the point of view of the spirit of love, which is opposed to law altogether—that Hegel is prepared finally to assimilate the conceptions of 'law' and 'life'. I must confess that I am not sure how the consciousness of being an 'organ' in a living whole can properly be called a 'law', though I suppose it does 'govern' one's behaviour. But it is probable, I think, that Hegel has in mind the attitude of one of his idealized Greeks toward the 'laws of the city'. In any case, the way in which he speaks of an 'enlivening law' here is one more sign that he did not regard the morality of pure love as final or sufficient.

The conception of God as spirit is identical with the vision of conscious life lived harmoniously and to the full. But in this conception, the dead world, the necessary inorganic background of life, is still excluded. In the living God we all live, move, and have our being. But in this 'spiritual' life there is nothing dead; spirit is 'absolutely opposed' to matter. Life as a self-maintaining process is the 'joining of opposition and relation' (i.e. of two distinct but fertile individuals of opposite sex); but life absolutely is the 'joining of joining and non-joining' (i.e. of spirit and matter, of the organic and the inorganic). God and nature, therefore, though they are opposed are somehow one. This unity is something that cannot be expressed reflectively without contradiction. In

---

[1] *absolute Entgegensetzung gilt*, Nohl, p. 347 (Knox, p. 311).

philosophy we cannot get beyond the *thought* of the living God; but that is the thought of something which *exists*. It is through the appeal to existence, to the actual experience of life that we avoid the infinite regress that is generated by thought's attempt to grasp its own opposite without contradiction. Religion is therefore higher than philosophy, because it is not simply a form of thought but a form of life. In philosophic thought we discover the finiteness of every part of nature and postulate what is needed to make it whole; to this end pure reason must criticize itself and recognize the transcendental illusions generated by its own infinite (the conception of nature as a *whole*). But as a result of this criticism the true infinite is shown to be something outside of the sphere of theoretical reason altogether.

Religion differs from philosophical theory in that the elevation of finite to infinite life in religious experience is not a matter of striving towards an ideal set up by reflective thought (whether it be an objective ideal, as in the case of obedience to the God of Moses, or a subjective one, as in the case of conformity with the Kantian 'holy will'). Any success in a rational striving of this sort is only an advance to a new point of view from which a further limit, a fresh imperfection to be overcome, is revealed. We advance perpetually towards a goal which by definition we can never reach. The infinite towards which we elevate ourselves exists *only* in thought, never in experience.

At this point the fragment breaks off—indeed my last sentence is really only a guess at what Hegel was about to say in the interrupted sentence.[1] Critics have generally been struck by two points in this discussion of the relation between religion and philosophy: the way in which the description of reflection anticipates Hegel's later conception of the dialectic, and the fact that philosophy is subordinated to religion. They point to the seeming revolution that occurs in this latter respect with the emergence of the ideal of 'absolute knowledge' within a year of Hegel's move to Jena. Richard Kroner's note expresses this general attitude very clearly, though perhaps in a rather extreme form:

[1] Kroner thinks Hegel was about to stigmatize the infinite of *Vernunft* as a 'false one'. Possibly he is right, although the fact that Hegel has just referred to Kant's achievement in the 'Dialectic' of the *Critique of Pure Reason* as 'placing the true infinite outside its sphere' makes me rather doubtful of this. In any case, if he is right my view that in the closing contrast between *Religion* and *Vernunft* Hegel is thinking of practical reason, becomes inescapable.

This statement [i.e. most immediately the sentence, 'Within the living whole there are posited at the same time death, opposition, and understanding, because there is posited a manifold that is alive itself and that, as alive, can posit itself as a whole', but the general reference seems to be to the whole paragraph down to this point], almost as dialectical as Hegel's later method, forecasts what Hutchison Stirling calls 'the secret of Hegel'—the reconciliation of understanding with life. But still he believes that this reconciliation is reserved to religion. Philosophical reflection always 'kills' life by distinguishing oppositions, and it cannot give up those distinctions without killing itself. Desperately but as yet unsuccessfully, Hegel gropes after a method which would understand life by both positing and uniting opposites. Nowhere else can the fountain-head of Hegel's dialectic be better studied than in the intellectual struggle reflected in this paper.[1]

It is because there is so much obvious truth in the first three sentences of this note that I feel moved to protest vigorously against the dangerous misrepresentation of Hegel's own position and attitude in the last two sentences. The claim that Hegel is 'desperately but as yet unsuccessfully' groping after a method is simply false; and the implied claim that we have in this passage 'the fountain-head of Hegel's dialectic', though not quite false, as we shall see, is at least dangerously misleading.

To begin with, what Hegel *is* 'desperately groping for' is a way of convincing the enlightened public of his time that Kant's critical philosophy cannot provide a 'rational faith' that is superior to other types of religious experience. His whole argument that 'philosophy stops short of religion' is directed against Kant's practical philosophy, and is founded on Kant's own conception of theoretical philosophy as Hegel understands it. As far as he is concerned, the *Critique of Pure Reason* has revealed once and for all the inevitably dialectical character (in Kant's sense of the word) of theoretical reflection about actual existence. It is in *practical* philosophy—when it tries to deal with life—that 'reflection is *driven on and on* without rest'; in theoretical philosophy it is only *thrown back and forth* between the thesis and antithesis of an antinomy. Hegel believes that the infinite progress of Kant's practical reason towards an unattainable ideal arises directly from the antinomic character of pure reason. This conviction is his only personal contribution to 'philosophy' as here portrayed. He was

[1] Knox, pp. 312–13 (n. 6).

not in the least concerned himself about the inevitable failure of reflection, *and he never changed his mind about it.*

As for the 'fountain-head of the dialectic' it is really a mistake to look for any such thing, because the word 'dialectic' means several different things in Hegel's mature thought. In one sense, the narrowest and most precise, but not the one most commonly intended by the critics who speak of it, what we have here is not so much the 'fountain-head of the dialectic' as the dialectic itself. This can be seen from Hegel's eventual distinction between 'dialectic' and 'reflection' in the *Encyclopedia*:

> In its proper character dialectic is . . . the real and true nature of the determinations of understanding, the nature of things and of the finite generally. To begin with, reflection is the movement out beyond the isolated determination and a relating [*Beziehen*] of it, whereby it is placed in connection [*Verhältnis*], but otherwise maintained in its isolated validity. Dialectic, on the other hand, is this *immanent* going beyond, wherein the onesidedness and limitedness of the determinations of understanding reveals itself as what it is, namely as their negation.[1]

It is clear, I think, that the conception of reflection in this passage from the mature system is identical with that expressed in *absolute Entgegensetzung gilt*; and the definition of dialectic corresponds perfectly with the attitude that Hegel adopts toward reflection in that fragment. We could hardly ask for a more graphic demonstration that Hegel's attitude toward 'philosophical reflection' did not change in later years. But the expression 'Hegel's dialectic' usually refers to 'what Hutchison Stirling calls "the secret of Hegel"—the reconciliation of understanding with life'. The 'fountain-head' of this, so far as there is one, is not to be found in anything that Hegel says here or elsewhere about 'reflection', but in the continuous evolution of his conceptions of 'life', 'religion', and particularly 'love'.

One of the most remarkable things about the development of Hegel's philosophy is that ideas mature in a sort of steady succession and, once matured, remain fairly stable even while other ideas are developing around and above them. His conception of 'reflection' is already mature in 1800. The conception of religion is not yet mature, for Hegel's ideal model is still the religion of the Greeks, or what he called in the *Phenomenology* the 'religion of art'. In the

---

[1] *Encyclopædia* (1830), section 81. I have translated the passage as faithfully as I can: cf. Wallace, p. 147, for a slightly more relaxed and readable rendering.

end this ideal is identified with 'art' simply, rather than with 'religion'. 'Absolute knowledge', the highest conception of all, develops out of the conception of 'love' as the self-consciousness of 'life', and hence as the reconciliation of thought (or 'reflection') with existence. In this development the already clarified conceptions of 'reflection', 'understanding', and 'representation' (*Vorstellung*) all play a part; but the role of the still-evolving notions of 'art' and 'religion' is more important.

We could perhaps say that the 'fountain-head' of it all is the dialectic between the Kantian and the Hellenic conceptions of reason. But 'dialectic' is used here in its reconciliatory sense to refer to what Hegel later calls the 'speculative or positively-rational phase' (which is not what 'dialectic' refers to in the strict sense).[1] It is the 'reconciliation of Reason (*Vernunft*), not of Understanding (*Verstand*), with life' that is the 'secret of Hegel'. And if we want to understand *that* secret we must not allow ourselves to be misled by the fact that the *words* 'philosophy' and 'religion' are put in one relation at this stage in his development, and in the opposite relation a year later; we must attend to what the words mean. When we do this we find that what is called 'philosophy' in the first instance does not subsequently change its status, and that what is called 'philosophy' later *grows out of* what was called 'religion' before.[2]

Confirmation of the view that the religion of the Greeks, not Christianity, is still for Hegel the 'absolute religion' in 1800, and some idea of what sort of experience it is that he looks to for a solution of the antinomies of practical reflection and 'rational faith' can be gained from the second surviving fragment of our present manuscript, *ein objektiven Mittelpunkt*. In this, the last quarto sheet of the essay, he seems to be finishing his description of an ideal system of religious worship.[3] He has reached the

---

[1] See *Encyclopædia*, sections 79 and 82.

[2] This point has been well taken and felicitously expressed by Peperzak (pp. 199–200).

[3] This is apparent when he reaches his conclusion: 'It only needs to be briefly touched on, that the remaining external spatial surroundings (of the place where the people assemble for worship) *ought* not so much to occupy the mind with purposeless beauty as point towards something else [i.e. the God] through purposeful adornment' (Nohl, p. 350; Knox, p. 316). Up to this point we might have taken his account of temple worship as part of a theoretical analysis of folk-religion rather than as a practical recommendation.

(Lukács, p. 275 n., has expressed doubt as to whether this really is the last

problem of the temple or church as the 'house of God', and of just
how and where God is conceived to dwell in it:

⟨The religious experience of a people has to have?⟩ an objective
centre. For all peoples [*Völkern*] it was the dawn-region [*Morgen-
gegend*] of the temple, and for the worshippers of an invisible God [the
Jews] only this emptiness [*Gestaltlose*] of the determinate space, only a
place. But this mere opposite, this purely objective, merely spatial
⟨centre⟩ need not necessarily remain in this imperfection [*Unvollständigkeit*] of perfect objectivity; it can itself, i.e. as self-maintaining,
revert to its own subjectivity through the figure [*durch die Gestalt*, sc.
of the God]. Divine feeling, the infinite sensed by the finite, is thereby
perfected [*vervollständigt*] for the first time, in that reflection is added
and dwells on it.[1]

Anyone who compares this passage with Hegel's critique of the
Eucharist in 'The Spirit of Christianity' will speedily perceive
that he is here making the same comparison between Jewish and
Greek worship that he there made between the love feast of the
early Christians and that of the Greek mysteries.[2] Religion is the
fulfilment of love because in religion reflection is satisfied by being
given an objective image of the divine being to focus upon. The
object abides and is not done away with or consumed, as it is in
love, or in the ordinary process of life, yet in its religious aspect it is
not set against the subject, for it is only the beauty of the *Vorstellung*
that is divine, and that was created entirely by the imaginative
genius of the artist, who is himself a member of the worshipping
communion. Love itself is, of course, a reflective state, but the
reflection is something separate from the actual feeling (that is
why Christian charity, the attempt to be faithful to life, leads in

sheet of the essay. Hegel did, of course, sometimes put the date into the margin
of work in progress when he *began* a new day's work (perhaps after an interval of
some days for study and reflection, or an interruption caused by the pressure
of other duties and concerns). See, for instance, the dates in *man mag die
widersprechendsten Betrachtungen*, Nohl, pp. 204 and 211. But he did not, I think,
ever put the date at the *end* of a sheet unless he wished to mark the completion
of a project: cf. Nohl's note at the end of *Das Leben Jesu* (Nohl, p. 136). Thus,
even if the sheet is full, as it may well be, the recording of the date 14 Sept.
1800 at the end of it proves fairly conclusively that in Hegel's mind some sort
of a terminus had here been reached.)

[1] Nohl, p. 349 (Knox, pp. 313–14). The addition at the beginning is, of course,
only a conjecture (upon which no weight should be placed). If *Morgen-gegend*
is translated simply as 'the east' we lose the echo of sun-worship which I am
confident that Hegel meant us to catch.

[2] *Der Abschied, den Jesus*, Nohl, pp. 297–301 (Knox, pp. 248–53).

the end only to the sacrifice of life). When religious consciousness is focused on the *Gestalt* of the divine, the unity and harmony of the whole community (its 'spirit') is not merely felt but known. The Jewish people could come together in the Temple and in that way feel their union. But they were expressly forbidden to 'make unto themselves any graven image'. The emptiness of the Holy of Holies offered for reflection only an 'actual objectivity', a *Vorstellung* of the non-living. Whereas in the Greek temple the people came together before the image of the God, an objectivity which 'is, at the same time, what it ought to be, in virtue of the subjectivity bound up with it [sc. that of the artist], not an actual but only a potential objectivity'. One could make this potential objectivity actual by smashing the statue or grinding it to powder, but then, as Hegel says in 'The Spirit of Christianity', one could not afterwards turn and worship the dust.[1]

Because it is the *Vorstellung* that matters, the presence of an actual physical work of art is not essential, but the fancy must have an image of beauty to play on. In Hegel's theory of 'life' we have seen how everything culminates in the conception of the child. The period between conception and birth is the period of 'oneness'. In the 'determinate space' of the womb the whole of life, the whole significance of the world, the infinity which the reflective ideal of 'nature as a whole' could not contain, actually is. Here we have the perfect image of that 'life in God' which Plato expressed in the myth of the soul's life before birth, and Jesus in the parable about the 'angels of the children'.[2] But we have also what Hegel calls 'the objective antinomy with respect to the *Gegenstand*'. The thing that 'stands against' life in its 'oneness' as its necessary objective complement is the womb of the mother, an environment which is itself alive; but the thing that 'stands against' life in the fulness of self-consciousness is the whole physical universe which is not alive. What reflection cannot grasp in its rational use, when it rises from the concept of 'Nature' to that of 'pure life', is the necessity of embodiment; this is what it captures, in its imaginative use, in the *Vorstellung* of God's Incarnation. But the gulf between the rational and the imaginative employment of reflection remains. This was the unsolved problem from which Hegel's conception

---

[1] *Der Abschied, den Jesus*, Nohl, pp. 300–1 (Knox, p. 252).

[2] See *Das Wesen des Jesus*, Nohl, pp. 315–16 (Knox, pp. 269–70), and B. Moral. *Bergpredigt*, Nohl, p. 400; compare the discussion above, pp. 366–7.

of 'absolute knowledge' sprang. The 'Father' and the 'Son', the two aspects of this antinomy, have yet to be united in the 'Spirit'.

Hegel mentions at this point another antinomy: 'just as, above the antinomy of time, the moment and the time of life, was posited as necessary'. He must have posited this antinomy in the part of the manuscript now lost. Just what it was depends on the meaning to be attached here to *die Zeit des Lebens*. At first sight it would seem that *der Moment des Lebens* can hardly be anything but an actual present moment of consciousness; if this is taken as the minimum requirement of life in its 'oneness' (the instant when the parents 'lose their individuality' in 'union' and a new life is conceived, but also every instant of consciousness in its 'purity', every instant in which we are or at least can be 'born again'), then *die Zeit des Lebens* must be the time required by life in its 'fullness'. But how long is this? Is it simply the normal life span of a healthy individual? Or is it rather the 'whole of time' (because only the immortal chain of the generations can properly be called a living *being*)? The analogy with the 'objective antinomy' suggests the latter view. But now that the alternative is squarely before us, we can see that *der Moment des Lebens* could quite easily be taken as a technical term for the 'individual life'. In that case what we have here is the antinomy between the immortal and the mortal aspects of life that was 'posited' in a passage of *absolute Entgegensetzung gilt* which we have already analysed: ' ⟨Life's⟩ relation is not more absolute, than ⟨the⟩ separation of the related ⟨manifold⟩'. Any of these three interpretations (or some combination of more than one of them) may be what Hegel means here by 'the antinomy of time'. We must resign ourselves to uncertainty on this point, and turn back again to the 'objective antinomy'.[1]

Religious experience makes us aware on the one hand that we

---

[1] It is in the highest degree unlikely that any more of this manuscript will turn up in the future. Rosenkranz does not appear to have possessed any more of it than we do (Rosenkranz, p. 94: 'einige mit Buchstaben bezeichnete Bogen vorhanden sind'). Haym, p. 492 n. 10, claims to be going 'back to the complete original manuscript' for the passage quoted and paraphrased on p. 85–6 of his book. But it is fairly clear that he only means the actual *text* of the *fragmentary* manuscript as against the paraphrased extract given by Rosenkranz. My own guess is that Hegel utilized much of the manuscript himself in later years in some way that made its destruction either necessary (e.g. he cut it up) or at least a matter of indifference to him subsequently. Some of it probably survives in the *Differenzschrift* and in *Glauben und Wissen*.

stand in a *living* relation to the world; but it also brings us face to face with the fact that we must admit the objectivity of the world. Judaism failed because it sought to deny the living relation; primitive Christianity failed because it sought to deny the objectivity, and set up the 'Kingdom of God' in opposition to the kingdom of Mammon. 'It may be', says Hegel, 'that in the relations of living beings, objectification [i.e. hostility or opposition] only has to last for a moment'; but it is nevertheless part of the human 'fate' to 'make living beings into objects'. From the way he speaks of the ending of this 'moment'—'life once more withdraws from ⟨making and being made an object⟩, frees itself therefrom, and leaves the oppressed to its own life and the resurrection of it'—it is probable that he is thinking here of ancient slavery and of the appeal of Christianity to a world where everyone was in bondage to the Roman Emperor.[1] We have here the first explicit declaration on Hegel's part that war to the death and the master–slave relation is a necessary phase in the natural development of human consciousness.

But apart from the moment of subjection on the part of life itself, we have to recognize the 'fate' of property. Life involves both the possession and the consumption of objects. In order to keep ourselves alive, we have to treat some living things as objects even to the point of actually destroying their life and consuming their dead bodies; and by building houses and cultivating the land (as Abraham refused to do) we admit the permanence and inevitability of life's dependence upon the non-living environment.

In religious experience, as we rise from finite to infinite life, we need to express somehow the fact that this relation to objects (the lower orders of organic life, and the inorganic world) is a universal relation. It belongs to life itself as the 'joining of joining and non-joining', not merely to us as finite individuals. This is the significance of the religious ceremony of sacrifice. At a Greek sacrifice the assembled people solemnly burned part of the offering (mainly

---

[1] Cf. *Jetzt braucht die Menge*, Nohl, pp. 70–1; *Unkunde der Geschichte*, Nohl, pp. 364–5; and *Jedes Volk hat ihm eigene Gegenstände*, Nohl, pp. 223–4 (Knox, pp. 157–8), for the continuous presence and gradual evolution of this idea in Hegel's mind from 1794 onwards. It seems not to be directly referred to in 'The Spirit of Christianity', which is concerned more directly with the resurrection of Jewish life from servitude to the Mosaic Law. Hegel can hardly be thinking of *that* here, because he certainly did not regard the Jewish 'fate' as the typical or natural fate of humanity.

the inedible part) as the share of the God, and then ate the rest in a communal feast. The love-feast aspect of this procedure is the closest approximation possible to 'spiritual' possession of the object: its character as *private* property is as nearly as possible destroyed; and the purposeless destruction of what is burned on the altar is 'the only religious relation to absolute objects', because it both makes us aware, and signifies our awareness, that in consuming things purposefully in order to live we are not simply maintaining ourselves till death comes in the ordinary course of nature, we are maintaining the immortal life of which 'the course of nature' is only an abstract image. In this sense the 'destruction for destruction's sake' that takes place on the altar 'makes good ⟨the⟩ other particular connection [*Verhältnis*] of ⟨man's⟩ purposeful destruction'.

Thus, at last, Hegel has justified the central position of communal sacrifice in the religious practice of his idealized Hellas. From the beginning, in *Religion ist eine* (1793), he had to face the fact that both the conservatives and the radicals, both the pious and the enlightened, in his own society were agreed that the practice of sacrifice was barbarous and superstitious. Furthermore, he himself agreed with the enlightened critics that much of the religious ceremonial of his own time which had an ascetic and quasi-sacrificial aspect was only fetishism and superstition. He maintained always that the sacrificial feasts of the Greeks were different, but it is only now that he has finally managed to show why.[1]

This was the climax of Hegel's account. Having shown why the God must be visibly present in the temple,[2] and what the people are to do in his presence, he turns briefly to externals. Physically the place of worship should be beautiful, but beautiful only in such a way as to focus attention upon the central *Gestalt* of the God; the forms of worship on the other hand should be such as to 'transcend' (*aufheben*) the passive contemplation (both rational and imaginative) of the 'objective God' which the whole physical design of the temple is calculated to encourage. *Aufheben*, which Hegel still uses primarily in a 'cancelling' sense, struck him as rather too

---

[1] Cf. *Religion ist eine*, Nohl, pp. 24–6 (pp. 503–4 below).

[2] Presumably *Joseph*, Mary, and the child Jesus would have to be before the worshipper's eyes in his Christian temple—or perhaps only the Risen Lord. Certainly not the Crucifixion, which sets before us the *fate* of Christianity that he wishes to overcome.

strong an expression here, so he adds: 'or rather to fuse [*ver-schmelzen*] it with the subjectivity of living beings in joy'. The people come before their God to sing, dance, and hear 'solemn orations'—more like Pericles' Funeral Oration, doubtless, than like a Lutheran sermon. In what Hegel says about dancing we get a glimpse, perhaps, of his reason for calling 'spirit' an 'enlivening law': he calls dancing 'a kind of subjective manifestation that becomes objective and beautiful through rules' (*durch Regel*). In the preface to the *Phenomenology*, we may remember, he finds the perfect image of the spirit in the most celebrated example of Greek religious dancing, the Bacchic revel; but there the emphasis is on spontaneity, rather than on the grace of voluntary control, for, as he says, all the revellers are drunk.[1] The ideal of worship here is more measured and Sophoclean. The whole order of worship is to be presided over by a priest 'who, if an outer life full of needs has greatly sundered man, will likewise be a sundered person', i.e. someone whose main social function is to be a priest. If we compare this relatively neutral remark with the polemical tone of Hegel's comments about the sundering of society into classes and professions in the fragments of 1794,[2] we shall see that his reflections upon the fate of the classless society of the 'Kingdom of God', have led to the removal from Hegel's own ideal of certain traits which were derived originally from the ideology of 1789 rather than from Periclean Athens.

In his last paragraph Hegel compares this ideal of the religion of a 'happy people' with the typical deformations that it undergoes among unhappy peoples. A happy people knows that the infinite life is *their* life; in their religious experience the opposition of subject and object is reduced to a minimum, since the beauty on which their attention is fixed is produced by the inspired imagination of one among them. 'Unhappy peoples' cannot achieve this: 'in the separation they have to take anxious care for the preservation of one of the separated terms, for independence'. In other words, their religious experience is the awareness of the infinite life as self-sufficient and independent; it is the reflective complement of their everyday life in which nothing is independent, everything

---

[1] *Phänomenologie des Geistes*, Hoffmeister, p. 39 (Baillie, p. 105).

[2] The present passage may be neutral in that a certain degree of 'sundering' is implicitly accepted as necessary. But it is clear that in the basic sense of a breach of natural familial ties 'sundering' is an evil. Hegel is not offering a justification for clerical celibacy.

is finite, causally determined, subject to law. The *Trennung* to which Hegel refers here is the *Trennung* between God and Nature which must exist for any man who has achieved reflective awareness of his own place in the natural order. For the reflective awareness of his dependence rests on a conscious contrast with an ideal standard of free and independent life that he has formulated for himself. He can conceive this contrast in two ways: positively or rationally. The *one* absolutely independent being set against the system of dependent creatures may be regarded as an inscrutable power, or as an independent rational subject. The more clearly and sharply one is aware of the *Trennung*, the more necessary it becomes to conceive of God both ways at once.[1] He is the absolute substance, the law of nature, and the absolute Ego, the law of duty. It does not make much difference in the end which of these roles is taken as fundamental to begin with. Positive religion and Kantian moral reason both arrive at the same terminus: the subjection of life to an almighty object (i.e. a commanding, compelling law). In both cases our human nature is taken as *absolutely* finite, and the divine nature as *absolutely* infinite (self-sufficient, independent). Our life, our experience, our world, is reduced to the status of a passing phenomenon, the existence or non-existence of which is ultimately indifferent so far as the one eternal being is concerned. When we rise towards the one eternal being we must leave that phenomenal nature behind us. We cannot draw near to God as individuals who share the powers of sensibility, and the capacity to exercise them creatively in imagination. We must be content to lose all of that, to rise above it and be purely rational beings. This exaltation of the Ego to 'blessedness' (in Kant, Fichte, and Schelling) is 'at bottom equivalent to' the original exaltation of an infinite Lord above all of Nature in the minds of Noah, Abraham, and Moses. Far from being modern and 'enlightened', therefore, the conception of God in 'rational religion' is elementary and primitive; it is the reflection of a life of hardship and 'need'. But even so it is nobler and more worthy than the orthodox Christian view, according to which the infinite power 'humbled itself', and in one unique

---

[1] This seems to me to be the upshot of that passage in Schelling's essay *Vom Ich* which made such an impression on Hegel's mind (see *Briefe*, i. 30, and Schelling, *Sämtliche Werke*, i. 201). But the immediate reference—the implicit quotation (Nohl, p. 351) which Kroner notices but cannot identify is to Fichte's *Appellation an das Publikum* (Jan. 1799). The quotation is supplied by Fuhrmans, pp. 459–60 n. 8.

historical event exhibited itself miraculously in a phenomenal life which was for it only 'the form of a servant'.[1]

11. *The 'ideal of my youth in reflective form'*

On 24 September 1800, just ten days after he had thus identified the achievements of Kant and Fichte with those of Abraham and Moses, and dismissed the orthodox conception of the Incarnation in a way which echoes the trenchant condemnation of 'faith in Christ' with which his long struggle with the Christian religion opened,[2] Hegel turned back again to his essay on 'The Positivity of the Christian Religion', which represents, if I am right, the fruition of the first stage of his inquiry. In the course of his Frankfurt researches he had gained a new insight into the relation between positive religion and the religion of reason. This insight did not affect his practical attitude towards either of them. But it did make it necessary for him to revise his original introduction to the essay of 1795, in which they were treated simply as opposite extremes.

The new introduction begins with the antithesis of 'natural' and 'positive' religion, because the ambiguities of this distinction enable Hegel to show up very clearly the contrast between his own integrated point of view and the two opposed reflective standpoints that he wishes to set aside. But whereas in the earlier version the main target of his criticism was the 'positive' religion of Storr and his followers at Tübingen, his criticism is now directed primarily against the enlightened religion of Lessing, Mendelssohn, Kant, Fichte, and Schelling. What is new in his discussion is the insistence that it is not enough to understand *that* a religion is 'positive', which is all that rational criticism can do. When we go further and ask how it came to be positive, how it came to deviate from the canons of reason, the right answer reveals not so much a superfluity in the religion analysed, as a lack in the standpoint of reflective criticism itself.

[1] Hegel consistently anticipates Feuerbach in his interpretation of all 'otherworldly' conceptions of the divine as reflections of physical need: cf. especially *Fortschreiten der Gesetzgebung*, Nohl, pp. 373–4, on the Judaic tradition. Christianity as a miracle-religion reflects a need which is spiritual as well as physical, because the culture to which it appealed was so much more developed. Freedom and spontaneity were frustrated, but the memory of a beautiful existence (not merely of 'a land flowing with milk and honey') was present.

[2] Compare the discussion of *Es sollte eine schwere Aufgabe* and *Wenn man von der christlichen Religion* (Nohl, pp. 50–69) in Chapter III above, pp. 177–83.

The antithesis of 'positive' and 'natural' religion (like that between 'positive' and 'natural' law) requires that all variation and multiplicity be assigned to the positive side. There can be only one 'natural' law or 'natural' religion, because the human nature that is governed by it or expressed in it is *ex hypothesi* uniform. From the point of view of a rational critic of positive religion, therefore, the natural norm must be defined before his critical attack can begin.[1] It was characteristic of the champions of 'enlightenment' to believe that they could define man's *Bestimmung* by the light of natural reason, and that in this concept they had a standard by which to define religion itself.[2] But from the standpoint of 'life in its integrity' which Hegel's investigations have now led him to adopt, it is apparent that the reflective concept of 'human nature as such' must have a long history of cultural development behind it. It is equally clear from either standpoint that 'pure human nature' has never actually existed. 'Pure human nature' is a universal concept, while actual humanity exists only in individuals. Something more than 'freedom of the will'—the standard which Fichte used to define man's *Bestimmung*—is needed to make a man.[3] Religion is man's consciousness of his humanity in its integrity. Hence it is bound to contain more than the pure rational principles of human morality which are the 'laws of freedom'. And so, once

[1] From the point of view of someone like Storr, who believed that religion must be positive, it was not strictly true that the concept of human nature must be defined *first*, though that concept and 'man's relation to God' were bound to play a crucial role in his argument to show that the positive revelation contained in the Bible was the *true* religion. From the way Hegel defines positive religion we can see that at this stage he does not any longer feel that he needs to take Storr's perversion of Kant seriously. It was only a further extension of the perversion of nature begun by Kant himself.

[2] *Der Begriff der Positivität*, Nohl, p. 139 (Knox, p. 167). It may well be that Hegel has the recent publication of Fichte's *Die Bestimmung des Menschen* in mind here, as Knox (p. 167 n. 44) suggests (see the following note). But we should remember that use of the term was widespread and fashionable for twenty years before the appearance of Fichte's book. Hegel seems to have encountered it for the first time in Moses Mendelssohn (see his excerpt of 31 May 1787 from Mendelssohn's article 'Was heißt aufklären?' of 1784: *Dok.*, pp. 140–3).

[3] *Der Begriff der Positivität*, Nohl, p. 141 (Knox, p. 169). There cannot be much doubt that Hegel is here thinking of Fichte's use of this 'one-sided standard' to show that man's *Bestimmung* is not really a thing of this world. See the whole argument in the last stages of *Die Bestimmung des Menschen* (Fichte, *Sämtliche Werke*, ed. I. H. Fichte, ii. 288–319; Chisholm, pp. 124–54) and particularly the following dictum: 'The absolute freedom of the will, which we bring down from the Infinite into the world of time, is the principle of this our life' (*Sämtliche Werke*, ii. 300; Chisholm, p. 125).

the integrity of life has been ruptured, once man has come to think of his life as governed by law, his religion is bound to assume a positive character. This 'positivity', however, is only the character that it has, as an external authority, for the reflective consciousness that has advanced to the point of recognizing the rupture—the opposition between existence and concept. For one who is simply *in* the state of rupture, the authoritative character of his religion is quite 'natural'. His religion provides him with a perfectly true and adequate consciousness of his actual condition as a living being. He is only conscious of it as 'positive', as an external authority, when this correspondence has ceased, when the 'spirit' that links his religion to his life has died or flown.[1]

This does not imply that we ought not to condemn any religion as positive or superstitious. It only means that our judgements about religion must be based on an 'ideal of human nature', not a definition of the 'human vocation'.[2] Haering has remarked on the difference between Hegel's concept of an 'ideal' here and the Kantian definition of an 'ideal' as distinct from an 'idea'.[3] There is in fact an important difference, but it has not generally been properly identified. Hegel's use of the term 'ideal' is fairly clearly derived from Kant's,[4] but whereas Kant says: 'By the ideal I understand the idea, not merely *in concreto* but *in individuo*', the ideal of which Hegel is speaking is concrete but *not* individual. Not Jesus or Socrates, but the 'Kingdom of God' or 'the City' is the ideal of human nature.

There is of course a tremendous difference in the *function* which the 'ideal' has in Hegel's theory as against Kant's; this is generally confused with the difference in character just pointed out. The

---

[1] Compare *Der immer sich vergrößernde Widerspruch* (Lasson, pp. 138–41) discussed on pp. 440–5 below.

[2] In the earlier version—*man mag die widersprechendsten Betrachtungen*, Nohl, p. 153 (Knox, p. 68)—Hegel lays it down as his *Grundsatz*, 'as a foundation for all judgements about the different form [*Gestalt*], modifications, and spirit of the Christian religion' that 'the *Zweck* and *Wesen* of all true religion is human morality'. This proposition still holds true, but it is no longer the 'Grundsatz' for all judgements. The 'foundation' for judgements is now human nature in its *fullness*; unlike human nature in its *purity*, this *Maßstab* cannot be contained in a *Grundsatz* at all—compare *Der Liebe versöhnt aber*, Nohl, pp. 294–5 (Knox, pp. 245–6).

[3] See Haering, i. 179; and cf. i. 454 and 580.

[4] Cf. *Abraham in Chaldäa geboren hatte schon*, Nohl, p. 247 (Knox, pp. 187–8). Knox quotes the relevant passage from the *Critique of Pure Reason*, A 568–9 in his note ad loc.

two differences are connected—for a 'personified ideal' such as Jesus could not perform the function Hegel assigns to the 'ideal of human nature'[1]—but they ought to be clearly distinguished. In Kant's theory it is the 'idea' (freedom, virtue, the moral law), not the ideal (the free, virtuous, rational man), that plays the decisive role. The ideal could not usurp this place because it is a work of imagination not of reason. But this is exactly why it becomes the more important of the two in Hegel's theory. Whereas Kant wanted to seat authority in the right place, Hegel wished from the beginning to eliminate the appeal to authority altogether. The ideal of the imagination does not command; it evokes love and a spontaneous desire to imitate. If anyone tries to make the ideal into a source of authority it immediately becomes 'positive'. In terms of 'authority' the imagination cannot set itself *against* the 'higher' functions of *Verstand* and *Vernunft*. But this is because the whole sphere of authority and hierarchy is 'lower'; the ordering of the inorganic world and of property generally is a function of reason and understanding; the sphere of life belongs rather to the imagination.[2]

The question to be asked about any religion, and in particular about our own, therefore, is not how far it meets the requirements of human reason, though it must do that, but how far it satisfies the highest longings of the human imagination. The claim that Christianity contains positive elements, that it commands things that are contrary to the law of reason or upon grounds that are not rational, is not in itself very interesting; for it does not touch upon the status of Christianity as *religion*. Where a claim of this sort is established as true, it only shows that in certain respects the religion has ceased to fulfil its proper function, that there is dead wood in it. We need rather to have the contrary proved, says Hegel: we need to be shown that all this 'discarded dogmatics'—which men like Storr have used to bolster up despotism—originally expressed an ideal of the imagination.[3] For to suppose that there was *never*

---

[1] Cf. *Es sollte eine schwere Aufgabe*, Nohl, p. 57, and *Wenn man von der christlichen Religion*, Nohl, p. 67; Hegel saw from the beginning that the 'ideal' has to be *übermenschlich*. Just for this reason it cannot be instantiated in a particular person.

[2] As Jesus said, one does not give stones to children crying for bread; but as Hegel adds, neither does one give bread to men who want to build a house. *Der Begriff der Positivität*, Nohl, p. 142 (Knox, p. 171).

[3] Ibid., Nohl, p. 143 (Knox, p. 172). Of course Hegel himself had already

anything but superstitious folly and shameless trickery in it, is the height of intellectual conceit.

Of course, if that ideal itself was a positive one, if authority, or lordship and bondage (*Herrschaft und Knechtschaft*), were the 'ideal of human nature' set forth by the Christian religion in its original form, then Christianity really would be a 'positive' *religion*. This is the ideal which Hegel ascribes to Noah, to Abraham, to Joseph, and to Moses.[1] But that the Christian religion was in fact grounded upon the accidental circumstance that Jesus claimed to be the Messiah, that something like this was the central core of Jesus' message, is a 'claim that would be rejected by reason and repudiated by freedom'. Hence the real object of Hegel's essay is the discovery of the particular circumstances which directly gave occasion to a positive interpretation.[2]

Thus Hegel shifts his ground. For although he announces that his purpose is to investigate *whether* the Christian religion *is* positive 'as a whole', he in fact takes it for granted that it is not positive in this sense; his real purpose is to show how something which was not positive originally, became positive because of the particular circumstances with which Jesus had to contend. He repeats this revised version of his purpose—which certainly corresponds with the actual content of the first part of the essay more closely than the programme taken over from the original

performed this task in 'The Spirit of Christianity'. The fact that he now asserts that it is a 'need of the time' shows that he regards the results of that investigation as co-ordinate with those of the present essay. Compare the division of the inquiry about Christianity as positive doctrine into a question about the religion 'as a whole' and another about its 'content', Nohl, p. 144 (Knox, pp. 173–4). See also the hypothesis and discussion above, pp. 379–82.

[1] For Noah see *Mit Abraham dem wahren Stammvater*, Nohl, p. 244 (Knox, p. 183); for Abraham, Joseph, and Moses see *Abraham in Chaldäa geboren hatte schon*, Nohl, p. 247 (Knox, p. 187); p. 248 (Knox, p. 188); and pp. 250–1 (Knox, pp. 191–3) respectively. The ideal of Jesus, of course, was exactly that 'love' which Abraham's religion compelled him to renounce in the sacrifice of Isaac.

[2] Hegel's question (Nohl, p. 145, first complete sentence) is whether there were particular circumstances which led to mere accidents being taken as eternally valid, and to the Christian religion's being founded on such an accident. He rejects this last claim out of hand (though it corresponds with the purpose that he has only just announced), but he goes on to explain that 'the accident from which a necessity has been supposed to proceed . . . is called in general authority'. I think that I am justified therefore in asserting that the particular 'accident' which he has in mind is Jesus' acceptance of the Messianic role. (Compare further the passage referred to below, p. 404 n. 2.)

introduction of 1795[1]—a little further on, at the end of his new introductory section.[2]

The perceptible wavering in Hegel's statement of his objective arises from the fact that orthodox Christianity, as a doctrine of salvation through grace, *is* a positive religion. It *does* rest on the claim that Jesus possessed a peculiar authority, that he was the eternal Lord himself in the 'form of a servant'; and this claim is based on the 'accidental circumstance' that Jesus made use of the Messianic hope. But Hegel was anxious to insist that this 'claim which reason would reject and freedom would repudiate' is not the whole truth about Christianity. Even though the accidental circumstance was given an absolute and fundamental significance, the substance of the Gospel, the 'spirit' or 'whole' of the religion of Jesus, which was distorted into the 'content' of positive Christianity, has always been there for those with eyes to see and ears to hear.[3] Jesus proclaimed one religion; his followers founded another. The 'Positivity' essay tells us how *this* came about, and 'The Spirit of Christianity' explains the fate that overtook the original religion of Jesus, within this accidental framework of authority.

By this time the new introduction has already impinged to some extent upon the substance of the earlier manuscript. The first part of the fourth section in the earlier version (which was headed 'Whence came the positive?') is directly incorporated into the new introductory section.[4] There is no need to say anything here about straightforward repetitions of this sort. Nor do we need to say much about the new versions of the second and third sections

---

[1] Only the first part of the essay corresponds directly with the purpose announced in either version of the introduction. With the section 'How a moral or religious society grows into a State' (Nohl, p. 173; Knox, p. 95) the topic begins to shift towards the related question of relations between the religious (voluntary) society of the Church, and the civil (compulsory, hence positive) society of the State. This part of the essay is the practical application of the historical investigation that precedes.

[2] Nohl, pp. 147–8 (Knox, p. 177).

[3] Thus the enlightened dismissal of the 'conviction of many centuries' as a 'relic of the dark ages' is unjustified on two counts. First it does not treat the millions of believers with the respect due to them as rational beings; and secondly it does not do justice to the ideal which enlightened thinkers have always recognized in the Gospels. (Compare Hegel's earliest statement of the problem in *Es sollte eine schwere Aufgabe*, which is guilty on the first count, perhaps, but not guilty on the second: see Nohl, pp. 51 and 58.)

[4] The passage beginning in the middle of Nohl, p. 145, from 'Daß die christ-

(on the 'state of Judaism' and 'Jesus') except that they reflect the greatly deepened understanding of the relation between Jesus and the tradition and spirit of Judaism that Hegel has now achieved; and they provide us with yet another source with which to fill the lacuna at the beginning of 'The Spirit of Christianity'.[1] But there is one other addition in the new introduction which deserves special notice because, as I indicated earlier, I think we can find in it a hint of what was in the lost manuscript that Hegel had just completed.

> It is obvious [he writes] that the investigation [of man's consciousness of the good and the divine] if it were carried out thoroughly on a conceptual basis [*durch Begriffe*] would pass over in the end into a metaphysical treatise on the relation of the finite to the infinite; but this is not the concern of this essay . . .

Since we have already seen that his remark about 'what the time needs', a few pages earlier, can be very plausibly construed as a reference to what he had done in 'The Spirit of Christianity', we are bound to wonder whether this is not another reference to something that he has himself just finished. Certainly the fragment *absolute Entgegensetzung gilt* would fit very neatly into the context of such a 'metaphysical treatise'; and the programme that Hegel implicitly lays out for the putative treatise provides a plausible bridge between that fragment and the Hellenic ideal of *ein objektiven Mittelpunkt*:

> But this is not the concern of this essay which assumes as a foundation that the need to recognize a higher being [*Wesen*] than human action as we are conscious of it, the need to make the intuition of its perfection into the enlivening spirit of life, and to devote time, institutions, and feelings simply to this intuition, quite unconnected [*ohne Verbindung*] with other purposes, is necessarily rooted in human nature itself. This

---

liche Religion sich auf Autorität gründe, usw.' to the middle of p. 146, '. . . in ihnen gewirkt werden könne', should be compared with *man mag die widersprechendsten Betrachtungen*, Nohl, pp. 155–7. (See Knox, pp. 174–6 and 71–3.)

[1] It is worthy of note, however, that the earlier claim, 'To the latter [i.e. obedience to the moral law] alone, not to descent from Abraham, did Jesus ascribe value in the eyes of God' (Nohl, p. 154; Knox, p. 70), disappears in the new version. From the standpoint of 'life' descent does have a significance. It helps one to recognize the union between one's own life and life as a whole. Hence this assertion in the first version is replaced by the comment that 'his [Jesus'] new teaching led to a religion for the world rather than for his nation alone' (Nohl, p. 149; Knox, p. 179). The earlier version stressed the

universal need of a religion contains within it many particular needs; how far the satisfaction of these needs belongs to nature, how far nature itself can provide the solution of the contradictions in which it becomes involved with itself, whether the Christian religion contains the only possible solution of them, and whether this solution lies altogether outside nature, whether man can grasp it only through passivity of faith—these questions, the investigation of their true significance, and their proper development may perhaps find a place somewhere else.[1]

Not all of these questions, probably, were dealt with fully in the missing manuscript. But we have here, if I am not mistaken, a fairly detailed prospectus of what Hegel meant when he told Schelling in November: 'In my scientific development, which began from the more subordinate needs of men, I was bound to be driven on to science, and the ideal of my youth had to be transformed at the same time into reflective form, into a system. I ask myself now, while I am still occupied with this, how I am to find a way back to intervention in the life of men.'[2]

The question Hegel asks himself here we must leave to our next chapter. But what he says about his 'scientific development' corresponds precisely with the whole course of his reflections and his labours, as we have reconstructed it from his last semester at Tübingen onwards. He began with an 'ideal of human nature', and a determination to 'intervene' effectively on its behalf 'in the life of men'. Both the ideal and the commitment to intervention caused him to focus his attention on the 'more subordinate needs of men', the needs of the heart, the imagination, and the senses. For on the one hand, it was in respect of these needs that the culture of his own society was most glaringly deficient in comparison with his ideal; and on the other hand, it was in these aspects of human nature that the motive forces, the means of effective intervention were to be found. Rational theory, the 'higher need' of

---

role of Jesus as a would-be national reformer (Nohl, p. 154; Knox, p. 69). (All these changes have to be considered together, otherwise we shall run the risk of mistaking a shift of emphasis for a material change in Hegel's own convictions.)

[1] *Der Begriff der Positivität*, Nohl, pp. 146–7 (Knox, p. 176) (this is the principal passage referred to in our earlier discussion, pp. 379–82 above). There is at least a half-promise to deal with these questions 'somewhere else' in the final sentence here; and we should note how all the themes that Hegel enumerates are present in the more 'theoretical' fragments of the Frankfurt period. It is only reasonable to suppose that all of these preliminary studies were utilized in the lost manuscript.

[2] Letter 29, 2 Nov. 1800 (*Briefe*, i. 59–60).

man, was the one respect in which his society seemed not to be deficient; and in so far as even the best rational theory (the rational religion of Kant and Fichte) reflected to some extent the defects of contemporary culture in respect of the 'more subordinate needs', that appeared to be fairly easy to correct in the light of his ideal. So he began his reconstructive effort at this higher level. But as soon as he began seriously trying to reintegrate the defective aspects of human nature in accordance with the ideal, he found that the whole body of theory that he had taken for granted needed re-setting in a wider context. The needs which were 'subordinate' in that theory were not subordinate, but were even in a sense 'higher' in the more general theory that his ideal required. Thus he was 'driven on to science', that is to the pure theorizing in which he had never hitherto had any personal interest, because the whole 'reflective' conception of the actual and the possible as 'separate' was mistaken. He found that he needed a conception of human religious experience which was not simply a 'deduction' of his ideal, but embraced the whole range of religious experience, from that ideal at one end to the positive supernaturalism of Herr Professor Storr with his new-printed manual of dogmatics at the other. So Hegel's ideal had to take on 'the form of reflection'; it had to become a 'system'—the 'system of life', the outlines of which were sketched in section 5 of this chapter. When he tells Schelling that he is still occupied with this in November, we may well believe him. But we need not on that account assume that he was then engaged on *another* manuscript of which we know nothing. All of the manuscripts that we have discussed, from the so-called 'Tübingen fragment' onwards, contribute something to the solution of the series of problems raised in the last of them that we know anything about before he wrote this letter to Schelling; and knowing, as we already do, how cautious he was in all that he said about his own researches to the spectacularly successful Schelling,[1]

---

[1] Thus, when he wrote to Schelling about his work in 1795, he spoke of sending a 'plan' for Schelling's criticism, although he may by that time have already written a large part of the 'Positivity' essay (Letter 14, 30 Aug. 1795, *Briefe*, i. 33; but see Chapter III, pp. 208-9, and p. 209 n. 2 above). To Hölderlin on the other hand he seems to have been ready to write about ideas which really were only half-formed plans in his mind (compare the remark of Hölderlin in Letter 15, 25 Nov. 1795, *Briefe*, i. 34, which is discussed above in the same place). Whatever the actual state of Hegel's researches may have been at the end of Aug. 1795, the contrast in his attitude to his two friends remains striking.

we can be certain that, as far as his reports to Schelling were concerned, he would continue to be 'occupied' with his 'system' until he had not one, but several interconnected manuscripts, completely ready for the press.

With this letter to Schelling in November 1800 we come to the end of Hegel's Frankfurt period, and almost to the end of the story of the 'ideal of his youth'. Only the tale of that political question about the 'way back to intervention in the life of men' remains to be told. Even this belongs in essence to the Frankfurt period, although the most important testament of it—the essay on the Constitution of Germany—was written after Hegel had gone on to Jena. At Jena his life enters on a new phase. In this new phase the practical dedication to an ideal was still present, but the place occupied by purely theoretical questions was much larger. At Jena Hegel could no longer refer to the theory that sufficed for his immediate needs, his theory of *human* life and of the *human* spirit as 'science' *sic et simpliciter*; nor could he call it a 'system', for it contained only part of what a system of philosophy had to contain according to the Jena professors—especially the young Herr Professor Schelling; and many of Hegel's closest concerns could hardly creep in among the footnotes of a 'system' as they understood it.

Schelling was already deeply involved in the 'philosophy of nature'. If Hegel wished to defend his theory of 'life' as a university professor, he could not avoid a similar involvement, which was no doubt attractive enough to him personally in any case.[1] Thus he became, of necessity, the author of a 'system' in the academic sense of the term. But I see no reason to suppose that he was thinking of anything like this when he wrote to Schelling about something that had *already happened* to his ideal by 1800. He certainly was not yet occupied with the production of his first 'academic' system.

---

[1] The original formulation of the ideal of the ἑν και παν was almost certainly related to Hegel's early interest in botany—which is still in evidence at Jena and was probably maintained throughout the intervening period. And Kroner may be right in suggesting that we have a testimony to Hegel's interest in Schelling's philosophy of Nature in the remark 'Die Natur nicht selbst Leben, sondern ein von der Reflexion ob zwar aufs würdigste behandeltes fixiertes Leben ist' (*absolute Entgegensetzung gilt*, Nohl, p. 347; Knox, p. 311 and n. 3).

1. *The third canon of folk-religion*

ACCORDING to Hegel's original formulation of the ideal of a folk-religion in 1793: 'It must be so constituted that all the needs [*Bedürfnisse*] of life—the public State activities [*Staatshandlungen*] are tied in with it.'[1] This was the third and final canon that he laid down, and from one point of view it was the minimal one. A folk-religion must express the people's consciousness of itself as a people. The requirements that *public* life must somehow be tied in with (*sich anschließen*) the common faith, would seem to follow more or less analytically from its being characterized as the religion of the 'folk'. Every faith that we do recognize, or could possibly recognize, as a *folk*-religion, must meet this requirement.

From this point of view, we might well be tempted to say that the young Hegel had his canons in reverse order. In order for a system of belief to qualify as a 'folk-religion', we could argue, it is *necessary* that it should satisfy the third canon, and at least *natural*, though not perhaps absolutely necessary, that it should satisfy the second: '*Phantasie, Herz,* and *Sinnlichkeit* must not go empty away.'[2] But it seems neither necessary nor natural, and perhaps

---

[1] *Religion ist eine*, Nohl, p. 20. (On the formulation of this canon see p. 345 n. 2 above.)

[2] Ibid. What we may, for convenience, call 'Temple Judaism'—i.e. Judaism from the time of Solomon to the Dispersion—was an example of a religion which satisfied the third canon, but in which the proper satisfaction of the second canon was effectively barred. Judaism was, in the most stringent sense of the word, a 'folk-religion'; it was the religion of a people who were aware of themselves as 'chosen' by their God; but when it became the religion of a settled nation the fundamental law against the making of graven images meant that *Phantasie*, at least, must be sent empty away. Abraham and Moses could experience *Erscheinungen* of their God in the course of nature without violating the law; but Pompey found to his amazement that the Holy of Holies was only an empty room. Cf. *Jedes Volk hat ihm eigene Gegenstände*, Nohl, pp. 218–19 n. (Knox,

not even possible, for an effective folk-religion to satisfy the first
canon properly: 'Its doctrines must be grounded on universal
reason.'

Hegel's answer to this objection is clear enough even in the
earliest formulation of his ideal, though he did not give it succinct
expression as a basic principle until late in 1795: 'the aim and
essence of *all* true religion . . . is human morality.'[1] Before a
system of beliefs and practices can count as a *folk*-religion it must
first qualify as a religion of any sort. In order to count as a religion
at all it must be such as to impress upon us the fear of God and the
hope of immortality in such a way as to forward the development
of moral reason. Otherwise it is 'mere superstition' or the 'fetish-
faith' which masquerades as folk-religion but which must be most
scrupulously avoided by the 'folk'.[2]

In fact, the order of the requirements is vitally important. The
ideal folk-religion must meet the needs of *Vernunft*, *Phantasie*,
Herz, and *Sinnlichkeit* in that order; and then finally it must inform
the whole of public life. It must meet the needs of *Vernunft* in
order to be a religion at all; it must be the ultimate controlling or
guiding power in the public life of an organized community in order
to count as a folk-religion; and only by keeping *Phantasie*, *Herz*,
and *Sinnlichkeit* in their proper order and due relationship can any
system of common belief and practice do both of these things at
once. This was the achievement of the Greeks, that they made the
supersensible world of reason sensible through the might of the
imagination and so gave it power over the heart of man, and control
over the lower self-seeking urges of his senses.

It is fairly clear that Hegel had all this in mind when he first
formulated his canons. For this would explain the central position

pp. 150-1 n.); *IV. Abraham in Chaldäa*, Nohl, p. 371; *Abraham in Chaldäa
geboren hatte schon*, Nohl, pp. 246 and 250-1 (Knox, pp. 186, 190-1); *ein
objektiven Mittelpunkt*, Nohl, p. 349 (Knox, pp. 313-14).

   Of course, Judaism did not send *Phantasie*, *Herz*, and *Sinnlichkeit* quite
empty away. But, as Hegel saw it at least, it took them in reverse order. *Phantasie*
and *Herz* were subordinated to the most primitive requirements of *Sinnlichkeit*.
The ideal of the Jews was to live long in a land 'given' to them by their God,
and 'flowing with milk and honey'; and their love of God was gratitude for this
bounty, 'Liebe um des Toten willen' (see *welchem Zwecke denn alles Übrige
dient*, Nohl, p. 378; and cf. *II. Abraham in Chaldäa*, Nohl, p. 369, and *Abraham
in Chaldäa geboren hatte schon*, Nohl, p. 250 (Knox, p. 191).

   [1] *man mag die widersprechendsten Betrachtungen*, Nohl, p. 153 (Knox, p. 68);
the italics are mine.

   [2] *Religion ist eine*, Nohl, pp. 9-10, 17, and 20; see below, pp. 487, 495, and 499.

that he gave to *Phantasie* even in the early stages, when he still conceived the primacy of moral reason as something absolute, and before there was any suggestion that religious experience is somehow superior to all forms of rational reflection. The opposition of the noumenal and phenomenal, the supersensible and the visible worlds, was a postulate which Hegel accepted initially from Plato and Kant; the idea that through the experience of beauty we are enabled to bridge the gulf between the phenomenal and the noumenal, to penetrate the veil between the visible and the intelligible, was one that he found in Plato and in Kant's disciple Schiller.[1] Thus Greek religion was the ideal folk-religion, precisely because it remained at the imaginative level; although it was 'grounded upon universal reason' it did not itself aspire to rational form:

The wet nurse [Religion] . . . did not rear him [the Greek spirit] or wish him to grow up in the leading reins of words which would have made him forever a minor—but she gave him to drink the cleaner and more wholesome milk of pure feelings [*Empfindungen*]—with the aid of free and beautiful fancy [*Phantasie*] she adorned with its flowers the impenetrable veil that withdraws divinity from our view—by enchantment she peopled the realm behind it with living images [*Bilder*] from

---

[1] Cf. *Es sollte eine schwere Aufgabe* (1794), Nohl, pp. 56–7, for definite evidence of Hegel's debt to Plato in this respect: 'If virtue, said Plato, appeared visibly among men, all mortals would be bound to love it.' The reference may well be, I think, to just that passage in the *Phaedrus* where Plato speaks most explicitly about the special position of beauty among the ideas in virtue of its direct availability to the sense of sight: 'Now beauty, as we said, shone bright amidst these visions, and in this world below we apprehend it through the clearest of our senses, clear and resplendent. For sight is the keenest mode of perception vouchsafed us through the body; wisdom, indeed, we cannot see thereby—how passionate had been our desire for her, if she had granted us so clear an image of herself to gaze upon—nor yet any other of those beloved objects, save only beauty; for beauty alone has been ordained, to be most manifest to sense and most lovely to them all.' Either because he was writing from memory, or deliberately, because he was applying Plato's view to Jesus (as an 'ideal' of virtue in the *Kantian* sense) Hegel put 'virtue' in the place of 'wisdom' here. Some years later (1797) he quoted from the *Phaedrus* the passage that immediately follows this one (in *so wie sie mehrere Gattungen*, Nohl, p. 377; cf. p. 298 n. 1 above). Probably the whole passage had stood in his excerpt collection since the Tübingen years.

Schiller's *Aesthetic Letters* appeared too late to have influenced Hegel at this early stage. But no doubt he found the same fundamental ideas in the earlier essays (e.g. *Über Anmut und Würde*) and poems that he did read. (If my hypothesis about the 'earliest system-programme' is right, Hegel's reading of the *Aesthetic Letters* in 1795 and 1796 was a catalyst for his view that the 'highest act of *Vernunft*' is an 'aesthetic act': see the Appendix to Chapter III above.)

which he carried forward the great Ideas of his own heart with all the
fullness of higher and more beautiful feelings.[1]

In this ideal, religion has the function of bringing man to full
rational consciousness. For someone who reaches that state of
spiritual maturity, religion is like the old nurse in a Greek household—a familiar friend but not a guardian or guide. Religion is
not one of the parents of the spirit: her role as *wet*-nurse is a vital
one, but only temporary. The concern of the grown man is with
politics—the affairs of his 'father', Chronos, 'on whom he remains
dependent in some degree [*in einiger Abhängigkeit*] all his life (the
circumstances of the time)', and of his 'mother', the constitution,
the stable structure of social life, which it is his task to maintain
against all the changes and chances of time that define the limits
of his free rational choice.[2]

The fundamental weakness of Christianity, in Hegel's eyes, at
the outset, was its failure to satisfy the third canon. His main
complaint against it in *Religion ist eine* was that it was a 'private'
religion, not a 'public' one. It did, in a way, inform all the activities
of private life, but the great ideals of public life—patriotic loyalty,
military courage, and the whole complex of cognate values—were
alien to it. In fact the whole of this visible world was alien to it,
so that Hegel was soon led to remark that in addition to failing in
respect of the third canon, Christianity fails in respect of the
second: it is 'not designed for the fancy—as among the Greeks—
it is sad and melancholy'.[3]

Only in respect of the first canon did Christianity seem fully
adequate. Here the task of the would-be reformer appeared simple,
and Hegel set to work with a will. In the development of Christian
doctrine the free play of the imagination, far from encouraging
the development of reason, had actually come to impede it. The
danger of this was already clearly present even in Greek experience;
and the remedy was pointed out by Plato in his rational criticism
of the poets and the traditional myths. But in Christianity the
danger was much greater, and the resulting evils were harder to
escape from, because the widely different functions of the inspired

---

[1] *Religion ist eine*, Nohl, p. 28. We should notice the influence of Hegel's
early theory of language and the two types of abstraction here. (The 'leading-
reins of words' are of course such formulas as the Decalogue and the Creeds.)

[2] Ibid., Nohl, p. 27 n. [*a*] (p. 506 below).

[3] (*a*) *Unter objektiver Religion* (1794), Nohl, p. 49 (p. 509 below).

messenger of the Gods (like Orpheus) who imaginatively creates a religion, and the religious sage (like Socrates in the *Phaedo*) who rationally interprets it, were here united in the single figure of Jesus. Thus the imaginative revelation of the truth came to have a kind of positive authority that is absolutely inimical to the proper functioning both of the fancy itself, and of reason. The first task therefore was to strip away from the Christian religion the whole overlay of positive authority that had arisen from this confusion.

Once this was done the possibility of a *public* religion founded on the Christian revelation could be assessed. This assessment Hegel attempted to make in the latter half of the 'Positivity' essay. His conclusion is outwardly completely negative. The rise of Christian sects, the inevitable privacy of Christian religious experience, is found to arise directly from the nature of rational freedom; a rational man can bind himself to act in preordained ways whenever certain defined conditions exist or come to pass, but he cannot bind himself to think or feel certain things. Hence, in any rational society, citizenship, membership in the political community, can only be contingently related with membership in the national church if church-membership is defined in terms of shared beliefs and feelings.

The further conclusion to be drawn, however, is that church-membership ought not to be so conceived. A folk-religion must be such that it can readily embrace a proliferation of sects. Theseus gave the Athenians both a monarchical constitution and a Pantheon. In *Religion ist eine* Hegel seems disposed to regard the second as subordinate to the first and primarily instrumental to its preservation. But, as a result of his study of the Judaic tradition and the gospel of Jesus, he came to regard this reconciliation of men's feelings at the level of *Phantasie* as the supreme achievement of political genius.[1] Paradoxically, the most significant result of his coming to terms with the deepest insights of Jesus, was an upward

---

[1] Of course this political genius has to be thought of as belonging to peoples rather than individuals. Theseus was not a greater genius than Jesus; but his people reacted differently to the pressures of physical need (*Not*): compare the first sentence of *so wie sie mehrere Gattungen* (Nohl, p. 377) with the remarks about Deucalion and Pyrrha in *Mit Abraham dem wahren Stammvater* (Nohl, p. 245; Knox, pp. 184–5), and about the Lares and Penates in *Abraham in Chaldäa geboren hatte schon* (Nohl, pp. 247–8; Knox, p. 188). (These last two passages show that whatever immediate range of reference the fragmentary opening clause of *so wie sie mehrere Gattungen* may have had, it can properly be applied to the Greeks and Romans.)

revaluation of just those aspects of religious and political experience in which he had always recognized that the Greeks were supreme. He always recognized that the unity of a folk-religion *must* exist at the level of spontaneous feeling and emotion, it *must* have its focus in *Phantasie*, because it can neither be commanded nor otherwise secured at the level of rational reflection. But through the gospel of love and the ideal of the Kingdom of God, Hegel was led to recognize that the spontaneity of feeling and fancy was not subordinate to the freedom of moral duty and rational reflection but superior to it.

On the plane of reflection Hegel recognized two levels of social co-operation and community: the State, as a system of civil rights and duties maintained by legally constituted authority; and the Church, as a paradigm case of an entirely voluntary, non-contractual type of collaboration for supra-personal ends. On the plane of life he found himself obliged to distinguish no less than four. First there was the realm of physical necessity (*Not*), where power is all that counts and legal compulsion is properly applicable. This is the sphere of external authority in general, and hence of the State as the central focus of all authority. Secondly there is the level of moral freedom. Here the rational man is still subject to authority, but not to compulsion, since he freely obeys his own reason. This level can be conceived in contractual terms, but only at the cost of a continual conflict of obligations (either possible or actual). Thirdly there is the level of love. Here two or more people are united in a whole in which all ideas of authority and contract have become irrelevant, because the union is at the level of feeling, and cannot possibly be expressed in reflective terms. Fourthly there is the level of religion, where the felt union is itself the object of aesthetic awareness for the group, and the direct focus of the common activity. Both the awareness and the activity must be imaginative rather than reflective, because reflective oppositions cannot be allowed to corrupt the union. At the reflective level, we must expect difference of opinion and argument. This will not threaten the imaginative union as long as we are prepared for it.

On the plane of *Phantasie* there is no question of an appeal to authority. The union is entirely voluntary and there is nothing in it that can give occasion for conflict. Wherever the feelings of love and friendship are present it can be readily extended to include other groups. When peoples or sects unite in this way their gods are first formed into a Pantheon, and then, where the Pantheon is already full, so to speak, or where it is a question of uniting Pantheons, the gods of the uniting peoples are identified one with another. What is requisite here is a fundamental willingness to be friends, a willingness on each side to treat with love and reverence what the other side regards as holy, and a general readiness to concede that the same god can be worshipped in different ways. All these things are practical matters rather than questions of intellectual belief; but they can hardly be reduced to moral duties of the Kantian type without the settlement of a great many intellectual questions about which dispute is always possible. Hence a religious union can only rest securely on the moral attitude which Hegel calls love, an attitude which has risen above the sense of duty and obligation altogether.

If, in the light of this conclusion, we ask ourselves now the question with which Hegel set out, 'How far is the Christian religion qualified to serve as a folk-religion?', we can see at once that the problem is to establish the right relation between Church and State. Jesus wished to have no relation to the State at all; as a result the fate of his Church was to become a sort of state in itself at a level of life where authority is impossible and compulsion illegitimate. Reflection on this situation can only reveal its inward contradiction. The Christian principle of love is corrupted on one side into rational anarchy, and on the other into positive tyranny. If we consider the voluntary character of the bond of love it ceases to have any effective binding power. If we consider it as binding we find ourselves obliged to employ force to maintain it. The Christian Church thus swings between two extremes, one where everyone is a heretic and there is no community, and the other where there is a community which has heresy-hunting as its essential common task. Religious union cannot exist on this reflective level at all. But we can escape from this reflective level only if the original *Trennung* between Church and State can somehow be healed. For authority has no place in religion; but it cannot be banished from life. Life has to maintain itself against a background of natural necessity; the organism must exert force in a great many ways in order to live. Men living together must regulate this exertion of force either morally or legally or in both ways. A free people must have a constitution as well as a religion; and only when the two together form a living whole will authority cease to be a problem at the religious level.[1] Thus when Hegel wrote to Schelling in November 1800 that, while still occupied with his 'system' at the reflective level, he was asking himself 'what way back to intervention in the life of men is to be found', he was following the natural sequence of his initial programme of research; he was referring to the studies of the constitution and political life of his own nation (the German *Volk*) which he had begun in 1799 and in which he was deeply engrossed by the time he wrote.[2]

2. *Hegel's first political studies*

An interest in economic and political affairs was by no means a new departure in Hegel's development. From the beginning Theseus was his hero, and Plato rather than Socrates was his model;[3] and, of course, we must never forget the extent to which his imagination was fired by the spectacle of the Revolution in France. He always took a keen interest in local political affairs wherever he found himself, and his comments regularly reflect his commitment both to the ideal of a representative democracy (a 'republic'), and to Rousseau's philosophical conception of the General Will. He observed the workings of the 'aristocratic' constitution of the Berne Canton with a keen but scarcely a dispassionate interest. How far his visit to Geneva in May 1795 may have been motivated

[1] Compare especially the comments cited by Rosenkranz from Hegel's critique of Kant's views on this subject. He there takes the Quakers and the Jesuits as representative of the two extremes and concludes: 'But if the principle of the State is a complete whole [*ein vollständiges Ganze*] then Church and State cannot possibly be distinct [*verschieden*]' (Rosenkranz, pp. 87–8: Aug. 1798).

[2] The first sketch for the *Verfassungsschrift* was probably written between the completion of the first version of 'The Spirit of Christianity' and the beginning of the revision. Rosenzweig has given fairly convincing reasons for holding that it was written before the end of the Congress of Rastatt (April, 1799). See *Sollte das Resultat des verderblichen Krieges* (*Dok.*, pp. 282–8) and Rosenzweig, i. 231–2. The fragments *über ihre Entstehung* (Lasson, pp. 141–2) and *Der immer sich vergrößernde Widerspruch* (Lasson, pp. 138–41) also belong to 1799 or 1800 (see *Dok.* pp. 468–70, and Schüler, p. 154). I think it not unlikely that Hegel began studying Pütter, Moser, and the rest as soon as he set *Der Begriff der Positivität* (the revised introduction of the 'Positivity' essay) aside (see Rosenzweig, i. 108 and 236–7). (For the ordering of the Jena fragments see H. Kimmerle in *Hegel-Studien*, iv. 125–76; corrected and augmented, ibid., Beiheft viii, 313–23.)

[3] See *Religion ist eine*, Nohl, p. 10, where Hegel at first wrote 'Theseus', then crossed it out and wrote instead 'the greatest men'; and *Dok.*, p. 174, for an excerpt from Tennemann (late 1793 or early 1794) about the respective roles of Socrates and Plato—I do not think there can be any question of Hegel's attitude to the contrast there drawn.

by a comparative interest we cannot be sure, for it appears to have left no visible mark in his surviving manuscripts. But the suspicion of some such a concern on his part is a natural one, in view of his attachment to Rousseau.[1]

Rosenkranz tells us that Hegel 'worked through the financial organization of Berne in the most minute detail, right down to the *Chausséegeld* etc.'.[2] From this one remark we know that Hegel's interest in 'political economy' dates back to the Berne period. But almost everything else that Rosenkranz says about Hegel's political and historical studies in the Swiss period has to be treated with considerable caution, because none of the manuscripts to which he refers has survived, and it is probable both on external and internal grounds that many of the extracts that he prints actually belong to the Frankfurt period, or even to the early years at Jena.[3]

The loss of these manuscripts and the consequent impossibility of an objective dating even for the extracts that we have, is the most serious lacuna in our knowledge of Hegel's early development. Thus, if we possessed the manuscript of those 'great carefully laid out tables' in which, so Rosenkranz tells us, 'he [Hegel] set out side by side chronologically the history of the *Kirchenstaat* in the left hand column, that of the German Empire on the right and in the middle between the two extremes the history of the different Italian States', we might find that Rosenkranz was right in assigning them to the Berne period.[4] If we also found that the fragment

---

[1] See Letter 11 (to Schelling, Apr. 1795, *Briefe*, i. 23) for Hegel's comments on the recent elections to the council in Berne. The surprisingly appreciative remark about Calvinism in *man mag der widersprechendsten Betrachtungen* (Nohl, p. 210; Knox, p. 142) is the one possible 'visible mark' of his visit to Geneva. See p. 224 n. 3 above.

[2] Rosenkranz, p. 61.

[3] The external grounds for this assertion are that Rosenkranz was demonstrably guilty of this sort of error in his classification of other manuscripts that were not dated by Hegel himself; and he seems always to have tended to date them too early. He assigned 'The Spirit of Christianity' to Berne and the first Jena system to Frankfurt (cf. Rosenkranz, pp. 58–9, 102).
The extracts that he prints are none of them dated, which strongly suggests that there were no dates on the manuscripts themselves; and in some cases the affinity with the Frankfurt essays in respect of content is so strong that one cannot escape the conclusion that the only reason that Rosenkranz had for assigning them to the Berne period was his belief that 'The Spirit of Christianity' was written there. This does not in itself prove that they were in fact written at Frankfurt; but it does mean that we have no reason to attach any weight at all to Rosenkranz's dating.

[4] The most probable view is that these *Tabellen* were made by Hegel for purposes of his comparison of the destinies of the different European nations,

In Italien, wo die politische Freiheit belonged to the Berne period, we could be fairly sure that Hegel was already contemplating the composition of something like the *Verfassungsschrift* then.[1] As it is, however, we have no definite knowledge of any such plan before 1798, and in the context of what we do know about the chronology of Hegel's manuscripts the likeliest date both for the *Tabellen* and the fragment appears to be 1801.[2]

Apart from the detailed study of the cantonal budget there is nothing that we know of among Hegel's political writings that can be assigned with certainty to the period before he moved to Frankfurt at the beginning of 1797. His translation of J. J. Cart's *Confidential Letters* was published at Easter 1798. It is likely that it was at least begun before he left Berne. But the task of preparing it for the press, reading the proofs, etc., belongs to the spring of 1798, and in the course of doing this Hegel appears to have been taken with the idea of becoming a political pamphleteer on his own account, for in the early months of the year he wrote an essay in support of the thesis 'That the magistrates of Württemberg should be chosen by the citizens'.[3] For reasons that will emerge, it seems

while he was working on the *Verfassungsschrift* (see n. 2 below). But the following alternatives can also be plausibly defended:

(i) That he made them in connection with one of Rösler's courses at Tübingen on Modern European or on Papal History (1789). (The difficulty with this view is that the evidence about the course that Hegel took is not very clear—cf. Rosenkranz, p. 26, and p. 74 n. 5 above).

(ii) That he made them in connection with one of Lebret's courses on Modern Church History (sometime between Sept. 1791 and June 1793).

(iii) That he made them at Berne in connection with his study of the problem of relations between Church and State. (This hypothesis is supported by the description that Rosenkranz provides).

(iv) That the tables were built up gradually, beginning in one of the above ways and receiving subsequent additions (or being redrafted in an enlarged form) when Hegel was working on the *Verfassungsschrift*.

[1] Rosenkranz, p. 526 (Fragment 12 in *Dok.*, p. 269). We can be fairly sure, at east, that there was no ostensible connection between the manuscript of this fragment and any part of the *Verfassungsschrift*, for Rosenkranz believed that the latter was written between 1806 and 1808.

[2] It is virtually certain that Hegel did at least lay out the history of the German Empire in tabular form while engaged with the *Verfassungsschrift* (cf. *Deutschland ist kein Staat mehr*: Lasson, p. 56); and for a parallel to *In Italien, wo die politische Freiheit*, see *Diese Form des deutschen Staatsrechts* (Lasson, pp. 109–10).

[3] *Daß die Magistrate*, Lasson, pp. 150–4. (See also Haym, pp. 65–8, for an outline of that part of the text which is now lost, with a few further quotations.) The title was at first: 'That the magistrates of Württemberg should be chosen by the people [*Volk*].' Hegel himself changed it to 'by the citizens [*Bürgern*]'; then

to me better to consider these two productions together in the context of the first notes and sketches on Judaism and the earliest fragments on love, than to study the Cart translation and notes separately against the background of *man mag die widersprechendsten Betrachtungen* and *Jedes Volk hat ihm eigene Gegenstände*.

There is reason to believe that both the Cart translation and the essay on the Württemberg constitution were occasioned by the political situation which Hegel found at home when he returned to Stuttgart for a few weeks in December 1796 and January 1797. Württemberg was remarkable among the German princedoms in that the old structure of feudal government had never collapsed into princely absolutism. Duke Karl Eugen managed, for more than twenty years, to give a very fair imitation of an enlightened despot, by not summoning the *Landtag* after 1770. But, before that, he had encountered serious opposition from that body, organized and led by the great jurist J. J. Moser—that same worthy whose death was recorded in the young Hegel's diary in 1785 with the epitaph 'He wrote more books than human life allows time to read'[1]—who was their official legal adviser. The Duke used his summary judicial powers to imprison Moser for more than five years (1759–65) on sedition charges, but the full constitutional rights of the Estates were maintained, so that looking round Europe shortly after Karl Eugen's death Charles James Fox could declare that Württemberg, alone in Europe, enjoyed a parliamentary constitution comparable to that of England.

Actually the comparison, popular as it no doubt was, was misleading. Württemberg did not have a constitution firmly founded upon parliamentary sovereignty, but rather one in which there were two separate sovereign powers. The *Landtag* had its own emissaries in foreign capitals, and under Moser's leadership they had even concluded their own agreements at the risk of civil war. The *Landtag* met in full session only at the call of the Duke, but it had a standing committee of eight members (the *Ausschuß*), 'which consented to taxation, and watched over the budget, controlled

someone else—probably one of the friends in Stuttgart to whom he sent the manuscript, for the change can hardly have been made much later—crossed out Hegel's title altogether and substituted: 'Concerning the most recent domestic affairs of Württemberg, especially the inadequacy of the municipal constitution.' (See Schüler, p. 148 n. 89, for this correction of the erroneous tradition which Lasson accepted from Rosenkranz, and Knox from Lasson.)

[1] *Dok.*, p. 24 (cf. p. 11 above).

foreign policy along with the Duke, and exercised a right of surveillance over the recruitment and command of the army'.[1]

After the death of Karl Eugen in 1793, his no more reactionary, but far less canny, brother Ludwig Eugen abandoned the policy of cautious neutrality that Karl had followed in foreign affairs, and joined the first coalition against the French Republic. In consequence, Württemberg, which had no army to speak of, and no revenue sufficient to raise or maintain one, was invaded and overrun by the army of Moreau in 1796. Ludwig's successor Friedrich Eugen (the third brother)—about whose 'enlightened disposition' Hegel and Schelling had entertained some hopes in the Tübingen days[2]—managed to conclude a separate peace with the Directory on 7 August 1796, and so secured the withdrawal of Moreau's troops. In some parts of the Duchy the French had been welcomed when they came, but their departure was regretted by none save a few Jacobin clubs and small groups of revolutionary enthusiasts, including, very probably, Hegel, Hölderlin, and Schelling, who were not, after all, actually in the Duchy when it was overrun.

The finances of the Duchy were by this time in a parlous condition. The various feudal dues and other sources of Ducal income over which the *Landtag* had no control were quite insufficient to pay the war indemnity levied by Moreau, and the *Ausschuß* which had done all that it could to resist the raising of military levies for the war, and had carried on its own separate peace negotiations, refused to consent to increases of taxation or to new taxes.[3] In these circumstances the Duke was compelled to summon the *Landtag*. No doubt he hoped to find the larger body more tractable,

---

[1] J. Droz, *L'Allemagne et la Révolution française*, P.U.F., Paris, 1949, p. 112. According to Hegel himself (in the article on the 'Württemberg Estates Assembly of 1815–1816' cited in n. 3 below) the source of all the power of the *Ausschuß* was its control of the Exchequer, which during the long period when the Estates were not summoned resulted in the outrageous abuses and speculations that came to light when the *Landtag* met in 1797. (See Lasson, pp. 193–5; Knox–Pelczynski, pp. 278–9.)

[2] Cf. Letter 13, Schelling to Hegel, 21 July 1795, *Briefe*, i. 27.

[3] 'Only too often the Estates have seen in times of crisis nothing but a favourable opportunity to put the Government in a difficulty, or to prescribe conditions for making the efforts it demanded for the sake of its own and its people's honour and welfare, and to acquire privileged rights against it' (Hegel, 'Proceedings of the Estates Assembly in the Kingdom of Württemberg 1815–1816', *Heidelbergische Jahrbücher*, 1817, Lasson, p. 181; Knox–Pelczynski, p. 267).

and to get a new *Ausschuß* elected which would be more co-opera-
tive.[1] The *Landtag* which opened in March 1797 contained fourteen prelates nominated by the Duke, and representatives chosen
by the local councils of towns and villages, which were generally
self-perpetuating bodies of magistrates in which vacancies were
filled by co-option. The power and effectiveness which it had
managed to retain—as compared, for example, with the *Landtag*
of Saxony, which was described by a satirical critic in 1795 as 'a
farce performed every six years, in which all the actors have to say
is "Yes" '[2]—was in large part due to its solid bourgeois homogeneity. The nobility had freed themselves from the Duke's
suzerainty, and so had not come to dominate the *Landtag* as they
did elsewhere. It was hardly a body in which sympathy for the
ideals of 1789 was to be looked for, but everyone knew that reforms
were in the offing, and its opening was greeted by a veritable flood
of pamphlets and open letters addressed to it.

It is as part of this flood that Hegel's Cart translation should be
viewed. To understand this we must add to the above summary
of events in Württemberg a thumbnail history of the Canton of
Vaud from 1790 to 1797. French-speaking Vaud had been under
the suzerainty of the German-speaking Canton of Berne since
1564, but in 1791 there was a popular uprising sparked by natural
sympathy with the Revolution in France. The uprising was quelled
in 1792, and the rule of the Berne oligarchy was restored and to all
outward appearances strengthened. The *Confidential Letters* of
J. J. Cart, which appeared in 1793, were, in essence, a protest
against the infringement or abrogation of various traditional or
constitutionally guaranteed rights and privileges of the inhabitants
of Vaud by the restored oligarchy. Most of the abuses of which
Cart complained were of long standing and in order to expose them
he went back to early charters or appealed to the traditional
customs of the territory; but the present stimulus and occasion of
his antiquarian zeal was the persecution of the 'Patriots'. Cart
himself fled to Paris, and travelled to North America before

---

[1] As Hegel himself records, the *Ausschuß* was, in fact, dissolved by this
last meeting of the *Landtag* before the dissolution of the Empire. The Duke
could reasonably count on a revulsion of public opinion against it, when its
accounts were examined. (See Lasson, pp. 92–5; Knox–Pelczynski, pp. 276–9.)

[2] Quoted in W. H. Bruford, *Germany in the Eighteenth Century*, Cambridge,
1935, p. 23. Compare further Bruford's description of the Diet of Weimar,
ibid., p. 35.

returning to Vaud in 1798.[1] By that time the revolutionary armies had fulfilled the hopes of the 'Patriots', and Vaud had broken away from the governance of Berne and was united with France.

It was this turn of events that prompted Hegel to publish his translation.[2] He wanted to underline the lesson that reaction and repression achieve nothing in the long run, in circumstances where reform is called for:

From the comparison of the contents of these letters with the latest events in Vaud, from the contrast between the semblance of peace imposed in 1792 and the pride of the government in its victory on the one hand, and its real weakness in the country and its sudden downfall there on the other, a multitude of useful lessons could be derived; but the events speak for themselves loudly enough; all that remains to be done is to appreciate them in all their fullness; they cry aloud over the whole earth:

Discite justitiam moniti,

but upon those who are deaf their fate will smite hard.[3]

Thus the publication of the translation should be viewed as the first shot in a campaign for 'justice' in Württemberg. Rosenzweig has pointed out that 'Gerechtigkeit' is the watchword of *Daß die Magistrate* just as it is of the translation; and several students have commented on the ambiguity of the term in both contexts.[4] Cart

---

[1] Hegel believed Cart was dead when the translation appeared. On the title-page the work was ascribed to a 'deceased Swiss'; and at the beginning of his *Vorerinnerung* Hegel says: 'The letters, from which this translation offers an excerpt, have as their author the advocate Cart, who has since died in Philadelphia' (*Dok.*, p. 247). A facsimile of the translation appeared in 1970 (see Bibliographical Index).

[2] This hypothesis is supported by the words '*Vormalige* Staatsrechtliche Verhältnis des Wadtlandes [(Pays de Vaud)] zur Stadt Bern' and '*ehemaligen* Oligarchie des Standes Bern' on the title-page as well as by the concluding sentences of the *Vorerinnerung* which are quoted below. According to Hoffmeister's notes (*Dok.*, pp. 458-9) Hegel could hardly have known about the revolution in Vaud before the translation appeared. But I assume that he was in direct touch with 'patriotic' sympathizers and that the idea of printing his translation (which he probably made for his own use while in Berne) occurred to him as soon as he heard of the uprising of Jan. 1798. In view of the direct involvement of French military power it would not have required prophetic powers or any great measure of political insight to see that this time the revolutionaries would be successful.

[3] *Dok.*, p. 348. The Latin tag comes from *Aeneid* vi. 620: 'Discite justitiam moniti et non temnere divos.' This appeal to 'learn justice and take warning not to despise the gods' is uttered by Phlegyas, the most unfortunate of those whom Aeneas sees being tormented in Hades.

[4] See Rosenzweig, i. 56-7; and for sample comments on the ambiguity of the term, Pelczynski in Knox-Pelczynski, pp. 32-3.

and Hegel both seem at times to be speaking of the justice of common law, the justice of precedent and custom, and the maintenance of old-established rights and privileges; but it is generally evident that they are in essence appealing to the justice of natural law and equity, and to the 'rights of man'. In Cart the appeal to precedent may well be a matter of practical expediency. He argues his case in terms of documents and customs, because that is how a case is established at law; but his own conviction of the rightness of his cause is grounded in Rousseau and the Declaration of the Rights of Man. In Hegel's case, however, it is a mistake to suppose that there was any real ambiguity or conflict involved. The laws and ways of life that a 'folk' establishes spontaneously in times of prosperity and amity *are* the direct expression of the 'law of nature'. Of course nothing is 'just' *simply* because one can cite legal precedent or ancient custom in defence of it, no matter how venerable its authority may be. But in a time of strife and faction it is natural to appeal to the laws and customs adopted in friendship in the old days before the strife and faction arose. Those laws and customs are 'just', because they express and articulate the unity and freedom of the folk at the level of economic existence, the level of physical dependence and property claims, where law and justice are inescapably necessary.[1]

The American War of Independence was in Hegel's view another example of the Nemesis that looms over all political authorities who are deaf to the voice of 'justice'. Both the nature and the strength of his republican sympathies can be judged from the way in which he takes issue with Cart for an admiring remark about the British constitution:

It is a very great mistake [writes Cart] to measure the goodness of a constitution by whether the levies paid under it are high or low. In this case the constitution of England would be the worst of all, for nowhere else do men pay so many taxes. And yet there is no people [*Volk*] in Europe which enjoys greater apparent prosperity or so much individual and national respect.—Because the Englishman is free, because he

---

[1] When Hegel found in one of his sources a defence of the nepotism of the Berne aristocracy on the grounds that it was 'an ancient usage of all times, all countries, and all places', he wrote in the margin of his excerpt 'An abuse, not a right' (see *Dok.*, p. 462, n. 2). The first canon of folk-religion applies *mutatis mutandis* to all institutions. Compare here Hegel's comments on the 'gute alte Recht' of Württemberg in 1817 (e.g. Lasson, pp. 199, 221–2; Knox–Pelczynski, pp. 282–3, 53 n.).

enjoys the rights inherent in freedom, in a word, because he taxes himself.[1]

Hegel comments rather acidly:

The author has not lived to see how gravely in these latest years the security of property has been compromised in many respects and the rights of domestic privacy restricted by the power conceded to the receivers of the higher taxes, how personal freedom has been limited by suspension of the constitution on the one hand [the allusion is doubtless to the suspension of the right of Habeas Corpus in 1794] and civil rights limited by positive laws on the other;—how strikingly clear it has become that a minister can scorn public opinion if he has a parliamentary majority at his command [*ein zu eigen gemachte Majorität*], that the nation is so inadequately represented that it cannot make its voice effective in Parliament, and its security depends more upon fear of its unconstitutional might, upon the prudence of the minister, or upon the discretion of the House of Lords [*der höhern Stände*]. Through this insight and on account of these facts even the respect toward the English nation itself of many of its strongest admirers, has fallen . . .

The tax, which the English Parliament imposed on tea imported into America, was very small; but the feeling of the Americans, that along with the quite insignificant sum which the tax would have cost them, their most important right would be lost to them, made the American Revolution.[2]

The 'justice' Hegel is concerned about is primarily the right of the people to govern itself. But it was not simply the principle of democratic representation on which he wished to focus attention.

[1] *Vertrauliche Briefe*, p. 71; *Dok.*, pp. 248–9. Pelczynski quotes this passage mistakenly as one of Hegel's own notes (Knox–Pelczynski, p. 11 n.).

[2] *Dok.*, p. 249. This passage, and the other reference to the English Crown (cited below), should be remembered when we are faced with Hoffmeister's contention that 'Hegels Führer ist durchaus *Montesquieu* nicht Rousseau' (ibid., p. 464). For, as Hoffmeister points out, Cart is here following Montesquieu (ibid., p. 463). The mistake here lies in opposing Montesquieu and Rousseau in a way which would never have occurred to Hegel himself. There can, of course, be no question of the enormous influence of Montesquieu upon Hegel's political and social thought from 1794 onwards. The first explicit reference is in *Wie wenig die objektive Religion* (1794; Nohl, p. 46); and the note on the election of the council at Berne (*Dok.*, pp. 255–7), in which Montesquieu's criteria for a healthy aristocracy are applied (see Hoffmeister's notes, ibid., p. 465), was almost certainly written in 1795 (cf. Letter 11 to Schelling, 16 Apr. 1795, *Briefe*, i. 23). See also the note to Cart's Ninth Letter (*Dok.*, p. 254), and the excerpt from *L'État et les délices de la Suisse* (ibid., p. 462).

One of Cart's basic complaints against the government of Berne was that it had robbed Vaud of 'the most precious right of freedom', representation in a national assembly. This was an abuse of long standing, since the Estates had not been summoned since 1536; but Hegel adds a long note on the way that the government functioned in those far off days when Vaud belonged to the Dukedom of Burgundy. The main body of the note is made up of direct quotations from two antiquarian sources (Seigneux's *Criminal Jurisprudence* and Müller's *History of Switzerland*), and it is clear I think that Hegel thought there was one point of contemporary relevance to be derived from each. Seigneux remarks: 'The German *Reichstag* is the closest model of these Estate Assemblies'; and Müller reports:

No venal baron could betray the land to the Prince in the hope of becoming a count, nor could the conceit of lesser nobles seeking the title of *Freiherr*; for the ratification of the Estates was necessary in the first case (it is well known [adds Hegel] what powerful influence the Crown has retained in the Parliament of England because it has the prerogative of creating Lords) and no one could take his place among the *Freiherren*, unless he had five and twenty vassals and at least three thousand pounds income. A resolution of the Estates did not become law unless confirmed in the Prince's Council; nor did an ordinance which was approved by the Prince become law, against the will of the Estates.[1]

It is, I think, clear that Hegel wished to see this particular model of an organic society re-established in his own time. His sympathy with the revolutionary aspirations of Vaud and of the American colonists might be taken to indicate a complete commitment to the ideals of 1789 and, in particular, to 'equality'. There are, however, many indications that he regarded 'liberty' and 'fraternity' as living ideals, but distrusted 'equality' as an abstract extreme. His Greek ideal, though it was primarily Athenian in origin, was always more aristocratic than democratic in its inspiration. He regarded class-consciousness as an evil, but he seems never to have doubted that certain natural divisions must exist in society which correspond

---

[1] *Dok.*, pp. 459–60 (*Vertrauliche Briefe*, pp. 58–60); Hegel gives the references to Seigneux, *Système abrégé de jurisprudence criminelle accommodée aux lois et à la constitution du pays* (Lausanne, 1756), and Müller, *Geschichte der Schweiz*, Book I, chapter 16, p. 463. (He certainly made these excerpts in the Berne period—compare Strahm, pp. 530 and 531–2).

to differences of function and must be separately represented in any effective expression of the popular will.[1] Every citizen must think of himself as an 'organ of a living whole', not as a member of a social class; but this does not alter the fact that the organs have distinguishable functions, and from the point of view of reflection these functions form a certain natural hierarchy. Pericles' Funeral Oration expressed for Hegel what it *felt like* to be an organ of a living whole; but Plato's *Republic* comes nearer to being a reflective picture of what the living whole *looks like*.[2] Throughout his life Hegel remained wedded to this ideal of a corporate society organized into 'Estates' with distinct functions. The essential thing, and the thing that is by no means clear in Plato's picture,[3] is that every part of the organism must operate with full spontaneity, and must speak with its own voice in the communion of the whole. It is in this respect that 'Justice' or 'giving to each his due' means more to Hegel than it did to Plato. No king, not even a philosopher-king, can be empowered to 'make Lords'; but neither can anyone, even a philosopher-king like Robespierre, altogether unmake them.[4] Society itself, the 'living whole', must make and unmake

[1] We might perhaps try to argue that Hegel simply believed that the *Volk* must govern itself in freedom in whatever way was natural to it in terms of its traditions as a nation (the heritage of Father Chronos imposing a certain form on Mother Politeia). Thus democratic equality would be right for the Americans while the distinction of the Estates was more appropriate for the Germans. Hegel did believe this. But there are passages in the various drafts of the *Verfassungsschrift* which indicate that he also believed that 'German freedom', properly restored, would be the most rational, and hence the stablest form of popular sovereignty. He may already have felt by 1800 that the Terror was the 'fate' of the abstract ideals of 1789; and it is quite likely that he would have said then, as he did twenty years later, that it was not yet possible to see what the 'fate' of the American Republic would be.

[2] Seigneux explains that the *Plait Général* was made up of the lords spiritual (*die Geistlichkeit*), the lords temporal (*der Adel*), and the commons (*das Gemeine*). If we remember Hegel's pedagogic conception of religion, the parallel with Plato's three classes (Guardians, Auxiliaries, and Citizens) becomes plain enough. Hegel himself indicates that *Adel* represents *milite* in Seigneux (*Dok.*, p. 460).

[3] It is more apparent in the *Laws* than in the *Republic* or the *Statesman*. But there is no way of establishing how far Hegel was acquainted with that work. (The *Lectures on the History of Philosophy* suggest that he was not.)

[4] Cf. the remark about the executing of Carrier in Letter 6 to Schelling, Christmas Eve 1794, *Briefe*, i. 12. When we examine the notes that Hegel added to Cart, we can hardly doubt that the reason for at least one of his omissions (Letter 1, 'über die Verwerflichkeit des Kriegs und des Königstums sowie des Adels', Rosenzweig, i. 51) was not so much fear of the censorship as the simple conviction that the doctrine contained in it was mistaken.

them, or perhaps we had better say that it must confirm that they have made or unmade themselves.[1]

We are now in a position to understand what Hegel meant when he wrote in his pamphlet on the Württemberg constitution that 'Justice is the unique criterion for deciding' what is untenable in it. It is plausible to suppose that he began to write his own pamphlet as soon as the Cart translation had gone to the printers. Certainly his defence of the thesis 'That the magistrates should be chosen by the citizens' was in the hands of friends in Stuttgart before the end of July, for on 7 August 1798 one of them sent him the dismaying verdict that its publication at that moment would be a disservice to the cause of popular freedom. This unknown referee also made some fairly trenchant criticisms of his proposals, and may very probably have suggested that he should concentrate on the critical part of his argument. Someone other than Hegel himself, certainly, wrote a new title on the manuscript: 'Concerning the most recent domestic affairs of Württemberg, especially the inadequacy of the municipal constitution [*Magistratsverfassung*].' The 'few fragments' that remained in Rosenkranz's time were probably those parts of the original manuscript that were most usable for this revised topic.[2]

Most of the contemporary pamphlets were addressed to the *Landtag*. But Hegel directed his essay 'To the people of Württemberg'.[3] He called on them to stop 'wobbling between fear and

[1] Hegel's notes on the *Tenth Letter* underline how essential this is for the 'spiritual order' as well as for the temporal (see *Dok.*, pp. 254 and 461; *Vertrauliche Briefe*, pp. 169–71).

[2] Rosenkranz, p. 91. In spite of Rosenkranz's assertion that the manuscript was fragmentary in 1844, Haym summarized the argument in 1857 without any explicit acknowledgement of lacunae. Possibly the 'few fragments' were more nearly complete than Rosenkranz realized; almost certainly the original essay was quite short. A more likely hypothesis, however, is that of Rosenzweig, who notes that Haym's summary says very little about the two major demands of the reforming pamphlets of this period—election (rather than co-option) of the magistrates and periodicity (rather than life tenure)—although Hegel's original title clearly indicates that these demands were in the forefront of his mind. Rosenzweig surmises that perhaps 'the text that Haym had before him was either incomplete or derives from a later state of the essay'. I take it that both of these alternatives were true (see Rosenzweig i. 61–2).

[3] The first change in the title (the substitution by Hegel himself of 'chosen by the citizens' for 'chosen by the people') I take to have no doctrinal significance. Having decided to address his pamphlet to the people of Württemberg (collectively) Hegel saw that he must refer to them distributively in his title in order to avoid a stylistically intolerable repetition of *Volk* ('That the magistrates should be chosen by the *people*. To the *people* of Württemberg'). Haering's hypothesis

hope, and oscillating between expectancy and disappointment'. Contemptuously dismissing those who think only of their personal interest or the interests of their *Stand*, Hegel appealed to 'men of nobler wishes and purer zeal' to direct their effort to the reform of 'those parts of the constitution that are based on injustice'. The summoning of the Estates after a lapse of twenty-seven years was itself evidence of a crisis which contented conservatives might dismiss as a 'fit of fever, but it is a fit that ends only in death or after the diseased matter has been sweated out. It is the straining of the still healthy force to expel the illness.'

The source of the sickness of the living whole must be identified and destroyed. Translated into the language of reflection this was the problem of reforming those parts of the constitution that 'no longer correspond to human habits, needs and attitudes [*den Sitten, den Bedürfnissen der Meinung der Menschen*]'. 'Justice is the unique criterion in making this decision.' If the reforms were not introduced in time, there would be 'a much more frightful outburst in which revenge joins hands with the need for reform and the mob [*die Menge*], ever deceived and oppressed, visits injustice with punishment'.

In these opening pages Hegel is quite transparently using the bogy of Robespierre and the Terror to frighten the self-interested into behaving 'justly'. The only hint of how 'der einzige Maßstab' is to be applied, comes at the end of the surviving manuscript, when he calls on 'every individual and every *Stand* to begin of its own accord to weigh up their relations [*Verhältnisse*] and their rights and if they find themselves possessed of inequitable rights let them strive to restore the balance between themselves and the rest'. Both the traditional Greek notion of 'giving each his due' and the Platonic definition of justice as 'minding one's own business and not meddling' are here in evidence; and we may note that the only 'individual' who needed to look specifically to his own rights and privileges was the Duke. For the rest justice consisted in a certain equilibrium of classes.[1]

that he did not want to set up the *Volk* and the magistrates as distinct is possible, but rather too fine-drawn for my taste (i. 588).

[1] All the quotations in the preceding two paragraphs are from Lasson, pp. 150–3 (Knox-Pelczynski, pp. 243–5). What follows derives from the summary and quotations of Haym. *Verhältnis* and *Recht* are corresponding terms on the plane of life and the plane of reflection respectively. (Anyone familiar with earlier discussions of this pamphlet will notice that I agree with Rosenkranz (p. 91) as against Haym (p. 66) about its Platonic inspiration.)

It is clear from Haym's account that Hegel went on to argue that this stock-taking was only a necessary preliminary to a thorough-going reform, in which the *Landtag* would have to take the initiative since the administration and civil service had a vested interest in maintaining things as they were. The root of the sick-ness was in the inequities and weaknesses of the representative system, so it was through the reform of the representative system that the sickness was to be cured. But reform was something to be tackled cautiously unless the reformer had the liberty of experi-menting and could withdraw reforms that did not produce the expected results. The safest way would be to concentrate on 'stop-ping up the sources of abuse', among which the principal one was the power enjoyed by legal and financial officials. These officials were like political 'father-confessors' of the *Ausschuß*, and when one of them was dismissed by the Permanent Committee he would demand to have his case heard before the Duke, 'to whom he had betrayed the interest of the country'.[1]

The administrative officials had lost 'all feeling for innate human rights'; and the whole constitution 'revolves around one man who *ex providentia majorum* unites all power in himself, and gives no guarantee of his recognition of or respect for the rights of man'. In order to cure this condition 'the essential thing is that the right of election [of the *Landtag* or possibly of the *Ausschuß*] be placed in the hands of a body of enlightened and upright men independent of the Court'.[2] But Hegel admits in despair that he

[1] This paragraph is founded on Haym, p. 65 and the excerpt he gives on pp. 483–5 (reprinted in Lasson, pp. 153–4, but not translated by Knox). The con-cluding remark quoted here should be compared with the comment about the 'venal barons' in the Estates Assembly of Vaud (quoted on p. 425 above).

[2] Quoted by Haym, p. 66. It is not quite clear what *Wahlrecht* Hegel is talking about. The natural and obvious assumption is that he is thinking of the election of the *Landtag* (which rested in the hands of the magistrates who 'should be elected by the citizens'). But Haym's earlier quotation about the dangers of giving the masses the right to choose their *Vertreter* suggests that Hegel may have had the right of the *Landtag* to choose the *Ausschuß* in mind. It was, in any case, the existing *Landtag* that he wanted to have replaced—for his Stuttgart correspondent objected that his proposal to dissolve it was 'nothing less than arbitrary'.

This objection is the strongest evidence for the view of Droz (pp. 124–6) that Hegel was the only real radical among the pamphleteers of 1797; and it is surprising, not to say ironic, that Lukács failed to recognize in Hegel's proposal the idea of a 'dictatorship of the bourgeoisie' which foreshadows Lenin's 'dictatorship of the proletariat'. But Droz certainly goes too far when he excepts Hegel from the general habit of 'resting on the ground of historic rights'. Hegel

does not know what sort of franchise or method of election could be expected to produce such a body in existing circumstances. To give 'an unenlightened mass of men, accustomed to blind obedience and at the mercy of every momentary impulse, suddenly the right to choose their defender' would merely complete the ruin of the constitution. In support of this view he cited a speech of Charles James Fox; and it is clear, I think, that the ruin Hegel foresaw in this radical democratic proposal was the one which in his view had overtaken the British Constitution; a 'pocket-majority' for the Duke thanks to an unholy alliance of throne and altar.[1]

If this was the explicit conclusion of the original essay, then Hegel must have abandoned in the end his initial assumption that the constitution of Württemberg was still healthy enough to heal its own infirmities. It is clear that what he wanted was a representative system based on indirect election, in which small communities elected their own councils, and those councils elected delegates

may have believed that 'it was necessary to create an entirely new political system'; but he wanted it to be constructed on the traditional model of 'German freedom'.

[1] See Haym, pp. 66–7. The speech of Fox which Hegel cited in this connection was almost certainly his oration of 26 May 1797 in support of 'Mr. Grey's motion for a reform in Parliament' (*Speeches*, vi. 339–70). There were many things in this speech which would have attracted Hegel's favourable attention; but in the present connection the following is especially noteworthy:

'I have always deprecated universal suffrage, not so much on account of the confusion to which it would lead, as because I think that we should in reality lose the very object which we desire to obtain; because I think it would in its nature embarrass, and prevent the deliberative voice of the country from being heard. I do not think that you augment the deliberative body of the people by counting all the heads, but that in truth you confer on individuals, by this means, the power of drawing forth numbers, who, without deliberation, would implicitly act upon their will. My opinion is, that the best plan of representation is that which shall bring into activity the greatest number of independent voters, and that that is defective which would bring forth those whose situation and condition take from them the power of deliberation. I can have no conception of that being a good plan of election which would enable individuals to bring regiments to the poll' (p. 363; cf. further p. 355).

Cf. also:

'I know well that a popular body of 558 gentlemen, *if truly independent of the crown, would be a strong barrier to the people*; but the House of Commons should not only be, but appear to be, the representatives of the people; the system should *satisfy the prejudices and the pride, as well as the reason of* the people; and you never can expect to give the just impression which a House of Commons ought to make on the people, until you derive it unequivocally from them' (p. 357; my italics).

Compare finally the way Fox speaks of the French example as a model to be followed rather than a 'Phantom' to be terrified by (pp. 352–5).

to the council of the realm, to represent the interests of the *Landschaft* advising and guiding the executive power of the *Herrschaft*. But he did not believe that this representative system would work properly if it was introduced directly, by a constitutional reform. The *Volk* did not 'know its rights' and 'no *Gemeingeist* was present'.[1] For this reason the enlightened bourgeoisie must look after the rights of the people until it was educated to proper political consciousness.

The clue to an explanation for Hegel's curiously ambivalent attitude towards his own central thesis in this essay is to be found in the circumstances of his life in Frankfurt, and in the recent vicissitudes of yet another German community, the city of Mainz.

We must remember, first, that at Frankfurt Hegel was no longer thinking and working in isolation, as he had been in Berne. He was now one of a group of young radicals who looked forward to the fulfilment of all the hopes of 1789 in Germany in the not too distant future. Writing to his young half-brother in February or March 1798,[2] Hölderlin remarks: 'How goes it then in your political world? The *Landtagsschriften* I have still not been able to find again. I have lent them to someone, and I don't know to whom.' The chances are very good indeed that the borrower was Hegel.[3]

---

[1] Quoted by Haym, p. 66. Notice that here again we have the same situation described from the two different viewpoints of 'reflection' and 'life'.

[2] The letter (Beck, Letter 152) was begun on 12 Feb. 1798 and sent on 14 Mar. 1798, and the manuscript is now lost so that stages in its composition cannot any longer be distinguished. But the part that begins with the passage here quoted, is markedly different from the first half both in topic and in tone. My own guess would be that it was written in March.

[3] Letter 152, lines 81–3. The idea that the borrower was Hegel has already occurred to Adolf Beck (see his notes ad loc., *GSA*, vi. 2, 867). If this view is accepted, my suggestion that Hegel began the pamphlet as soon as the Cart translation went to the printer can be taken as confirmed. There is no way of knowing just which *Landtagsschriften* were involved. But Hölderlin's library at the time of his death contained the anonymous pamphlet (ascribed by Hölzle to the radical leader K. F. Baz) *Über das Petitionsrecht der Wirtembergischen Landstande* (1797); and in view of the fairly close and enduring tie that was formed between Hölderlin and J. F. Gutscher it is reasonable to suppose that he had Gutscher's *Die wichtigsten Reformen der landständischen Ausschüsse Wirtembergs* (1797). Gutscher's pamphlet of 1798, *Unparteyische Beleuchtung der neuesten Staatseinrichtung in dem Herzogthum Würtemburg*, was presumably published too late to have been read by Hegel before he began his own, but I think it is highly likely that Gutscher was one of Hegel's Stuttgart referees. He was certainly a typical moderate, and he survived the political crisis of 1797–1800 without losing his place in the civil service of the Duchy: see Beck's note to Letter 209, line 23, in *GSA* vi. 1028–30.

For the rest of the group (whose existence is attested, *inter alia*, by Hölderlin's very uncertainty) were less concerned about constitutional developments in Stuttgart than about the progress of the Congress of Rastatt. They hoped for nothing less than a Swabian Republic, to be established like the revolutionary republics in Italy and Switzerland through French intervention.

At that particular moment their eyes were fixed on Mainz. Hegel himself visited Mainz in the spring of 1798; and both Hölderlin and his friend Sinclair knew personally several members of the Jacobin Club there,[1] which under the leadership of Georg Forster had declared Mainz to be part of the French Republic and the left bank of the Rhine to be its natural and proper boundary. Forster himself was a convinced democrat; but the Mainz 'Convention' of March 1793 which authorized him to announce this decision to the National Convention in Paris, was a far from representative one. The bulk of the bourgeoisie were certainly opposed to the annexation, and the peasantry were indifferent at best. The 'Convention' was only made possible by the presence of the army of Custine; and its work had been speedily undone by the army of Frederick William of Prussia. But now the Congress of Rastatt had reconfirmed it; and Hölderlin ends this same letter to his brother with the hope that 'the *Cisrhenaner* will soon become more really and actively [*lebendiger*] republican. In Mainz, particularly, the military despotism which itself sought to stifle every seed of freedom, will now soon be stopped.'[2]

Just what Hegel thought about these events at the time we cannot be sure. He did not sympathize with the Kantian cosmopolitanism of Forster as much as Hölderlin; and it is hard to believe that he would have conceded that the Rhine was the natural boundary of the French Republic, though we cannot be too sure about this.[3] But he did certainly approve of the way in which

[1] For Hegel's visit see Letter 27 to Nanette Endel, 25 May 1798, *Briefe*, i. 58. The main link between Homburg and Mainz was F. W. Jung. For the Mainz connections of Hölderlin and Sinclair see Beck's notes to the following passages from Hölderlin's *Letters*: Letter 115, line 48, and Letter 183, line 6 (on F. W. Jung); Letter 138, line 26 (on N. Vogt); Letter 190, line 11 (on J. Neeb); and Letter 206, introduction (on F. Emerich). Hegel went to Mainz again in Sept. 1800, but no one, as far as I know, has traced *his* personal connections there. The Frankfurt 'pass' for this later journey is in *Briefe*, iv. 90.

[2] Letter 152, lines 105–8.

[3] One might think this point was settled by the sorrowful way in which he speaks of the consequences of the Congress of Rastatt in *Sollte das Resultat*. But

a group of intellectuals had seized the initiative at Mainz and he did believe that in the period when an old *Gemeingeist* was dying and a new one was being born, such a group could better represent the interests of the 'people' than anyone whom the people themselves might be persuaded to elect. It is virtually certain, as we shall see presently, that he shared the hope of the group that a renewal of the war would lead to a revolution in Southern Germany, and he was ready and eager to support a minority government of 'patriots' in a Republic of Württemberg established by French arms. A group of this sort is in all likelihood what he is thinking of, when he speaks of 'a body of enlightened and upright men, independent of the court'.[1]

It is reasonable to suppose that Hegel agreed with his Stuttgart correspondents[2] that the publication of his pamphlet at that time would do more harm than good. In any case, he returned for the time being to his theoretical studies, both antiquarian and contemporary. He made notes on Kant and wrote the first draft of 'The Spirit of Christianity' before he turned again to current political problems. The passage which Rosenkranz quotes from his commentary on Kant's *Rechtslehre* shows how his mind continued to revolve around the reintegration of the 'spiritual' and 'temporal' estates. Having summed up Kant's doctrine in the thesis 'Church and State should leave one another alone', he argues that once they are conceived as separate entities this policy is quite impossible

---

it is by no means clear that he really means to bewail the losses of the Empire in that fragment. What is truly lamentable in his eyes is that the war had no *positive* consequences. It did not make Germans conscious of themselves as a nation. The *Volk*, we should remember, was not strictly a *natural* entity for Hegel. His hero was Theseus, who made one city out of a collection of warring tribes.

[1] The driving force of the conspiracy in Württemberg itself was probably K. F. Baz. But the man whom the conspirators planned to put at the helm of the new Republic was none other than Councillor Georgii, who had inherited the mantle of J. J. Moser. Georgii himself was far too circumspect to express any really radical sentiments publicly. (Cf. Beck's notes to Letter 155, line 20, Letter 168, line 9, Letter 175, line 15, and Letter 209, line 23, in *GSA*, vi. 2, 872, 898, 923, 1028–30; and Droz, pp. 126–7, 129.)

[2] There were actually *three* friends in Stuttgart who were allowed to see Hegel's manuscript. The fact that Rosenkranz failed to name them, though he must have known their names, is one more indication of the conspiratorial background of the pamphlet. The correspondents 'added to his stock of materials' among other things. Probably they gave him anonymous pamphlets of their own. The preservation of *this* anonymity may well have been one reason for Rosenkranz's reluctance to identify them.

to follow, because their laws with respect to the material world as a whole are absolutely opposed.

But the principle of the State is a perfect whole, so that Church and State cannot possibly be separated. What for the State is the sovereign power, recognized by reflection, that same thing is for the Church a living whole, set forth by the fancy. This living whole of the Church becomes just a mere fragment, if man in his wholeness is shattered into the two distinct roles of citizen and churchman.[1]

We can easily understand, in the light of this passage, why, until religion itself had been reintegrated, Hegel anticipated only political ruin from a democratic extension of the suffrage.

3. The genesis of the Verfassungsschrift

From 19 February till 16 May 1799 Hegel occupied himself (for at least some part of his spare time) in making a commentary on the *Political Economy* of Sir James Steuart.[2] In the light of Miss Schüler's ordering of the manuscripts it is a plausible hypothesis that he had completed the first draft of 'The Spirit of Christianity' and was moving on logically to the next step in his theoretical investigation.[3] For in his study of Christianity Hegel had recognized from the beginning that the crucial difficulty in the transformation of the religion of Jesus from a 'private' to a 'public' one, was the attitude of the founder towards property and 'the things of this world' generally.[4] He had now reached the point where this problem posed itself for him as that of the relation between the

---

[1] Rosenkranz, p. 88; reprinted in *Dok.*, p. 281. The significance of this passage in relation to the Berne essays has already been alluded to (see pp. 415-16 above).

[2] Rosenkranz, p. 86. The *Inquiry into the Principles of Political Economy* (2 vols., London, 1767) appeared twice in German (2 vols., Hamburg, 1769; and 2 vols., Tübingen, Cotta, 1769-72). On the relationship between the two versions see Chamley in *Hegel-Studien*, iii. 235-9.

[3] The reader should be warned that the appeal to Miss Schüler's ordering of the manuscripts here is to some extent circular, since her *dating* is partly guided by a similar hypothesis. Almost all of the firmly dated manuscripts of this period (e.g. the commentaries on Kant and on Steuart) have been lost. Thus the relating of these *dated* works to the definite *order* of the surviving manuscripts is necessarily rather hypothetical (see Schüler, pp. 151-3).

[4] Cf. *Wie wenig die objektive Religion*, Nohl, p. 41; for the extremely trenchant critique of Jesus' views in 'The Spirit of Christianity' itself, and for Hegel's recognition of the problem involved, see Nohl, pp. 273-4 (Knox, pp. 221-2). (It is not possible from examination of the printed texts to say with certainty whether this passage belongs to the first or to the second draft. My own guess is that it belongs to the first, but the point is of no great importance.)

living community and its indispensable material, economic, and legal base. That was why he concentrated on the *transition* from the theory of law to the theory of morality in his study of Kant's *Tugendlehre*; and it is in this light that Rosenkranz's account of the Steuart commentary, and of Hegel's political and economic studies in this period generally,[1] should be read:

All of Hegel's reflections about the nature of civil society, about need [*Bedürfnis*] and labour, about the division of labour and resources among the classes, about poor relief [*Armenwesen*] and the police, about taxes etc. were concentrated finally in a running commentary on the German translation of Stewart's [*sic*] *Political Economy.* . . . In it there are many impressive views on politics and history, many fine observations. Stewart was still a supporter of the mercantile system. With noble feeling, with a wealth of interesting examples Hegel fought against what was dead in it, as he strove to save the heart [*Gemüt*] of man amidst the competition and mechanical interaction of labour and of commerce.[2]

While I am ready enough to join in the laments of Hoffmeister and Lukács over the loss of this manuscript, I do not feel there is any reason to hold, as Lukács does, that Rosenkranz has misunderstood and misrepresented it.[3] What Rosenkranz says does not imply that Hegel adopted any position opposed to that of Steuart in economic theory, but only that he had a certain purpose in studying economics. It is not hard, in my view, to see what that purpose was, but it is virtually impossible for us now to gain any clear idea of how he achieved it.[4] The economic world of competition and mechanical interaction is presumably all that is left of political life when the living spirit of the State dies. Thus the best guide that we have to Hegel's conception of economic life is to be found in his account of Judaism in its decadence as a religion of self-preservation through obedience to law. When we compare

---

[1] Of course we do not know how far Rosenkranz's dating of all the other studies which he takes to have culminated in the Steuart commentary is correct. A concern with the Prussian criminal code fits in well enough both with the study of Kant's philosophy of law and with the essay on punishment in 'The Spirit of Christianity'; and Hegel's interest in the English Constitution and in Poor Law reform at this time is attested by the notes to the Cart translation. But both of these concerns doubtless continued throughout the following years in which he was occupied with the *Verfassungsschrift*.

[2] Rosenkranz, p. 86.

[3] Lukács, pp. 228–9.

[4] Hoffmeister has, however, drawn attention to a few passages in Steuart that were bound to have aroused Hegel's interest (*Dok.* pp. 466–7).

the analysis of Judaism with all that we know of his views on economic theory in later years, there is every reason to suppose that Hegel himself adopted the most 'satanic view' (the adjective is one that Hoffmeister applies to Steuart's work) of the contemporary economic scene. Such a view was the appropriate logical counterpart to Christian other-worldliness; and thus, in studying Steuart Hegel could feel certain that he had before him the problem of the sundering of human nature in its starkest form. To reintegrate human nature was his problem.

Hegel's study of Steuart was preceded or accompanied by the writing of the first draft of what eventually became the introductory section of the essay on the German Constitution.[1] But at this stage Hegel seems to have regarded what he was writing as another occasional pamphlet rather than as a logical development of his own research. The occasion for it was the news he received through Hölderlin of the latest developments at the Congress of Rastatt.

Hölderlin had left the house of the Gontards in Frankfurt in September 1798 and moved to Homburg at the instance of his friend Isaac von Sinclair.[2] In November Sinclair was sent to Rastatt on official business for the Count of Hessen-Homburg and he took Hölderlin with him. Hölderlin stayed only about two weeks, but Sinclair remained in Rastatt until early February 1799. Both of them, while in Rastatt, met and talked with the emissaries of the Württemberg *Landtag* at the Congress, as well as with other young radicals, some of whom subsequently visited them in Homburg. In the months following his return to Homburg in December 1798, Hölderlin was certainly buoyed up by the belief that once hostilities began again, new French victories would lead to a political revolution in Swabia. He wrote to his mother early in March 1799:

It is likely that the war which is just now breaking out again will not

---

[1] *Sollte das Resultat, Dok.*, pp. 282–8. The dating is much less conjectural than that of 'The Spirit of Christianity' drafts because of the references to the Congress of Rastatt. Even so Haering has tried to cast doubt on Rosenzweig's arguments. I hope that by connecting the fragment with Hölderlin's return from Rastatt in Dec. 1798 and indicating who the German 'patriots' were whom Hegel had in mind, I have finally disposed of all doubts on this point. My own guess is that the fragment was written in Dec. 1798 and/or Jan. 1799 *before* Hegel began to study Steuart. But in any case it was certainly begun before the *renewal* of hostilities in March (see Rosenzweig, i. 231–3; Haering, ii. 316–17).

[2] See Letter 165, line 21, and Beck's notes, *GSA*, vi. 283 and 888–9.

leave our Württemberg in peace, though I have it upon sure authority that the French will respect the neutrality of the Imperial states [*Reichländer*] including, of course, Württemberg, as long as possible. . . . In the event that the French are victorious there may perhaps be some changes in our fatherland [i.e. Württemberg]. . . . That you may not in certain possible circumstances come to any harm, for this I would look to it with all my might, and perhaps not without avail. But all this is still very far off.[1]

It is obvious that Hölderlin's 'sure authority' was Sinclair, and that, even if not actively involved in any plotting, Hölderlin was privy to a great part of Sinclair's dealings, and expected, in one way or another, to have some influence with the revolutionary government once it was established. He was not any longer in frequent contact with Hegel,[2] but they must surely have been eager to see one another and discuss the latest news when he came back from Rastatt. It was from their meeting and talking then that the spur for yet another political pamphlet came.

Hegel begins by speaking of the bitter disappointment of 'many German patriots' that the outcome of the war (and of the Congress) was so negative in relation to all their hopes. Germany had suffered grievous losses in territory, population, and material resources, and the fact that 'no higher aims' were pursued at the Congress 'has *almost wholly* deprived them [i.e. the patriots] of the hope ⟨of what would be⟩ the stopping of the source of all ills, a fundamental improvement of the defects of the constitution'.[3] Of his own attitude he wrote:

The following pages are the voice of a heart [*Gemüt*] that is unwilling to bid farewell to its hope of seeing the German State raised up from its utter insignificance, and before being absolutely parted from its hopes would like once more to recall to life its gradually failing wishes,

---

[1] Letter 175, lines 8–15, 26–9, *GSA*, vi. 317–18. For Hölderlin's stay in Rastatt see Letters 167–70 and Letter 200, lines 14–22 (with Beck's notes throughout).

[2] He wrote to his sister in February that his circle was now 'mainly restricted to just two friends Sinclair and Muhrbeck' (a young philosophy professor from Greifswald who had come back from Rastatt with Sinclair for a visit of some months). See Letter 174, lines 48–59, *GSA*, vi. 316.

[3] *Sollte das Resultat, Dok.*, pp. 282–3 (italics mine). Compare the remarks of the anonymous correspondent of 7 Aug. 1788 (Rosenkranz, p. 91); and for the *Verstopfung alles Übels* compare also *Daß die Magistrate* (Lasson, p. 153, or Haym, p. 484). It is not quite true, as Lukács claims, that there is no trace of resentment towards the French in Hegel's notes. He fairly clearly associates himself here with the strictures of 'German patriots' like his unknown correspondent (Lukács, p. 188).

and once more to nourish with a mental image [*im Bilde genießen*] its willing faith in the fulfilment of those hopes.

Even while he was writing he cancelled this passage, and in the revision of 1800 he cancelled all reference to these patriotic 'hopes' and roundly asserted that the lesson of the Congress of Rastatt was that Germany was not a State at all.[1] Probably, like Hölderlin, he was 'absolutely parted from his hopes' by the defeats which befell the French armies in the renewed fighting.[2] But he may have continued working on his pamphlet—if that is indeed what it was—for some time, for we have another fragment, which seems quite definitely to belong to it, but which Miss Schüler is tentatively inclined to place some months later.[3]

The bulk of what remains to us from the pamphlet is concerned with the historical origins of the German Constitution. Hegel analyses the feudal system as 'the saga of German freedom'. In the beginning 'the individual' (*der Einzelne*, the feudal lord who established his lordship by force of arms, the *Herr* who triumphs over the *Knecht* in the *Phenomenology*) was 'unbowed before the Universal'. The feudal lord 'belonged to a whole' (i.e. to the German nation) but he did not realize this fact. He carved out his own fief for himself with his sword, or he died in the attempt. The nation as a whole was ruled by customs which grew up naturally, and acquired the force of law as the situation became stabilized and the victorious fathers bequeathed their conquests to their children as a kind of property. Thus it was that, as men came to be directly aware of their membership in a wider society, the rights of property and of inheritance became the foundation of all political association. Towns, guilds, and 'Estates' (*Stände*) came later and established

---

[1] The dictum 'Deutschland ist kein Staat mehr' which is the opening theme and a recurrent *leitmotiv* in later drafts, first occurs as a marginal comment in the revision which probably took place in the winter of 1800–1.

[2] This is certainly true for Hölderlin. Sometime in the summer—perhaps in June, perhaps in August, the date depends on which French defeat he was bewailing—he wrote to Susette Gontard that he and Muhrbeck wept and comforted each other over 'another defeat for the French in Italy' (Letter 182, lines 27–32, *GSA*, vi. 337. The presence of Muhrbeck makes the June date more likely—see Beck's note, *GSA*, vi. 2, 943.) Hegel's emotions were no doubt calmer, but we cannot doubt that they were fairly similar.

[3] *über ihre Entstehung*, Lasson, pp. 141–2. Miss Schüler thinks the handwriting is contemporary with the revision of 'The Spirit of Christianity'. But Hegel's handwriting was relatively stable all through 1799 so nothing very definite can be said about the interval (if any) between this fragment and *Sollte das Resultat*.

their place in the system in the same way, by seizing whatever they could, and getting their possession legalized afterwards.

A political system that is based in this way on private rights is inevitably at the mercy of the centrifugal tendency that is innate in 'German freedom'. Everyone tries to make their own authority as absolute as possible. In the second fragment Hegel describes the resulting situation as being like that of a mob on a frozen river, where everyone is engaged in grabbing as much of the ice as he can, and is breaking it up in the process, quite oblivious of the fact that all of them will drown in the end if they do not stop before it is too late. He still believed, however, that it was not too late, that there were forces which could arrest the fatal trend towards isolation:

If this tendency toward isolation is the only moving principle in the German Empire then Germany is now sinking irresistibly into the abyss of her dissolution, and to utter a cry of warning is a sign of zeal, but only of the foolish zeal of a wasted effort. But may not Germany still be at the cross roads between the fate of Italy and unification [*Verbindung*] into one State? There are notably two circumstances that raise hope for the second alternative, two circumstances which can be viewed as a tendency opposed to its dissolving principle.[1]

The manuscript breaks off in the middle of the next sentence, so we cannot tell what the circumstances were that raised Hegel's hopes, but it looks rather as if one of them was the alienation between the prince and his people since the time of the Peace of Augsburg.[2] One of the things which had kept the Estates of Württemberg alive as a genuinely representative body, for example, was the accession of a Catholic Duke in that very Protestant Duchy in 1733;[3] and certainly resentful contempt for dynastic politics and

---

[1] *über ihre Entstehung*, Lasson, p. 142. For the significance of the term *Verbindung* in Hegel's thought at this time see the discussion of *absolute Entgegensetzung gilt* in Chapter IV, pp. 383–8 above.

[2] From the way the fragmentary last sentence begins it looks as if Hegel was going to argue that whereas in former times 'German freedom' really was in harmony with the freedom of the *Volk*, this is no longer the case (and hence the urge toward popular freedom would be one force that could be harnessed against feudal particularism): 'Of old on the one hand the local majesty [*Landeshöheit*] of the prince or the town flowed together with freedom, especially with religious freedom, on the other hand the *Verbindung* of the Empire . . .' In the margin, against the word *Landeshöheit*, Hegel added (in the revision of 1800/1?) the even more explicit comment: 'Religious and political freedom were contained in it.'

[3] Cf. F. L. Carsten, *Princes and Parliaments in Germany*, Oxford, 1959, pp. 123–4.

traditional privilege was one of the most potent sources of bourgeois intellectual sympathy with the ideals of 1789 in Germany.

The next political fragment, *Der immer sich vergrößernde
Widerspruch*,[1] belongs, fairly certainly, to the year 1800, and is
quite different in style and character from all of the other fragments
and drafts that are in any way connected with the *Verfassungsschrift*.
In its general tone it is more reminiscent of 'The Spirit of
Christianity' and of the so-called 'System-fragment' (*absolute
Entgegensetzung gilt* and *ein objektiven Mittelpunkt*) than of anything else,[2] and it really ought to be regarded as a restatement of
Hegel's political views in the theoretical vocabulary of his 'system'.
Perhaps it was precisely of this endeavour that Hegel was thinking
when he wrote to Schelling that even while still engaged with his
system he was asking himself about a 'way back to influencing the
life of men'.[3] But, be this as it may, one thing is clear: we are not
any longer dealing with a political pamphlet but with an essay
meant for the eyes of professors.

There is, according to the manuscript, an ever increasing contrast
—Hegel says 'contradiction'—between the unknown goal which
men generally—we soon discover that he means specifically the

---

[1] Lasson, pp. 138-41. I have learned a great deal from Luporini's extended
analysis of the very difficult opening paragraphs of this fragment, though I do
not agree with his interpretations of some of the key terms.

[2] Haering recognized this, but wished to assign the fragment to the Jena period
because he could not reconcile the doctrines of the two manuscripts to his own
satisfaction. He hesitated, and finally hedged altogether about the dating because
he could also see the essential continuity of the doctrine with that of the other
Frankfurt fragments on politics (i. 595-6 and 785 n. 2). I do not myself find
any serious difficulty in reconciling this fragment with *ein objektiven Mittelpunkt*,
so I see no reason to doubt, and every reason to accept, Miss Schüler's conclusion
that *Der immer sich vergrößernde Widerspruch* comes between the second version
of 'The Spirit of Christianity' and the *Systemfragment* (Schüler, p. 154; cf.
Hoffmeister in *Dok.*, pp. 469-70).

[3] If we could accept a very fine-drawn inference from the handwriting,
proposed by Hoffmeister (*Dok.*, p. 470), we might claim that the first sheet of
Der immer sich vergrößernde Widerspruch was a fair copy or revision of the
original opening and was made later than the rest, precisely in Nov. 1800. But,
unless some more definite evidence of a break in the manuscript, or of a later
revision, can be produced, the argument from handwriting alone must be set
aside as too speculative. There is a general tendency to write the opening pages
of a well-pondered manuscript more self-consciously and deliberately; and it is
natural to find that the handwriting grows freer as the ideas themselves begin to
flow spontaneously. Newer habits of writing, which are not firmly established,
may well give way to older ones when this happens. (Of course it is also probable
that the letter of 2 Nov. 1800 was long-pondered and carefully written; see
Fuhrmans, i. 453 ff.)

people of Germany—are unconsciously seeking, and the actual life which existing social conditions permit. This unconscious 'contradiction' has come to full consciousness in the minds of a few isolated individuals who have 'elaborated Nature within themselves to the level of the *Idee*'. These few have a *known* goal, but it is merely an object of 'yearning', not of effective action. But the two situations involve, as Hegel says, a 'straining towards one another'; each side has what the other needs. The enlightened minority know the end, the ignorant populace has the means to overcome the 'limits' of existing society and make a life in accordance with the ideal of 'Nature' possible.

The enlightened individual cannot live alone in enjoyment of his ideal—as the 'beautiful soul' strives to do. He must either endure 'perpetual death', not even trying to express his vision in his outer behaviour but simply living by routine and doing what is socially required or expected; or he must strive to 'overcome (*aufheben*) the negative power of the subsisting world'.[1] Either way his life will be one of suffering, consciously willed and accepted, because everything he does is frustrated, or compromised and made ambiguous, and in general limited by the social context. He suffers precisely because he *will not accept* the limits from which he cannot escape—his attitude towards the social order is one of contempt. By the moral standards of that order, therefore, he deserves to be unhappy, he brings it all on himself.

On the other hand the ordinary man is unhappy too, but not by any deliberate fault of his own. He suffers without knowing why,

---

[1] It may be that Hegel holds that all men equally are 'driven by the time into an inner world'. In that case the 'perpetual death' of routine is the lot of the ordinary man, who has no *conscious* inner life at all, while the conscious minority are all of them 'driven to life by Nature ⟨which they have elaborated in themselves to the level of *Idee*⟩'. This interpretation is very attractive—there is a parallel for it in *Der Begriff der Positivität* (Nohl, p. 148; Knox, p. 178) where the mass of the Jewish people are contrasted with 'men of finer clay'. But I think that in the present context Hegel wants to make clear that someone 'of finer clay' who is 'driven into an inner world' has then the *choice* of enduring the 'perpetual death' of ordinary life or else of reacting in some practical way. I am not sure that it would make sense to say that the state of the ordinary man is 'perpetual death' *wenn er sich in dieser erhalten will*; for the ordinary man seems to have no choice in the matter. But perhaps I am oversimplifying the issue. It may be rather that Hegel sees everyone as having the choice that he describes—thus the 'Messiahs' mentioned in *Der Begriff der Positivität* might well belong to the group who have elaborated an ideal of Nature in themselves, but certainly not all of the 'robber bands' were led by a Karl Moor—even if the hypothesis, so often adopted by novelists, that Barabbas was a Jewish national patriot is correct!

and certainly without deserving it, for he respects all the existing social values and accepts willingly all the sacrifices that they impose upon himself and others. He does not understand his fate, he does not recognize that he has brought it upon himself, so how can he be said to will it? Whereas one of the marks of something that we recognize as our *destiny* is that we do willingly accept it.

'The overcoming of what is from the point of view of Nature negative, but from that of the moral will positive, is not to be brought about by violence, neither by the violence which a man does to his own fate, nor by that which is done to it from without.'[1] Violence done to fate from without fails because the intent is not understood, and the act is regarded as unwarranted interference, as a breach of private property rights or of social privilege or prerogative. Robin Hood or Karl Moor, even Gustavus Adolphus leading the German Protestants against the Catholic League, is only one 'particular' element of the universal social structure set against another, and whatever successes he may achieve are merely momentary disturbances of the balance of destiny which steadily returns to its old equilibrium until the time is ripe for a genuine change in the pattern of life.

The violence of a people or an individual against its (or his) own fate fails for the same reason but with a rather different result. For in trying to do violence to our own fate we raise it to consciousness, we discover that what we are trying to set aside or do away with is our own substance, our most cherished possession, 'forgotten' but not 'dead' as it appeared to us to be when we rebelled against it. Thus the moment of 'enthusiasm' in which we seek to throw off our 'bonds' is a moment of fearful self-discovery, and the hoped-for revolution, whether personal or social, perishes in a failure of nerve.

This was, of course, to be the fate of the German Revolution that Hegel and his friends were dreaming of and working for—so far as it can be said to have come to pass at all. Instead of making the unknown known and the unconscious self-conscious, they were labouring on the *Begeisterung eines Gebundenen*. Thus, when he declares magisterially that the 'feeling of the contradiction between

---

[1] Lasson, p. 139. It seems to me that Luporini goes quite wrong in his interpretation of 'external violence' here (pp. 90–3) and that the value of his commentary is gravely vitiated at some points subsequently as a consequence of his metaphysical analysis of *Schicksal*.

Nature and the subsisting life is the need that it should be overcome; and it gets to this point [of being an actual need] when the
subsisting life has lost its power and all its worth, when it has
become a pure negative', he is forecasting his own failure. But he
knows that he can show (as he does later in the *Verfassungsschrift*)
that the 'universal' structure of Germany has 'lost its power and
all its worth'. This causes him to believe that the time is now ripe:

All the manifestations of the present age show that satisfaction is no
longer to be found in the old life; the old life was one of restriction
[*Beschränkung*] to an orderly dominion over one's property, a contemplation and enjoyment of one's completely subservient little world, and
then finally, to make the restriction palatable [*diese Beschränkung
versöhnende*], a self-annihilation and ascension into Heaven in thought.[1]

The 'subservient little world' has been corrupted by the increase
of poverty on the one side, and luxury on the other. In this 'dry
Verstandesleben' the pretence of a divinely ordained order has
broken down, and man himself stands revealed as the *Herr* whose
personal right of property is the only thing that is sacrosanct.
Hence the trend of the time is towards a new life altogether; and
this tendency is 'nourished by the actions of individual men of
greatness' (i.e. probably Napoleon, but also some earlier heroes of
the National Convention), 'by the movements of whole peoples'
(we should think here not only of France, but of Switzerland,
Italy, and the Rhineland), 'by the expression [*Darstellung*] of
human nature and human destiny by poets' (Goethe, Schiller,
Hölderlin). 'Through metaphysics the bounds are set to the
restrictions themselves'—or in other words the standards of 'Life'
and 'Reason' as interpreted by Hegel and other children of the
Kantian Revolution, provide criteria for the evaluation of the
'gute alte Recht'.

This revolutionary situation is bound to involve violence
(*Gewalt*). For as soon as the ideal of Nature 'comes to power' and
can begin to affect real life it has to face repressive violence on the
part of the old order. The replacement of the old order by the new
will normally begin spontaneously (as in 1789) and so far as there
is a 'plan' it will have the appearance of an external interference
with the pattern of destiny that hitherto existed. It will be a case
of 'particular against particular'. But when the defenders of the

[1] Lasson, p. 140.

old order as a whole are forced to enter the lists as partisans, the truth is made manifest that the old 'universal' has perished, and a new basis for social rights is being proclaimed. This was the 'truth' of the old order—that it was the basis of all 'rights'—which can be 'refuted' only by 'Nature' (i.e. by the actual expression of popular feeling, as in the storming of the Bastille, not by putting forward proposals for a new constitution, as for instance in the work of Sièyes).

Lukács finds here a proof that Hegel viewed the struggle against feudalism in a way that was typical of 'ideological champions of the bourgeoisie'.[1] That is to say, he admitted it was a class struggle, but insisted nevertheless that it was not a struggle merely of class interests. In the light of his known sympathy for the 'patriots' of Switzerland and Germany, this is a very plausible interpretation. But I think it should be added that Hegel's ideal of 'Nature' as the harmony of unrestricted life did provide for him a standard for non-partisan political activity. He was not a radical bourgeois partisan because his acceptance of the ideals of 1789 stopped short of 'égalité'. The life that he looked for was a 'harmony' of all the warring 'classes'.

As he saw it, political life in Germany had decayed into a class war because the 'universal sovereign power' (*machthabende Allgemeinheit*) had disappeared, or decayed into a partisan force. The 'universal' is present only as a 'thought', not as an 'actuality'. He seems almost ready to say in 1800, what he did not yet say in 1799, that 'Germany is a state no longer'. But once more, as he broke off,[2] he was restating his view that Germany was still at the cross-roads between the fate of Italy and the establishment of genuine national unity.

The use of the term 'negative' as a dialectical correlate of 'positive' in this fragment is a novelty; but there is nothing very startling about it, if we view it in the context of Hegel's critique of Kant in 'The Spirit of Christianity'. If even the moral law, conceived rigorously, is a *positive* authority, then anything which is

---

[1] Lukács, p. 195.

[2] From the descriptions of the manuscript given by Schüler and Hoffmeister, it seems natural to suppose, though I may be wrong about this, that there is a blank space remaining on the third sheet. In that case Hegel laid down his pen, for some reason, at the very beginning of a sentence, and never returned to complete it (see Schüler, p. 145, and *Dok.*, p. 470). The manuscript is a *Reinschrift* (*Dok.*, p. 469).

'positive' (i.e. authoritative) for the will is 'negative' (i.e. restrictive) for 'Nature', and in these circumstances what is 'negative' for the will (rebellion against authority) may be 'positive' (liberating) for 'Nature'. We must beware of saying, however, that what is positive for the will must always or necessarily be negative for Nature and vice versa. That would be the extreme of 'love' (exemplified by Jesus) as opposed to the extreme of 'reflection' (exemplified by Kantian rigorism). The proper harmony of life only exists when what is positive for the will (or on the plane of reflection) is *not* negative for Nature (or on the plane of life) and vice versa. Only then is freedom actually achieved.

During most of this same year 1800 Hegel was occupied with the long manuscript of which the 'System-fragment' is all that now remains. It seems clear from the concluding sheet which has survived that he described in it at least the 'conscious' or 'religious' aspect of the completely fulfilled life, the ideal which he refers to as 'Nature' in *Der immer sich vergrößernde Widerspruch*. In view of what we have now discovered about his studies in economics and politics, it may be that he also sketched the 'actual' (economic and political) aspects of the ideal in that manuscript—though the fact that he turned directly from it to the revision of the 'Positivity' essay, and the way in which he expressed himself in that revision, suggests rather that the whole 'system' was concerned with 'consciousness', or in plain language that it was a philosophy of religion and a theory of human values. In any case, when it was done, the problem of its 'application', or of a 'way back to influence in the life of men', was finally posed for Hegel as the logical next step in his own programme. In the winter of 1800—after a second visit to Mainz of which all we know is that he spent some time studying geometry and began to revise his introduction to the 'Positivity' essay[1]—Hegel began to work

[1] See the 'Geometrische Studien' in *Dok.*, pp. 288–300, the first of which is dated from Mainz, 23 Sept. 1800. The ordering of these two fragments is a case where the danger of relying on some of Hoffmeister's more fine-drawn inferences about the order in which manuscripts were written (cf. p. 440 n. 3 above) has been clearly brought out by Miss Schüler (compare *Dok.*, pp. 469–70; Schüler, p. 155).

The revision of the 'Positivity' essay, *Der Begriff der Positivität*, is dated 24 Sept. 1800 at the head. Travelling conditions being what they were I think Hegel could hardly have written anything on that day unless he were still in Mainz. (He travelled to Mainz on 19 Sept.: see the 'pass' from Frankfurt in *Briefe*, iv. 90.)

seriously on the problem of how the constitution of Germany was to be reconstructed. He read and made notes from Pütter's *Historical Development of the Present Constitution*[1] and from other authors,[2] he revised his draft of 1799 to serve as the introduction for his new study, he began in his usual way to write fragmentary drafts for different sections of it, and finally he made a plan and wrote a continuous essay.

4. The 'Constitution of the German Empire': Part I

It is possible to distinguish three phases in the composition of the essay on the German Constitution.[3] But the basic conception was already fairly definitely fixed in the plan that Hegel made early in the second phase. We can see this if we compare that first plan with the final structure of the manuscript in its latest condition as is done in the following table:

Initial Plan (about May 1801)[4]	*Final State* (late 1802)
Germany is no longer a State	[Introduction *b*] 'Germany is no longer a State' etc. (Lasson, pp. 3–7)
(*a*) Is no improvement to be hoped for in the Peace [i.e. the Treaty of Lunéville]?	

[1] See *Versuche der katholischen Religion, Dok.*, pp. 309–12. J. S. Pütter's *Historische Entwickelung der heutigen Staatsverfassung des teutschen Reichs* appeared in three volumes at Göttingen in 1786 and 1787, and in an English translation at London in 1790.

[2] Notes from other authors are not preserved. But the manuscripts attest to their existence, and Rosenzweig has managed to identify with a considerable degree of plausibility many of the works and authors that Hegel consulted (see the notes in Rosenzweig, i. 237–40).

[3] The first phase begins with the sketch *Religion. 2. In Rüksicht auf*—which may have been written before Hegel moved to Jena—and embraces a group of sketches, and some fragments of a larger whole which seems to have possessed a modicum of continuity. This phase ends about Mar. 1801. But it was not sharply divided from the second phase—the first continuous manuscript that survives—which began in May 1801 and was completed before August. There is then a considerable break before the final phase—the second draft of the manuscript as a fair copy which was begun about Nov. 1802 and abandoned unfinished. (The ordering of the manuscripts is given by H. Kimmerle in *Hegel-Studien*, iv. 137–41; see also Rosenzweig, i. 236–7, and Haering, ii. 317–19, for earlier discussions of the chronology of the *Verfassungsschrift*).

[4] *Deutschland kein Staat mehr*, Lasson, p. 138. Kimmerle places this little piece *after* the main manuscript of the second phase, but the objective ground for his ordering is very slight here (he has to date it in terms of the excerpt that was subsequently added on the back of the sheet) and cannot outweigh the *a priori* probability that it was written before the main manuscript. This probability is strengthened by the clear reference to the Treaty of Lunéville (9 Feb. 1801) which it contains.

Initial Plan (about May 1801)	*Final State* (late 1802)
Staatsrecht has passed into *Privatrecht*	[Introduction *a*] 'The form of German *Staatsrecht*' etc. (Lasson, 7–16)[1]
(*b*) What is essential to a State? Not community of religion, etc.	1. *Begriff* of the State (Lasson, pp. 17–32)
(*c*) There is no supreme authority in Germany:	(Lacuna in our text)
(*a*) The apportioning of constitutional authority is inheritable and judicial, courts of judgement	
(*β*) Power (Aleph) Military	2. [Military Power] (Lasson, pp. 32–9)[2]
(Beth) Financial	3. [Finances] (Lasson, pp. 39–49)
(Gimel) War and Peace	4. [Territories of the Realm] (Lasson, pp. 49–57)[3]
(*d*) (*a*) Judiciary	5. [The organization of justice] (Lasson, pp. 58–73)
	6. [Religion][4] (Lasson, pp. 73–82)
	7. [The power of the Estates] (Lasson, pp. 82–97)
	8. [The independence of the Estates] (Lasson, pp. 97–106)
	9. [The formation of States in the rest of Europe] (Lasson, pp. 106–16)

[1] The two headings 'Deutschland kein Staat mehr' and 'Deutsches Staatsrecht ist Privatrecht' were inserted in the margin of *Sollte das politische Resultat* (see Lasson, pp. [3] and [10]. The first is the theme of *Deutschland ist kein Staat mehr* (Lasson, pp. 3–7), the introduction to the final quarto-manuscript; and the second that of *Diese Form des deutschen Staatsrechts* (Lasson, pp. 7–16), with which the earlier folio manuscript begins. That Lasson is probably right in linking the two versions into a single continuous introduction in the way that he does is borne out by the marginal transition indicated at the beginning of *Wir können eine Menschenmenge* (see Lasson, p. [17]).

[2] The beginning of this section is fragmentary. Perhaps along with its opening pages a chapter corresponding to section C, subsection *a*, of the initial plan has been lost.

[3] What Lasson takes to be the history of the *Reich*-boundaries is actually the history of the wars it has made and the peaces it has concluded, regarded as an index of its existence as a recognized sovereign power in international relations. Thus the parallel holds good here still.

[4] From this point onwards only the earlier draft of the manuscript exists. The fact that the plan marches so well with the second draft, and both cease at the same point, can hardly be more than a coincidence, however, since upon any reckoning there must have been a lapse of more than a year between them.

Initial Plan (about May 1801)   *Final State* (late 1802)

10. [The two German major powers] (Lasson, pp. 116–27)
11. [Freedom of Citizens and Estates] (Lasson, pp. 128–32)
12. [The unification of Germany] (Lasson, pp. 133–6)

In analysing the manuscripts it seems best therefore, to follow the basic plan common to all stages and to discuss any notable developments in the successive drafts as we consider the separate topics. It is clear from the plan that Hegel had two complementary critical (or theoretical) aims; and from the structure of the manuscript itself it emerges that he had a third aim, which we might call his constructive (or practical) purpose. By the method of comparative historical analysis he wanted first to show what was necessary for the existence of a State, and secondly to prove that it was at present lacking in the constitution of the German Empire; and finally he wanted to point out how what was lacking could best be brought into existence or restored to life.

It is true that there is one difficult passage in the introduction to the final draft which seems to suggest that Hegel had, by that time, only the theoretical aims, and not the practical aim in mind:

The thoughts contained in this essay cannot by their public expression have any other aim or effect than to promote the understanding of things as they are and thereby lead to a calmer outlook and a sensible acceptance [*gemäßigtes Ertragen*] of things as they are, both in our practical dealings and in our discussion. For it is not the way things are that makes us passionately disturbed, but the fact that they are not as they ought to be; but when we realize that things are the way they have to be, i.e. that it is not chance or caprice that makes them so, we realize also that they ought to be just the way they are.[1]

But a little reflection upon this passage in its context will be enough to convince the reader that Hegel is not here abandoning the ideal of 'Nature' that he has been striving to bring into being for ten years. I do not myself believe that he ever abandoned it, but in any case even a cursory analysis of the *Verfassungsschrift* will suffice to prove that he had not given it up at the end of 1802. His point in the introduction is that the whole attitude of reflective moral judgement has to be abandoned if that ideal is to be achieved.

[1] Lasson, p. 5; cf. Knox–Pelczynski, p. 145.

'Germany is a State no longer.' The life has gone out of a certain political structure, and it is dead. This is the fact that has to be reckoned with, and to say that it ought not to be so is not a sensible way of reckoning with it. If we understand how it came to be so we shall not be tempted either to pretend that it is not so, or to repine because it is so. Only then will the new life come into existence and into consciousness. Like Spinoza, Hegel holds that rational understanding, once it is achieved, becomes itself the actuality of freedom. So he can quite truthfully say at the beginning of his essay that he seeks only to advance rational understanding of things as they are, without ceasing to believe that things can come to be otherwise as a result of that understanding. There can be life where there was death, free creative action where there was passion and suffering. This regeneration will not occur, however, as the result of preaching.

To realize that the object of political essayists must be to teach, not to exhort, to advance understanding, not to advocate action, is a great step forward; for this recognition is itself the achievement of freedom on the side of 'consciousness'. The 'life' of the mind itself, begins with the surrender of all claims to exercise moral authority. Thus Hegel *logically could not* have any other aim, or claim to do more than advance the understanding of things as they are, if he wished to be faithful to his ideal of 'Nature' and to contribute as much as he could to the regeneration of Germany as a 'living whole'. It was precisely because he could not do more than this with his pen—i.e. show people that 'Germany is a State no longer'—that he *had* to look for a new Theseus to create the new Germany.[1]

In fact, Hegel emphasizes in his introduction what an enormous practical difference there is between understanding one's experience, and merely suffering it, at a time when everything has gone wrong. He seems to be thinking of the creation of that group of 'enlightened and upright men independent of the Court', of whom he had written in his Württemberg pamphlet, when he says:

From the experience of mistakes which is an outburst of inner weakness and ineptitude, those who have made the mistakes are less likely

---

[1] Rosenzweig infers that Hegel is addressing private citizens and *not* the new Theseus (i. 129). If I am right this is a false distinction. Hegel could not appeal to his Theseus except as one free citizen to another. His appeal *is* different from Machiavelli's appeal to the Prince, in that his Theseus can only be a leader of free men.

to learn than others—indeed they only build up even further the habit of making mistakes. Others [i.e. the new men unconnected with the Court?] can recognize the mistakes [instead of reacting with panic and ineptitude and so making more] and through this insight put themselves into a position to benefit from the experience.[1]

That Germany is not a State is the lesson of the war with France. War is the experience in which such a lesson can be learned, for we can know the strength of a bond only when it is tested, and we feel the lack of power and authority only when it is needed. The German Constitution is no longer a real bond but only a memory, no longer a focus of force or authority but only a system of legal forms by recourse to which any action or policy can be either clothed in legitimacy or assailed as unjust according to the interests of the constitutional theorist concerned.

Hegel argues, reasonably enough, that this fate has overtaken the German Constitution because in the rest of Europe the feudal system (with the earlier tribal life and organization out of which it developed) has given place to a system of sovereign national States. In the old days each baron spoke for his 'people', and thus through him personally the people had a share in the sovereign power of the Empire. Elsewhere the system of personal fealties has given place to a system of public legal obligations, but in Germany the tendency has rather been for every baron or vassal to become a little emperor on his own, a despot whose will is not opposed to law because it is not subject to it.

In the picture Hegel gives of the 'German freedom' from which the feudal constitution developed, the outlines of the dialectic of 'Lordship and Bondage' as developed later in the *Phenomenology* are even clearer than they were in *Sollte das Resultat*, though most of the substance of his discussion is directly taken over from the earlier drafts.[2] The 'makeshift' law of the Empire, the 'justice'

---

[1] Lasson, p. 5 (Knox–Pelczynski, pp. 144–5).

[2] Some sentences are taken over more or less intact, and some material simply disappears (for example the comment that it is a mistake either to idealize the era of tribal freedom as a 'state of nature' or to vilify it as 'barbarism', which was added in the revision of 1800–1: *Dok.*, p. 284 n. 10). But for the most part the earlier discussion is enriched or amplified along lines already suggested in that earlier revision. For example *Sollte das Resultat* (spring 1799) reads:

'The individual . . . without fear or self-doubt set his own boundaries by his own lights [*durch seinen Sinn*]; this state of things in which character without laws was lord of the world, is rightly called "German freedom". The sphere [*Kreis*] of possessions which each created for himself, the gains he

that consists simply in adjusting political rights as if they were private property rights, was originally only a legalization of a *de facto* situation; but when what was once a matter of life and death became a matter of private property, the living unity of the old life perished. From the earliest draft onwards Hegel pours scorn upon the efforts of legal theorists to make sense out of the political and legal dealings of the Empire. But in the final version his irony rises to a new pitch of violence because their activity is now seen as a kind of active deceit by which a fictional political life is maintained.[1] He declares at the outset that 'Germany is *no longer* a State'; but his real view is that Germany *never became* a State in the modern sense of a society founded on law. It existed once as a living whole, but in those days custom, not law, was the bond of the *Volk* in peace, and common interest, not a sovereign command,

> earned, were fixed bit by bit with the passage of time which brought men's needs and individualities closer together, even while they smote one another in enmity. For all enemies as they fight with one another become more like one another.'

In *Sollte das politische Resultat* (Feb.–Mar. 1801) this became:

> 'The individual . . . without fear or self-doubt set his own boundaries by his own lights. This state, in which a mass of men was bound into one people not by laws but by customs, and the people as a State represented similarity of interest not a universal command, is rightly called "German freedom". The sphere of authority which each by character and fortune made for himself, the possessions which each gained for himself, these variable things were fixed bit by bit by the passage of time, and inasmuch as the exclusive rights of property wholly sundered the individuals from one another, concepts became the bonds by which they were bound together and makeshift [*notdürftige*] laws began to govern.'

(Here the remark about its being equally mistaken to vilify or to idealize this condition was added in the margin.)

Finally, in *Diese Form des deutschen Staatsrechts* (about June 1801) we find a considerably expanded version (translated in Knox–Pelczynski, pp. 147–8) in which the following passage is specially notable: 'He [the individual] set his own boundaries all by himself without fear or doubt; but what lay within his sphere was so much and so completely himself, that we could not even call it his property. For what belonged in his eyes to his sphere—for something which we would call a part [of our property or our rights] and so would risk only a part of ourself [i.e. of our energies and efforts]—he risked life and limb, soul and salvation, etc.'

[1] It looks as if the fragmentary last sentence of *Sollte das politische Resultat* may have been leading into a peroration something like that which is before us in revised form in the closing paragraphs of *Diese Form des deutschen Staatsrechts* (beginning with 'Der Staatsrechtslehrer, der Deutschland usw.', Lasson, p. 15). But it is a fair inference in any case that the closing pages of this later version were largely new.

was the effective unity of the State in war.[1] The view of Pütter, which was generally accepted, was that Germany was a 'Staat aus Staaten'. Hegel's view was rather that the old Germany was a community of *Estates*, which could not now become a State precisely because it did now consist of States.[2]

Unity for the common defence of all property belonging to members of the group is what Hegel takes to be the conceptual minimum of Statehood. As long as this *Staatsmacht* exists and is effective, everything else in the constitution can vary freely over a wide range even within the political life of one *Volk*; and it is clearly Hegel's view that local autonomy with consequent variety in almost all directions, is something that ought to be preserved and fostered.

Even the form of the central authority itself 'belongs to chance'. It does not matter whether the government is a hereditary or an elected monarchy, an aristocratic or an elected assembly, or whether all citizens have equal rights or there are many recognized types of civic status. There need not even be one single system of law in the State, says Hegel, citing the example of France before the Revolution.[3] It is a little surprising to find him taking this view, since he seems generally to distinguish fairly sharply between the undeveloped society founded on custom and the fully developed State that is founded on law. Of course, he is only talking about the essential or minimal unity, which even the old Reich had once

[1] *Sollte das politische Resultat, Dok.*, p. 284 n. 6. For a translation of the passage see p. 450 n. 2 above. Compare also *Da die deutsche Verfassung*, Lasson, p. 147, where the dialectic of lordship and bondage is again briefly alluded to; and the concluding paragraphs of the final draft (Lasson, pp. [70]-[71]) cited on p. 463 below.

[2] The ambiguity of the question whether Germany is 'no longer' a State or 'not yet' a State is illustrated in the two drafts of his Introduction which Hegel finally yoked into one. In the final version, as in all the preceding ones, Hegel brings out two points about the peace with France. First that the burden of war debts is unequally borne (being more severe for the South than the North) and secondly that apart from territories ceded to the conquerors 'many States will lose what is their supreme good, namely their existence as independent States' (*Deutschland ist kein Staat mehr*, Lasson, p. 4; Knox-Pelczynski, p. 144). But in *Diese Form des deutschen Staatsrechts*, Lasson, p. 14 (Knox-Pelczynski, p. 151), the emphasis falls on the unequal war effort of different 'Estates'. The ambivalence of terminology reflects the ambivalence of the situation.

[3] *I. Begriff des Staats*, Lasson, p. 21 (Knox-Pelczynski, p. 156); cf. *II. 3. Die Publicisten selbst*, Lasson, p. [21]. (This latter fragment originally belonged to the first phase in the evolution of the manuscript—Feb.-Apr. 1801—but was subsequently revised to stand as part of the first continuous draft—cf. Rosenzweig, i. 108 and 236.)

possessed and which a feudal empire like Russia still possessed. He clearly believed that as the national consciousness developed, a coherent legal system must be created and customary barriers to free change of social status must be swept away. But we should remember that Hegel's conception of society was organic rather than egalitarian; against his undoubted sympathy with the Revolution, we have to weigh both his trenchant criticisms of rational legal theories like that of Fichte, and the fact that in his Hellenic ideal serfdom was accepted as a social status that was both necessary to society and natural to man.[1]

The maintenance of a central authority presupposes secure possession of the necessary financial and material resources. About this problem Hegel's view is slightly clearer. It is not absolutely necessary that the central authority should have the right to levy taxes, for a feudal authority could maintain itself without this right. But it is essential in a modern State. As we shall see presently, however, Hegel thinks that the centralized financial organization of the 'modern' State has the seeds of many dangers within it. Here again, in spite of his criticisms, he displays a sympathy with feudal modes of thought which ceases to be surprising when we reflect upon his conception of society as a 'living whole'.[2]

Apart from these essentials—the *Staatsmacht*, which is a concentration of power and resources sufficient to defend the property of the community, and the *Staatsgewalt*, which is a central authority that controls and administers this power—everything else in the structure of a political constitution belongs on the theoretical side (*für den Begriff*) to the 'sphere of the better or worse', and on the practical side (*für die Wirklichkeit*) to the 'sphere of chance and caprice'. But the criterion of what is better rather than worse, the criterion that raises *Willkür* to rationality, is the fostering of the

---

[1] Hegel may well have believed, with Aristotle, that serfdom is a proper or 'natural' condition for many men. His political theory of rural life always remained aristocratic. The proper 'representative' of the land in his eyes was the hereditary landlord. But the existence of serfdom as an unchangeable *legal* status is hard to reconcile with his ideal of 'Nature'. Hegel must have held from the beginning therefore that this aspect of the feudal system *had* to be overthrown.

[2] Lasson, p. 24; cf. Knox–Pelczynski, p. 157 and especially n. 3. The fact that Hegel was the son of a financial official and was always interested in public finance makes the loss of all his manuscripts concerned with economic matters especially regrettable.

'living freedom and personal will [*Wille*]' of the citizens.[1] This principle governs and explains Hegel's treatment of all the 'non-essential' aspects of the constitution. The original unity of the *Volk* was built on a cultural community of language and religion; but the conscious union of a large modern State cannot rest on this foundation. Europe was briefly united in the great Crusades of Christendom to save the Holy Land from the infidels, but, since the Reformation, Church and State have had to be separated as they were when the Church began; and quite apart from empires that embrace many tongues, every national language contains a variety of dialects which are often more divisive than different languages would be. Government and administration should be decentralized as far as possible, because this variety of life and culture, which was impossible in an ancient city-state, must be preserved and developed. The reconciliation of differences, which is essential if peace is to be preserved, must be achieved at the level of *Phantasie* rather than at the level of intellect.[2] This is the suppressed premiss which explains why Hegel shows throughout his discussion a marked preference for the Athenian model of the Hapsburgs as against the Spartan model of the Hohenzollerns; and it is also why he condemns both the practical experiments of Robespierre and the rationalist theories of Fichte in the same breath.[3]

Hegel's position is grounded explicitly in his own revision of enlightened moral reason: 'Quite apart from considerations of utility, nothing should be so sacred for it [the Government] as guaranteeing and safeguarding the free activity of citizens in such affairs [as do not touch the security of the State]. For this freedom is in itself sacred.'[4] He declares himself to be quite prepared to argue his case for the free organic society as against the 'machine-

---

[1] Lasson, p. 19 (Knox–Pelczynski, pp. 154–5). This paragraph appears only in the final version. (The Kantian contrast of *Willkür* and *Wille* should be carefully attended to here.)

[2] Hegel does not say this in the *Verfassungsschrift*; but it is the burden of all his studies of the relation of Church and State from *man mag die widersprechendsten Betrachtungen* to *ein objektiven Mittelpunkt*.

[3] Lasson, p. 26 (Knox–Pelczynski, p. 159). No earlier draft of these closing pages of the first section have survived. (Thus, as far as our evidence goes, no explicit contrast between the 'living' State and the 'machine State' was drawn by Hegel before the last months of 1802. But possibly the unpublished fragment *Der Nahme für die Staatsverfassung* will fill this lacuna.)

[4] Lasson, p. 29 (Knox–Pelczynski, pp. 161–2).

State' on grounds of utility and economic efficiency as well. But
the real purpose of his supplementary argument is to show *why*
civic freedom is the *summum bonum* of political life.

He claims first that a completely centralized administration is
more expensive because motives of charity and public recognition
cannot be enlisted in the public service. But what is important in
Hegel's eyes is clearly not the supposed monetary saving, but the
different quality of civic experience when public service is performed for love rather than for money, and the people is 'treated
with trust and freedom' rather than, as in the 'machine-State',
'with reason and according to necessity'.[1]

When he turns from the calculation of material costs and savings
to what he calls 'the second and third mode of reckoning', he says
explicitly that the different quality of experience is what is important. The 'second mode of reckoning' is concerned with the development of *Verstand* and technical competence, and the third with
Lebendigkeit and 'free self-respect'. But Hegel does not discuss
the second mode separately at any length. He merely remarks that
it is bad for a government to act on the assumption that private
citizens do not have the intellectual capacity to do what is in their
own best interests, because public spirit can only be founded on
self-confidence, and thus he comes to his 'third mode'. The 'free
loyalty [*Anhänglichkeit*], the self-awareness, and the individual
effort of the people' is

an all-powerful invincible spirit which that hierarchy [of the machine-
State] has renounced, and which has its life only where the supreme
State authority leaves as much as possible to the personal charge of the
citizens. How dull and spiritless a life is engendered in a modern State
of the sort where everything is regulated from the top downwards,

---

[1] Lasson, p. 30. Knox's translation of this tangled sentence is not easy to
follow. I construe it thus:

'Both circumstances [i.e. points (i) and (ii) in Knox] make a difference—
even if in connection with the first more money might have to be contributed
by the people, which is not really to be credited. The first makes the difference
that no one pays out money for something that *he* does not need, for something
that is a non-universal need of the State [i.e. not a matter for legislation by the
General Will]; the second produces an actual saving for everybody. Both
together make the difference that the people feels itself treated in the one case
[*dort*—over there in the machine-State] with reason and according to necessity
[compare Fichte's *Geschlossene Handelstaat*] and in the other case [*hier*—
here, in the living state] with trust and freedom. ⟨This last point is⟩ a circumstance which constitutes the most important difference in the second and third
modes of reckoning.'

where nothing which has implications for the community as a whole [*was eine allgemeine Seite hat*] is left to the management and execution of those parts of the people that have an interest in it—in a State such as the French Republic has made itself into—this we have still to experience in the future, if indeed mastery can maintain itself at this pitch of pedantry. But what life and what sterility reigns in another equally regulated State—in Prussia—strikes anyone who sets foot in the first village across the border or considers the complete lack of scientific or artistic genius in Prussia, and does not assess its strength by the ephemeral level of energy which a single man of genius was able to force it up to for a time.[1]

This attack on Prussia forms the rhetorical climax of Hegel's opening chapter on the 'Concept of the State'. But just when he seems to be about to embark on the next topic in his plan—'There is no supreme authority in Germany (*a*) Apportioning of sovereign authority is inheritable and judicial'—there is a break in our manuscript. The continuous drafts begin again at different points in the section on the military power of Germany. Lasson says comfortably that the lacuna here is clearly not a great one.[2] But there seem to be no grounds of his confidence. All the evidence points rather to the existence of a fairly considerable gap. That Hegel was in all likelihood following his plan is attested first by the final paragraph of the fragment *Deutschland ist kein Staat mehr*, and secondly by the cancellation of a paragraph about Germany's failure to meet the minimal criterion of Statehood in the revision of the earlier fragment *II. 3. Die Publicisten selbst*.[3] Finally, and most important of all, the account of Hegel's argument given by Rosenkranz makes it clear that he possessed more of the manuscript than we do; and the fact that some of the information he provides can be assigned with reasonable confidence to the lost part of the section on 'Military power', provides strong support for the already plausible supposition that what he had before him was the content of the lacuna as a whole.[4]

---

[1] Lasson, p. 31 (Knox–Pelczynski, pp. 163–4).

[2] See his 'Feststellung des Textes', p. 505.

[3] Lasson, p. [21]. This fragment was first written, probably, before the plan was made. But in its revised form (which begins *Wir können eine Menschenmenge*: Lasson, p. [17]) it served as the answer to the question 'What is essential to a State?' in the first continuous draft.

[4] This hypothesis seems preferable to the suggestion of Kimmerle (*Hegel-Studien*, v. 86–7, 93) that Rosenkranz may have been depending on another draft of the introduction which is now lost. The evidence that there ever *was* another

The report of Rosenkranz clearly shows that Hegel's manuscript originally contained a discussion of feudal Germany that is now lost:

Hegel asked in his essay whether the decadence [*Untergang*] of the German Empire should rightly be ascribed to lack of *courage* [*Tapferkeit*] or personal morale? This view, he answered, is contradicted by history which justified the renown of the individual soldier for military proficiency everywhere, even in the army of the Empire. Hence military defeat must be laid to the charge of the fragmented character of Germany and the bad leadership of the troops. [Compare Lasson, p. 39.]

He asked further whether the decadence had perhaps arisen from a *national bankruptcy*? This, he thought, was just as far from being the case. For with all the bad housekeeping of the individual States, Germany was still not acquainted with all those serious problems which sprang in other States from a *National debt*, whose management occupied the most oustanding minds, and in which even small errors could lead to the most fearful consequences. [Compare Lasson, pp. 40–1.]

Finally he asked whether perhaps lack of *ethics* [*Sittlichkeit*], of *education* [*Bildung*], of *religious feeling* [*Religiosität*] could be the cause of the weakness? This, he countered, could least of all be asserted. *Not in the individual, therefore, but in the mechanism of the whole must the principle of corruption lie.*[1]

draft for the introduction is very slight and unreliable. The report of Rosenkranz (p. 236) that Hegel rewrote his *Eingang* 'three or four times', beginning always with the words 'Deutschland ist kein Staat mehr', is sufficiently accounted for by the following data in the manuscripts that we have:

(*a*) the fact that the final draft (Chronological Index, item 131) does begin with these words precisely.

(*b*) *Deutschland kein Staat mehr* is the *incipit* of Hegel's outline-plan (item 125).

(*c*) Hegel cancelled the second and third paragraphs of *Sollte das politische Resultat* (item 116) and inserted the words *Deutschland kein Staat mehr* in the margin beside paragraph 4. This was taken as marking a new beginning by Lasson [3] and almost certainly by Rosenkranz before him.

My own guess is that Rosenkranz himself created the lacuna in our text by removing one or two sheets which struck him as interesting enough to deserve summary notice in the biography. (Kimmerle also mentions the possibility that Rosenkranz was using some pages now lost from the still unpublished draft *Der Nahme für die Staatsverfassung*. But in view of what Rosenkranz says about the constancy of Hegel's *Eingang* I am more inclined to believe that he was completely unacquainted with this draft.)

[1] This paragraph *could* be regarded as a confused account of Lasson, pp. 31–2; but, in spite of the other parallels indicated in square brackets, the order in which Rosenkranz puts Hegel's 'questions' strongly suggests that he is *not* working from any of the manuscripts that we possess. The guide-line that he used in summarizing all of Hegel's discussion of military prowess, finance, and religion may well have been the sentence immediately before the break in the

This principle of corruption Hegel now found in the fact that the German Empire still sought to operate always in the *form of the medieval feudal system* in which the relatively sovereign vassal had to furnish to his sovereign the contingent that was fixed by his contract, and thus the sovereign was more or less dependent on the goodwill of his liegeman. In *actuality*, however, feudalism had long since disappeared; the petty princes had in effect become sovereign and their dependence on the Empire was a mere sham. The art of war [*Kriegführung*] had been wholly transformed by the ever more widespread use of *gunpowder*, as a result of which the form of battle as a *personal combat* between two opponents was done away with [*aufgehoben*], and the disciplined movement of the individual as an element in a mass [*Glied einer Masse*] became essential. With this change the patchwork-quilt formation of an army from a multitude of contingents with different uniforms, different weapons and so on, had come into contradiction with the absolute instrument of death, gunpowder.—On the *financial* side the middle ages still kept in many respects the form of contributions in the *form of natural produce*, whereas the modern era has everywhere made the *power of money* central in this realm as the universal worth of *all* things and as the *most readily transferred* medium.—Finally, with respect to *education* and *religion*, in the middle ages the latter had been politically important and had for this reason dominated culture. The German Empire had never been able to free itself from this attitude. Almost all of its wars had had a religious tinge . . .[1]

From this point onwards, Rosenkranz's account is clearly based on the text that we have—except for one isolated remark about Mainz which we shall have to consider later.[2] Only what he says about the military revolution produced by gunpowder is quite without parallel in our text. But I am inclined to think that the contrast between the medieval and the modern economic system, and the remarks about the authority of the medieval Church, also come from the missing text.[3]

manuscript: 'Daß also in Deutschland die unfreie Forderung nicht erfüllt ist, Gesetze, Rechtspflege, *Auflegung und Erhebung der Abgaben* usw., Sprache, *Sitten, Bildung, Religion* von einem Mittelpunkt reguliert und guberniert zu wissen, sondern darüber die disparateste Mannigfaltigkeit stattfindet, *dies würde nicht hindern, daß Deutschland einen Staat konstituierte*, wenn es anders als eine Staatsgewalt organisiert ⟨wäre⟩. . . ' (for an English version see Knox–Pelczynski, p. 164). And it seems very likely that the order of Rosenkranz's 'questions' was suggested by the order of topics, military, financial, religious, in the lost discussion of feudal Germany summarized in the next paragraph of the quotation.

[1] Rosenkranz, pp. 236–8.   [2] See below, p. 475 n. 1.

[3] If we accept the plan *Deutschland kein Staat mehr* as our guide to Hegel's objectives in this lost discussion of the feudal system we can get some further

At the point where the main manuscript begins again,[1] Hegel is speaking of the military reputation of the Germans as mercenaries. The German states, even the larger ones, had been turning their military resources into money for generations. Yet Germany as a political unit was quite unable to defend itself properly. Foreign hints of its probable content from the drafts and sketches which have survived from the first phase in the development of the manuscript. The set of notes on the feudal constitution of the Reich *Da die deutsche Verfassung* (for which see p. 461 n. 1 below) and the fragment of the first continuous discussion of this topic *C. Die Lehensverfassung ist durch* (Lasson, pp. 144–9 and [83]–[87]) are obviously relevant in this connection. But the most interesting piece is the fragment *d. politischer Grundsatz* (Lasson, pp. [62]–[65]) which is, in essence, a meditation on the theme 'German constitutional law is private law'. (Lasson took this fragment to be an early draft for the section on the juridical organization of the Empire. Some of the points that it contains are taken up in that section, and some are also echoed in the later section on the independence of the 'Estates'. But the degree of overlap and repetition is no greater than that between Hegel's own opening chapter on the *Begriff* of the State, and the subsequent chapters in which he develops and deploys his argument in detail.)

Briefly the argument of *d. politischer Grundsatz* is as follows: There is a fundamental difference between matters of political authority (*Staatsgewalt*) and matters of judicial right (*Rechtsgegenstand*). For this reason claims for constitutional sovereignty are not subject to judicial settlement. The first examples that Hegel considers—the way in which the German princes have arrogated to themselves the right to make war on one another and *not* to support, or even to oppose, the *Reich* in its wars belong properly to the topic 'War and Peace' in a later subsection of Hegel's plan. But they could well receive notice in a preliminary statement of the main thesis 'There is no supreme authority in Germany'; and the remaining topic of this fragment fits almost perfectly under subhead *alpha*—'The apportioning of constitutional authority in inheritable and judicial'. 'State authority', says Hegel, 'cannot be private property; it flows from the State and there is no right to it save that of the State; its extent and its possession depends on the State and is only valid in relation to the State; it is not an object for judicial settlement [*Behandlung*]. Inheritance of private property is a matter of chance and caprice. State authority must remain intimately connected with the whole; the State is the supreme ruler—though only in One Respect—of the defence of the laws, and ⟨of the people⟩ against foreign ⟨powers⟩—so then in this matter all right derives from it, it must decide, not chance, not charters or other legal titles.' (In the 'Other Respect'—Consciousness as opposed to actuality—the Church would be the guardian, but hardly the 'ruler', of the religious values of the community.)

The fragment continues by analysing how the Imperial Courts, in seeking to make decisions about inheritance and other legal claims to political authority, are at the mercy of a powerful claimant, even where, as in the case of a foreign monarch, the claim ought to be rejected on political grounds regardless of its legality. This example (which is taken up several times in later sections of our surviving manuscripts) reveals the most serious weakness involved in treating political authority as a matter of private property and legal right.

[1] *Die Fortpflanzung dieses kriegerischen Talents* (Lasson, p. 32) is the *incipit* of the first draft. The final draft begins again with *jedes Gesicht auf* at the top of Lasson, p. 34. From the middle of page 34 to page 48 the first draft is printed at

powers were quite eager to hire German soldiers, yet the Imperial Army of Germany was a laughing-stock. This was because the free cities and smaller States, on the one hand, could not maintain forces large enough to generate a military tradition or *esprit de corps*. Their armies were only princely playthings, quite unfit for active service, as the call to battle regularly revealed. The larger States, on the other hand, only answered the Empire's call if it suited them, so that, in fact, the contending parties in the civil wars which tore Germany to pieces could and did raise more formidable armies than the Empire ever raised in its own defence. Even if the larger contingents came, they remained under separate commands, so that the army was not one but several mutually jealous forces.[1]

The same situation, Hegel goes on, prevails in the financial sphere. In this field the centralized administration of the 'machine-State' lies at one extreme, and the anarchy of the Empire at the other. Because of its decentralization the finances of the central authority of the Empire are simple, and 'no Pitt is required for their management'.[2] The smaller Estates had finally begun to commute their feudal military obligations to money payments, and in this Hegel saw the beginning of the transformation of the older society into a modern State. But this transformation had begun too late and had not gone far enough: and the existing constitution was full of loop-holes by which the payment of contributions to the imperial treasury could be avoided.

One of the methods by which the Diet sought to fill the Imperial treasury without actual cost to themselves offered an irresistible target for ironic humour. The Diet had voted that the revenues of

the foot of the page. It breaks off very near the end of the section on finances. *jedes Gesicht auf* continues unbroken to page 68 and its final paragraphs are reprinted at the foot of pages 68 to 71. The first draft begins at the foot of page 66 ⟨wer⟩*den kann, wodurch die Freyheit* and continues unbroken to the end. From the foot of page 68 onwards Lasson treats it as the principal text; and from page 71 onwards it is the only text we have (apart from a few sketches from the first phase).

[1] Lasson, pp. 32–9 (Knox–Pelczynski, pp. 164–9). Cf. also *Reichsfeind, der dritte*, Lasson, pp. 142–3. The references to the Thirty Years' war and the Seven Years' war are made explicit in the first draft (Lasson, pp. [34]–[35]).

[2] Lasson, p. 41 (Knox–Pelczynski, p. 169). Cf. *Die Fortpflanzung dieses kriegerischen Talents*, Lasson, p. [41]. Behind this remark there lies, almost certainly, bitter resentment of the way Pitt manipulated the coalition against France by means of subsidies, thus contriving to combat the Revolution with German blood and English money.

lost provinces should go to the Imperial Treasury when those provinces were recovered. As Hegel remarks: 'The Empire has managed always so to arrange matters as to lose more territory and so to increase the Imperial fund. Consequently the loss of the left bank of the Rhine has its more comforting aspect: it is a route to the possibility of founding an Imperial exchequer.'[1] This curious piece of never-never-land finance provided a natural transition to the sad tale of the Empire's ever-shrinking boundaries. Hegel takes as his starting-point, in this connection, the Peace of Westphalia (1648) at the conclusion of the Thirty Years' War. We can reasonably infer, I think, that in his view the older spontaneous natural unity of the *Volk* perished in that war. From that time the principle was accepted that a Protestant minority was not bound by a majority decision of the *Reichstag*; and thereby the very possibility of real federal union and centralized authority was destroyed.[2] The impotence of the State thereafter showed itself in two ways: first in actual loss of territories ceded to victorious enemies, and secondly in the acceptance of foreign princes as fief-holders of the Reich. The kings of France and Sweden had seats in the Diet under the settlement of 1648, and with the accession of the Elector of Hanover as George I in 1714, the English king arrived also.[3]

---

[1] Lasson, p. 46 (Knox–Pelczynski, p. 172). The earlier draft for this section (*Die Fortpflanzung dieses kriegerischen Talents*, Lasson, pp. [39]–[48]) contains rather fuller discussions of the old feudal arrangements, and some remarks about the judicial system of the *Reich* which may have been eliminated from the revised version because Hegel felt they were, or could be, sufficiently dealt with in the fuller discussions in later sections. The earliest draft, *Da die deutsche Verfassung*, Lasson, pp. 144–9, is actually a set of notes for the discussion of:

[A: Finance], pp. 144–5.
[B: Justice and judicial finance], pp. 145–6.
C: Lack of supreme power in Germany
    (a) in theory [legal rights of the Estates], pp. 146–8.
    (b) in practice [religious divisions], p. 148.
[D: Cultural and economic divisions], p. 149.
E: History since the Peace of Westphalia, p. 149.

(The unbracketed headings are used by Hegel himself. Compare further the account quoted from Rosenkranz on pp. 457–8 and p. 458 n. 3 above.)

[2] See especially *Da die deutsche Verfassung* section C (b), Lasson, p. 148. In this section of his essay Hegel depends heavily on J. S. Pütter. A fairly clear idea of how critical he was in his use of Pütter's work can be gained by comparing the notes in *Dok.*, pp. 309–12 (and Hoffmeister's notes, *Dok.*, p. 474) with the text in Lasson, pp. 52–7 (Knox–Pelczynski, pp. 175–9).

[3] Compare the following passages in the final drafts: Lasson, pp. 53–7 (Knox–Pelczynski, pp. 175–8); Lasson, pp. 87–92 (Knox–Pelczynski, pp. 197–201).

Among these 'foreign sovereigns' Hegel counts Prussia.[1] Elector
Frederick II forced the Emperor to recognize him as 'King' of
Prussia in 1701, but it was really the achievement of his father, the
'Great Elector', in holding together the various scattered in-
heritances of the Hohenzollern house from 1640 onwards, which
made Brandenburg–Prussia to all intents and purposes an independent power in the north of Germany. With Prussia on the one
side, Austria on the other, and several foreign powers liable to
become involved in any domestic quarrel, the constitutional
justice meted out to the Estates by the Imperial courts, virtually
the last surviving vestige of central authority, could hardly be very
even-handed. Every smaller princedom speedily realized that it
was better to have powerful allies than a costly and dilatory
judgement which could not be executed. Thus the German
Empire became after 1648 a *Gedankenstaat*: all the forms of
constitutional unity remained, but in reality several of the estates
managed to make themselves into viable independent states, and the
existence of the rest was at the mercy of circumstance.[2]

The *Gedankenstaat* is essentially a legal fiction. Its natural and
proper sphere is the courts. But even within this sphere the
sovereign authority of Germany was only a thought, not a reality.
Even where the legal situation was clear, the actual process of
delivering judgement could be paralysed by legal and diplomatic
means; the courts were absolutely clogged with litigation, some
of which had dragged on for generations, and though the Diet
resolved to increase the number of judges it failed to find any money
to pay them with.

The administration of the law is so constituted that if the legal
verdict is declared in constitutional relations it cannot be executed
except where the interests concerned are those of an estate without
political power; but if this is not the case, as it usually is not, the case
does not come up for legal settlement, but is decided by power and
political relations.[3]

At this point in his final draft, Hegel began a new chapter with
the heading 'Legitimacy [*Rechtmäßigkeit*] ⟨of the fact⟩ that the
execution of the constitutional laws does not come to pass.' The

[1] Lasson, p. 53 (Knox–Pelczynski, p. 176); cf. also Lasson, p. 88 (Knox–
Pelczynski, p. 198).
[2] Lasson, pp. 70–2 (Knox–Pelczynski, pp. 187–9).
[3] Lasson, p. [68].

manuscript breaks off soon afterwards, but it was clearly his intention to argue that Germany had returned in a quite constitutional way to the state of anarchy that preceded the establishment of the 'imperial peace' (the *Landfriede* of 1495). Unlike the rest of Europe, Germany failed to make the transition from barbarism to civilization:

In the struggle out of savagery into culture, the crucial question was which of the two, the universal, the State, or the individual, would gain the upper hand; in most European countries the State has won a complete victory here, in some its victory is incomplete, in none so inadequate as in Germany with its mere pretence of being a State. The state of barbarism consists precisely in this, that a mass of men [*eine Menge*] is a people without being at the same time a State, that the State and the individual exist in opposition and in a state of separation [*in einer Trennung*]; the ruler is in his own person the State authority; and the bulwark [*Rettung*] against his personality is nothing but the opposition of ⟨the baron's⟩ personality. In a civilized [*gebildeten*] State the laws, or universality, stand between the personality of the monarch, and the individual ⟨burgher⟩; the individual deed of the monarch concerns all, it burdens or injures all, or it benefits all. But that the monarch should *eo ipso* be the State authority, that he should have the sovereign power, that the State should in fact exist, all come to the same thing. The contradiction ⟨between the requirement⟩ that the State should be the sovereign authority, and ⟨the requirement⟩ that the individual should not be oppressed by it, is resolved by the power of the laws. Lack of faith in the power of the laws is what stems from that failure of wisdom which wavers between the necessity of giving sovereign power to the State, and the fear that the individual will be oppressed by it. All wisdom in the organization of States turns on the solution of this problem; but the first essential is that the State should exist, hence the first essential is that its power should be sovereign, and that directly implies also that there are laws . . . (*breaks off*)[1]

'German freedom' was originally the arbitary power of a local lord; when this was embodied in a system of law it represented

---

[1] Lasson, pp. [70]–[71]. For the relation of the two drafts in Lasson's edition see p. 459 n. 1 above. The manuscript of the final version was 'uncompleted' (*unvollendet*), Rosenzweig, i. 237. The germ of this new 'chapter' (the only chapter heading given in the manuscript after 'I. Begriff des Staats') is plainly to be seen in a marginal insertion in the final paragraph of the section on constitutional law in the first draft (Lasson, p. [72]). The justification for holding that 'individual' refers initially to the baron is provided by his account of Germany in the days before the Imperial Peace, which follows almost immediately and is discussed below.

nothing but a 'failure of wisdom' and a lack of faith in the law, which perpetually justified itself because it effectively prevented the growth of a constitutional monarchy or sovereign power.

5. The 'Constitution of the German Empire': Part II

Probably Hegel meant to illustrate this thesis by comparing the fate of Germany with that of Italy—the other exception in Europe —as he does in the first draft. In any case there is no reason to suppose that the course of the discussion in his second draft, if he had completed it, would have been very different from the argument of the first draft, which continues unbroken from slightly before this point to the end. But whereas the first half of the treatise is mainly concerned with the 'fate' of Germany, the second half is devoted rather to the regeneration of the 'spirit of German freedom' which Hegel identifies with the 'spirit' of Europe as a whole.[1]

In the days before the imperial peace, when the Germans knew that they were a nation but did not yet pretend to be a State, there was a certain *Zusammenhang* of all the conflicting parties which arose from the homogeneity of their interests and the essential similarity of their characters. They were all of them free lords, not driven by economic need to think of their own private interests separately from the interests of the whole, as free 'Bürgers' are.[2] Thus Germany was closer to becoming a State at the inception of the *Landfriede* than it ever was afterwards. The Reformation and the wars of religion 'divided the peoples for ever', just when the diversification of society made the establishment of constitutional sovereignty essential. Hegel clearly implies that it was precisely because of its *Unbändigkeit* that Germany became the cockpit of the religious upheaval. All of the causes that historians might appeal to in an account of German history are only 'tools in the hands of higher powers, of primordial fate and of time that conquers all things'.[3]

---

[1] In this latter half of the essay we have therefore the first statement of the reasons why Hegel called the modern period the 'Christian-Teutonic World' in his lectures on the philosophy of history twenty years later. (The structure of the *Verfassungsschrift*—a negative, critical analysis, followed by a positive, reconstructive one—should be compared with that of the 'Positivity' essay of 1795.)

[2] The marginal addition, 'The prince⟨ly⟩ and noble sense ⟨is⟩ freer, not subjected to the need of earning [*Not des Erwerbs*]' (Lasson, p. [73]), is another hint of the dialectic of *Herr* and *Knecht*. Cf. p. 450 above (with n. 2).

[3] Lasson, p. 74 (Knox–Pelczynski, p. 190).

The settlement of the religious question in the treaty of Westphalia was in the main a reaffirmation of the basic premiss of the Peace of Augsburg. Every princedom had its own 'established religion' and civil recognition was denied to other faiths. Hegel's attitude to this problem of religious toleration and the civil rights of dissenters is by no means easy to expound, because he applies his own doctrine of the relation of the realm of 'right' to the realm of 'love' in more than one way. On the one hand religious toleration ought to be a matter of 'grace', not of 'right', because the 'community of religion is deeper than community of physical needs, of property, or of gain', and 'grace' is higher than 'right'. This leads Hegel to say that the 'grace' extended by Prussia to Catholics and by Austria to Protestants was 'infinitely higher' than the 'rights' guaranteed by the treaty. But he also says that this grace of religious toleration 'accords with the higher *natural rights* of freedom of conscience and the non-dependence of civil rights on faith'. This latter statement is the general burden of the essay on 'The Positivity of Christianity', and it is clear from the argument in that essay that the proper interpretation of the superiority of 'grace' is that matters of grace should not be regulated by law at all. The Nemesis of the claim for 'religious rights' was the doctrine of *itio in partes*, by which a religious minority could refuse to accept a majority decision of the Diet. The failure to resolve the religious division properly by making a clear separation of Church and State reduced the sovereign power itself to a partisan position.

It is fair to say, I think, that Hegel viewed the Peace of Augsburg itself as a necessary transition from primitive spontaneity to conscious freedom of conscience. 'The times were not ripe' for a proper separation of Church and State,[1]—and in that context the 'grace' extended by the Prince in violation of the 'rights' of the established religion was 'higher'. But it is only by legal recognition that religion does not ultimately concern the State at all—the proper fulfilment of the right of *itio in partes*—that the realm of 'right' is brought into its true harmony with the realm of 'grace'.[2]

Freedom of conscience in combination with the principles of private property, produced finally a breach in the constitutional

---

[1] Cf. Lasson, pp. 77 and 80.

[2] In this connection Hegel's remarks about the contrast between Richelieu's policy in France and his policy in Germany (quoted on p. 469 below) are illuminating.

theory of 'German freedom'. The maxim *cuius regio eius religio* presupposed that the prince would be at one with his people in all fundamental matters of conscience. But by the natural operation of the rights of free inheritance a Catholic prince could succeed to a Protestant princedom and vice versa. In this event the prince could no longer be a natural 'representative' of his people. However the problem might be politically or legally resolved, the personality of the prince was then clearly distinct from and opposed to the unity of the people. Thus religion—which is the foundation of the natural unity of the *Volk*, and ought to be, as it was in the work of Theseus, the foundation of their political union into a State—was for Germany not only the most effective barrier against her becoming a State, but even a force which disrupted the natural unity that was originally possessed by the parts. And yet, as Hegel says, the fact that Germany is nevertheless *supposed* to be a State, shows that in principle the possibility of a separation of Church and State is acknowledged.[1]

The religious division alone would not have been sufficient to prevent Germany from advancing from a feudal community into a national State. The crucial development that prevented this was the emergence in Prussia of a single power capable of standing alone against all the might that the Emperor could muster. Hegel speaks in the plural of 'disproportionate aggrandisement of single Estates', and he draws an analogy with the peculiar case of Poland, where an alliance of vassals exercised an influence which ultimately led to the downfall of the kingdom; but it is quite clear that in his eyes the unity of Germany was effectively prevented by the emergence of Brandenburg–Prussia, and its impossibility demonstrated by Frederick the Great's successful defiance of the Imperial ban.

Prussia represents that aspect of the German spirit which appears in the alien guise of 'fate'. She was the closest of the 'Teutonic'

---

[1] Lasson, p. 79 (Knox–Pelczynski, pp. 193–4). Hegel never alludes explicitly to the 'secularization' of the ecclesiastical principalities, discussed at the Congress of Rastatt and carried into effect by the Peace of Lunéville. Yet the way in which the various states holding territory on the left bank of the Rhine were 'compensated' for their loss by receiving ecclesiastical lands within the body of the Empire is as ludicrous from the point of view of the 'whole' as the financial resolutions that he pokes fun at. The natural inference is that he regarded this aspect of the negotiations and treaties as a definite gain for the *Reich* (compare further p. 473 n. 1 below).

but external powers who were able to use the normal channels of dynastic politics to become fief-holders within the Empire.[1] Even the power of Austria—through which the feudal constitution of Germany was preserved, so far as it survived at all—was an alien power. Ignoring, for the moment, the influence of France,[2] Hegel views the history of Germany as a struggle among the Teutonic nations Denmark, Sweden, England, Prussia, and Austria. He speaks in terms of glowing admiration of the intervention of Gustavus Adolphus on behalf of the Protestants in the Thirty Years' War; but in the next breath he condemns those who believe that a 'human work of justice and dreams realized' could be 'secure against the higher justice of nature and truth'. A foreign hero could only bring about the triumph of foreign power.[3]

The foreign powers whose influence in Germany Hegel chooses to consider are just the ones he is primarily thinking of when he says that 'most of the European States were founded by Germanic peoples, and out of the spirit of these peoples their constitution has developed'.[4] In the tribal system of the German forests, and even in the early days of the feudal system, before the development of the towns, 'every free man's arm was counted on. . . . Princes

[1] Hegel's theory of fate as the nature of a man (or a community) separated from him (or it) by his (or its) own act, and appearing over against him (or it) as an *alien* force, explains the ambivalence that is continually apparent in his treatment of Prussia. Prussia was inside the *Reich*, yet outside it, not only in practice but in constitutional theory (the same was true of Austria, of course). But the way Hegel switches from speaking of Prussia's refusal to pay the *Kammerzieler*, or of the status of the Margrave of Brandenburg within the *Reich*, to discussing the role of Prussia as one of the 'foreign powers from the North' is bewildering, unless we realize that for Hegel all of those powers are 'Germanic' and Prussia is simply the latest of the states 'founded by Germanic peoples'. Its constitution, moreover, is the extreme of modernity and economic efficiency. The 'machine-State' is the 'fate' of 'German freedom'. (Cf. Lasson, pp. 83, 85–6, 88, 92; Knox–Pelczynski, pp. 196–202.)

[2] Since Hegel mentions France first among the national states of Europe (Lasson, p. 92; Knox–Pelczynski, p. 202), and alludes also (Lasson, p. 85; Knox–Pelczynski, pp. 196–7) to the use of Charlemagne's regalia in the coronation of the Emperor, he does not mean to slight the Frankish contribution to European history. He presumably counts the Franks as 'Germanic peoples' of some sort. But the fate of France, like that of Germany itself, was peculiar. The feudal system did not develop properly, and the spirit of 'German freedom' was lost as the monarchy became absolute and the nobility lost its 'representative' character (cf. Lasson, pp. 95–6; Knox–Pelczynski, pp. 205–6). All the same, France did manage to become a viable State and overcome its crisis (Lasson, pp. 107–9; Knox–Pelczynski, pp. 215–17).

[3] Lasson, pp. 89–90 (Knox–Pelczynski, p. 199).

[4] Lasson, p. 92 (Knox–Pelczynski, p. 202).

were chosen by the people, and . . . anyone who wished took part in the council.' The development of free towns broke this pattern, for the burghers were no longer 'free' in the sense of having serfs to labour and provide for them economically. But also, as the feudal system itself developed, the political business of the nation grew further and further away from the immediate concerns of noble landlords. Hence a system of parliamentary representation developed in which the different Estates of the realm were represented. This is the ideal mean between the extremes of despotism (the universal slavery of oriental empires) and republicanism (the civic equality of the Roman Empire).[1] When the empire of the Romans gave place in the West to that of the Germans, parliamentary representation was the form that the principle of 'German freedom' had to assume.

The feudal system itself was only a transitional phase. The arrival on the scene of free men other than nobles, meant that two *types* of 'Estates' had to be represented. In the case of the noble representative of a landed estate, primogeniture was the natural principle of representation. But in the case of the free commoners, free election and a career open to talent were equally natural. Hegel has a good word here for both England and Austria, and he finds in the decay of Estates-General the reason for the 'misfortune' of the *ancien régime* in France. In a marginal addition to his text he condemns the 'new États Généraux' (i.e. the National Convention) for abolishing the distinction of Estates altogether. In his view the two principles of noble birth ('character') and bourgeois equality of opportunity ('skill and expertise') have to be harmonized together. 'Nature and most modern States' tend to diminish the distinction between the nobility and the ordinary burghers; in France 'that which is purely personal [i.e. the skill and expertise that an individual acquires for himself, not the 'character' that he has as one link in an immortal life-line] has been made into a principle and the career of public service has been closed to the nobility altogether.[2]

---

[1] Lasson, p. 93 (Knox–Pelczynski, p. 203). The Greeks cannot have a place in this schema because they did not create a world empire. But they expressed the ideal in its fully developed form at the level of the face-to-face society. Hegel is careful to point out that the German tribes in their forests did not and could not do this. Theirs was the simple life of the ἀναγκαιοτάτη πόλις of which Plato speaks in *Republic* ii.

[2] Lasson, pp. 94–6 (Knox–Pelczynski, pp. 204–6). The two principles of

In Germany itself German freedom was institutionalized as the spirit of constitutional legality. All problems were thought of as questions of established 'rights'. But the assumption that any system of rights can be absolutely stable ignores the many-sidedness of human relations which renders conflicts of rights inevitable.[1] There are situations where the opposed parties have both a 'just cause' for war, and war is the only way to settle the issue, precisely because the right of both sides is well grounded. Hegel speaks with bitter contempt of the pretexts which the German princes found for some of their wars after the *Landfriede*. But he clearly holds that in the absence of a central authority strong enough to impose a judicial settlement, nothing better could be expected. His contempt springs from the fact that the pretexts were found and the wars were fought in pursuit of *private* interests, since political power had been reduced to a kind of private property.

At this point Hegel embarks on a comparison of the 'fate' of Germany with that of France and that of Italy. Both France and Germany had faced the same problem of religious division; and one man, Richelieu, had been the architect both of unity for France and of dissolution for Germany:

While annihilating the Huguenot state, he left them freedom of conscience, churches, worship, civil and political rights on a parity with the Catholics. By doing what was logical for him as a statesman, he discovered and exercised the toleration which was finally recognized as rationally valid [*geltend gemacht*] more than a hundred years later as the product of a more civilized age and as the most brilliant achievement of philosophy and of more humane manners [*Milderung der Sitten*]; and it was not ignorance and fanaticism in the French, when, in the war and in the Peace of Westphalia, they did not think of the separation of State and Church in Germany, but made religion the basis of a distinction in political and civil rights, thereby granting validity to a principle in Germany which they cancelled [*aufgehoben*] in their own country.[2]

representation were united in the tribal society in which 'the people chose the princes', and their joint influence was still evident in the ceremonial election of the Emperor.

[1] The whole section on 'The Independence of the Estates' should be read as an exemplar of Hegel's critique of Kant's ethics in 'The Spirit of Christianity'. Hegel himself refers, as is natural at this point, to the political application of Kant's philosophy in *Perpetual Peace* (Lasson, p. 99; Knox–Pelczynski, p. 208).

[2] Lasson, p. 108 (Knox–Pelczynski, p. 217). Of course France and Germany were opposite extremes that needed to be reconciled now that the *ancien régime* had perished—see further, p. 467 n. 2 above.

France and Germany were opposites. Italy, on the other hand, had followed 'the same course' as Germany somewhat earlier. 'The desire of the Emperors to keep both countries [Germany and Italy] under their rule has destroyed their power in both.'[1] Times had changed but Hegel thought that nevertheless there was a valid parallel between the Guelphs and Ghibellines, and the 'parties' of Prussia and Austria among the German States; and the fate that had overtaken the Italian city-states and petty princedoms, of being subjected to foreign domination, now loomed over Germany.

When Italy stood at the cross-roads of fate that Germany had only just now reached, Machiavelli had analysed her situation and pointed the way to national union as the only path of salvation. By quoting from his appeal at the end of the *Prince* and by insisting (rightly) that Machiavelli's essay was 'the following through of an idea [*Idee*] generated directly from insight [*Anschauung*] into the situation of Italy', not a 'compendium of moral-political principles equally suited to all situations, or in other words suitable for none', Hegel manages implicitly to point to the parallel between Machiavelli's endeavours and his own; and by pointing out that no prince—not even Machiavelli's most famous princely critic Frederick the Great—has yet lived up to the *ideal* requirements that Machiavelli lays down for his prince, Hegel strikes another blow at the villain of his story, Prussia. Everything that appears immoral in what Machiavelli counsels his prince to do, is justifiable as punishment for the crime of 'engineering anarchy', which is the ultimate crime against the State, the sum and epitome of all civil offences.[2]

After his brief excursion on the fate of Italy, and the example of

[1] Lasson, p. 109 (Knox–Pelczynski, p. 218). This whole section is concerned more with the fate of Germany and Italy, which had *not* become States, than with 'The formation of States in the rest of Europe'.

[2] Lasson, pp. 110–16 (Knox–Pelczynski, pp. 219–23: the excerpt from *The Prince* was among the earliest notes that Hegel made for the *Verfassungsschrift*. (Hegel does not think, however, that Machiavelli showed a sound insight in supposing that Cesare Borgia might have been the saviour of Italy had it not been for accidental circumstances. Cesare Borgia was not, like Richelieu, a statesman, but only 'an instrument for the founding of a State'—the State which his uncle Alexander VI acquired for the Papacy. Hegel seems to have had a higher opinion of the statesmanship of Julius II, the enemy who inherited the Borgia's work. The Papal State, however, was not a creation upon which Hegel could look with any great favour, for reasons which must, by now, be obvious.)

Machiavelli,[1] neither of which is ever out of his mind from this point onwards, Hegel comes to grips finally with the actual situation of Germany. Although he has said that Italy's fate followed 'the same course' as Germany's, he does not deny that the changing of the times has actually introduced important differences in the German situation. The Italian states could survive in their time, even when attacked by much greater powers; and in particular no one or two of them could gain a preponderance of power over all the rest. Neither of these conditions held true for Germany, in which two major powers could now be distinguished, a group of middle-sized 'neutrals', and a large mass of small States, whose very existence depended absolutely on the maintenance of the Imperial constitution in some form.[2]

Of the two great powers Prussia possessed greater freedom of political manœuvre and could exercise its power freely in pursuit of its own interests, without instantly arousing universal suspicion and a reaction of defensive solidarity such as was generated by any 'unconstitutional' action on the part of Austria in its relations with the rest of the *Reich*. Just for this reason, because of the long tradition of constitutional relations, Hegel feels that the salvation of the *Reich* must lie with Austria. Prussia (like the French Republic) was a 'modern' State where all that counted was

[1] In the course of his discussion of Machiavelli Hegel interjects a comment upon the suicide of Cato of Utica which took place at a comparable moment in the history of Rome, when the structure of the old Republic had broken down into anarchy, but the new imperial constitution was not yet established. Cato killed himself, says Hegel, 'not because what the Romans still called freedom, i.e. anarchy, had been suppressed' but simply because he wished Pompey to have supreme power and could not endure to see it fall to Octavius (Lasson, p. 114; Knox–Pelczynski, p. 222).

This verdict is a correction of his own earlier view, that Cato sought death because the free Republic upon which his whole existence depended had perished, and hence life had no meaning for him any more (*Jedes Volk hat ihm eigene Gegenstände* (1796), Nohl, p. 222; Knox, p. 155). Apart from increased knowledge of the circumstances, the probable ground for Hegel's change of opinion lies in his new conception of world history in terms of the sequence of Empires (cf. p. 468 n. 1 above). Whereas previously he had thought primarily of the analogy between the Roman Republic and the Greek city states, he now thought rather of the Empire as a 'State' on a different level of political existence altogether, and he was willing to suppose that Cato did likewise.

[2] Hegel only noted the existence of the 'neutral' group (Bavaria, Baden, Saxony) in a revision of his manuscript. Originally he sought to treat Germany as a collection of small units all clinging uneasily to their constitutional 'rights' as best they could between two major powers, one Protestant, the other Catholic (cf. Lasson's note, p. 117; Knox–Pelczynski, p. 225).

efficiency, the foresighted calculation of physical necessity. A Germany unified by the power of Prussia could only be founded on force and authority; it would be without real freedom because the modern world of the Enlightenment knew no freedom save that of rational calculation:

> Prussia's modern politics has not proceeded from the kingly majestic principle, but from the *bourgeoisie*, and in contrast to the Austrian power, for instance, she is now like a *bourgeois* who has made his fortune [*Schätze*] toilsomely penny by penny, by his own labour, as compared with the free nobleman who has inherited wealth, whose income [*Besitz*] rests on his land and remains the same even if he lets his servants or neighbours look after the details of arrangements. His wealth is not a sum—which of course is diminished by the subtraction of a single part—but something permanent and unchangeable.[1]

In the body of his essay Hegel's attitude towards 'German freedom', especially in its institutionalized form, is critical to the point of being merciless. He insists continually that the survival of any political organization depends on the maintenance of its *Macht* against enemies or transgressors and the effective recognition of its *Gewalt* by its own members. This makes it easy to overlook the fact that for Hegel, *Macht* and *Gewalt*, force and authority, are not ends in themselves—they are only instruments of freedom. Their existence in a political organization is justified, first, by natural needs and the unavoidable necessities of physical existence; but once they are securely established they should be so employed as to make possible a kind of life that is free from the pressure of need and the compulsion of necessity. The Greeks had shown how the State which comes into existence for the sake of life, could continue to exist for the sake of the good life; and the institutionalization of 'German freedom' in the other Germanic nations pointed the way by which this lesson could be applied in national States. Hegel recognized and apparently approved (as productive of harmony) a certain tendency toward the assimilation of the nobility with the bourgeoisie. But he thought of the monarchy, the 'majestic principle', as a point of balance between these two

---

[1] Lasson, pp. 122-3 (Knox–Pelczynski, pp. 229–30). Note the contrast between the personal fortune of the bourgeois and the family patrimony of the noble. We can see in this passage why Hegel's conception of the human spirit and its immortality made it impossible for him to be an ideological partisan of the *bourgeoisie*.

classes, and he preferred to see it resting more on the nobility, as the Austrian monarchy did, than on the bourgeoisie, as was the case in Prussia and in revolutionary France. This preference reveals once more the essentially Platonic origins of his inspiration. It was in this way that he hoped to save the *Gemüt* of man amid the mechanical necessities of mercantilist economics.

In pleading the cause of Austria, however, he faced one serious problem. It was the religious issue which had divided Germany in a way which made the rise of Prussia possible, by reducing Imperial House itself to the status of a partisan. Individual statesmen like Richelieu had perceived the path of wisdom in this matter, but religious mistrust could never perish as long as there was the fear that a new ruler or a new situation might lead to a reversal of the policy of toleration. Hegel argued that there was no reason to believe that the liberal reforms of Joseph II in the 1780s could be undone in this way. Presumably he felt that the spreading of the ideals of 1789 had now made them irreversible. He also pointed out that the religious problem in the Palatinate had now been settled finally, and that long experience had shown that the acceptance of a Catholic prince need not pose any threat to the Protestant faith of his subjects.[1]

Hegel's argument in defence of religious toleration is, as we know from his theoretical 'system', only the negative side of his own philosophy of religion. He seems to have cherished the hope that the liberal policies of Joseph II would make it possible for some equally enlightened successor to establish a national Church within which Protestants and Catholics could worship side by side, conscious of their community at the level of *Phantasie* and mutually respectful or even sympathetically appreciative of their differences at the level of *Verstand*.[2]

This was the 'revolution to be produced by philosophy' for

[1] Lasson, pp. 124–6 (Knox-Pelczynski, pp. 231–3). Toleration was established in the Palatinate and elsewhere by the French annexation and 'compensations'. For Hegel's reflections on the problem of Catholic persecution of Protestants, compare his notes on Pütter (*Im Deutschen Reich, Dok.*, p. 310): 'The examples are too old; litany against Catholic principles, but the Catholic princes make this separation [*Trennung*: sc. of Church and State] ever increasingly.' Where the prince was a bishop, however, the 'separation of Church and State' was 'especially hindered'.

[2] Some ideal of this sort was the goal of his 'way back to influence in the life of men', unless our reconstruction of what he called his 'system' is radically mistaken.

which the French Revolution had opened the way.[1] But the Revolution did not only mark the end of religious intolerance; it was also the death knell of the old European pattern of dynastic politics, in which the 'Universal monarchy' of the Emperor was something that had to be continually guarded against. 'Universal monarchy' had always been an imaginary bugaboo, or so Hegel affects to think; but now men had realized that political freedom was not merely a negative thing, but a concept that had positive content. This positive content, which the terror and the depredations of the warring armies had made clear, consists of a strong central government operating in accordance with laws made by a body that represents the people. In particular, the representative assembly must have control of the public purse, the modern equivalent of the feudal service which the council of vassals voted upon in the old time. Austria, Bohemia, and Hungary had this kind of representative system, whereas in Prussia the power of the old Estates Assembly had been nullified.

The French armies had taught most of the German 'Estates' the folly of their anarchic independence; and by the standards of the Revolution itself it was apparent that the older system of representative government had decayed into oligarchic corruption, or autocratic tyranny, ever since princely independence had been established absolutely by the Peace of Westphalia. 'German freedom', as interpreted by the Germans, had proved the worst enemy of 'German freedom', as interpreted and achieved by the rest of Europe. 'To whom does Germany mean anything, where could patriotic feeling for Germany come from?', asks Hegel bitterly, at the very moment when he is about to lay down the conditions for the regeneration of the *Reich*.[2]

Germany, if it is to be a State, must first of all have a single national army, in which every prince is a general by right of birth, and commander of his own regiment. Secondly, in order to secure constitutional control of this national army, there must be a

---

[1] The phrase occurs in Letter 13, Schelling to Hegel 21 July 1795, *Briefe*, i. 28 (for the interpretation of Schelling's pessimism in this letter see above, Chapter III, pp. 209–10).

[2] Lasson, p. 132 (Knox–Pelczynski, 238). It seems entirely likely to me that the whole section about the Peace of Westphalia (from Lasson, p. 129 bottom to the end of p. 132; Knox–Pelczynski, pp. 236–8) was originally written quite separately from the rather more positive—not to say optimistic—diagnosis of the preceding and following pages.

national parliament of representatives elected from constituencies of equal population, which are themselves subdivisions of the provincial divisions which would be needed for the levying and administration of the national army. This new 'House of Commons' (so to speak) could be created through an enlargement of the 'College of Cities' in the existing Diet of the realm.[1]

There are three points to be noted about this proposal. First we should observe how Hegel links the political organization of the *Reich* with its military organization; secondly, that he explicitly acknowledges the principle of noble birth in what he says about the officer-corps of the army; and thirdly, that he emphasizes the elective principle in what he says about the national Diet. He clearly envisages that his new 'House of Commons' will have the power of the purse, and that in this way the deadlock of the Diet when the three Colleges (Electors, Princes, Cities) disagreed would be avoided.

Along these lines some modern Theseus could adapt the principles of ancient Greek democracy to modern circumstances.[2] He would have to use force because, as Hegel says in his concluding paragraph:

Once the social nature of man is distorted and compelled to throw itself into private particular concerns [*Eigentümlichkeiten*], such a radical perversion comes over it, that it spends its strength now upon this alienation [*Entzweiung*] from others, and in the maintenance of its separation [*Absonderung*] it goes to the pitch of madness [*Wahnsinn*]; for madness is nothing else but the complete separation of the individual from his kind [*Geschlecht*]. And though the German nation is not capable of pushing its stubborn adherence to particularism [*Hartnäckigkeit*

---

[1] Rosenkranz, p. 238, says: 'For foreign affairs an *administrative centre* should be established, perhaps at *Mainz*, in which all the federated states would have a common government.' Except for the reference to Mainz the context plainly shows that he is summarizing the present passage (Lasson, pp. 133–5; Knox–Pelczynski, pp. 239–41). It is just possible that he noticed some chance reference to Mainz in an aside in the lost discussion of feudal Germany. But my own guess is that he has injected into his summary some remark made by Hegel in a letter of the period 1806–8 (the period to which Rosenkranz believed the *Verfassungsschrift* belonged). We may note that if Hegel made some such remark, even at that date, his sympathy with the policy of Forster in 1798 must be considered doubtful.

[2] Hegel speaks of 'a democratic constitution such as Theseus gave his people' (Lasson, pp. 135–6; Knox–Pelczynski, p. 241). But the constitution he describes owes more to Plato than to any Athenian statesman after Theseus himself. For the work of Theseus and his fate, Hegel's authority is almost certainly Thucydides, ii. 15.

in dem Besondern] to the pitch of madness achieved by the Jewish nation, the nation that cannot be united with others in friendly companionship and community of life [*Geselligkeit und Gemeinschaftlichkeit*] —though they cannot arrive at such a frenzy of separation as to murder and be murdered till the State is wiped out, yet particular interest and prerogative and precedence are so intimately personal to them, that conceptual understanding [*der Begriff*] or insight into necessity is far too weak to produce action by itself. Conceptual insight brings with it such mistrust and opposition that it has to be validated by authoritative power [*Gewalt*]; only then does man submit to it.[1]

But this Theseus would also have to have the courage and magnanimity to trust those who mistrusted him, and share power with those who resented what he had done. Dilthey thought that Hegel's hopes were focused on Napoleon.[2] But in the light of his comments about the achievements of Gustavus Adolphus, whom he greatly admired, it seems clear that he could not put much faith in the lasting power of anything created by a foreign lawgiver. The whole tenor of his discourse indicates that he was hoping rather for a worthy successor to Joseph II in the Imperial House itself. Archduke Karl is, as Rosenzweig says, the only possible candidate.[3] Still, the example set by Napoleon was no doubt in Hegel's mind. He hoped that the native German military hero, the outstanding representative of the old order of things, would be inspired to copy the First Consul. Instead it was the First Consul who became an Emperor.

Indeed, if there was any reason, apart from the pressure of his University work, that caused Hegel to stop working on his essay with the fair copy half finished, around the end of 1802, it was almost certainly the decisive intervention of Napoleon in German politics. The First Consul followed the example of Richelieu by seeking to stabilize the fragmented situation of Germany. The settlement which the *Reichsdeputation* produced under his aegis, in fulfilment of the terms of the Peace of Lunéville, abolished a large number of the smallest, worst governed and least viable states, especially the ecclesiastical ones, which were most prone to look to the leadership of Austria. But the surviving small states,

---

[1] Lasson, p. 136 (Knox–Pelczynski, p. 242). With the remarks about the Jewish resistance to the emperor Titus compare especially *Abraham in Chaldäa geboren hatte schon* (Nohl, p. 260; Knox, pp. 204–5).

[2] Dilthey, iv. 136–7.

[3] Rosenzweig, i. 126–7.

and those of middle size, were strengthened and confirmed in their independence, and inclined to be grateful to their benefactor. Both of the German great powers profited materially, but the prestige of Austria suffered a bad blow, and it was made abundantly clear that no German Theseus would be suffered to arise either in the north or in the south.[1]

Thus *der Begriff und die Einsicht* gave way before *Gewalt*. The German Machiavelli fared no better than his Florentine predecessor. His 'way back to intervention in the life of men' was blocked; and at Jena he began on quite a new path toward the sunlight, not of Plato's City but of the Idea. In that new journey, however, which took Hegel so far from the *agora*, the earlier Odyssey was by no means forgotten. It reappeared transmuted into an ideal pilgrimage, the 'Phenomenology of the Spirit'.

[1] The proposals of France and Russia were put before the Deputation on 8 Sept. 1802; with modifications mainly designed to make them more palatable to Austria, they were accepted by the Diet on 25 Feb. 1803, and finally ratified by the Emperor on 27 Apr. (The last excerpts in Hegel's papers connected with the *Verfassungsschrift* are from a *Votum* of Brandenburg in the Deputation, 14 Sept. 1802, and from other diplomatic exchanges on that day or the previous one; and finally extracts from speeches by Bonaparte and Fox, reported in French newspapers in Nov. 1802: see Rosenzweig, i. 237, and Kimmerle, p. 151. Hegel probably began writing his final draft at about this time and abandoned it early in 1803.)

APPENDIX

Texts

PREFATORY NOTE TO THE TRANSLATIONS

I HAVE added here translations of the so-called 'Tübingen fragment' and of three other short pieces that have not been translated into English before. All of them are rough drafts or even (in parts) rough notes in Hegel's manuscript, and I have done my best not to 'improve' them in any way, preferring faithfulness to elegance even in such purely stylistic matters as the use of the dash (—) in place of normal punctuation. I have had to make *some* insertions in order to get a translatable sense at all, but I have tried scrupulously to indicate these by the use of brackets. Words which I believe Hegel omitted accidentally are enclosed in angled parentheses ⟨ ⟩; additions which merely indicate my interpretation of what he wrote are enclosed in square brackets [ ]; normal parentheses ( ) represent the brackets which are part of the text: i.e. they belong to Hegel's own very rough and ready system of punctuation. (I have 'improved' this very slightly by adding some necessary commas and deleting a few superfluous ones.)

For ease of reference I have also inserted (in square brackets) the page numbers of the German text from which the translations were made (except for the 'earliest system-programme' which was not printed by Nohl); and in the case of the shorter fragments I have numbered the paragraphs.

Last of all, I have translated the two paragraphs 'On Judgement and Being' which Hölderlin wrote on opposite sides of the flyleaf of a book early in 1795. It seems to me that Henrich is right in arguing that this piece marks the beginning of a new approach toward the critical theory of knowledge in which Hegel subsequently participated. It should be compared carefully with the sketch on 'Faith and Being' that he wrote about three years later.

I. THE TÜBINGEN ESSAY OF 1793:
Religion ist eine

[3] Religion is one of the most important concerns of our life—already as infants we were taught to lisp our prayers to the divinity, shown how to place our hands together in order to raise them to the Supreme Being, and had our memories burdened with a heap of then still unintelligible formulas intended for our future use and comfort in life—

As we grow older, the business of religion occupies a great part of our life, indeed for many the whole cycle of their thoughts and inclinations turns ⟨on it⟩—even as the outer rim of a wheel turns on the hub.— Apart from other feast days in between, we devote the first day of every week to it, and from our youth up that day shines with a more beautiful, more festal light, than all the others. We see among us a special class of men, who are called exclusively to the service of religion; in all the more important events and activities of the life of man, those on which his personal happiness depends, such as birth, marriage, death and burial, a religious element is mingled—[*The following sentence was cancelled by Hegel:* The sick and the afflicted are supported by the comfort of religion, which sustains and enlivens their hope,⟨—⟩how many still sentiments of thanks and compassion rise up to God—feelings that are known only to the soul who prays and to God.]

But then, when he is older, does man reflect upon the nature and attributes of this Being to which all his feelings are directed, and especially upon the relation of the world to it?—Human nature is so constituted, that the practical aspects of the doctrine of God, the aspects that can become mainsprings of action, sources of the knowledge of [our] duties, and sources of solace—quickly present themselves to the uncorrupted mind [*Menschensinne*]—and the instruction that we are given about this from youth up, the concepts, and all the external [trappings] pertaining to it [4] which make such an impression on us, are of the sort that can be grafted on to a natural need of the human spirit —often immediately, but all too frequently alas, it is attached only by bonds rooted in arbitrariness, and not in the nature of the soul, or in truths engendered and developed from the concepts themselves.

[*Here there is a lacuna of four pages in the manuscript. The inner half of Hegel's first folded quarto sheet is missing.*]

... to set ⟨the whole?⟩ of human life in motion—The sublime demand that Reason imposes on mankind, whose legitimacy we recognize with whole heart whenever our heart is filled with it, and the alluring descriptions of guiltless or wise men which a pure and beautiful fancy may

produce—these must never so far overpower us that we begin hoping
to find many such men in the actual world, or believing we can see and
catch hold of this beauteous cloud picture as a solid reality here or somewhere else; ⟨then we shall be less subject to⟩ dissatisfaction with what
we do find, and ill humour will less often cloud our minds—Hence we
shall not be shocked when we are obliged to admit that sensibility [i.e.
the needs and pleasures of the senses] is the principal factor in all the
action and striving of men; how hard it is to decide—whether mere
prudence or actual morality is the determining ground of the will.
If the satisfaction of the drive toward happiness is taken as the highest
goal of life, then if one only knows how to calculate the means to it
properly the same pattern of action will result to all outward appearance, as if the law of Reason were determining our will. Just as [on the
one hand] pure morality must in the abstract be sharply distinguished
from sensibility in a system of morals, since sensibility is placed far
below it—even so [on the other hand] in dealing with human nature and
human life in general we must take particular account of man's sensibility, his dependence on external and internal nature, upon his surroundings and the environment in which he lives, and upon sense
impulses and blind instinct—the nature of man is, as it were, only
pregnant with the Ideas [*Ideen*] of Reason—just as salt permeates a
dish, and if it be well prepared, never reveals itself all in a lump, but
spreads its savour through the whole, or as the light penetrates and fills
all spaces and has its effect throughout the whole of nature; yet it
cannot be conceived as a substance, and still it gives objects their shape,
and is reflected from each differently, and from the plants it evolves
wholesome air, even so the Ideas of Reason enliven the whole web of
his [i.e. man's] feelings, even so as a result of their influence his actions
appear to him in a special light,⟨—⟩they themselves [the Ideas] seldom
reveal their essence, but still their operation penetrates everything [i.e.
every human feeling] like a subtle matter and gives a peculiar tinge to
every inclination and impulse—

[5] It is inherent in the concept of religion that it is not mere science
of God, of his attributes, of our relation and the relation of the world to
him and of the enduring survival of our souls—all of this might be
admitted by mere Reason, or known to us in some other way—but
religion is not a merely historical or rational knowledge, it is a concern
of the heart, it has an influence on our feelings and on the determination
of our will—partly because our duties and the laws make a stronger
impression on us when they are presented to us as the laws of God;
and partly because the image [*Vorstellung*] of the sublimity and the
goodness of God towards us fills our hearts with wonder and with a
sense of humility and gratitude.

Thus religion gives to morality and its motive powers a new and a more exalted light, it furnishes a new and a more solid barrier against the might of the sensual impulses. For men whose experience is all at the level of sense [*sinnlichen Menschen*] religion also is at that level—the religious motives to good action must be sensible in order that they may work upon the senses; because of this, of course, they generally lose some part of their proper worth as moral motives—but they have thereby taken on such a human aspect, they are so exactly adapted to our feelings that we are led on by our hearts and beguiled by the beauty of fancy, and we frequently and easily forget that a cool reason disapproves of picture images of this kind or even forbids saying anything about them.

Where we speak of public religion—we mean to include in it the concepts of God and immortality and all that goes with them, so far as they make up the conviction of a people, and so far as they influence the actions and mode of thought of that people—and further there belongs to it also the means whereby these Ideas [*Ideen*] are on the one hand taught to the people, and on the other hand enabled to penetrate their hearts—this operative aspect involves not merely the immediate [consequence] that I do not steal because God has forbidden it—the more distant [consequences] should be given special consideration, and have often to be accorded the most weight. These more distant consequences are, above all, the elevation, the ennobling of the spirit of a nation—the fact that the all-too-often slumbering sense of its dignity is awakened in the soul, that the people does not degrade itself or allow itself to be degraded, that it does not merely feel itself to be ⟨a community of⟩ men, but also that gentler tints of humanity and goodness are brought into the picture.

The principal doctrines of the Christian religion have [6] indeed remained the same since the beginning, but, according to the circumstances of the time, one doctrine would be pushed completely into the shadows while another was specially emphasized, and placed in the limelight, and distorted at the expense of the eclipsed doctrine, being either stretched too far or restricted too narrowly—

The whole mass of religious principles, and of feelings that spring from them, and particularly the degree to which they can influence how men act, is the main thing in a folk-religion.—Religious ideas [*Ideen*] can make but little impression upon an oppressed spirit which has lost its youthful vigour under the burden of its chains and is beginning to grow old—

The youthful genius of a people—[in contrast with one that is] growing old—the former senses itself and rejoices in its strength, it falls ravenously upon anything new and is most vitally concerned with

it, but turns again perhaps and leaves it to seize on something else, but
never can this be something that would put fetters on its own proud
and free neck—the ageing genius is marked out particularly by firm
adherence to tradition in every respect, it gets its fetters from there like
an old man with the gout, grumbling about it but unable ever to have
done with it—it allows itself to be pushed around as its ruler [*Herrscher*]
wills—but it takes its pleasures only semiconsciously, not freely and
openly, with the more serene and beautiful joy that invites the sympathy of others—its festivals are gossip times, like an old man it does
not get beyond a quiet chat—no loud outcry—no full-blooded enjoyment.

Exposition of the distinction between objective and subjective religion; the
importance of this exposition in the context of the total problem.

Objective religion is *fides quae creditur* [the faith that is held], the
understanding and the memory are the powers that are operative in it,
they examine evidences, think it through and preserve it or, if you like,
believe it—Practical evidences may also form part of objective religion,
but then they are only an unemployed capital fund—objective religion
suffers itself to be arranged in one's mind, organized into a system, set
forth in a book, and expounded to others in discourse; subjective
religion expresses itself only in feelings and actions—if I say of a man
that he has religion, this does not mean that he has much knowledge
about it, but rather that he feels in his heart the deeds, the miracles, the
nearness of the Deity, his heart knows and sees God in its own nature,
in the destinies [*Schicksalen*] of men, that he casts himself down before
God, gives praise and thanks to him in his own deeds—that in his
actions he does not merely consider whether some course is good or
prudent, but also the thought 'It is pleasing to God' is a motive for
him—and often his strongest motive; when he feels happy or [7] when
he has good fortune he looks also to God and gives him thanks for it—
Subjective religion is alive, it is effective in the inwardness of our being,
and active in our outward behaviour. Subjective religion is fully indivi-
duated [*etwas Individuelles*], objective religion is abstraction⟨:⟩ the
former is the living book of nature, plants, insects, birds and beasts, as
they live with one another and upon one another, each living its life
and getting its pleasure, all mixed together, so that one comes across
all kinds everywhere—the latter is the cabinet of the naturalist wherein
the insects have been killed, the plants dried, the animals stuffed or
pickled—and the things that Nature divided [*trennte*] are put side by
side—all organized for one single end where nature had interlaced an
infinite variety of ends in a friendly bond—
The whole mass of religious evidences that go to make up objective

religion may be the same for a great people, in principle they might be the same over the whole earth; it is interwoven in subjective religion, but makes up only a small and rather ineffective part of it—it takes a different form in every man—the most important point at issue in subjective religion is whether, and to what extent, the mind [Gemüt] is disposed to let itself be controlled by religious motives—how far it is susceptible to religion; and further what kinds of images [Vorstellungen] make a special impression on the heart—what kinds of feelings have been most cultivated and are most easily produced in the soul—the one man has no sense for the gentler images of love; motives derived from the love of God do not strike upon his heart—his organs of feeling, being coarser, are only stirred up by the arousing of fear, by thunder and lightning; the strings of his heart sound not at the gentle touch of love; other ears are deaf to the voice of duty—it is useless to draw their attention to conscience, to the inward judge of actions who has set up his court right in the heart of man—this voice never sounds in them— self-interest is the pendulum whose swinging keeps their machine going.

Upon this disposition—upon this receptivity depends the character that subjective religion takes on in each particular person. We are taught objective religion in the schools from our youth up; they stuff our memories with it quite early enough, so that often the still immature understanding, the fair and delicate plant of the free and open mind [Sinn], is borne down by the burden, or just as roots work their way through a light soil, and are entwined in it and get their nourishment from it, but are turned aside by a stone and seek another path, so the burden laid on the memory remains lying there unbroken until the mature intellectual faculties [Seelenkräfte] [8] either shake it right off or let it lie on one side and draw no nourishing sap from it.

Nature has buried in every man a seed of the finer feeling that springs from morality, it has placed in him a sense for what is moral, for ends that go beyond the range of mere sense; to see that this seed of beauty is not choked, that a real receptivity for moral Ideas [Ideen] and feelings actually grows out of it, this is the task of education, of culture [Bildung] —religion is not the first thing that can put down roots in the mind [Gemüt], it must have a cultivated plot there before it can flourish.

Everything depends on subjective religion—it is this that has true and genuine worth—let the theologians contend about the dogmas, about all that belongs to objective religion, about the more precise interpretation of the propositions; a few fundamental propositions lie at the base of every religion; they are merely modified or deformed to a greater or lesser degree in the different religions, expressed more or less purely [rein]—they constitute the basis of all the faith and all the hopes that religion offers to us. When I speak of religion here, I abstract absolutely from all scientific or, more precisely, metaphysical knowledge of God, and of our relation to him, or that of the whole world, etc. Evidence of this sort, with which only the discursive understanding is concerned, is theology, not religion any longer. I include here under religion only such knowledge of God and immortality as the need of practical reason demands, and all that stands in an easily perceived connection with it—Thus more precise deductions about special arrangements of God for the benefit of man are not excluded.

With objective religion I am concerned only in as much as it constitutes one factor in subjective religion—

It is not my object to investigate what religious doctrines are most appealing to the heart, ⟨or⟩ most apt to elevate and give comfort to the soul—not how the doctrines of a religion should be constituted in order to make a people better and happier—but rather to inquire what institutions are requisite in order that the doctrines and the force of religion should enter into the web of human feelings, become associated with human impulses to action, and prove living and active in them— in order that religion should become wholly subjective—When it is subjective it does not manifest its presence merely in putting the hands together, bending the knees, and abasing the heart before that which is holy; rather it spreads out into every budding branch of human impulse (without the soul being even quite aware of it) and is everywhere active —though only indirectly—it is active *negatively*, so to speak, in the gay fulfilment of human joys—or in the doing of high [9] deeds and the exercise of the gentler virtues of benevolence [*Menschenliebe*]; even if it does not operate directly here, still it has this subtler influence, that at least it lets the soul express itself [*fortwirken*] freely and openly, and does not distort the longing of its activity—the expression of a human capacity, be it courage or compassion [*Menschlichkeit*], is like gaiety and enjoyment of life—it involves freedom from an evil disposition of the soul toward envy—and things of that sort, it involves innocence and a clear conscience, and religion helps to foster these two qualities [innocence and freedom from evil tendencies]. In the same way, too, religion has an influence such that innocence when combined with it knows precisely how to recognize the point at which gaiety passes over into debauchery, and courage and resolution into aggression against the rights of others.

[*Here follows a cancelled heading and two subheads:*

How Religion acts

(a) What the mind must be like for religion to gain entry to it,

(b) How it acts when it gains entry.]

Subjective Religion

If theology is a matter of the understanding and the memory—no matter where it originates from—⟨even⟩ from religion itself—while religion is a matter of the heart, important on account of a requirement of practical reason, then it is self-evident that different psychological faculties are operative in religion and in theology, and that different mental preparation is required for each of them—In order to justify the hope that the supreme good, of which the realization of a constituent part is laid upon us as our duty, will be realized as a whole, practical reason requires faith in a Deity—⟨and⟩ in immortality.

This is at least the seed from which religion springs—and conscience, the inward sense of right and wrong and the feeling that punishment must attend upon wrongdoing and happiness upon righteousness—is analysed into clear concepts in this deduction of religion only in its essential structure. Whether the Idea [*Idee*] of a mighty, but invisible Being was generated in the soul of man through some fearful natural phenomenon, whether God first revealed himself to men in the tempest where everyone senses the near proximity of God, or in the gentle murmur of the evening breeze, the Idea linked itself to that moral sense, which found it wholly concordant with its own requirement—

Religion becomes mere superstition if one derives one's determining grounds for action from it in situations where simple prudence ought to be one's guide, or if the fear of God causes one to do certain actions through which one believes his displeasure can be averted. [10] This is precisely the character of religion among many sense-oriented [*sinnlich*] people. Their image [*Vorstellung*] of God and of his dealings with man is restricted to this, that he acts according to the laws of human sensibility and only upon our sensible nature—and the moral element in this concept is very slight—⟨but⟩ the *concept* of God and of devoting onself to him (worship) is already rather moralized, i.e. it points already more toward the consciousness of a higher order directed to ends greater than those that are determined by sense—and though indeed the superstition referred to above is mixed in with it—yet the feeling that everything depends on God's decisions goes along with questioning him about the future⟨,⟩ or calling upon him to aid the success of an undertaking, and in general there lies at the root the faith that God allots happiness only to the just, and ordains unhappiness for the unjust and the overweening—or at least this faith has its place beside the faith in destiny [*Schicksal*], and natural necessity—wherever moral motives for action are derived from religion.

In good men subjective religion is very nearly the same, while their objective religion may be of almost any stripe—'What makes me to you a Christian, makes you to me a Jew' says Nathan [Act IV, Scene 7]

—since religion is a matter of the heart which often acts in a way inconsistent with the dogmas that are accepted in the understanding or the memory—the men most worthy of veneration are indeed not always those who have speculated most about religion, for all too often they transform their religion into theology, i.e. they often substitute frigid arguments and verbal exercises for the full and heartfelt experience of faith.—

Religion gains very little from the understanding, whose operations, whose doubts, are on the contrary more apt to numb the heart than to warm it—and the man who has discovered that the ways in which other nations, the heathens as they are called, represent ⟨their religious beliefs⟩ contain much that is absurd, and for this reason congratulates himself heartily upon his own higher insights, his understanding which allows him to see further than [Theseus—*deleted*] the greatest men saw—that man does not know what religion is. The man who calls his Jehova 'Jupiter' or 'Brahma'—and is a true worshipper of God—brings his thanks and his offering as childlike as the true Christian—⟨he knows what religion is.⟩ Who is there that is not moved by the beautiful simplicity with which innocence is mindful of its greatest benefactor amid all the good things that nature supplies, and offers him the best, the most spotless, the first fruits of corn and flock—who does not admire Coriolanus, who feared Nemesis at the height of his fortune, and besought the gods to humble him and not the spirit of Roman greatness, [11] just as Gustavus Adolphus humbled himself before God at the battle of Lützen.—

Signs of this kind are for the heart, and are to be appreciated by the heart, in simplicity of spirit and of feeling, not coldly and critically evaluated by the understanding—Only the self-conceit of a sect, which accounts itself wiser than all men of other parties, can let the guiltless last wish of Socrates to offer a cock to the god of health, his noble sense that he should thank the gods for his death, which he saw as a healing, go unappreciated, and produce the ugly comment that Tertullian makes about it in Chapter 46 of the *Apologeticum*.[1]

Where the heart does not speak louder than the understanding, as it did for the Friar in that scene from *Nathan* from which our earlier quotation was borrowed, where it remains closed, and leaves the understanding time to syllogize about an action—such a heart is not worth

---

[1] The remark Hegel refers to is as follows: 'He ordered a cock to be sacrificed to Aesculapius, at the very last, I think for the honour of Aesculapius' father, because Apollo prophesied that Socrates was the wisest of all. Oh heedless Apollo! He awarded the palm of wisdom to that fellow who denied that the gods existed!' (No doubt this chapter of Tertullian was excerpted in Hegel's collection under the heading: 'Socrates' Cock': see Chapter I, pp. 14–15 above).

much, love does not dwell in it. Nowhere is the voice of the pure heart
and of uncorrupted feeling more beautifully set against the righteousness of the understanding than in the story in the Gospel where Jesus
accepted with love and goodwill the anointing of his body by a woman
who had formerly lived a life of ill fame, accepting it as the free out-
pouring of a beautiful soul pierced by repentance, faith, and love, and
not allowing itself to be turned aside by the surrounding company, while
some of his apostles were too cold-hearted to empathize with the depth
of her womanly feeling, her beautiful offering of faith, and made
marginal comments in which their coldness was bedecked with a
pretended concern for charitable purposes.—What a cold and unnatural comment is the good Gellert's remark somewhere—that a small
child today knows more of God—than the wisest pagan; just like
Tertullian with his *deum quilibet opifex* in the *Apologeticum* chapter 46.[1]
As if the compendium of morals that I have here on my bookshelf,
which I may use, since I have it at hand, as the wrapping for a stinking
cheese, had more worth than the perhaps sometimes unrighteous heart
of a Frederick II; for the difference between Tertullian's craftsman or
Gellert's child who has been imprinted with the catechism, stuffed with
the theological sourdough—and the paper, on which the morality is
printed, is on the whole [12] not very great from this point of view—
both of them lack precisely and almost to the same degree the consciousness that is acquired through experience.

[*Here sheet* d *ends. The next sheet in the manuscript that we have is
marked* f. *Thus sheet* e, *if there was one, is missing*]

Enlightenment—the intent to work through understanding

The understanding serves only objective religion.—To clarify the
principles, to set them forth in their purity—it has brought forth noble
fruits, Lessing's *Nathan*, and it deserves the eulogies which are continually offered in its honour—

But it is never through understanding that the principles are rendered
practical.

The understanding is a courtier who adapts himself complaisantly to
the caprices of his lord. It knows how to scare up justifying arguments
for every passion, and every undertaking—it is especially a servant to
self-love, which is always on the lookout for ways to set faults already

---

[1] This is another reference to the same source (and probably to the same
excerpt): 'Any Christian craftsman both finds God and points him out . . .
although Plato can assert that the creator of the universe is not easy to find, and
is difficult to describe to everyone once he is found.' (This passage identifies who
the 'wisest pagan'—of Gellert's poem 'Der Christ'—was in Hegel's mind.)

committed or about to be committed in a good light, and often takes credit to itself for this—that it has thus found a good excuse for itself.

Enlightenment of the understanding makes us cleverer certainly, but not better. And if we reduce virtue to prudent cleverness, if we reckon it up that man cannot be happy without virtue, the reckoning is too cold and too hairsplitting to be effective in the moment of action or in general to have influence on our lives.

Anyone who picked up the best manual of morality, made himself conversant with the most exact definitions both of the general principles and of the particular duties and virtues, and then wanted to reflect on this heap of rules and exceptions at the moment of actual decision, would produce such a tangled pattern of behaviour—a pattern of perpetual anxiety and inner conflict.—Even the author of a moral manual would not expect to find a man who would either learn the book by heart, or consult his manual about everything he did or every impulse that he had to see whether it was ethical or whether it was permitted—And yet it is precisely this demand that one makes upon the reader of one's manual—No printed manual can bring it about that evil impulses should never arise at all, or that they should not develop to any great extent—no enlightenment of the understanding can achieve this—this negative effect⟨—⟩Campe's *Theophron*[1]—a man must act for himself, [13] do his own work, make up his own mind, not let others act for him—for then he is no more than a piece of machinery.

When we speak of 'enlightening a people' that presupposes that errors are prevalent among them—popular prejudices—errors in the matter of religion—and for the most part they are more of less or this character, they are based on sensibility, on the blindly irrational expectation that something will happen which has absolutely no connection with the cause which is supposed to bring it about as an effect—among a people that has many ⟨such⟩ prejudices, the concept of cause seems mainly to be based still on the concept of mere succession—for ⟨not⟩ infrequently too, when they speak of causes they leave out and fail to notice the intervening links in the chain of causal succession—Sense and fancy [*Phantasie*] are the source of prejudice, and even right opinions are prejudices in the popular mind if they are held prior to investigation by

---

[1] Hegel read J. H. Campe's *Theophron or the Experienced Adviser for Inexperienced Youth* (Hamburg, 1783, and elsewhere) while he was at the Gymnasium in Stuttgart. His note here probably indicates that he intended to appeal to his own experience in trying to use it as a guide of life as an example when he filled in the brief outline given here (compare what he writes a little further on, p. 493 [Nohl, pp. 15–16]).

the understanding, inasmuch as people can only have faith in them since they do not have any cognitive grounds for them.

Thus prejudices can be of two kinds:

(*a*) actual errors,

(*b*) beliefs which are actually true, but which are not grasped as truths, not known by reason simply but recognized by faith and taken on trust —and in this case no greater benefit ⟨than before⟩ comes to pass on the subjective side ⟨through their establishment as truths⟩—Since we are not here discussing prejudices of the practical sort, i.e. those that influence the basic orientation of the will, and have quite different origins and consequences, popular enlightenment, the removal of popular prejudices means so forming the popular understanding in respect of certain objects that, on the one hand, it is actually set free from the belief in and subjection to errors—and, on the other hand, it is given grounds for its convictions of actual truth—But in the first place, what mortal man can definitively distinguish what is true? Well, let us grant here, as we must if we are going to speak of human knowledge in a concrete sense, and one must grant it simply from the political point of view too, if human society is to be establishable, that there are universally valid principles which are not only evident to healthy common sense, but which must also lie at the basis of every religion that is worthy of the name, even though they may be rather deformed ⟨in it⟩—

(α) it is certain, then, that there are only a few of them, and that just for this reason, since for one thing they are so general and abstract, and for another if they are to be set forth purely, as reason demands,—they do not ⟨agree⟩ with experience and sense appearance, since they are not a rule for sense appearance but [14] can only agree with an opposed [i.e. non-sensible] order of things—they are not easily adapted for a living recognition on the part of the people, and even if they have been learned by heart—they still do not form any part of the spiritual system of human desires,

(β) since it is impossible to constitute a religion for the general populace out of universal truths, which only outstanding men in every age have arrived at and have grasped with whole heart and cloven to with love—so that, on the one hand, additional elements always have to be mixed in which have to be taken on trust as matters of faith—or [to put it another way] the pure principles must be made coarser, embedded in a sensible shell, if they are to be understood and made palpable to the senses,—and, on the other hand, religious practices must be introduced, whose necessity or utility is persuasively established by the sincerity of faith once more, or by habituation from youth upwards: because of this it is evident that a folk-religion whose doctrines are to be effective in life and work (which is something that is already involved in the very concept of religion) cannot possibly be founded on mere Reason—Positive religion rests necessarily on faith in the traditions through which it has been transmitted to us—and so with its religious practices, it is only on this same ground that we can be convinced of our obligation to perform them, or have the faith that God requires them of us as duties because they are pleasing to him. But from the point of view of Reason pure and simple, we can only say this much about them, that they serve to arouse and build up the sense of holiness, and their aptness for this purpose can be investigated. And as soon as I have become convinced that God is not really honoured by these practices, by our 'service',—that right action is the service that is most pleasing to him, though I am still aware that these practices serve the purpose of edification, yet even so these practices have lost a great part of the influence that they could formerly have had on me.

Since religion in general is a thing of the heart, the question might be raised, how far abstract argument [*Räsonnement*] can be involved in it, if it is to go on being religion at all. When one thinks a lot about the genesis of one's emotions, about the practices that one must join in, and through which feelings of holiness are to be aroused, about their historical origin, about their aptness to their purpose and so forth, they are certainly deprived of the aura of sanctity, within which we were ever wont to view them, just as the dogmas of theology lose their authority when we examine them in the light of Church history—How little such cold reflection helps to sustain men, we see frequently enough where they get into situations where the heart is rent and needs a stronger staff, where despair [15] often then tries to seize once more on that which gave it comfort of old, and to which it cleaves all the more tightly and anxiously now, so that it shall not be deprived of it again, and shuts its ears diligently against the sophistries of the understanding.

Wisdom is something different from enlightenment, from abstract argument—But wisdom is not science—it is an elevation of the soul, which has raised itself above dependence on opinions and upon the impressions of sensibility through experience conjoined with reflection, and if it is practical wisdom and not mere self-satisfaction or ostentation, it must necessarily be accompanied by a quiet heat, a gentle fire; it argues little, and it does not begin from concepts with a 'mathematical method', and arrive at what it takes for truth through a string of syllogisms like *Barbara* and *Baroco*—it has not purchased its conviction at the general market where they give out knowledge to everyone who pays the fair price, nor would it know how to pay for it in the current hard cash that gleams on the counter[1]—it speaks rather from the fullness of the heart.

The cultivation of the understanding and its application to the objects that attract our interest to themselves—for this enlightenment remains a great advantage, as does clear knowledge of duties, enlightenment about practical truths—but these types of enlightenment are not the kind of thing that can make men moral—they stand infinitely far below goodness and purity of heart in moral worth, they are ⟨not⟩ properly even *commensurable* with it.

To be cheerful is a basic trait in the character of a well-natured youth; if circumstances hinder its expression so that he has to withdraw mainly into himself, and he makes the resolution to mould himself into a man of virtue, and he has not yet enough experience to know that books cannot make him one—then, perhaps, he may take Campe's *Theophron* in hand—with the idea of making these counsels of wisdom and prudence the guide-line of his life—he reads a section of it night and morning, and thinks upon it all day long—what will the result be? Actual perfection of character perhaps? Knowledge of men? Practical competence? For these the experience and usage of years is needed— and the meditation on Campe and Campe's straight-edge will become intolerable in a week! Gloomy and anxious he goes out into society, where no one is welcome save he who knows how to be amusing, hesitantly he tastes of some pleasure which satisfies only one who brings a cheerful heart to it—Pierced right through by the sense of his own imperfection, he abases himself before everyone—The company of the other sex does not amuse him, [16] because he is afraid that the light touch of some girl or other may set a blazing fire coursing through his veins—and this makes him stiff and gauche—but he will not put up with it for long, he will shake off the control of this surly tutor, and will find himself better off as a result.

If enlightenment really does produce all that its greatest encomiasts claim for it, if it does deserve its praises, then it is true wisdom, but otherwise it is usually sham wisdom that gives itself airs, and plumes itself upon its *manières* in which it supposes itself to have the advantage over so many weaker brethren. This conceit is commonly found in most youths or men who get new points of view from books, and are begin- ning to give up the beliefs that they formerly shared with most of the people around them,—vanity often plays an especially important part here—The man who can talk at length about the unbelievable stupidity

[1] Nohl rightly detects here an echo of *Nathan the Wise*, Act III, Scene 6:
. . . I came prepared
For money, and he asks for truth—for truth!
And wants it paid in ready cash, as though
The truth were coinage.
(Trans. W. A. Steel, Everyman, p. 165.)

of men, the man who demonstrates to one with absolute precision that it is the very height of folly for a people to have such-and-such a prejudice, the man who is always throwing around such terms as 'enlightenment', 'knowledge of men', 'history of mankind', 'happiness', 'perfection', is nothing else but a gossip of the Enlightenment, a market huckster crying stale panaceas for sale—these folk feed one another on cold words, and overlook the holy, delicate web of human feeling—Everyone, perhaps, has heard chatter of this kind going on around him; and many, probably, have found themselves involved in it personally, since this trend of culture is very widespread in our hyper-literary times.—If one or another learns through life itself to understand better something that previously lay in his soul like unemployed capital, yet still in every stomach there remains a clutter of undigested book learning—and since this gives the stomach quite enough to do, it gets in the way of any more healthy nourishment—it will not let any nourishing sap flow to the rest of the body—the swelled-up appearance gives perhaps the illusion of health, but in every limb a sapless phlegm cripples free movement—

It is one task of the enlightening understanding to sift objective religion—But just as the power ⟨of understanding⟩ is of no great moment where human betterment, education to great and mighty dispositions, to noble emotions, to a resolute independence is what is in issue—so likewise the product, objective religion, has little weight in this connection.

It is a delight to the human understanding to look upon its work—a great high edifice of divine knowledge and of the knowledge of human [17] duties and of nature—And, to be sure, it has, itself, assembled the building materials and equipment for this; it has made a building with them, and it goes on ornamenting it all the time, and even making florid designs on it; but the more extensive and the solider the building becomes, on which humanity as a whole is working, the less it belongs to each single individual privately—The man who only copies this universal building, and simply gets material from it for his own use, the man who does not build in and from his own personality, a little house of his own to dwell in, so as to be at home within his own walls and under his own roof, where if he has not hewn every stone from the rough himself—at least he has turned it over in his hands and laid it in its proper place—this man [i.e. one who has not built for himself] is a *Buchstabenmensch*[1]—he has not lived his own life and woven his own character—The man who builds himself a palace on the model of the great house

---

[1] Literally 'man-of-the-letter'. The term was coined, or at least it was first used in print, by Moses Mendelssohn. The implicit contrast is with a 'man-of-the-spirit' and the underlying reference is to St. Paul's remark that 'the letter killeth, but the spirit giveth life'.

—lives in it like Louis XIV in Versailles, he hardly knows all the rooms in his property, and occupies only a very small sitting-room—whereas the father of a family is better informed in every way about his ancestral home, he knows every screw and every tiny cupboard, and can explain its use and tell its story—Lessing's *Nathan*—'In most cases I still can tell, how, where, and why I learned it' [Act V, Scene 6].[1]—

Religion must help man build his own little house, a home which he can call his own, how much can it help him in this?

Given that the difference between pure rational religion, which worships God in spirit and in truth, and makes his service consist only in virtue—and the fetish faith that believes it can gain God's love for itself through something ⟨other⟩ than a will that is good in itself—is so great that the latter [fetish faith] is of absolutely no worth as against the former, the two of them are of quite distinct species, and it is quite crucial for mankind, that it be led up ever closer to rational religion and that fetish faith should be got rid of; and since a universal Church of the spirit is only an ideal of reason, and it is not really possible that a public religion should be established which removed every possibility of reviving a fetish faith from it; the question arises as to how a folk-religion has to be set up in order (*a*) negatively, to give as little occasion as possible for cleaving to the letter and the ceremonial observance, and (*b*) positively—that the people may be led to rational religion, and become receptive to it.

When the Idea [*Idee*] of holiness, is set up in moral philosophy as the ultimate apex of ethical conduct and the ultimate limit of all striving, the objections of those who say that such an ideal is [18] not attainable by man (which our moralists themselves grant anyway), but that, apart from pure respect for the law, he needs other motives, motives which affect his sensibility—these objections do not so much go to show that man ought not to strive to come ever closer to that ideal even for all eternity, but only that in savagery [*Roheit*] and when there is a powerful propensity toward sensibility—we frequently have to be content to produce only a law abiding habit in most men, and no purely ethical motives, for which they have little sense, are required to produce this (compare *Matthew* 19: 16)[2]—and that it is already a gain if grosser

---

[1] In this scene Nathan's adopted daughter Recha is discussing with Saladin's sister, Sittah, the way Nathan brought her up. She has not learned to read well because 'My father loves not much / That cold book learning, which dead letters cram / Into the brain'. But she knows many things 'from his mouth . . . and of most of them etc.'. She thinks Sittah also has not read much because she is genuine and unaffected, and 'Books, you know, / Too seldom leave us so, my father says'. All this occurs in the context of Recha's new-made discovery that Nathan is *not* her father in the literal sense (Steel, pp. 210–11).

[2] The reference here is to the story of the young man who asked Jesus what he

sensibility is merely refined—or at the lowest just if concern for something higher is awakened—and in place of strictly animal drives, feelings which are more apt to come under the influence of reason, and closer in themselves to moral feelings are awakened, or merely those whose presence makes it possible for moral feelings to germinate as well, once the loud outcry of the senses is somewhat damped down—in short, sheer culture is already something gained—they [the objectors] claim just this much, that it is certainly not probable, that anywhere on this earth, either mankind generally or even any individual man could altogether dispense with non-moral motives—and in our nature itself [i.e. our character as *rational* beings] this kind of feeling is woven— feelings, which though they are not moral, they do not spring from respect for the law, and hence they are neither quite fixed and reliable nor do they have a [moral] worth in themselves so as to be themselves deserving of respect, yet they are worthy of love, they inhibit evil tendencies and they further the highest development [*das Beste*] of man—of this type are all benign tendencies, such as compassion, benevolence, friendship, etc. To this empirical character, enclosed within the circle of the inclinations, the moral feeling also belongs, which must send out its delicate threads through the whole web; the fundamental principle of the empirical character is love—which has something analogous to Reason in it, thus far—just as love finds itself in other men, or rather by forgetting itself—puts itself outside of its own existence, and, so to speak, lives, feels, and acts in others—even so Reason as the principle of universally valid laws knows itself again in every rational being, recognizing itself as fellow citizens of an intelligible world. The empirical character of man is certainly affected by desire and aversion,—love, even if it is a pathological principle of action, is disinterested, it does not do good actions, because it has calculated that ⟨the⟩ joys that arise from its actions will be less mixed and longer lasting than those of sensibility or those that spring from the satisfaction of any passion—thus it is not the principle of refined self-love, where the ego is in the end always the ultimate goal—

[19] In the establishment of principles, empirical evidence [*Empirismus*] is certainly not worth anything at all—but when we are discussing how to influence men, we must take them as they are, and seek out all the good impulses and sentiments through which their nature can be

---

must do to gain eternal life. Jesus said first that he should keep the command- ments, and when he claimed that he was already doing this, instructed him to sell all he had and give to the poor and then come and follow him. The way Hegel here assimilates Jesus' instructions to the Kantian distinction between *Legalität* and *Moralität* shows that he was already interpreting the Gospel in rather narrowly Kantian terms before he left Tübingen.

ennobled even if their freedom is not directly increased—In a folk-religion particularly, it is of the greatest moment, that heart and fancy should not go unsatisfied, that fancy should be fulfilled with great and pure images, and that the more beneficent feelings should be aroused in the heart—That both should be well directed is all the more important in religion, whose object is so great and so sublime, [and lies in a region] where both can all too easily make their own way, or let themselves be led astray, either because the heart, misled by false opinions or by its own convenience, hangs upon externals or nourishes itself on base feelings of mock-humility, and believes it is serving God thereby—or because the fancy connects things as cause and effect, whose sequence is merely accidental, and promises extraordinary effects that are against nature. Man is such a many-sided being that one can make anything of him, the web of his feelings is interwoven so many ways with so many loose ends that anything can be tied on to it—if not in one place then in another. That is why he is capable of the most stupid super-stition, of the most abject ecclesiastical [*hierarchischen*] and political slavery—to weave these beautiful threads into a bond concordant with his nature—this must be the special task of folk-religion—

Folk-religion is distinguished from private religion particularly in this respect, that inasmuch as it powerfully affects the imagination and the heart, its aim inspires the whole soul with power and enthusiasm—with the spirit that is indispensable for greatness and sublimity in virtue—The development of the individual in accord with his character, instruction about cases of conflict of duties, the particular means for the advancement of virtue, comfort, and support in particular states of suffering and calamity, these things must be left to private religion for development—that they do not qualify as part of a public folk-religion is plain from the following considerations:

(*a*) Instruction about cases of conflict of duties—these are so various that I can only help myself out of them in a way that satisfies my conscience either through the counsel of just and experienced men—or through the conviction that duty and virtue are the supreme principle—a conviction which has in any case been firmly established already, and made capable of becoming the maxim of my action through public religion: public instruction like instruction in morality—discussed above—is too dry and just as incapable as moral instruction of con-trolling [20] with its rules of casuistry, the way we make up our minds at the moment of action; or else an endless train of scruples would arise, which is absolutely opposed to the resolution and strength that is requisite for virtue—

(*b*) Since virtue is not a product of teaching and preaching, but a plant which—though it needs proper care—develops in its own direction and under its own power—therefore the manifold arts which have supposedly been discovered for producing virtue in a greenhouse where it virtually cannot fail, do more to corrupt it in man, than if it were left to grow wild[1]—Public religious instruction essentially involves not just the enlightening of the understanding about the Idea of God and our relation to him, but also an attempt to deduce all other duties from the obligations that we have ⟨to⟩ God—an attempt to make us feel them more keenly, to bring their binding force before our eyes [*sie als desto bindender vorzustellen*]—But this deduction has already something *recherché*, something far-fetched about it, it is the sort of tie where only the understanding perceives the connection—a connection which is often very artificial or at any rate not apparent to ordinary common sense—and what usually happens is that the more moving grounds one adduces for a duty, the cooler one becomes towards it.

(*c*) The one true comfort in suffering [*Leiden*] (for sorrows [*Schmerzen*] there is no comfort—against them one can only set strength of soul)[2]

---

[1] In the excerpts that he printed in 1842, Rosenkranz here inserted the following sentence, which does not appear in the manuscript as we have it: 'Men bathed early in the dead sea of moral preachments, go forth again invulnerable like Achilles, certainly, but their human power has been drowned in it as well.' He probably found this sentence in a sheet that is now lost; see further, p. 132 n. 1 above.

[2] The opposition between *Leiden* and *Schmerzen* here is not easy to interpret, since it is not referred to elsewhere in this essay. Lacorte takes it to refer to a contrast between mental distress [*Leiden*] and physical pain [*Schmerzen*]. It seems more likely to me that the contrast is between two ways in which the will of the sufferer is related to his suffering generally. There is 'suffering' which is perceived as imposed simply by external power, and 'sorrow' which arises from a spontaneous emotional commitment on the part of the sufferer. (If my interpretation is right Hegel's thoughts have already begun to move along the lines that led to his theory of 'spirit' and 'fate' in the Frankfurt period.) It is interesting to note that the term *Schmerz* recurs in *so wie sie mehrere Gattungen*— Hegel still seems to regard it as something for which there is no legitimate form of comfort or consolation. What he there says is natural, and consistent with my interpretation of the concept here, but cannot be said to require it: 'Where the *Trennung* between impulse and actuality is so great that actual *Schmerz* arises, union [die *Vereinigung*] is impossible and if man has still strength enough to bear this *Trennung* he sets himself against fate without submitting to it; if he has not the strength, he posits this *Vereinigung* in a future state, and hopes to get it from an alien unifying object . . . ' (about July 1797).
Some time later (about a year as in the case of the fragment on 'Love'?) Hegel rewrote the passage as follows:
'Where the *Trennung* between impulse and actuality is so great that actual *Schmerz* arises, he posits an independent activity as the ground of this suffering [*Leiden*], and enlivens it, but since union with the *Schmerz* is impossible, since it is suffering [*ein Leiden*], so also is union with that cause of suffering impossible, and he sets it over against himself as a hostile being; had he never enjoyed any favour from it, he would ascribe to it a hostile nature that never changes;

is trust in the providence of God, all the rest is empty preaching that slides off of the heart [without affecting it].

How must folk-religion be constituted? (Folk-religion is here taken objectively.)

(*a*) With respect to objective doctrines
(*b*) With respect to ceremonies.

> A. I. Its doctrines must be grounded on universal Reason.
>   II. Fancy, heart, and sensibility must not thereby go empty away.
>   III. It must be so constituted that all the needs of life—the public affairs of the State are tied in with it.

> B. What must it steer clear of?

Fetish faith—under this head especially the faith so common in our word-rich epoch that one has done enough to meet the requirement of Reason through [21] tirades about enlightenment etc.—so that men are forever at loggerheads about dogmas and do less than no good to themselves and others in the process.

I

Even if their authority rests on a divine revelation the doctrines must necessarily be so constituted that they are authorized really by the universal Reason of mankind, so that every man sees and feels their obligatory force when it is drawn to his attention—for ⟨otherwise⟩ such doctrines [the doctrines of a folk-religion], apart from either furnishing us with a special means of obtaining God's goodwill, or else promising to provide us with some special higher knowledge, more precise information about unattainable objects, and that too for the purpose of Reason, not just those of fancy—apart from sooner or later becoming an object of critical attack for thinking men, and an object of controversy, which always means the loss of their practical import or the setting up of precise—intolerant—symbols on account of the controversy—since their linkage with the true needs and requirements of Reason remains always unnatural and they give easy occasion for

but if he has already had joy from it, if he has loved it, then he must think of the hostile disposition as merely transient, and if he is conscious of any guilt within himself, then he recognizes in his *Schmerz* the punishing hand of God, with whom he lived once in amity—But if he is conscious of his own purity, and has strength enough to bear this complete *Trennung*, he confronts an unknown power, mighty over his fate, in which there is nothing human, without submitting to it, or finding any other kind of union with it, since union with a mightier being could only be slavery of some sort' (Nohl, p. 377).

Cf. also the undated 'historical' fragment *Klageweiber bei der öffentlichen Toten-feier* (Berne, summer 1796?, *Dok.*, pp. 262–3).

misuse even where this connection has been firmly fixed by custom—
[for all these reasons doctrines not directly authorized by Reason] can
certainly never acquire in our feelings the significance of a pure and
authentic practical moment that has direct bearing upon morality—

But these doctrines must also be simple, for if they are truths of
Reason, they must be simple on that account alone, since as such they
cannot be in need either of a scholarly apparatus or of a great display
of laborious proofs; and by reason of this property of simplicity they
will exercise all the more power and impact upon the mind [*Gemüt*],
and upon the determination of the will to action—being thus concentrated they will have far more influence, they will play a much greater
part in the formation of the spirit of a people, than if the commandments
are piled high, and artificially organized and precisely for that reason
need an ever increasing number of exceptions—

These universal doctrines must at the same time be humane
[*menschlich*]—a requirement which is both important and hard to
satisfy—they must be humane in the sense that they are appropriate
to the spiritual culture and stage of morality that a people has reached—
some of the most sublime Ideas, and those which are of the greatest
import for humanity, are just the ones which are hardly in any way fit
to be adopted as universal maxims—they appear rather to be the private
possession of a few men who have proven themselves and forced their
way through to wisdom over long experience, and for whom these
Ideas have come to be not a quaking conviction but a firm faith, a
faith that is operative in just those situations where it [22] ought to be—
Of this kind particularly is the faith in a wise and clement Providence,
which is bound up with complete resignation to God's will whenever
it is a genuine living faith.

Certainly this doctrine and everything that goes with it is a basic one
within the Christian community, since all that is ever talked about within
it reduces to the surpassing love of God and it all comes out to that—
and furthermore God is presented to us year in, year out, as ever near
and ever present, as the agent in all that happens around us—and certainly
the doctrine is not just presented to us as something that is necessarily
connected with our morality and with the things that are holiest for us,
but is also rendered perfectly certain by heaps of assurances from God
himself and by other deeds [of his] which ought to convince us of it in-
controvertibly—yet we see in experience—among the masses—that a
stroke of bad weather, a night frost, will suffice to bring this trust in
Providence and patient resignation to the will of God to a very low ebb—
that it is in general the part of a wise man to put aside impatience,
vexation over frustrated hopes, and low spirits in misfortune—

The sudden downfall of trust in God, and rapid transition to dissatisfaction with him—is made all the easier by the fact that the Christian congregation is not merely accustomed to pray incessantly from youth up, but also the attempt is always made to persuade them of the supreme necessity of this practice by promising them the fulfilment of their prayers.

Furthermore such a heap of reasons for comfort in misfortune has been brought together from all corners of the earth for the use and benefit of suffering humanity, that it might well be a cause for grief to one in the end that one does not lose one's father or mother or is not stricken with blindness every week—the argument has here taken the tack of following out physical and moral effects to the limit with incredible precision and in hairsplitting detail; and since these effects are then set out as the goals of Providence, the belief that we have thereby achieved clearer insight into God's plans, not only for mankind generally, but even for particular individuals is fostered—

In this connection, as soon as we are no longer content to put our finger to our lips and keep silence, full of reverential awe, nothing is more common than for the most arrogant knowingness to put itself forward, presuming to be master of the ways of Providence, a tendency which is strongly reinforced, though not indeed among the common people, by the many idealistic notions [*Ideen*] that are current. All of which [the idealistic *Ideen*] has very little to do with the furtherance of resignation to God's [23] will and of contentment. It would be very interesting to compare the faith of the Greeks [with this contemporary attitude]—On the one hand they had the basic faith that the Gods are gracious to the good man and subject the evil-doer to the terror of Nemesis—built upon the deep moral need of Reason, and enlivened with love through the warm breath of their feelings—not on the cold conviction, deduced from particular cases, that everything will turn out for the best—[a conviction] which can never be brought into real life— on the other hand misfortune for them was misfortune—sorrow was sorrow—something that had happened and could not be altered—they could not puzzle over the inner meaning of these things, for their μοιρα, their ἀναγκαια τυχη was blind—but they submitted willingly and with all possible resignation to this necessity, and gained at least this advantage, that men can more easily bear what they have been accustomed to regard as necessary from youth up, and that, apart from the sorrow or suffering to which it gives birth, misfortune does not also bring forth that multitude of heavier, more intolerable [evils, such as] anger, sullenness, discontent—This faith, since it ⟨is⟩ reverence for the flow of natural necessity on the one hand, and at the same time the conviction that men are ruled by the Gods according to moral laws— seems to be humanly appropriate [both] to the sublimity of the Deity, and to man's weakness, his dependence upon nature, and his limited range of vision—

Simple doctrines founded on universal Reason are compatible with every level of folk-culture, and the culture will gradually modify the doctrines in accord with its changes, though mainly in respect of their outward expression, all the imaginative paintwork of the fancy—

These doctrines, if they are doctrines founded on universal human Reason, must be characterized by reference to no other aim than this, that they affect the spirit of the people only in great matters, partly directly, and partly through the wonder of profoundly impressive ceremonies that are bound up with them; so that they are not involved in the practice of civic justice, they do not presume to become a private code of judgement, and since they are formulated simply they do not easily give occasion for strife about their interpretation—and since they require and establish but little in the way of positive [institutions], the lawgiving of Reason being only formal, the thirst for power [*Herrschsucht*] of the priests in a religion of this sort is limited.

II

Every religion that is to count as a folk-religion, must necessarily be so constituted as to keep heart and fancy occupied—Even the purest [24] religion of Reason becomes embodied in the soul of [the individual] man—still more in that of the people—and it would surely be a good thing to link myths with the religion itself from the start, in order to avoid adventurous rovings of the fancy by showing it at the least a beautiful path for it to strew with flowers—the doctrines of the Christian religion are for the most part bound up with history or set forth in history, and the theatre is this earth, even if the actors in the play are not mere men; thus an easily comprehended goal is here presented in the fancy—but there remains still plenty of spare room to allow it free play, and if it is tempered with black gall it can paint for itself a fearful world, but on the other side it falls easily into childishness, for it is just the fair and lovely colours derived from [mature] sensibility that are excluded by our religion—and we are generally too much men of Reason and of words to love beautiful images. As far as ceremonies are concerned, on the one hand a folk-religion is quite unthinkable without them, and on the other hand nothing is more difficult certainly than to prevent them from being taken as the essence of religion by the general populace [*dem Pöbel*]—

Religion is made up of three elements, (*a*) concepts, (*b*) essential practices, (*c*) ceremonies. If we regard baptism and the Eucharist as rites, to which certain extraordinary benefits and graces are attached, the performance of which is laid upon us as a duty in itself, and makes us more moral and more perfect as Christians, then they belong to the second class—But if we regard them merely as means, the purpose and effect of which is only the arousing of pious feelings, then they belong in the third class—

Sacrifices too belong here [in this ambiguous category], but they cannot properly be called ceremonies since they are essential to the religion with which they are connected—they belong to the structure itself—whereas ceremonies are only the decorations—the formal aspects of the structure.

Still sacrifices too can be considered from a double point of view.
(a) In part they were brought to the altars of the Gods as atonement offerings, indulgence fees, commutations of a physical or moral punishment that was feared into a money payment, or as a way of sneaking back into the lost good graces of the overlord, the dispenser of rewards and punishments—from this point of view the irrational absurdity and the perversion of the concept of morality is properly condemned in judgements of the unworthiness of any such practice—but at the same time it must be remembered that the Idea of sacrifice has never in fact existed anywhere in such an utterly crass form (except perhaps in the Christian church)[1] [25]—and then too the worth of the feelings that were at work in it should not go quite unrecognized, even if they were not quite unmixed—the reverent awe before the holy Being, the humble prostration and contrition of the heart before him—the trust that drew the oppressed soul, yearning for peace back to this harbour—A pilgrim borne down by the burden of his sins—one who leaves comfort, wife and child, and the soil of his fatherland—to wander barefoot through the world in a hair shirt, who seeks trackless regions to make torments for his feet—and bedews the holy place with his tears, seeking peace for his strife-torn spirit—with every tear shed, with every penance— with every sacrifice he is solaced—and by the thought that here has Christ passed, here was he crucified for me—he is cheered, he regains a little strength—a little confidence in himself—should such a pilgrim as this with his simplicity of heart call forth in us the response of the Pharisee: 'I am wiser than such men as he' just because a way of life such as his is no longer possible for us on account of the different intellectual climate [anderer Begriffe] of our time—should his holy feelings be an object of scorn for us.—Such penances as his are a sub-species of the type of sacrifices to which I was referring here,

---

[1] Hegel added here the following marginal note: 'Outside the Christian Church it was at the most a drop of balsam for the soul of the transgressor (for certainly no example of the moral corruption of a whole people in this way can be given), and his conscience was not set at rest by this means [alone].'

sacrifices which are offered in the very same spirit as that in which those penances were performed—

(*b*) another, gentler, form in which sacrifice appears, and one that sprang up in a milder climate, is probably more primitive and more universal—it is founded on thanfulness and goodwill—where there is the sense of a Being that is more exalted than man—the consciousness that we have to thank it for everything, and that it does not disdain anything that we offer it in a spirit of innocence—and the disposition to implore its aid first at the inception of every undertaking—to think of it first in every joy, and in every achieved good fortune, of Nemesis first before every allotted pleasure—to it the first fruits, the first flower of every good is offered, this Being we invite [to share with us], and we hope that it will tarry with us men in amity—the disposition in which a sacrifice such as this was offered—was far removed from the thought of having done penance for some part of one's sins and the punishments that they deserve, nor did conscience persuade him [who made the sacrifice] that by this means Nemesis would be satisfied, and would [26] surrender its claims on him for this reason, and suspend its laws by which moral equilibrium was maintained—

The essential practices of religion—such as this, do not have to be more closely concordant with it than they are with the spirit of the people, and it is from the latter that they really ought to spring— otherwise they are gone through without life, coldly, without force, the emotions to which they give rise are artificially pumped up—or there are practices which are not essential to the folk-religion—though they may be essential to private religion—thus the Eucharist in the form that it now has among Christians [is one such] in spite of its original character as a meal to be enjoyed in company.

Necessary properties of the ceremonies of a folk-religion are: (*a*) and in chief, that they give as little as possible occasion for fetish worship, that ⟨as far as possible⟩ they ⟨are not so⟩ constituted, that the outward act, the mechanical performance, stands by itself—and the spirit disappears—their purpose must only be to enhance devotion, and heighten pious feelings—and as one such pure means, which is only minimally capable of misuse, but produces this effect, sacred music and the song of a whole people is perhaps all that there is—or perhaps also there are folk festivals, in which religion should be involved—

III

As soon as there is a dividing wall between life and doctrine—or even just a severance [*Trennung*] and long distance between the two of them— there arises the suspicion that the form of religion is defective—either it is too much occupied with idle word-games, or it demands a level of piety from men that is hypocritical because it is too high [*an die Menschen zu große frömmelnde Forderungen macht*]—it is in conflict with their natural needs, with the impulses of a well-ordered sensibility—της σωφροσυνης—or it is a case of both [faults] together—If the joys, the gaiety of men have to be ashamed before religion—if one who makes merry at a public festival—must sneak into the temple unobtrusively—then the form of religion is too gloomy on its outward side to dare give any pledge that men would surrender the joys of life in response to its demands—

It must abide in amity with all the emotions of life—not want to force its way in—but be everywhere welcome. If religion is to be able to work on the people it must go along with them amicably everywhere—stand beside them in their [public?] business and on the more serious occasions of life as well as at their festivals and rejoicings—but not so that it appears to be intruding or is like a harsh school-governess—rather as if it were the ring leader urging things on—The popular festivals of the [27] Greeks were indeed all religious festivals in the honour of a god, or of a man who had been deified because he had deserved well of the State—Everything, even the excesses of the Bacchants, was sacred to a god—even their public theatrical performances had a religious origin—which was never disavowed in their later development—Agathon did not forget the gods when he gained the prize for tragedy at one of them—the next day he held a festival for the gods. *Symposium*, p. 168.[1]

Folk-religion—which generates and nourishes noble dispositions—goes hand in hand with freedom.

Our religion aims to educate men to be citizens of Heaven whose gaze is ever directed thither so that human feelings become alien to them. At our greatest public festival, one draws near to enjoy the heavenly gifts, in a garb of mourning and with lowered gaze—at the festival—which ought to be the feast of universal brotherhood—many a man is afraid he will catch from the common cup the venereal infection of the one who drank before him, so that his mind is not attentive, not occupied with holy feelings, and during the function itself he must reach into his pocket and lay his offering on the plate—unlike the Greeks with the friendly gifts of nature—crowned with flowers and arrayed in joyful colours—radiating gaiety from open faces that invited

---

[1] Hegel's reference is to the introductory discussion of the dialogue in the Stephanus edition. The clearest evidence on this point in the text itself is at 173 a: 'It was given, I [Apollodorus] told him [Glaucon], when you and I were in the nursery, the day after Agathon's celebrations with the players when he had won the prize with his first tragedy.' Socrates himself (174 bc) compares the party to a Homeric celebration after a sacrifice.

all to love and friendship—[thus] they approached the altars of their benevolent gods.

The spirit of the people ⟨is⟩ its history, its religion, the level of its political freedom—[these things] cannot be treated separately either with respect to their mutual influence, or in characterizing them [each by itself]—they are woven together in a single bond—as when among three expert colleagues none can do anything without the others but each gets something [essential] from the others—to form the moral character of individual men is a matter of private religion, of parental training, of personal effort, and of particular circumstances—to form the spirit of the people is in part again a matter of the folk-religion, in part of political relations—

[*The following paragraph was cancelled by Hegel some time after he had written it:*] The father of this Genius is Time on which he remains dependent in a way all his life (the circumstances of the time)—his mother the πολιτεια, the Constitution—his midwife, his wet-nurse, Religion—who took the fine arts into her service to aid in his education—and the music of physical and spiritual motion—an aetherial essence—that is drawn down to the earth and held fast by a light bond which resists through a magic spell all attempts to break it, for it is completely intertwined in his essence. This bond, whose main foundations are our needs, is [28] woven together from the manifold threads of nature; and because he [the *Volksgeist*] binds himself more firmly to nature with every new thread, he is so far from feeling any constraint, that he rather finds an amplification of his enjoyment, an extension of his range of life in this voluntary augmentation, this multiplying variety of the threads. All the finer and fairer feelings have developed within him [in this way], and they bring a thousand differing shades of delight to experience and joy.

[*The uncancelled text continues thus:*] Ah yes! from the far-off days that are gone a radiant picture shines for the soul that has a feeling for human beauty, for greatness in great men—the picture of a Genius among the peoples—a son of fortune and of freedom, a pupil of beautiful fancy. The brazen bond of his needs fetters him too [like other *Volksgeister*] to Mother Earth, but he worked over it, refined it, beautified it with feeling and fancy, twining it with roses by the aid of the Graces, so that he could delight in these fetters as his own work, as a part of himself. His servants were joy, gaiety, and grace; his soul filled with the consciousness of its power and its freedom, his more serious companions at play [were] friendship and love, not the woodland faun, but the sensitive and soulful *Amor* adorned with all the charms of the heart and of sweet dreams.

From his father, a darling of fortune and a son of force, he received as his heritage faith in his fortune and pride in his deeds. His indulgent mother, no scolding, harsh woman, left her son to the education of nature, and did not swaddle his delicate limbs in tight bands—and like a good mother she fell in with the whims and humours of her darling more than she repressed them—In harmony with her the wet-nurse could not rear the child of nature, or seek to bring him up to adolescence with [such methods as] the fear of the rod or of a ghost in the dark, nor [did she feed him] on the sour-sweet sugar-bread of mysticism that weakens the stomach—nor did she keep him in the leading reins of words, which would have made him forever a minor—but she gave him the cleaner more wholesome milk of pure feelings to drink—with the aid of fancy, fair and free, she adorned with its flowers the impenetrable veil that withdraws divinity from our view—by enchantment she peopled the realm behind it with living images [*Bilder*] from which he carried forward the great Ideas of his own heart with all the fullness of higher and more beautiful feelings—As the nurse in a Greek household remained in the family circle and was a friend to her charge all his life, so was she [Religion] ever his [the Greek spirit's] friend, and he offered her his thanks and his love with unspoiled spontaneity, he shared his joy and his games with her as a friendly comrade and was not kept from his joys by her [29]—but she kept her dignity inviolate, and his own conscience punished every slight to it—she kept her authority [*Herrschaft*] always, for it was founded on love and gratitude, on the noblest emotions of her charge—she flattered his finery—heeded the humours of his fancy—but she taught him to respect iron necessity, she taught him to follow the path of unalterable destiny [*Schicksal*] without grumbling.—

We know this Genius only by hearsay, only a few traits of his character are we permitted to gaze on in love and wonder in surviving copies of his form, [traces] which merely awaken a sorrowful yearning for the original—He is the beautiful youth, whom we love even in his thought-less moments, along with the whole company of the Graces, and with them the balsam breath of nature, the soul, which is inspired by them, he sucked from every flower, he is flown from the earth.—

[*Hegel began the following paragraph but cancelled it in midsentence, leaving the above as his peroration:*] A different Genius of the nations has the West hatched—his form is aged—beautiful he never was—but some slight touches of manliness remain still faintly traceable in him—his father is bowed [with age]—he [i.e. the Western Genius?] dares not stand up straight either to look round gaily at the world nor from a sense of his own dignity [*Gefühl seiner selbst*]—he is short-sighted and can see only little things one at a time⟨—⟩without courage, without confidence in his own strength, he hazards no bold throw, iron fetters raw and [*here the manuscript ends*].

2. THE BERNE PLAN OF 1794
(a) *Unter objektiver Religion*

[page 48] [paragraph 1] (Alpha) Under the heading 'objective religion' I take to be included this whole system of the connection of our duties and wishes with the Idea [*Idee*] of God and of the immortality of the soul—and thus it may also be called 'Theology', as long as 'Theology' does not merely concern itself with the knowledge of the existence and attributes of God, but deals with this problem in relation to men and to the needs of their reason—

[2] (Beta) So far as this theory does not merely exist in books, but embraces the actual concepts of men [*die Begriffe von Menschen begriffen*], love of duty and respect for the moral law, so far as they are enlivened [*verstärkt*] by the Idea—[so far as] they are actually felt, to that extent religion is subjective—But now since the public legal system [*die bürgerliche Gesetzgebung*] does not have morality, but only legality as its immediate purpose—and no specific institutions [*Anstalten*] are established with a view to the advancement of respect for the moral law and of the disposition to fulfil the laws in spirit [not just according to the letter]—since this is rather to be regarded as belonging also to religion, we do not want to separate these topics [i.e. subjective religion and moral education] from one another here, but to treat morality in general as the purpose of religious institutions, not just the advancement of morality through the Idea of God.

[3] (Gamma) Not all the instincts of human nature, for instance the reproductive instinct and so on, have morality as their purpose—but the supreme purpose of man is to be moral, and among the tendencies [*Anlagen*] that contribute to this end, his tendency toward religion is one of the most important—Of its own nature, the knowledge of God cannot be dead, it has its origin in the moral nature of man, in his practical needs, and from it [the knowledge of God] in turn springs [49] moral life—or if the spreading of the name and fame of Christ—or Mahomet⟨—⟩ought to be its ultimate purpose, then Orpheus and Homer deserved to be celebrated and honoured in Greece just as much as Jupiter and Pallas—and they [the Christians] have reason to be most proud of Karl the converter of Saxony—or the Spanish missionaries in America, or the Jew-seeker Schulz—or [should the ultimate purpose of religion be] the absolute authority of the name of God? in that case there would be no better Christians than the hymn-singing *Brigitten-schwalben*—and the Pope at High Mass in St. Peter's would be a more worthy object of God's favour than the corporal ([in Jacobi's novel]

Woldemar) who saved thirteen persons in the shipwreck by the sacrifice of his own life, and died with the fourteenth in the service of mankind.

[4] (Delta) To make objective religion subjective must be the great concern of the State, the institutions must be compatible with freedom of moral dispositions [*Gesinnungen*], they must not do violence to conscience and freedom, but must operate indirectly on the determining grounds of the will—how much can the State do? How much must be left to every man?

[5] (Epsilon) Advancement of morality, this purpose of religion is achieved (*a*) through its teachings (*b*) ceremonies. Every religion has always had a care for both of these and always involves a tendency towards both—the State through the constitution, through the spirit of the government.

[6] (Zeta) How far is the Christian religion qualified for this purpose? The Christian religion is originally a private religion, modified according to the requirements of the circumstances of its establishment, the requirements of men, and the requirements of prejudice—

(*a*) [With respect to teachings]:

   (*a*) Its practical teachings are pure and have the advantage of being expressed mainly in examples—for where, [as in] Matthew 5: 6 ff., the spirit of morality is expressed in universal terms— and the expression is not limited to the formal aspect, but contains material prescriptions—it is subject to misunderstandings and has in fact been misunderstood.

   (*β*) Historical truths upon which it is founded—therein the miraculous element is always subject to incredulity; as long as it is a private religion—it remains open to everyone to believe or not, but as a public religion there are always bound to be unbelievers.

   (Gimel) Not designed for the imagination—as with the Greeks— it is sad and melancholy—oriental, not grown on our soil, cannot be assimilated therewith.

(*b*) [With respect to ceremonies]:

   The ceremonies appropriate to it as private religion have quite lost their sense and spirit, since it has become a public religion— apart from their function as means of grace—they are not fraternal in a spirit of joyfulness—for then they would be public—but they could have been promoters of tolerance if they had not [50] been bound up by force with exclusive hypotheses—now, alas, they are distinguishing marks for sects, when they could have been just the opposite.

(c) Other commands concerning the way of life:

(a) Withdrawal from public affairs.

(b) Distribution of alms—the collecting together of a common fund possible in a private religion, not feasible in the State— also what was once a work of piety—now bound up with public honour.

3. THE 'EARLIEST SYSTEM-PROGRAMME OF GERMAN IDEALISM' (BERNE, 1796)[1]

eine Ethik

[1] . . . an *Ethics*. Since the whole of metaphysics falls for the future within *moral theory*—of which Kant with his pair of practical postulates has given only an *example*, and not *exhausted* it,⟨—⟩this Ethics will be nothing less than a complete system of all Ideas [*Ideen*] or of all practical postulates (which is the same thing). The first Idea is, of course, the presentation [*Vorst⟨ellung⟩*] *of my* self as an absolutely free entity [*Wesen*]. Along with the free, self-conscious essence there stands forth— out of nothing—an entire *world*—the one true and thinkable creation out of nothing.—Here I shall descend into the realms of physics; the question is this: how must a world be constituted for a moral entity? I would like to give wings once more to our backward physics, that advances laboriously by experiments.

[2] Thus—if philosophy supplies the Ideas, and experience the data, we may at last come to have in essentials the physics that I look forward to for later times. It does not appear that our present-day physics can satisfy a creative spirit such as ours is or ought to be.

[3] From nature I come to the *work of man*. The Idea of mankind [being] premised—I shall prove that it gives us no Idea of the *State*, since the State is a mechanical thing, any more than it gives us an Idea of a *machine*. Only something that is an objective [*Gegenstand*] of *freedom* is called an *Idea*. So we must go even beyond the State!—for every State must treat free men as cogs in a machine; and this it ought not to do; so it must *stop*. It is self-evident that in this sphere all the Ideas, of perpetual peace etc., are only *subordinate* Ideas under a higher one. At

---

[1] For the curious background of this piece see the Appendix to Chapter III (p. 249 above). It has been reprinted among the works of Hegel (*Dok.*, pp. 219– 21), the works of Hölderlin (*GSA*, iv. 297–9), and those of Schelling (Fuhrmans, i. 69–71). The present translation has been made from Fuhrmans's text because the meticulously exact 'Lesarten' of Beissner (*GSA*, iv. 801–2) show that Fuhrmans's text is in letter-perfect accord with the manuscript.

the same time I shall here lay down the principles for a *history of mankind*, and strip the whole wretched human work of State, constitution, government, legal system—naked to the skin. Finally come the Ideas of a moral world, divinity, immortality—uprooting of all superstition, the prosecution of the priesthood which of late poses as rational, at the bar of Reason itself.—Absolute freedom of all spirits who bear the intellectual world in themselves, and cannot seek either God or immortality outside themselves.

[4] Last of all the Idea that unites all the rest, the Idea of *beauty* taking the word in its higher Platonic sense. I am now convinced that the highest act of Reason, the one through which it encompasses all Ideas, is an aesthetic act, and that *truth and goodness only become sisters in beauty*—the philosopher must possess just as much aesthetic power as the poet. Men without aesthetic sense is what the philosophers-of-the-letter of our times [*unsre Buchstabenphilosophen*] are. The philosophy of the spirit is an aesthetic philosophy. One cannot be creative [*geistreich*] in any way, even about history one cannot argue creatively—without aesthetic sense. Here it ought to become clear what it is that men lack, who understand no ideas—and who confess honestly enough that they find everything obscure as soon as it goes beyond the table of contents and the index.

[5] Poetry gains thereby a higher dignity, she becomes at the end once more, what she was in the beginning—the *teacher of mankind*; for there is no philosophy, no history left, the maker's art alone will survive all other sciences and arts.

[6] At the same time we are told so often that the great mob must have a *religion of the senses*. But not only does the great mob need it, the philosopher needs it too. Monotheism of Reason and heart, polytheism of the imagination and of art, this is what we need.

[7] Here I shall discuss particularly an idea which, as far as I know, has never occurred to anyone else—we must have a new mythology, but this mythology must be in the service of the Ideas, it must be a mythology of *Reason*.

[8] Until we express the Ideas aesthetically, i.e. mythologically, they have no interest for the *people*, and conversely until mythology is rational the philosopher must be ashamed of it. Thus in the end enlightened and unenlightened must clasp hands, mythology must become philosophical in order to[1] make the people rational, and philosophy

---

[1] Here I read *um* in place of the MS. *und*. The correction was proposed by Ludwig Strauss, and the reasons for adopting it are obvious enough. But, of course, I do not believe, as he did, that it is a *copying* error (or at least not one that arose from the difficulties of copying from *someone else's* script). See further, p. 255 n. 2.

must become mythological in order to make the philosophers sensible [*sinnl⟨ich⟩*]. Then reigns eternal unity among us. No more the look of scorn [of the enlightened philosopher looking down on the mob], no more the blind trembling of the people before its wise men and priests. Then first awaits us *equal* development of *all* powers, of what is peculiar to each and what is common to all. No power shall any longer be suppressed for universal freedom and equality of spirits will reign!—A higher spirit sent from heaven must found this new religion among us, it will be the last ⟨and⟩ greatest work of mankind.

4. THE FRANKFURT SKETCH ON 'FAITH AND BEING' (1798)
Glauben ist die Art[1]

[1] [382] Faith [Belief] is the mode, in which the unity, whereby an antinomy has been united, is present in our *Vorstellung*. The union is the activity; this activity reflected as object is what is believed. In order to unite, the terms of the antinomy must be felt as conflicting, their relation to one another as an antinomy must be recognized; but what is conflicting can only be recognized as conflicting because it has already been united; the union is the standard [measuring rod] against which the comparison is made, against which the opposites appear as such, appear as unsatisfied [unfulfilled]. So if it is shown that the opposed limited terms could not subsist as such, that they would have to cancel themselves [or one another—*sich aufheben müßten*], and that even to be possible they [383] presuppose a union (just to be able to show that they are opposed, the union is presupposed) then it is thereby proven, that they have to [*müssen*] be united, that the union ought to exist [*sein soll*]. But that the union itself does exist, is not thereby proven, rather this mode of presence of the *Vorstellung* of it is believed [matter of faith]; and it cannot be proved, since the opposites are the dependent terms, [and] in respect to them the union is what is independent [self-subsistent]; and to prove means ⟨to show⟩ the dependence; what is independent in respect to these opposite [dependent terms] may certainly be in another respect a dependent term, an opposite, in its turn; and then there has to be once more a progression to a new union which is now once more what is believed [a matter of faith].

[1] In the translation of this piece I have received much helpful advice from my colleague, Dr. Walter Beringer, with whom I have discussed the text at length. But he cannot be held responsible for any mistakes that there may be in my interpretation since his own views about the argument of the sketch are in many respects different from mine.

[2] Union and Being are synonymous; in every proposition the copula 'is' expresses the union of subject and predicate—a being; being can only be believed in; belief [faith] presupposes a being [as its content]; it is therefore contradictory to say that in order to believe [in something] one must first be convinced of [its] being. This independence [self-subsistence], the absoluteness of being is what people stumble over; it [the independent being] is certainly assumed to be, but just because it is [on its *own* account] it need not on that account be for us; the independence [self-subsistence] of being is assumed to [*soll*] consist precisely in the fact that it *is*, be it for us or not, being is supposed to be something that may be utterly sundered from us, something in which there lies no necessity that we should enter into relation with it; how far can something be, of which it would yet be possible that we did not believe [in] it? i.e. it is something possible, thinkable, which yet we do not believe [in], i.e. which is still not on that account [as merely thinkable] necessary—from thinkability being does not follow; it [the thinkable something] *is* indeed so far as it is something thought of; but something thought of is a sundered thing, opposed to the thinker; it is no existent being. Only through this [way of arguing] can a mistaken view arise, that there are different modes of union, of being, and hence that one can in virtue of that say: 'there is something, but it is not on that account necessary that I should believe [in] it'—along with one mode of being it is not *eo ipso* entitled to acquire another mode of being; furthermore belief [faith] is not being, but a reflected being; and in virtue of this one may say that that which is, still is not on that account [i.e. just because it *simply* is] bound ⟨to be⟩ reflected, it is not bound to come to consciousness. That which is, does not have to be believed [in], but what is believed [in] does have to be. Thus, what is thought of as a sundered thing must become something united, and only then can it be believed [in]; the thinking is a union, and is believed, but what is thought of [is] not yet.

[3] The sundered thing finds only in One Being its union; for a distinct being in One Respect presupposes a nature, which would also not be nature, hence a contradiction; a union could in the same respect [i.e. the respect in which the being is distinct] also not be a union; thus a positive faith [belief] is a union of the sort that in the place of the one and only possible union sets up another one; in the place of the one and only possible being it puts [posits] another being; and thus it unites the opposites in a mode whereby they are indeed united, but incompletely, i.e. they are not united in the respect in which they ought to be united.

[4] [384] In positive religion any union is supposed [*soll*] to be something given; [but] what is given, that one still does not have till one

receives [accepts] it; and after the reception something given is still supposed to be able to remain on the one side. But from this point of view something given is nothing else but an opposed term, and consequently the union would be an opposed term, and that too just so far as it is united, which is a contradiction. The contradiction arises from an illusion: [these are] less complete modes of union, which in another respect are still opposed, an imperfect being ⟨is substituted for⟩ the being which in the respect in which it is supposed to be united is perfect, and one mode of being is substituted for another. The different modes of being are the more complete or incomplete unions. In every union there is a determining and a being determined, which are one, but in positive religion the determining factor is supposed, even so far as it determines, to be determined; its doing is not supposed to be an activity, but a suffering; but the determining factor, whereby it suffers, is again something united, [and] in this union the doing might have been active; but this is a lower form of union; for in the deed, which is done out of positive faith, that which has been united is itself once more an opposite, which determines its opposite, and [so] there is here only imperfect [incomplete] union, since both terms remain opposed, the one is the determining factor and the other the determined; and the determining factor itself is [what it is] *qua* active, but the form of the activity is determined by another; i.e. what has been given, the active factor, so far as it is active, is supposed to be a determined factor; that which determines the activity must [*muß*] as an existent being have previously been united, and if in this union too the determining factor is supposed to have determined, then it was determined by another and so on, [and] the positive believer would have to be an exclusively passive thing, an absolutely determined factor, which is contradictory.—Hence all positive religions set up a more or less narrow boundary within which they confine [human] activity; they allot certain unions to it, e.g. [sensible] intuition, they concede a certain being to men, e.g. that he is a being that sees—hears—moves, is an agent, but with an empty activity, in every determinate activity the active factor has not determined [what is], but since it is active only up to a point it is a determined agent.

[5] The determining factor is a power, through which the activity receives its direction, its form; even if there is believing and doing on the basis of trust—trust is identity of person, of will, of ideal, with difference of accidental aspect—if I, in the case where I am not he and he is not I, believe in him and act according to his will, then I am determined, he is a power facing me and I assume a positive relation in the face of him.

[6] Positive faith requires faith in something that is not—that which is not, can only either come to be—or not come to be—the factor that is determined [as something that is not] is so far no existing being, but since it is supposed to be believed in, it is supposed none the less to be an existing being. A power is felt, one [385] suffers in the face of it, and it is not [it does not have its being] in this feeling, but in the sundering of the feeling, in which the suffering party, which in this passive mode becomes [the] object, is opposed to the party that produces the suffering (which becomes from this point of view [the] subject).

[7] All positive religion starts from something opposed, a thing that we are not, and we ought to be; it sets up an ideal prior to its own being; in order for faith in the ideal to be possible, it must be a power—in positive religion the existent thing, the union is only a *Vorstellung*, a something thought of—'I believe that it is' means 'I believe in the *Vorstellung*', 'I believe that I am presenting something to myself', 'I believe in something that has been believed [something that has been formulated in the mode of faith]' (Kant, [the] Divinity); Kant⟨ian⟩ philosophy—positive religion. (Divinity holy will, man absolute negation; in the *Vorstellung* it [this antinomy] is united, *Vorstellungen* are unified—*Vorstellung* is a thinking process, but the thing thought of is no existent being.)

5. HÖLDERLIN:
[*Über Urtheil und Seyn*]
(Jena, April? 1795)[1]

[1] *Being* [*Seyn*]—expresses the joining [*Verbindung*] of Subject and Object.

Where Subject and Object are absolutely, not just partially united [*vereiniget*], and hence so united that no division can be undertaken, without destroying the essence [*Wesen*] of the thing that is to be sundered

---

[1] This piece was written on the flyleaf of a book and subsequently torn out. The section on Judgement was written on the recto of the leaf and the section on Being on the verso. For this reason Beissner—who supplied the title—prints them in that order (*GSA*, iv. 216–17). But I agree with Henrich (*Hölderlin-Jahrbuch*, xiv (1965/6), 84) that Hölderlin almost certainly began writing on the verso—as one very naturally might when writing one's reflections on the flyleaf of a book one has been studying—and continued on the recto. Beissner hazards the conjecture that the book was Fichte's *Wissenschaftslehre*. It is not possible to confirm this because the book was published in parts (beginning June 1794) so that the binding would vary with the whims of buyer and binder. But Henrich says the hypothesis is 'not excluded' by the dimensions of the sheet.

[*getrennt*], there and not otherwise can we talk of an *absolute* Being, as is the case in intellectual intuition.

But this Being must not be equated [*verwechselt*] with Identity. When I say: I am I, the Subject (Ego) and the Object (Ego) are not so united that absolutely no sundering can be undertaken, without destroying the essence of the thing that is to be sundered; on the contrary the Ego is only possible through this sundering of Ego from Ego. How can I say 'I' without self-consciousness? But how is self-consciousness possible? Precisely because I oppose myself to myself; I sunder myself from myself, but in spite of this sundering I recognize myself as the same in the opposites. But how far as the same? I can raise this question and I must; for in another respect [*Rüksicht*] it ⟨i.e. the Ego⟩ is opposed to itself. So identity is not a uniting of Subject and Object that takes place absolutely, and so Identity is not equal to absolute Being.

[2] *Judgement*: is in the highest and strictest sense the original sundering of Subject and Object most intimately united in intellectual intuition, the very sundering which first makes Object and Subject possible, the *Ur-Theilung*. In the concept of division [*Theilung*] there lies already the concept of the reciprocal relation [*Beziehung*] of Object and Subject to one another, and the necessary presupposition of a whole of which Object and Subject are the parts. 'I am I' is the most appropriate example for this concept of *Urtheilung* in its *theoretical* form, but in practical *Urtheilung*, it [the ego] posits itself as opposed to the *Non-ego*, not to itself.

Actuality and possibility are to be distinguished, as mediate and immediate consciousness. When I think of an object [*Gegenstand*] as possible, I merely duplicate the previous consciousness in virtue of which it is actual. There is for us no thinkable possibility, which was not an actuality. For this reason the concept of possibility has absolutely no valid application to the objects of Reason, since they come into consciousness as nothing but what they ought to be, but only the concept of necessity ⟨applies to them⟩. The concept of possibility has valid application to the objects of the understanding, that of actuality to the objects of perception and intuition.

A CHRONOLOGICAL INDEX
TO HEGEL'S EARLY WRITINGS
AS CITED IN THIS BOOK

Note: All items are identified (as far as possible) by the titles used by Hegel himself or by the opening words of the text as it now survives. (In the case of some excerpts the *incipit* here given is preceded by a date and/or indication of source. I have generally preferred not to use these for identification because of the ambiguities that would arise where two excerpts were made on the same day or from the same source.)

I. THE STUTTGART PERIOD

(For this period only the texts that survive are here listed. The full calendar of Hegel's known scholarly activities as a schoolboy is given in Appendix II to Chapter I.)

1. *Erziehung. Plan der Normal-Schulen in Rußland* [excerpt], 22 Apr. 1785 (*Dok.*, pp. 54–5), 4 n., 43, 44 n., 51, 52.
2. *Philosophie. Pädagogik. Feders neuer Emil* [excerpt], begun 5 May 1785 (*Dok.*, pp. 55–81), 4 n., 17 n., 24, 26–7, 50 n., 51, 53, 175.
3. *Unterredung zwischen Dreien* [Dramatic Scene], 30 May 1785 (*Dok.*, pp. 3–6), 4 n., 30–1, 43 n., 53.
4. *Definitionen von allerhand Gegenständen*, begun 10 June 1785 (see Rosenkranz, pp. 14–15), 51, 52, 53.
5. *Tagebuch*, 26 June 1785–7 Jan. 1787 (*Dok.*, pp. 6–41), 1 n., 2–3, 7–14, 16, 17–18, 22–3, 30, 31, 44, 46, 47, 48, 50, 52–5, 59 n., 68, 87, 134 n., 137 n., 140 n., 157 n., 419.
6. *Excerpta e Praefatione Gesneri*, 6–17 Feb. 1786 (*Dok.*, pp. 82–6), 11, 54.
7. *Über das Excipieren* [essay in the *Tagebuch*], 8–21 Mar. 1786 (*Dok.*, pp. 31–5), 12, 54, 87 n.
8. *Hahn des Sokrates* [excerpt], 6 Apr. 1786 (*Dok.*, pp. 86–7), xxiv, 9 n., 14–16, 22 n., 48, 54, 134 n., 488 n.
9. *Stoiker* [excerpt], 5 June 1786 (*Dok.*, p. 87), 54.
10. *Wahre Glückseligkeit* [excerpt], 17–22 June 1786 (*Dok.*, pp. 87–100), 22 n., 23–6, 28, 49, 54, 101 n.
11. *Plurimos vitae prosperae* [excerpt], 27 June 1786 (*Dok.*, p. 100), 51, 54.
12. *Seele* [excerpt], 10 Oct. 1786 (*Dok.*, pp. 101–4), 27, 50, 54, 175.
13. *Weg zum Glück in der großen Welt* [excerpt], 16 Oct. 1786 (*Dok.*, p. 100), 22 n., 24, 49, 54.

37. *Philosophie. Verhältnis der Metaphysik zur Religion* [excerpt], 29 Sept. 1788 (*Dok.*, pp. 156–66), 34 n., 56.

II. THE TÜBINGEN PERIOD

38. *Über einige Vorteile* [oration or essay], Dec. 1788 (*Dok.*, pp. 169–72), 72, 75–7, 81, 86.
39. (a) *Über das Urteil des gemeinen Menschenverstands*,
    (b) *Über das Studium der Geschichte der Philosophie* [essays], summer 1790 (*specimina* for *Magisterexamen*, Sept. 1790: see *Briefe*, i. 169), 72, 77, 85 n., 86–7.
40. *Jes. 61: 7. 8* [sermon outline], 10 Jan. 1792 (*Dok.*, pp. 175–9), 109.
41. *Am Feiertag Phil. u. Jak.* [sermon outline], 1 May 1793 (*Dok.*, pp. 182–4), 109–11.
42. *Predigt über Matth. 5, 1–16* [sermon outline], 16 June 1793 (*Dok.*, pp. 179–82), 111–13.
43. *Inwiefern ist Religion* [outline], ⟨early 1793?⟩ (Nohl, pp. 355–7), 119, 127 n., 129 n., 131–2 nn., 139–41 nn., 164–5 nn., 169–70 nn., 284 n.
44. *Aber die Hauptmasse* [outline], ⟨early 1793?⟩ (Nohl, pp. 357–8), 131 n., 134 n., 145–6 nn., 235 n., 268 n.
45. *Die Formen der andern Bilder* [outline], ⟨early 1793?⟩ (Nohl, pp. 358–9), 128 n., 141 n., 145 n., 148 n., 236 n.
46. *Religion ist eine* [essay: the 'Tübingen fragment'], July–Aug. 1793? (Nohl, pp. 3–29; see pp. 481–507 above). See Analytical Index, s.v. Tübingen fragment.
47. *Man lehrt unsre Kinder* [outline], ⟨September 1793?⟩ (Nohl, p. 359), 127 n., 163 n.
48. *Eins der vorzüglichsten Verdienste* [sermon], ⟨September 1793?⟩ (*Dok.*, pp. 184–92), 117–19.

III. THE BERNE PERIOD

49. *Nicht zu leugnen sind* [outline], ⟨late 1793?⟩ (Nohl, pp. 359–60), 129 n., 163 n., 166 n., 168, 173.
50. *Außer dem mündlichen Unterricht* [draft], ⟨late 1793 or early 1794?⟩ (Nohl, pp. 30–2), 162–3, 173 n., 240 n., 269.
51. *Christus hatte zwölf Apostel* [draft], ⟨early 1794?⟩ (Nohl, pp. 32–5), 162–4, 167, 170 n., 176 n., 185 n., 217, 268–9.
52. *Sokrates' Zweck ging nicht* [excerpt], ⟨early 1794?⟩ (*Dok.*, p. 174), 146 n., 170 n., 176 n., 185 n., 198 n., 239 n., 416 n.
53. *Die Staatsverfassungen* [draft], ⟨1794⟩ (Nohl, pp. 36–9), 165–6, 166 n., 168, 268.
54. *Wie wenig die objektive Religion* [draft], ⟨1794⟩ (Nohl, pp. 39–42), 166, 173, 424 n., 434 n.
55. *öffentliche Gewalt* [draft fragment], ⟨1794⟩ (Nohl, pp. 42–4), 166, 174, 219 n., 224 n.
56. *So kann in einem Staate* [draft], ⟨1794⟩ (Nohl, pp. 44–5), 167, 168, 219 n., 224 n.

(d) *Daß auch Jesus den Zusammenhang* [bridge fragment? There is a break here and the sequence is uncertain] (Nohl, pp. 289–90; Knox, pp. 239–40), 338 n., 354.

(e) *Kühnheit, die Zuversicht* [second bridge fragment?] (Nohl, p. 290; Knox, p. 240), 338 n., 355.

(f) *Im Geiste der Juden* [second essay, part 2] (Nohl, pp. 290–3; Knox, pp. 240–4), 338 n., 355–6.

(g) *Die Liebe versöhnt aber* [second essay, part 3] (Nohl, pp. 293–6; Knox, pp. 244–7), 317 n., 318 n., 337–9, 341, 401 n.

(h) *Der Abschied, den Jesus* [second essay, part 4] (Nohl, pp. 297–301; Knox, pp. 248–53), 318 n., 338 n., 356–7, 392, 393.

(i) *Am interessantesten wird es sein* [third essay, connecting prelude] (Nohl, p. 302; Knox, p. 253), 357, 369 n.

(j) *Reines Leben zu denken* [third essay, part 1] (Nohl, pp. 302–11; Knox, pp. 254–64. Probably this section ought to be further divided at *Man kann den Zustand*: Nohl, p. 306; Knox, p. 256), 357–64, 365 n., 367 n., 376 n., 383–4 n.

(k) *Wenn Jesus so sprach* [bridge passage?] (Nohl, p. 312; Knox, p. 265), 364, 365 n.

(l) *Das Wesen des Jesus* [third essay, part 2] (Nohl, pp. 312–24; Knox, pp. 266–81), 319, 358 n., 363–4 nn., 365–70, 372 n., 378 n., 381, 393.

(m) *Mit dem Mute und dem Glauben* [fourth essay, part 1] (Nohl, pp. 325–30; Knox, pp. 281–8. Nohl believes there is a lacuna in the manuscript at the end of this part), 333 n., 358 n., 365 n., 370–2, 374, 376 n.

(n) *Der negativen Seite* [fourth essay, part 2] (Nohl, pp. 332–3; Knox, pp. 289–91), 374–5.

(o) *Die lebenverachtende Schwärmerei* [displaced fragment of first draft; not clearly disposed of in the revision] (Nohl, p. 331; Knox, pp. 288–9, footnote), 372 n., 378 n.

(p) *Nach dem Tode Jesu* [fourth essay, part 2 continued: the opening is that part of the first draft which was preceded by (o) above] (Nohl, pp. 333–5; Knox, pp. 291–3), 372–4, 376 n.

(q) *Es ist nicht die Knechtgestalt* [fourth essay, part 3] (Nohl, pp. 335–42; Knox, pp. 293–301), 372–3 nn., 376–9, 382–3.

108. *Der immer sich vergrößernde Widerspruch* [unfinished essay], ⟨early 1800?⟩ (Lasson, pp. 138–41), 401 n., 416 n., 440–5.

109. *Gegen des Stromes* [opening of a poem], 21 Aug. 1800 (Rosenkranz, p. 81; or *Dok.*, p. 384).

110. (a) *absolute Entgegensetzung gilt* [fragment of essay], ⟨before Sept. 1800⟩ (Nohl, pp. 345–8; Knox, pp. 309–13), xxviii, xxxii, 250, 256, 288, 296 n., 379–92, 394, 405–8, 439 n., 440, 445.

(b) *ein objektiven Mittelpunkt* [concluding fragment of essay], finished 14 Sept. 1800 (Nohl, pp. 349–51; Knox, pp. 313–19), 379–82, 391–9, 405–8, 410 n., 440, 454 n.

111. *1 B 1. S dient* [geometrical studies], 23 Sept. 1800 (*Dok.*, pp. 288–300.)

112. *Der Begriff der Positivität* [revised introduction for 69 above], begun 24 Sept. 1800 (Nohl, pp. 139–51; Knox, pp. 167–81), 379–80, 382, 399–407, 416 n., 445.

113. *Der unmittelbare Eindruck* [essay], ⟨late 1800 or possibly early 1801⟩ (*Jub.*, xx. 456–8).

V. THE JENA PERIOD

(Only the essays and fragments discussed in the present volume are here listed.)

114. *Religion. 2. in Rücksicht auf* [fragment of a draft], ⟨Jan.–Feb. 1801⟩ (Lasson, pp. [75–82]), 446 n.

115. *Macch. richtet sich an Laurent.* [excerpt in French], ⟨Jan.–Feb. 1801?⟩ (Lasson, pp. 111–12, in German; Knox–Pelczynski, pp. 219–20, in English. The dating is doubtful since the handwriting provides no reliable evidence in this case. The excerpt is on the back of one sheet of 114. There *may* be a considerable lapse of time between them), 470.

116. *Sollte das politische Resultat* [revision of 104], ⟨Feb.–Mar. 1801⟩ (*Dok.*, pp. 282–8), 438–9, 446, 447, 451–2, 457 n.

117. *Im deutschen Reich gibts* [outline], ⟨Feb.–Mar. 1801⟩ (Lasson, p. 149; or *Dok.*, p. 309).

118. *Versuche der katholischen Religion* [notes and excerpts], ⟨Feb.–Mar. 1801⟩ (*Dok.*, pp. 309–12), 446, 473 n.

119. *II. 3. Die Publicisten selbst* [draft complex], ⟨Feb.–Mar. 1801⟩ (see below), 452 n., 456.

The following fragments are distinguished in Chapter V above:

(a) *Wir können eine Menschenmenge* [fragment of introduction] (Lasson, pp. [17–25]), 447 n., 456 n.

(b) *d. politischer Grundsatz* [fragment] (Lasson, pp. [62–5]), 459 n.

(c) *Reichsfeind, der dritte* [fragment] (Lasson, pp. 142–3), 460 n.

(d) *Da die deutsche Verfassung* [fragment] (Lasson, pp. 144–9), 452 n., 459 n., 461 n.

(e) *C. Die Lehensverfassung ist durch* [fragment] (Lasson, pp. [83–7]), 459 n.

(f) *II. Ein Staat, dem die Kraft* [fragment] (Lasson, pp. [49–56]).

120. *Ich* § (a) *Menschenliebe, Freundschaft* [outline], ⟨Feb.–Mar. 1801⟩ (*Dok.*, p. 467; the date is determined by the fact that 121 begins on the back of the sheet).

121. (a) and (b) *Kaiserliches KommissionsDekret* [excerpts from decrees of 5 and 7 Apr. 1801], ⟨Apr. 1801⟩ (unpublished).

122. *Schreiben der Reichsstände* [excerpts from a brief of 8 May 1801], ⟨May 1801⟩ (unpublished).

123. *Diese Form des deutschen Staatsrechts* [draft], ⟨June–July 1801⟩ (Lasson, pp. 7–16), 447, 450–2.

124. (a) and (b) *Der Nahme für die Staatsverfassung* [fragments of a draft], ⟨June–July 1801⟩ (unpublished), 454 n., 457 n.

125. *Deutschland kein Staat mehr* [outline plan], ⟨June–July 1801⟩

(Lasson, p. 138). (See p. 446 n. 4 above. This may be earlier than 123 but 127 is on reverse side), 446–7, 457–8 nn.

126. *Die Fortpflanzung des kriegerischen Talents* [fragments of essay sequence], ⟨June–July 1801⟩ (Lasson, pp. 32–4, [34–48], [66–8], 68–136), xxix–xxxi, 251, 256, 418 n., 447, 453 n., 459 n., 460–77.

127. *Gustav hatte kaum die Schlacht* [excerpts], ⟨June–July 1801⟩ (unpublished).

(At this point there was a break of rather more than a year before Hegel returned to the *Verfassungsschrift*. The essays and manuscripts of this period are here omitted.)

128. *Sitzung 14ten Sept. 1802* [excerpts], ⟨Sept. 1802⟩ (unpublished) 477 n.

129. (*a*) and (*b*) *Nouvelles de Paris 2 Nov.* [excerpts], ⟨Nov. 1802⟩ (unpublished). (129(*b*) is from a French report of a speech of C. J. Fox on 23 Nov. 1802 [but there is no parliamentary address recorded or printed for any date in the month in Fox's *Speeches*]. 130 is on the back of the sheet), 477 n.

130. *Botschaft der Regierung* [excerpt], ⟨Dec. 1802⟩ (unpublished), 477 n.

131. *Deutschland ist kein Staat mehr* [fragments of fair copy. Revision of 126], ⟨Dec. 1802 or early 1803⟩ (Lasson, pp. 3–7, 17–32, 34–68, [68–71]), xxix–xxxi, 251, 256, 418 n., 447, 448–50, 452–7, 459 n., 460–4, 476, 477 n.

VI. UNDATED WRITINGS

The following items cannot be dated with certainty or with any degree of precision. The order in which they are here placed, and even the assignment to a particular period, are in most instances conjectural.

132. Translation of Tacitus' *Agricola*, ⟨Stuttgart period?⟩ (mentioned by Rosenkranz, p. 12), 48.

133. Analysis of Schiller's *Fiesko*, ⟨Stuttgart period?⟩ (mentioned by Rosenkranz, p. 13), 41 n., 43 n.

134. Oration: *De utilitate poeseos*, ⟨Stuttgart period?⟩ (mentioned by Rosenkranz, p. 16), 12 n.

135. Excerpts from Locke, Hume, Kant's *Critique of Pure Reason*, etc., ⟨Tübingen, 1789–90?⟩ (mentioned by Rosenkranz, pp. 14, 86–7), 46, 83.

136. Translations from Plato, ⟨Tübingen, 1789? and after⟩ (mentioned by Rosenkranz, p. 40), 85, 98.

137. Translations from Sophocles (especially *Antigone*), ⟨Tübingen, 1791? and after⟩ (mentioned by Rosenkranz, p. 11) 48 n., 56 n.

138. *Ich las neulich Lessings Briefwechsel*, ⟨Berne, 1794?⟩(*Jub.*, xx. 451–5), 174 n.

139. Notes and excerpts from Kant's *Critique of Practical Reason*, ⟨Berne, 1795?⟩ (mentioned by Rosenkranz, pp. 86–7), 195.

140. Studies of the finances of the Canton of Berne, ⟨Berne period⟩ (described by Rosenkranz, p. 61), 158, 233 n., 244, 252, 417, 418.

141. (*a*) *L'État et les délices de la Suisse* [excerpts], ⟨Berne period⟩ (*Dok.* pp. 462–3), 423 n., 424 n.

BIBLIOGRAPHICAL INDEX

Note: What follows is an index for the sources and references in this book, not an exhaustive survey of the literature—or even of the works that I have myself used and consulted. All sources I have actually used which are explicitly referred to in the text or the notes (except classical authors) are here listed by author in alphabetical order. Translations are listed immediately after the texts translated. In cases where an editor's or translator's name has been used to identify a work in the footnotes the necessary cross references are here supplied.

(For a key to Abbreviations the reader should consult the note on page xiii.)

ALLISON, HENRY E., *Lessing and the Enlightenment*, U. of Michigan Press, Ann Arbor, 1966.

ASVELD, PAUL, *La Pensée religieuse du jeune Hegel*, Publications Universitaires, Louvain, and Desclée de Brouwer, Paris, 1953.

BAILLIE, SIR JAMES BLACK (translator), *see* HEGEL, *Phenomenology*.

BECK, ADOLF (ed.), *see* HÖLDERLIN.

BECK, LEWIS WHITE, *Early German philosophy*, Harvard (Belknap), Cambridge, Mass., 1969. (*See also* KANT.)

—— (translator): *See* KANT, *Critique of practical reason*.

BETZENDÖRFER, WALTER, *Hölderlins Studienjahre im Tübinger Stift*, Salzer, Heilbronn, 1922.

BRECHT, MARTIN, and SANDBERGER, JÖRG, 'Hegels Begegnung mit der Theologie im Tübinger Stift', *Hegel-Studien*, v (1969), 47–81.

BRUFORD, WALTER HORACE, *Germany in the eighteenth century*, C.U.P., Cambridge, 1935 (paperback, 1965).

—— *Culture and society in classical Weimar*, C.U.P., Cambridge, 1962.

BURKHARDT, FREDERICK H. (translator), *see* HERDER, *God*.

CARSTEN, F. L., *Princes and parliaments in Germany*, Clarendon Press, Oxford, 1959.

CHAMLEY, PAUL, 'Les origines de la pensée économique de Hegel', *Hegel-Studien*, iii (1965), 225–61.

CHISHOLM, RODERICK M. (ed.), *see* FICHTE, *The vocation of man*.

CHRISTENSEN, DARRELL E. (ed.), *Hegel and the philosophy of religion*, Nijhoff, The Hague, 1970.

D'HONDT, JACQUES, *Hegel secret*, P.U.F., Paris, 1968.

DILTHEY, WILHELM, 'Die Jugendgeschichte Hegels', in vol. iv of *Gesammelte Schriften*, B. G. Teubner, Stuttgart, 1962–5.

DÖDERLEIN, JOHANN LUDWIG, *see* HENRICH.

DROZ, JACQUES, *L'Allemagne et la Révolution française*, P.U.F., Paris, 1949.

Edinburgh Review: 'The States of Wirtemberg', *Edinburgh Review*, xxix (Feb. 1818), 337–63.

HEGEL, GEORG WILHELM FRIEDRICH, *Phänomenologie des Geistes*, ed. J. Hoffmeister, F. Meiner, Hamburg, 1952.
—— *Phenomenology of mind*, translated by J. B. Baillie, 2nd edn., Allen & Unwin, London, 1931.
—— *Sämtliche Werke*, ed. H. Glockner, Jubilee edn. in 20 vols., a Hegel-Monograph and a Lexicon, Frommann, Stuttgart, 1927– (*Jub.*).
—— *Schriften zur Politik und Rechtsphilosophie*, ed. G. Lasson, F. Meiner, Leipzig, 1913 (Lasson).
—— *Hegel's political writings*, translated by T. M. Knox, with an introductory essay by Z. A. Pelczynski, Clarendon Press, Oxford, 1964.
—— *Theologische Jugendschriften*, ed. H. Nohl, J. C. B. Mohr, Tübingen, 1907.
—— *Early theological writings*, translated by T. M. Knox, with an introduction and fragments translated by R. Kroner, University of Chicago Press, Chicago, 1948 (paperback, Harper and Row Torchbooks,) New York, 1961).
—— *Vertrauliche Briefe* (von Jean-Jacques Cart) aus dem Französischen übersetzt und kommentiert. Faksimiledruck der Ausgabe von 1798 herausgegeben von Wolfgang Wieland, Vandenhoeck & Ruprecht, 1970.
—— *Werke*, complete edn. by a group of friends of the deceased, 17 vols., Duncker and Humblot, Berlin, 1832 ff.
Hegel-Studien, ed. F. Nicolin and O. Pöggeler, Bouvier, Bonn, 1961– .
HENRICH, DIETER, 'Leutwein über Hegel. Ein Dokument zu Hegels Biographie', *Hegel-Studien*, iii (1965), 39–77.
—— 'Hölderlin über Urteil und Sein', *Hölderlin-Jahrbuch*, xiv (1965/6), 73–96.
—— 'Some presuppositions of Hegel's System', in D. Christensen (ed.), *Hegel and the philosophy of religion*, Nijhoff, The Hague, 1970.
—— and DÖDERLEIN, JOHANN LUDWIG, 'Carl Immanuel Diez. Ankündigung einer Ausgabe seiner Schriften und Briefe', *Hegel-Studien*, iii (1965), 276–86.
HERDER, JOHANN GOTTFRIED, *Sämtliche Werke*, 33 vols., ed. B. Suphan and others, Weidmann, Berlin, 1877–1913.
—— *God, some conversations*, translated by F. H. Burkhardt, Bobbs-Merrill (Library of Liberal Arts), Indianapolis–New York, 1940.
HERMES, JOHANN TIMOTHEUS, *Sophiens Reise*, ed. F. Brüggemann, Reclam, Leipzig, 1940.
HIPPEL, THEODOR GOTTLIEB VON, *Sämtliche Werke*, 14 vols., Reimer, Berlin, 1827–39.
HOČEVAR, ROLF K., *Stände und Repräsentation beim jungen Hegel*, C. H. Beck, Munich, 1968.
HOFFMEISTER, JOHANNES (ed.), see HEGEL, *Briefe*, *Dokumente*, and *Phänomenologie*.
HÖLDERLIN, JOHANN CHRISTIAN FRIEDRICH, *Sämtliche Werke* (Große Stuttgarter Ausgabe), ed. F. Beissner and A. Beck (to be completed in 8 vols.), Kohlhammer, Stuttgart, 1943– (*GSA*).
KANT, IMMANUEL, *Kritik der reinen Vernunft*, ed. Raymund Schmidt, F. Meiner, Hamburg, 1930.

KANT, IMMANUEL, *Critique of pure reason*, translated by N. Kemp Smith, Macmillan, London, 1929.
—— *Gesammelte Schriften*, edited by the Royal Prussian Academy of Sciences, Reimer, Berlin, 1902–38 (*Akad.*).
—— *Critique of practical reason*, translated by L. W. Beck, Bobbs-Merrill (Library of Liberal Arts), Indianapolis–New York, 1956.
—— *Foundations of the metaphysics of morals* and *What is enlightenment*, translated by L. W. Beck, Bobbs-Merrill (Library of Liberal Arts), Indianapolis–New York, 1959.
—— *The metaphysical elements of justice*, translated by John Ladd, Bobbs-Merrill (Library of Liberal Arts), Indianapolis–New York, 1965.
—— *The doctrine of virtue*, translated by M. J. Gregor, Harper and Row Torchbooks, New York, 1964. (Another translation by J. Ellington is available in the Library of Liberal Arts.)
—— *Religion within the limits of reason alone*, translated by T. M. Greene and H. H. Hudson, 2nd edn., Harper and Row Torchbooks, New York, 1960.
KAUFMANN, WALTER, *Hegel, a reinterpretation*, Doubleday, New York, 1965 (paperback, Anchor Books, 1966).
KELLY, GEORGE ARMSTRONG, *Idealism, politics and history*, C.U.P., Cambridge, 1969.
KIMMERLE, HEINZ, 'Zur Chronologie von Hegels Jenaer Schriften', *Hegel-Studien*, iv (1967), 125–76.
—— 'Die von Rosenkranz überlieferten Texte Hegels aus der Jenaer Zeit', *Hegel-Studien*, v (1969), 83–94.
—— *Das Problem der Abgeschlossenheit des Denkens*, Bouvier, Bonn, 1970 (Hegel-Studien, Beiheft 8).
KLAIBER, JULIUS, *Hölderlin, Hegel und Schelling in ihren schwäbischen Jugendjahren*, Stuttgart, 1877.
KNOX, SIR T. MALCOLM, 'Hegel's attitude to Kant's ethics', *Kant-Studien*, 49 (1957–8), 70–81. (*See also* HEGEL, *Early theological writings* and *Political writings*.)
LACORTE, CARMELO, *Il primo Hegel*, Sansoni, Florence, 1959.
LASSON, GEORG (ed.), see HEGEL, *Schriften zur Politik*.
LESSING, GOTTHOLD EPHRAIM, *Sämtliche Schriften*, ed. K. Lachmann, 3rd edn. revised by F. Muncker, 23 vols., De Gruyter, Berlin and Leipzig, 1886–1924 [reprint of 1968].
—— *Laocoon, Nathan the Wise, Minna von Barnhelm*, translated by W. A. Steel and A. Dent, Dent (Everyman), London, 1930. (There is a more adequate translation of *Laocoon* in the Library of Liberal Arts.)
—— *Theological writings*, translated by Henry Chadwick, A. & C. Black, London, 1956 [includes 'The Education of the Human Race'].
LUKÁCS, GYORGY, *Der junge Hegel* (Über die Beziehungen von Dialektik und Ökonomie) (*Werke*, vol. 8), Luchterhand, Neuwied and Berlin, 1948.
LUPORINI, CESARE, 'Un frammento politico giovanile di G. F. Hegel', in *Filosofi vecchi e nuovi*, Sansoni, Florence, 1949.
MENDELSSOHN, MOSES, *Gesammelte Schriften*, ed. G. B. Mendelssohn, 7 vols. in 8, Brockhaus, Leipzig, 1843–5.

—— *Briefe und Dokumente*, vol. i, ed. H. Fuhrmans, Bouvier, Bonn, 1962.

SCHILLER, JOHANN CHRISTOPH FRIEDRICH, *Werke* (Nationalausgabe), ed. L. Blumenthal and B. von Wiese, H. Bohlau, Weimar, 1943– (in progress). (The principal philosophical treatises are in volume 20.)

—— *Sämtliche Schriften*, Historisch-kritische Ausgabe, ed. K. Goedeke, Cotta, Stuttgart, 1867–76 [vol. x contains the text of 'Über die Ästhetische Erziehung des Menschen' as it first appeared in *Die Hören*].

—— *On the aesthetic education of man*, edited and translated by E. M. Wilkinson and L. A. Willoughby, Clarendon Press, Oxford, 1967.

SCHOLZ, HEINRICH (ed.), *Die Hauptschriften zum Pantheismusstreit zwischen Jacobi und Mendelssohn*, Reuther & Reichard, Berlin, 1916.

SCHÜLER, GISELA, 'Zur Chronologie von Hegels Jugendschriften', *Hegel-Studien*, ii (1963), 111–59.

SHAFTESBURY, A. A. COOPER, 3RD EARL, *Characteristics*, Bobbs-Merrill (Library of Liberal Arts), Indianapolis–New York, 1964.

STEUART, SIR JAMES DENHAM, *An inquiry into the principles of political economy*, 2 vols., Millar & Cadell, London, 1767.

STIRLING, JAMES HUTCHISON, *The secret of Hegel*, 2nd edn., Oliver & Boyd, Edinburgh, 1898.

STORR, GOTTLOB CHRISTIAN, *Annotationes quaedam theologicae ad philosophicam Kantii de religione doctrinam*, apud Bornium, Tübingen, 1793.

—— *Bemerkungen über Kant's philosophische Religionslehre*, Nebst einigen Bemerkungen des Uebersetzers ⟨F. G. Süskind⟩, über den aus Principien der praktischen Vernunft hergeleiteten Ueberzeugungs-grund von der Möglichkeit und Wirklichkeit einer Offenbarung in Beziehung auf Fichte's Versuch einer Kritik aller Offenbarung, Cotta, Tübingen, 1794; reprinted photographically in the series Aetas Kantiana, Culture et Civilisation, Brussels, 1968.

—— *An elementary course of biblical theology*, translated from the work of Professors Storr and ⟨K. C.⟩ Flatt, with additions by S. S. Schmucker, D.D. Reprinted from the second American edition (1836), T. Ward & Co., London.

STRAHM, HANS, 'Aus Hegel's Berner Zeit', *Archiv für Geschichte der Philosophie*, xli (1932), 514–33.

VANNI-ROVIGHI, SOFIA, 'Osservazioni sulla cronologia dei primi scritti di Hegel', *Il Pensiero*, v (1960), 157–75.

WALLACE, WILLIAM (translator), *see* HEGEL, *Logic*.

WIEDMANN, FRANZ, *Hegel, an illustrated biography*, translated by J. Neugroschel, Pegasus, New York, 1968.

WILKINSON, ELIZABETH M., and WILLOUGHBY, L. A. (translators), *see* SCHILLER, *On the aesthetic education of man*.

ANALYTICAL INDEX

P p